40.76
4.08
2.00
46.84

Church and State in America

CHURCH AND STATE IN AMERICA

A Bibliographical Guide

The Colonial and Early National Periods

EDITED BY

John F. Wilson

GREENWOOD PRESS

NEW YORK · WESTPORT, CONNECTICUT · LONDON

Library of Congress Cataloging-in-Publication Data
Main entry under title:

Church and state in America.

   Includes index.
   Contents: v. 1. The Colonial and early national
periods.
   1. Church and state—United States—Bibliography.
I. Wilson, John Frederick.
Z7776.72.C48 1986 [BR516] 016.322'1'0973   85-31698
ISBN 0-313-25236-X (lib. bdg. : v. 1 : alk. paper)

Library of Congress Catalog Card Number: 85-31698
ISBN: 0-313-25236-X

First published in 1986

Greenwood Press, Inc.
88 Post Road West, Westport, Connecticut 06881

Printed in the United States of America

The paper used in this book complies with the
Permanent Paper Standard issued by the National
Information Standards Organization (Z39.48-1984).

10 9 8 7 6 5 4 3 2 1

Contents

Introduction

John F. Wilson

This volume and its sequel are designed to survey the historiographical resources that bear on the church-state issue in American culture. Taken together, they will contain twenty-two chapters, sixteen devoted to review of
largely period-defined literatures, and three double chapters concerned with
education, law, and gender relations as fundamental to structures of authority in the society. The chapters of this first volume concern the subject from
the colonial settlements to the Civil War and those of the second volume
pursue it in the subsequent century and more. Each of these twenty-two
chapters consists of both an essay, which analyzes the literature relevant to
the church-state question in the period or topic under review, and a listing of
selected books, journal articles, primary sources, and critical bibliographies.
In general, references are to works of the last quarter century, supplemented
by a very few older publications which continue to be important. The authors
are current or recent graduate students familiar with the respective periods
or topics because of their specialized studies.

Attention to the church-state issue has been episodic in our national history,
often directly reflecting the social tension aroused when religious interests
have been manifestly linked to political controversies. What we clearly lack is
responsible literature, written from historical and comparative perspectives,
on the relation of religious authorities and actions to political regimes and
interests in America. With this in mind, the Princeton Project on Church and
State, under the guidance of a steering committee of historians, has sought to
make a start in creating the library that will meet that need. In so doing, we
hope to permit a fuller appreciation not only of our past but also of our present,
and perhaps make a contribution to our collective futures. The resources to be
developed, which will include a number of monographs, an overall survey, and
a legal casebook, will provide a more nuanced and self-conscious understanding of the issue in American history than has hitherto been available. The

framework adopted by the project is frankly more broad than narrow, and
strongly represents critical rather than prescriptive approaches.

Both inside and outside observers of American society generally concur
that the nation has found a unique resolution to the church-state question.
Outsiders think that religious freedom and the absence of an established
church are important factors, along with economic opportunity, political
liberty, and artistic freedom, in defining what is distinctive about this country. Insiders believe that America has solved the perennial church-state problem. Whether we describe this solution in terms of the "wall of separation"
metaphor, or choose instead to emphasize the latitude our society affords
religious behavior and belief, we assume that certain issues of long standing
(at least in Western history) have been settled in and through the American
polity. Both outsiders and insiders have no doubt that our society has taken a
pioneering route, so to speak, to arrive at its own formulas concerning the
interaction of religious and political authority.

Yet in such discussions the terms "church" and "state" are often too strictly construed to have much relevance to actual social institutions and practices. Intuitively we know that our society is highly plural in both political
and religious terms. On the religious side, not only are formal institutions—
the denominations—multiple, but we readily recognize that authentic religious impulses also flow through alternative movements, center on charismatic figures, and entail various ritual transactions that extend well beyond
the conventional reference of the "church." On the political side, although
seldom acknowledged, the life of the society is no less complex and dynamic.
The several branches of the federal, state, regional, and local governments
overlap and intertwine. They are supplemented by quasi-public agencies and
private enterprises also dedicated to addressing the requirements of the public life. Yet even when these elements of government are directed by dynamic
partisan actors and agencies they do not sum to anything like the "state" of
traditional thought or perhaps recent European experience. Thus a strict
construction of this term too is wholly inappropriate because it misrepre-
sents the political dimensions of our social reality.

At the same time, we should not fail to recognize that the term "church and
state" has always had a more expansive reference. For behind and beyond
the narrow institutions denominated "church" and "state" lurk enduring
questions such as where authority within a culture is to be found, and what
forms it takes. Where cultural authority is located in easily identified and
discrete institutions, "church and state" may seem to describe an evident set
of relationships. Where the boundaries of institutions are less clear cut, as in
the American national experience, the deeper issue of cultural authority
nonetheless remains. How does religious power establish its authority

against governmental claims to legitimacy? And how much scope do governments permit to actions taken in the name of religion? Understood in terms of this wider definition, the concept of church and state has a continuing relevance to American social experience. But it is a relevance obscured by beguiling metaphors ("the wall") that substitute for thought, or constraining doctrines ("strict separation") that fail to take account of social variety and change.

One theme that emerges from the bibliographies in this volume and its sequel is the contrast between the very limited attention given to the church-state question construed narrowly, and the extremely broad and wide-ranging, essentially amorphous, literature that relates to the question when it is viewed more inclusively. In one respect this is another way of commenting that we lack an effective formulation accurately to designate the subject which is our chief concern. But that observation also leads us to highlight the few authors who have attempted systematically to address the issue as we have defined it. One, whose name will appear in a number of the bibliographies, is Mark DeWolfe Howe. His Weil Lectures, published with the title *The Garden and the Wilderness*, show how studying American law in its cultural setting offers new perspectives on the church-state issue.[1] Of course, his casebook, which circulated in extremely limited numbers, also remains a valuable resource three decades after its appearance.[2] Frequent citation of articles or essays by Sidney E. Mead in many of the following chapters will identify him as an author who has repeatedly formulated this issue in challenging ways. His essays collected in *The Lively Experiment* and *The Nation With the Soul of a Church*, when taken together, offer a remarkable series of insights into the topic so central to the social experiment that is America.[3] In *The Old Religion in the Brave New World* Professor Mead offers further sustained reflection on this matter.[4] The remarkable compilation by Anson Phelps Stokes, *Church and State in the United States*, provided the initial impetus for the Princeton Project.[5] While Stokes's work lacks a theoretical framework and does not address problems of definition, his omnibus three-volume collection of materials proves how the culture has shaped the church-state question in America. Much of the volumes' richness remains in the abridgement that Leo Pfeffer developed some years later.[6]

Explicit reference to these few individuals and their writings does not suggest that the work of this project is redundant. Rather, it is to indicate that despite the manifest importance of the subject, very few authors have sought to develop a cultural interpretation of the church-state question. The Princeton Project is under no illusion it can discharge such a large assignment to its own satisfaction, let alone that of others. But it does intend that the publications it sponsors, beginning with this volume, will both establish the signifi-

cance of the church-state question when set in the context of the dynamic
culture of America and direct scholarly interests to the ample relevant resources that are available.

The essays in this volume, because of their diversity of subject matter and
approach, vary in their respective forms and designs, though the purpose in
every case remains the same: to lead the interested reader into the primary
and secondary publications that bear on the church-state issue in the context
of the encompassing culture. They also reflect the difficulty of defining areas
and periods, particularly in the early years. Maryland, for instance, may be
seen as belonging in the colonial period either to the middle colonies or to
the south. The choice for its location must be arbitrary: at the time, religious
and political divisions were not congruent. Moreover, the bibliographic listings show that scholarship has been unevenly distributed over the spectrum
of American history. Thus, the field of education is represented here more in
terms of primary than secondary sources, reflecting the relative lack of recent activity on the topic. In addition, lack of sufficient work on other potentially interesting topics has made it impossible for us to include them as the
subjects of bibliographies. We should emphasize that citation of the same
items in more than one bibliography is deliberate: the reader should expect to
find everything he or she requires within the listings on a single topic or
period. At the same time, we hope that browsing across the chapters will
bring new and fruitful viewpoints on the general subject.

Finally it is important to reiterate that this is the initial publication in what
is conceived as a broad and ambitious venture. The sequel to this bibliography, covering the remaining century and more of the national experience, will
be issued approximately a year after this volume. The legal casebook and
various monographs will follow in due course. We hope that these publications will stimulate other authors, as well as students, to take a broader,
cultural view of this vexing question in the American experience. Such a
renewed and deepened interest in the issue is the ultimate objective of this
Project.

At all stages of planning and execution, the steering committee has offered
advice, counsel, and direction. Robert T. Handy, of Union Theological Seminary, and my colleagues at Princeton University, Stanley N. Katz and Albert J.
Raboteau, have consistently suggested, stimulated, criticized, and assisted in
constructive ways. John Fitzmier, the author of one chapter, has also served
as technical consultant in the use of computing technology. His ingenious
and dedicated contributions have made the venture work. Above all, Yoma
Ullman, as coordinator of the Project, has stood at the center of the bibliographical endeavor. Her contribution has gone well beyond the managerial
and editorial. In becoming herself a collaborator, she has made possible a

publication that otherwise would have been problematic. The project as a whole is being financed through a generous grant from the Lilly Endowment. Dr. Robert W. Lynn, Senior Vice President for Religion, has been a valued and consistent supporter throughout.

NOTES

1. Mark DeWolfe Howe, *The Garden and the Wilderness: Religion and Government in American Constitutional History* (Chicago: University of Chicago Press, 1965).

2. Mark DeWolfe Howe, comp. *Cases on Church and State in the United States*, prelim. ed. (Cambridge, Mass.: Harvard University Press, 1952).

3. Sidney E. Mead, *The Lively Experiment: The Shaping of Christianity in America* (New York: Harper & Row, 1963): *The Nation With the Soul of a Church* (New York: Harper & Row, 1975).

4. Sidney E. Mead, *The Old Religion in the Brave New World: Reflections on the Relation Between Christendom and the Republic* (Berkeley: University of California Press, 1977).

5. Anson Phelps Stokes, *Church and State in the United States*, 3 vols. (New York: Harper & Brothers, 1950).

6. Anson Phelps Stokes and Leo Pfeffer, *Church and State in the United States*, rev. ed. in 1 vol. (New York: Harper & Row, 1964).

Church-State Issues in the Middle Colonies from Colonization to the Mid–Eighteenth Century

Randall H. Balmer

No area of colonial America boasted more heterogeneity than the Middle Colonies. Ranging from Catholic Maryland to Dutch New York to Quaker Pennsylvania, Swedish Delaware, and polyglot New Jersey, the Middle Colonies provide a veritable laboratory for the study of church-state relations in the colonial period. Wars (both in Europe and America), political takeovers, and changing demographics further complicated the picture, with the result that diverse interests and ideologies competed against one another for ascendance. Although each colony dealt with the church-state issue autonomously, most governments eschewed religious establishment in order to accommodate the lack of religious consensus within their jurisdictions.

MARYLAND

Of all religious groups in the English-speaking world of the seventeenth and eighteenth centuries, none met with less toleration than Roman Catholics. Recusancy laws drove Elizabethan Catholics underground and established patterns of discrimination and persecution that reached their apogee during the English Revolution. Through marriage or personal confession all Stuart monarchs at one time or another fell under suspicion for their alleged Catholic sympathies; one lost his head to the Puritans in 1649 and another his throne to a Dutch Protestant in 1688.

The English colonization of North America in the seventeenth century provided a new theater for playing out these tensions. On June 30, 1632, King Charles I granted Cecil Calvert, second baron of Baltimore, a charter for an American colony which eventually came to be called Maryland, named for the king's Spanish wife. In November 1633 the *Ark* and *Dove* pulled out of London down the Thames and, after taking on additional passengers at the Isle of Wight, sailed west toward the New World. Lord Baltimore's directive to the first settlers established the tenor of religious toleration in the new colony. Baltimore instructed Catholics on the expedition to "suffer no scandall nor offense to be given to any of the Protestants" and to "be silent upon all occasions of discourse concerning matters of Religion."[1]

Several historians, among them most notably John D. Krugler, have offered insights into the English background of the Calverts in general and their religious and political views in particular. Krugler's "Calvert Family, Catholicism, and Court Politics" examines in general the English political background for the colonization of Maryland. "'Face of a Protestant'" considers the political career of George Calvert, the first Lord Baltimore, and illustrates the difficulties of a Catholic in early Stuart England. In 1625 Calvert stepped down as one of the principal secretaries of state and declared publicly his allegiance to Roman Catholicism. The relationship between Calvert's resignation and his resolve to form a colony devoted to religious freedom has engaged Krugler's attention in "Sir George Calvert's Resignation." After reviewing various interpretations, Krugler concludes that Calvert resigned more for political than religious reasons.

Krugler finds that the priority of pragmatic considerations over religious idealism also extended to the Maryland enterprise itself. In "Lord Baltimore, Roman Catholics, and Toleration," Krugler insists that Cecil Calvert, while not entirely indifferent to religion, "was not involved in founding a Catholic refuge as such. At no time did he ever put the interests of the Catholic Church above the interests of his colony. Uppermost in his mind was the establishment of a colony that would return some dividend on the family investment" (p. 75). In his essay "'With Promise of Liberty in Religion,'" Krugler reviews the contrasting historiographical interpretations of Maryland's past. The first school credited the Calverts with founding religious liberty in the New World because of their own ill treatment back in England. The contrasting interpretation held that toleration in Maryland grew not out of conviction, but of expediency. Finding both views inadequate, Krugler suggests that the Calverts' scheme "was based on gaining the loyalty of Marylanders of differing religious affiliations and tying them to the proprietary government" (p. 39). The growth of anti-Catholicism over the course of the seventeenth century, however, foiled the plan. Nevertheless, Krugler characterizes the Calvert experiment as "daring and resourceful," and finds that the proprietors' "efforts to implement religious toleration cannot be diminished by its ultimate failure, for they pointed to the future" (p. 39).

"The Catholic Contribution to Religious Liberty" by J. Moss Ives also treats the English career of George Calvert, although the author devotes the preponderance of his argument to Catholicism in the New World. Ives celebrates the modernity of Maryland under Catholic rule—its broad franchise, its simple law code—and attributes these to religious liberty because, in Ives's words, "religious liberty is the parent of civil liberty" (p. 289). Even the 1649 Act of Toleration, which legislated severe penalties for blasphemy against the Holy Trinity, Ives contends, was a concession to the growing number of zealous Protestants and did not substantially blemish the colony's religious liberty. Ives's larger work, *The Ark and the Dove*, emphasizes the radical mission of Maryland's founders. Whereas the *Mayflower* crossed the Atlantic heavily laden with Old World ideology, with fairly traditional notions about the relation of church and state, the voyage of the *Ark* and the *Dove*, with the commitment of its passengers to religious freedom, "was quite without precedent in the history of the Christian era" (p. vi).

Indeed, of all the English colonies Maryland proved perhaps the most tolerant of religious diversity, a fact not lost on historians, especially Roman Catholic historians who have openly admired the farsightedness of Maryland's founder. In "Maryland and the Controversies as to Her Early History," John Gilmary Shea reviews the nineteenth-century views of Maryland's religious policies and concludes that the interpretations that exalt Catholics for their modernity and liberality "have been triumphantly established" (p. 677). Thomas O'Brien Hanley's rather whiggish contributions to this genre include *Their Rights and Liberties* and "Church and State in the Maryland Ordinance," which examines the 1639 legislative measure that codified Baltimore's toleration policies and provided a precedent for the Toleration Act of 1649.

R. J. Lahey pursues a somewhat different tack in "The Role of Religion in Lord Baltimore's Colonial Enterprise." Lahey examines Sir George Calvert's earlier attempts to settle a colony in Newfoundland and finds that, although Baltimore tried to fashion a haven for Catholicism, he accepted "the practice of more than one expression of Christianity under the same civil government" and thereby took "one of the first positive steps in the English speaking world towards recognition of the individual's right freely and openly to profess his religious beliefs" (p. 511). While Lahey stresses Baltimore's role in obviating the post-Reformation dictum *cuius regio, eius religio*, others have emphasized the modernity of Maryland's toleration. Arthur Pierce Middleton has argued in "Toleration and the Established Church" that the Calverts' vision of religious freedom was ill-suited to the theological temper of the seventeenth century; it was an idea before its time. Especially in the early part of this century historians of Maryland pointed to the colony's religious policies as roughly parallel to those in Rhode Island and as harbingers of the formulation later embodied in the Constitution that sought to disengage religious institutions and civil government. Examples of this argument include George Petrie's "Church and State in Early Maryland" and William T. Russell's *Land of Sanctuary*. In "Separation of Church and State in Early Maryland," Matthew Page Andrews writes that in proprietary Maryland "there is no record of any proscription or persecution because of any religious belief, or lack of belief" (p. 175).

Dennis M. Moran's account of the developments in seventeenth-century Maryland emphasizes the interrelation of colonial and British politics. In "Anti-Catholicism in Early Maryland Politics: The Puritan Influence," Moran traces the first disruption of religious toleration in Maryland to Ingle's rebellion in 1645 (see also "Richard Ingle in Maryland" by Henry F. Thompson). Richard Ingle, an English mariner and outspoken Puritan, seized the capital city of St. Mary's, plundered Catholic households, and sent many Catholics into exile. Although the proprietary party regained control the next year, Ingle's insurrection fed sentiments back in England for a Protestant magistrate. The clamor for Protestant rule prompted Cecil Calvert to appoint William Stone, a Protestant, as governor in 1648. Moran finds that "Protestant intolerance was growing in the colony as Puritan political power grew in England" (p. 147). This surge of Puritan activity resulted in the exclusion of Catholics from office in 1654, the deprivation of religious freedom for virtually everyone but the Puritans, and attempts to deprive Cecil Calvert of his charter.

Indeed, demographic changes lay behind much of the turmoil. By the mid-seventeenth century the halcyon days of religious toleration in Maryland were threatened by the arrival of non-Catholic immigrants; as the century wore on, George B. Scriven notes in "Religious Affiliation in Seventeenth Century Maryland," Catholics quickly faded into a minority. In " 'God's Candle' within Government," David W. Jordan shows that Quakers participated actively—and cooperatively—in the colonial government, and, according to Kenneth L. Carroll's "Quaker Opposition," they joined with Catholics in opposing religious establishment.

Maryland's 1649 Act of Toleration, which provided religious freedom to all forms of trinitarian Christianity, suffered a mortal blow when news of England's Glorious Revolution reached the colony. Anglicans, as Lawrence C. Wroth illustrates in "The First Sixty Years of the Church of England in Maryland," had been present from the beginning and had steadily chipped away at the influence of the Catholic proprietary government.

The wave of anti-Catholicism emanating from the Glorious Revolution, as Lois Green Carr and David Jordan point out in *Maryland's Revolution of Government*, provided the immediate catalyst for rebellion in 1689. Richard A. Gleissner ("Religious Causes of the Glorious Revolution") believes that religion provided only a pretext for John Coode and the Protestant Associators to harass Catholics, deprive them of their political rights, and drive many of them into exile. The Settlement of 1691, John H. Seabrook shows in

"The Establishment of Anglicanism" and Spencer Ervin recounts in "The
Established Church of Colonial Maryland," excluded Catholics from political
office, established the Church of England, and imposed a tax on all free-
holders to support the established religion. Even Protestants found this English rule arbitrary and highhanded; many joined with Catholics in opposing
it, and Don Manuel Coloma, Spain's ambassador to England, petitioned the
English crown on behalf of Maryland's Catholics (see David Jordan, "Plea for
Maryland Catholics"). In "Anti-Catholicism in Early Maryland Politics: The
Protestant Revolution," Dennis Moran continues the saga of Catholic difficulties begun in his study of the Puritan influence in seventeenth-century Maryland. Once the Glorious Revolution in England made Maryland a royal
province in 1691 and paved the way for Anglican establishment, Maryland's
tradition of religious freedom finally was eclipsed. "The Calverts had not only
lost control of their colony," Moran writes, "but they had seen the liberal
religious laws of Maryland supplanted by the narrowness of English religious
policy" (p. 236).

Anglicans quickly set about the task of fashioning their own political
hegemony, an undertaking augmented considerably by the formation of the
Society for the Propagation of the Gospel in Foreign Parts. In 1696 Anglicans
founded King William's School with the support of public taxes (see Charlotte Fletcher, "King William's School"). But the taproots of Anglicanism in
Maryland politics reached far deeper than that. Gerald E. Hartdagen's considerable research into Maryland vestries shows that these ecclesiastical bodies
in Maryland's thirty parishes actually assumed many of the functions of
government. His article "The Vestry as a Unit of Local Government" and Alan
L. Clem's "Vestries and Local Government" detail the vestries' wide powers
in the administration of secular affairs: collection of taxes, keeping parish
records, operating Maryland's tobacco economy.

For nearly a century, until the American Revolution, Anglicanism retained
its political ascendency in Maryland, and the Catholic minority, Thomas
O'Brien Hanley shows in "Catholic and Anglican Gentry," had little choice
but to cooperate. But Hanley also contends that the Catholic gentry worked
subtly to reverse the religious intolerance brought on by the Glorious Revolution. Indeed, the Catholics had grievances to avenge. According to "Eighteenth-Century Suffrage" by Thornton Anderson, Catholics struggled in vain
for voting privileges accorded other religious groups. Suspicions about Catholics, Timothy W. Bosworth argues in "Anti-Catholicism as a Political
Tool," fed on paranoia coming from England and added to the volatility of
colonial politics. Fear of the French, especially during the Seven Years War,
according to Bosworth, further animated anti-Catholic sentiments, an assertion supported by "Maryland's Fear of Insurrection" by Mark J. Stegmaier.

The Church of England itself, by its established status and the benefits it

enjoyed from general taxation, goaded many non-Anglicans into rebellion
during the Revolutionary era (see Nelson Rightmyer, "Anglican Church in
Maryland" and Anne Y. Zimmer, "'Paper War' in Maryland"). In *Charles
Carroll of Carrollton*, Thomas O'Brien Hanley offers an almost hagiographi-
cal account of one Catholic's decision to join the Patriot cause, a story
continued in Hanley's *Revolutionary Statesman* and in *Charles Carroll of
Carrollton* by Ellen Hart Smith.

Hanley's *American Revolution and Religion* discusses the church-state
issue during the Revolution and says that "the American Revolutionary War
brought an era of religious growth and vitality in Maryland." Hanley exults in
the emergence of what he calls a "Christian state" in Maryland, a product, it
seems, of Anglican disestablishment and the fact that, in the author's words,
"religious life was better" (p. 3). John Corbin Rainbolt's "Struggle to Define
'Religious Liberty'" traces the final process of disestablishing religion in
colonial Maryland, a cause abetted by such unlikely bedfellows as John Carroll, archbishop of Baltimore, and Jonathan Boucher, an Anglican clergyman
and erstwhile Loyalist. Indeed, as the case of Jonathan Boucher illustrates
(see Michael D. Clark, "Jonathan Boucher and Toleration"), many Anglicans,
in fact, welcomed disestablishment. Arthur Pierce Middleton's "Daughter
Church to Sister Church" describes the transition following the disestablishment of the Church of England after the Revolution and the dislocations this
caused. Anglican laymen supported disestablishment, Middleton suggests,
because it afforded the opportunity to distance their church from the un-
popular policies of England and allowed the Anglican denizens of Maryland
greater control over ecclesiastical affairs. The formation of a Maryland diocese in the 1780s reorganized the Episcopalians independently of public
support and autonomously within the Anglican communion.

The 350th anniversary of Maryland's founding has prompted reviews of the
colony's checkered history of religious toleration. In "Maryland's Toleration
Act," Carl N. Everstine praises the 1649 measure as a "notable piece of
legislation and a commendable accomplishment," but he tempers his ap-
proval somewhat by pointing out the political realities that forced the bill and
the outright intolerance of the ensuing decades (p. 114). Maxine N. Lurie's
"Theory and Practice of Religious Toleration" also remarks on the difficulties
brought about by religious diversity in the seventeenth-century colonies. Religion divided people more often than it united them, Lurie concludes, no
matter how noble the ideals of the proprietors.

At least two Catholic scholars, James Hennesey and John Courtney Murray, have tried to place the Catholic experience in the New World against the
background of European church-state relations. In *We Hold These Truths*,
Murray argues that the American situation was unique because "pluralism

was the native condition of American society," not the result of a shattered consensus, as in Europe and England (p. x). Such singularity called for a new proposition, one that came to be embodied in the Constitution. But Murray also stresses the antecedents found in the free-exercise provision in English common law, the natural law tradition, and in the institutional discreteness of church and state, the two kingdoms, during the Middle Ages. Hennesey's essay, "Roman Catholicism: The Maryland Tradition," more firmly anchored in the Maryland experience, also recalls medieval traditions, but this time in an attempt to explain the motivations of Maryland's founders. Hennesey does not find strong theoretical underpinnings in their thought, but he attributes the colony's early religious policies to the influence of the Anglo-American environment on Catholicism. This environment, he argues, prompted Catholics to accommodate to religious pluralism and thereby abandon the "unitary medieval image" that asserted the subservience of the state to the church.

NEW JERSEY

New Jersey's polyglot composition and its notorious lack of comity set it apart even from the rest of the Middle Colonies. Divided into East and West Jersey and ruled by proprietors after the English Conquest of 1664, the two regions united as a royal colony in 1702 under the governorship of Lord Cornbury.

Even in its history prior to English rule, issues of church and state assumed some importance. Donald Einar Bjarnson's "Swedish-Finnish Settlement in New Jersey" recounts the career of Lars Tolstadius, a young dissident minister who arrived from Sweden in 1702 to challenge the hierarchy of the Swedish Lutheran Church. Tolstadius proceeded to form his own parish in Raccoon, New Jersey, amidst the outraged denunciations of Swedish ecclesiastical authorities both in Uppsala, Sweden, and in the New World.

Another exceedingly strong religious group in colonial New Jersey, the Quakers, exerted considerable political influence. Arthur Zilversmit's "Liberty and Property" traces the early movements of abolitionism in New Jersey and the impact of Quakers in the legislature. In "'Quaker' Politics," Larry R. Gerlach describes the divisive character of eighteenth-century politics in New Jersey by examining a document purporting to coordinate political strategy among Quakers in 1772. Gerlach asserts that Quakers remained a force in New Jersey politics for as long as they did because of the colony's factionalism. (On the political divisiveness in New Jersey, see John R. McCreary, "Governors, Politicians, and the Sources of Instability.").

When the English took over the Jerseys, Anglicanism was virtually nonexistent; but the consolidation of East and West Jersey under royal government, coincident with the formation of the Society for the Propagation of the Gospel, led to attempts on the part of young and zealous Anglican clergy to secure a favored legal standing with the new authorities. Some of the central figures in the Anglicans' early attempts to establish a foothold in New Jersey include John Talbot, Thorowgood Moore, George Keith (see Ethyn Williams Kirby, *George Keith;* Charles Smith Lewis, "George Keith, the Missionary"), and Governor Cornbury himself. Wallace N. Jamison's *Religion in New Jersey* and Leonard J. Trinterud's *Forming of an American Tradition* review the travail of Francis Makemie, a Presbyterian minister who was arrested, tried, and eventually acquitted on Cornbury's charge of preaching without a license. Despite his incessant attempts to establish the Church of England, the mercurial Cornbury occasionally turned his wrath upon fellow Anglicans. According to Gordon Turner in "Church-State Relationships in Early New Jersey" (which, regrettably, lacks historical documentation), one early breach of church-state separation occurred when Thorowgood Moore, Anglican rector at Burlington, censured Cornbury for his corruptions, whereupon the governor had Moore arrested.

Nelson R. Burr's *Anglican Church in New Jersey* and his article, "New Jersey: An Anglican Venture" outline the history of Anglicanism in the colony from 1664 into the twentieth century. Burr argues that the seventeenth-century Jersey proprietors granted religious liberty and the privileges of self-government in order to attract tenants. The formation of the royal colony in 1702, then, offered negligible support for the Anglicans who, according to Lewis Morris writing in 1700, numbered not more than a dozen in the entire colony. Burr then recounts the rise of the Church of England in the eighteenth century (through the efforts of George Keith and others) as well as its crisis during the Revolutionary Period. On the issue of a colonial bishop, New Jersey Anglicans, Burr says, "were in the front line of the battle to establish an American diocese" ("Anglican Venture," p. 12).

The role of the College of New Jersey in the church-state question concerns Alison B. Olson in "The Founding of Princeton University." Olson sees the school's origins "as a chapter in New Jersey's political history, for the College was deeply involved in provincial politics during the first years after its creation" (p. 133). Contemporary political disputes, Olson maintains, pitted the Anglican East Jersey proprietors against the "Presbyterian interest" of Elizabeth and Newark liberals. Princeton's first two presidents, Jonathan Dickinson and Aaron Burr, were champions of the Newark and Elizabeth settlers and bitter opponents of the proprietary party. In *Princeton, 1746–1896,* Thomas Jefferson Wertenbaker points out the college's role, and particularly that of John Witherspoon, in the move toward independence, in the Revolution, and in the providing of statesmen for the new nation. Witherspoon's part in the Patriot cause is discussed in "John Witherspoon as Sage" by L. Gordon Tait. The matter receives fuller treatment in the first volume of Varnum Lansing Collins's biography, *President Witherspoon*, and in Martha Lou Lemmon Stohlman's *John Witherspoon*.

Trinterud's *Forming of an American Tradition*, published in 1949, remains the best history of colonial Presbyterianism. The latter half of the book addresses the threat of an American episcopate and the role of Presbyterians in the American Revolution and beyond. While united in their opposition to an American bishop, the Presbyterians were divided in their allegiance to the Revolution, although the Patriot group, led by Witherspoon, was the more numerous. (According to Howard Miller's "Grammar of Liberty," Presbyterians also divided on the matter of constitutions.) After the Revolution, Trinterud argues, Presbyterians abandoned their animus against other religious traditions, especially Anglicanism, in favor of, in the words of a contemporary Presbyterian document, "a high respect for the other Protestant Churches of the Country, though several of them differ from her [Presbyterianism] in some forms of government and modes of Worship" (p. 278).

The correlation between Evangelicals during the Great Awakening and Patriots during the American Revolution has received a great deal of attention in the recent historiography, especially in New England. Indeed, George H. Ingram's "Presbytery of New Brunswick" emphasizes the pivotal role of revivalists in the Revolutionary cause. The Baptists, too, according to Norman H. Maring's *Baptists in New Jersey*, generally lined up with the Patriots. "Francis Alison and John Witherspoon" by James L. McAllister Jr., however, serves as a reminder of the perils of such generalizations. Both Alison and Witherspoon—Old Side and New Side Presbyterians, respectively—supported the Revolutionary cause. (Alison, moreover, according to McAllister, recognized the civil threat inherent in an American bishop.) Mark A. Noll's "Observations on the Reconciliation of Politics and Religion in Revolutionary New Jersey" takes a different tack in exploring the connection between Evangelical and Patriot. Looking at the career of Jacob Green, a New Side Presbyterian, Noll recounts Green's many efforts on behalf of the Revolutionary cause but says that it was "not in a translation of religious into political views that his theology played a central role but rather in an application of his Christian beliefs themselves to social problems in the colonies" (p. 225). The ground of Green's activity in the Revolutionary era, then, lay in Edwardsean rather than whig ideology.

How did New Jersey come to toleration as the formula for relations of church and state? The best explanation seems to be, simply, that no one religion came anywhere close to hegemony or to mustering the political power necessary to win establishment status. Toleration, therefore, was merely a concession to the colony's diversity. Edward J. Cody in "The Growth of Toleration and Church-State Relations in New Jersey," however, attempts a different, more circuitous explanation. Cody reviews the different cases of Cornbury's meddling in the ecclesiastical affairs of Quakers, Presbyterians, and Anglicans, and refers to the early colonists' ideals of "religious purity," or religious homogeneity. He then goes on to argue that the Great Awakening gave New Jersey colonists assurance of God's blessing and assuaged their guilt about "ignoring the quest for denominational religious purity" (p. 57). At the same time, he says, the Awakening's emphasis on religious experience reduced sectarian hostility, because religion came increasingly to be viewed as a private matter, and an antiauthoritarian climate was born in the revival's tendency to transcend denominational barriers.

NEW YORK

Even as early as 1628, Jonas Michaelius, the first clergyman in New Netherland (New York), advocated a calculated distance between church and state in the newly founded colony. Writing to a friend in the Netherlands, Michaelius commented that although "political and ecclesiastical persons can greatly assist each other, nevertheless the matters and offices belonging together must not be mixed but kept separate, in order to prevent all confusion and disorder."[2] Michaelius's sentiments doubtless derived from the "two kingdoms" configuration of religion and politics back in the Netherlands. According to Douglas Nobbs, whose *Theocracy and Toleration* offers a detailed treatment of church-state relations in seventeenth-century Holland, "Calvinist theory had been clearly elaborated in favour of a church independent of political interference" (p. ix). Although the Netherlands configuration changed with the Arminian disputes as the century wore on, the two kingdoms theory provided the model for ecclesiastical and political relations in New Netherland. (This is not to say that the two realms never found themselves at odds; indeed, as Quirinus Breen narrates in "Dominie Everhardus Bogardus," a Dutch Reformed clergyman, Bogardus, and Willem Kieft, director-general of the colony, feuded bitterly.)

Although the Dutch West India Company maintained formally that the Dutch Reformed Church was the only religion tolerated in the colony, as early as 1638 the Company allowed that in matters of conscience "every man shall be free to live up to his own in peace and decorum." By 1663 Pieter Stuyvesant received word (as part of the official response to the Flushing Remonstrance of 1657) to "shut your eyes, at least not force people's consciences, but allow every one to have his own belief, as long as he behaves quietly and legally, gives no offense to his neighbors and does not oppose the government."[3]

This question of establishment religion in New Netherland has provoked some debate in the secondary literature. In "Guilders and Godliness," George L. Smith finds that the economic interests of the colony dictated religious policies. "Where a Reformed establishment did not interfere with the successful pursuit of economic profit," Smith writes, "the West India Company supported and sanctioned the Church, though it always claimed for itself the final say in ecclesiastical as well as civil matters in its colonies" (p. 28). Smith enlarges his argument in *Religion and Trade in New Netherland,* where he posits that a preoccupation with commerce in both the Netherlands and New Netherland made both Dutch societies tolerant of religious diversity, which in effect disestablished the Reformed religion. Such an interpretation sees New Netherland as the earliest harbinger of disestablishment. Historians have been slow to recognize this, Smith explains, for two reasons: the general historiographical neglect of New Netherland and the lack of any one figure, such as William Penn in Pennsylvania, Roger Williams in Rhode Island, or Cecil Calvert in Maryland, who stands out as the architect of such a policy.

Smith's interpretation conflicts with that of Frederick J. Zwierlein (*Religion in New Netherland* and "New Netherland Intolerance"). Zwierlein finds the Dutch exceedingly intolerant, but he fails to explain why, in the face of such intolerance, New Netherland harbored Jews, Catholics, Quakers, Mennonites, Lutherans, and Huguenots, among others, and allowed all of them freedom of religious expression.

The English Conquest of 1664 immediately altered the colony's political landscape and augured changes in its religious configuration. Edward T. Corwin's "Ecclesiastical Condition of New York" provides a general survey of ecclesiastical relations from the New Netherland period to the end of the seventeenth century. Thomas F. O'Connor and others have interpreted the duke of York's kindly treatment of Catholics (among whom he numbered himself) as evidence of a broad and general liberality in religious affairs. O'Connor's "Religious Toleration in New York" traces the history of church-state relations from the Conquest through the end of the century and attributes the relative toleration the English granted in the early years to their magnanimity.

Such a generous construction, however, belies the fact that the English realized they were badly outnumbered in the colony by other ethnic groups, especially the Dutch, and it fails to account for English actions in the Van Rensselaer affair. Nicholas Van Rensselaer, a renegade Dutchman who held Anglican orders, arrived in New York in 1675 with instructions from the Catholic duke of York to Governor Edmund Andros to place him in a Dutch church. Andros assigned the young minister to the Dutch Reformed church at Albany, even though Albany already had a minister. Such a procedure violated both Reformed polity and the ecclesiastical autonomy guaranteed by the Articles of Capitulation signed by the Dutch at their surrender in 1664. The action aroused the opposition of several Dutch ministers and also raised the ire of Jacob Leisler and Jacob Milborne (see Lawrence H. Leder, "Unorthodox Dominie" and, for the broader context, Robert C. Ritchie, *The Duke's Province*). The event doubtless fueled Leisler's suspicions of English rule, suspicions that erupted into open rebellion in 1689 with news of the Glorious Revolution back in England.

A considerably less subtle assault on non-Anglican religions followed quickly on the heels of Leisler's Rebellion and the restoration of English rule. Governor Benjamin Fletcher, acting on instructions from London, sought from the Assembly a bill that provided for the maintenance of an Anglican minister in New York City and the surrounding counties. After some temporizing, the Assembly passed the Ministry Act in 1693, which, in Fletcher's judgment, established the Church of England. The bill's language was sufficiently vague, however, to invite several "dissenting" congregations to appropriate the public funds to support non-Anglican clergy, and the bill never achieved the effects that Fletcher had envisioned. R. Townsend Henshaw's "The New York Ministry Act" examines the bill itself and the circumstances surrounding its passage. Perhaps the best treatment of the Ministry Act in particular and Anglican attempts at establishment in general is Cynthia A. Kierner's "A Concept Rejected." Kierner sets the Ministry Act in New York against the background of English politics and attributes its ultimate failure to several causes: the colonial church's inability to fulfill the same social functions as the church in England, its utter dependence upon royal magistrates and the Society for the Propagation of the Gospel, and New York's religious heterogeneity.

In "The Vestry in the Middle Colonies," Borden W. Painter suggests that the failure of the Anglicans to secure full establishment provided the basis for stronger lay leadership. The vestries in the Middle Colonies, he finds, "really had more freedom than those in Maryland and Virginia where the Church was established by law. They did not have to worry about interference from the government, and their charters gave them a clear legal authority which left them free to work out their own problems" (p. 36).

For New York, at least, Painter may be overstating the case. The success of Anglicanism in the colony in the early decades of the eighteenth century had much to do with the beneficence of successive English governors and the arrival of missionaries from the Society for the Propagation of the Gospel. Indeed, the formation of the Society in 1701 (see Samuel Clyde McCulloch,

"Foundation and Early Work") transpired with the blessings of the English crown, and its success relied in great measure upon the cooperation of colonial magistrates. E. Clowes Chorley's "The Beginnings of the Church in the Province of New York" recounts the early history of Anglicanism in the colony, especially the efforts of various governors on behalf of the Church of England.

Of all the colonial governors in New York, none was more relentless in his attempts to favor Anglicanism and in his hectoring of non-Anglican religions than Edward Hyde, Lord Cornbury, who served concurrently as governor of New Jersey. Cornbury, who frequently dressed as a woman and paraded through the streets of New York, has often been dismissed as a buffoon. But such an interpretation overlooks his determined and often ingenious strategies for promoting the Church of England. During Cornbury's administration several measures were enacted that enhanced the legal standing of Anglicanism. But the Church of England's sallies met with the most success among religious traditions that were already weakened in one way or another. The French Huguenots, to cite one prominent example, lacked any Old World base or effective clerical leadership (see William A. Bultmann, "S.P.G. and the French Huguenots"; Robert M. Kingdon, "Why Did the Huguenot Refugees in the American Colonies Become Episcopalian?"; Jon Butler, *Huguenots in America*). The state-supported S.P.G. stepped in and provided them with schools and clergy as well as an opportunity to assimilate into the dominant colonial culture. The Dutch met a similar fate. In "The Episcopal Church and the Dutch" Nelson R. Burr reviews the effects of English rule on the Dutch, the battles of Reformed churchmen against Anglican attempts at establishment, and the divisions that opened in the Dutch church over its posture toward the Church of England. As the eighteenth century wore on, Anglicanism became a retreat for many of the more conservative Reformed church members.

Cornbury's venality and his meddling in colonial ecclesiastical affairs eventually cost him his office; virtually no one regretted his departure, not even fellow Anglicans, who recognized that his antics and high-handedness had undermined the Church of England's credibility. But when Robert Hunter, a successor, tried to modulate the intensive political efforts to promote the Church of England, he found himself at odds with prominent Anglicans, notably William Vesey, rector of Trinity Church (see Alison Gilbert Olson, "Governor Robert Hunter and the Anglican Church in New York"; Lawrence H. Leder, "Robert Hunter's *Androboros*").

As the eighteenth century wore on, the Church of England increasingly became identified with Britain's metropolitan policies. As in other colonies, much of the agitation centered around speculation about the crown's intentions to establish an American episcopate. On the attempts to locate an Anglican bishop in the American colonies and the opposition such a plan engendered, see Arthur Lyon Cross, *The Anglican Episcopate* and Jordan D. Fiore, "Jonathan Swift and the American Episcopate." Non-Anglicans especially opposed such a move as a threat to religious liberties, although, as Frederick V. Mills demonstrates in "The Internal Anglican Controversy," many Anglicans also harbored reservations.

The controversy over the threat of an Anglican establishment reached its apogee in the eighteenth century over the founding of King's College. *From King's College to Columbia* by David C. Humphrey and "Samuel Johnson and the Founding of King's College" by Don R. Gerlach and George E. DeMille review the origins of the college, including the heated dispute between the so-called Anglican and Presbyterian parties. The Presbyterians, who opposed the use of public funds to support an Anglican school, were led by a Dutchman-turned-Presbyterian, William Livingston, who published several treatises in *The Independent Reflector.* John M. Mulder's "William Livingston" recounts Livingston's career and his role in the King's College controversy as well as his opposition to an Anglican bishop in the American colonies. Livingston condemned all established churches as "the most fatal engine ever invented by satan for promoting human wretchedness" (p. 100). Milton M. Klein, among others, has recognized in Livingston a major theorist of the doctrine of church-state separation. Klein's "Church, State, and Education" argues that Presbyterian opposition—and particularly that of Livingston—to an Anglican college and their support for public financing of education was "strikingly original and remarkably liberal" (p. 301). Although Livingston's ideas met with immediate failure in the establishment of King's College in 1754 under Anglican auspices, they were eventually vindicated in the formation of the University of the State of New York after the American Revolution.

The King's College dispute engendered bitternesses that extended into the Revolutionary period. "The Whigs of Colonial New York" by Charles H. Levermore asserts that the animosities between Anglicans and Presbyterians that erupted in the middle of the eighteenth century grew out of Anglican attempts at establishment earlier in the century and their continued political imperiousness. More recently, James S. Olson's article, "The New York Assembly, the Politics of Religion, and the Origins of the American Revolution," traces the evolution of the religious issues and parties of the 1750s and 1760s into the political disputes that fueled the Revolution.

An article by David L. Holmes, "The Episcopal Church and the American Revolution," surveys the condition of Anglicanism before the Revolution, reviews the reasons for Anglican affiliations on both sides (although most sided with the Loyalists), and assesses the ecclesiastical damage to Anglicanism in the wake of the Revolution. Holmes credits the Patriot clergy, admittedly a minority, with recognizing "that Oaths, liturgies, even governments are lesser things than the commission of Christ, and that the Church of God can exist faithfully and separately without formal connection with the government of a particular nation" (p. 288). In "The Role of the Anglicans in the American Revolution," William Warren Sweet seeks to reconcile two seemingly contradictory facts: not only did the Church of England contribute the largest proportion of Loyalists, but it also contributed the largest proportion of signatories to the Declaration of Independence. The Anglicans divided, he decides, because "they possessed no over-all organization such as the Presbyterians had in their Synods and Presbyteries, or as the Congregationalists or Baptists possessed in their Associations" (p. 69). Independence finally provided the opportunity to build a more cohesive, indigenous organization.

Other works that address religion in the Revolutionary era include Alice P. Kenney, *Stubborn for Liberty*, George De Vries, "The Dutch in the American Revolution," and John W. Beardslee's "Dutch Reformed Church and the American Revolution." Beardslee focuses on the history of the Dutch Reformed church from Leisler's Rebellion to the Great Awakening in an effort to account for the deep divisions between Loyalist and Patriot during the Revolution. He concludes that Dutch revivalists during the Awakening tended toward the Patriot cause, while opponents of the revival favored the Loyalists. Kenney's *Stubborn for Liberty* underlines Dutch contributions to American culture and to the Revolutionary cause, and George De Vries expends a great deal of energy filtering the Dutch experience during the Revolution through his own Calvinistic scruples. Although he offers no evidence to support his assertions, De Vries accuses Dutch Patriots of deriving their religious justification for revolution "from English Puritanism with its messianic view of America and its emphasis on the laws of God in human society, interpreted in covenantal terms" (p. 52).

Several historians have attempted broad and synthetic interpretations of colonial New York with special attention to the church-state theme. Carl Bridenbaugh's *Mitre and Sceptre* plots the various forays of Anglicanism into the colonies, the resistance it encountered, and the independence of church from state hammered out in the Revolutionary period. Several chapters detail the ecclesiastical-political struggle in the Middle Colonies, a struggle waged fiercely by New Side Presbyterians, principally William Livingston. Only the constitution of 1777, Bridenbaugh says, fully repudiated the Ministry Act of 1693. In "New York in the American Colonies," Milton Klein, who judges the Ministry Act an utter failure, argues that religious toleration in New York, from the Flushing Remonstrance of 1657 to the Articles of Capitulation at the English conquest to the Duke's Laws, was a pragmatic response on the part of first the Dutch and then the English to the colony's diversity. In its reluctant accommodation to religious pluralism, Klein argues, colonial New York anticipated the American solution of free exercise embodied in the First Amendment.

Finally, John Webb Pratt's *Religion, Politics, and Diversity*, which extends the analysis through the nineteenth century, argues that the roots of religious freedom and separation of church and state "ran far back into New York's colonial past" (p. 1). Pratt finds a benign toleration in New Netherland but then subtitles his treatment of the years 1664–1701 "The Roots of Religious Liberty," ignoring altogether the Van Rensselaer ordeal and minimizing the Ministry Act of 1693. The failure of Anglicans to win establishment status in the eighteenth century, Pratt says, was due to the Church of England's weakness and lack of popular appeal as well as its "close identification with the policies and practices of the English crown" (p. 78). The state constitution of 1777 accommodated New York's long tradition of religious diversity, even though it limited somewhat the religious freedom of Roman Catholics by imposing an anti-Catholic naturalization oath.

PENNSYLVANIA

The very nature and ambitions of William Penn's "holy experiment" in the American colonies set it apart from other colonial ventures. Penn envisioned a society founded upon religious principles and yet tolerant of religious diversity. Pennsylvania would be governed, moreover, by the pariahs of English society, the Society of Friends, better known as Quakers, who eschewed violence. This unique configuration of church and state has attracted a great deal of historical attention. From their confident beginnings in 1681 to their formal withdrawal from colonial government in 1756, Quakers tried to come to terms with governing a diverse colony while adhering to strict religious scruples. In the end, of course, they failed to harmonize the two, but along the way they strove gamely to attain the precarious balance that finally eluded them.

Several historians have focused on the founding and early years of the "holy experiment." Fulmer Mood's "William Penn and English Politics" underscores the king's political motives in granting Penn's charter. In "Religious Liberty in Early Pennsylvania," J. William Frost argues that Penn's own experience in England prompted his desire for religious liberty in the New World, but that in the course of early settlement "a non-coercive Quaker establishment" actually emerged (p. 449). With the influx of other religious groups and nationalities into the colony, Frost says, Quakers came to accept limitations on their political authority, and the "Pennsylvania pattern" eventually became a model for the new nation. *Quakers and Politics* by Gary B. Nash, perhaps the best work on early Pennsylvania, chronicles the search on the part of Friends for political stability.

Controversy came early to Pennsylvania, with the first visitation taking the form of George Keith. Keith, a sort of religious journeyman and at that time a Quaker, questioned the propriety of Friends holding political office. His movement for pietistic vitality among the Quakers represented a thinly veiled challenge to Friends in political power and touched off what became known as the Keithian Schism. Jon Butler's work on Keith and his "Christian Quakers" ("'Gospel Order Improved'" and "Into Pennsylvania's Spiritual Abyss") demonstrates the interaction of religious and political themes.

Although the Quakers sought determinedly to maintain friendly relations with the Indians, the encroachment of settlers onto Indian lands together with imperial machinations led Pennsylvania into colonial wars and the Quakers to a crisis of conscience. The government's equivocal response to frontier bellicosity, moreover, prompted political maneuverings. The colonial crisis occasioned by King George's War in the 1730s, Alan Tully contends in "King George's War and the Quakers," realigned Pennsylvania politics and identified the Quaker party with popular rights and legislative privilege. In "The Philadelphia Election Riot of 1742," Norman S. Cohen narrates another episode in the increasingly heated dispute between the Quaker and Proprietary parties.

Jack D. Marietta's "Conscience, the Quaker Community, and the French and Indian War" examines the effects of the frontier war on the Quakers. The Society of Friends, Marietta finds, was buffeted by "struggle, acrimony, equivocation" because of internal divisions over their political and religious postures (p. 27). In "The Political Dilemma of the Quakers," Hermann Wellenreuther asserts that what divided the Quakers by the middle of the eighteenth century "was not that a number of Quakers gave up the peace testimony." Rather, Friends split over their interpretation of pacifism, whether or not support for the government violated the peace testimony. Ralph L. Ketcham's "Conscience, War, and Politics" examines the circumstances surrounding the final decision of Quakers in the Assembly to resign their seats in 1756 amidst the conflict between their pacifist consciences and the colony's military obligations. Ketcham concludes that these Friends "did not mean that they would sacrifice all to assure conduct of government according to religious principles; they meant rather that they would relinquish public office before they would endanger the vitality or unity of the Society of Friends" (p. 437).

Indeed, there are indications that the decision to quit government had salutary effects on Quaker piety. Manning Marable argues in "Death of the Quaker Slave Trade" that sanctions of Friends against their slave-trading brethren began in earnest only after the Quakers' withdrawal from colonial politics. In "A Look at the 'Quaker Revival of 1756,'" Kenneth L. Carroll contends that while the revival of piety and moral fervor among Quakers in 1756 may have been catalyzed by the decision to leave government, there had been signs of renewal and awakening many years earlier. This reawakening, nevertheless, "enabled American Quakerism to come through the intense crisis of the Revolution as a living and growing movement" (p. 80).

By the middle of the eighteenth century Presbyterians, Anglicans, and German groups had begun to influence colonial politics, and the intersection of religion and politics remained formidable. One such example concerns the College of Philadelphia. Several historians have examined the relationship between Benjamin Franklin and William Smith, provost of the College (see Ralph L. Ketcham, "Benjamin Franklin and William Smith: New Light on an Old Philadelphia Quarrel"; James H. Hutson, "Benjamin Franklin and William Smith: More Light on an Old Philadelphia Quarrel"; Bruce Richard Lively, "William Smith, the College and Academy of Philadelphia and Pennsylvania Politics"; Melvin H. Buxbaum, "Benjamin Franklin and William Smith: Their School and Their Dispute"). Although Franklin had supported Smith's appointment as provost, Smith soon became a propagandist for the Proprietary party and forced Franklin's ouster from the board of trustees. Far from fulfilling Franklin's original intent as an institution free from sectarian and political interests, the college had become, in Franklin's eyes, an engine for Proprietary interests against liberal Quaker rule.

In the winter of 1763–64 a band of unruly frontiersmen, aroused by the colony's inadequate provisions for defense against the Indians, stormed Philadelphia. In the ensuing riots many Quakers took up arms in self-defense against the backcountry malcontents, the majority of whom were Presbyterian. According to Robert F. Ulle in "Pacifists, Paxton, and Politics," unrest on the frontier had placed Quakers, Mennonites, and other peace churches on the defensive as Presbyterians and others justified the killings of Indians as a legitimate response on the part of frontiersmen left defenseless by a pacifist-dominated Assembly. In "March of the Paxton Boys," Brooke Hindle interprets the Paxton Riots primarily as a backcountry-versus-urban revolt, although he also acknowledges the religious dimension of the episode. Later studies have made more of religion in their interpretations. Peter A. Butzin argues in "Politics, Presbyterians and the Paxton Riots," that the political alignments during the uprising can best be understood in terms of religious affiliations. David Sloan examines the effects of the Paxton disturbances on the Society of Friends in " 'A Time of Sifting and Winnowing.' " The Riots prompted many Quakers to take up arms and triggered a great deal of soul-searching, Sloan says. This self-examination, however, prepared the Society for the Revolutionary era.

With the outbreak of hostilities at Lexington and Concord in 1775 many Quakers again questioned the pacifism of their faith, thus prompting another crisis within the Society of Friends. In the three counties of southeastern Pennsylvania, according to Kenneth A. Radbill in "Quaker Politics," the Society expelled over four hundred belligerent Quakers, many of whom became active participants in the struggle for independence. In "The Relation of the Quakers to the American Revolution," Arthur J. Mekeel reviews the questions of conscience—from military service to paying taxes to accepting colonial paper currency—faced by Quakers in the Revolutionary era. The Revolution severed the connection between British and Pennsylvania Quakers and, in Mekeel's words, "caused the final retirement by the Friends from any participation in political life wherever they had been formerly active" (p. 18). Those who remained true to Quaker principles often faced ostracism and reprisal. "Philadelphians in Exile" by Robert F. Oaks reviews the plight of Quakers during the war, with many forced into exile for refusing to take oaths of allegiance.

The Revolution "challenged the Quakers either to find a new role in American society or to accept a futile isolation from it," Sydney V. James argues in "The Impact of the American Revolution on Quakers' Ideas about Their Sect" (p. 360). Quakers tempered their isolationist tendencies during the Revolution and came to see that they "had to enter the life of the whole civil community" (p. 382). According to Jack Michel in "Philadelphia Quakers and the American Revolution," the movement for independence triggered the final abandonment of the "holy experiment" even as it prompted reform in the Philadelphia monthly meeting. "Until the war, Quaker interest was largely directed to the preservation of their power," Michel writes. "After it, social reforms—especially the abolition of slavery and the advocacy of temperance—were the principle public concerns of the meeting" (p. 54).

With the subtraction of Quakers from the political equation in Pennsylvania, government took a different form. Using quantitative methods, Wayne L. Bockelman and Owen S. Ireland document the realignment of political power in Pennsylvania as a result of the Revolution ("Internal Revolution in Pennsylvania"). Scotch-Irish Presbyterians, German Lutherans, and the Reformed displaced English and Welsh Quakers and Anglicans. In "The Anglican Clergy of Pennsylvania," Edgar Legare Pennington finds a cleavage within Anglicanism between the rural and the Philadelphia clergy. The rural clergy were Loyalist to a man, while the sentiments of the Philadelphians tended toward the Patriots. The author attributes the position of the latter to their lack of formal affiliation with the Society for the Propagation of the Gospel and to their direct accountability to local vestries. He explains the attitudes of the former as "the inability of clergymen of the Church of England to overcome the Erastian outlook upon their religion" (p. 429). Lutherans generally supported the Patriot cause (see David L. Scheidt, "The Lutherans in Revolutionary Philadelphia"), but the Mennonites, true to their pacifist tradition, sought to remain aloof from politics. According to Wilbur J. Bender's *Nonresistance in Colonial Pennsylvania,* Mennonites saw no reason for dissatisfaction with British rule, an interpretation corroborated in "Religion and Revolution" by Donald F. Durnbaugh. Although ostensibly neutral during the war, the Mennonites' posture had a pro-Loyalist cast that rendered them chary of accepting the new government.

Several historians have reached for broader interpretations of the church-state configuration in colonial Pennsylvania. Sydney V. James's *A People Among Peoples* and Frederick B. Tolles's *Meeting House and Counting House* both trace the Quaker reassessments of their mission in the New World. "Religious Freedom in the Constitutions" by John Casey recounts the history of religious toleration in Pennsylvania from William Penn's "Plan of Government" in 1681 through the constitution of 1790. Casey concludes that "the provisions regarding religious freedom in the present Constitution of Pennsylvania show to a marked degree the influence of the legislation prepared for his colony by William Penn" (p. 180). Jon Butler's *Power, Authority, and the Origins of the American Denominational Order* examines four Protestant groups in the Delaware Valley—Quakers, Baptists, Anglicans, and Presbyterians—between the colony's founding in 1681 and the Great Awakening. Butler finds that, contrary to prevailing views of American denominations as purveyors of nascent forms of democracy and lay leadership, churches in the Delaware Valley were dominated by strong ministers who transplanted English ecclesiastical institutions and sensibilities to the New World. These denominations, Butler concludes, "were largely oligarchic and hierarchical rather than democratic," but they nevertheless survived "because these non-democratic Old World institutions continually responded with creativity to the New World problems they faced" (p. 78).

In "Pacifism and the State in Colonial Pennsylvania," Guy Franklin Hershberger takes on the issue of religious nonresistance. After examining the various forms of pacifism, Hershberger contends that William Penn envisioned "an attempt to combine an uncompromising testimony of peace with an active political life" (p. 57). Penn's "holy experiment" failed, the author believes, not so much because of military concerns, but because "the practical demands of statecraft required methods so out of line with Quaker morals that the men in the provincial government of Pennsylvania could not be good Quakers and good politicians at the same time" (p. 73). "Quakers and Non-Violence in Pennsylvania" by Edwin B. Bronner emphasizes Penn's expectation that his colony, guided by Quaker peace principles and populated with a virtuous people, would avoid warfare. Bronner concludes that, from the very beginning, "Friends had to decide whether they would remain firm in their convictions or make small compromises with their principles in order to carry out their program for the colony. Pennsylvania existed in a world at war, and the Quakers were fortunate to be able to govern as long as they did in such an environment" (pp. 21–22).

DELAWARE

With some notable exceptions, the writing of Delaware's colonial history has devolved, by default, upon antiquarians rather than critical historians. Nevertheless, several topics relating to the church-state question emerge from a survey of the historiography. For a background of Delaware in the colonial period, John A. Munroe's *Colonial Delaware—A History* provides a useful point of departure as well as a good bibliography. Other general studies of particular seventeenth-century communities include *Swedish Settlements on the Delaware* by Amandus Johnson, "Quakers in Delaware" by Herbert Standing, and, of more limited value, "The City of Amsterdam's Colony on the Delaware" by C. A. Weslager. Sally Swartz's "Society and Culture in the Seventeenth-Century Delaware Valley" includes a brief discussion of the religious-political configurations through successive regimes.

Several historians have explored the relationship of the Lutheran church of New Sweden (Delaware) with, successively, Sweden, the Dutch, and the English. Johan Printz, governor of New Sweden from 1642 to 1653, jealously protected church interests, according to Nelson R. Burr in "The Early History of the Swedes and the Episcopal Church on the Delaware." Burr chronicles the Swedes' cooperation with and gradual assimilation to the Anglicans after the English Conquest of 1664, an account elaborated, parish by parish, in Joyce L. White's "Affiliation of Seven Swedish Lutheran Churches." Nelson Waite Rightmyer's "Swedish-English Relations" also reviews the cooperation of Swedish Lutherans and the Anglicans. Rightmyer suggests that the reasons for their alliance lay more in their common status as national churches and their Erastian principles than in their common episcopal polity. "The Swedish Church on the Delaware" by Conrad J. I. Bergendoff surveys the history of the Swedish Lutheran Church from the founding of the first New World settlement in 1638 through the Revolution. Even in the eighteenth century, although their political presence had long ago been eclipsed, the government of Sweden subsidized mission efforts in the New World. Finally, Grant W. Andresen's "The American Revolution and the Swedish Church in the Delaware Valley" reviews the difficulty the Swedish churches faced in maintaining their neutrality during the American Revolution. Andresen also charts the gradual Anglicization of the Swedes in the eighteenth century, which led to the severing of ties with the Swedish state church and the eventual assimilation with the Episcopalians.

In July 1663 an enigmatic figure named Pieter Corneliszoon Plockhoy arrived at Zwaanendael on the mouth of the Delaware to establish an exclusive, though non-sectarian community. In 1659, according to Irvin B. Horst in "Pieter Cornelisz Plockhoy: An Apostle of the Collegiants," Plockhoy had appealed to the Cromwellian government in England for universal toleration and freedom of religious expression and warned of the dangers of a state-church system. Plockhoy's appeal fell on deaf ears; nevertheless, Horst counts him as "one of the heralds of that religious freedom which modern nations accept and cherish" (p. 166). According to Leland Harder in "Plockhoy and His Settlement at Zwaanendael, 1663," the experimental community in the New World represented a challenge to the nominal Dutch Reformed establishment, although Plockhoy, as it turned out, had little time to test his ideals. Sir Robert Carr plundered the Zwaanendael settlement in 1664 in his quest to secure the Delaware region for the English crown.

Another question of church and state in colonial Delaware pertains to the establishment and the procurement of a charter for Newark Academy, an Old Side Presbyterian institution that was known in successive incarnations as the New London Academy, Newark Academy, Newark College, and Delaware College. Several articles explore the founding and early years of the Academy, including "The Colonial Origin of Newark Academy" by George Morgan, "Francis Alison, Colonial Educator" by Thomas Clinton Pears, Beverly McAnear's "The Charter of the Academy of Newark," and George H. Ryden's "The Newark Academy of Delaware in Colonial Days" and "The Relation of Newark Academy to the Presbyterian Church and to Higher Education in the American Colonies." John Munroe's short booklet, *Church vs. State*, provides the fullest treatment of the church-state issues surrounding the institution's early history, although most of the controversy begins in the years after the Revolution and extends into the nineteenth century.

As in all the colonies, the onset of the American Revolution in Delaware placed the matter of church and state into bold relief and often presented both churches and individuals with difficult and painful choices. Elizabeth Waterston's *Churches in Delaware During the Revolution* provides a comprehensive, if unsophisticated, overview of the postures of various religious traditions toward the Revolution. *The Anglican Church in Delaware* by

Nelson Rightmyer includes sections entitled "Support of the Clergy" and "Through Revolution to Independence." A brief article by Dorothy Colburn, " 'No More Passive Obedience and Non-Resistance,' " recounts the difficulties of an Anglican clergyman in Delaware, Philip Reading, during the Revolution. Similarly, "Francis Asbury and Thomas White" by James W. May addresses Asbury's plight in the Revolutionary era. The Methodist bishop took refuge in Delaware primarily because Thomas White, a Tory, sheltered him there, but also because Delaware did not require a test oath of the clergy.

NOTES

1. Clayton Colman Hall, ed., *Narratives of Early Maryland, 1633–1684* (New York: Charles Scribner's Sons, 1910), 16.

2. Edward T. Corwin, ed., *Ecclesiastical Records: State of New York*, 7 vols. (Albany: James B. Lyon, 1901–1916), 1:55.

3. *Ibid.*, 1:120, 530.

BIBLIOGRAPHY

MARYLAND

Anderson, Thornton. "Eighteenth-Century Suffrage: The Case of Maryland." _Maryland Historical Magazine_ 76 (Summer 1981), 141-158.

Andrews, Matthew Page. "Separation of Church and State in Maryland." _Catholic Historical Review_ 21 (July 1935), 164-176.

Beitzell, Edwin W. "St. Mary's County, Maryland, the 'Cradle of Catholicity.'" _Chronicles of St. Mary's_ 30 (October 1982), 489-490.

Bosworth, Timothy W. "Anti-Catholicism as a Political Tool in Mid-Eighteenth-Century Maryland." _Catholic Historical Review_ 61 (October 1975), 539-563.

Browne, William Hand, ed. _Archives of Maryland_. 32 vols. Baltimore: Maryland Historical Society, 1883-1912.

Carr, Lois Green. "Sources of Political Stability and Upheaval in Seventeenth-Century Maryland." _Maryland Historical Magazine_ 79 (Spring 1984), 44-70.

Carr, Lois Green, and Jordan, David W. _Maryland's Revolution of Government, 1689-1692_. Ithaca, N.Y.: Cornell University Press, 1974.

Carroll, John. _The John Carroll Papers_. Edited by Thomas O'Brien Hanley. 3 vols. Notre Dame, Ind.: University of Notre Dame Press, 1976.

Carroll, Kenneth L. "The Nicholites and Slavery in Eighteenth-Century Maryland." _Maryland Historical Magazine_ 79 (Summer 1984), 126-133.

Carroll, Kenneth L. "The Quaker Opposition to the
     Establishment of a State Church in Maryland." Maryland
     Historical Magazine 65 (Summer 1970), 149-170.

Clark, Michael D. "Jonathan Boucher and the Toleration of
     Roman Catholics in Maryland." Maryland Historical Magazine
     71 (Summer 1976), 194-204.

Clem, Alan L. "The Vestries and Local Government in Colonial
     Maryland." Historical Magazine of the Protestant Episcopal
     Church 31 (September 1962), 219-229.

Curran, Francis X. Catholics in Colonial Law. Chicago: Loyola
     University Press, 1963.

Cushing, John D., comp. The Laws of the Province of Maryland.
     Wilmington, Del.: Michael Glazier, 1978.

Deibert, William E. "Thomas Bacon, Colonial Clergyman."
     Maryland Historical Magazine 73 (Spring 1978), 79-86.

Ellis, John Tracy, ed. Documents of American Catholic History.
     rev. ed. 2 vols. Chicago: Henry Regnery, 1967.

Ervin, Spencer. "The Established Church of Colonial Maryland."
     Historical Magazine of the Protestant Episcopal Church 24
     (September 1955), 232-292.

Everstine, Carl N. The General Assembly of Maryland, 1634-
     1776. Charlottesville, Va.: Michie, 1980.

Everstine, Carl N. "Maryland's Toleration Act: An Appraisal."
     Maryland Historical Magazine 79 (Summer 1984), 99-116.

Falb, Susan Rosenfeld. "Proxy Voting in Early Maryland
     Assemblies." Maryland Historical Magazine 73 (Fall 1978),
     217-225.

Fletcher, Charlotte. "King William's School and the College of
     William and Mary." Maryland Historical Magazine 78 (Summer
     1983), 118-128.

Gleissner, Richard A. "Religious Causes of the Glorious
     Revolution in Maryland." Maryland Historical Magazine 64
     (Winter 1969), 327-341.

Gleissner, Richard A. "The Revolutionary Settlement of 1691 in
     Maryland." Maryland Historical Magazine 66 (Winter 1971),
     405-419.

Guilday, Peter. The Life and Times of John Carroll, Archbishop
     of Baltimore (1735-1815). 2 vols. New York: Encyclopedia
     Press, 1922.

Hall, Clayton Colman, ed. Narratives of Early Maryland, 1633-
1684. New York: Charles Scribner's Sons, 1910.

Hall, Michael G.; Leder, Lawrence H.; and Kammen, Michael G.,
eds. The Glorious Revolution in America: Documents on the
Colonial Crisis of 1689. Chapel Hill: University of North
Carolina Press, 1964.

Hanley, Thomas O'Brien. The American Revolution and Religion:
Maryland 1770-1800. Washington, D.C.: Catholic University
of America Press, 1971.

Hanley, Thomas O'Brien. "The Catholic and Anglican Gentry in
Maryland Politics." Historical Magazine of the Protestant
Episcopal Church 38 (June 1969), 143-151.

Hanley, Thomas O'Brien. Charles Carroll of Carrollton: The
Making of a Revolutionary Gentleman. rev. ed. Chicago:
Loyola University Press, 1982.

Hanley, Thomas O'Brien. "Church and State in the Maryland
Ordinance of 1639." Church History 26 (December 1957), 325-
341.

Hanley, Thomas O'Brien. Revolutionary Statesman: Charles
Carroll and the War. Chicago: Loyola University Press,
1983.

Hanley, Thomas O'Brien. Their Rights and Liberties: The
Beginnings of Religious and Political Freedom in Maryland.
Westminster, Md.: Newman Press, 1959.

Hartdagen, Gerald E. "The Anglican Vestry in Colonial
Maryland: Organizational Structure and Problems."
Historical Magazine of the Protestant Episcopal Church 38
(December 1969), 349-360.

Hartdagen, Gerald E. "The Anglican Vestry in Colonial
Maryland: A Study in Corporate Responsibility." Historical
Magazine of the Protestant Episcopal Church 40 (September
1971), 315-355; (December 1971), 461-479.

Hartdagen, Gerald E. "Vestry and Clergy in the Anglican Church
of Colonial Maryland." Historical Magazine of the
Protestant Episcopal Church 37 (December 1968), 371-396.

Hartdagen, Gerald E. "The Vestry as a Unit of Local Government
in Colonial Maryland." Maryland Historical Magazine 67
(Winter 1972), 363-388.

Hennesey, James. "Roman Catholicism: The Maryland Tradition."
Thought: A Review of Culture and Idea 51 (September 1976),
282-295.

Ives, J. Moss. <u>The Ark and the Dove: The Beginning of Civil and Religious Liberties in America</u>. New York: Cooper Square, 1969.

Ives, J. Moss. "The Catholic Contribution to Religious Liberty in Colonial America." <u>Catholic Historical Review</u> 21 (October 1935), 283-298.

Jordan, David W. "'God's Candle' within Government: Quakers and Politics in Early Maryland." <u>William and Mary Quarterly</u>, 3d ser., 39 (October 1982), 628-654.

Jordan, David W. "John Coode, Perennial Rebel." <u>Maryland Historical Magazine</u> 70 (Spring 1975), 1-28.

Jordan, David W. "A Plea for Maryland Catholics." <u>Maryland Historical Magazine</u> 67 (Winter 1972), 429-435.

Krugler, John D. "The Calvert Family, Catholicism, and Court Politics in Early Seventeenth-Century England." <u>Historian</u> 13 (May 1981), 378-392.

Krugler, John D. "'The Face of a Protestant, and the Heart of a Papist': A Reexamination of Sir George Calvert's Conversion to Roman Catholicism." <u>Journal of Church and State</u> 20 (Autumn 1978), 507-531.

Krugler, John D. "Lord Baltimore, Roman Catholics, and Toleration: Religious Policy in Maryland During the Early Catholic Years, 1634-1649." <u>Catholic Historical Review</u> 65 (January 1979), 49-75.

Krugler, John D. "Sir George Calvert's Resignation as Secretary of State and the Founding of Maryland." <u>Maryland Historical Magazine</u> 68 (Fall 1973), 239-254.

Krugler, John D. "'With Promise of Liberty in Religion': The Catholic Lords Baltimore and Toleration in Seventeenth-Century Maryland, 1634-1692." <u>Maryland Historical Magazine</u> 79 (Spring 1984), 21-43.

Lahey, R. J. "The Role of Religion in Lord Baltimore's Colonial Enterprise." <u>Maryland Historical Magazine</u> 72 (Winter 1977), 492-511.

Land, Aubrey C.; Carr, Lois Green; and Papenfuse, Edward C., eds. <u>Law, Society, and Politics in Early Maryland: Proceedings of the First Conference on Maryland History, June 14-15, 1974</u>. Baltimore: John Hopkins University Press, 1977.

Lehman, James O. "The Mennonites of Maryland During the Revolutionary War." <u>Mennonite Quarterly Review</u> 50 (July 1976), 200-229.

Lurie, Maxine N. "Theory and Practice of Religious Toleration
in the Seventeenth Century: The Proprietary Colonies as a
Case Study." Maryland Historical Magazine 79 (Summer 1984),
117-125.

McIlvain, James William. "Early Presbyterianism in Maryland."
Johns Hopkins University Studies 8, pt. 5-6 (Baltimore,
1890), 313-345.

Melville, Annabelle M. John Carroll of Baltimore, Founder of
the American Catholic Hierarchy. New York: Charles
Scribner's Sons, 1955.

Middleton, Arthur Pierce. "From Daughter Church to Sister
Church: The Disestablishment of the Church of England and
the Organization of the Diocese of Maryland." Maryland
Historical Magazine 79 (Fall 1984), 189-196.

Middleton, Arthur Pierce. "Toleration and the Established
Church in Maryland." Historical Magazine of the Protestant
Episcopal Church 53 (March 1984), 13-24.

Miller, Rodney K. "The Influence of the Socio-Economic Status
of the Anglican Clergy of Revolutionary Maryland on Their
Political Orientation." Historical Magazine of the
Protestant Episcopal Church 47 (June 1978), 197-210.

Miller, Rodney K. "The Political Ideology of the American
Clergy." Historical Magazine of the Protestant Episcopal
Church 45 (September 1976), 227-236.

Moran, Dennis M. "Anti-Catholicism in Early Maryland Politics:
The Protestant Revolution." Records of the American
Catholic Historical Society of Philadelphia 61 (December
1950), 213-236.

Moran, Dennis M. "Anti-Catholicism in Early Maryland Politics:
The Puritan Influence." Records of the American Catholic
Historical Society of Philadelphia 61 (September 1950), 139-
154.

Murray, John Courtney. We Hold These Truths: Catholic
Reflections on the American Proposition. New York: Sheed &
Ward, 1960.

Petrie, George. "Church and State in Early Maryland." Johns
Hopkins University Studies in Historical and Political
Science 4 (April 1892), 1-50.

Rainbolt, John Corbin. "The Struggle to Define 'Religious
Liberty' in Maryland, 1776-85." Journal of Church and State
17 (Autumn 1975) 443-458.

Rightmyer, Nelson Waite. "The Anglican Church in Maryland:
    Factors Contributory to the American Revolution." Church
    History 19 (September 1950), 187-198.

Rightmyer, Nelson Waite. Maryland's Established Church.
    Baltimore: Church Historical Society for the Diocese of
    Maryland, 1956.

Russell, William T. The Land of Sanctuary: A History of
    Religious Toleration in Maryland from the First Settlement
    until the American Revolution. Baltimore: J. H. Furst,
    1907.

Scriven, George B. "Religious Affiliation in Seventeenth
    Century Maryland." Historical Magazine of the Protestant
    Episcopal Church 25 (September 1956), 220-229.

Seabrook, John H. "The Establishment of Anglicanism in
    Colonial Maryland." Historical Magazine of the Protestant
    Episcopal Church 39 (September 1970), 287-294.

Shea, John Gilmary. "Maryland and the Controversies as to Her
    Early History." American Catholic Quarterly Review 10
    (October 1885), 658-677.

Smith, Ellen Hart. Charles Carroll of Carrollton. Cambridge,
    Mass.: Harvard University Press, 1942.

Stegmaier, Mark J. "Maryland's Fear of Insurrection at the
    Time of Braddock's Defeat." Maryland Historical Magazine 71
    (Winter 1976), 467-483.

Thompson, Henry F. "Richard Ingle in Maryland." Maryland
    Historical Magazine 1 (June 1906), 125-140.

Thompson, Tommy R. "The Country and Court Parties in
    Eighteenth Century Maryland." North Dakota Quarterly 47
    (1979), 43-53.

Vivian, James F., and Vivian, Jean H. "The Reverend Isaac
    Campbell: An Anti-Lockean Whig." Historical Magazine of the
    Protestant Episcopal Church 39 (Spring 1970), 71-89.

Vivian, Jean H. "The Poll Tax Controversy in Maryland, 1770-
    76: A Case of Taxation with Representation." Maryland
    Historical Magazine 71 (Summer 1976), 151-176.

Wennersten, John R. "The Travail of a Tory Parson: Reverend
    Philip Hughes and Maryland Colonial Politics 1767-1777."
    Historical Magazine of the Protestant Episcopal Church 44
    (December 1975), 409-416.

Werline, Albert. Problems of Church and State in Maryland
    During the Seventeenth and Eighteenth Centuries. South
    Lancaster, Mass.: College Press, 1948.

Wroth, Lawrence C. "The First Sixty Years of the Church of
    England in Maryland, 1632-1692." Maryland Historical
    Magazine 11 (March 1916), 1-41.

Yackel, Peter G. "The Benefit of Clergy in Colonial Maryland."
    Maryland Historical Magazine 69 (Winter 1974), 383-397.

Zimmer, Anne Y. "The 'Paper War' in Maryland, 1772-73: The
    Paca-Chase Political Philosophy Tested." Maryland
    Historical Magazine 71 (Summer 1976), 177-193.

NEW JERSEY

Bjarnson, Donald Einar. "Swedish-Finnish Settlement in New
    Jersey in the Seventeenth Century." Swedish Pioneer
    Historical Quarterly 27 (October 1976), 238-246.

Burr, Nelson R. The Anglican Church in New Jersey.
    Philadelphia: Church Historical Society, 1954.

Burr, Nelson R. "The Episcopal Church and the Dutch in
    Colonial New York and New Jersey--1664-1784." Historical
    Magazine of the Protestant Episcopal Church 19 (June 1950),
    90-111.

Burr, Nelson R. "New Jersey: An Anglican Venture in Religious
    Freedom." Historical Magazine of the Protestant Episcopal
    Church 34 (March 1965), 3-34.

Bush, Bernard, comp. Laws of the Royal Colony of New Jersey,
    1702-1745. Trenton, N.J.: New Jersey State Library, 1977.

Cody, Edward J. "The Growth of Toleration and Church-State
    Relations in New Jersey, 1689-1763: From Holy Men to Holy
    War." In Economic and Social History of Colonial New
    Jersey, edited by William C. Wright, 42-63. Trenton, N.J.:
    New Jersey Historical Commission, 1974.

Collins, Varnum Lansing. President Witherspoon: A Biography.
    2 vols. Princeton, N.J.: Princeton University Press, 1925.

Cushing, John D., ed. The Earliest Printed Laws of New Jersey,
    1703-1722. Wilmington, Del.: Michael Glazier, 1978.

Gerlach, Larry R. "'Quaker' Politics in Eighteenth Century New
    Jersey: A Documentary Account." Journal of the Rutgers
    University Library 34 (December 1970), 1-12.

Hood, John. Index of Colonial and State Laws of New Jersey
    Between the Years 1663 and 1903 Inclusive. Camden, N.J.:
    Sinnickson Chew & Sons, 1905.

Ingram, George H. "The Presbytery of New Brunswick in the
    Struggle for American Independence." Journal of the
    Presbyterian Historical Society 9 (June 1917), 49-64.

Jamison, Wallace N. Religion in New Jersey: A Brief History.
    Princeton, N.J.: D. Van Nostrand Co., 1964.

Kirby, Ethyn Williams. George Keith (1638-1716). New York: D.
    Appleton Century Co., 1942.

Lewis, Charles Smith. "George Keith, the Missionary." New
    Jersey Historical Society, Proceedings, n.s., 13 (January
    1928), 38-45.

McAllister, James L., Jr. "Francis Alison and John
    Witherspoon: Political Philosophers and Revolutionaries."
    Journal of Presbyterian History 54 (Spring 1976), 33-60.

McCreary, John R. "Governors, Politicians, and the Sources of
    Instability in the Colonies: New Jersey as a Test Case."
    Journal of the Alabama Academy of Science 42 (1971), 215-
    227.

Maring, Norman H. Baptists in New Jersey: A Study in
    Transition. Valley Forge, Pa.: Judson Press, 1964.

Miller, Howard. "The Grammar of Liberty: Presbyterians and the
    First American Constitutions." Journal of Presbyterian
    History 54 (Spring 1976), 142-164.

Noll, Mark A. "Observations on the Reconciliation of Politics
    and Religion in Revolutionary New Jersey: The Case of Jacob
    Green." Journal of Presbyterian History 54 (Summer 1976),
    217-237.

Olson, Alison B. "The Founding of Princeton University:
    Religion and Politics in Eighteenth-Century New Jersey."
    New Jersey History 87 (1969), 133-150.

Stohlman, Martha Lou Lemmon. John Witherspoon: Parson,
    Politician, Patriot. Philadelphia: Westminster Press, 1976.

Tait, L. Gordon. "John Witherspoon as Sage: 'The Druid' Essays
    of 1776." New Jersey History 100 (Fall-Winter 1982), 31-46.

Trinterud, Leonard J. The Forming of an American Tradition: A
    Re-examination of Colonial Presbyterianism. Philadelphia:
    Westminster Press, 1949.

Turner, Gordon. "Church-State Relationships in Early New
    Jersey." New Jersey Historical Society, Proceedings 69
    (July 1951), 212-223.

Wertenbaker, Thomas Jefferson. Princeton, 1746-1896.
    Princeton, N.J.: Princeton University Press, 1946.

Whitehead, William A., ed. Archives of the State of New
    Jersey: Documents Relating to the Colonial History of the
    State of New Jersey. 1st ser. 42 vols. Newark: Daily
    Journal, 1880-1949.

Zilversmit, Arthur. "Liberty and Property: New Jersey and the
    Abolition of Slavery." New Jersey History 88 (Winter 1970),
    215-226.

                              NEW YORK

Beardslee, John W., III. "The Dutch Reformed Church and the
    American Revolution." Journal of Presbyterian History 54
    (Spring 1976), 165-181.

Breen, Quirinus. "Dominie Everhardus Bogardus." Church
    History 2 (June 1933), 78-90.

Bridenbaugh, Carl. Mitre and Sceptre: Transatlantic Faiths,
    Ideas, Personalities, and Politics. New York: Oxford
    University Press, 1962.

Bultmann, William A. "The S.P.G. and the French Huguenots in
    Colonial America." Historical Magazine of the Protestant
    Episcopal Church 20 (June 1951), 156-172.

Burr, Nelson R. "The Episcopal Church and the Dutch in
    Colonial New York and New Jersey--1664-1784." Historical
    Magazine of the Protestant Episcopal Church 19 (June 1950),
    90-111.

Butler, Jon. The Huguenots in America: A Refugee People in New
    World Society. Cambridge, Mass.: Harvard University Press,
    1983.

Chorley, E. Clowes. "The Beginnings of the Church in the
    Province of New York." Historical Magazine of the
    Protestant Episcopal Church 13 (March 1944), 5-25.

The Colonial Laws of New York from the Year 1664 to the
    Revolution. 5 vols. Albany: James B. Lyon, 1894-1896.

Corwin, Edward T. "The Ecclesiastical Condition of New York at
    the Opening of the Eighteenth Century." American Society of
    Church History, Papers, 2d ser., 3 (1912), 79-115.

Corwin, Edward T., ed. Ecclesiastical Records: State of New
    York. 7 vols. Albany: James B. Lyon, 1901-1916.

Cross, Arthur Lyon. The Anglican Episcopate and the American
    Colonies. New York: Longmans, Green & Co., 1902.

Cushing, John D., ed. The Earliest Printed Laws of New York,
1665-1693. Wilmington, Del.: Michael Glazier, 1978.

Davidson, Elizabeth. The Establishment of the English Church
in Continental American Colonies. Durham, N.C.: Duke
University Press, 1936.

De Vries, George, Jr. "The Dutch in the American Revolution:
Reflections and Observations." Fides et Historia 10 (Fall
1977), 43-57.

Fiore, Jordan D. "Jonathan Swift and the American Episcopate."
William and Mary Quarterly, 3d ser., 11 (July 1954), 425-
433.

Gerlach, Don R., and DeMille, George E. "Samuel Johnson and
the Founding of King's College, 1751-1755." Historical
Magazine of the Protestant Episcopal Church 44 (September
1975), 335-352.

Henshaw, R. Townsend. "The New York Ministry Act of 1693."
Historical Magazine of the Protestant Episcopal Church 2
(December 1933), 199-204.

Holmes, David L. "The Episcopal Church and the American
Revolution." Historical Magazine of the Protestant
Episcopal Church 47 (September 1978), 261-291.

Humphrey, David C. From King's College to Columbia, 1746-1800.
New York: Columbia University Press, 1976.

Johnson, Samuel. Samuel Johnson, President of King's College:
His Career and Writings. Vol 4, Founding King's College.
Edited by Herbert Schneider and Carol Schneider. Foreword
by Nicholas Murray Butler. New York: Columbia University
Press, 1929.

Kenney, Alice P. Stubborn for Liberty: The Dutch in New York.
Syracuse, N.Y.: Syracuse University Press, 1975.

Kierner, Cynthia A. "A Concept Rejected: New York's Anglican
'Establishment,' 1693-1715." Essays in History 26 (1982),
71-100.

Kingdon, Robert M. "Why Did the Huguenot Refugees in the
American Colonies Become Episcopalian?" Historical Magazine
of the Protestant Episcopal Church 49 (December 1980), 317-
335.

Klein, Milton M. "Church, State, and Education: Testing the
Issue in Colonial New York." New York History 45 (October
1964), 291-303.

Klein, Milton M. "New York in the American Colonies: A New
Look." New York History 53 (April 1972), 132-156.

Klein, Milton M. The Politics of Diversity: Essays in the
   History of Colonial New York. Port Washington, N.Y.:
   Kennikat Press, 1974.

Leder, Lawrence H. "Robert Hunter's Androboros." Bulletin of
   the New York Public Library 68 (March 1964), 153-160.

Leder, Lawrence H. "The Unorthodox Dominie: Nicholas Van
   Rensselaer." New York History 35 (April 1954), 166-176.

Levermore, Charles H. "The Whigs of Colonial New York."
   American Historical Review 1 (January 1896), 238-250.

Livingston, William. The Independent Reflector; Or, Weekly
   Essays on Sundry Important Subjects More Particularly
   Adapted to the Province of New-York. Edited by Milton M.
   Klein. Cambridge, Mass.: Harvard University Press, 1963.

McCulloch, Samuel Clyde. "The Foundation and Early Work of the
   Society for the Propagation of the Gospel in Foreign Parts."
   Huntington Library Quarterly 8 (May 1945), 241-258.

Mead, Nelson P. "The Growth of Religious Liberty in New York
   City." New York State Historical Association, Proceedings
   17 (1919), 141-153.

Mills, Frederick V., Sr. "The Internal Anglican Controversy
   Over an American Episcopate." Historical Magazine of the
   Protestant Episcopal Church 44 (September 1975), 257-276.

Mulder, John M. "William Livingston: Propagandist Against
   Episcopacy." Journal of Presbyterian History 54 (Spring
   1976), 83-104.

Nobbs, Douglas. Theocracy and Toleration: A Study of the
   Disputes in Dutch Calvinism from 1600 to 1650. Cambridge:
   Cambridge University Press, 1938.

O'Callaghan, E. B., ed. Documentary History of the State of
   New-York. 4 vols. Albany: Weed, Parsons & Co., 1850-1851.

O'Callaghan, E. B., ed. Documents Relative to the Colonial
   History of the State of New-York. 15 vols. Albany: Weed,
   Parsons & Co., 1853-1887.

O'Connor, Thomas F. "A Jesuit School in Seventeenth Century
   New York." Mid-America, n.s., 3 (January 1932), 265-268.

O'Connor, Thomas F. "Religious Toleration in New York, 1664-
   1700." New York History 17 (October 1936), 391-410.

Olson, Alison Gilbert. "Governor Robert Hunter and the
     Anglican Church in New York." In <u>Statesmen, Scholars and</u>
     <u>Merchants: Essays in Eighteenth-Century History Presented to</u>
     <u>Dame Lucy Sutherland</u>, edited by Anne Whiteman, J. S.
     Bromley, and P. G. M. Dickson, 44-64. Oxford: Oxford
     University Press, 1973.

Olson, James S. "The New York Assembly, the Politics of
     Religion, and the Origins of the American Revolution, 1768-
     1771." <u>Historical Magazine of the Protestant Episcopal</u>
     <u>Church</u> 43 (March 1974), 21-28.

Painter, Borden W. "The Vestry in the Middle Colonies."
     <u>Historical Magazine of the Protestant Episcopal Church</u> 47
     (March 1978), 5-36.

Pratt, John Webb. <u>Religion, Politics, and Diversity: The</u>
     <u>Church-State Theme in New York History</u>. Ithaca, N.Y.:
     Cornell University Press, 1967.

Ritchie, Robert C. <u>The Duke's Province: A Study of New York</u>
     <u>Politics and Society, 1664-1691</u>. Chapel Hill: University of
     North Carolina Press, 1977.

Ritchie, Robert C. "God and Mammon in New Netherland."
     <u>Reviews in American History</u> 2 (September 1974), 353-357.

Rossiter, Clinton. "The Shaping of the American Tradition."
     <u>William and Mary Quarterly</u>, 3d ser., 11 (October 1954), 519-
     535.

Smith, George L. "Guilders and Godliness: The Dutch Colonial
     Contribution to American Religious Pluralism." <u>Journal of</u>
     <u>Presbyterian History</u> 47 (March 1969), 1-30.

Smith, George L. <u>Religion and Trade in New Netherland: Dutch</u>
     <u>Origins and American Development</u>. Ithaca, N.Y.: Cornell
     University Press, 1973.

Sweet, William Warren. "The Role of the Anglicans in the
     American Revolution." <u>Huntington Library Quarterly</u> 11
     (November 1947), 51-70.

Weaver, Glenn. "John Frederick Haeger: S.P.G. Missionary to
     the Palatines." <u>Historical Magazine of the Protestant</u>
     <u>Episcopal Church</u> 27 (June 1958), 112-125.

West, Kenneth B. "Quakers and the State: The Controversy Over
     Oaths in the Colony of New York." <u>Michigan Academician</u> 2
     (1970), 431-443.

Zwierlein, Frederick J. "New Netherland Intolerance."
     <u>Catholic Historical Review</u> 4 (April 1918), 186-216.

Zwierlein, Frederick J. Religion in New Netherland: A History
    of the Development of the Religious Conditions in the
    Province of New Netherland, 1623-1664. Rochester, N.Y.:
    John P. Smith, 1910.

                              PENNSYLVANIA

Baumann, Richard. For the Reputation of Truth: Politics,
    Religion and Conflict Among the Pennsylvania Quakers, 1750-
    1800. Baltimore: Johns Hopkins University Press, 1971.

Bender, Wilbur J. Nonresistance in Colonial Pennsylvania.
    Scottdale, Pa.: Herald Press, 1934.

Bockelman, Wayne L., and Ireland, Owen S. "The Internal
    Revolution in Pennsylvania: An Ethnic-Religious
    Interpretation." Pennsylvania History 41 (April 1974), 125-
    159.

Bronner, Edwin B. "The Quakers and Non-Violence in
    Pennsylvania." Pennsylvania History 35 (January 1968), 1-
    22.

Bronner, Edwin B. William Penn's "Holy Experiment": The
    Founding of Pennsylvania, 1681-1701. New York: Columbia
    University Press, 1962.

Butler, Jon. "'Gospel Order Improved': The Keithian Schism and
    the Exercise of Quaker Ministerial Authority in
    Pennsylvania." William and Mary Quarterly, 3d ser., 31
    (July 1974), 431-452.

Butler, Jon. "Into Pennsylvania's Spiritual Abyss: The Rise
    and Fall of the Later Keithians, 1693-1703." Pennsylvania
    Magazine of History and Biography 101 (April 1977), 151-170.

Butler, Jon. Power, Authority, and the Origins of the American
    Denominational Order: The English Churches in the Delaware
    Valley, 1680-1730. American Philosophical Society,
    Transactions 68, pt. 2 (Philadelphia, 1978).

Butzin, Peter A. "Politics, Presbyterians and the Paxton
    Riots, 1763-64." Journal of Presbyterian History 51 (Spring
    1973), 70-84.

Buxbaum, Melvin H. "Benjamin Franklin and William Smith: Their
    School and Their Dispute." Historical Magazine of the
    Protestant Episcopal Church 39 (December 1970), 361-382.

Carroll, Kenneth L. "A Look at the 'Quaker Revival of 1756.'"
    Quaker History 65 (Autumn 1976), 63-80.

Casey, John. "Religious Freedom in the Constitutions of the Commonwealth of Pennsylvania." Records of the American Catholic Historical Society of Philadelphia 60 (September 1949), 167-180.

Casino, Joseph J. "Anti-Popery in Colonial Pennsylvania." Pennsylvania Magazine of History and Biography 105 (July 1981), 279-309.

Cheyney, Edward P. History of the University of Pennsylvania, 1740-1940. Philadelphia: University of Pennsylvania Press, 1940.

Cohen, Norman S. "The Philadelphia Election Riot of 1742." Pennsylvania Magazine of History and Biography 92 (July 1968), 306-319.

Currey, Cecil B. "Eighteenth-Century Evangelical Opposition to the American Revolution: The Case of the Quakers." Fides et Historia 4 (Fall 1971), 17-35.

Cushing, John D., comp. The Earliest Printed Laws of Pennsylvania, 1681-1713. Wilmington, Del.: Michael Glazier, 1978.

Durnbaugh, Donald F. "Religion and Revolution: Options in 1776." Pennsylvania Mennonite Heritage 1 (July 1978), 2-9.

Frost, J. William. "Religious Liberty in Early Pennsylvania." Pennsylvania Magazine of History and Biography 105 (October 1981), 419-451.

Frost, J. William. "Unlikely Controversialists: Caleb Pusey and George Keith." Quaker History 64 (1975), 16-36.

Gross, Leonard, ed. "Mennonites and the Revolutionary Era." Mennonite History Bulletin 35 (January 1974), 3-11.

Hershberger, Guy Franklin. "Pacifism and the State in Colonial Pennsylvania." Church History 8 (March 1939), 54-74.

Hindle, Brooke. "The March of the Paxton Boys." William and Mary Quarterly, 3d ser., 3 (October 1946), 461-486.

Hutson, James H. "Benjamin Franklin and William Smith: More Light on an Old Philadelphia Quarrel." Pennsylvania Magazine of History and Biography 93 (January 1969), 109-113.

Jable, J. Thomas. "Pennsylvania's Early Blue Laws: A Quaker Experiment in the Suppression of Sports and Amusements, 1682-1740." Journal of Sports History 1 (1974), 107-122.

Jable, J. Thomas. "The Pennsylvania Sunday Blue Laws of 1779:
A View of Pennsylvania Society and Politics During the
American Revolution." Pennsylvania History 40 (October
1973), 413-426.

James, Sydney V. "The Impact of the American Revolution on
Quakers' Ideas about Their Sect." William and Mary
Quarterly, 3d ser., 19 (July 1962), 360-382.

James, Sydney V. A People Among Peoples: Quaker Benevolence in
Eighteenth Century America. Cambridge, Mass.: Harvard
University Press, 1963.

Ketcham, Ralph L. "Benjamin Franklin and William Smith: New
Light on an Old Philadelphia Quarrel." Pennsylvania
Magazine of History and Biography 88 (April 1964), 142-163.

Ketcham, Ralph L. "Conscience, War, and Politics in
Pennsylvania, 1755-1757." William and Mary Quarterly, 3d
ser., 20 (July 1963), 416-439.

Lively, Bruce Richard. "William Smith, the College and Academy
of Philadelphia and Pennsylvania Politics." Historical
Magazine of the Protestant Episcopal Church 38 (September
1969), 237-258.

MacMaster, Richard K. Conscience in Crisis: Mennonites and
Other Peace Churches in America, 1739-1789: Interpretation
and Documents. Scottdale, Pa.: Herald Press, 1979.

Marable, Manning. "Death of the Quaker Slave Trade." Quaker
History 63 (1974), 17-33.

Marietta, Jack D. "Conscience, the Quaker Community, and the
French and Indian War." Pennsylvania Magazine of History
and Biography 95 (January 1971), 3-27.

Marietta, Jack D. The Reformation of American Quakerism, 1748-
1783. Philadelphia: University of Pennsylvania Press, 1984.

Mekeel, Arthur J. "The Relation of the Quakers to the American
Revolution." Quaker History 65 (Spring 1976), 3-18.

Metcalf, Michael F. "Dr. Carl Magnus Wrangel and
Prerevolutionary Pennsylvania Politics." Swedish Pioneer
Historical Quarterly 27 (October 1976), 247-260.

Michel, Jack. "The Philadelphia Quakers and the American
Revolution: Reform in the Philadelphia Monthly Meeting."
Working Papers from the Regional Economic History Research
Center 3, no. 4 (1980), 53-109.

Mood, Fulmer. "William Penn and English Politics, 1680-81: New
Light on the Granting of the Pennsylvania Charter." Journal
of the Friends Historical Society 32 (1935), 3-21.

Nash, Gary B. Quakers and Politics: Pennsylvania, 1681-1726.
     Princeton, N.J.: Princeton University Press, 1968.

Oaks, Robert F. "Philadelphians in Exile: The Problem of
     Loyalty During the American Revolution." Pennsylvania
     Magazine of History and Biography 96 (July 1972), 298-325.

Pennington, Edgar Legare. "The Anglican Clergy of Pennsylvania
     in the American Revolution." Pennsylvania Magazine of
     History and Biography 63 (October 1939), 401-431.

Pennsylvania Archives. 9 ser. Philadelphia: J. Severns & Co.,
     1852-1856; Harrisburg, 1874-1919.

Radbill, Kenneth A. "Quaker Politics: The Leadership of Owen
     Biddle and John Lacey, Jr." Pennsylvania History 45
     (January 1978), 47-60.

Rau, Albert G. "Moravian Missions and Colonial Politics."
     Moravian Historical Society, Transactions 11 (Bethlehem,
     Pa., 1934), 137-145.

Rothermund, Dietmar. "The German Problem of Colonial
     Pennsylvania." Pennsylvania Magazine of History and
     Biography 84 (January 1960), 3-21.

Rothermund, Dietmar. "Political Factions and the Great
     Awakening." Pennsylvania History 26 (October 1959), 317-
     331.

Salomon, Richard G., ed. "William White's 'The Case of the
     Episcopal Churches in the United States Considered' (1782)."
     Historical Magazine of the Protestant Episcopal Church 22
     (December 1953), 435-506.

Scheidt, David L. "The Lutherans in Revolutionary
     Philadelphia." Concordia Historical Institute Quarterly 49
     (Winter 1976), 148-159.

Simmons, Richard. "The Quakers' American Proprietaries."
     History Today 22 (July 1972), 506-512.

Sloan, David. "'A Time of Sifting and Winnowing': The Paxton
     Riots and Quaker Non-Violence in Pennsylvania." Quaker
     History 66 (Spring 1977), 3-22.

Smith, William. Account of the College, Academy and Charitable
     School of Philadelphia in Pennsylvania. Edited by Thomas R.
     Adams. Philadelphia: University of Pennsylvania Library,
     1951.

Stowe, Walter H. "William White: Ecclesiastical Statesman."
     Historical Magazine of the Protestant Episcopal Church 22
     (December 1953), 372-378.

Stowe, Walter H., ed. "The Autobiography of Bishop William White." <u>Historical Magazine of the Protestant Episcopal Church</u> 22 (December 1953), 380-432.

Tolles, Frederick B. <u>Meeting House and Counting House: The Quaker Merchants of Colonial Philadelphia, 1682-1763</u>. Chapel Hill: University of North Carolina Press, 1948.

Tolles, Frederick B. "William Penn's Prayer for Philadelphia." <u>Pennsylvania Magazine of History and Biography</u> 90 (1966), 517-519.

Tully, Alan. "King George's War and the Quakers: The Defense Crisis of 1732-1742 in Pennsylvania Politics." <u>Journal of the Lancaster County Historical Society</u> 82 (Michaelmas 1978), 174-198.

Tully, Alan. <u>William Penn's Legacy: Politics and Social Structure in Provincial Pennsylvania, 1726-1755</u>. Baltimore: Johns Hopkins University Press, 1977.

Ulle, Robert F. "Pacifists, Paxton, and Politics: Colonial Pennsylvania, 1763-1768." <u>Pennsylvania Mennonite Heritage</u> 1 (October 1978), 18-21.

Washburn, Louis C. "The Church in Pennsylvania." <u>Historical Magazine of the Protestant Episcopal Church</u> 4 (June 1935), 116-127.

Wax, Darold D. "Reform and Revolution: The Movement Against Slavery and the Slave Trade in Revolutionary Pennsylvania." <u>Western Pennsylvania Historical Magazine</u> 57 (October 1974), 403-429.

Weinlick, John R. "The Moravians and the American Revolution: An Overview." Moravian Historical Society, <u>Transactions</u> 23 (Bethlehem, Pa., 1977), 1-16.

Wellenreuther, Hermann. "The Political Dilemma of the Quakers in Pennsylvania, 1681-1748." <u>Pennsylvania Magazine of History and Biography</u> 94 (April 1970), 135-172.

Woolman, John. <u>The Journal and Major Essays of John Woolman</u>. Edited by Phillips P. Moulton. New York: Oxford University Press, 1971.

DELAWARE

Andresen, Grant W. "The American Revolution and the Swedish Church in the Delaware Valley." <u>Swedish Pioneer Historical Quarterly</u> 27 (October 1976), 261-269.

Bergendoff, Conrad J. I. "The Swedish Church on the Delaware." Church History 7 (September 1938), 215-230.

Burr, Nelson R. "The Early History of the Swedes and the Episcopal Church in America." Historical Magazine of the Protestant Episcopal Church 7 (June 1938), 113-132.

Colburn, Dorothy. "'No More Passive Obedience and Non-Resistance.'" Historical Magazine of the Protestant Episcopal Church 46 (December 1977), 455-461.

Cushing, John D., ed. The Earliest Printed Laws of Delaware, 1704-1741. Wilmington, Del.: Michael Glazier, 1978.

Eckman, Jeannette. Crane Hook on the Delaware, 1667-1699: An Early Swedish Lutheran Church and Community. Newark: University of Delaware, 1958.

Harder, Leland. "Plockhoy and His Settlement at Zwaanendael, 1663." Delaware History 3 (March 1949), 138-154.

Harder, Leland, and Harder, Marvin. Plockhoy from Zurik-zee. Newton, Kan.: Mennonite Board of Education and Publication, 1952.

Horst, Irvin B. "Pieter Cornelisz Plockhoy: An Apostle of the Collegiants." Mennonite Quarterly Review 23 (July 1949), 161-185.

Johnson, Amandus. The Swedish Settlements on the Delaware: Their History and Relation to the Indians, Dutch and English, 1638-1664. 2 vols. Philadelphia: University of Pennsylvania Press, 1911.

Lewis, William D. "The University of Delaware and Its Predecessors: A Bibliography." Delaware Notes 17 (1944), 111-125.

McAnear, Beverly. "The Charter of the Academy of Newark." Delaware History 4 (September 1950), 149-156.

May, James W. "Francis Asbury and Thomas White: A Refugee Preacher and His Tory Patron." Methodist History 14 (April 1976), 141-164.

Morgan, George. "The Colonial Origin of Newark Academy." Delaware Notes 8 (1934), 7-30.

Munroe, John A. Church vs. State: The Early Struggle for Control of Delaware College. Newark: University of Delaware, 1982.

Munroe, John A. Colonial Delaware--A History. Millwood, N.Y.: KTO Press, 1978.

Pears, Thomas Clinton, Jr. "Francis Alison, Colonial
   Educator." Delaware Notes 17 (1944), 9-22.

Rightmyer, Nelson Waite. The Anglican Church in Delaware.
   Philadelphia: Church Historical Society, 1947.

Rightmyer, Nelson Waite. "Swedish-English Relations in
   Northern Delaware." Church History 15 (June 1946), 101-115.

Ryden, George H. "The Newark Academy of Delaware in Colonial
   Days." Pennsylvania History 2 (October 1935), 205-224.

Ryden, George H. "The Relation of Newark Academy to the
   Presbyterian Church and to Higher Education in the American
   Colonies." Delaware Notes 9 (1935), 7-42.

Standing, Herbert. "Quakers in Delaware in the Time of William
   Penn." Delaware History 20 (Fall-Winter 1982), 123-147.

Swartz, Sally. "Society and Culture in the Seventeenth-Century
   Delaware Valley." Delaware History 20 (Fall-Winter 1982),
   98-122.

Waterston, Elizabeth. Churches in Delaware During the
   Revolution, With a Brief Account of Their Settlement and
   Growth. Wilmington, Del.: Historical Society of Delaware,
   1925.

Weslager, C. A. "The City of Amsterdam's Colony on the
   Delaware, 1656-1664; With Unpublished Dutch Notarial
   Abstracts." Delaware History 20 (Spring-Summer 1982), 1-26;
   (Fall-Winter 1982), 73-97.

White, Joyce L. "The Affiliation of Seven Swedish Lutheran
   Churches with the Episcopal Church." Historical Magazine of
   the Protestant Episcopal Church 46 (June 1977), 171-186.

2

Puritanism and the Civil Order
in New England from the First
Settlements
to the Great Awakening

Mark Valeri

Early New England has been one of the most thoroughly studied of colonial societies in the New World for at least two, interconnected reasons. First, much of the social and cultural activity of the English settlements north and east of New York took place within a well-defined and clearly articulated ideological context—Puritanism. Accordingly New England has been seen as an ideal case study of the interaction between religious ideas and social practice in early America. Second, there is a wealth of literary evidence from early New England, which has given scholars access to the smallest details of life there. Intent on building a civic order that accorded with both the Bible and English legal traditions, the settlers of Plymouth, Massachusetts Bay, Rhode Island, Connecticut, and New Haven placed a high premium on literacy. With extraordinary thoroughness they wrote personal journals, compiled ecclesiastical accounts, maintained private libraries, preserved civic records, and published books, tracts, and sermons. Many of the original documents are extant, maintained by such repositories as the American Antiquarian Society (Worcester, Massachusetts), the Connecticut State Library (Hartford), Harvard University's Houghton Library (Cambridge, Massachusetts), Yale University's Beinecke Library (New Haven), the Massachusetts Historical Society (Boston), and the individual collections of many church parishes.

In consequence, this essay concerns a scholarly literature that encompasses hundreds of general essays, monographs, and journal articles interpreting some facet of church-state issues in the New England colonies from 1630 to 1740. Given the abundance of this material, and the fact that historians have seemed unable to discuss almost any aspect of New England's early development without reference to the close association that the Puritans made between religious and social institutions, the following discussion serves only as an introduction to representative approaches to this period. In order to provide some degree of direction through the literature, somewhat artificial divisions have been made between types of studies that are usually considered together because of their particular methodologies and interpretations. Works cited in the following bibliography, then, are grouped around four basic issues: first, Puritan theology and its relation to congregational polity; second, the role of religious dissent within early New England; third, New England's political institutions and the legal dimensions of church-state issues; and fourth, the relation between local social affairs, communal authority, and religion.

PURITAN THEOLOGY AND POLITICAL THEORY

The writings of Perry Miller, focused on the development of New England in terms of Puritanism as a collective mind, have had an enormous influence on subsequent historians. Three of Miller's essays in *Errand Into the Wilderness*, "Errand Into the Wilderness" (1952), "The Marrow of Puritan Divinity" (1935), and "The Puritan State and Puritan Society" (1938) condense many of his more lengthy discussions contained in *Orthodoxy in Massachusetts* and in *The New England Mind*. Against what he saw as an anti-intellectual pragmatism within Progressive historiography, Miller argued that New Englanders were motivated by an ideological consensus, which originated with the reforming efforts of English Calvinists such as William Perkins (1558–1602). According to Miller, the social ideals of the first generation of New England's clergy and magistracy derived from the concepts of covenant, or federal, theology. Individuals were to submit voluntarily to the covenant of redemption as the condition for salvation, the covenant of grace as the rule of ecclesiastical practice, and the covenant of works as the moral law for society. The idea of voluntary submission, however, implied no acceptance of religious pluralism or political democracy. Miller maintained that the founders of New England took as revealed by biblical and natural law Calvinist soteriology, congregational polity (which required a public demonstration of conversion for full church membership), and godly standards for political rule. Social prosperity depended on maintaining the conditions associated with the various covenants. New England's later acceptance of more accommodating forms of church membership and of religious pluralism, Miller contended, were declensions from the intentions of the leaders of the Great Migration. They reflected a theological capitulation to the internal social pressures created by cultural, social, and economic individualism.

Miller's theses have been modified and contested by several other studies of Puritan ideology. In his "Understanding the Puritans," David D. Hall surveys some of the recent work on English Calvinism and early New England theology, and concludes that the New England Puritans represented a far more internally diverse group than the preachers discussed by Miller. Along the lines suggested by Geoffrey Nuttall's analysis of English Puritanism, *The Holy Spirit in Puritan Faith and Experience*, Hall maintains that Puritans were characterized less by specific political and ecclesiastical traditions than by their emphasis on the Holy Spirit's intervention in human affairs. This insistence on an experience of the Spirit led some Puritans to attempt to purify the church of worldly elements. In the extreme, this evolved into Separatism, i.e., the insistence that genuinely reformed congregations would condone neither civil intervention into religious affairs (the violation of congregational autonomy) nor church practices that allowed unregenerate membership. Most recently, Philip F. Gura's *A Glimpse of Sion's Glory* has posited an ideological instability within Puritanism. According to Gura, the purist and reformist impulse within Puritanism, enhanced in New England by contact with radical English dissenters, found its logical extensions in the Baptist and Antinomian movements. Gura maintains that what New Englanders did do consistently was to attempt by ousting extremists to curb the inherent radicalism of Puritanism.

Other scholars have pointed out that changes in Puritan religion were compelled not necessarily by theological capitulation, but by the application of genuinely Reformed ideals to shifting social circumstances. Beginning with their first formal statement of ecclesiastical principles in the 1648 Cambridge Platform, New England's first generation of religious leaders increasingly lamented the growth of social schism, moral apathy, and religious dissent. Most troublesome, however, was the relatively small number of conversions among members of the second and third generations. While unregenerate children of saints could be baptized, they were not granted full membership in the churches. They were denied voting privileges, participation in the Lord's Supper, and baptism for their children. In contrast to previously strict interpretations of congregational theory, the Half-way Covenant (officially recognized in 1662) extended the right of baptism to the grandchildren of saints. During the subsequent three or four decades, more liberalizing policies were adopted. By the end of the seventeenth century, some churches had opened full membership, including sacramental privileges, to any members of the community who acknowledged the truth of Christian doctrine (i.e., professed to have historical faith) and lived uprightly. By the time of the Great Awakening New England's churches had adopted the idea that church membership, once limited to those who claimed to possess the requisites of sainthood, was virtually coterminous with the territorial boundaries of the church parish.

Because of this important transition in the definition of church membership, several studies of seventeenth-century New England have focused

on the Half-way Covenant and related developments as the key to understanding the eventual settlement of the churches' place in New England
society. As he also argues in his study of John Winthrop (1588–1649), *The
Puritan Dilemma*, Edmund Morgan maintains in his *Visible Saints* that the
leaders of Massachusetts continually struggled against the separatist impulse. Winthrop's fight against Antinomianism represented the early phase of
this struggle; the Half-way Covenant marked the further efforts of the churches to maintain their presence within an impure society. By allowing baptism
to children of those who could not visibly demonstrate their sainthood, Morgan contends, pastors were attempting to promote the reform of society.
Robert Pope's *The Half-Way Covenant* examines the actual practice and use
of the Half-way Covenant in four Massachusetts churches. According to
Pope, second and third generation New Englanders were reluctant to use the
Half-way Covenant until a series of social crises, chiefly King Philip's War and
the revocation of Massachusetts' charter, provoked a sense of need for communal religious experience. The covenant became the means by which the
churches, whose favored status had been threatened by royal pressure upon
the magistracy to tolerate Baptists and Anglicans, moved themselves into the
secular sphere. Hall's study of developments within the Puritan ministry, *The
Faithful Shepherd*, reinforces the idea that during the seventeenth century
New England's clergy forcefully rejected separatism in order to extend their
authority over a religiously heterogeneous society. In his study of Richard
Mather (1596–1669), Increase Mather (1639–1723), and Cotton Mather
(1662–1727), *The Mathers*, Robert Middlekauff describes how intellectual
developments across three successive generations of Puritan preachers involved changing conceptions of the relations between New England society
and Reformed doctrine, yet continued to include elements of Puritan piety.

While the New England church tradition eventually acknowledged that the
society was composed of sinners as well as saints, Puritan ideology continued to aspire to the sacralization of the civic order. Much of the work on
New England thought describes this aspiration in terms of Puritan interpretations of history and providence. In his "Experiments Holy and Unholy,"
Richard S. Dunn contrasts Puritan motives for American colonization to
English activities in Ireland and the Caribbean. The settlers of New England,
suggests Dunn, perceived themselves as agents of divine activity, instituting
in the New World a godly, social refuge from European apostasy. Sacvan
Bercovitch's *The American Jeremiad* and "Rhetoric as Authority" concentrate on New England's literary reflections on America. Using Cotton Mather's writings as typical expressions of the New England mentality, Bercovitch
interprets Puritan rhetoric as millenarianism wedded to the myth of a divinely elected nation. Mather's belief that America was the antitype of the

Biblical Israel, according to Bercovitch, involved a collective (and imaginative!) assertion of a sacred past and a promised destiny for America. In *The Language of Canaan*, Mason I. Lowance, Jr., examines the Puritan development of typology in a theological context. J. F. Maclear's "New England and the Fifth Monarchy" posits a link between Puritan political aspirations and millennial convictions about the institution of a godly society in New England. Other interpretations of millennial motifs in Puritan literature, such as Lyman Tower Sargent's "Utopianism in Colonial America," describe the Puritan impulse in terms of that strand of idealism.

RELIGIOUS DISSENT IN EARLY NEW ENGLAND

Most of the studies already mentioned in this introductory essay concentrate on developments within Puritan congregational theory and on the relations between the churches established (or settled) according to that pattern and the governments of Massachusetts and Connecticut. Other works in the bibliography provide a different perspective by focusing on groups that dissented from the established order: William G. McLoughlin's *New England Dissent* and Jacob Rader Marcus's *Early American Jewry* are two examples. Other scholars have addressed the issue of dissent by examining the ideas and activities of the separatist and antinomian groups which contributed to the founding of Rhode Island.

New England separatism took its most celebrated form in the career of Roger Williams (1603–1693), whose movements, debates, and writings revealed the full implications of separatist ideas. One of the first settlers in Boston, Williams rejected many of the practices of the established church, which was eventually organized on congregational principles, including its refusal to denounce the validity of the Church of England. Williams's purist ideals led him to Plymouth. There he openly criticized some of the political principles upon which the General Court of Massachusetts had negotiated its charter from the King, especially the King's moral mandate to evangelize Indian lands and the Court's right to require from Massachusetts citizens an oath of loyalty to the crown. Forced by the Court to leave Massachusetts, Williams briefly settled in Providence and in 1643 sailed to England to obtain a charter for what became Rhode Island. While in England, he wrote *The Bloudy Tenant of Persecution* (1644), in which he advocated the complete separation of church and state on the grounds of the sanctity of private religious conscience. Many of his arguments were directed against the apologies for New England's practices written by Boston's John Cotton (1584–1652).

Studies of Williams by Perry Miller and Edmund Morgan, while sympathetic to the democratic implications of Williams's insistence on separation of church and state, point out that separatism challenged the basic premises upon which New England functioned. In his *Roger Williams*, Morgan maintains that Williams's ideas derived from a genuinely Puritan suspicion of governmental power, but also contradicted the Puritan notion of the reforming mission of the true church. Miller contends in his *Roger Williams* that Williams's doctrines derived from consistent application of a method of biblical interpretation that took Old Testament social institutions to be types of spiritual realities rather than legitimations of particular links between godliness and political affairs. Both Miller and Morgan, however, show that the position taken by Cotton and the Court, and the charges against Williams, were based on a genuine concern to maintain the commonwealth, not on irrational propensities towards persecution. Jesper Rosenmeier's "The Teacher and the Witness" describes differences beween Cotton and Williams in terms of contrasting eschatologies. Rosenmeier's essay and Bruce C. Daniels's "Dissent and Disorder" both indicate that despite his spiritualized interpretation of the Bible, Williams attempted to exercise a moral influence over social affairs in Providence. In "John Cotton and Roger Williams," Elizabeth Hirsch discusses the Reformed theological background to the separatist positions.

Antinomianism, i.e., a denial of the importance of obedience to the moral law, also presented an immense challenge to the social order in early New England. Encouraged by the evangelical teachings of Cotton, Anne Hutchinson (1591–1643) began in 1635 to hold private meetings in which she taught doctrines that in effect disparaged the legal and moral implications of covenant theology. Brought to trial, she was accused of heresy (technically for claiming to have had immediate revelations from Christ) and banished to Rhode Island. Several conflicting assessments have been made of the Antinomian Crisis. William K. B. Stoever's "*A Faire and Easie Way to Heaven*" is an attempt to set the discussion within the context of Reformed theology and the historical roots of Antinomianism. In "Church and State in Seventeenth-Century Massachusetts," Ronald D. Cohen contends that the heresy did indeed threaten early New England: the severe action of the General Court was in defense of a precarious social stability. According to Emery Battis's account in *Saints and Sectaries*, Hutchinson had supporters among Boston's merchants, many of whom resented the anti-commercial mentality of the clergy. Hutchinson's story has also provided a case study in response to the recent interest in the status of women in colonial America. In "The Case of the American Jezebels," for example, Lyle Koehler attempts to demonstrate that those who condemned Hutchinson did so in part because of their opposition to the idea of a female teacher of doctrine.

CIVIL LAW, GOVERNMENT, AND POLITICAL PRACTICE

Covenant theology and Puritan aspirations towards the institution of a godly commonwealth reflected the common conviction in New England that civil and religious affairs were interdependent. The above-mentioned studies of Puritan thought and of the prevalent attitudes of New England's leaders towards religious dissent and separatism, then, provide some of the ideological background for an examination of church-state legislation and political theory in early New England.

One approach to this set of issues has been to discuss the official posture of colonial governments vis-à-vis churches that were not officially settled. As a whole, the literature that deals with the question of religious toleration indicates that policies greatly differed from one colony to another. Bruce C. Daniels's "Dissent and Disorder" shows that Rhode Island's liberal policies quite self-consciously emerged in contradiction to the power of non-separating congregationalism in Massachusetts Bay. New Haven rigidly adhered to the Puritan standard of a monopoly on ecclesiastical establishments, while Connecticut congregational churches were less successful in maintaining religious homogeneity in the colony. A straightforward account of events in Connecticut is M. Louise Greene's *The Development of Religious Liberty in Connecticut.* Three studies of the "Pilgrim" colony, John M. Bumsted's "A Well-Bounded Toleration," George D. Langdon's *Pilgrim Colony,* and Harry M. Ward's *Statism in Plymouth Colony,* discuss the social and historical conditions that led the separatist founders of Plymouth to a relatively tolerant position vis-à-vis religious dissent.

The policies of Massachusetts Bay towards religious dissent have received an enormous amount of scholarly attention. Susan M. Reed's *Church and State in Massachusetts* provides a clear, if whiggish, narrative. Developments such as the 1631 law which limited freemanship to members of settled churches, the 1641 Body of Liberties that gave to civil magistrates the authority to enforce observance of orthodoxy within Massachusetts churches, the expulsion of Roger Williams and Anne Hutchinson, and the sporadic persecutions of Quakers and Baptists have been interpreted by earlier historians such as Reed as the result of a regressive conception of civil liberties on the part of the clergy. Truly democratic ideals triumphed, according to this point of view, as Massachusetts began to accept the notion of religious toleration during the 1680s and to permit Anglicans and Baptists to establish and maintain their own churches. In contrast to this interpretation, Aaron B. Seidman maintains in his "Church and State in the Early Years of the Massachusetts Bay Colony" that the clergy's 1648 Cambridge Platform clearly enunciated the essential principles of the separation of church and state: previous laws against religious dissent derived from the magistracy's attempts to use the churches as tools against political and social disorder. Several other studies follow Seidman's line of argument. Thomas E. Buckley's "Church and State in Massachusetts Bay" suggests that during the 1650s Baptists were ousted only when they began to pose a public threat to the established social order. Buckley argues that Puritan clergy feared the civic dangers of dissent far more than the idea of the freedom of private conscience and worship. In "The Social Context of Religious Heterodoxy," Jonathan M. Chu contends that Quakers were harassed more for their economic and political practices than for their religious doctrines. Timothy J. Sehr's "Defending Orthodoxy in Massachusetts" further explains the social occasions of legal restrictions on heterodoxy. In his "On Toleration in Massachusetts," E. Brooks Holifield shows that disputes over the Half-way Covenant frequently allied conservative pastors with evangelical Baptists. According to Holifield, Massachusetts' gradual toleration of Baptists resulted in part from such localized divisions within the congregational structure.

Related to the question of religious toleration is the problem of interpreting the nature of Puritan politics. During the first decades of the twentieth century, American historians such as James Truslow Adams and Vernon L. Parrington impugned early New England as an oligarchy of self-selected saints. Later works such as Thomas Jefferson Wertenbaker's *The Puritan Oligarchy* also claimed that New England's government tended towards a theocratic conception of civic authority. Sydney Ahlstrom's essay on the political principles of Connecticut's Thomas Hooker (1586–1647), however, points to a different interpretation. According to Ahlstrom, the Puritans' emphasis on law and participatory politics fostered the ideals of democratic responsibility. Much of the debate on democracy in Massachusetts has focused on religious qualifications for suffrage, voting patterns, and the boundaries of the franchise. For example, in "Democracy in Colonial Massachusetts," Robert E. Brown contends that 80 to 90 percent of the adult males in Stockbridge voted, while in "Godliness, Property, and the Franchise in Puritan Massachusetts," Richard C. Simmons argues that the percentage of freemen steadily declined after 1640, as an increasing number of New Englanders failed to meet the property and religious qualifications for voting. B. Katherine Brown's "The Controversy over the Franchise in Puritan Massachusetts, 1954–1975" provides a helpful review of this debate.

A third approach to the issue of Puritanism's relation to civic affairs examines the understanding and function of law in early New England. George Lee Haskins's *Law and Authority in Early Massachusetts* remains one of the most thorough and nuanced studies of this problem. In this book and in several related articles, Haskins maintains that the Puritan leaders of Massachusetts intentionally developed a legal system that would both defend the civil liberties of New Englanders according to the precedents of English law, and institute biblical polity wherever applicable to social affairs. Haskins contends that Puritan religiosity provided the ethical values by which the magistracy interpreted the common and civil laws of England. Accordingly he posits in early New England an incipient system of American liberties.

Several other legal histories complement Haskins's work. In his "Crime, Law Enforcement, and Social Control in Colonial America," Douglas Greenberg describes how Connecticut's criminal laws reflected an intense effort to uphold what the magistracy understood to be the mandate for maintaining social control by means of biblical law. Richard Gaskins's "Changes in Criminal Law in Eighteenth-Century Connecticut" suggests that between 1700 and 1750 the nature of criminal law cases had more to do with economic grievances than with moral offenses. David Thomas Konig's careful examination of civil disputes in Essex County during the seventeenth century, *Law and Society in Puritan Massachusetts*, demonstrates the importance of legal practices on a local scale. Konig concludes that in the civil courts New Englanders had a mechanism for solving social disputes and maintaining some semblance of the cohesive communities towards which Puritanism aspired. In his "Rationality, Legal Change, and Community in Connecticut," Bruce H. Mann points to a similar pattern during the first half of the eighteenth century in Connecticut. Mann suggests that changes in Connecticut law were attempts to rationalize and order increasingly diverse social aspirations.

A fourth approach interprets colonial developments within the trans-Atlantic context of imperial politics, rather than exclusively from a perspective of the native evolution of law. Several general studies discuss the impact on New England of English colonial policy. Viola F. Barnes's *The Dominion of New England*, Leonard W. Labaree's *Royal Government in America*, Jack M. Sosin's *English America and the Restoration Monarchy of Charles II*, and Richard R. Johnson's *Adjustment to Empire* provide perspectives on the Navigation Acts, the revocation of Massachusetts' charter, the establishment of the Dominion, the role of royal governors in New England, and English pressures on colonial assemblies to tolerate Anglican, Baptist, and Quaker dissent. Robert S. Bosher's *The Making of the Restoration Settlement* contains a useful discussion of church-state affairs in England during this period. In *The Glorious Revolution in America*, David S. Lovejoy maintains that Massachusetts' resistance to the royal policies favoring Anglicanism involved an assertion of the right to self-governance: the Puritans' hostility towards royal governors manifested the English constitutional crisis that erupted in the revolution of 1688. George Allen Cook's *John Wise* [1652–1725] is the

standard biography of an important colonial writer who combined Puritan
legal theory and political constitutionalism in defending Massachusetts'
charter against the claims of royal prerogative.

Against the English background, colonial attitudes towards the role of
religion in social affairs are illumined in various ways. Timothy H. Breen's
The Character of the Good Ruler is an examination of New England perceptions about the requirements of political authority. Breen maintains that only
with the Restoration, and the consequent dissipation of hopes for a Reformed
England, did New Englanders finally accept the notion that their magistrates
should be judged according to codified principles of law rather than according to personal standards of godliness. Breen's most recent book, *Puritans
and Adventurers*, and David Grayson Allen's *In English Ways* illustrate the
current scholarly interest in setting colonial legal practice within the English
context. According to both Breen and Allen, the social, cultural, and religious
localism of village life in Stuart England was transferred to New England. In
Connecticut and Massachusetts settlers attempted to defend local prerogatives against provincial and royal intervention. Congregational autonomy, variations between towns in the acceptance of Baptists or Quakers, and
diverse attitudes towards the official proclamations of the magistracy each
reflected this localism.

LOCAL PATTERNS OF RELIGION AND SOCIAL AFFAIRS

The work of Breen and Allen indicates the importance of approaching
church-state issues in early New England not only from the vantage point of
Puritan theology and legal practice but also from the perspective of local
social developments. During the previous two decades, social historians have
produced an immense literature that deals with such issues as communal
conflict, social growth, and local or even family patterns of authority in
colonial life. Drawing on local ecclesiastical and court records, private journals, and demographic data, social historians emphasize the formation and
operation of New England's towns and villages under the stress of intra-
communal conflicts such as economic class and conflicting loyalties such as
family, church, and town. With respect to church-state issues, these types of
studies explore the relation of religion to local patterns of social authority
and communal schism.

One interpretation within this historiographical genre posits deeply rooted
contradictions within New England societies that over the course of the
seventeenth century evolved into social fragmentation. Three general essays
contain variations of this thesis in condensed forms. In "The Locus of Authority in Colonial Massachusetts," Clifford K. Shipton stresses the contrast be-

tween decentralized notions of authority and provincial political structures. In "New England and the Challenge of Heresy," Stephen Foster points to the inherent tension created by an ideology of covenant fidelity existing alongside ecclesiastical institutions that readily accommodated heresy. Darrett Rutman maintains in his "The Mirror of Puritan Authority" that magistrates and ministers continually competed for power while Puritanism was inherently individualistic and anti-authoritarian.

Foster's essay contains observations he made earlier in *Their Solitary Way*, a study of the Puritan social ethic. Foster there argued that New England was founded on pairs of mutually exclusive ideals: submission to a hierarchically arranged authority and voluntary participation in civic life, rule by divine law and rule by popular elections, the purity of the Church and the necessity for social discipline, and contentment in one's native social condition and the calling to increase one's worldly estate. Foster concludes that moral reform efforts by third-generation preachers, such as Cotton Mather and Solomon Stoddard (1643–1729), were based on the supposition that the Church had to extend itself into secular society rather than to pursue visible purity. In *Valley of Discord*, a description of social affairs in the Connecticut Valley from 1636 to 1725, Paul R. Lucas asserts that ecclesiastical debates ruined (from the start) any attempts by the churches to exercise a unifying authority over common life. Rutman's important analysis of the development of Boston during its first decades, *Winthrop's Boston*, contains an explanation of lay/clerical conflicts in New England's largest town. According to Rutman, social schism and economic competition made it impossible to realize the kind of social solidarity and Christian unity idealized in the *Arbella* speech of Governor John Winthrop (1606–1676). Rutman interprets the settlement of new villages, divisions between Boston's selectmen and the populace, and antinomian resistance to clerical authority as manifestations of class divisions. Such conflicts, he concludes, represented an acceptance of modern notions of contractualism, individualism, and pluralism. Bernard Bailyn's *The New England Merchants in the Seventeenth Century* describes conflicts between Puritan leaders, who attempted to isolate New England from English social practice, and merchants, who sought freedom from Calvinist economic prohibitions and who wanted to extend commercial activities across the Atlantic.

A second focus for the study of social developments in New England is the growth of individual communities. Among the many local histories, three stand out in their relevance to church-state issues. In *A New England Town*, Kenneth A. Lockridge concentrates on Dedham, Massachusetts, from its founding in 1636 to 1736. Relying on voting records, court cases, population figures, and church lists, Lockridge argues that during its first fifty years

Dedham achieved a remarkable amount of social solidarity and religious cohesion. Most of the residents submitted to the town covenant, joined the church, voted, and lived in relative peace. After 1686, however, centrifugal forces such as distant land grants (sometimes settled by distinctly non-Puritan types) divided Dedham. Outlying settlers contested the authority of the town's selectmen, and successfully appealed to the General Court to allow the establishment of new churches. Social fragmentation, aggravated by the need for land, forced Dedham to accept class divisions and religious diversity. In his *Puritan Village,* Sumner Chilton Powell shows a similar developmental pattern in Sudbury, Massachusetts. Local factionalism over the use of land, Powell maintains, spilled over into religious quarrels in Sudbury. Philip Greven's *Four Generations* is a historical-demographic study of Andover, Massachusetts. Like Lockridge's Dedham, the Andover Greven presents initially attained a tight-knit social order based on religious ideals. Greven however, links the disintegration of this utopia to generational shifts in family patterns. In his view, communal authority in Andover resided in control over partially extended families established by the first generation. This patrilineal pattern, buttressed by the longevity of the founders and by the proportionately high percentage of church membership among them, broke down under the pressure of rising population. As the grandchildren of the first settlers began to seek their own lands, they moved out of the original homestead and married at a younger age than did their parents. Nuclear, individualistic family structures, maintains Greven, increasingly resulted in a shift in the locus of communal authority. Several other local histories (e.g., John J. Waters's "Hingham, Massachusetts," John Frye's "Class, Generation, and Social Change") and synthetic treatments of the social development of New England towns (e.g. Bruce C. Daniels's *The Connecticut Town* and Michael Zuckerman's *Peaceable Kingdoms*) address issues similar to those raised by Lockridge, Powell, and Greven.

Puritanism's impact on domestic relations (the moral force it exercised in structuring family practices, providing rules for domestic conduct, and contributing to nuclear-family loyalties) is examined in Edmund S. Morgan's *The Puritan Family* and John Demos's *A Little Commonwealth.* During the seventeenth century, the use of slaves and indentured servants became more widespread in New England. As Lawrence W. Towner argues in his "A Fondness for Freedom," new laws regulating slave-master relations were intended to inject Puritan morality into an otherwise unjustifiable system. Winthrop D. Jordan's *White Over Black* remains the most substantial account of New England's accommodation to black slavery.

A third and related discussion within the social history of New England revolves around the place of Puritanism in social conflicts such as the Salem witchcraft trials. Drawing on Morgan's assessment that Puritan religiosity fostered a kind of family tribalism, Demos contends that Calvinist ethics tended to inhibit expressions of disobedience, independence, or conflict in the nuclear family. Repressed adolescent aggression, he asserts, later manifested itself in social conflicts. In his *Entertaining Satan,* Demos extends this argument into one explanation for the witchcraft hysteria and trials that staggered New England in the 1690s. Such outbursts, Demos maintains, resulted from the lack of institutional channels for voicing anger, discontent, and jealousies. Deprived of a public forum for conflict by the churches' insistence on obedience to authority and submission to the common good, New Englanders tried to legitimate their social hostilities by accusations of supernatural evil. In *Salem Possessed,* Paul Boyer and Stephen Nissenbaum assessed the social origins of the witchcraft trials in terms of economic class divisions in Salem Village. As described by Boyer and Nissenbaum, Salem Village was divided into two distinct social groups: a middle- to upper-income class with commercial interests in the town center, and a lower-income class of farmers who sought to maintain an isolated community with cohesive moral values. The latter group, fearful of the socially disruptive effects of commercial activism, defended their communal order by accusing members of the former group of witchcraft. Demos's conclusions, and those of Boyer and Nissenbaum, support the central thesis of Kai T. Erikson's social-psychological analysis of Puritan conceptions of deviant behavior, *Wayward Puritans.* Erikson contends that Puritan legal and moral conventions were ambiguous about the relation between individual freedom and social discipline. By resorting to the idea of supernatural malevolence, Erikson asserts, Puritans formed a new frame of reference with which to define deviance. Salem's witches, Boston's Anne Hutchinson, and Rhode Island's Quakers were judged to be satanically criminal because their behavior violated perceived yet inadequately rationalized rules of normative social conduct.

A fourth area for the study of the relation between the Puritan churches and colonial social institutions covers the impact of English settlements on New England's Indians. Much of the debate here has centered on the causes and consequences of violent confrontations such as King Philip's War (1675–1676). Douglas E. Leach's *Flintlock and Tomahawk* narrates the war itself. In *New England Frontier,* Alden T. Vaughan argues that the fighting resulted from conflicts between Puritan conceptions of legal justice and Pequot understandings of the territorial rights of their tribe and competing Indian groups. Kenneth M. Morrison maintains in "The Bias of Colonial Law" that the New England settlers' reaction to Abenaki legal traditions stemmed from a fear of native barbarism and that white racism, predicated on the supposed superiority of English law, aggravated Indian antipathies towards settlers. In

The Invasion of America, Francis Jennings attempts to show that Puritan missionary activity among the Indians, including the organization of Massachusetts' Praying Town Indians, was inseparable from New England's quest for Indian lands. Most recently, Neal Salisbury's *Manitou and Providence* provides an analysis of European settlement in New England from the emerging perspective of historical ecology.

In his concise essay on differences between seventeenth-century institutions in Geneva and those in Boston, entitled "Protestant Parishes in the Old World and the New," Robert M. Kingdon points out the distinctive character of the New England parish system. In contrast to European Calvinism, which maintained the practice of identifying a parish as a geographical unit under the authority of a state-supported church, New England congregationalists located ecclesiastical control within the parish itself. Almost unrelated to geographical boundaries, Kingdon contends, Boston's congregational parishes consisted of voluntary members drawn from different parts of the city. According to Kingdon, sectarianism, the hostility of royal government, and ethnic diversity created competition for religious loyalties and reinforced the voluntaryism and individualism of American church "parishes." Kingdon's reflections and the above social and local histories of colonial New England suggest a summary observation: while New England congregationalist churches gradually lost much of their control over provincial politics—and thereby began to accept the idea of a religiously plural society subject to political principles that did not acknowledge the civic authority of orthodox Puritanism—they continually struggled to assert moral and spiritual prerogatives on local levels. Accordingly, examination of local practices and of the relation between religious authority and public affairs in various social settings has greatly benefited interpretations of church-state issues in early New England.

BIBLIOGRAPHY

PRIMARY SOURCE EDITIONS

Bradford, William. Of Plymouth Plantation, 1620-1647. Edited by Samuel Eliot Morison. New York: Knopf, 1952.

Hall, David D., ed. The Antinomian Controversy, 1636-1638: A Documentary History. Middletown, Conn.: Wesleyan University Press, 1968.

Heimert, Alan, and Delbanco, Nicholas, eds. The Puritans in America: A Narrative Anthology. Cambridge, Mass.: Harvard University Press, 1985.

Mather, Cotton. Magnalia Christi Americana. Books I and II. Edited by Kenneth B. Murdock with the assistance of Elizabeth W. Miller. Cambridge, Mass.: Belknap Press, 1977.

Miller, Perry, and Johnson, Thomas H., eds. The Puritans. 2 vols. 1938. rev. ed. New York: Harper and Row, 1963.

Morgan, Edmund S., ed. Puritan Political Ideas, 1558-1794. Indianapolis: Bobbs-Merrill, 1965.

Sewall, Samuel. The Diary of Samuel Sewall, 1674-1729. Edited by Halsey Thomas. 2 vols. New York: Farrar, Straus and Giroux, 1973.

Williams, Roger. The Complete Writings. 7 vols. Edited by Perry Miller. New York: Russell and Russell, 1963.

SECONDARY SOURCES

Ahlstrom, Sydney E. "The Saybrook Platform: A 250th
    Anniversary Retrospect." American Congregational
    Association, Boston. Library. Bulletin of the
    Congregational Library 9 (October 1959), 5-10.

Ahlstrom, Sydney E. "Thomas Hooker--Puritanism and Democratic
    Citizenship: A Preliminary Enquiry into Some of the
    Relationships of Religion and American Civic
    Responsibility." Church History 32 (December 1963), 415-
    431.

Allen, David Grayson. In English Ways: The Movement of
    Societies and the Transferal of English Local Law and Custom
    to Massachusetts Bay in the Seventeenth Century. Chapel
    Hill: University of North Carolina Press, 1981.

Allen, David Grayson. "A Tale of Two Towns: Persistent English
    Localism in Seventeenth-Century Massachusetts." In Contrast
    and Connection: Bicentennial Essays in Anglo-American
    History, edited by H. C. Allen and Roger Thompson, 1-35.
    London: Bell, 1976.

Andrews, Charles M. The Colonial Period of American History.
    4 vols. New Haven: Yale University Press, 1933-1938.

Axtell, James. The School upon a Hill: Education and Society
    in Colonial New England. New Haven: Yale University Press,
    1974.

Axtell, James. "The White Indians of Colonial America."
    William and Mary Quarterly, 3d ser., 32 (January 1975), 55-
    88.

Bailyn, Bernard. The New England Merchants in the Seventeenth
    Century. Cambridge, Mass.: Harvard University Press, 1955.

Bailyn, Bernard. The Origins of American Politics. New York:
    Knopf, 1968.

Barnes, Viola F. The Dominion of New England: A Study in
    British Colonial Policy. New Haven: Yale University Press,
    1923.

Battis, Emery. Saints and Sectaries: Anne Hutchinson and the
    Antinomian Controversy. Chapel Hill: University of North
    Carolina Press, 1962.

Beales, Ross W., Jr. "The Half-Way Covenant and Religious
    Scrupulosity: The First Church of Dorchester, Massachusetts,
    as a Test Case." William and Mary Quarterly, 3d ser., 31
    (July 1974), 465-480.

Beaver, R. Pierce. "Methods in American Missions to the Indians in the Seventeenth and Eighteenth Centuries: Calvinist Models for Protestant Foreign Missions." Journal of Presbyterian History 47 (June 1969), 124-148.

Bercovitch, Sacvan. "The Historiography of Johnson's Wonder-Working Providence." Essex Institute Historical Collections 104 (April 1968), 138-161.

Bercovitch, Sacvan. The Puritan Origins of the American Self. New Haven: Yale University Press, 1975.

Bercovitch, Sacvan. "Rhetoric as Authority: Puritanism, the Bible, and the Myth of America." Social Science Information (Great Britain) 21, no. 1 (1982), 5-17.

Bercovitch, Sacvan. "Typology in Puritan New England: The Williams-Cotton Controversy Reassessed." American Quarterly 19 (Summer 1967), 166-191.

Bosher, Robert S. The Making of the Restoration Settlement: The Influence of the Laudians, 1649-1662. Westminster, England: Dacre Press, 1951.

Boyer, Paul, and Nissenbaum, Stephen. Salem Possessed: The Social Origins of Witchcraft. Cambridge, Mass.: Harvard University Press, 1974.

Breen, Timothy H. The Character of the Good Ruler: A Study of Puritan Political Ideas in New England, 1630-1730. New Haven: Yale University Press, 1970.

Breen, Timothy H. Puritans and Adventurers: Change and Persistence in Early America. New York: Oxford University Press, 1980.

Breen, Timothy H. "Who Governs: The Town Franchise in Seventeenth-Century Massachusetts." William and Mary Quarterly, 3d ser., 27 (July 1970), 460-474.

Brenner, Elise M. "To Pray or to Be Prey: That is the Question: Strategies for Cultural Autonomy of Massachusetts Praying Town Indians." Ethnohistory 27 (Spring 1980), 135-152.

Bridenbaugh, Carl. Cities in the Wilderness: The First Century of Urban Life in America, 1625-1742. 1938. 2d ed. New York: Knopf, 1955.

Brockunier, Samuel H. The Irrepressible Democrat, Roger Williams. New York: Ronald Press, 1940.

Brown, B. Katherine. "The Controversy over the Franchise in Puritan Massachusetts, 1954-1974." William and Mary Quarterly, 3d ser., 33 (April 1976), 212-241.

Brown, B. Katherine. "Freemanship in Puritan Massachusetts."
     American Historical Review 49 (July 1954), 865-883.

Brown, Robert E. "Democracy in Colonial Massachusetts." _New
     England Quarterly_ 25 (September 1952), 291-313.

Buckley, Thomas E. "Church and State in Massachusetts Bay: A
     Case Study of Baptist Dissenters, 1651." _Journal of Church
     and State_ 23 (Spring 1981), 309-322.

Bumsted, John M. "A Well-Bounded Toleration: Church and State
     in the Plymouth Colony." _Journal of Church and State_ 10
     (Spring 1968), 265-279.

Bumsted, John M. "The Pilgrim's Progress: The Ecclesiastical
     History of the Old Colony, 1620-1775." Ph.D. diss., Brown
     University, 1965.

Bushman, Richard. _From Puritan to Yankee: Character and the
     Social Order in Connecticut, 1680-1765_. Cambridge, Mass.:
     Harvard University Press, 1967.

Butler, Jon. "Magic, Astrology, and the Early American
     Religious Heritage, 1600-1760." _American Historical Review_,
     84 (April 1979), 317-346.

Carroll, Peter N. _Puritanism and the Wilderness: The
     Intellectual Significance of the New England Frontier, 1629-
     1700_. New York: Columbia University Press, 1969.

Chadwick, Hansen. "The Metamorphosis of Tituba, or Why
     American Intellectuals Can't Tell an Indian Witch from a
     Negro." _New England Quarterly_ 47 (March 1974), 3-12.

Chu, Jonathan M. "The Social Context of Religious Heterodoxy:
     The Challenge of Seventeenth-Century Quakerism to Orthodoxy
     in Massachusetts." _Essex Institute Historical Collections_
     118 (April 1982), 119-150.

Clark, Charles E. _The Eastern Frontier: The Settlement of
     Northern New England, 1610-1763_. New York: Knopf, 1970.

Cobb, Sanford H. _The Rise of Religious Liberty in America_.
     New York: Macmillan, 1902.

Cohen, Ronald D. "Church and State in Seventeenth-Century
     Massachusetts: Another Look at the Antinomian Controversy."
     Journal of Church and State 12 (Autumn 1970), 475-494.

Cook, Edward M., Jr. _The Fathers of the Towns: Leadership and
     Community Structure in Eighteenth-Century New England_.
     Baltimore: Johns Hopkins University Press, 1976.

Cook, George Allen. _John Wise: Early American Democrat_. New
     York: King's Crown Press, 1952.

Cott, Nancy F. "Divorce and the Changing Status of Women in Eighteenth-Century Massachusetts." William and Mary Quarterly, 3d ser., 33 (October 1976), 586-614.

Covey, Cyclone. The Gentle Radical: A Biography of Roger Williams. New York: Macmillan, 1966.

Craven, Wesley Frank. The Colonies in Transition, 1660-1713. New York: Harper and Row, 1968.

Cross, Arthur Lyon. The Anglican Episcopate and the American Colonies. New York: Longmans, Green, and Co., 1902.

Curran, Francis X. Catholics in Colonial Law. Chicago: Loyola University Press, 1963.

Daly, Robert. God's Altar: The World and the Flesh in Puritan Poetry. Berkeley: University of California Press, 1978.

Daniels, Bruce C. The Connecticut Town: Growth and Development, 1635-1790. Middletown, Conn.: Wesleyan University Press, 1979.

Daniels, Bruce C. "Dissent and Disorder: The Radical Impulse and Early Government in the Founding of Rhode Island." Journal of Church and State 24 (Spring 1982), 357-378.

Demos, John. Entertaining Satan: Witchcraft and the Culture of Early New England. New York: Oxford University Press, 1982.

Demos, John. A Little Commonwealth: Family Life in Plymouth Colony. New York: Oxford University Press, 1970.

Demos, John. "Underlying Themes in the Witchcraft of Seventeenth-Century New England." American Historical Review 75 (June 1970), 1311-1326.

Dunn, Mary Maples. "Saints and Sisters: Congregational and Quaker Women in the Early Colonial Period." American Quarterly 30 (Winter 1978), 582-601.

Dunn, Richard S. "Experiments Holy and Unholy." In The Westward Enterprise: English Activities in Ireland, the Atlantic, and America, 1480-1630, edited by K. R. Andrews, N. P. Canny, and P. E. H. Hair, 271-289. Liverpool, England: Liverpool University Press, 1978.

Dunn, Richard S. Puritans and Yankees: The Winthrop Dynasty of New England, 1630-1717. Princeton, N.J.: Princeton University Press, 1962.

Elliott, Emory. Power and the Pulpit in Puritan New England. Princeton, N.J.: Princeton University Press, 1975.

Ellis, John Tracy. <u>Catholics in Colonial America</u>. Benedictine Studies, vol. 8. Baltimore: Helicon Press, 1965.

Erikson, Kai T. <u>Wayward Puritans: A Study in the Sociology of Deviance</u>. New York: John Wiley & Sons, 1966.

Eusden, John D. "Natural Law and Covenant Theology in New England, 1620-1670." <u>Natural Law Forum</u> 5 (1960), 1-30.

Fiering, Norman. <u>Moral Philosophy at Seventeenth-Century Harvard: A Discipline in Transition</u>. Chapel Hill: University of North Carolina Press, 1981.

Flaherty, David H. <u>Privacy in Colonial New England</u>. Charlottesville: University Press of Virginia, 1972.

Flaherty, David H., ed. <u>Essays in the History of Early American Law</u>. Chapel Hill: University of North Carolina Press, 1969.

Foster, Stephen. "The Massachusetts Franchise in the Seventeenth Century." <u>William and Mary Quarterly</u>, 3d ser., 24 (October 1967), 613-623.

Foster, Stephen. "New England and the Challenge of Heresy, 1630-1660: The Puritan Crisis in Transatlantic Perspective." <u>William and Mary Quarterly</u>, 3d ser., 38 (October 1981), 624-660.

Foster, Stephen. <u>Their Solitary Way: The Puritan Social Ethic in the First Century of Settlement in New England</u>. New Haven: Yale University Press, 1971.

Frye, John. "Class, Generation, and Social Change: A Case in Salem, Massachusetts, 1636-1656." <u>Journal of Popular Culture</u> 11 (Winter 1977), 743-751.

Gaskins, Richard. "Changes in Criminal Law in Eighteenth-Century Connecticut." <u>American Journal of Legal History</u> 25 (October 1981), 309-342.

Gay, Peter. <u>A Loss of Mastery: Puritan Historians in Colonial America</u>. Berkeley: University of California Press, 1966.

Gildrie, Richard. "The Ceremonial Puritan Days of Humiliation and Thanksgiving." <u>New England Historical and Genealogical Register</u> 136 (January 1982), 3-16.

Gildrie, Richard. <u>Salem, Massachusetts, 1626-1683: A Covenant Community</u>. Charlottesville: University Press of Virginia, 1975.

Greaves, Richard L. "A Colonial Fifth Monarchist? John Clarke of Rhode Island." <u>Rhode Island History</u> 40 (May 1981), 43-47.

Greenberg, Douglas. "Crime, Law Enforcement, and Social Control in Colonial America." _American Journal of Legal History_ 26 (October 1982), 293-325.

Greene, M. Louise. _The Development of Religious Liberty in Connecticut_. Boston: Houghton, Mifflin & Co., 1905.

Greven, Philip. _Four Generations: Land and Family in Colonial Andover, Massachusetts_. Ithaca, N.Y.: Cornell University Press, 1970.

Greven, Philip. _The Protestant Temperament: Patterns of Child-Rearing, Religious Experience, and the Self in Early America_. New York: Knopf, 1977.

Gura, Philip F. _A Glimpse of Sion's Glory: Puritan Radicalism in New England, 1620-1660_. Middletown, Conn.: Wesleyan University Press, 1984.

Haffenden, Philip S. _New England in the English Nation, 1689-1713_. Oxford: Clarendon Press, 1974.

Hall, David D. _The Faithful Shepherd: A History of the New England Ministry in the Seventeenth Century_. Chapel Hill: University of North Carolina Press, 1972.

Hall, David D. "The Mental World of Samuel Sewell." Massachusetts Historical Society, _Proceedings_ 92 (Boston, 1980), 21-44.

Hall, David D. "Toward A History of Popular Religion in Early New England." _William and Mary Quarterly_, 3d ser., 41 (January 1984), 49-55.

Hall, David D. "Understanding the Puritans." In _The State of American History_, edited by Herbert J. Bass, 330-349. Chicago: Quadrangle Books, 1970.

Hall, Michael G. _Edward Randolph and the American Colonies, 1676-1703_. Chapel Hill: University of North Carolina Press, 1960.

Hambrick-Stowe, Charles E. _The Practice of Piety: Puritan Devotional Disciplines in Seventeenth-Century New England_. Chapel Hill: University of North Carolina Press, 1982.

Hammond, Jeffrey A. "The Bride in Redemptive Time: John Cotton and the Canticles Controversy." _New England Quarterly_ 56 (March 1983), 78-102.

Hansen, Chadwick. _Witchcraft at Salem_. New York: George Braziller, 1969.

Haskins, George Lee. _Law and Authority in Early Massachusetts: A Study in Tradition and Design_. New York: MacMillan, 1960.

Haskins, George Lee. "Reception of the Common Law in
    Seventeenth-Century Massachusetts: A Case Study." In Law
    and Authority in Colonial America, edited by George Athan
    Billias, 17-31. Barre, Mass.: Barre Publishers, 1965.

Haskins, George Lee. "Representative Government and Biblical
    Rule in the First Years of the Massachusetts Bay Colony."
    University of Akron Law Review 9 (Fall 1975), 207-222.

Heyrman, Christine Leigh. "The Fashion Among More Superior
    People: Charity and Social Change in Provincial New England,
    1700-1740." American Quarterly 34 (Summer 1982), 107-124.

Hirsch, Elizabeth. "John Cotton and Roger Williams: Their
    Controversy Concerning Religious Liberty." Church History
    10 (March 1941), 38-51.

Holifield, E. Brooks. "On Toleration in Massachusetts."
    Church History 38 (June 1969), 188-200.

Howe, Mark DeWolfe. "The Sources and Nature of Law in Colonial
    Massachusetts." In Law and Authority in Colonial America,
    edited by George Athan Billias, 1-16. Barre, Mass.: Barre
    Publishers, 1965.

Illick, Joseph E. "Child-Rearing in Seventeenth-Century
    England and America." In The History of Childhood, edited
    by Lloyd deMause, 303-350. New York: Psychohistory Press,
    1974.

Innes, Stephen. "Land Tenancy and Social Order in Springfield,
    Massachusetts, 1652 to 1702." William and Mary Quarterly,
    3d ser., 35 (January 1978), 33-56.

James, Sydney V. Colonial Rhode Island: A History. New York:
    Scribners, 1975.

James, Sydney V. "The Worlds of Roger Williams." Rhode Island
    History 37 (November 1978), 99-109.

Jennings, Francis. The Invasion of America: Indians,
    Colonialism, and the Cant of Conquest. Chapel Hill:
    University of North Carolina Press, 1975.

Johnson, Parker H. "Humiliation Followed by Deliverance:
    Metaphor and Plot in Cotton Mather's Magnalia." Early
    American Literature 15 (Winter 1980-1981), 237-246.

Johnson, Richard R. Adjustment to Empire: The New England
    Colonies, 1675-1715. New Brunswick, N.J.: Rutgers
    University Press, 1981.

Jordan, Winthrop D. White Over Black: American Attitudes
    toward the Negro, 1550-1812. Chapel Hill: University of
    North Carolina Press, 1968.

Keller, Karl. "The Loose, Large Principles of Solomon Stoddard." Early American Literature 16 (Spring 1981), 27-41.

Kibbey, Ann. "Mutations of the Supernatural: Witchcraft, Remarkable Providences, and the Power of Puritan Men." American Quarterly 34 (Summer 1982), 125-148.

Kingdon, Robert M. "Protestant Parishes in the Old World and the New: The Case of Geneva and Boston." Church History 48 (September 1979), 290-309.

Kittredge, George L. Witchcraft in Old and New England. New York: Russell and Russell, 1956.

Knott, John R., Jr. The Sword of the Spirit: Puritan Responses to the Bible. Chicago: University of Chicago Press, 1980.

Koehler, Lyle. "The Case of the American Jezebels: Anne Hutchinson and Female Agitation During the Years of Antinomian Turmoil, 1636-1640." William and Mary Quarterly, 3d ser., 31 (January 1974), 55-78.

Konig, David Thomas. Law and Society in Puritan Massachusetts: Essex County, 1629-1692. Chapel Hill: University of North Carolina Press, 1979.

Labaree, Leonard W. Royal Government in America: A Study of the British Colonial System before 1783. New Haven: Yale University Press, 1930.

Lamont, William M. Godly Rule: Politics and Religion, 1603-60. New York: St. Martin's Press, 1969.

Langdon, George D., Jr. Pilgrim Colony: A History of New Plymouth, 1620-1691. New Haven: Yale University Press, 1966.

Lauer, Paul E. Church and State in New England. 1892. Reprint. New York: Johnson Reprint Corp., 1973.

Lawrence, David. "Jonathan Edwards, Solomon Stoddard, and the Preparationist Model of Conversion." Harvard Theological Review 72 (July-October 1979), 267-283.

Leach, Douglas E. Flintlock and Tomahawk: New England in King Philip's War. New York: MacMillan, 1958.

Leder, Lawrence H. Liberty and Authority: Early American Political Ideology, 1689-1763. Chicago: Quadrangle Books, 1968.

Lee, Charles R. "Public Poor Relief and the Massachusetts Community, 1620-1715." New England Quarterly 55 (December 1982), 564-585.

Levin, David. <u>Cotton Mather: The Young Life of the Lord's
    Remembrancer, 1663-1703</u>. Cambridge, Mass.: Harvard
    University Press, 1978.

Lockridge, Kenneth A. <u>A New England Town, The First Hundred
    Years: Dedham, Massachusetts, 1636-1736</u>. New York: W. W.
    Norton and Co., 1970.

Lockridge, Kenneth A., and Kreider, Alan. "The Evolution of
    Massachusetts Town Government, 1640-1740." <u>William and Mary
    Quarterly</u>, 3d ser., 23 (October 1966), 549-574.

Lokken, Roy N. "The Concept of Democracy in Colonial Political
    Thought." <u>William and Mary Quarterly</u>, 3d ser., 16 (October
    1959), 568-580.

Love, William Deloss. <u>The Fast and Thanksgiving Days of New
    England</u>. Boston: Houghton, Mifflin, 1895.

Lovejoy, David S. <u>The Glorious Revolution in America</u>. New
    York: Harper and Row, 1972.

Lowance, Mason I., Jr. <u>Increase Mather</u>. New York: Twayne
    Publishers, 1974.

Lowance, Mason I., Jr. <u>The Language of Canaan: Metaphor and
    Symbol in New England from the Puritans to the
    Transcendentalists</u>. Cambridge, Mass.: Harvard University
    Press, 1980.

Lucas, Paul R. "An Appeal to the Learned: The Mind of Solomon
    Stoddard." <u>William and Mary Quarterly</u>, 3d ser., 30 (April
    1973), 257-292.

Lucas, Paul R. "Colony or Commonwealth: Massachusetts Bay,
    1661-1666." <u>William and Mary Quarterly</u>, 3d ser., 24
    (January 1967), 88-107.

Lucas, Paul R. <u>Valley of Discord: Church and Society Along the
    Connecticut River, 1636-1725</u>. Hanover, N.H.: University
    Press of New England, 1976.

Maclear, J. F. "New England and the Fifth Monarchy: The Quest
    for the Millennium in Early American Puritanism." <u>William
    and Mary Quarterly</u>, 3d ser., 32 (April 1975), 223-260.

McLoughlin, William G. <u>New England Dissent 1630-1833: The
    Baptists and the Separation of Church and State</u>. 2 vols.
    Cambridge, Mass.: Harvard University Press, 1971.

Mann, Bruce H. "Rationality, Legal Change, and Community in
    Connecticut, 1690-1760." <u>Law and Society Review</u> 14 (Winter
    1980), 187-221.

Marcus, Jacob Rader. _Early American Jewry_. 2 vols. Philadelphia: Jewish Publication Society of America, 1951-53.

Martin, Calvin. "The European Impact on the Culture of a Northeastern Algonquian Tribe: An Ecological Interpretation." _William and Mary Quarterly_, 3d ser., 31 (January 1974), 3-26.

Middlekauff, Robert. _The Mathers: Three Generations of Puritan Intellectuals_. New York: Oxford University Press, 1971.

Miller, Perry. "The Contribution of the Protestant Churches to Religious Liberty in Colonial America." _Church History_ 4 (March 1935), 57-66.

Miller, Perry. _Errand into the Wilderness_. Cambridge, Mass: Harvard University Press, 1956.

Miller, Perry. _The New England Mind: From Colony to Province_. 1953. Reprint. Boston: Beacon Press, 1963.

Miller, Perry. _The New England Mind: The Seventeenth Century_. 1939. Reprint. Boston: Beacon Press, 1963.

Miller, Perry. _Orthodoxy in Massachusetts, 1630-1650_. 1933. Reprint. Gloucester, Mass.: Peter Smith, 1965.

Miller, Perry. _Roger Williams: His Contribution to the American Tradition_. Indianapolis: Bobbs-Merrill, 1953.

Miller, Perry. "Solomon Stoddard, 1643-1729." _Harvard Theological Review_ 34 (October 1941), 277-320.

Moore, LeRoy. "Religious Liberty: Roger Williams and the Revolutionary Era." _Church History_ 34 (March 1965), 57-76.

Moran, Gerald F. "Religious Renewal, Puritan Tribalism, and the Family in Seventeenth-Century Milford, Connecticut." _William and Mary Quarterly_, 3d ser., 36 (April 1979), 236-254.

Morgan, Edmund S. _The Puritan Dilemma: The Story of John Winthrop_. Boston: Little, Brown, 1958.

Morgan, Edmund S. _The Puritan Family: Religion and Domestic Relations in Seventeenth-Century New England_. 1944. rev. ed. New York: Harper and Row, 1966.

Morgan, Edmund S. _Roger Williams: The Church and the State_. New York: Harcourt, Brace and World, 1967.

Morgan, Edmund S. _Visible Saints: The History of a Puritan Idea_. Ithaca, N.Y.: Cornell University Press, 1963.

Morison, Samuel Eliot. _Builders of the Bay Colony_. Cambridge,
    Mass.: Harvard University Press, 1930.

Morison, Samuel Eliot. _Harvard College in the Seventeenth
    Century_. 2 vols. Cambridge, Mass.: Harvard University
    Press, 1936.

Morison, Samuel Eliot. _The Puritan Pronaos_. 1936. Reprinted
    as _The Intellectual Life of Colonial New England_. Ithaca,
    N.Y.: Cornell University Press, 1956.

Morris, Richard B. "Civil Liberties and Jewish Tradition in
    Early America." _American Jewish Historical Society
    Publications_ 46 (September 1956), 20-39.

Morris, Richard B. _Studies in the History of American Law,
    with Special Reference to the Seventeenth and Eighteenth
    Centuries_. 1930. 2d ed. Philadelphia: Mitchell, 1959.

Morrison, Kenneth M. "The Bias of Colonial Law: English
    Paranoia and the Abenaki Arena of King Philip's War, 1675-
    1678." _New England Quarterly_ 53 (September 1980), 363-387.

Murdock, Kenneth B. _Increase Mather, Foremost American
    Puritan_. Cambridge, Mass.: Harvard University Press, 1925.

Nelsen, Anne Kusener. "King Philip's War and the Hubbard-
    Mather Rivalry." _William and Mary Quarterly_, 3d ser., 27
    (October 1970), 615-629.

Nuttall, Geoffrey. _The Holy Spirit in Puritan Faith and
    Experience_. Oxford: Blackwell, 1946.

Oberholzer, Emil, Jr. _Delinquent Saints: Disciplinary Action
    in the Early Congregational Churches of Massachusetts_. New
    York: Columbia University Press, 1956.

Park, Charles E. "Puritans and Quakers." _New England
    Quarterly_ 27 (March 1954), 53-74.

Parkes, Henry Bamford. "John Cotton and Roger Williams Debate
    Toleration." _New England Quarterly_ 4 (October 1931), 735-
    756.

Peacock, John. "Liberty and Discipline in Covenant Theology."
    Canadian Review of American Studies 15 (Spring 1984), 1-16.

Pettit, Norman. _The Heart Prepared: Grace and Conversion in
    Puritan Spiritual Life_. New Haven: Yale University Press,
    1966.

Pope, Robert G. _The Half-Way Covenant: Church Membership in
    Puritan New England_. Princeton, N.J.: Princeton University
    Press, 1968.

Pope, Robert. "New England Versus the New England Mind: The
     Myth of Declension." _Journal of Social History_ 3 (Winter
     1969-1970), 95-108.

Powell, Sumner Chilton. _Puritan Village: The Formation of a_
     New England Town. Middletown, Conn.: Wesleyan University
     Press, 1963.

Reed, Susan M. _Church and State in Massachusetts, 1691-1740_.
     University of Illinois Studies in the Social Sciences, vol.
     3, no. 4. Urbana: University of Illinois Press, 1914.

Reinitz, Richard. "The Typological Arguments for Religious
     Toleration: The Separatist Tradition and Roger Williams."
     Early American Literature 5 (Spring 1970), 74-97.

Riley, Arthur J. _Catholicism in New England to 1788_.
     Washington, D.C.: Catholic University of America, 1936.

Rosenmeier, Jesper. "New England's Perfection: The Image of
     Adam and the Image of Christ in the Antinomian Crisis, 1634
     to 1639." _William and Mary Quarterly_, 3d ser., 27 (July
     1970), 435-459.

Rosenmeier, Jesper. "The Teacher and the Witness: John Cotton
     and Roger Williams." _William and Mary Quarterly_, 3d ser.,
     25 (July 1968), 408-431.

Rutman, Darrett. _American Puritanism: Faith and Practice_.
     Philadelphia: Lippincott, 1970.

Rutman, Darrett. "The Mirror of Puritan Authority." In _Law_
     and Authority in Colonial America, edited by George Athan
     Billias, 149-167. Barre, Mass.: Barre Publishers, 1965.

Rutman, Darrett. "The Social Web: A Prospectus for the Study
     of the Early American Community." In _Insights and_
     Parallels: Problems and Issues of American Social History,
     edited by William L. O'Neill, 57-88. Minneapolis: Burgess
     Pub. Co., 1973.

Rutman, Darrett. _Winthrop's Boston: Portrait of a Puritan_
     Town, 1630-1649. Chapel Hill: University of North Carolina
     Press, 1965.

Salisbury, Neal. _Manitou and Providence: Indians, Europeans,_
     and the Making of New England, 1500-1643. New York: Oxford
     University Press, 1982.

Salisbury, Neal. "Red Puritans: The 'Praying Indians' of
     Massachusetts and John Eliot." _William and Mary Quarterly_,
     3d ser., 31 (January 1974), 27-54.

Sargent, Lyman Tower. "Utopianism in Colonial America." History of Political Thought (Great Britain) 4 (Winter 1983), 483-522.

Sehr, Timothy J. "Defending Orthodoxy in Massachusetts, 1650-1652." Historical Journal of Massachusetts 9 (January 1981), 30-40.

Seidman, Aaron B. "Church and State in the Early Years of the Massachusetts Bay Colony." New England Quarterly 18 (June 1945), 211-233.

Selement, George. "The Meeting of the Elite and Popular Minds at Cambridge, New England, 1638-1645." William and Mary Quarterly, 3d ser., 41 (January 1984), 32-48.

Shipton, Clifford K. "The Locus of Authority in Colonial Massachusetts." In Law and Authority in Colonial America, edited by George Athan Billias, 136-148. Barre, Mass.: Barre Publishers, 1965.

Shuffelton, Frank. Thomas Hooker, 1586-1647. Princeton, N.J.: Princeton University Press, 1977.

Silverman, Kenneth. The Life and Times of Cotton Mather. New York: Harper and Row, 1984.

Simmons, Richard C. "The Founding of the Third Church in Boston." William and Mary Quarterly, 3d ser., 26 (April 1969), 241-252.

Simmons, Richard C. "Godliness, Property, and the Franchise in Puritan Massachusetts: An Interpretation." Journal of American History 55 (December 1968), 495-511.

Simmons, William S. "Conversion from Indian to Puritan." New England Quarterly 52 (June 1979), 197-218.

Simpson, Alan. Puritanism in Old and New England. Chicago: University of Chicago Press, 1955.

Slotkin, Richard. "Narratives of Negro Crime in New England, 1675-1800." American Quarterly 25 (March 1973), 3-31.

Slotkin, Richard. Regeneration through Violence: The Mythology of the American Frontier, 1600-1860. Middletown, Conn.: Wesleyan University Press, 1973.

Smith, Daniel Scott. "Parental Power and Marriage Patterns: An Analysis of Historical Trends in Hingham, Massachusetts." Journal of Marriage and the Family 35 (August 1973), 419-439.

Smith, Peter H. "Politics and Sainthood: Biography by Cotton Mather." *William and Mary Quarterly*, 3d ser., 20 (April 1963), 186-206.

Solberg, Winton U. *Redeem the Time: The Puritan Sabbath in Early America*. Cambridge, Mass.: Harvard University Press, 1977.

Sosin, Jack M. *English America and the Restoration Monarchy of Charles II: Transatlantic Politics, Commerce, and Kinship*. Lincoln: University of Nebraska Press, 1980.

Sosin, Jack M. *English America and the Revolution of 1688: Royal Administration and the Structure of Provincial Government*. Lincoln: University of Nebraska Press, 1982.

Stanford, Ann. "Anne Bradstreet: Dogmatist as Rebel." *New England Quarterly* 39 (September 1966), 373-389.

Starkey, Marion. *The Devil in Massachusetts: A Modern Enquiry into the Salem Witch Trials*. New York: Knopf, 1969.

Stead, G. A. "Roger Williams and the Massachusetts Bay." *New England Quarterly* 7 (June 1934), 235-257.

Stoever, William K. B. *"A Faire and Easie Way to Heaven": Covenant Theology and Antinomianism in Early Massachusetts*. Middletown, Conn.: Wesleyan University Press, 1978.

Swift, Lindsay. "The Massachusetts Election Sermons." Colonial Society of Massachusetts, *Transactions* 1 (Boston, 1895), 388-451.

Thomas, G. E. "Puritans, Indians, and the Concept of Race." *New England Quarterly* 48 (March 1975), 3-27.

Tichi, Cecilia. *New World, New Earth: Environmental Reform in American Literature*. New Haven: Yale University Press, 1979.

Towner, Lawrence W. "A Fondness for Freedom: Servant Protest in Puritan Society." *William and Mary Quarterly*, 3d ser., 19 (April 1962), 201-219.

Tucker, Bruce. "Beyond Reason and Revelation: Perspectives on the Puritan Enlightenment." *Studies in Eighteenth-Century Culture* 10 (1981), 165-179.

Tucker, Bruce. "The Reinterpretation of Puritan History in Provincial New England." *New England Quarterly* 54 (December 1981), 481-498.

Turner, Eldron R. "Peasants and Parsons: John Wise's Churches Quarrel Espoused." *Early American Literature* 18 (Fall 1983), 146-170.

Twombly, Robert C., and Moore, Robert H. "Black Puritan: The Negro in Seventeenth-Century Massachusetts." William and Mary Quarterly, 3d ser., 24 (April 1967), 224-242.

Van Deventer, David E. The Emergence of Provincial New Hampshire, 1623-1741. Baltimore: Johns Hopkins University Press, 1976.

Van de Wetering, Maxine. "Moralizing in Puritan Natural Science: Mysteriousness in Earthquake Sermons." Journal of the History of Ideas 43 (July-September 1982), 417-438.

Vaughan, Alden T. New England Frontier: Puritans and Indians, 1620-1675. Boston: Little, Brown, 1965.

Vaughan, Alden T. "Peqots and Puritans: The Causes of the War of 1637." William and Mary Quarterly, 3d ser., 21 (April 1964), 256-269.

Waerden, G. B. "Law Reform in England and New England, 1620-1660." William and Mary Quarterly, 3d ser., 35 (October 1978), 668-690.

Wall, Robert E. "The Decline of the Massachusetts Franchise, 1647-1666." Journal of American History 59 (September 1982), 303-310.

Wall, Robert E. Massachusetts Bay: The Crucial Decade, 1640-1650. New Haven: Yale University Press, 1972.

Walsh, James P. "Holy Time and Sacred Space in Puritan New England." American Quarterly 32 (Spring 1980), 79-95.

Walzer, Michael. "Puritanism as a Revolutionary Ideology." History and Theory 3 (1965), 59-90.

Warch, Richard. School of the Prophets: Yale College, 1701-1740. New Haven: Yale University Press, 1973.

Ward, Harry M. Statism in Plymouth Colony. Port Washington, N.Y.: Kennikat Press, 1973.

Waters, John J. "Hingham, Massachusetts, 1631-1661: An East Anglican Oligarchy in the New World." Journal of Social History 1 (Summer 1968), 351-370.

Weisberg, D. Kelly. "'Under Greet Temptations Heer': Women and Divorce in Puritan Massachusetts." Feminist Studies 2, no. 2/3 (1975), 183-194.

Wertenbaker, Thomas Jefferson. The Puritan Oligarchy: The Founding of American Civilization. New York: Charles Scribner's Sons, 1947.

Williams, Selma R. <u>Divine Rebel: The Life of Anne Marbury Hutchinson</u>. New York: Holt, Reinhart and Winston, 1981.

Winslow, Ola Elizabeth. <u>Master Roger Williams: A Biography</u>. New York: Macmillan, 1957.

Youngs, J. William T., Jr. "Congregational Clericalism: New England Ordinations before the Great Awakening." <u>William and Mary Quarterly</u>, 3d ser., 31 (July 1974), 481-90.

Zanger, Jules. "Crime and Punishment in Early Massachusetts." <u>William and Mary Quarterly</u>, 3d ser., 22 (July 1965).

Zemsky, Robert M. <u>Merchants, Farmers, and River Gods: An Essay on Eighteenth-Century American Politics</u>. Boston: Gambit, 1971.

Ziff, Larzer. <u>The Career of John Cotton: Puritanism and the American Experience</u>. Princeton, N.J.: Princeton University Press, 1962.

Ziff, Larzer. <u>Puritanism in America: New Culture in a New World</u>. New York: Viking Press, 1973.

Ziff, Larzer. "The Social Bond of the Church Covenant." <u>American Quarterly</u> 10 (Winter 1958), 454-462.

Zuckerman, Michael. <u>Peaceable Kingdoms: New England Towns in the Eighteenth Century</u>. New York: Knopf, 1970.

3

Church-State Relations
in the Colonial South

Leigh Eric Schmidt

From the settling of Jamestown in 1607 the Church of England occupied a privileged and important place in the society of the southern colonies. By 1758, with the formal establishment of Anglicanism in Georgia, the Church was the officially preferred religion throughout the colonial South. Preferment and establishment, however, did not necessarily result in strength and uniformity. The Anglican establishments faced problems and challenges throughout the colonial era. Church-state issues—particularly the scope of religious toleration and the range of privileges to be accorded the establishment—were among the most perplexing of these problems and debates, whether in Virginia, the Carolinas, or Georgia. These issues, coalescing around the relationship between Anglicanism and dissent, have spawned a rich and voluminous literature. Some of the writing has been synoptic, attempting to analyze the experience of the southern colonies as a whole. More often scholars have subdivided their treatment of church-state relations in the colonial South, colony by colony, with Virginia being the primary beneficiary of this approach. Other students of the southern colonies have dealt with exemplary figures like Samuel Davies or James Blair and through them have attempted to illumine the broader debates on church and state. Still others have concentrated not so much on individual colonies or on particular figures but instead given their attention to specific issues—slavery most extensively. In surveying the literature on religion and politics in the southern colonies each of these approaches will be discussed and salient examples of each lifted out of the bibliography for discussion. In this way the introductory essay serves here as both historiographical overview and guide to the bibliography.

Of the general works covering relations between church and state in the American colonies, Sanford H. Cobb's *The Rise of Religious Liberty in America* remains the best overall survey of the colonial period. Though

Whiggish in its orientation, it is less tendentious in this regard than Anson Phelps Stokes's three-volume *Church and State in the United States*, which, along with its Whiggishness, also slights the development of church-state relations in the colonial era. Unlike Stokes, Cobb manages to moderate his satisfaction with the fall of the Anglican establishments, even as he heralds the triumph of religious liberty. While fullest in his narrative of Virginia's experience, Cobb also adequately sketches the church-state issues for the Carolinas and somewhat less adequately for Georgia. His work is a good starting point for a general delineation of church-state relations in the colonies. To Cobb's early study, one should add the broadly interpretive work of Sidney Mead. His second essay in *The Lively Experiment*, "From Coercion to Persuasion: Another Look at the Rise of Religious Liberty," is particularly apposite for church-state issues in the colonial South.

Many of the more recent synoptic works on the southern colonies have involved church-state relations only tangentially, but they are nonetheless valuable for establishing a broader context in which to pursue church-state issues. Carl Bridenbaugh in his *Myths and Realities: Societies of the Colonial South* offers one of the most concise and cogent portrayals of the diverse cultures of the Chesapeake, the Carolinas, and the backcountry. In the colonial era, Bridenbaugh argues, there was not one South, but several Souths— each with distinctive religious, economic, and social patterns. *Religion in the Southern States*, edited by Samuel Hill, is another survey which adds to Bridenbaugh's picture of a plural and heterogeneous South. While the essays in Hill's volume focus on post-colonial periods, the authors begin their stories where appropriate in the colonial era. A more important, yet less variegated, synthesis is Donald Mathews's *Religion in the Old South*. His analysis concentrates almost exclusively on nineteenth-century southern Evangelicalism, but by way of introduction he offers a trenchant discussion of Anglicanism's decline in the eighteenth century and of the rise of the Baptists and Methodists to dominance in its stead. Mathews's monograph is a stalwart achievement in its synthesis of early Evangelical history in the South. In a different vein, Richard B. Davis's monumental three-volume *Intellectual Life in the Colonial South* presents not so much synthetic distillation as encyclopedic coverage. His detailed chapters on religion are the most complete renderings available of the theological and spiritual life of the southern colonies. His volumes simply dwarf anything else on the intellectual history of the colonial South. Finally, Philip Greven's far-ranging study, *The Protestant Temperament*, offers unusual psychological insight into three paradigmatic religious orientations in colonial America: the genteel, the Evangelical, and the moderate. Greven's work shows considerable analytical acumen in probing the religious experience and social practices of the southern gentry, moderates like the Presbyterians, and militant backcountry dissenters like the Baptists. Again, as with the other works, Greven's study is a place to begin, a way to gain hold of a wider social and religious context in which to set the more particular studies of church-state relations.

Most writers have veered away from synoptic studies and found the narrower confines of individual colonies to be the better and more navigable approach. America's earliest and largest colony, Virginia, has received the lion's share of attention from those who have taken this line. The Church of England took root early in colonial Virginia, and religion—or at least religious rhetoric—suffused the venture from the first. In a rare glance southward, Perry Miller limned what he pictured as a deep religious wellspring empowering the Virginia enterprise as surely as one had, in Miller's opinion, driven the New England experiment. His two articles on "The Religious Impulse in the Founding of Virginia" set out the intellectual history of the first decades of the colony—a history that in a sense makes the earliest Virginians over into the image of the Puritans, but also recaptures an essential spiritual dynamic too often overlooked in studies of seventeenth-century Virginia.

Miller's articles are something of an exception. Generally when historians have taken up the religious history of early Virginia, a marked institutional and ecclesiological, instead of intellectual, bent has characterized their work. This predilection has made the ecclesiastical and political workings of Anglicanism the preferred subject. Exemplary of the best in this historiography are the studies by William Seiler and Arthur Middleton, who have both examined the colonial Anglican parish and vestry. Within this category as well are George Brydon's works, notably his *Virginia's Mother Church*—the most comprehensive study of Virginian Anglicanism, though not the most dispassionate. Numerous additional articles in this ecclesiological vein (for example, those of Spencer Ervin and William Perry) can be culled from the *Historical Magazine of the Protestant Episcopal Church*, a cornucopia for detailed institutional studies of colonial Anglicanism. This bibliography has listed only the most salient and valuable examples, and the *Historical Magazine* itself should be consulted for still further accounts.

Recently historians have shown signs of moving beyond Miller's brief anatomizing of Virginia's Puritan mind and beyond the many institutional histories that have treated Anglicanism as the sole religious force in seventeenth-century Virginia. One indication of this new direction is the work of Darrett Rutman and Jon Butler. Both Rutman's "The Evolution of Religious Life in Early Virginia," and Butler's "Magic, Astrology, and the Early American Religious Heritage" stress the presence of extra-institutional forms of religious experience and practice in the colonies that could complement or compete with the churches. They point to a rich current of popular religion, involving, for example, spells, charms, alchemy, astrology, and witchcraft. "To understand what many colonists meant by religion," Butler maintains, "historians need to move beyond the study of ecclesiology, theology, and the ministry to recover non-institutional religious practices" (p. 318). As one illustration, Butler uses the case of the seventeenth-century Virginian cleric, Thomas Teackle, who appears to have blended his Anglicanism with a broad-based Hermeticism and occultism. Teackle is but one example of the colonists' continued fascination with various European forms of magic and heterodoxy. Both Butler and Rutman underline this fascination and attempt to push historians to broader conceptions of religion in colonial America—in Rutman's case in seventeenth-century Virginia in particular. In turn their broadening of the religious spectrum should raise new questions for those examining issues of church and state: for example, did the Anglican establishment ever really gain hegemony at a popular level, or, more concretely, how did popular religious beliefs affect witchcraft trials and accusations (nineteen examples of which, Rutman reminds us, remain on record for Virginia to 1705)?

Students of the Quakers have also pointed to another side of the religious life of seventeenth-century Virginia. The Quakers found persecution in Virginia as they did in New England. A number of stringent laws were passed against them in the Old Dominion beginning in 1659, and they only gained marginal toleration over the next sixty years through a combination of boldness and persistence. Kenneth L. Carroll's "Quakerism on the Eastern Shore of Virginia" traces the Quakers' disturbing appearance in Virginia from the 1650s through their gradual disappearance from the Eastern Shore by the end of the colonial era. In between their rise and decline, he depicts the shift in their reputation from "'an unreasonable and turbulent sort of people'" in the 1660s to that of a group of "'industrious inhabitants'" by the 1710s (pp. 172, 184). Warren M. Billings's introduction to the "Four Remonstrances" by the roving Friend, George Wilson, adds helpful detail to Carroll's survey. Wilson, "an ardent champion of religious toleration," became to his fellow Friends something of a martyr at the hands of Anglican intolerance after he died in "'a dirty dungeon . . . a nasty stinking prison'" in Jamestown in ca. 1662 (pp. 129–130). The carefully edited remonstrances remain the substance of Billings's piece and furnish a useful source for hearing the early pleas of the Quakers for toleration and for understanding their challenge to the Anglican social and ecclesiastical order. Another article of note is Carroll's reflection on "George Fox's Visit to America in 1672"—a tour which, though centered on Maryland, stimulated Quaker growth throughout colonial America and during which Fox spent eight weeks in Virginia and North Carolina. Finally, Rufus Jones's venerable survey of colonial Quakerism remains a standard and is not superseded in coverage by these more recent articles. In sum, the Quakers of the seventeenth century are critical for church-state issues throughout the colonies. Not only does their treatment pose most poignantly the problem of religious intolerance, but their zeal presages the development of the Evangelical challenge to the standing orders of the eighteenth century.

By 1720, Anglicanism, like the gentry it most fully represented, had become entrenched in the Old Dominion. The Church of England had weathered Quakerism, few Presbyterians had yet arrived, and even alternative popular forms of religion and magic were reportedly on the wane. The Anglican gentry seemed to have gained a well-nigh undisputed dominance over colonial Virginian society and religion. Yet, even as the Anglican gentry were in the process of consolidating their power, cracks in the social and religious order became apparent. The cracks became cleavages in the Great Awakening: from the 1740s through the 1770s Virginia, more than any other colony, faced a sustained Evangelical attack on its established church and the prevailing order that that church represented. Given the significance of the Awakening in Virginia, it has understandably resulted in an abundant literature. Wesley Gewehr's older study, *The Great Awakening in Virginia*, remains the best overall account of the revival movement in the Old Dominion and his narrative has informed the structure of later chronicles. More than an institutional or denominational history, Gewehr's work is also sensitive to the political, educational, and social consequences of the revival, which he views as a primary force in the rise of democracy and religious liberty.

In Gewehr's work the Baptists, perhaps the most important insurgents, occupied only one chapter; a number of other works have to good effect put them at the center of their story. For example, the studies of the Baptist contribution to religious liberty in Virginia by William Thom and Lewis Little remain valuable, though whiggish. Little particularly tends to celebrate the noble achievement of the Baptists in their quest for the separation of church and state, but nonetheless his *Imprisoned Preachers and Religious Liberty in Virginia* is useful, especially for its abundant citation of primary materials. Indeed, the animosity provoked by the incendiary Baptist preachers— like Samuel Harriss, James Ireland, and dozens of others—finds full documentation in Little's volume. Harriss, for example, was repeatedly set upon while preaching and his meetings frequently broken up by gangs with whips and clubs. Ireland's problems were still more severe, especially because of his insistence on preaching from his jail cell. To quiet him, his enemies tried to blow him up with gunpowder and to suffocate him with the smoke of brimstone and Indian pepper. Once when Ireland was preaching the Gospel from his cell, his opposers went to "a height of arrogance and wickedness" in their efforts to humiliate and silence him: they "got a table, bench, or something else, stood upon it, and made their water in my face!" (pp. 163–164). These incidents surrounding Harriss and Ireland indicate how Little in his narrative managed not only to compile a colorful collection of materials, but also, as with Thom's account, to capture the challenge of the Baptists to the establishment and their persecution by those they challenged.

More recent scholarship on the Awakening in Virginia has gained much in methodological sophistication and interpretive insight over its earlier counterparts. This new scholarship is epitomized by the work of Rhys Isaac— especially his book, *The Transformation of Virginia*, though his several articles have maintained an importance in and of themselves. The focus of Isaac's work has been on Virginia's two revolutions—the Awakening and the coming of American independence—and their interrelations. More broadly, Isaac has sought to convey the texture and fabric of the social, political, and religious life of eighteenth-century Virginia and in doing so has shown profound sensitivity to the complexity and diversity of a past culture. Borrowing his methodological orientation from the cultural anthropology of Mary Douglas, Clifford Geertz, and Victor Turner, Isaac carefully describes and analyzes a wide range of social actions and encounters from cockfights to elections to revivals. He attempts to discern in the carriage, costumes, scripts, and gestures of representative figures engaged in these various actions the underlying patterns of order and authority at work in the culture. His ethnographic history has particularly helped establish the contours of the Evangelical challenge to the prevailing power and authority of the gentry. His scholarly writing stands among the most important for interpreters of the colonial South and his approach to the Awakening shows promise of reshaping the study of the revival in other parts of the colonies. Also, for an extensive discussion of Isaac's history of eighteenth-century Virginia and his method, one should consult Philip Morgan's "The Medium and the Message."

Isaac has, of course, not stood alone in his enterprise of nuancing the religious and political history of eighteenth-century Virginia. Both Richard Beeman and A. G. Roeber have contributed to Isaac's method and extended its uses. Beeman has probed at the local level Isaac's basic premises about the cultural conflict between the Anglican gentry and the insurgent Evangelicals. In his "Social Change and Cultural Conflict in Virginia: Lunenburg County, 1746 to 1774" and in a companion piece written with Isaac, Beeman sets out the battle between the two different cultural camps for hegemony in a particular frontier parish. By the 1770s the Baptists had taken over the county, shifting the locus of political and religious authority from the gentry's courthouse and their parish church to the Baptist meetinghouse. Additionally, Beeman has recently extended his study of Lunenburg county into the antebellum period in his book, *The Evolution of the Southern Backcountry*. For the eighteenth century, his findings at the level of case study fit tongue and groove with Isaac's broader work. Similarly, A. G. Roeber in "Authority, Law, and Custom" shares in Isaac's method and gives a full dramaturgic rendering of the rituals of court day—an analysis which anticipated Isaac's extension of his own method to topics beyond the core conflict of the Anglicans and Evangelicals.

Less directly tied to Isaac's method and work are three additional studies of the colonial Baptists: J. Stephen Kroll-Smith's "Tobacco and Belief," William Lumpkin's *The Baptist Foundations in the South*, and Sandra Rennie's "Virginia's Baptist Persecution." The last, in quantifying the incidence of Baptist persecution, argues that in the majority of cases the violent mobs encountered by Baptist preachers were led by the local gentry, whose deep anxieties over status and revolt fueled desperate attempts to preserve the old order. In his turn, Kroll-Smith adopts a Weberian view of the Virginia Baptists in which their theology (e.g., finding assurance through sanctification) helped corroborate an ideology congenial to the rising middle class of yeoman planters. This aspiring class found in the Baptists a way to ratify a new middle-class social order over against that of the gentry. Kroll-Smith's article remains Weberian in perspective but does not directly engage the debate over a Puritan versus a Southern ethic as well it might. Finally, Lumpkin's work does for the South something akin to what C. C. Goen's study of revivalism and separatism in New England did for the northern colonies; namely, it traces the revival's legacy through the separate Baptists who began to make significant inroads in the southern colonies in the 1750s.

The Awakening in Virginia was by most accounts an important precursor to the overthrow of Britain's royal and ecclesiastical authority. One of the more prominent results of these overturnings was the disestablishment of Virginia's Mother Church. The Awakening had given considerable impetus to the movement, but only in the revolutionary era, when the Evangelicals formed an uneasy coalition with Enlightenment men like Jefferson and Madison, was disestablishment effected. Several historians have made this final period in Virginia's colonial church-state struggle their domain: Sidney Mead, of course, has made the study of that coalition of rationalists and pietists one of his special themes, particularly in *The Lively Experiment*. In addition to Mead's frequently cited work, another study, Thomas Buckley's *Church and State in Revolutionary Virginia*, stands out. In his close analysis of the years 1776 to 1787, Buckley finds Virginia's working-out of the church-state issues to be "a politicoreligious microcosm in which the whole nation could study the alternatives for a church-state relationship" (p. 6). To Buckley, revolutionary Virginia was the crucible in which a variety of church-state models were tested: Patrick Henry's proposal for a multiple Protestant establishment; plans for refurbishing and perpetuating the colonial Anglican establishment; the theocratic designs and visions of Presbyterians like John Blair Smith; and a variety of separationist schemes advocated in turn by Baptists or Jeffersonians. Buckley's book is no doubt the most detailed examination of this decade-long drive toward disestablishment, but it has its limitations. Buckley has little to say, for example, about the prologue to this final struggle and his treatment of the coalition of "the rationalists and the religionists" is slightly imbalanced (p. 164). Only in the conclusion does he begin to assess in earnest the Evangelical contribution. Another important study of church-state issues in revolutionary Virginia is Fred Hood's "Revolution and Religious Liberty" in which the theocratic conceptions of the Presbyterians are probed. Here the ideas of such Presbyterian stalwarts as John Witherspoon, Thomas Reese, and John Blair Smith are seen to point ahead to the ideology that came to underlie the de facto establishment of the Evangelicals in the nineteenth century.

Besides all of the studies discussed which have carved out pieces of the whole to consider, a few historians have tried to relate the rise of religious liberty in Virginia on a larger scale. Three of these studies are of some note; all three were published before 1910 and share to some degree in a Whiggish view of religious liberty's rise and triumph. The works are: H. J. Eckenrode's *Separation of Church and State in Virginia,* Charles James's *Documentary History of the Struggle for Religious Liberty in Virginia,* and Henry McIlwaine's *The Struggle of Protestant Dissenters for Religious Toleration in Virginia.* Of these general histories of Virginia's church-state relations, Eckenrode's remains the standard.

Though Virginia has received more attention than any of the other southern colonies, significant work has also been done on the Carolinas. For South Carolina, a number of works address church-state issues directly. S. Charles Bolton's *Southern Anglicanism: The Church of England in Colonial South Carolina* is the best exploration of South Carolina's established church. Bolton broadly refashions and reverses the prevailing perceptions of the Anglicans' clerical leadership as immoral and incompetent and insists on the effectiveness of the South Carolina Church as an administrative and stabilizing body. He emphasizes the power of the laity (more particularly the vestry) in ecclesiastical affairs and stresses the benefits of this lay power to the church in such matters as improved clerical discipline. In short, he eschews the conventional wisdom that the power accorded the vestries, coupled with the absence of episcopal authority in the colonies, hampered the church and its clerics. On the whole, what emerges from Bolton's study is a South Carolina establishment which was effective, latitudinarian yet disciplined, but which failed to incorporate those settlers of the backcountry into its membership and which left the black majority almost entirely outside its fold. In other words, for all its strength, it was an establishment unusually vulnerable to the Evangelical insurgency.

A second work, John Brinsfield's *Religion and Politics in Colonial South Carolina*, addresses church-state relations still more directly. Brinsfield admits his work makes much of "the Whig view of history" and hence his study comes at the issues from the side of the dissenters (p. 136). With "the quest for religious freedom in colonial South Carolina" as a guiding theme, Brinsfield works his way through five distinct periods of church-state configurations in the colony: the proprietary system (1663–1704), under which full religious toleration was granted to all orderly dissenters; the proprietary establishment of the Church of England (1704–1706), with dissenters excluded from public office; the royal establishment of the Church of England (1719–1778), with provisions for general religious toleration; the establishment of Protestant Christianity (1778–1790); and the formal separation of church and state (1790–). Brinsfield's work, with its emphasis on the dissenters, is a useful complement to Bolton's study. A third work, of less note, is George Rogers's *Church and State in Eighteenth-Century South Carolina*, which summarizes the important features of the church-state issues and charts particularly the simultaneous decline of Anglican and royal authority in the colony.

For North Carolina the older works of Stephen Weeks remain best for the specific issues of church-state relations. In his first study, *The Religious Development in the Province of North Carolina*, Weeks studies the relations between church and state as formulated by the Carolina Proprietors to 1711 with theoretical, if not practical, establishment coming by means of a vestry act passed in 1701. In his second study, *Church and State in North Carolina*, Weeks carries the story forward through the fall of the establishment during the Revolution. Together these two volumes, while hardly exhaustive, provide a helpful outline of church-state relations for the colony. Haskell Monroe's article, "Religious Toleration and Politics in Early North Carolina" is a useful supplement to Weeks's delineation. Monroe attributes the general religious toleration prevailing in the Carolinas through 1704 to the economic ambitions of the Proprietors, the Lockean ideal of liberty of conscience, and the prevalence of religious indifference. Indicative of this toleration in early Carolina is the treatment of the Quakers, who fared far better there than in Virginia or New England. Indeed, in 1686 two Quaker missionaries were given funding by the Carolina government—one indication, Monroe suggests, of Quaker acceptance and Carolinian tolerance.

Two other notable articles on church-state relations in colonial North Carolina deal with the frailty of the Anglican establishment on the eve of the Revolution. Paul Conkin's "The Church Establishment in North Carolina" and Gary Freeze's "Like a House Built upon Sand" both assess the Church of England's failing efforts in the years 1765 to 1776 to strengthen its establishment and to ward off dissent. In the long run, Anglican attempts to bolster the establishment, led in particular by Governor William Tryon, ended only in intensifying anti-Anglican sentiment and in hastening the church's downfall. Finally, Roger Ekirch's *"Poor Carolina": Politics and Society in Colonial North Carolina, 1729–1776* studies the factious political life of North Carolina as a royal colony within a broad social, economic, and cultural context. While religion figures only peripherally in Ekirch's analysis, his history nonetheless recreates, more fully than any other, the social and political milieu in which church-state issues in the colony took shape.

The Great Awakening in the Carolinas has not received the critical attention that it has in Virginia and elsewhere in the colonies. David Morgan in "The Great Awakening in South Carolina, 1740–1775" and in "The Great Awakening in North Carolina, 1740–1775" offers useful narratives of the revival movement in the two colonies. In both pieces Morgan stresses the importance of the separate Baptists as the group embodying the Awakening impulse in the Carolinas. To Morgan, they are the true heirs of George Whitefield's early Evangelicalism, notwithstanding the aging itinerant's desire to disinherit them by the 1760s. Indeed, the heirs far outdid their progenitor. The core of the Awakening in the Carolinas is not Whitefield's early excursions in 1739 and 1740, but instead the Baptist advances of the 1760s. These gains were personified in the brothers-in-law Shubal Stearns and Daniel Marshall, who, in their roving ministries, became the patriarchs of the separate Baptist movement in the South.

While David Morgan has provided needed narratives recounting the Awakening's course in both Carolinas (and, as we will see, in Georgia), William Kenney has offered suggestive analysis of the initial stages of the Awakening in South Carolina in particular. In "Alexander Garden and George Whitefield: The Significance of Revivalism in South Carolina, 1738–1741," Kenney argues that these early years were critical for revitalizing dissent in South Carolina and for invigorating the assault on the Anglican establishment and its political buttresses. To Kenney, the Awakening sparked a widescale attack on British ecclesiastical and political authority—an attack which found embodiment in Whitefield. In him, colonists discovered a young Anglican priest who reenforced and compounded their worst suspicions of Anglican tyranny as he used "his own church as a whipping-post to reject the time-worn viability of exclusive ecclesiastical establishments" (p. 16). As in Virginia, awakened dissenters in the Carolinas pushed the colonies toward disestablishment, if not revolution. In addition to the articles of Kenney and Morgan, Richard Hooker's edition of the journal of the Anglican missionary, Charles Woodmason, is an indispensable primary source for grasping Anglican revulsion in the face of the backcountry dissenters. *The Carolina Backcountry* is certainly the most colorful and perhaps the most essential document for the study of Carolinian Evangelicals and Anglican responses to them on the eve of the revolution.

The relevant historiography for church-state relations in America's youngest colony, Georgia—chartered only in 1732—is scanty by comparison to its older southern counterparts. Sanford Cobb in his synoptic account of church-state issues in colonial America went so far as to dismiss Georgia's "religious story" as "without much importance in the development of our present theme" (p. 301). Even the fullest chronicle of its church-state relations, Reba Strickland's *Religion and the State in Georgia in the Eighteenth Century*, concludes that Georgia "contributed little that was original to the development of church-state relations" (p. 185). But these judgments, coupled with the relative dearth of literature, do not mean one should pass quickly over Georgia's forty-four-year colonial history and the religious and political events that transpired there. Despite its self-effacing conclusion, Reba Strickland's account reveals a rich generation of religious ferment in the colony. By the 1740s a wide variety of religious groups—Lutherans (the Salzburgers), Moravians, Jews, Presbyterians, Huguenots, and, of course, Anglicans—had settled in the broadly tolerant colony headed by Proprietor James Oglethorpe. Only Catholics were consistently denied religious liberty in Georgia—an inveterate intolerance in the British colonies at large and one only aggravated by Georgia's proximity to Spanish Florida. Strickland's study surveys the whole of colonial Georgia's religious and political experience, first under the proprietors and after 1752 under the royal governors. Establishment of Anglicanism came in 1758, but it remained weak and fell easily during the Revolution. Strickland's study, published in 1939, remains a solid and solitary account of church-state relations in Georgia. One supplement to her work, however, is Harold Davis's *The Fledgling Province*, which contains a chapter on Georgia's religious life. Davis does not push his analysis of the colony's religion beyond Strickland's, but instead stresses rather simply the unchurched and irreligious quality of colonial Georgia. The strength of his work lies in its provision of a social and cultural matrix in which to view the religiopolitical developments documented by Strickland.

While colonial Georgia's church-state relations have not received much treatment at a general level, a few incidents in its early religious history have. One of the more notorious and exemplary is John Wesley's brief stint in Georgia from 1736 to 1737. Strickland offers extended discussion of Wesley's problems in the colony, while two articles, David Morgan's "John Wesley's Sojourn in Georgia Revisited" and William Cannon's "John Wesley's Years in Georgia" focus solely on his stay in the colony. The articles, however, add but little to Strickland's account of the church-state dimensions of Wesley's case. In Georgia, Wesley in his early formalism ran afoul of his congregants' desire to observe loosely several ecclesiastical rubrics such as certain baptismal rules and particular requirements for receiving communion. One woman, annoyed by Wesley's rigor, even tried to shoot him and when that failed went after him with a pair of scissors. The situation only grew worse after Wesley denied communion to a woman whom he had courted, Sophia Hopkey, after her marriage to another suitor. Wesley was arrested and indicted not only for defaming Sophia's character, but also for several ecclesiastical violations involving his putatively excessive stringency. In the ensuing legal struggle, which divided Savannah and which ended in his surreptitious exit from Georgia, Wesley "would come into court and harangue the people crying 'Liberty'," speculate in a sermon on the lawfulness of giving tribute to Caesar, and urge the denizens of Savannah to "resist oppression" (Strickland, p. 62). Two years before the advent of the Awakening in the South, Wesley in his own antics was demonstrating how religion—in this case High Church Anglicanism, not Evangelicalism—could challenge existing civil and ecclesiastical authorities and could encourage the people to maintain their liberties. More than a curious tale of Wesley's early failure as a missionary, his problems in Georgia, evident more in Strickland's account than in the other two, reveal a notable church-state dimension.

Shortly after John Wesley's departure, Georgia played host to another great leader of eighteenth-century Evangelicalism, George Whitefield. As was the case with Wesley's, Whitefield's efforts there, particularly his founding of the Bethesda orphanage and his attempts to stir up revival, have received considerable attention, indeed have attained notoriety. In addition to Harold Davis's account in *The Fledgling Province*, Neil O'Connell's "George Whitefield and Bethesda Orphan-House" and Theda Perdue's "George Whitefield in Georgia: Philanthropy" offer good assessments of Whitefield's orphanage, which served simultaneously as an eleemosynary institution, a pet money-raising cause for the itinerant in his wayfaring tours, and a bastion of Evangelical dissent within Georgia itself. This last aspect was especially unnerving to the Anglicans. The leaders of the orphanage in Whitefield's absence, James Habersham and Jonathan Barber, were noted for their harassment of unconverted Anglican priests and one critic saw the operation as "a Nest for the Enemies of the Church" (quoted in Strickland, p. 136). In short, Whitefield's House of Mercy served as a center for the Evangelicals in their challenge to Anglicanism in Georgia and South Carolina. More broadly, in a pair of articles on Whitefield and the Awakening in Georgia and the Carolinas, David Morgan chronicles the grand itinerant's stoking of the revival in the colony. Again Morgan provides useful narratives on these neglected phases of the revival and suggests how Whitefield helped spearhead the initial Evangelical assault on the traditional order. A final note on Georgia's religious life concerns the settlement of Lutheran refugees, the Salzburgers, at Ebenezer. These pietists, who formed an unusually cohesive and initially theocratic community near Savannah, were perhaps the most successful and distinctive religious group in the colony. Their story has been most recently told and reexamined in George Jones's *Salzburger Saga.*

In discussing Wesley and Whitefield in Georgia, another approach to church-state issues has been raised: namely, the study of an exemplary individual and his significance for church-state relations in the colonial South. Several historians have adopted this approach, which has resulted in the emergence of a number of figures as critically important in the historiography. Among these James Blair, Alexander Garden, Samuel Davies, Patrick Henry, and John Zubly stand out as representative. As a group they have, on the whole, received more attention for their contributions to church-state relations in the South than any other figures before Jefferson and Madison in the Constitutional period. A brief survey of the historiography surrounding them should serve to introduce these significant individuals and to document the fruits of this approach.

James Blair and Alexander Garden were two of the most important Anglican leaders in the American colonies and both repeatedly exercised significant roles in the political and ecclesiastical life of the colonial South. As Commissaries of the Bishop of London, they headed the church in their respective provinces—Blair in Virginia, Garden in South Carolina. Blair is most fully treated in Parke Rouse's biography, *James Blair of Virginia,* out of which emerges a fine portrait of this missionary and preacher, organizer and president of William and Mary College, religiopolitical writer and leader. Garden has not been the subject of a published book-length monograph, though S. Charles Bolton's *Southern Anglicanism* contains a thorough chapter on him. Together two articles, William Kenney's "Alexander Garden and George Whitefield" and Quentin Keen's "The Problems of a Commissary," suggest the array of difficulties facing Garden as the leader of South Carolina's established church—such problems as the lack of missionaries, the threat of slave insurrection, the weakness of educational enterprises, and, of course, the outbreak of the Awakening. Finally, an article, "The Commissaries of the Bishop of London in Colonial Politics," by Alison Olson suggests broadly the political significance of the office held by Blair and Garden. Blair, for example, used his office to put considerable pressure on Virginia Governors Alexander Spotswood and Francis Nicholson, and repeatedly commissary and governor clashed over the extent of their respective powers and authority. As Olson concludes, the commissary often encouraged factions by leading one group of colonists against another led by the governor and thereby aided in the formation of the concept and practice of party politics. Not surprisingly, to Spotswood, Blair was "the constant Instrument of Faction" (quoted in Rouse, p. 194). In short, the Anglican commissaries, like Blair, assisted in the legitimation of political factionalism "within an accepted structure of government" (Olson, p. 124). For the study of southern Anglicanism through an important figure, one would be hard-pressed to do better than to begin with either Commissary Blair or Commissary Garden.

For the colonial South, one Presbyterian, Samuel Davies, stands out as the acknowledged early leader and promoter of his denomination in the region. Distinguished as a preacher, hymnist, poet, and educator, Davies was one of the most important religious leaders of eighteenth-century America and has been singled out particularly as an early advocate of religious toleration in Virginia. This singling out has been accomplished preeminently by George Pilcher whose biography, *Samuel Davies: Apostle of Dissent in Colonial Virginia*, and article, "Samuel Davies and Religious Toleration," are critical for assessing Davies's role among Virginia dissenters. Unlike early denominational historians, Pilcher is careful not to apotheosize Davies's efforts and cautions that Davies as a Presbyterian was "working primarily for the benefits of his church" ("Davies and Toleration," p. 49). Nevertheless, the circumspect and silver-tongued Davies was instrumental in securing toleration for Presbyterian meetings and ministers under the terms of the Act of Toleration of 1689 and in turn helped broaden dissent's foothold in Virginia. In addition to Pilcher, Rhys Isaac in his wide-ranging work has commented considerably on Davies and has corrected both Pilcher and the denominational historians in a number of places by way of revising "the legend of Samuel Davies" ("Religion and Authority," p. 30). Finally, Michael Greenberg offers further commentary on Davies in "Revival, Reform, Revolution: Samuel Davies and the Great Awakening in Virginia" and treats particularly the contribution of Davies's theology and preaching to revolutionary and anti-slavery ideologies.

Samuel Davies's influence on colonial Virginian culture was manifold and was decisively felt by the patriot-preacher, Patrick Henry. Socially and politically situated in the refined circle of the gentry, but linked by oratorical style and fervor to the swelling ranks of the Evangelicals, Henry has received growing scholarly attention because of his evident synthesis of the two worlds—the Evangelical and gentry—which competed for hegemony in eighteenth-century Virginia. Alan Heimert in his *Religion and the American Mind* was among the first to suggest the significance of the Evangelical dimensions of Henry's rhetoric and found in him an epitome of his own thesis that the

New Lights of the 1740s issued in the revolutionaries of the 1770s. Others have considerably expanded and nuanced Heimert's suggestion. Charles Cohen in his "The 'Liberty or Death' Speech: A Note on Religion and Revolutionary Rhetoric" adds significantly to an understanding of Henry's fusion of Whig and Evangelical ideologies. In an unusually strong and sprightly analysis, Cohen assesses Henry's famous speech as a jeremiad—"a political harangue suffused with religious imagery" (p. 704). Rhys Isaac has addressed Henry's role in several works, notably in "Preachers and Patriots," "Patrick Henry: Patriot and Preacher?," and in *The Transformation of Virginia*. For Isaac as for Cohen, Henry's success and distinctiveness lay in his ability to move easily between Virginia's two revolutions in religion and politics. "He achieved a harmony," Isaac concludes, "above the clashing discords of the old traditional culture and the new evangelical counterculture" ("Patrick Henry," p. 175). While these syntheses of Evangelical-Whig and Evangelical-gentry world views have, as motifs, dominated much of the recent historiography on Henry, Richard Beeman's biography offers a full account of Henry's distinguished political career. Also of importance—particularly for its primary material—is William Wirt Henry's three-volume *Patrick Henry: Life, Correspondence, and Speeches*.

If Henry stands as a paragon of the unabashed patriot, the Georgia preacher and pamphleteer, John Zubly, could stand as the epitome of the torn and tragic Loyalist. Ordained as a German Reformed minister in 1744, Zubly settled the next year in Georgia, where he was to become the spokesman for Georgia Whiggery between 1765 and 1775, only to end an outcast because of his final refusal to support American independence. In the decade preceding the Revolution, Zubly wrote pamphlets that combined both religious and political grievances against Britain and her established church and exuded a command of both Puritan and Whig rhetoric. Yet, although he had forcefully articulated the colonial position over against the Crown and had attended the Continental Congress, he suffered the fate of a moderate caught in the storm of revolution and ended his life in banishment for his lingering conservatism. Randall Miller's selected edition of Zubly's writings, *"A Warm and Zealous Spirit": John J. Zubly and the American Revolution*, provides easy access to important primary materials and is the best introduction to Zubly's life and work. In "Tragic Hero: Loyalist John J. Zubly," William Pauley probes Zubly's loyalism and demonstrates his double bind: by 1777 Zubly was spurned by both the patriots, who had moved beyond him in their militant zeal, and the Tories, who continued to see Zubly's previous decade of writings as rebellious. Of note also is Roger Martin's account, "John J. Zubly Comes to America," which depicts Zubly's early life in the colonies to 1758 and sets the stage for his rise to prominence thereafter.

Obviously these five figures—Blair, Garden, Davies, Henry, Zubly—do not

begin to exhaust for the colonial South the array of important figures whom
historians have lifted out and studied. They are certainly representative, but
the bibliography by no means stops with them. For example, Harry Porter's
"Alexander Whitaker: Cambridge Apostle to Virginia" and Charles Smith's
"Chaplain Robert Hunt" offer detailed portrayals of two of Virginia's earliest
and most distinguished clerics. Similarly, the zealous Anglican, Devereux
Jarratt, has received marked attention, notably in Rhys Isaac's work and in
Harry Rabe's "The Reverend Devereux Jarratt and the Virginia Social Order."
Jarratt's own autobiography remains an invaluable source for understanding
eighteenth-century Anglicanism and the rise from within of Methodism. Revolutionary and Constitutional leaders in the South are treated primarily in
other bibliographies in this volume, but three studies should nevertheless be
noted here: Paul Boller's *George Washington and Religion*, Dickinson W.
Adams's edition of *Jefferson's Extracts from the Gospels*, and Marvin
Zahniser's *Charles Cotesworth Pinckney, Founding Father*. The early development of the religious views of these men sheds light broadly on the religious life of the gentry in the colonial South, particularly illumining the
gradual permeation of southern culture with Enlightenment ideas.

A final aspect of the colonial South demands comment: that is, the growth
and entrenchment of slavery and its impact on the configurations of church
and state in the southern colonies. The volume and quality of literature on
slavery in the South defies simple summary or cursory presentation; only a
core of the most relevant works, therefore, has been included in the bibliography. (For a recent and thorough historiographical essay on colonial
black history, Peter Wood's "'I Did the Best I Could for My Day'" is unusually
valuable.) Still, several works should be lifted out here. Of seminal importance is Edmund Morgan's *American Slavery, American Freedom* which
sets out as the central paradox of American history the ongoing tension
between enslavement and liberty. As a history of seventeenth-century Virginia and as an interpretive essay on American culture, Morgan's work has
few peers. Jack Greene's "'Slavery or Independence'" offers a compact extension of Morgan's theme to South Carolina. Two other works, Winthrop
Jordan's *White over Black* and David Brion Davis's *The Problem of Slavery in
Western Culture*, have been the starting-points for probing the attitudes of
whites toward the enslaved. Davis takes a longer historical view than Jordan,
but both are essential for understanding white perceptions of slaves and
slavery in the colonial era. Recent work has shifted from attempts at understanding the ideology and attitudes of whites to discerning the experience of
the slaves themselves. Three exemplary works in this vanguard, which include much important material for the colonial era as well as the antebellum
period, are: John Blassingame's *The Slave Community;* Eugene Genovese's

Roll, Jordan, Roll; and Albert Raboteau's *Slave Religion.* Innovatively using sources such as songs, folk tales, aphorisms, and slave narratives long overlooked by institutional and economic historians like U. B. Phillips and Kenneth Stampp, these works have reanimated much of the slave experience.

In the narrower realm of church-state issues, two topics emerge from this literature on slavery as particularly germane: first, religion as a wellspring of slave resistance and revolt and second, the impact of Christian catechesis and conversion on the slave's social and civil status. For the first point, Herbert Aptheker's *American Negro Slave Revolts* and Gerald Mullin's *Flight and Rebellion: Slave Resistance in Eighteenth-Century Virginia* add valuable detail to the more general works of Blassingame, Genovese, and Raboteau. (Genovese has, however, taken on this theme specifically in a published set of lectures, entitled *From Rebellion to Revolt,* which includes an exhaustive bibliographical essay on slave resistance.) While religion played a primary role in the great revolts and conspiracies of the nineteenth century (notably those of Nat Turner and Denmark Vesey), religious visions—whether informed by traditional African cosmologies, or by Christian prophecy, or both—also sustained slave resistance and plots in the colonial era. Slave religion, it was altogether clear to an anxious gentry, could inspire revolt and undermine the social order. To protect themselves and to undergird their hegemony, the gentry in their political assemblies often found it prudent to enact legislation that severely limited religious meetings among the slaves. This was true, for example, in South Carolina in the wake of the Stono Rebellion in 1739 as it would be again in the aftermath of Nat Turner's apocalypse in Virginia. On the second issue of Christian catechesis for the slaves and its relation to their civil status, slaveholders were broadly wary of what impact Christianity—for example, baptism—would have on their property. Colonial governments early on took up this problem and "by 1706 at least six colonial legislatures had passed acts denying that baptism altered the condition of a slave 'as to his bondage or freedom'" (Raboteau, p. 99). Again civil law tried to define the scope of slave religion.

The rise of slavery as an institution in the colonial South was perhaps the most important and foreboding development in the colonial era. For the area of church-state relations, however, it was only one significant development among many in the southern colonies. Anglicanism had taken root and flourished in Virginia and South Carolina as the established religion; in North Carolina and Georgia the ground was less fertile for England's Mother Church and, in the eyes of its faithful, the tares far outnumbered the stocks of wheat in these provinces. Yet in all four cases, whether strong or weak, the establishments fell with the coming of the Revolution. The Evangelical insurgents paired with advocates of an enlightened Whig ideology to spark the drive toward disestablishment. But to end simply with disestablishment as a grand culmination of sorts would obscure what has gone before in this essay. The development of church-state relations in the colonial South, it is clear, is not to be seen merely as prologue to disestablishment, but instead as part of a variegated and rich history significant on its own terms. The literature surveyed here (and in the following bibliography—with still more variety) points persuasively to that mottled diversity and that significance.

BIBLIOGRAPHY

Abbot, W. W. The Royal Governors of Georgia, 1754-1775.
   Chapel Hill: University of North Carolina Press, 1959.

Adams, Dickinson, W., ed. Jefferson's Extracts from the
   Gospels: "The Philosophy of Jesus" and "The Life and Morals
   of Jesus." Princeton, N.J.: Princeton University Press,
   1983.

Alden, John R. Robert Dinwiddie, Servant of the Crown.
   Charlottesville: University Press of Virginia, 1973.

Anderson, James D. "Thomas Wharton, Exile in Virginia, 1777-
   1778." Virginia Magazine of History and Biography 89
   (October 1981), 425-447.

Aptheker, Herbert. American Negro Slave Revolts. New York:
   Columbia University Press, 1943.

Ashe, Samuel A.; Weeks, Stephen B.; and Van Noppen, Claude L.,
   eds. Biographical History of North Carolina: From Colonial
   Times to the Present. 8 vols. Greensboro, N.C.: C. L. Van
   Noppen, 1905-17.

Axtell, James. The European and the Indian: Essays in the
   Ethnohistory of Colonial North America. New York: Oxford
   University Press, 1981.

Bailey, Kenneth K. "Protestantism and Afro-Americans in the
   Old South: Another Look." Journal of Southern History 41
   (November 1975), 451-472.

Bailey, Raymond C. Popular Influence upon Public Policy:
   Petitioning in Eighteenth-Century Virginia. Westport,
   Conn.: Greenwood Press, 1979.

Bailey, Raymond C.   "Popular Petitions and Religion in
  Eighteenth-Century Colonial Virginia." Historical Magazine
  of the Protestant Episcopal Church 46 (December 1977), 419-
  428.

Baldwin, Alice M.   "Sowers of Sedition: The Political Theories
  of Some of the New Light Presbyterian Clergy of Virginia and
  North Carolina." William and Mary Quarterly, 3d ser., 5
  (January 1948), 52-76.

Bauer, Gerald.   "The Quest for Religious Freedom in Virginia."
  Historical Magazine of the Protestant Episcopal Church 41
  (March 1972), 85-93.

Beeman, Richard R.   The Evolution of the Southern Backcountry:
  A Case Study of Lunenburg County, Virginia, 1746-1832.
  Philadelphia: University of Pennsylvania Press, 1984.

Beeman, Richard R.   Patrick Henry: A Biography. New York:
  McGraw-Hill, 1974.

Beeman, Richard R.   "Social Change and Cultural Conflict in
  Virginia: Lunenburg County, 1746 to 1774." William and Mary
  Quarterly, 3d ser., 35 (July 1978), 455-476.

Beeman, Richard R., and Isaac, Rhys.   "Cultural Conflict and
  Social Change in the Revolutionary South: Lunenburg County,
  Virginia." Journal of Southern History 46 (November 1980),
  525-550.

Berens, John F.   "Religion and Revolution Reconsidered: Recent
  Literature on Religion and Nationalism in Eighteenth-Century
  America." Canadian Review of Studies in Nationalism 6 (Fall
  1979), 233-245.

Bertelson, David.   The Lazy South. New York: Oxford University
  Press, 1967.

Billings, Warren M.   "The Growth of Political Institutions in
  Virginia, 1634 to 1676." William and Mary Quarterly, 3d
  ser., 31 (April 1974), 225-242.

Billings, Warren M., ed.   The Old Dominion in the Seventeenth
  Century: A Documentary History of Virginia, 1606-1689.
  Chapel Hill: University of North Carolina Press, 1975.

Billings, Warren M.   "A Quaker in Seventeenth-Century Virginia:
  Four Remonstrances by George Wilson." William and Mary
  Quarterly, 3d ser., 33 (January 1976), 127-140.

Blassingame, John W.   The Slave Community: Plantation Life in
  the Antebellum South. New York: Oxford University Press,
  1972.

Boller, Paul F., Jr. George Washington and Religion. Dallas:
Southern Methodist University Press, 1963.

Bolton, S. Charles. "South Carolina and the Reverend Doctor
Francis Le Jau: Southern Society and the Conscience of an
Anglican Missionary." Historical Magazine of the Protestant
Episcopal Church 40 (March 1971), 63-80.

Bolton, S. Charles. Southern Anglicanism: The Church of
England in Colonial South Carolina. Westport, Conn.:
Greenwood, 1982.

Bonomi, Patricia U., and Eisenstadt, Peter R. "Church
Adherence in the Eighteenth-Century British American
Colonies." William and Mary Quarterly, 3d ser., 39 (April
1982), 245-286.

Bowler, Clara A. "Carted Whores and White Shrouded Apologies:
Slander in the County Courts of Seventeenth-Century
Virginia." Virginia Magazine of History and Biography 85
(July 1977), 274-288.

Boyd, Julian P., and Cullen, Charles T., eds. The Papers of
Thomas Jefferson. 1st ser., 21 vols.; 2d ser., 1 vol.
Princeton, N.J.: Princeton University Press, 1950.

Bradley, Michael R. "The Role of the Black Church in the
Colonial Slave Society." Louisiana Studies 14 (Winter
1975), 413-421.

Breen, T. H. "Looking Out for Number One: Conflicting Values
in Early Seventeenth-Century Virginia." South Atlantic
Quarterly 78 (Summer 1979), 342-360.

Breen, T. H. Puritans and Adventurers: Change and Persistence
in Early America. New York: Oxford University Press, 1980.

Breen, T. H., and Innes, Stephen. "Myne Owne Ground": Race and
Freedom on Virginia's Eastern Shore, 1640-1676. New York:
Oxford University Press, 1980.

Breen, T. H.; Lewis, James H.; and Schlesinger, Keith. "Motive
for Murder: A Servant's Life in Virginia, 1678." William
and Mary Quarterly, 3d ser., 40 (January 1983), 106-120.

Bridenbaugh, Carl. Jamestown, 1544-1699. New York: Oxford
University Press, 1980.

Bridenbaugh, Carl. Mitre and Sceptre: Transatlantic Faiths,
Ideas, Personalities, and Politics, 1689-1775. New York:
Oxford University Press, 1962.

Bridenbaugh, Carl. Myths and Realities: Societies of the
Colonial South. Baton Rouge: Louisiana State University
Press, 1952.

Brinsfield, John W. "Daniel Defoe: Writer, Statesman, and
   Advocate of Religious Liberty in South Carolina." South
   Carolina Historical Magazine 76 (July 1975), 107-111.

Brinsfield, John W. Religion and Politics in Colonial South
   Carolina. Easley, S.C.: Southern Historical Press, 1983.

Brock, Peter. "Colonel Washington and the Quaker Conscientious
   Objectors." Quaker History 53 (Spring 1964), 12-26.

Brock, Robert K. Archibald Cary of Ampthill, Wheelhorse of the
   Revolution. Richmond: Garrett and Massie, 1937.

Brown, Richard M. The South Carolina Regulators. Cambridge,
   Mass.: Harvard University Press, 1963.

Brown, Robert E., and Brown, B. Katherine. Virginia 1705-1786:
   Democracy or Aristocracy? East Lansing: Michigan State
   University Press, 1964.

Brunk, Ivan W. "Mennonites in the Carolinas." Pennsylvania
   Mennonite Heritage 5, no.1 (1982), 14-21.

Brydon, George M. The Established Church in Virginia and the
   Revolution. Richmond: Virginia Diocesan Library, 1930.

Brydon, George M. Virginia's Mother Church and The Political
   Conditions Under Which It Grew. 2 vols. Richmond: Virginia
   Historical Society, 1947-52.

Buckley, Thomas E. Church and State in Revolutionary Virginia,
   1776-1787. Charlottesville: University Press of Virginia,
   1977.

Butler, Jon. The Huguenots in America: A Refugee People in New
   World Society. Cambridge, Mass.: Harvard University Press,
   1983.

Butler, Jon. "Magic, Astrology, and the Early American
   Religious Heritage." American Historical Review 84 (April
   1979), 317-346.

Calam, John. Parsons and Pedagogues: The S.P.G. Adventure in
   American Education. New York: Columbia University Press,
   1971.

Calhoon, Robert M. Religion and the American Revolution in
   North Carolina. Raleigh: North Carolina Department of
   Cultural Resources, 1976.

Candler, Allen D. The Colonial Records of the State of
   Georgia. 19 vols. New York: AMS Press, 1970.

Cannon, William B. "John Wesley's Years in Georgia."
   Methodist History 1 (July 1963), 1-7.

Carroll, Kenneth L.   "Quakerism on the Eastern Shore of
     Virginia." Virginia Magazine of History and Biography 84
     (April 1966), 170-189.

Carroll, Kenneth L.   "Some Thoughts on George Fox's Visit to
     America in 1672." Quaker History 61 (Autumn 1972), 82-90.

Cart, Theodore W., and Pruden, George B., Jr.   "Rich and Poor
     in the Port City." South Carolina Historical Association,
     Proceedings (1980), 31-35.

Chapin, Bradley. Criminal Justice in Colonial America, 1606-
     1660. Athens, Ga.: University of Georgia Press, 1983.

Chumbley, George L. Colonial Justice in Virginia: The
     Development of a Judicial System, Typical Laws and Cases of
     the Period. Richmond: The Dietz Press, 1938.

Clifton, Denzil T.   "Anglicanism and Negro Slavery in Colonial
     America." Historical Magazine of the Protestant Episcopal
     Church 39 (March 1970), 29-70.

Cobb, Sanford H. The Rise of Religious Liberty in America: A
     History. New York: Macmillan, 1902.

Cohen, Charles L.   "The 'Liberty or Death' Speech: A Note on
     Religion and Revolutionary Rhetoric." William and Mary
     Quarterly, 3d ser., 38 (October 1981), 702-717.

Coleman, Kenneth. The American Revolution in Georgia, 1763-
     1789. Athens, Ga.: University of Georgia Press, 1958.

Conkin, Paul.   "The Church Establishment in North Carolina,
     1765-1776." North Carolina Historical Review 32 (January
     1955), 1-30.

Crane, Verner W. The Southern Frontier, 1670-1732. Ann Arbor:
     University of Michigan Press, 1929.

Craven, Wesley F. The Dissolution of the Virginia Company: The
     Failure of a Colonial Experiment. New York: Oxford
     University Press, 1932.

Craven, Wesley F. The Southern Colonies in the Seventeenth
     Century, 1607-1689. Baton Rouge: Louisiana State University
     Press, 1949.

Cross, Arthur L. The Anglican Episcopate and the American
     Colonies. New York: Longmans, Green and Co., 1902.

Crow, Jeffrey J., and Tise, Larry E., eds. The Southern
     Experience in the American Revolution. Chapel Hill:
     University of North Carolina Press, 1978.

Crowe, Charles. "The Reverend James Madison in Williamsburg
    and London, 1768-1771." West Virginia History 25 (July
    1964), 270-278.

Curran, Francis X. Catholics in Colonial Law. Chicago: Loyola
    University Press, 1963.

Davidson, Elizabeth H. The Establishment of the English Church
    in Continental American Colonies. Durham, N.C.: Duke
    University Press, 1936.

Davis, David Brion. The Problem of Slavery in Western Culture.
    Ithaca, N.Y.: Cornell University Press, 1966.

Davis, Harold E. The Fledgling Province: Social and Cultural
    Life in Colonial Georgia, 1733-1776. Chapel Hill:
    University of North Carolina Press, 1976.

Davis, Richard B. "The Devil in Virginia in the Seventeenth
    Century." Virginia Magazine of History and Biography 65
    (April 1957), 131-149.

Davis, Richard B. Intellectual Life in the Colonial South,
    1585-1763. 3 vols. Knoxville: University of Tennessee
    Press, 1978.

Davis, Robert S., Jr. "The Other Side of the Coin: Georgia
    Baptists who Fought for the King." Viewpoints: Georgia
    Baptist History 7 (1980), 47-57.

Detweiler, Robert. "Robert Rose, 1704-1751: Effective and
    Popular Minister of Colonial Virginia." Historical Magazine
    of the Protestant Episcopal Church 41 (June 1972), 153-162.

Easterby, J. H., and Green, Ruth S., eds. The Colonial Records
    of South Carolina. 9 vols. Columbia, S.C.: The Historical
    Commission of South Carolina, 1951-62.

Eckenrode, H. J. The Separation of Church and State in
    Virginia: A Study in the Development of the Revolution.
    Richmond: Department of Archives and History, 1909.

Egnal, Marc. "The Origins of the Revolution in Virginia: A
    Reinterpretation." William and Mary Quarterly, 3d ser., 37
    (July 1980), 401-428.

Ekirch, A. Roger. "Poor Carolina": Politics and Society in
    Colonial North Carolina, 1729-1776. Chapel Hill: University
    of North Carolina Press, 1981.

Ellis, John T. Catholics in Colonial America. Baltimore:
    Helicon Press, 1965.

Ervin, Spencer. "The Anglican Church in North Carolina, 1663-1823." _Historical Magazine of the Protestant Episcopal Church_ 25 (June 1956), 102-161.

Ervin, Spencer. "The Establishment, Government, and Functioning of the Church in Colonial Virginia." _Historical Magazine of the Protestant Episcopal Church_ 26 (March 1957), 65-110.

Essig, James D. "A Very Wintry Season: Virginia Baptists and Slavery, 1785-1797." _Virginia Magazine of History and Biography_ 88 (April 1980), 170-185.

Fall, Ralph E., ed. _The Diary of Robert Rose: A View of Virginia by a Scottish Colonial Parson, 1746-1751_. Verona, Va.: McClure, 1977.

Farish, Hunter D., ed. _Journal and Letters of Philip Vickers Fithian, 1773-1774: A Plantation Tutor of the Old Dominion_. Chapel Hill: University of North Carolina Press, 1957.

Fenn, Elizabeth A., and Wood, Peter H. _Natives and Newcomers: The Way We Lived in North Carolina before 1770_. Chapel Hill: University of North Carolina Press, 1983.

Fiering, Norman. "The First American Enlightenment: Tillotson, Leverett, and Philosophical Anglicanism." _New England Quarterly_ 54 (September 1981), 307-344.

Flaherty, David H. "A Select Guide to the Manuscript Court Records of Colonial Virginia." _American Journal of Legal History_ 19 (April 1975), 112-137.

Foote, William H. _Sketches of North Carolina, Historical and Biographical_. New York: R. Carter, 1846.

Foote, William H. _Sketches of Virginia, Historical and Biographical_. 1850-55. Reprint. Richmond: John Knox Press, 1966.

Fraser, Walter J., Jr. "Controlling the Poor in Colonial Charles Town." South Carolina Historical Association, _Proceedings_ (1980), 13-30.

Freeze, Gary. "Like a House Built Upon Sand: The Anglican Church and Establishment in North Carolina, 1765-1776." _Historical Magazine of the Protestant Episcopal Church_ 48 (December 1979), 405-432.

Friedlander, Amy, ed. "Commissary Johnston's Report, 1713." _South Carolina Historical Magazine_ 83 (October 1982), 259-271.

Garrison, Webb B. _Oglethorpe's Folly: The Birth of Georgia_. Lakemont, Ga.: Copple House Books, 1982.

86902

Gaustad, Edwin S. "A Disestablished Society: Origins of the
    First Amendment." Journal of Church and State 11 (Autumn
    1969), 409-425.

Genovese, Eugene D. From Rebellion to Revolution: Afro-
    American Slave Revolts in the Making of the Modern World.
    Baton Rouge: Louisiana University Press, 1979.

Genovese, Eugene D. Roll, Jordan, Roll: The World the Slaves
    Made. New York: Pantheon, 1974.

Gewehr, Wesley M. The Great Awakening in Virginia, 1740-1790.
    Durham, N.C.: Duke University Press, 1930.

Gilborn, Craig. "Samuel Davies' Sacred Muse." Journal of
    Presbyterian History 41 (June 1963), 63-79.

Goodman, Abram V. American Overture: Jewish Rights in Colonial
    Times. Philadelphia: Jewish Publication Society of America,
    1947.

Goodwin, Gerald J. "The Anglican Reaction to the Great
    Awakening." Historical Magazine of the Protestant Episcopal
    Church 35 (December 1966), 343-371.

Goodwin, Gerald J. "Christianity, Civilization and the Savage:
    The Anglican Mission to the American Indian." Historical
    Magazine of the Protestant Episcopal Church 42 (June 1973),
    93-110.

Gragg, Larry D. Migration in Early America: The Virginia
    Quaker Experience. Ann Arbor: UMI Research Press, 1980.

Greenberg, Michael. "Revival, Reform, Revolution: Samuel
    Davies and the Great Awakening in Virginia." Marxist
    Perspectives 3 (Summer 1980), 102-119.

Greene, Jack P. The Quest for Power: The Lower Houses of
    Assembly in the Southern Royal Colonies, 1689-1776. Chapel
    Hill: University of North Carolina Press, 1963.

Greene, Jack P. "'Slavery or Independence': Some Reflections
    on the Relationship Among Liberty, Black Bondage, and
    Equality in Revolutionary South Carolina." South Carolina
    Historical Magazine 80 (July 1979), 193-214.

Greven, Philip. The Protestant Temperament: Patterns of Child-
    Rearing, Religious Experience, and the Self in Early
    America. New York: Knopf, 1977.

Guice, John D. W. "Log Colleges and the Legacies of the Great
    Awakening." Southern Quarterly 10 (January 1972), 117-136.

Gunderson, Joan R. "The Myth of the Independent Virginia
     Vestry." Historical Magazine of the Protestant Episcopal
     Church 44 (June 1975), 133-141.

Harris, Waldo P., III. "Daniel Marshall: Lone Georgia
     Revolutionary Pastor." Viewpoints: Georgia Baptist History
     5 (1976), 51-64.

Hart, Freeman H. The Valley of Virginia in the American
     Revolution, 1763-1789. Chapel Hill: University of North
     Carolina Press, 1942.

Heimert, Alan. Religion and the American Mind: From the Great
     Awakening to the Revolution. Cambridge, Mass.: Harvard
     University Press, 1966.

Hening, William W., ed. The Statutes at Large; Being a
     Collection of all the Laws of Virginia, from the First
     Session of the Legislature, in the Year 1619. 1819-23.
     Reprint. Charlottesville: University Press of Virginia,
     1969.

Henry, William Wirt. Patrick Henry: Life, Correspondence and
     Speeches. 3 vols. 1891. Reprint. New York: B. Franklin
     Press, 1969.

Hill, A. Shrady. "The Parson's Cause." Historical Magazine of
     the Protestant Episcopal Church 46 (March 1977), 5-35.

Hill, Samuel S., ed. Religion in the Southern States: A
     Historical Survey. Macon, Ga.: Mercer University Press,
     1983.

Hiner, Ray, Jr. "Samuel Henley and Thomas Gwatkin: Partners in
     Protest." Historical Magazine of the Protestant Episcopal
     Church 38 (March 1968), 39-50.

Hoffman, Paul E. "Legend, Religious Idealism, and Colonies:
     The Point of Santa Elena in History, 1552-1566." South
     Carolina Historical Magazine 84 (April 1983), 59-71.

Hogue, William M. "The Religious Conspiracy Theory of the
     American Revolution: Anglican Motive." Church History 45
     (September 1976), 277-292.

Holmes, David. "The Episcopal Church and the American
     Revolution." Historical Magazine of the Protestant
     Episcopal Church 47 (September 1978), 261-291.

Hood, Fred J. "Revolution and Religious Liberty: The
     Conservation of the Theocratic Concept in Virginia." Church
     History 40 (June 1971), 170-181.

Hooker, Richard J., ed. The Carolina Backcountry on the Eve of
     the Revolution: The Journal and Other Writings of Charles
     Woodmason, Anglican Itinerant. Chapel Hill: University of
     North Carolina Press, 1953.

Howe, George. History of the Presbyterian Church in South
     Carolina. 2 vols. Columbia, S.C.: Duffie and Chapman,
     1870-83.

Huhner, Leon. Jews in America in Colonial and Revolutionary
     Times. New York: Gertz Brothers, 1959.

Hurley, James M. "The Political Status of Roman Catholics in
     North Carolina." Records of the American Catholic
     Historical Society 38 (March 1927), 237-296.

Hutchinson, William T., and Rachal, William M. E., eds. The
     Papers of James Madison. Chicago: University of Chicago
     Press, 1962.

Isaac, Rhys. "Dramatizing the Ideology of the Revolution:
     Popular Mobilization--Virginia, 1744 to 1776." William and
     Mary Quarterly, 3d ser., 33 (July 1976), 357-385.

 Isaac, Rhys. "Evangelical Revolt: The Nature of the Baptists'
     Challenge to the Traditional Order in Virginia, 1765-1775."
     William and Mary Quarterly, 3d ser., 31 (July 1974), 345-
     368.

Isaac, Rhys. "Patrick Henry: Patriot and Preacher?" Virginia
     Cavalcade 31 (Winter 1982), 168-175.

Isaac, Rhys. "Preachers and Patriots: Popular Culture and the
     Revolution in Virginia." In The American Revolution:
     Explorations in the History of American Radicalism, edited
     by Alfred Young. De Kalb, Ill.: Northern Illinois
     University Press, 1976.

Isaac, Rhys. "Religion and Authority: Problems of the Anglican
     Establishment in Virginia in the Era of the Great Awakening
     and the Parson's Cause." William and Mary Quarterly, 3d
     ser., 30 (January 1973), 3-36.

Isaac, Rhys. The Transformation of Virginia, 1740-1790.
     Chapel Hill: University of North Carolina Press, 1982.

Ives, J. Moss. "The Catholic Contribution to Religious Liberty
     in Colonial America." Catholic Historical Review 21
     (October 1935), 283-298.

James, Charles F. Documentary History of the Struggle for
     Religious Liberty in Virginia. Lynchburg, Va.: J. P. Bell,
     1900.

Jarratt, Devereux. The Life of the Reverend Devereux Jarratt, Rector of Bath Parish, Virginia, Written by Himself in a Series of Letters Addressed to the Rev. John Coleman. Baltimore: Warner and Hanna, 1806.

Jellison, Richard M., ed. Society, Freedom, and Conscience: The Coming of the Revolution in Virginia, Maryland, and New York. New York: Norton, 1976.

Johnson, Thomas C. Virginia Presbyterianism and Religious Liberty in Colonial and Revolutionary Times. Richmond: Presbyterian Committee of Publication, 1907.

Jones, George F. "John Martin Boltzius' Trip to Charleston, October 1742." South Carolina Historical Magazine 82 (April 1981), 87-110.

Jones, George F. The Salzburger Saga: Religious Exiles and Other Germans along the Savannah. Athens, Ga.: University of Georgia Press, 1984.

Jones, Jerome W. "The Established Virginia Church and the Conversion of Negroes and Indians, 1620-1740." Journal of Negro History 46 (January 1961), 12-23.

Jones, Newton B., ed. "Writings of the Reverend William B. Tennent, 1740-1777." South Carolina Historical Magazine 61 (July 1960), 129-145; (October 1960), 189-209.

Jones, Rufus. The Quakers in the American Colonies. London: Macmillan, 1911.

Jordan, Winthrop. White over Black: American Attitudes toward the Negro, 1550-1812. Chapel Hill: University of North Carolina Press, 1968.

Kammen, Michael G., ed. "Virginia at the Close of the Seventeenth Century: An Appraisal by James Blair and John Locke." Virginia Magazine of History and Biography 74 (January 1966), 141-169.

Katz, Stanley N., and Murrin, John M., eds. Colonial America: Essays in Politics and Social Development. 3d ed. New York: Knopf, 1983.

Keen, Quentin B. "The Problems of a Commissary: The Reverend Alexander Garden of South Carolina." Historical Magazine of the Protestant Episcopal Church 20 (June 1951), 136-155.

Kenney, William H., III. "Alexander Garden and George Whitefield: The Significance of Revivalism in South Carolina, 1738-1741." South Carolina Historical Magazine 71 (January 1970), 1-16.

Kenney, William H., III. "George Whitefield, Dissenter Priest ofthe Great Awakening, 1739-1741." William and Mary Quarterly, 3d ser., 26 (January 1969), 75-93.

Ketcham, Ralph L. "James Madison and Religion--A New Hypothesis." Journal of the Presbyterian Historical Society 38 (June 1960), 65-90.

Kingdon, Robert M. "Why did the Huguenot Refugees in the American Colonies become Episcopal?" Historical Magazine of the Protestant Episcopal Church 49 (December 1980), 317-335.

Klein, Rachel N. "Ordering the Backcountry: The South Carolina Regulation." William and Mary Quarterly, 3d ser., 38 (October 1981), 661-680.

Klingberg, Frank J., ed. Carolina Chronicle: The Papers of Commissary Gideon Johnston, 1707-1716. Berkeley: University of California Press, 1946.

Klingberg, Frank J., ed. The Carolina Chronicle of Dr. Francis Le Jau, 1706-1717. Berkeley: University of California Press,1956.

Kroll-Smith, J. Stephen. "Tobacco and Belief: Baptist Ideology and the Yeoman Planter in Eighteenth-Century Virginia." Southern Studies 21 (Winter 1982), 353-368.

Kroll-Smith, J. Stephen. "Transmitting a Revival Culture: The Organizational Dynamic of the Baptist Movement in Colonial Virginia, 1760-1777." Journal of Southern History 50 (November 1984), 551-568.

Kupperman, Karen O. Settling with the Indians: The Meeting of English and Indian Cultures in America, 1580-1640. Totowa, N.J.: Rowman and Littlefield, 1980.

Lewis, Andrew W., ed. "Henry Muhlenberg's Georgia Correspondence." Georgia Historical Quarterly 49 (December 1965), 424-454.

Lewis, Jan. "Domestic Tranquility and the Management of Emotion among the Gentry of Prerevolutionary Virginia." William and Mary Quarterly, 3d ser., 39 (January 1982), 135-149.

Little, Lewis Peyton. Imprisoned Preachers and Religious Liberty in Virginia: A Narrative Drawn Largely from the Official Records of Virginia Counties. Lynchburg, Va.: J. P. Bell, 1938.

Lockridge, Kenneth A. Settlement and Unsettlement in Early America: The Crisis of Political Legitimacy before the Revolution. New York: Cambridge University Press, 1981.

Lohrenz, Otto. "The Right Reverend William Harrison of
    Revolutionary Virginia, First 'Lord Archbishop of America.'"
    Historical Magazine of the Protestant Episcopal Church 53
    (March 1984), 25-43.

Loomie, Albert J. The Spanish Jesuit Mission in Virginia,
    1570-1572. Chapel Hill: University of North Carolina Press,
    1953.

Lumpkin, Henry. From Savannah to Yorktown: The American
    Revolution in the South. Columbia, S.C.: University of
    South Carolina Press, 1981.

Lumpkin, William L. The Baptist Foundations in the South:
    Tracing through the Separates the Influence of the Great
    Awakening, 1754-1787. Nashville: Broadman Press, 1961.

Lurie, Maxine N. "Theory and Practice of Religious Toleration
    in the Seventeenth Century: The Proprietary Colonies as a
    Case Study." Maryland Historical Magazine 79 (Summer 1984),
    117-125.

McCaul, Robert L. "Whitefield's Bethesda College Projects and
    Other Major Attempts to Found Colonial Colleges." Georgia
    Historical Quarterly 44 (September 1960), 263-277; (December
    1960), 381-398.

McColley, Robert. Slavery and Jeffersonian Virginia. Urbana:
    University of Illinois Press, 1964.

McCully, Bruce T. "Governor Francis Nicholson, Patron par
    excellence of Religion and Learning in Colonial America."
    William and Mary Quarterly, 3d ser., 39 (April 1982), 310-
    333.

McIlwaine, Henry R. The Struggle of Protestant Dissenters for
    Religious Toleration in Virginia. Baltimore: Johns Hopkins
    Press, 1894.

McKibbens, Thomas R., and Smith, Kenneth L. The Life and Works
    of Morgan Edwards: First Baptist Historian in the United
    States. New York: Arno Press, 1980.

McLoughlin, William G., and Jordan, Winthrop D., eds.
    "Baptists Face the Barbarities of Slavery in 1710." Journal
    of Southern History 29 (November 1963), 495-501.

Maier, Pauline. "Popular Uprisings and Civil Authority in
    Eighteenth-Century America." William and Mary Quarterly, 3d
    ser., 27 (January 1970), 3-35.

Malone, Michael T. "Sketches of the Anglican Clergy Who Served
    in North Carolina During the Period, 1765-1776." Historical
    Magazine of the Protestant Episcopal Church 39 (June 1970),
    137-161; (December 1970), 399-429.

Mariner, Kirk. Revival's Children: A Religious History of
    Virginia's Eastern Shore. Salisbury, Md.: Peninsula, 1979.

Marshall, Abraham. "Biography of the Late Rev. Daniel
    Marshall." Georgia Analytical Repository 1 (May-June 1802),
    23-31.

Martin, Roger A. "John J. Zubly Comes to America." Georgia
    Historical Quarterly 61 (Summer 1977), 125-139.

Mathews, Donald G. Religion in the Old South. Chicago:
    University of Chicago Press, 1977.

May, Henry R. The Enlightenment in America. New York: Oxford
    University Press, 1976.

Mays, David J., ed. The Letters and Papers of Edmund
    Pendleton, 1734-1803. 2 vols. Charlottesville: University
    Press of Virginia, 1967.

Mead, Sidney E. The Lively Experiment: The Shaping of
    Christianity in America. New York: Harper and Row, 1963.

Micklus, Robert. "'The History of the Tuesday Club': A Mock-
    Jeremiad of the Colonial South." William and Mary
    Quarterly, 3d ser., 40 (January 1983), 42-61.

Middleton, Arthur P. "The Colonial Virginia Parish."
    Historical Magazine of the Protestant Episcopal Church 40
    (December 1971), 431-446.

Middleton, Arthur P. "The Colonial Virginia Parson." William
    and Mary Quarterly, 3d ser., 26 (July 1969), 425-440.

Miller, Helen H. George Mason: Gentleman Revolutionary.
    Chapel Hill: University of North Carolina Press, 1975.

Miller, Perry. "Religion and Society in the Early Literature:
    The Religious Impulse in the Founding of Virginia." William
    and Mary Quarterly, 3d ser., 5 (October 1948), 492-522; 6
    (January 1949), 24-41.

Miller, Randall M., ed. "A Warm and Zealous Spirit": John J.
    Zubly and the American Revolution: A Selection of His
    Writings. Macon, Ga.: Mercer University Press, 1982.

Mills, Frederick V. Bishops By Ballot: An Eighteenth-Century
    Ecclesiastical Revolution. New York: Oxford University
    Press, 1978.

Monk, Robert C. "Unity and Diversity Among Eighteenth-Century
    Colonial Anglicans and Methodists." Historical Magazine of
    the Protestant Episcopal Church 38 (March 1969), 51-69.

Monroe, Haskell. "Religious Toleration and Politics in Early North Carolina." North Carolina Historical Review 29 (July 1962), 267-283.

Morgan, David T. "The Consequences of George Whitefield's Ministry in the Carolinas and Georgia, 1739-1740." Georgia Historical Quarterly 55 (Spring 1971), 62-82.

Morgan, David T. "George Whitefield and the Great Awakening in the Carolinas and Georgia, 1739-1740." Georgia Historical Quarterly 54 (Winter 1970), 517-539.

Morgan, David T. "The Great Awakening in North Carolina, 1740-1775: The Baptist Phase." North Carolina Historical Review 45 (Summer 1968), 264-283.

Morgan, David T. "The Great Awakening in South Carolina, 1740-1775." South Atlantic Quarterly 70 (Autumn 1971), 595-606.

Morgan, David T. "John Wesley's Sojourn in Georgia Revisited." Georgia Historical Quarterly 64 (Fall 1980), 253-262.

Morgan, Edmund S. American Slavery, American Freedom: The Ordeal of Colonial Virginia. New York: Norton, 1975.

Morgan, Edmund S. "Slavery and Freedom: The American Paradox." Journal of American History 59 (June 1972), 5-29.

Morgan, Philip D. "The Medium and the Message: The Transformation of Virginia." Historical Studies 20 (October 1983), 590-599.

Mullin, Gerald W. Flight and Rebellion: Slave Resistance in Eighteenth-Century Virginia. New York: Oxford University Press, 1972.

Nadelhaft, Jerome J. The Disorders of War: The Revolution in South Carolina. Orono, Me.: University of Maine Press, 1981.

Nash, Gary B. "The Image of the Indian in the Southern Colonial Mind." William and Mary Quarterly, 3d ser., 29 (April 1972), 197-230.

O'Connell, Neil J. "George Whitefield and Bethesda Orphan-House." Georgia Historical Quarterly 54 (Spring 1970), 41-62.

Olson, Alison G. "The Commissaries of the Bishop of London in Colonial Politics." In Anglo-American Political Relations, 1675-1775, edited by Alison G. Olson and Richard M. Brown. New Brunswick, N.J.: Rutgers University Press, 1970.

Parker, Mattie E. E., ed. North Carolina Charters and Constitutions, 1578-1698. Raleigh: Carolina Charter Tercentenary Commission, 1963.

Pauley, William E., Jr. "Tragic Hero: Loyalist John J. Zubly." Journal of Presbyterian History 54 (Spring 1976), 61-81.

Perdue, Theda. "George Whitefield in Georgia: Evangelism." Atlanta Historical Quarterly 22 (Spring 1978), 43-51.

Perdue, Theda. "George Whitefield in Georgia: Philanthropy." Atlanta Historical Quarterly 22 (Fall-Winter 1978), 53-62.

Perry, William S. "The Foundations of Church and State in Virginia." Historical Magazine of the Protestant Episcopal Church 26 (March 1957), 34-64.

Pilcher, George W. "Samuel Davies and Religious Toleration in Virginia." Historian 28 (November 1965), 48-71.

Pilcher, George W. Samuel Davies, Apostle of Dissent in Colonial Virginia. Knoxville: University of Tennessee Press, 1971.

Porter, Harry C. "Alexander Whitaker: Cambridge Apostle to Virginia." William and Mary Quarterly, 3d ser., 14 (July 1957), 317-343.

Powell, William S., ed. Dictionary of North Carolina Biography. Chapel Hill: University of North Carolina Press, 1979-.

Quinlivan, Mary E. "From Pragmatic Accommodation to Principled Action: The Revolution and Religious Establishment in Virginia." West Georgia College Studies in the Social Sciences 15 (June 1976), 55-64.

Rabe, Harry G. "The Reverend Devereux Jarratt and the Virginia Social Order." Historical Magazine of the Protestant Episcopal Church 33 (December 1964), 299-336.

Raboteau, Albert J. Slave Religion: The "Invisible Institution" in the Antebellum South. New York: Oxford University Press, 1978.

Ramsay, David. The History of South Carolina from Its First Settlement in 1670 to the Year 1808. 2 vols. Charleston, S.C.: David Longworth, 1809.

Ramsey, Robert W. Carolina Cradle: Settlement of the Northwest Carolina Frontier, 1747-1762. Chapel Hill: University of North Carolina Press, 1964.

Ray, Mary A. *American Opinion of Roman Catholicism in the Eighteenth Century*. New York: Columbia University Press, 1936.

Rennie, Sandra. "The Role of the Preacher: Index to the Consolidation of the Baptist Movement in Virginia from 1760 to 1790." *Virginia Magazine of History and Biography* 88 (October 1980), 430-441.

Rennie, Sandra. "Virginia's Baptist Persecution, 1765-1778." *Journal of Religious History* 12 (June 1982), 48-61.

Ritchie, Carson I. A. *Frontier Parish: An Account of the Society for the Propagation of the Gospel and the Anglican Church in America, Drawn from the Records of the Bishop of London*. Rutherford, N.J.: Fairleigh Dickinson University Press, 1976.

Robertson, Heard. "The Reverend James Seymour, Frontier Parson, 1771-1783." *Historical Magazine of the Protestant Episcopal Church* 45 (June 1976), 145-153.

Robinson, W. Stitt, Jr. "Indian Education and Missions in Colonial Virginia." *Journal of Southern History* 18 (May 1952), 152-168.

Robinson, W. Stitt, Jr. "The Legal Status of the Indian in Colonial Virginia." *Virginia Magazine of History and Biography* 61 (July 1953), 247-259.

Roeber, A. G. "Authority, Law, and Custom: The Rituals of Court Day in Tidewater Virginia, 1720-1750." *William and Mary Quarterly*, 3d ser., 37 (January 1980), 29-52.

Roeber, A. G. *Faithful Magistrates and Republican Lawyers: Creators of Virginia Legal Culture, 1680-1810*. Chapel Hill: University of North Carolina Press, 1981.

Roediger, David R. "And Die in Dixie: Funerals, Death, and Heaven in the Slave Community, 1700-1865." *Massachusetts Review* 22 (Spring 1981), 163-183.

Rogers, George C., Jr. *Charleston in the Age of the Pinckneys*. Norman, Okla.: University of Oklahoma Press, 1969.

Rogers, George C., Jr. *Church and State in Eighteenth-Century South Carolina*. Charleston, S.C.: Dalcho Historical Society, 1959.

Ronda, James P. "'We are Well as We Are': An Indian Critique of Seventeenth-Century Christian Missions." *William and Mary Quarterly*, 3d ser., 34 (January 1977), 66-82.

Rouse, Parke, Jr. *James Blair of Virginia*. Chapel Hill: University of North Carolina Press, 1971.

Rutland, Robert A., ed. The Papers of George Mason. 3 vols. Chapel Hill: University of North Carolina Press, 1970.

Rutman, Darrett B. "The Evolution of Religious Life in Early Virginia." Lex et Scientia: International Journal of Law and Science 14 (October-December 1978), 190-214.

Rutman, Darrett B., ed. The Old Dominion: Essays for Thomas Perkins Abernathy. Charlottesville: University Press of Virginia, 1964.

Rutman, Darrett B., and Rutman, Anita H. A Place in Time: Explicatus. New York: Norton, 1984.

Rutman, Darrett B., and Rutman, Anita H. A Place in Time: Middlesex County, Virginia, 1650-1750. New York: Norton, 1984.

Sappington, Roger E. "North Carolina and the Non-Resistant Sects During the American War of Independence." Quaker History 60 (Spring 1971), 29-47.

Saunders, William L., ed. The Colonial Records of North Carolina. 10 vols. Raleigh: P. M. Hale, 1886-90.

Schelbert, Leo. "The American Revolution: A Lesson in Dissent: The Case of John Joachim Zubly." Swiss American Historical Society Newsletter 12, no. 3 (1976), 3-11.

Scherer, Lester B. Slavery and the Churches in Early America, 1619-1819. Grand Rapids: Eerdmans, 1975.

Scott, Arthur P. "The Constitutional Aspects of the 'Parson's Cause.'" Political Science Quarterly 31 (December 1916), 558-577.

Scott, P. G. "James Blair and the Scottish Church: A New Source." William and Mary Quarterly, 3d ser., 33 (April 1976), 300-308.

Scott, Robert F. "Colonial Presbyterianism in the Valley of Virginia, 1727-1775." Journal of the Presbyterian Historical Society 25 (June 1957), 71-92; (September 1957), 171-192.

Seiler, William H. "The Anglican Parish in Virginia." In Seventeenth-Century America: Essays in Colonial History, edited by James M. Smith. Chapel Hill: University of North Carolina Press, 1959.

Seiler, William H. "The Anglican Parish Vestry in Colonial Virginia." Journal of Southern History 22 (August 1956), 310-337.

Seiler, William H. "The Church of England as the Established
    Church in Seventeenth-Century Virginia." Journal of
    Southern History 15 (November 1949), 478-508.

Sellers, Charles G., Jr. "John Blair Smith." Journal of the
    Presbyterian Historical Society 34 (December 1956), 201-225.

Semple, Robert B. A History of the Rise and Progress of the
    Baptists in Virginia. 1810. rev. ed. Richmond: Pitt and
    Dickinson, 1894.

Sheehan, Bernard. Savagism and Civility: Indians and
    Englishmen in Colonial Virginia. Cambridge: Cambridge
    University Press, 1980.

Singleton, Marvin K. "Colonial Virginia as First Amendment
    Matrix: Henry, Madison, and Assessment Establishment."
    Journal of Church and State 8 (Autumn 1966), 344-364.

Sirmans, M. Eugene. Colonial South Carolina: A Political
    History, 1663-1763. Chapel Hill: University of North
    Carolina Press, 1966.

Sloan, Herbert, and Onuf, Peter. "Politics, Culture, and the
    Revolution in Virginia: A Review of Recent Work." Virginia
    Magazine of History and Biography 91 (July 1983), 259-284.

Smith, Charles W. F. "Chaplain Robert Hunt and His Parish in
    Kent." Historical Magazine of the Protestant Episcopal
    Church 26 (March 1957), 15-33.

Smith, Daniel B. Inside the Great House: Planter Family Life
    in Eighteenth-Century Chesapeake Society. Ithaca, N.Y.:
    Cornell University Press, 1980.

Smith, Timothy L. "Congregation, State, and Denomination: The
    Forming of the American Religious Structure." William and
    Mary Quarterly, 3d ser., 25 (April 1968), 155-176.

Smylie, James H. "Presbyterian Clergy and Problems of
    'Dominion' in the Revolutionary Generation." Journal of
    Presbyterian History 48 (Fall 1970), 161-175.

Spalding, Phinizy. Oglethorpe in America. Chicago: University
    of Chicago Press, 1977.

Stein, Stephen J. "George Whitefield on Slavery: Some New
    Evidence." Church History 42 (June 1973), 243-256.

Stern, Malcolm H. "New Light on the Jewish Settlement of
    Savannah." American Jewish Historical Quarterly 52 (March
    1963), 169-199.

Stokes, Anson Phelps. _Church and State in the United States:_
The Development of Church-State Thought Since the
Revolutionary Era. 3 vols. New York: Harper & Brothers,
1950.

Stokes, Durward T. "The Baptist and Methodist Clergy in South
Carolina and the American Revolution." _South Carolina_
Historical Magazine 73 (April 1973), 87-96.

Stokes, Durward T. "Different Concepts of Government Expressed
in the Sermons of Two Eighteenth-Century Clergymen."
Historical Magazine of the Protestant Episcopal Church 40
(March 1971), 81-94.

Stokes, Durward T. "The Presbyterian Clergy in South Carolina
and the American Revolution." _South Carolina Historical_
Magazine 71 (1970), 270-282.

Stowe, Walter H. "The Reverend Richard Hakluyt (c. 1553-1616)
and the First Charter of Virginia (1606)." _Historical_
Magazine of the Protestant Episcopal Church 26 (March 1957),
10-14.

Strickland, Reba C. _Religion and the State in Georgia in the_
Eighteenth Century. New York: Columbia University Press,
1939.

Sydnor, Charles S. _American Revolutionaries in the Making:_
Political Practices in Washington's Virginia. Chapel Hill:
University of North Carolina Press, 1952.

Sykes, Norman. _Church and State in England in the Eighteenth_
Century. Cambridge: Cambridge University Press, 1934.

Tarver, Jerry L. "Baptist Preaching from Virginia Jails, 1768-
1778." _Southern Speech Journal_ 30 (Winter 1964), 139-148.

Tate, Thad W., and Ammerman, David L., eds. _The Chesapeake in_
the Seventeenth Century: Essays on Anglo-American Society.
Chapel Hill: University of North Carolina Press, 1979.

Thom, William T. _The Struggle for Religious Freedom in_
Virginia: The Baptists. Baltimore: The Johns Hopkins Press,
1900.

Thompson, Ernest T. _The Presbyterians in the South_. 2 vols.
Richmond: John Knox Press, 1963.

Thompson, H. P. _Into All Lands: The History of the Society for_
the Propagation of the Gospel in Foreign Parts. London:
Society for the Propagation of the Gospel, 1950.

Thompson, J. Earl, Jr. "Slavery and Presbyterianism in the
Revolutionary Era." _Journal of Presbyterian History_ 54
(Spring 1976), 121-141.

Thorpe, Francis N., ed. The Federal and State Constitutions.
7 vols. Washington, D.C.: Government Printing Office, 1909.

Tresch, John W., Jr. "The Reception Accorded George Whitefield
in the Southern Colonies." Methodist History 61 (January
1968), 17-26.

Trinterud, Leonard J. The Forming of an American Tradition: A
Re-examination of Colonial Presbyterianism. Philadelphia:
Westminster Press, 1949.

Tyler, Lyon G., ed. Encyclopedia of Virginia Biography. 5
vols. New York: Lewis Historical Publishing Co., 1915.

Ulmer, Barbara. "Benevolence in Colonial Charleston." South
Carolina Historical Association, Proceedings (1980), 1-12.

Van Horne, John C. "Impediments to the Christianization and
Education of Blacks in Colonial America: The Case of the
Associates of Dr. Bray." Historical Magazine of the
Protestant Episcopal Church 50 (September 1981), 243-269.

Van Horne, John C. "Joseph Solomon Ottolenghe (ca. 1711-1775):
Catechist to the Negroes, Superintendent of the Silk
Culture, and Public Servant in Colonial Georgia." American
Philosophical Society, Proceedings 125 (October 1981), 398-
409.

Voigt, Gilbert D. "Religious Conditions Among German-Speaking
Settlers in South Carolina, 1732-1774." South Carolina
Historical Magazine 56 (April 1955), 59-66.

Walker, Charles O. "Georgia's Religion in the Colonial Era,
1733-1790." Viewpoints: Georgia Baptist History 5 (1976),
17-44.

Walsh, James P. "'Black Cotted Raskolls': Anti-Anglican
Criticism in Colonial Virginia." Virginia Magazine of
History and Biography 88 (January 1980), 21-36.

Waterhouse, Richard. "The Development of Elite Culture in the
Colonial American South: A Study of Charles Town, 1670-
1770." Australian Journal of Politics and History 28, no. 3
(1982), 391-404.

Watson, Alan D. "The Anglican Parish in Royal North Carolina,
1729-1775." Historical Magazine of the Protestant Episcopal
Church 48 (September 1979), 303-319.

Weaver, C. Douglas. "David Thomas and the Regular Baptists in
Colonial Virginia." Baptist History and Heritage 18
(December 1983), 3-19.

Weeks, Stephen B. Church and State in North Carolina.
Baltimore: Johns Hopkins Press, 1893.

Weeks, Stephen B. The Religious Development in the Province of
    North Carolina. Baltimore: Johns Hopkins Press, 1892.

Weir, Robert M. "'The Harmony We Were Famous For': An
    Interpretation of Pre-Revolutionary South Carolina
    Politics." William and Mary Quarterly, 3d ser., 26 (October
    1969), 473-501.

Weis, Frederick L. The Colonial Clergy of Virginia, North
    Carolina, and South Carolina. Boston: Publications of the
    Society of the Descendants of the Colonial Clergy, 1955.

Wells, Guy F. Parish Education in Colonial Virginia. New
    York: Columbia University Press, 1923.

Wertenbaker, Thomas J. "The Attempt to Reform the Church of
    Colonial Virginia." Sewanee Review 25 (July 1917), 257-282.

Wood, Peter H. Black Majority: Negroes in Colonial South
    Carolina from 1670 through the Stono Rebellion. New York:
    Knopf, 1974.

Wood, Peter H. "'I Did the Best I Could For My Day': The Study
    of Early Black History During the Second Reconstruction,
    1960-1976." William and Mary Quarterly, 3d ser., 35 (April
    1978), 185-225.

Wood, Peter H. "'Jesus Christ Has Got Thee at Last': Afro-
    American Conversion as a Forgotten Chapter in Eighteenth-
    Century Southern Intellectual History." Bulletin of the
    Center for the Study of Southern Culture and Religion 3
    (November 1979), 2-7.

Wood, Sandra T. "The Reverend John Urmstone: A Portrait of
    North Carolina." Historical Magazine of the Protestant
    Episcopal Church 41 (September 1972), 263-285.

Woodward, C. Vann. "The Southern Ethic in a Puritan World."
    William and Mary Quarterly, 3d ser., 25 (July 1968), 343-
    370.

Woolverton, John F. Colonial Anglicanism in North America.
    Detroit, Mich.: Wayne State University Press, 1984.

Wright, J. Leitch. Anglo-Spanish Rivalry in North America.
    Athens, Ga.: University of Georgia Press, 1971.

Wright, Louis B. Religion and Empire: The Alliance Between
    Piety and Commerce in English Expansion, 1558-1625. Chapel
    Hill: University of North Carolina Press, 1943.

Zahniser, Marvin R. Charles Cotesworth Pinckney, Founding
    Father. Chapel Hill: University of North Carolina Press,
    1967.

4

Church and State in America from the Great Awakening to the American Revolution

Mark Valeri

Prior to the mid-eighteenth century, relations between church establishments and provincial and royal powers differed widely from colony to colony, reflecting the diverse affiliations of individual colonies to European nations. In the decades from the Great Awakening to the American Revolution, this trend towards colonial differentiation was reversed. Two powerful, intercolonial movements demarcate this period. At the start stands what to its advocates (known as New Lights) seemed an extraordinary revival of religion, the Great Awakening. Adumbrated in localized revivals in New Jersey and Pennsylvania in the late 1720s, which were followed by a revival in the Connecticut River Valley in 1734 and 1735, the Awakening became a *cause célèbre* with the 1739–1741 evangelistic tour of the Englishman George Whitefield. A year of American-led revivals followed Whitefield's itinerations. Spreading throughout the colonies, the Awakening reached the southern backcountry during the 1760s. At the close of this period, some thirty years after the height of the revivals, political conflicts between colonists and imperial rule erupted in the American Revolution (1775–1783). During the war, colonists debated about and began to establish the political, social, and religious patterns that provided the context for perspectives on church and state in the constitution-making period.

This essay thus concerns the period when colonists began to identify themselves as belonging to a single nation, which encompassed the social, political, and religious institutions existing from New Hampshire to Georgia. Other bibliographies in this series concentrate on the early history of New England, the middle colonies, and the South; this discussion addresses crucial developments in the colonies at large, with particular attention to New England. The development of state constitutions during the war, the ideals of those political leaders (such as Jefferson and Madison) whose activities culminated in the legal constructs of the new nation, and the writing and ratification of the federal constitution are issues to be discussed in other bibliographic essays.

In one of the many books produced in celebration of the nation's Bicentennial, *Religion and the American Revolution* (edited by Jerald C. Brauer) three noted scholars each gave a short analysis of the relationship between American religion and the new nation. These essays represent three distinct and prevailing perspectives on the proper formulation of the subject. First, in his "Christendom, Enlightenment, and the Revolution," Sidney E. Mead argues that by the time of the formation of the Republic, the Enlightenment had conquered orthodox Christianity in America. This view reflects Mead's earlier conclusions, given at length in his *The Lively Experiment*, that the geographical and intellectual spaciousness of the New World allowed Americans to settle once and for all on a pluralistic, voluntary, and individualistic society. Mead thinks that the Republic, in which Americans wholeheartedly rejected the idea of an established church, was united as a political unit that embodied no common religion. Second, by way of contrast, Brauer writes in his essay, "Puritanism, Revivalism, and the Revolution," that the nationalism which emerged in the Revolution was predicated on a repristinized Puritanism—in the form of the Great Awakening. Brauer contends that American democracy was born not of the rationalized individualism of the Enlightenment, but of the intensely pietistic and critical religion exemplified in the thought of Jonathan Edwards. Yet a third position is taken by Robert N. Bellah, in his "The Revolution and Civil Religion." Beneath the multiplicity of theologies and ecclesiastical forms that were encompassed by the new nation, he argues, there was a "lowest common denominator" [p. 57]. This common set of values, which Bellah calls "civil religion," was neither exclusively the Enlightenment nor a revived Puritanism; it was a common morality formed by the confluence of biblical notions of covenant and a utilitarian ethics. It implied loyalty to the common life as the essence of a generic American religion.

These essays are not necessarily the most useful statements about church and state, but they do concisely indicate three common starting points from which scholars have approached the late colonial era. First, this period indicates to some the Enlightenment's profound influence on American society. As a movement of religious and political significance, the Enlightenment may be described in various ways: as humanocentric in focus, rationalistic or empiricist in method, critical of orthodox dogma, individualistic in social vision, or liberal (and in some form democratic) in terms of eighteenth-century political thought. In the context of the issues of church and state, it is enough to describe the Enlightenment as the conviction, born of a confluence of rationalist theologies and democratic political sentiments, that the commonweal depended on no particular body of religious thought or practice, save only a uniformly accepted political ethic. Since no single doctrinal system or ecclesiastical form could claim to be an authority over national institutions, common loyalties fell to non-religious social institutions. Second, those who agree with Brauer's line of argument think that American nationalism and democracy, whatever their specific traits, arose out of a Calvinist, Puritan, and revivalistic vision for common life. In this interpretation, the Great Awakening was a formative national experience, manifesting a widespread conviction that divine intentions were integral to social values; religious ideals were to shape political institutions. Bellah's essay represents a third perspective, from which a peculiarly American form of civil religiosity appears in the emergence of colonists' loyalties to uniquely American social traditions and political institutions. Religious sentiment, according to this interpretation, was directed towards civic forms of life; patriotism became the American orthodoxy as the nation became an object of ultimate value. Although much of the current literature on this period does not directly address these three issues, it does address questions raised by them.

THE IMPACT OF ENLIGHTENMENT THOUGHT
ON COLONIAL SOCIETY

Within the historiography of the American Enlightenment, several works describe the inroads that rationalist thought made in late colonial America. In *The Beginnings of Unitarianism in America* Conrad Wright investigates the theological genesis of liberal religion in New England. Herbert H. Morais's *Deism in America* and G. Adolph Koch's *Republican Religion* describe some of the central features of more radical rationalism. Henry May's *The Enlightenment in America*, however, is the most thorough and sophisticated analysis of the subject. May shows that the moderate and revolutionary forms of the Enlightenment, deriving respectively from Locke and Rousseau, became popular in America, while the skepticism of Hume and Voltaire was disregarded. A. Owen Aldridge's monograph on Thomas Paine, *Thomas Paine's American Ideology*, supports May's thesis that the revolutionary Enlightenment tended towards a secular millennialism. May also posits a fourth strand, a didactic Enlightenment. Centered in debates in moral philosophy and grounded in the social theories of Scottish rationalists such as Francis Hutcheson, this tradition has been seen as important for both Jeffersonian politics and theological ethics in the eighteenth century. Garry Wills's *Inventing America* and Morton White's *The Philosophy of the American Revolution* are crucial for understanding the political import of May's didactic Enlightenment. Norman Fiering's *Jonathan Edwards's Moral Thought,* although focused on the relation between Calvinist theology and rationalist or sensationalist ethical theories, provides a clear picture of the trans-Atlantic nature of American moral and social discourse during this period. There are several reliable biographies of leading Congregational clergymen who were influenced by Enlightenment ideology. Many describe the pastoral and intellectual complications that attended liberalism and that cautiously moved some preachers to accommodate Puritan orthodoxy to rationalism: Charles Akers's book on Jonathan Mayhew, *Called Unto Liberty*, Edward Griffin's study of Charles Chauncy, *Old Brick*, and Robert Wilson III's work on Ebenezer Gay, *The Benevolent Deity*.

From the perspective of a supposed spread of Enlightenment ideals in the colonies, events seem to cluster around three foci: developments in colonial law that favored religious toleration, alliances between Whig ideology and clerical patriotism, and secular motivations for revolutionary activism. One traditional approach, then, has been to define "church and state" as a question of the juridical status of religious groups. New England's church-state relations were complicated by the incongruity between colonial sentiments and the directives of the crown, and by disparities between popular practice and provincial statutes. For example, throughout this period Baptists were officially protected in Connecticut under the 1689 Act of Toleration, yet were hampered by Connecticut laws that obligated them to pay ecclesiastical taxes in support of the Congregational church. Through appeals to local justices who were sympathetic, moreover, some Baptist congregations met for years without fulfilling their tax requirements. Sanford H. Cobb's *The Rise of Religious Liberty in America* celebrates the classically liberal view of the separation of church and state. Cobb argues that during the revolutionary period Jeffersonian ideas finally overcame a dogmatic Calvinism that was theocratically authoritarian. Other histories provide more balanced narratives of institutional and legal developments in religious affairs. The most thorough and straightforward are Paul E. Lauer's *Church and State in New England*, M. Louise Greene's *The Development of Religious Liberty in Connecticut*, and Jacob Meyer's *Church and State in Massachusetts*. This approach has tended towards a Whig historicism, looking for developments in the colonial law that indicate the struggle for and eventual triumph of Lockean ideas of natural law and religious toleration. Charles Kinney's study of New Hampshire, *Church and State*, however, reaches further to describe diversity in local practices. Historians of Catholicism in colonial America have pointed out that New England granted civil liberties to Catholics only after a long and complex process of accepting the full implications of the ideal of the freedom of religion. In *Catholicism in New England to 1788*, Arthur J. Riley recounts the gradual erosion of anti-Catholic legislation and reprints most of the original laws against the Church of Rome in New England. John Tracy Ellis has shown in *Catholics in Colonial America* that only with the success of the Revolution did Protestant America begin to abandon its official prohibitions against Catholic churches. Tracy suggests that traditional fears of an alliance between Catholicism and European forms of political tyranny were challenged by the assistance given the patriots by French forces.

The Church of England occupied an awkward position in New England. Officially the church of the Crown, it provoked enormous fear and resentment among protectors of the Congregationalist establishment and radical forms of dissent. Royal pressure compelled Massachusetts and Connecticut to permit Anglican congregations the right of worship without its members being required to support locally established churches as well. As Bruce Steiner has shown in his "Anglican Officeholding in Pre-Revolutionary Connecticut," members of the Church of England did not hold high office in the elected governments of Connecticut and Massachusetts, although they managed to win some local elections. During the 1750s, as some Anglican missionaries in New England began to advocate the establishment of an Anglican bishopric in America, Congregationalist leaders of almost every theological party flew into anti-Anglican rages. Arthur L. Cross relates these developments with great detail in *The Anglican Episcopate and the American Colonies*. Jonathan Mayhew and Charles Chauncy, Boston preachers greatly influenced by rationalist religion, led the fight against the Anglican bishopric. Akers's biography of Mayhew and Charles Lippy's study of Chauncy, *Seasonable Revolutionary*, argue that the furor over Anglicanism did not stem from religious bigotry on the part of the liberals. Akers and Lippy attempt to show that the Boston clergy feared the political implications of an alliance between royal policy and Episcopalian polity. Claude H. Van Tyne's "Influence of the Clergy" stresses a union between Puritanism, ideals of religious liberty, and anti-Anglicanism. In *Mitre and Sceptre*, Carl Bridenbaugh similarly contends that the Anglican campaign represented such a specter of England's encroachment upon New England's religious liberties and natural rights that it provoked revolutionary fervor among the clergy.

A second type of study of the religious-political impact of liberal thought describes the participation of the clergy (taken as a whole) and the churches in the Revolution itself. Alice M. Baldwin's *The New England Clergy and the American Revolution* is still an important and useful representative of this approach. Understanding the Revolution as the fruition of Lockean ideas of natural rights and social contractualism, Baldwin maintains that Puritan covenant thought was easily accommodated to political liberalism and that clerical support of independence devolved from Whig political values among most of New England's preachers. Several other works follow in Baldwin's tracks and find additional evidence gleaned (frequently out of context) from sermonic literature: John G. Buchanan's "Drumfire from the Pulpit," Sheldon H. Cohen and Larry Gerlach's "Princeton in the Coming of the Revolution," Leonard J. Kramer's "Presbyterians Approach the American Revolution" and "Muskits in the Pulpit," and Karl Reichenbach's "The Connecticut Clergy and the Stamp Act." Stronger support for Baldwin's position is found in Stephen Botein's "Religion and Politics in Revolutionary New England." Richard D. Brown's studies of popular politics show the clergy as providing a network for the dissemination of Whig radicalism; see his *Revolutionary Politics in Massachusetts* and "Spreading the Word." Denominational historians often have attempted to demonstrate that the Americanization of their traditions eventuated in a democratization of ecclesiastical polity; examples are Leonard Trinterud's study of Presbyterianism, *The Forming of An American Tradition,* Robert F. Scott's "Colonial Presbyterianism in the Valley of Virginia," and a recent study of colonial Episcopalianism by Frederick V. Mills, Sr., *Bishops by Ballot.*

The assumption that a unified Enlightenment ideology suffused both the Revolution and religious perceptions of the position of churches in civil society has been challenged on several grounds. Toryism among Anglicans, pacifism among Quakers, and political variations among Calvinists denoted conflicting political views among the clergy. For studies that explain Loyalism as the result of Anglican and Catholic fears of Congregational hegemony, see Charles Mampoteng, "The New England Anglican Clergy" and Charles H. Metzger, *Catholics and the American Revolution.* Other works have demonstrated contradictory political sympathies within religious groups, and search for ethnic or economic occasions for such differences. "The Dutch Reformed Church" by John W. Beardslee III and "The Internal Revolution in Pennsylvania" by Wayne L. Bockelman and Owen S. Ireland point to the former; Lester Douglas Joyce's *Church and Clergy in the American Revolution* is a tendentious yet clear example of the latter. A better study of economic factors is Jonathan Powell's "Presbyterian Loyalists." Mark Noll's *Christians in the American Revolution* gives a simplified schema for understanding some of the theological sources of political diversity among the clergy.

A third concern within the literature of the American Enlightenment focuses on the nature of revolutionary activity, finding the sources of late colonial politics not in classical Whig political theory, but in a profound mistrust of governmental authority and power. In his "Towards a Republican Synthesis," Robert Shalhope surveys the recent historiography of this so-called Republican Ideology. According to this interpretation, most influentially given in Bernard Bailyn's *The Ideological Origins of the American*

Revolution, in Pauline Maier's *From Resistance to Revolution*, and in Gordon Wood's *The Creation of the American Republic*, several ideological traditions, including Puritanism, English common law, classicism, and—most importantly—the opposition politics of seventeenth-century English dissenters known as the Commonwealthmen, combined to create a perception that the established government was tyrannical and corrupt. This perception in itself, not precise theories of constitutional propriety, controlled the revolutionary impulse. Bailyn's interpretation, while undercutting both the older Whig view and the economic reductionism of Progressive historians, does attribute the social ideals of Americans during this period to the eventual triumph of secularized and religiously indifferent, if not necessarily Lockean, values. In his "Religion and Revolution," Bailyn argues that American clergymen did not interject religion into their politics. Positing a dichotomy between political and religious ideology, he reads the revolutionary statements of the liberal Mayhew and the Calvinist Stephen Johnson as uniformly controlled by Republican or opposition thought. Wood's magisterial book and J. G. A. Pocock's *The Machiavellian Moment* both maintain that the dominant values of republicanism were a secularized notion of civic virtue. Contending that Patriot leaders manipulated clerical loyalties to enhance partisan political activities, other analyses support the idea that the Revolution signaled the eclipse of religion's power over American society; see Philip Davidson's *Propaganda and the American Revolution*, Frank Dean Giffort's "The Influence of the Clergy," Emory Elliott's "The Dove and the Serpent," Timothy W. Bosworth's "Anti-Catholicism as a Political Tool," and Larzer Ziff's "Revolutionary Rhetoric and Puritanism." The implication of this line of thought is that the churches accommodated themselves to political reality by accepting the essentially non-religious nature of the social body. Edmund Morgan thus contends in "The American Revolution Considered as an Intellectual Movement" that in the revolutionary period politicians replaced clergymen as the most dominant public spokesmen for American values.

Many writers who understand the late colonial era as a triumph of Lockean ideals of religious toleration, as an emergence of individualist social values, or as a secularization of politics, applaud this putative acceptance of religious pluralism and voluntaryism. They suggest that the colonists associated popular sovereignty with natural liberty. They accordingly assert that patriots were implicitly motivated by a desire to defend the idea of social heterogeneity against social constrictions. Besides Mead's works cited above, other studies in this vein are Edward Frank Humphrey's *Nationalism and Religion in America*, Max Savelle's *Seeds of Liberty*, Clinton Rossiter's *Seedtime of the Republic*, and Franklin Littel's *From State Church to Pluralism*. In their perspective, the Enlightenment failed to remake Europe, but found its definitive social expression in America.

THE GREAT AWAKENING AND THE REVOLUTION

Rather than emphasizing American manifestations of the Enlightenment, much of the historiography of the late colonial period takes its departure from considering the impact of religious values upon the revolutionary movement. For this approach, the central issue is the meaning and implication of the Great Awakening. Several narrative overviews of the event provide introductions: Edwin Scott Gaustad's *The Great Awakening in New England*, Wesley M. Gewehr's *The Great Awakening in Virginia*, and Dietmar Rothermund's study of the middle colonies, *The Layman's Progress*. If, as these studies claim, the revivals were widespread, popular, and a turning point for colonial religion, then they manifested a vigorous Calvinism and/or pietism among colonists. Several important interpretations of the Revolution posit a causal link between the religiosity of the Awakening and the nationalist loyalties and moral cohesiveness that were integral to the intercolonial coalescence of American identities. Among these interpretations are Bridenbaugh's *The Spirit of '76*, Cedric Cowing's *The Great Awakening and the American Revolution*, and Robert Middlekauff's recent *The Glorious Cause*.

The thesis that a great and general movement of religious renewal fed the Revolution has been challenged. In his "No Awakening, No Revolution?" John Murrin contends that New Lights may have helped to win the war, but that the Declaration of Independence would have gained colonial support even if there had been no Jonathan Edwards, George Whitefield, or Gilbert Tennent to spread and popularize the Awakening. Jon Butler has even maintained that there was no great and general evangelical mobilization. In his "Enthusiasm Described and Decried," he argues that we should not claim revolutionary significance for events that were essentially apolitical, especially since they happened thirty years before independence. By the 1770s, Butler claims, leading New Lights had conflicting political views; furthermore, many of the adult participants in the revivals really were too old to have exercised a significant influence on events after the Stamp Act crisis.

Proponents of the view that the Awakening was a socially and politically formative event, however, have not based their arguments on assumptions that the Awakening was a monolithic movement with clearly defined parameters. Nor do they claim that New Light activity in the 1740s directly occasioned Patriot campaigns in the 1770s. Most of the arguments describe broad cultural influences or long-ranged shifts in social values. Generally, these interpretations have focused on three issues: first, the impact of Puritan ideas (frequently seen as reformulated by the Awakening) on beliefs in a peculiar destiny for an American nation; second, the relation between evangelical and/or Calvinist mentalities and motivations for social and political reform;

and third, the import of the Awakening for questions of authority and social control—particularly on a local level.

First, accordingly, Puritanism's place in the growth of an American identity has been a central interest in the historiography of this period. In his seminal essays, *The Social Sources of Denominationalism*, *The Kingdom of God in America*, and "The Idea of Covenant and American Democracy," H. Richard Niebuhr argued that in the Great Awakening Calvinist theologians such as Jonathan Edwards took a central tradition within Puritanism—the conviction that divine rule was to be instituted in social policy—and began to apply it to the concept of an American nation. Animated by millennial expectations that arose out of the revivals, maintains Niebuhr, Edwards and other clergymen believed that the church should attempt to shape American society into conformity with what they conceived as the earthly manifestation of the Kingdom of God: a harmonious society knit together by divine love. Perry Miller took the central concept in this conviction to be the Puritan notion of covenant. According to Miller, Puritans believed that the Lord had a unique mission for America. America's privileged status was embodied in a divine covenant, in which the Lord promised to favor America with providential blessing upon the condition that the society pursue godliness and charity. *Nature's Nation* contains several of Miller's essays in support of this thesis. In "From the Covenant to the Revival" Miller contends that after the Awakening colonists finally became convinced that years of providential chastisement in the form of political oppression and social disorder had come to an end; the time was ripe for God's vindication of America's calling and thus for victory over the British empire. Sacvan Bercovitch gives a literary analysis of the jeremiad as a form of rhetoric within the covenant motif. Warnings against religious apathy and social sins, Bercovitch contends in *The American Jeremiad*, were a vehicle to affirm America's importance. Divine chastisement portended eventual salvation on a social scale. The Awakening strengthened these convictions and enhanced the religious rationale for nationalist sentiments. In "How the Puritans Won the American Revolution," Bercovitch argues that in the fight against the British, profane events consequently became symbols of sacred activity and intention, encouraging Patriots.

Bercovitch also points out that Puritan typological exegesis of scripture could lead to expectations that Christ would establish in America the millennial reign. As many historians have indicated, the Awakening fueled such expectations. In "Jonathan Edwards: A New Departure in Eschatology," C. C. Goen maintains that Edwards broke with traditional Reformed eschatology. In standard Calvinist interpretations, Goen suggests, Christ's temporal reign (a thousand-year period of earthly felicity for the godly) would be initiated only by divine intervention into human history, i.e., by the Second Coming. According to Goen, Edwards made an important innovation in asserting that the Second Coming would happen after the millennium. If the millennium was to be established before Christ returned, then godly people were to turn their hopes for the millennium away from cataclysmic events, towards earthly activity. Edwards's views, Goen asserts, consequently justified a belief that Americans were working for the institution of God's kingdom on earth. The Awakening was one such activity; social and political reforms were others. Other interpretations, such as Stephen Stein's "An Apocalyptic Rationale for the American Revolution" and Charles Royster's *A Revolutionary People at War*, hold that Patriot clergy encouraged the struggle for independence by assuring the rebels that America's cause would be imminently vindicated by the millennial reign of God—who intended America to be a national example of godliness, liberty, and righteousness. While James West Davidson's *The Logic of Millennial Thought* and John F. Wilson's "Jonathan Edwards as Historian" indicate that Edwards directed his millennial writings less to predicting immediate political affairs than to providing a theological interpretation of history, both Davidson and Wilson show that New Light eschatology placed special emphasis on the place of America within divinely guided history.

Other scholars maintain that Puritanism strengthened the moral resolve of revolutionary activism. Such interpretations have drawn on Max Weber's analysis of Protestant notions of vocation, seeing Puritanism as providing an ethic that supported political activism. According to Edmund Morgan in "The Puritan Ethic and the American Revolution," Calvinist ideas of economic self-discipline enhanced colonial motives for resisting British importation in the 1770s. Sydney Ahlstrom ("The Puritan Ethic and the Spirit of American Democracy") and Charles Constantin ("The Puritan Ethic and the Dignity of Labor") relate American democratic ideals to the implicit egalitarianism of Puritan concepts of calling and human nature.

Second, the Awakening has received abundant attention as a religious movement that implied and encouraged the kind of social and political reformism that led to democratic revolution. Perry Miller defined the American mind at the Awakening by focusing on the dominant intellectual among New Lights. In *Jonathan Edwards* Miller argues that Edwards was the first American to grasp the anthropological implications of the New Science, integrating empiricist philosophy into a Calvinist critique of the individualism and greed of liberal culture. Patricia Tracy's study of Edwards's career in Northampton, *Jonathan Edwards, Pastor*, shows Edwards's role in the Northampton revivals: his appeal to youth and the social factionalization in Northampton that eventuated in Edwards's pastoral failure and dismissal.

Several studies, including Fiering's *Jonathan Edwards's Moral Thought*, Clyde A. Holbrook's *The Ethics of Jonathan Edwards*, and Roland A. Delattre's "Beauty and Politics," attempt to show how Edwards's theology might be seen to relate to public ethics and political values.

One of the most detailed, extended, and substantial works on the relation between the Awakening and the Revolution is Alan Heimert's *Religion and the American Mind*. Heimert surveys the sermons and tracts of eighteenth-century clergymen and concludes that controversies over the Awakening manifested profoundly contrasting mentalities: a rationalistic, Arminian, and hierarchical sensibility that idealized law and authority, and an evangelical, Calvinist, and populist sensibility that pursued an egalitarian society united by universal fraternalism. Thus extending Miller's thesis into a study of the transmission of evangelical ideas throughout the eighteenth and early nineteenth centuries, Heimert sees democratic nationalism as stemming from Calvinist evangelicalism. Old Lights (opponents of the revivals) and liberals, Heimert thinks, may have voiced Whig ideals; but they did so without democratic convictions or revolutionary force. Outside of a handful of elite political leaders from Virginia, America's proponents of Republican virtue were not the hesitant spokesmen of moderation and order. They were evangelical preachers. The political fruition of the Awakening, Heimert contends, was the populism of Jacksonian society.

Heimert's thesis has been supported by several other types of analyses. Harry S. Stout examines revival rhetoric, and interprets it as a populist mode of communication that encouraged widespread political criticism; see Stout's "Religion, Communications, and the Ideological Origins of the American Revolution." Robert Sklar's "The Great Awakening and Colonial Politics" finds a similar pattern of evangelical populism in Connecticut. James C. Spalding's "Loyalist as Royalist" and Gerald J. Goodwin's "The Anglican Reaction to the Great Awakening" reinforce Heimert's position on rationalist Arminianism. In *Jonathan Edwards to Aaron Burr, Jr.*, Suzanne Geissler attempts to apply Heimert's thesis to the career of a New Light who became a politician. Eldon Eisenach's "Cultural Politics and Political Thought" describes evangelical and millenarian views of history as more conducive to political radicalism than were Whig and liberal concerns about constitutional propriety. Philip Greven's investigation of the social-psychological dimensions of colonial child-rearing, *The Protestant Temperament*, posits three types of colonial personalities. Evangelicals preferred nuclear family units, were oriented towards religious conversion, and were strict in discipline. Moderates characteristically lived in extended families, were theological liberals, and emphasized familial love and duty over punishment. The genteel used servants or nurses for child-rearing, were religiously indifferent, and were personally indulgent towards children. Greven is unsympathetic with what he sees as evangelical authoritarianism, but he argues that evangelicals were more likely to become revolutionaries than were moderates or the genteel, because their suppressed anger eventually expressed itself in manifest rebelliousness. Edwin G. Burrows and Michael Wallace's "The Ideology and Psychology of National Liberation" shows that Patriot hostility towards Britain involved colonial charges of imperial infanticide and desires for a political form of adulthood, i.e., independence. Greven's evangelicals seem to fit into Wallace and Burrows's group of Patriot parricides.

Calvinist social reformism, however, became most apparent in the careers of the transmitters of Edwardsean thought in the late eighteenth century. This New Divinity school, led by Joseph Bellamy, Samuel Hopkins, and Jonathan Edwards, Jr., not only supported the Revolution but also consistently opposed slavery. In his classic study, *Piety Versus Moralism*, Joseph Haroutunian finds in the New Divinity a decline of classically Edwardsean and Calvinist religiosity. More recent writers, however, have seen the moral concerns of the heirs to Edwards as indications of a profound mistrust of the individualist, rationalist, and secularized ethics of liberal society. Important studies here are Joseph A. Conforti's biography of Hopkins, *Samuel Hopkins and the New Divinity Movement*, William Breitenbach's "Unregenerate Doings," and Richard P. Birdsall's "Ezra Stiles versus the New Divinity Men."

According to the interpretations given by Perry Miller, Alan Heimert, and the other writers mentioned above, the Awakening was integral to the making of the nation. The evangelical heirs to Puritanism, and other New Lights, helped to form the American character by attempting to channel corporate activity and remake political institutions according to religious values. The Awakening revived Puritan assumptions about divine intentions for the nation. It stimulated, or became the vehicle of expression for, a democratic egalitarianism and social reformism. The colonial period, in this perspective, did not mark the triumph of liberalism, rationalism, individualism, or secularism; indeed, it was characterized by increasingly popular efforts on the part of Calvinists to apply spiritual convictions to social events.

A third approach to the New Light movement has been to focus on the impact of the revivals on relations between social groups in the colonies. Here the Awakening is seen as crucial for the parameters of church and state in the revolutionary period. The emphasis is placed on questions of popular resistance to local hierarchies, religious dissent, and challenges to established patterns of social authority, instead of on the development of nationalist loyalties or revolutionary social and political reform. While the historians discussed above rely on printed sources and examine the ideological implications of the revivals, scholars who address this third question are more concerned about local patterns of behavior and social dynamics on the popular level.

Much of the emphasis in the historiography of religious dissent has been on Baptist and separatist movements. In *Revivalism and Separatism in New England*, Goen describes the proliferation of Baptist churches in areas that were previously monopolized by Congregationalism. He also narrates the rise of separatism, i.e., the post-Awakening phenomenon of ecclesiastical schism. In debates over the revivals, congregations often split into factions. Old Lights within churches controlled by New Lights, or—more commonly— New Lights in churches controlled by Old Lights, formed new congregations and called their own pastors, operating in contravention of ecclesiastical and civil regulations. William G. McLoughlin's two-volumed *New England Dissent* details the development of evangelical dissent by focusing on the Baptists. According to McLoughlin, dissenting movements challenged the traditional pattern of religious authority and thereby catalyzed opposition to both local political oligarchies and hierarchical social values embedded in colonial law. He contends that Baptist leaders such as Isaac Backus consistently defended the civil rights of dissenters in response to colonial prohibitions against radical New Light activities. Backus's arguments, as McLoughlin describes them, were not chiefly based on Whig political theories. Backus and other New Lights feared that civil intervention in religious affairs would dampen the pursuit of godliness by restricting the divine right of private conscience.

One of the theses embedded in McLoughlin's *New England Dissent*, which he elaborates in "The Role of Religion in the Revolution," is that evangelical piety was intensely anti-authoritarian and individualistic. The conclusions of several social historians reinforce McLoughlin's thesis. Richard Bushman's study of Connecticut from 1690 to 1765, *Puritan to Yankee*, has influenced the views of McLoughlin and many other historians. Bushman argues that the Awakening eroded the kind of Puritan political consensus that, as Michael Zuckerman contends in *Peaceable Kingdoms*, restrained social dissent for most of the seventeenth and eighteenth centuries in New England. Bushman maintains that the evangelical message of repentance and forgiveness relieved New Lights of the sense of guilt that often attended the transgression of conservative, hierarchical, and restrictive social values. The revivals, he argues, were supported largely by new merchants, debtors, and recent immigrants, most of whom favored economic expansion and opposed established interests. Containing an implicit justification of economic activism and social individualism, New Light activities led to an assault on both authoritarian ecclesiastical structures and anti-commercialistic institutions in pre-revolutionary Connecticut. Rhys Isaac's study of colonial Virginia, *The Transforma-tion of Virginia*, examines popular culture. Isaac sees movements against the Anglican, genteel, and wealthy aristocracy of Virginia as characterized by Baptist, evangelical, and lower-class cultural styles. The Baptist and Pres-byterian-led revivals of the 1760s, according to Isaac, were part of the coloni-al revolution against traditional social hierarchies. In "Evangelical Revolt," he sees Virginia Baptists as gaining social control by advocating an evan-gelical fraternalism that encompassed slaves and by encouraging social disci-pline and moral reform to challenge the behavior of the elite. Isaac's conclu-sions are similar to those in James A. Henretta's *The Evolution of American Society*. Henretta argues that the Awakening involved an inversion of author-ity; dispossessed peoples, encouraged by the revivalists' critique of religious authorities, identified genuine social leadership with previously ostracized social groups. In *Settlement and Unsettlement in Early America*, Kenneth A. Lockridge adds to this picture of the anti-authoritarian nature of the revivals by linking the Awakening to a supposed rebirth of Puritan localism. Lock-ridge asserts that the Awakening was an inter-colonial movement charac-terized by the defense of local prerogatives against colonial authorities. John W. Jeffries's "The Separation in the Canterbury Congregational Church" shows how New Light separatism entailed opposition to a local political elite in one Connecticut village.

Other local studies attempt to demonstrate that the revivals contributed to dissent against dominant ecclesiastical establishments. John M. Bumsted's analysis of Norwich, Connecticut, "Revivalism and Separatism in New En-gland," emphasizes the breakdown of the characteristic territorial parish system under the impact of New Light separatism. Martin E. Lodge ("The Crisis of Churches in the Middle Colonies") and James Walsh ("The Great Awakening in the First Congregational Church of Woodbury, Connecticut") contend that New Light adherents were not opposed to traditional doctrine or formal church practice. According to Lodge and Walsh, however, the Awakening created a kind of ecclesiastical competition as settlers in areas without established churches sought to create their own religious organi-zations.

THE RISE OF CIVIL RELIGION

A third general perspective on church and state in the late colonial period, introduced in this essay with reference to Bellah's "The Revolution and Civil Religion," regards the movement for American independence as entailing a fusion of nationalist and religious sentiments. According to this interpreta-tion, during the political crises of the revolutionary period particular eccle-siastical or theological traditions—whether indebted to the Enlightenment,

Puritanism, or evangelicalism—fostered a common belief in the divine status of the nation. Civic loyalty, regardless of the different modes by which it was articulated, became the expression of a common American religion.

One focus for the study of civil religion is the role of providential and millenarian rhetoric in the period. The kind of eschatological convictions that were heightened by the Awakening and that rose to revolutionary fervor could become attached not simply to the triumph of a Calvinist (or Baptist), democratic society in the New World, but also to the success of the nation itself. Accordingly, Nathan Hatch argues in *The Sacred Cause of Liberty* that civil millennialism differed from the evangelical variety in that it subsumed competing theological perspectives under patriotic aspirations. Hatch asserts that Edwards, Bellamy, and other Calvinists remained aloof from political idealization. The French and Indian Wars created such a social crisis, however, that some Old Lights and New Lights, oblivious to religious incompatibilities, commonly attached sacred significance to America's civic welfare. When these patriotic preachers took to millennial themes, Hatch maintains, they linked the idea of providential rule to Whig theories of Republican virtue. In *The Puritan Origins of the American Self* and "The Typology of America's Mission," Bercovitch makes a similar point about the uses of biblical-millennial motifs. Bercovitch interprets Edwards as holding to an Augustinian distinction between sacred and profane events; preachers such as Cotton Mather represent the tendency of other writers to adopt a providential understanding of history, in which divine action was closely identified with temporal affairs. In *Providence and Patriotism in Early America*, John F. Berens finds a similar development. American patriots, Berens argues, accommodated the idea of providential action to their assumptions that America was a divinely ordained nation. That is, Hatch, Bercovitch, and Berens each assert that millennial ideas were often transposed into civic religiosity; the evidence for this transposition lay in the common application of such images to the state by preachers of conflicting religious traditions. Ernest Lee Tuveson's study of the rhetoric of national self-glorification, *Redeemer Nation*, describes some of the ways in which millennial visions of America's destiny reflected colonial convictions that America would become the center of a divinely inspired utopia. In "William Smith and the Rising Glory of America," William D. Andrews shows that Smith, an Anglican and friend of Benjamin Franklin, participated in the ecstatic nationalism of which Tuveson writes. J. F. Maclear's "The Republic and the Millennium" further supports the thesis that Patriots often expected a literal and political form of millennial reign in America.

Hatch, Bercovitch, and Maclear emphasize the presence of civil millennialism before the Revolution, contending that religious patriotism enhanced the movement for independence. In "Images of the Future in Eighteenth

Century American Theology," Glenn T. Miller argues that clerical millennialism was only vaguely addressed to an American state before the Declaration of Independence. Miller contends that truly nationalist millennialism did not flourish until the last decades of the eighteenth century and the first decades of the nineteenth. According to Miller, the poetic nationalism of Timothy Dwight was far more akin to civil religiosity than were earlier clerical eschatologies—grounded as they were in an Augustinian conception of history. The Revolution, in other words, created civil millennialism; not vice versa. Cushing Strout's *The New Heavens and the New Earth* also posits an alliance in the Revolution between religious and nationalist values. Strout stresses the idea that American Calvinists, who in defending the Awakening against civil prosecution had unwittingly accepted the assumptions of liberalism, became evangelists for Whig ideology only when the revolutionary crisis reached irreversible proportions—in the 1770s. Then, Strout maintains, a moral nationalism emerged, in which religious values were attached to the corporate welfare.

Miller and Strout's arguments lead to a second approach to civil religiosity, which looks for religious devotion to the nation in the public rituals and popular sentiments attending the formation of the United States. Employing the broad definition of religion that has emerged among proponents of the History of Religions school (i.e., religion is a set of symbols by which individuals find historical events meaningful and through which individuals locate their place in the world), Catherine Albanese's *Sons of the Fathers* is a full exposition of this method. Albanese maintains that in the social crises of the revolutionary period, colonists from different ethnic, economic, and ecclesiastical backgrounds found common meaning in the Patriot cause. Attaching symbolic value to events that signaled the formation of an American community, they developed public rituals in celebration of American independence: the planting of Liberty Trees, the singing of patriotic songs, the preaching of Whig values. Reverence for the nation, she emphasizes, gave meaning to Americans' struggles. Patriotism, replete with a full symbol system, was religious, as Americans defined their history by reference to national figures and events; George Washington was celebrated as the country's Father, the war as America's Exodus, Bunker Hill as a shrine of holy significance, and the Constitution as Scripture. In his *American Patriots and the Rituals of Revolution*, Peter Shaw comes to similar conclusions about the emergence of civil religiosity during the Revolution.

CONCLUSION

The period under discussion here has attracted diverse historical methodologies and conflicting conclusions. In part, this is due to the fact that between the Awakening and the Revolution, when colonists first began to identify themselves as a discrete nation, much of the American character and mentality was supposedly formed. Students of colonial periods see the late colonial era as the fruition of earlier events; interpreters of the constitution-making period see in these revolutionary decades the formation of American intentions regarding the place of religion within the public order. Interpretations of subsequent developments in church and state relations must, in some way, come to some prior conclusion about the kinds of issues discussed here. Does this period indicate the triumph of the Enlightenment, the powerful impact of the churches upon public affairs, or a coalescence of a civil religiosity on a national scale? Answers to these questions are crucial for providing some of the context in which to understand church-state issues in the new nation.

BIBLIOGRAPHY

PRIMARY SOURCE EDITIONS

Bailyn, Bernard, ed. <u>Pamphlets of the American Revolution,</u> <u>1750-1771</u>, vol. 1. Cambridge, Mass.: Harvard University Press, 1965.

Carroll, Peter N., ed. <u>Religion and the Coming of the American</u> <u>Revolution</u>. Waltham, Mass.: Ginn-Blaisdell, 1970.

Goen, C. C., ed. <u>The Works of Jonathan Edwards</u>. Vol. 4, <u>The</u> <u>Great Awakening</u>. New Haven: Yale University Press, 1972.

Heimert, Alan, and Miller, Perry, eds. <u>The Great Awakening:</u> <u>Documents Illustrating the Crisis and its Consequences</u>. Indianapolis: Bobbs-Merrill, 1967.

McLoughlin, William G., ed. <u>Isaac Backus on Church, State and</u> <u>Calvinism: Pamphlets, 1754-1789</u>. Cambridge, Mass.: Harvard University Press, 1969.

Mayhew, Jonathan. <u>Sermons: Seven Sermons, A Discourse</u> <u>Concerning the Unlimited Submission and Non-resistance to</u> <u>the Higher Powers, The Snare Broken</u>. Reprint. New York: Arno Press and the New York Times, 1968.

Morgan, Edmund S., ed. <u>Puritan Political Ideas, 1558-1794</u>. Indianapolis: Bobbs-Merrill, 1965.

Smylie, James H., ed. "Presbyterians and the American Revolution: A Documentary Account." <u>Journal of Presbyterian</u> <u>History</u> 52 (Winter 1974), 303-487.

SECONDARY SOURCES

Adams, Willi Paul. The First American Constitutions:
Republican Ideology and the Making of the State
Constitutions in the Revolutionary Era. Translated by Rita
and Robert Kimber. Chapel Hill: University of North
Carolina Press, 1980.

Ahlstrom, Sydney E. "The Puritan Ethic and the Spirit of
American Democracy." In Calvinism and the Political Order:
Essays Prepared for the Woodrow Wilson Lectureship of the
National Presbyterian Center, Washington, D.C., edited by
George Laird Hunt, 88-107. Philadelphia: Westminster Press,
1965.

Akers, Charles W. Called Unto Liberty: A Life of Jonathan
Mayhew, 1720-1766. Cambridge, Mass.: Harvard University
Press, 1964.

Akers, Charles W. The Divine Politician: Samuel Cooper and the
American Revolution in Boston. Boston: Northeastern
University Press, 1982.

Albanese, Catherine L. Sons of the Fathers: The Civil Religion
of the American Revolution. Philadelphia: Temple University
Press, 1976.

Aldridge, A. Owen. Thomas Paine's American Ideology. Newark,
Del.: University of Delaware Press, 1984.

Andrews, William D. "William Smith and the Rising Glory of
America." Early American Literature 8 (Spring 1973), 33-43.

Appleby, Joyce. "Liberalism and the American Revolution." New
England Quarterly 49 (March-December 1976), 3-26.

Appleby, Joyce. "The Social Origins of American Revolutionary
Ideology." Journal of American History 64 (March 1978),
935-958.

Bailyn, Bernard. The Ideological Origins of the American
Revolution. Cambridge, Mass.: Harvard University Press,
1967.

Bailyn, Bernard. "Political Experience and Enlightenment Ideas
in Eighteenth-Century America." American Historical Review
67 (January 1962), 339-351.

Bailyn, Bernard. "Religion and Revolution: Three Biographical
Studies." Perspectives in American History 4 (1970), 85-
169.

Baldwin, Alice M. The New England Clergy and the American
    Revolution. Durham, N.C.: Duke University Press, 1928.

Baldwin, Alice M. "Sowers of Sedition: The Political Theories
    of Some of the New Light Presbyterian Clergy of Virginia and
    North Carolina." William and Mary Quarterly, 3d ser., 5
    (January 1948), 52-76.

Barker, Charles A. "Maryland Before the Revolution: Society
    and Thought." American Historical Review 46 (October 1940),
    1-20.

Beam, Christopher M. "Millennialism and American Nationalism,
    1740-1800." Journal of Presbyterian History 54 (Spring
    1976), 182-199.

Beardslee, John W., III. "The Dutch Reformed Church and the
    American Revolution." Journal of Presbyterian History 54
    (Spring 1976), 165-181.

Becker, Carl. The Declaration of Independence: A Study in the
    History of Political Ideas. 1922. Reprint. New York:
    Knopf, 1942.

Bellah, Robert N. "The Revolution and Civil Religion." In
    Religion and the American Revolution, edited by Jerald C.
    Brauer, 55-73. Philadelphia: Fortress Press, 1976.

Bercovitch, Sacvan. The American Jeremiad. Madison:
    University of Wisconsin Press, 1978.

Bercovitch, Sacvan. "How the Puritans Won the American
    Revolution." Massachusetts Review 17 (Winter 1976), 597-
    630.

Bercovitch, Sacvan. The Puritan Origins of the American Self.
    New Haven: Yale University Press, 1975.

Bercovitch, Sacvan. "The Typology of America's Mission."
    American Quarterly 30 (Summer 1978), 135-155.

Berens, John F. Providence and Patriotism in Early America,
    1640-1815. Charlottesville: University Press of Virginia,
    1978.

Berens, John F. "Religion and Revolution Reconsidered: Recent
    Literature on Religion and Nationalism in Eighteenth-Century
    America." Canadian Review of Studies in Nationalism
    (Canada) 6 (Fall 1979), 233-245.

Berk, Stephen E. Calvinism versus Democracy: Timothy Dwight
    and the Origins of American Evangelical Orthodoxy. Hamden,
    Conn.: Archon Books, 1974.

Birdsall, Richard P. "Ezra Stiles versus the New Divinity Men." _American Quarterly_ 17 (Summer 1965), 248-258.

Bloch, Ruth Hedi. "Visionary Republic: Millennial Themes in American Ideology, 1756-1800." Ph.D. diss., University of California at Berkeley, 1980.

Bockelman, Wayne L., and Ireland, Owen S. "The Internal Revolution in Pennsylvania: An Ethnic-Religious Interpretation." _Pennsylvania History_ 41 (April 1974), 125-159.

Bonomi, Patricia. _A Factious People: Politics and Society in Colonial New York_. New York: Columbia University Press, 1971.

Bosworth, Timothy W. "Anti-Catholicism as a Political Tool in Mid-Eighteenth Century Maryland." _Catholic Historical Review_ 61 (October 1975), 539-563.

Botein, Stephen. "Income and Ideology: Harvard-Trained Clergymen in the Eighteenth Century." _Eighteenth-Century Studies_ 13 (Summer 1980), 396-413.

Botein, Stephen. "Religion and Politics in Revolutionary New England: Natural Rights Reconsidered." In _Political Opposition in Revolutionary America_, edited by Patricia Bonomi, 13-34. New York: Sleepy Hollow Press, 1980.

Brauer, Jerald C. "Puritanism, Revivalism, and the Revolution." In _Religion and the American Revolution_, edited by Jerald C. Brauer, 1-27. Philadelphia: Fortress Press, 1976.

Breitenbach, William. "Unregenerate Doings: Selflessness and Selfishness in New Divinity Theology." _American Quarterly_ 34 (Winter 1982), 479-502.

Bridenbaugh, Carl. _Mitre & Sceptre: Transatlantic Faiths, Ideas, Personalities and Politics, 1689-1775_. New York: Oxford University Press, 1962.

Bridenbaugh, Carl. _The Spirit of '76: The Growth of American Patriotism Before Independence_. New York: Oxford University Press, 1975.

Brinsfield, John Wesley. _Religion and Politics in Colonial South Carolina_. Easley, S.C.: Southern Historical Press, 1983.

Brown, Richard D. _Revolutionary Politics in Massachusetts: The Boston Committee of Correspondence and the Towns, 1772-74_. Cambridge, Mass.: Harvard University Press, 1970.

Brown, Richard D. "Spreading the Word: Rural Clergymen and the Communication Network of Eighteenth-Century New England." Massachusetts Historical Society, _Proceedings_ 94 (Boston, 1982), 1-14.

Brumm, Ursula. _American Thought and Religious Typology_. New Brunswick, N.J.: Rutgers University Press, 1970.

Buchanan, John G. "Drumfire from the Pulpit: Natural Law in Colonial Election Sermons of Massachusetts." _American Journal of Legal History_ 12 (July 1968), 232-244.

Buchanan, John G. "The Justice of America's Cause: Revolutionary Rhetoric in the Sermons of Samuel Cooper." _New England Quarterly_ 50 (March 1977), 101-124.

Buckley, Thomas E. _Church and State in Revolutionary Virginia, 1776-1787_. Charlottesville: University Press of Virginia, 1977.

Bumsted, John M. "Religion, Finance, and Democracy in Massachusetts: The Town of Norton as a Case Study." _Journal of American History_ 57 (March 1971), 817-831.

Bumsted, John M. "Revivalism and Separatism in New England: The First Society of Norwich, Connecticut, as a Case Study." _William and Mary Quarterly_, 3d ser., 24 (October 1967), 588-612.

Bumsted, John M. "'Things in the Womb of Time': Ideas of American Independence, 1633 to 1763." _William and Mary Quarterly_, 3d ser., 31 (October 1974), 533-564.

Bumsted, John M., and Van de Wetering, John E. _What Must I Do To Be Saved?_ Berkshire Studies in History. Hinsdale, Ill.: The Dryden Press, 1976.

Burrows, Edwin G., and Wallace, Michael. "The Ideology and Psychology of National Liberation." _Perspectives in American History_ 6 (1972), 167-306.

Burton, David H. "The Jesuit as American Patriot: Fathers Robert Harding and Robert Molyneux." _Pennsylvania History_ 48 (January 1981), 51-61.

Bushman, Richard L. _From Puritan to Yankee: Character and the Social Order in Connecticut, 1690-1765_. Cambridge, Mass.: Harvard University Press, 1967.

Butler, Jon. "Enthusiasm Described and Decried: The Great Awakening as Interpretive Fiction." _Journal of American History_ 69 (September 1982), 305-325.

Cherry, Conrad. _Nature and Religious Imagination: From Edwards to Bushnell_. Philadelphia: Fortress Press, 1980.

Clark, Harry Hayden. "Toward a Reinterpretation of Thomas Paine." American Literature 5 (May 1933), 133-145.

Clebsch, William A. From Sacred to Profane in America: The Role of Religion in American History. New York: Harper and Row, 1968.

Cobb, Sanford H. "The Period of the Revolution." Chap. 9 in The Rise of Religious Liberty in America. New York: Macmillan, 1902.

Cohen, Sheldon S., and Gerlach, Larry R. "Princeton in the Coming of the American Revolution." New Jersey History 92 (Summer 1974), 69-92.

Colbourn, H. Trevor. The Lamp of Experience: Whig History and the Intellectual Origins of the American Revolution. Chapel Hill: University of North Carolina Press, 1965.

Conforti, Joseph A. "The Rise of the New Divinity in Western New England, 1740-1800." Historical Journal of Western Massachusetts 8 (January 1980), 37-47.

Conforti, Joseph A. Samuel Hopkins and the New Divinity Movement: Calvinism, the Congregational Ministry, and Reform in New England Between the Great Awakenings. Grand Rapids: Eerdmans, 1981.

Constantin, Charles. "The Puritan Ethic and the Dignity of Labor: Hierarchy vs. Equality." Journal of the History of Ideas 40 (October-December 1979), 543-561.

Cowing, Cedric B. The Great Awakening and the American Revolution: Colonial Thought in the Eighteenth Century. Chicago: Rand McNally, 1971.

Cross, Arthur L. The Anglican Episcopate and the American Colonies. New York: Longmans, Green, and Co., 1902.

Dargo, George. "The Relations Between Church and State." Chap. 4 in Roots of the Republic: A New Perspective on Early American Constitutionalism. New York: Praeger, 1974.

Davidson, James West. The Logic of Millennial Thought: Eighteenth-Century New England. New Haven: Yale University Press, 1977.

Davidson, Philip. Propaganda and the American Revolution, 1763-1783. Chapel Hill: University of North Carolina Press, 1941.

Delattre, Roland A. "Beauty and Politics: A Problematic Legacy of Jonathan Edwards." In American Philosophy from Edwards to Quine, edited by R. W. Shahan and K. R. Merrill, 20-48. Norman: University of Oklahoma Press, 1977.

Eisenach, Eldon J. "Cultural Politics and Political Thought:
The American Revolution Made and Remembered." American
Studies 20 (Spring 1979), 71-97.

Elliott, Emory. "The Dove and the Serpent: The Clergy in the
American Revolution." American Quarterly 31 (Summer 1979),
187-203.

Ellis, John Tracy. Catholics in Colonial America. Benedictine
Studies, vol. 8. Baltimore: Helicon Press, 1965.

Endy, Melvin B., Jr. "Just War, Holy War, and Millennialism in
Revolutionary America." William and Mary Quarterly, 3d
ser., 42 (January 1985), 3-25.

Ferm, Robert L. Jonathan Edwards the Younger: 1745-1801, A
Colonial Pastor. Grand Rapids: Eerdmans, 1976.

Fiering, Norman S. "Benjamin Franklin and the Way to Virtue."
American Quarterly 30 (Summer 1978), 199-223.

Fiering, Norman. Jonathan Edwards's Moral Thought and Its
British Context. Chapel Hill: University of North Carolina
Press, 1981.

Foner, Eric. Tom Paine and Revolutionary America. New York:
Oxford University Press, 1976.

Gaustad, Edwin Scott. The Great Awakening in New England. New
York: Harper and Row, 1957.

Gaustad, Edwin Scott. "Restitution, Revolution, and the
American Dream." Journal of the American Academy of
Religion 44 (March 1976), 77-86.

Geissler, Suzanne. Jonathan Edwards to Aaron Burr, Jr.: From
The Great Awakening to Democratic Politics. Studies in
American Religion, vol. 1. New York: Edwin Mellen Press,
1981.

Gerardi, Donald F. M. "The King's College Controversy, 1753-
1765, and the Ideological Roots of Toryism in New York."
Perspectives in American History 11 (1977-78), 145-196.

Gerlach, Larry R. Prologue to Independence: New Jersey in the
Coming of the American Revolution. New Brunswick, N.J.:
Rutgers University Press, 1976.

Gewehr, Wesley M. The Great Awakening in Virginia, 1740-1790.
Durham, N.C.: Duke University Press, 1930.

Giffort, Frank Dean. "The Influence of the Clergy on American
Politics from 1763 to 1776." Historical Magazine of the
Protestant Episcopal Church 10 (June 1941), 104-123.

Goen, C. C. "Editor's Introduction." In The Works of Jonathan Edwards, vol. 4, The Great Awakening, edited by C. C. Goen. New Haven: Yale University Press, 1972.

Goen, C. C. "Jonathan Edwards: A New Departure in Eschatology." Church History 28 (March 1959), 25-40.

Goen, C. C. Revivalism and Separatism in New England, 1740-1800: Strict Congregationalists and Separate Baptists in the Great Awakening. New Haven: Yale University Press, 1962.

Goodwin, Gerald J. "The Anglican Reaction to the Great Awakening." Historical Magazine of the Protestant Episcopal Church 35 (December 1966), 352-357.

Grant, Charles S. Democracy in the Connecticut Frontier Town of Kent. New York: Columbia University Press, 1961.

Greene, Evarts B. Religion and the State: The Making and Testing of an American Tradition. New York: New York University Press, 1941.

Greene, Jack P. All Men Are Created Equal: Some Reflections on the Character of the American Revolution. Oxford University Inaugural Lecture, 1976. Oxford: Oxford University Press, 1976.

Greene, M. Louise. The Development of Religious Liberty in Connecticut. Boston: Houghton, Mifflin & Co., 1905.

Greven, Philip. Four Generations: Land and Family in Colonial Andover, Massachusetts. Ithaca, N.Y.: Cornell University Press, 1970.

Greven, Philip. The Protestant Temperament: Patterns of Child-Rearing, Religious Experience, and the Self in Early America. New York: Knopf, 1977.

Griffin, Edward M. Old Brick: Charles Chauncy of Boston, 1705-1787. Minneapolis: University of Minnesota Press, 1980.

Gross, Robert A. The Minutemen and Their World. New York: Hill and Wang, 1976.

Hanley, Thomas O. The American Revolution and Religion: Maryland, 1770-1800. Washington, D.C.: Catholic University of America Press, 1971.

Haroutunian, Joseph. Piety Versus Moralism: The Passing of the New England Theology. 1932. Reprint. New York: Harper and Row, 1970.

Hatch, Nathan O. The Sacred Cause of Liberty: Republican Thought and the Millennium in Revolutionary New England. New Haven: Yale University Press, 1977.

Heimert, Alan. Religion and the American Mind: From the Great
     Awakening to the Revolution. Cambridge, Mass.: Harvard
     University Press, 1966.

Heimert, Alan, and Miller, Perry. "Introduction" to The Great
     Awakening: Documents Illustrating the Crisis and Its
     Consequences. New York: Bobbs-Merrill Co., 1967.

Henretta, James A. The Evolution of American Society, 1700-
     1815: An Interdisciplinary Analysis. Lexington, Mass.: D.
     C. Heath, 1973.

Hogue, William M. "The Religious Conspiracy Theory of the
     American Revolution: Anglican Motive." Church History 45
     (September 1976), 277-292.

Holbrook, Clyde A. The Ethics of Jonathan Edwards: Morality
     and Aesthetics. Ann Arbor: University of Michigan Press,
     1973.

Holmes, David L. "The Episcopal Church and the American
     Revolution." Historical Magazine of the Protestant
     Episcopal Church 47 (September 1978), 261-291.

Horne, Thomas A. "Bourgeois Virtue, Property and Moral
     Philosophy in America, 1750-1800." History of Political
     Thought (Great Britain) 4 (Summer 1983), 317-340.

Humphrey, Edward Frank. Nationalism and Religion in America,
     1774-1781. Boston: Chipman Law, 1924.

Hutson, James H. Pennsylvania Politics, 1746-1770: The
     Movement for Royal Government and Its Consequences.
     Princeton, N.J.: Princeton University Press, 1972.

Isaac, Rhys. "Evangelical Revolt: The Nature of the Baptists'
     Challenge to the Traditional Order in Virginia, 1765-1775."
     William and Mary Quarterly, 3d ser., 31 (July 1974), 345-
     368.

Isaac, Rhys. "Religion and Authority: Problems of the Anglican
     Establishment in the Era of the Great Awakening and the
     Parson's Cause." William and Mary Quarterly, 3d. ser, 30
     (January 1973), 3-36.

Isaac, Rhys. The Transformation of Virginia, 1740-1790.
     Chapel Hill: University of North Carolina Press, 1982.

Jedrey, Christopher M. The World of John Cleaveland: A Family
     and Community in Eighteenth-Century New England. New York:
     W. W. Norton, 1979.

Jeffries, John W. "The Separation in the Canterbury
     Congregational Church." New England Quarterly 52 (December
     1979), 522-549.

Joyce, Lester Douglas. <u>Church and Clergy in the American Revolution: A Study in Group Behavior</u>. New York: Exposition Press, 1966.

Kenyon, Cecilia M. "Republicanism and Radicalism in the American Revolution: An Old-Fashioned Interpretation." <u>William and Mary Quarterly</u>, 3d ser., 19 (April 1962), 143-182.

Kerr, Harry P. "Politics and Religion in Colonial Fast and Thanksgiving Sermons, 1763-1783." <u>Quarterly Journal of Speech</u> 46 (December 1960), 372-382.

Kershaw, Gordon E. "A Question of Orthodoxy: Religious Controversy in a Speculative Land Company: 1759-1775." <u>New England Quarterly</u> 46 (June 1973), 205-235.

Kettner, James H. <u>The Development of American Citizenship, 1608-1870</u>. Chapel Hill: University of North Carolina Press, 1978.

Kinney, Charles B. <u>Church and State: The Struggle for Separation in New Hampshire, 1630-1900</u>. New York: Teachers College, Columbia University, 1955.

Koch, G. Adolph. <u>Republican Religion: The American Revolution and the Cult of Reason</u>. 1933. Reprinted as <u>Religion of the American Enlightenment</u>. New York: Crowell, 1968.

Kramer, Leonard J. "Muskits in the Pulpit: 1776-1783." <u>Journal of the Presbyterian Historical Society</u> 31 (December 1953), 229-241; 32 (March 1954), 37-51.

Kramer, Leonard J. "Presbyterians Approach the American Revolution." <u>Journal of the Presbyterian Historical Society</u> 31 (June 1953), 71-86; (September 1953), 167-180.

Labaree, Leonard Woods. <u>Conservatism in Early American History</u>. 1948. Reprint. Ithaca, N.Y.: Great Seal Books, Cornell University Press, 1959.

Landsman, Ned. "Revivalism and Nativism in the Middle Colonies: The Great Awakening and the Scots Community in East Jersey." <u>American Quarterly</u> 34 (Summer 1982), 149-164.

Lauer, Paul E. <u>Church and State in New England</u>. 1892. Reprint. New York: Johnson Reprint Corp., 1973.

Launitz-Shurer, Leopold, Jr. "A Loyalist Clergyman's Response to the Imperial Crisis in the American Colonies: A Note on Samuel Seabury's <u>Letters of a Westchester Farmer</u>." <u>Historical Magazine of the Protestant Episcopal Church</u> 44 (June 1975), 107-119.

Leder, Lawrence H. Liberty and Authority: Early American
    Political Ideology, 1689-1763. Chicago: Quadrangle Books,
    1968.

Library of Congress. The Development of a Revolutionary
    Mentality. Essays by Henry Steele Commager, Caroline
    Robbins, J. H. Plumb, Richard Bushman, Edmund S. Morgan,
    Pauline Maier, Jack P. Greene, Mary Beth Norton, and Esmond
    Wright. Washington, D.C.: Library of Congress, 1972.

Lippy, Charles. Seasonable Revolutionary: The Mind of Charles
    Chauncy. Chicago: Nelson Hall, 1982.

Lippy, Charles H. "Trans-Atlantic Dissent and the Revolution:
    Richard Price and Charles Chauncy." Eighteenth-Century Life
    4 (December 1977), 31-37.

Littell, Franklin H. From State Church to Pluralism. Chicago:
    Aldine Publishing Co., 1962.

Lockridge, Kenneth A. Settlement and Unsettlement in Early
    America: The Crisis of Political Legitimacy before the
    Revolution. Cambridge: Cambridge University Press, 1981.

Lodge, Martin E. "The Crisis of Churches in the Middle
    Colonies, 1720-1750." Pennsylvania Magazine of History and
    Biography 95 (April 1971), 195-210.

Love, William Deloss. The Fast and Thanksgiving Days of New
    England. Boston: Houghton, Mifflin, 1895.

Lovejoy, David S. Rhode Island Politics and the American
    Revolution, 1760-1776. Providence: Brown University Press,
    1958.

Lovejoy, David S. "Samuel Hopkins: Religion, Slavery, and the
    Revolution." New England Quarterly 40 (June 1967), 227-243.

Lowance, Mason I., Jr. The Language of Canaan: Metaphor and
    Symbol in New England from the Puritans to the
    Transcendentalists. Cambridge, Mass.: Harvard University
    Press, 1980.

Lynd, Staughton. The Intellectual Origins of American
    Radicalism. New York: Pantheon Books, 1968.

McCallum, James Dow. Eleazer Wheelock: Founder of Dartmouth
    College. Hanover, N.H.: Dartmouth College Publications,
    1939.

Maclear, J. F. "The Republic and the Millennium." In The
    Religion of the Republic, edited by Elwyn A. Smith, 189-194.
    Philadelphia: Fortress Press, 1971.

McLoughlin, William G. "'Enthusiasm for Liberty': The Great Awakening as the Key to the Revolution." American Antiquarian Society, Proceedings 87, part 1 (April 1977), 69-95.

McLoughlin, William G. New England Dissent 1630-1833: The Baptists and the Separation of Church and State. 2 vols. Cambridge, Mass.: Harvard University Press, 1971.

McLoughlin, William G. Revivals, Awakenings and Reform: An Essay on Religion and Social Change in America, 1607-1977. Chicago: University of Chicago Press, 1978.

McLoughlin, William G. "The Role of Religion in the Revolution: Liberty of Conscience and Cultural Cohesion in the New Nation." In Essays on the American Revolution, edited by Stephen G. Kurtz and James H. Hutson, 197-255. Chapel Hill: University of North Carolina Press, 1973.

Maier, Pauline. From Resistance to Revolution: Colonial Radicals and the Development of American Opposition to Britain, 1765-1776. New York: Knopf, 1972.

Maier, Pauline. The Old Revolutionaries: Political Lives in the Age of Samuel Adams. New York: Knopf, 1980.

Mampoteng, Charles. "The New England Anglican Clergy in the American Revolution." Historical Magazine of the Protestant Episcopal Church 9 (December 1940), 267-304.

Marcus, Jacob Rader. "Jews and the American Revolution: A Bicentennial Documentary." American Jewish Archives 27 (November 1975), 103-276.

Marini, Stephen A. Radical Sects of Revolutionary New England. Cambridge, Mass.: Harvard University Press, 1982.

Marsdon, George. "The American Revolution: Partisanship, 'Just Wars,' and Crusades." In The Wars of America: Christian Views, edited by Ronald A. Wells, 11-24. Grand Rapids: Eerdmans, 1981.

Marty, Martin. Religion, Awakenings and Revolution. Wilmington, N.C.: Consortium Press, 1977.

Marty, Martin. Righteous Empire. New York: Dial Press, 1970.

Maxson, Charles H. The Great Awakening in the Middle Colonies. 1920. Reprint. Gloucester, Mass.: Peter Smith, 1958.

May, Henry F. The Enlightenment in America. New York: Oxford University Press, 1976.

Mead, Sidney E.   "Christendom, Enlightenment, and the
    Revolution." In Religion and the Revolution, edited by
    Jerald C. Brauer, 29-54. Philadelphia: Fortress Press,
    1976.

Mead, Sidney E.   The Lively Experiment: The Shaping of
    Christianity in America. New York: Harper and Row, 1963.

Mekeel, Arthur J.   "The Relation of the Quakers to the American
    Revolution." Quaker History 65 (Spring 1976), 3-18.

Metzger, Charles H.   Catholics and the American Revolution: A
    Study in Religious Climate. Chicago: Loyola University
    Press, 1962.

Meyer, Donald H.   The Democratic Enlightenment. New York:
    Capricorn Books, 1976.

Meyer, Freeman W.   Connecticut Congregationalism in the
    Revolutionary Era. Hartford: American Revolution
    Bicentennial Commission of Connecticut, 1977.

Meyer, Jacob C.   Church and State in Massachusetts from 1740 to
    1833: A Chapter in the History of Individual Freedom.
    Cleveland: Western Reserve University Press, 1930.

Middlekauff, Robert.   The Glorious Cause: The American
    Revolution, 1763-1789. New York: Oxford University Press,
    1982.

Miller, Glenn T.   "Fear God and Honor the King: The Failure of
    Loyalist Civil Theology in the Revolutionary Crisis."
    Historical Magazine of the Protestant Episcopal Church 47
    (June 1978), 221-242.

Miller, Glenn T.   "Images of the Future in Eighteenth Century
    American Theology." Amerikastudien/American Studies (West
    Germany) 20, no. 1 (1975), 87-100.

Miller, John C.   "Religion, Finance, and Democracy in
    Massachusetts." New England Quarterly 6 (March 1933), 29-
    58.

Miller, Perry.   "From the Covenant to the Revival." In
    Religion in American Life, vol. 1, The Shaping of American
    Religion, 322-368. Princeton Studies in American
    Civilization, edited by James Ward Smith and A. Leland
    Jamison, no. 5. Princeton, N.J.: Princeton University
    Press, 1961.

Miller, Perry.   Jonathan Edwards. New York: William Sloan
    Associates, Inc., 1947.

Miller, Perry.   "Jonathan Edwards' Sociology of the Great
    Awakening." New England Quarterly 21 (March 1948), 50-77.

Miller, Perry. _Nature's Nation_. Cambridge, Mass.: Harvard University Press, 1967.

Mills, Frederick V., Sr. _Bishops by Ballot: An Eighteenth Century Ecclesiastical Revolution_. New York: Oxford University Press, 1975.

Moore, LeRoy. "Religious Liberty: Roger Williams and the Revolutionary Era." _Church History_ 34 (March 1965), 57-76.

Morais, Herbert M. _Deism in Eighteenth Century America_. New York: Columbia University Press, 1934.

Morgan, Edmund S. "The American Revolution Considered as an Intellectual Movement." In _Paths of American Thought_, edited by Morton White and Arthur M. Schlesinger, Jr., 11-33. Boston: Houghton Mifflin Co., 1963.

Morgan, Edmund S. _The Gentle Puritan: A Life of Ezra Stiles, 1727-1795_. New Haven: Yale University Press, 1962.

Morgan, Edmund S. "The Puritan Ethic and the American Revolution." _William and Mary Quarterly_, 3d ser., 24 (January 1967), 3-43.

Morgan, Edmund S., and Helen M. _The Stamp Act Crisis: Prologue to Revolution_. Chapel Hill: University of North Carolina Press, 1953. rev. ed. New York: Collier MacMillan, 1962.

Mulder, John M. "William Livingston: Propagandist Against Episcopacy." _Journal of Presbyterian History_ 54 (Spring 1976), 83-104.

Murrin, John M. "No Awakening, No Revolution? More Counterfactual Speculations." _Reviews in American History_ 11 (June 1983), 161-171.

Nash, Gary. _The Urban Crucible: Social Change, Political Consciousness, and the Origins of the American Revolution_. Cambridge, Mass.: Harvard University Press, 1979.

Nelson, William E. _The Americanization of the Common Law: The Impact of Legal Change on Massachusetts Society, 1760-1830_. Cambridge, Mass.: Harvard University Press, 1975.

Niebuhr, H. Richard. "The Idea of Covenant and American Democracy." _Church History_ 23 (June 1954), 126-135.

Niebuhr, H. Richard. _The Kingdom of God in America_. New York: Harper and Row, 1937.

Niebuhr, H. Richard. _The Social Sources of Denominationalism_. 1929. Reprint. New York: Henry Holt, 1957.

Nobles, Gregory H. Divisions Throughout the Whole: Politics
and Society in Hampshire County, Massachusetts, 1740-1775.
New York: Cambridge University Press, 1983.

Noll, Mark A. Christians in the American Revolution. Grand
Rapids: Eerdmans, 1977.

Noll, Mark A. "Ebenezer Devotion: Religion and Society in
Revolutionary Connecticut." Church History 45 (September
1976), 293-307.

Noll, Mark A. "Observations on the Reconciliation of Politics
and Religion in Revolutionary New Jersey: The Case of Jacob
Green." Journal of Presbyterian History 54 (Summer 1976),
217-237.

Olson, Alison B. "The Founding of Princeton University:
Religion and Politics in Eighteenth-Century New Jersey."
New Jersey History 87 (Fall 1969), 133-150.

Pearson, Samuel C., Jr. "Nature's God: A Reassessment of the
Religion of the Founding Fathers." Religion in Life 46
(Summer 1977), 152-165.

Pocock, J. G. A. The Machiavellian Moment: Florentine
Political Thought and the Atlantic Republican Tradition.
Princeton, N.J.: Princeton University Press, 1975.

Powell, Jonathan. "Presbyterian Loyalists: A Chain of Interest
in Philadelphia." Journal of Presbyterian History 57
(Summer 1979), 135-160.

Pratt, John Webb. Religion, Politics, and Diversity: The
Church-State Theme in New York History. Ithaca, N.Y.:
Cornell University Press, 1967.

Reichenbach, Karl. "The Connecticut Clergy and the Stamp Act."
In University of Michigan Historical Essays, edited by A. E.
Boak, 148-158. Ann Arbor: University of Michigan Press,
1937.

Reid, Ronald F. The American Revolution and the Rhetoric of
History. Falls Church, Va.: Speech Communication
Association, 1978.

Riley, Arthur J. Catholicism in New England to 1788.
Washington, D.C.: Catholic University of America, 1936.

Ritter, Kurt, and Andrews, James P. The American Ideology:
Reflections of the Revolution in American Rhetoric. Falls
Church, Va.: Speech Communication Association, 1978.

Robbins, Caroline. The Eighteenth-Century Commonwealth Man:
     Studies in the Transmission, Development and Circumstance of
     English Liberal Thought from the Restoration of Charles II
     until the War with the Thirteen Colonies. Cambridge, Mass.:
     Harvard University Press, 1959.

Rossiter, Clinton. Seedtime of the Republic: The Origins of
     the American Tradition of Political Liberty. New York:
     Harcourt, Brace, 1953.

Rothermund, Dietmar. The Layman's Progress: Religious and
     Political Experience in Colonial Pennsylvania, 1740-1770.
     Philadelphia: University of Pennsylvania Press, 1962.

Royster, Charles. A Revolutionary People at War: The
     Continental Army and the American Character, 1775-1783.
     Chapel Hill: University of North Carolina Press, 1979.

Ryerson, R. A. "Political Mobilization and the American
     Revolution: The Resistance Movement in Philadelphia, 1765 to
     1776." William and Mary Quarterly, 3d ser., 31 (October
     1974), 565-588.

Savelle, Max. "Nationalism and Other Loyalties in the American
     Revolution." American Historical Review 67 (July 1962),
     901-923.

Savelle, Max. Seeds of Liberty: The Genesis of the American
     Mind. New York: Knopf, 1948.

Schmotter, James W. "Ministerial Careers in Eighteenth-Century
     New England: The Social Context, 1700-1760." Journal of
     Social History 9 (Winter 1975), 249-267.

Scott, Donald M. From Office to Profession: The New England
     Ministry, 1750-1850. Philadelphia: University of
     Pennsylvania Press, 1978.

Scott, Robert F. "Colonial Presbyterianism in the Valley of
     Virginia, 1727-1775." Journal of the Presbyterian
     Historical Society 35 (March 1957), 71-92; (September 1957),
     171-92.

Shalhope, Robert. "Toward a Republican Synthesis." William
     and Mary Quarterly, 3d ser., 29 (January 1972), 49-80.

Shapiro, Darlene. "Ethan Allen: Philosopher-Theologian to a
     Generation of American Revolutionaries." William and Mary
     Quarterly, 3d ser., 21 (April 1964), 236-255.

Shaw, Peter. American Patriots and the Rituals of Revolution.
     Cambridge, Mass.: Harvard University Press, 1981.

Sklar, Robert. "The Great Awakening and Colonial Politics:
    Connecticut's Revolution in the Minds of Men." Connecticut
    Historical Society Bulletin 28 (July 1963), 81-95.

Spalding, James C. "Loyalist as Royalist, Patriot as Puritan:
    The American Revolution as a Repetition of the English Civil
    Wars." Church History 45 (September 1976), 329-340.

Spurlin, Paul M. The French Enlightenment in America: Essays
    on the Times of the Founding Fathers. Athens, Ga.:
    University of Georgia Press, 1984.

Stein, Stephen J. "An Apocalyptic Rationale for the American
    Revolution." Early American Literature 9 (Winter 1972),
    211-225.

Stein, Stephen J. "Editor's Introduction." In The Works of
    Jonathan Edwards, vol. 5, The Apocalyptic Writings, edited
    by Stephen J. Stein. New Haven: Yale University Press,
    1977.

Steiner, Bruce E. "Anglican Officeholding in Pre-Revolutionary
    Connecticut: The Parameters of New England Community."
    William and Mary Quarterly, 3d ser., 31 (July 1974), 369-
    406.

Stout, Harry S. "The Great Awakening in New England
    Reconsidered: The New England Clergy." Journal of Social
    History 8 (Spring 1974), 21-48.

Stout, Harry S. "Religion, Communications, and the Ideological
    Origins of the American Revolution." William and Mary
    Quarterly, 3d ser., 34 (July 1977), 519-541.

Stout, Harry, and Onuf, Peter. "James Davenport and the Great
    Awakening in New London." Journal of American History 70
    (December 1983), 556-578.

Strout, Cushing. The New Heavens and the New Earth: Political
    Religion in America. New York: Harper and Row, 1975.

Sweet, Douglas H. "One Glorious Temple of God: Eighteenth-
    Century Accommodation to Changing Reality in New England."
    Studies in Eighteenth-Century Culture 11 (1982), 311-320.

Swift, David E. "Samuel Hopkins: Calvinist Social Concern in
    Eighteenth-Century New England." Journal of Presbyterian
    History 47 (March 1969), 31-54.

Swift, Lindsay. "The Massachusetts Election Sermons."
    Colonial Society of Massachusetts, Transactions 1 (Boston,
    1895), 388-451.

Sykes, Norman. Church and State in England in the Eighteenth
    Century. Cambridge: Cambridge University Press, 1934.

Tait, Gordon J. "John Witherspoon and the Scottish Loyalists."
     Journal of Presbyterian History 61 (Fall 1983), 299-315.

Tolles, Frederick B. Meeting House and Counting House: The
     Quaker Merchants of Colonial Philadelphia. Chapel Hill:
     University of North Carolina, 1948.

Tracy, Patricia J. Jonathan Edwards, Pastor: Religion and
     Society in Eighteenth-Century Northampton. New York: Hill
     and Wang, 1980.

Trinterud, Leonard J. The Forming of An American Tradition: A
     Re-examination of Colonial Presbyterianism. Philadelphia:
     Westminster Press, 1949.

Tucker, Louis Leonard. Puritan Protagonist: President Thomas
     Clap of Yale College. Chapel Hill: University of North
     Carolina Press, 1962.

Tuveson, Ernest Lee. Redeemer Nation: The Idea of America's
     Millennial Role. Chicago: University of Chicago Press,
     1968.

Van Tyne, Claude H. "Influence of the Clergy, and of Religious
     and Sectarian Forces on the American Revolution." American
     Historical Review 19 (October 1913), 44-64.

Walsh, James. "The Great Awakening in the First Congregational
     Church of Woodbury, Connecticut." William and Mary
     Quarterly, 3d ser., 28 (October 1971), 543-562.

Warch, Richard. "The Shepherd's Tent: Education and Enthusiasm
     in the Great Awakening." American Quarterly 30 (Summer
     1978), 177-198.

Waters, John J. "Patrimony, Succession and Social Stability in
     Guilford, Connecticut." Perspectives in American History 10
     (1976), 131-160.

Weaver, Glenn. "Anglican-Congregationalist Tensions in Pre-
     Revolutionary Connecticut." Historical Magazine of the
     Protestant Episcopal Church 26 (June 1957), 169-285.

Westbrook, Robert B. "Social Criticism and the Heavenly City
     of Jonathan Edwards." Soundings 59 (Winter 1976), 396-412.

White, Eugene E. "Decline of the Great Awakening in New
     England: 1741 to 1746." New England Quarterly 24 (March
     1951), 35-52.

White, Morton. The Philosophy of the American Revolution. New
     York: Oxford University Press, 1978.

Willingham, William F. "Deference, Democracy, and Town
Government in Windham, 1758-1786." William and Mary
Quarterly, 3d ser., 30 (July 1973), 401-422.

Wills, Garry. Inventing America: Jefferson's Declaration of
Independence. Garden City, N.Y.: Doubleday & Co., 1978.

Wilson, John F. "Jonathan Edwards as Historian." Church
History 46 (March 1977), 5-18.

Wilson, Robert, III. The Benevolent Deity: Ebenezer Gay and
the Rise of Rational Religion in New England, 1696-1787.
Philadelphia: University of Pennsylvania Press, 1984.

Wood, Gordon S. Creation of the American Republic, 1776-1787.
Chapel Hill: University of North Carolina Press, 1969.

Wood, Gordon S. "Rhetoric and Reality in the American
Revolution." William and Mary Quarterly, 3d ser., 23
(January 1966), 3-32.

Wright, Conrad. The Beginnings of Unitarianism in America.
Boston: Starr King Press, 1955.

Wright, Conrad Edick. "Christian Compassion and Corporate
Beneficence: The Institutionalization of Charity in New
England, 1720-1800." Ph.D. diss., Brown University, 1980.

Yodelis, M. A. "Boston's First Major Newspaper War: A 'Great
Awakening' of Freedom." Journalism Quarterly 51 (Summer
1974), 207-212.

Youngs, J. William T., Jr. God's Messengers: Religious
Leadership in Colonial New England, 1700-1750. Baltimore:
Johns Hopkins University Press, 1976.

Zeichner, Oscar. Connecticut's Years of Controversy: 1750-
1770. Chapel Hill: University of North Carolina Press,
1949.

Ziff, Larzer. "Revolutionary Rhetoric and Puritanism." Early
American Literature 13 (Spring 1978), 45-49.

Zuckerman, Michael. Peaceable Kingdoms: New England Towns in
the Eighteenth Century. New York: Knopf, 1970.

5

Church-State Relations in the Constitution-Making Period

Elizabeth B. Clark

When the Supreme Court handed down its landmark decision in the well-known *Everson* case of 1947 (330 U.S. 1), it relied on a method of constitutional interpretation which drew heavily from history. That opinion gave great weight to the thought of the Founding Fathers, and in particular of Thomas Jefferson, whose metaphor of the "wall of separation" between church and state the Court interpreted as mandating a radical and complete estrangement between government and religion. In the nearly forty years since *Everson*, the Court's historical method and doctrine of absolute separation have remained keystones of federal adjudication on church-state matters. Both the method and the principle, however, have come under serious attack from groups on both ends of the political spectrum, and today more than ever the Jeffersonian wall of separation is a subject of intense public scrutiny and debate. The history of any subject which has a volatile contemporary life will be politically charged, and this is especially true in the study of church-state relations, where history has the power to decide issues. For those who rely on the Framers' intent to settle current disputes, the interpretation of that intent will be critical. For those on either side with a political agenda, the tendency to ignore historical complexity in favor of persuasive simplicity will be great.

This tendency must be taken into account in evaluating the literature on church-state relations during the constitution-making period. Section 3a of the appended bibliography presents much of the historical and legal literature on the provisions for religion contained in the Constitution and the Bill of Rights, including the most important works of scholarship. This literature, although it reflects substantial disagreement over the *content* of the Framers' thought, agrees by and large on certain canons of constitutional interpretation. Most writers cited in this section work from the assumption that the Framers had arrived at a common understanding, a single intent which can be discerned by careful study of the significant texts—in this case state and federal constitutions, constitutional debates, state statutes concerning religion and the treatment of dissenters, and the private papers of the Framers, particularly Jefferson and Madison, the most deeply involved in the church-state debate. Some of this writing is careful and useful, and has provided great insight into the drafters' attitudes toward these issues. But in many cases scholars of the Constitution are producing an openly utilitarian or whiggish history designed to buttress their views on the proper relationship between civic and religious institutions today. Much of the historical writing on religion in the Constitution is contained in brief prefaces or appendices to analyses of contemporary church-state policy entitled "Epilogue: History Speaks" or "Deductions from History", which serve mainly to legitimate their authors' positions on current questions.

History of this kind is always suspect, and in this case methodological weaknesses are manifest in the outcome. Constitutional history has produced two schools whose extreme elements stand in flat contradiction to each other, yielding the kind of "yes-they-did-no-they-didn't" type of historical debate which generally indicates that the wrong questions are being asked. Both schools are in some sense a departure from the nineteenth-century tradition of the celebration of church-state separation as an American innovation which has produced healthy civic and religious institutions. Philip Schaff is one of the fathers of this American success story, and he sees church-state separation as the natural outcome of the American struggle for freedom, and as beneficial to church and state both. For Schaff, "[L]iberty, both civil and religious, is an American instinct. All natives suck it in with the mother's milk" (p. 10). Schaff's view did not encompass the strict separation which exists today, though, but allowed for a more accommodating approach by government to religion. The state in Schaff's view was separate but friendly to the church, and the two flourished side by side in mutually beneficial amity.

Although they do support absolute separation, scholars such as Anson Phelps Stokes, whose massive work is still one of the main sources on church and state, have in part picked up on Schaff's celebration of liberty. The happy nineteenth-century optimism about the health of American churches was tempered by the prospect of declining membership and waning influence in this century, but Stokes and many others continued to picture the present separation as the inevitable outcome of the rational, enlightened quest for liberty whose principles were expressed in the Declaration of Independence. Such work relies heavily on Jefferson as the architect of church-state relations, as does Leo Pfeffer's. Pfeffer, a distinguished constitutional lawyer and historian, has produced a massive and influential body of work in support of the Supreme Court's arguments and reasoning as first set out in the *Everson* case. Pfeffer is sensitive to the historical context, although only insofar as it supports his argument. But for him and others, the bottom line is that history proves that the ideal of complete separation attributed to Thomas Jefferson accurately represented the intent of the Framers, was embodied in the First Amendment and, having been properly interpreted by the Court, remains our benchmark today.

On the other side of this debate stands a group of scholars and judges who, with the same historical evidence, have sought to prove that the First Amendment historically construed did *not* mandate the absolute separation implied by the Jeffersonian wall. They also assume that the intent of the Framers is controlling, but do not see that intent as resting on deistic or rationalistic assumptions about the separability of religion and government. Historians and constitutional scholars in this group argue rather that America was a deeply religious society with a common, shared understanding of the importance of the practice of religion and the teaching of moral values in the life of the new nation. They agree that religious liberty was a paramount value, and that by common consensus the Constitution properly sought to restrain the federal government from establishing a single state church. This school asserts for a variety of reasons, though, that the Constitution never intended the standard of absolute separation imposed by the Supreme Court on American society today. In its view, the Bill of Rights was added not only to restrain federal government from establishing a state church, but also to keep it from interfering with the states' jurisdiction over religious matters: in fact the First Amendment was an important part of the working out of federalism, and by restraining the federal government left the states completely free to establish or disestablish state churches, promote or ignore religion, as they chose. Many of these writers contend that the application of the Bill of Rights to state governments through incorporation by the courts into the Fourteenth Amendment was a grave error, substantially changing the constitutional configuration of states' rights over religion. Many feel too that the First Amendment in no way prohibits nondiscriminatory federal aid to churches, or a friendly accommodation of religion. The First Amendment religion clauses are commonly interpreted in these works as separate entities rather than as a unitary whole, with the provision for religious liberty as the primary clause, and separation only necessary to the extent required to achieve that goal. These authors attack as based on an erroneous view of history the historical reasoning of the Supreme Court cases which establishes our current model of complete separation. The intent of the Framers, they concede, should be controlling: but that intent was to establish federal and state governments friendly to religious institutions, and accommodating in a nondiscriminatory way.

Both of these schools of constitutional interpretation, which between them comprise much of what has been written, rely heavily on historical interpretation, on discerning what exactly the Framers of the Constitution meant, how they provided for particular current problems and contingencies. As suggested earlier, this method generally produces a flattened and rather simplistic history, as it must: its assumption is that there was one intent, one agreement, one amendment expressing one mind. But we know that this was not so: the social, political, religious, and cultural historiography of the last two decades has shown the richness and complexity of competing and coexisting traditions, and the impoverishment of the school of history which emphasizes great texts and great men. This is no less true for the Constitution: it was not exempt from popular consideration and participation by virtue of being a great text. On the contrary, as the highest expression of federal will, it was assented to by motley groups of citizens; and socially, religiously, and regionally diverse thought went into its making. By the standards of good history, then, the interpretivist approach, the attempt to depict a single true meaning or intent, is a questionable enterprise.

Section 3b of this bibliography cites a number of recent articles on constitutional interpretation which have explored this problem. This is not an exhaustive catalog by any means, but it includes a sample of recent work on the problems involved in relying on historical interpretation in adjudicating current constitutional questions. Many of these articles are highly critical of the interpretivist approach, and deem it a failure—as Kelly says, the Court "has attempted to sit on two stools at once and has fallen between them" (155). Reliance on a partial or partisan history destroys the usefulness of the intent standard, and even the fullest history could not predict the views of Jefferson and Madison on civic crèches and parochial school busing: here we are asking questions of the Constitution which it was not designed to answer. Further, as Powell points out, the Framers themselves did have a theory of binding intent. It was not their *own* intent as drafters which they saw as controlling, however. Rather, the Framers themselves considered the binding intent to be the understanding of the states which were party to the compact, altogether a much broader standard.

The question of the force of the Framers' intent also dovetails with the touchy subject of judicial activism: to what extent are judges bound by intent in constitutional issues, and to what extent are they free effectively to "legislate" new policy through the judicial process? Interpretivism seeks to reduce the discretionary power of the judge to make policy according to personal conviction rather than democratic norms. This view has been criticized by a number of scholars. Schlag, for instance, attacks judges' reliance on the intent of the Framers ("a group of people who cannot respond") because it "appears to reprieve judges, practitioners, and legal scholars from responsibility for the moral and political character of their actions . . . (and) insulate those actors from criticism by transforming them into mere conduits for decisions made by others" (285). As we have seen, if history may be manipulated in any direction, unrestrained judicial activism is possible under the cloak of interpretivism.

Our reliance on intent makes sacred a small piece of our history at the expense of the rest. Brest suggests that *any* revolutionary constitution is of questionable authority at the time of its inception, and that "it is only through a history of continuing assent or acquiescence that the document could become law" (225). This view stresses the Constitution as a dynamic and vital compact, into which we incorporate through continual adjudication the evolving principles and values of a democratic society. It sees the Constitution, not as inerrant script, but as part of an ongoing democratic process. As one scholar of church-state relations wrote recently, "the 'constitutional' tradition is at once a matter of the written constitution of the United States and the struggling of the whole American society to arrive at a viable social understanding of the interaction of religion and civil authority" (Smith, *Religious Liberty*, p. xi).

In fact, what history takes with one hand it can give back with the other. It cannot provide a single theory on which to rest current policy decisions, but it can illuminate the historical processes through which ideas of religious liberty and church-state separation gained acceptance and support. These ideas took root early: as Perry Miller suggested in *The Life of the Mind*, "nobody regards this principle (of separation) as having been violently or suddenly promulgated by the Revolution itself. Every denomination saw it as the logical culmination of native experience" (p. 36). This suggestion certainly runs counter to popular supposition in early nineteenth-century Europe, which saw the American Revolution as simultaneously sweeping away entrenched parallel systems of civil and religious authority. Scholars of the period tend to agree with Miller, though, that even at the start of the Revolution there flourished a large measure of toleration and of support for free exercise of religion throughout the colonies. These attitudes, especially support for full religious liberty, grew stronger during the course of the war, and formed the social concord on which the First Amendment rested.

This commitment to religious liberty reflected both an ideological stance (or stances) and pragmatic acceptance of colonial conditions, where religious pluralism was a fact of life. Immigration, growth, and perhaps a natural cooling of religious fervor overwhelmed the theocracy of early New England and the religious homogeneity of Virginia. By the time of the Revolution no locality's dominant religious order remained unchallenged, and in many places members of different sects coexisted happily. Crèvecoeur in his *Let-*

ters from an American Farmer (J. M. Dent and Sons, London, 1912, pp. 49–50) imagines a country road on which a German Lutheran, a seceder, a Catholic, and a Dutch Reformed farmer live, all sober, modest, and industrious. Their neighborly patterns, including perhaps the intermarriage of their children, nurtured what Crèvecoeur called "religious indifference," or the loosening of strict and exclusive sectarian ties. The war-time service records of men from Baptist and other dissenting groups went a good way further to legitimate their choice of religion in the eyes of their countrymen. This kind of experience, common throughout the colonies in the eighteenth century, made tolerance a practical necessity in daily life. It also took away the taste for persecution required to maintain an established religion: increasingly colonists felt that no doctrinal difference, least of all between Protestants, warranted harrying or persecution.

The Great Awakening of the mid-eighteenth century had contributed to this pattern of religious pluralism in the colonies. Although evangelical revivalism produced little by way of a theology or philosophy justifying religious freedom, the call to individual conscience, the emphasis on the personal relationship with God, and the debunking of ecclesiastical hierarchy and authority, all tended to undermine the idea of any one true established church or single revealed truth. The revivals worked cracks and fissures in even the most firmly founded religious bodies, splitting many churches into competing congregations, especially in New England. The Great Awakening closed the door permanently on religious uniformity. Although the Congregationalists, the Anglicans, and the Quakers were still formally or informally established in different areas, no group would be able to dominate the others convincingly enough to maintain primacy throughout the colonies: the forging of a federal union precluded the establishment of any single church, although multiple establishment remained a possibility.

A final strand of support for free exercise was Enlightenment thought. Religious liberty had a powerful analog in claims for political liberty, as the individual's right to be free from coercion of conscience formed the core of both. Parliament itself had passed a Toleration Act in 1689, and Locke's letter on toleration was influential with his followers in America. Jefferson's and Madison's religious beliefs remain a subject for debate, but it is clear that for them, as for many of their peers and followers, civil and religious liberty were cut from the same cloth.

This is not to say that the success of ideas of free exercise and disestablishment represented a coup for deism or for anti-religious forces. Far more churchmen than philosophes worked for disestablishment, and although circumstances varied from colony to colony, many clergymen felt that they and their churches stood to gain substantially from limits on local and national power to regulate or establish religion. The legacy of Roger Williams's strict separationist views was still alive in New England. As Mark DeWolfe Howe points out in his classic study, *The Garden and the Wilderness*, Williams's vision of the "wall of separation" was of a structure which would protect the church from the encroachments of civil authority, a view quite different from Jefferson's wall, which by contrast sought to protect the state from the corrupting influence of religion. This desire to keep churches free from worldly entanglement was probably reinforced by eighteenth-century political thought: the many clergy who supported the federal constitution or disestablishment at the state level surely shared in the understanding of their day that power must be controlled and diffused, a basic premise of the Constitution and the Bill of Rights. Indeed, the churches themselves were going through their own processes of re-formation. Cut off, like the colonies, from their European parent organizations and subject to increasing division and dissension, the churches, too, went into a period of constitution-making in an attempt to order their own houses, a job they presumably felt they could do better than the federal government. Clearly, then, the tradition of religious separation was not unique to the enlightened mind: many churchmen espoused it as well and saw themselves acting in concert with statesmen to create better civil and religious institutions both.

Within the Protestant ranks there was struggle too. The process of disestablishment in many places tracked social, political, and religious alignments to reveal local, state, and regional variations on the church-state pattern. An examination of American church-state relations of the eighteenth and nineteenth centuries must include state and local as well as the federal government, because it is on the state level that most religious regulation took place. The puzzling silences of the federal constitution make more sense if seen in this light: one important function of the First Amendment was to restrain the federal government's power to interfere with the state regulation of religion. The state was the appropriate overseer of religion under the federal system, and states were assumed to have been left free to establish, disestablish, or partially establish religion as they saw fit. Nor did the movement toward religious liberty seem to require federal encouragement in 1787. By that time, virtually every colony practiced toleration, or had at least enacted a noncoercion or toleration provision into their constitutions or statute law, and some states had gone much further. No state was moving in the direction of greater coercion.

The middle colonies by and large had little formal establishment, and, at least in the case of Pennsylvania, a strong heritage of liberty of conscience. Their struggles were less severe.

By contrast, the Anglican church was at least nominally established in all the southern colonies, and was especially strong in Virginia. Although it was powerful in only a few states and reduced to itinerant status in the rest, the specter of Anglican establishment, an old enemy, still weighed heavily on colonists fearful of English encroachments on liberty. The Anglican church in the south served as a constant reminder of the evils of establishment, and the possible installation of an Anglican bishop in North America, which would free the church to grow and take root there, became a highly sensitive political issue. The Anglican clergy were a weedy and penurious group lacking the respect and status within the community accorded their New England counterparts. But Anglicanism in its social form was strong: it was the religion of the elite in Virginia, a hierarchical society, and functioned as much as a form of social authority as it did as a religion. Those gentry within the Anglican fold had remained largely untouched by revivalistic fervor, and were content with their own less sensational liturgical forms.

The Great Awakening, though, helped to inspire pietism and discontent particularly among the middling and lower classes. By the 1760s the Baptists in the Tidewater area had grown strong enough to challenge Anglican supremacy, a simultaneous challenge to social and religious authority. Nor did this challenge go unmet: to the ruling class, a spontaneous mass movement of "social nobodies" (Smith, *Religious Liberty*, p. 32) posed a threat of social disorder and chaos. The two groups engaged in a protracted struggle over the interpretation and enforcement of the Toleration Act of 1689. Anglicans sought to use it to check the spread of religious enthusiasm, while Baptist dissenters pressed on all sides for freedom to expand—more meeting houses, licenses for more itinerant preachers to reach the scattered back-country population, and greater participation in the affairs of local government handled at the parish level.

The dissenting movement lacked a mature theory of rights or a theological justification for separation. It provided the social impetus, however, for the religious liberty article of the Virginia Declaration of Rights of 1776, a document which greatly influenced the national church-state debate. During the debates on the Declaration of Rights, Jefferson and Madison developed a philosophical doctrine of religious liberty based on Enlightenment precepts of reason, conscience, and natural rights. The philosophes and the more pragmatic dissenters agreed on the goal of religious liberty and disestablishment, although they had different visions of the world they were trying to create. But although the language formally incorporated by the Virginia Declaration was ultimately that of the philosophes, both strains had contributed to the forging of Virginia's church-state tradition.

In New England, too, the Congregationalist Standing Order fought off attacks by dissenters, but in this case with more success: disestablishment was not final in Connecticut and Massachusetts until well into the nineteenth century. Orthodoxy in New England was treading a very fine line: victims of religious intolerance themselves, the Congregationalists had strong beliefs about the inviolability of conscience. But although most measures coercive of orthodox belief and participation had been dropped, the New England colonies maintained a strong de facto establishment supported by a universal tax. Various provisions sought to exempt dissenters from this tax, but the difficulty of ascertaining genuine dissenter status to certify exemption (distinguishing dissenters from habitual late sleepers, who got no quarter), and the problem of which of the many new sects to extend this benefit to, meant that conscientious dissenters often paid double their assessment, or were jailed or distrained for failure to pay. This problem was at the root of Baptist attacks on orthodoxy in New England.

But again, more was at stake than tax revenues. The Congregational order was rooted more deeply in New England than the Anglican order in Virginia. The clergy were powerful in local and state affairs, often acting both as civil and religious officers in the towns. A number of works suggest a strong identification between the bench, the church, and the Federalist party, whose members were bound together by ties of mutual dependence and a common social vision. One member of the Standing Order openly branded the Baptist campaign for religious liberty "a rebellion against the STATE" (quoted in McLoughlin, *Isaac Backus and the American Pietistic Tradition*, p. xi). The Republican party in some places took on church and state as one in electoral battles, relying on a platform of religious liberty to gain political points.

In addition, New England had its own Baptist tradition, which William McLoughlin's body of work, capped by the massive and scholarly *New England Dissent*, describes in detail. He refutes the notion that American church-state theory had two schools only, the high-minded Jeffersonians who sought complete isolation to protect the virtue of the state, and the followers of Roger Williams, who saw the wall of separation as equally impermeable but existing for the benefit of the church, to keep it free of worldly taint. Rather, McLoughlin describes a third tradition, that of evangelical pietism, which he sees as the dominant strain until the twentieth century. Initially a pragmatic rather than a scholarly tradition, like its counterpart in Virginia it grew up out of the experience of living as second class citizens under the reigning orthodoxy—self-interest with a spark of righteous indignation at injustice. In part disestablishment in New England was a contest between Puritan and pietistic forces and signaled not a reordering of civil power but a sharing of power within Protestantism itself.

The Baptists and their most articulate spokesman, Isaac Backus, were Republicans and followers of Jefferson. Although socially more conservative than he was ("the Baptists did not agree with Jefferson that a little revolution every now and then was a good thing" [McLoughlin, *Isaac Backus and the American Pietistic Tradition*, p. 196]) they saw in him a fighter against the common enemies of privilege, aristocracy, and coercive institutions, and a proponent of freedom of conscience and republican values. For Baptists, the seeds of religious liberty had been planted well before the Revolution, starting with the legacy of Roger Williams. But the social upheaval and prevailing democratic ethos helped to transform that struggle into a unique product of its time and place. The Baptists and other religious groups were swept up in the general revolt against hierarchy. In churches as well as in governments, theories of power changed; institutions and their leaders became, not the delegates of God, but the delegates of the people, from whom power flowed. Unlike Jefferson, the Baptist dissenters in New England did not necessarily promote absolute separation, and retained the desire for some kind of corporate Christian state. But their experience with Congregationalism and the personal nature of their faith led them to value religious liberty and disestablishment highly, and on this basis they made common cause with him.

These were some of the diverse strains of thought which went into the making of the constitutional church-state tradition. Each state worked out, on the basis of its own religious traditions and constituencies, an individual settlement on questions like general assessment, support of clergy or teachers of religion, and oaths of office. For fully one hundred years after the framing, the issues of church and state were negotiated not in the Supreme Court but in the state courts and legislatures, churches and town halls throughout the country. Disestablishment was the rule in state constitutions, too. But each state, in some cases each town, played its own variations on that theme. The Bill of Rights represented a restraint on the federal government's power to abridge civil liberties. But in the case of the religion clauses, which were replicated in most state constitutions, it also testified to the willingness of most sects to give up the possible benefits of establishment and the hope of supremacy and to cooperate with Americans of all religious persuasions in order to form a union. The necessary adjustments and realignments meant that the First Amendment in its first century had a rich life of its own outside the courts.

Contrary to the fears of some clergymen, notably Congregationalists and Anglicans, the process of disestablishment and the movement for religious liberty did not create a secular society. In fact, they set the stage for a Protestant revival and worked a momentous change in the relationship of religious groups to each other. The revolutionary and early federal periods saw the growth of denominationalism, or a move away from the sectarian conviction of a single holy truth embodied in one group's doctrine, toward religious pluralism, or the harmonious coexistence of Protestant groups of different stripes. Under the denominational system groups would compete for members, but were willing to acknowledge other denominations as a part of the larger church of God. For some statesmen of the period, denominationalism had an economic analog: it was a desirable way of securing individual religious choice through the free competition of religious groups. Others saw it as a practical necessity for survival, or the price to be paid for freedom from government regulation.

Whatever the rationale for denominationalism, it allowed Americans to maintain strong religious beliefs while working in harness with others of different theological bents toward common social goals. Of course this accommodation was easier in the context of a nation still relatively homogeneous: even most of those who ardently supported religious liberty and legal disestablishment could only imagine it in the context of a Christian, or more specifically a Protestant, nation. As Benjamin Gale wrote in 1775, "Liberty (of conscience) may be indulg'd to every person . . . whose religious principles are not incompatible with a Protestant country, or destructive to the community, such as Roman Catholics, Deists, Atheists or . . . men of 'no religion'" (quoted in Thomas Curry, p. 333), and many shared Gale's views.

This homogeneity and the resurgence of religious feeling in the first years of the nineteenth century allowed for a de facto establishment of Protestantism which, largely through the medium of voluntary associations, was to act as a force both of cultural cohesion and of social change. While allowing doctrinal latitude, the "benevolent empire," as the phalanx of voluntary associations has been called, had an extraordinary influence on the moral and social life of the nation through its network of charitable, missionary, temperance, anti-slavery, and other societies; Justice Holmes was said to have remarked of his boyhood Boston that "you could deny the divinity of Christ but you would be overwhelmed by the utmost social opprobrium if you advocated sports on Sunday" (Perry Miller, "The Location of American Religious Freedom", p. 16). Participants in voluntary associations de-emphasized theological wrangling, a popular eighteenth-century pastime, in favor of a concerted effort to bring about the moral regeneration of America. Millennial aspirations for a moral nation and hopes for the success of the federal union meshed. Protestantism indeed became a national religion in the sense that its moral values and precepts, which became hallmarks of the emerging middle classes, defined the dominant cultural mode. In the context of antebellum America, the voluntary associations wielded far more power than similar groups do today; such organizations served as political interest groups, helping to shape public policy, as well as performing quasi-governmental functions later subsumed under the welfare state.

This extraordinary influence rested on a base of voluntary activity and support, with little help from governmental regulation. Most citizens in antebellum America probably envisioned their government, not as a secular state, but as one friendly to Christian teachings, and as embodying in some general way Christianity's moral and religious values. But religious groups did not seek to use the state's power to implement their programs. Many Americans, including many judges and lawyers, acknowledged a belief that Christian principles were incorporated into the common law. But these principles, like those of justice and equity, stood behind the law as a general support: no case turned on Christian doctrine, and it was extremely rare for judges to cite biblical or religious sources in legal opinions. There was no active or systematic attempt to incorporate religious doctrine into law. In fact, courts were moving rapidly away from the punishment of moral crimes such as fornication, adultery, and blasphemy. It was not until after the Civil War that evangelical groups turned to federal, state, and local legislatures, and then with limited success, to seek regulation of what they considered immoral and antisocial behavior, the censorship of printed material, the establishment of prayer in schools, and other similar legislative goals which have since been the subject of debate.

This turn to moral legislation in the last decades of the nineteenth century in many respects signaled a tremendous departure from the early federal understanding of church and state. The makers (not just the Framers) of the constitution had sought to do away with exactly the kind of restraints on liberty which moral legislation imposed. The original church-state settlement had arisen out of an understanding of human nature that stressed two critical elements: the vital, personal nature of the individual's relationship with God, unmediated, uncoerced, and uncorrupted by human institutions; and the liberation of the human will, the capacity for *self* government and the possession of the moral means to work for salvation. These were the tenets of early federal theology which fueled the great antebellum moral crusades. In a society in the throes of revivalistic fervor and still quite homogeneous, before the influx of non-Protestant groups in significant numbers, there was little need to resort to governmental regulation to implement moral and religious values. The move toward regulatory legislation came only with the diversification of American society in the later nineteenth century, when religious and cultural cohesion had broken down. And, aside from the Mormon polygamy cases, it is only in the twentieth century that the religion clauses have been fully tested in the courts, which have had to interpret them in light of the prevailing religious diversity representing not just a Protestant pluralism but an amalgam of Protestant, Catholic, Jewish, and many other groups.

The quest for the Framers' intent, as this essay has tried to show, is an elusive enterprise, and an unsatisfying one when undertaken to bolster current policies. The profusion of ideologies, theologies, and motivations which lies behind the First Amendment's religion clauses precludes settling on a single correct interpretation. As scholars continue to draw a fuller and more complex picture of the different traditions within the development of church-state separation, it becomes less and less possible to establish the Framers' intent as controlling, and more important to acknowledge the democratic nature of our constitution-making process. That process rests on the initial compact and the ongoing assent of diverse groups of people, as well as on the continual restating of constitutional norms in light of changes in our society over time.

BIBLIOGRAPHY

1. RELIGIOUS LIBERTY AND THE CONDITIONS OF SEPARATION

Baker, Robert A. "Baptists and the American Revolution."
Baptist History and Heritage 11, no. 3 (1976), 149-159.

Bridenbaugh, Carl. Mitre and Sceptre: Transatlantic Faiths,
Ideas, Personalities, and Politics, 1689-1775. New York:
Oxford University Press, 1963.

Cobb, Sanford H. The Rise of Religious Liberty In America: A
History. 1902. Reprint. New York: Cooper Square
Publications, 1968.

Curry, Thomas J. "The First Freedoms: The Development of the
Concepts of Freedom of Religion and Establishment of
Religion in America From the Early Settlements to the
Passage of the First Amendment to the Constitution." Ph.D.
diss., Claremont Graduate School, 1983.

Dargo, George. Roots of the Republic: A New Perspective on
Early American Constitutionalism. New York: Praeger
Publishers, 1974.

Dawson, Joseph M. America's Way in Church, State, and Society.
Westport, Conn.: Greenwood Press, 1979.

Greene, Evarts B. Church and State. Indianapolis: National
Foundation Press, 1947.

Greene, Evarts B. Religion and the State: The Making and
Testing of an American Tradition. 1941. Reprint. New
York: AMS Press, 1976.

Haller, William. "The Puritan Background of the First
Amendment." In The Constitution Reconsidered, edited by
Richard B. Morris. rev. ed. New York: Harper & Row, 1968.

Handy, Robert T. "The American Tradition of Religious Freedom:
An Historical Analysis." Journal of Public Law 13 (1969),
247-266.

Handy, Robert T. A Christian America: Protestant Hopes and
Historical Realities. New York: Oxford University Press,
1971.

Hofstader, Richard. America at 1750: A Social Portrait. New
York: Knopf, 1971.

Holmes, David. "The Episcopal Church and the American
Revolution." Historical Magazine of the Protestant
Episcopal Church 47, no. 3 (1978), 261-291.

Hudson, Winthrop S. The Great Tradition of the American
Churches. New York: Harper & Brothers, 1953.

Ives, Joseph Moss. The Ark and the Dove: The Beginnings of
Civil and Religious Liberty in America. New York: Cooper
Square Publications, 1936.

Katz, Wilbur G. "The Case for Religious Liberty." In Religion
in America, edited by John Cogley. New York: Meridian
Books, 1958.

Kraft, Virgil A. The Freedom Story. Tujunga, Calif.:
Parthenon Books, 1977.

Krinsky, Fred, ed. The Politics of Religion in America.
Beverly Hills: Glencoe Press, 1968.

Leder, Lawrence. Liberty and Authority: Early American
Political Ideology, 1689-1763. Chicago: Quadrangle Books,
1968.

Littell, Franklin H. "The Basis of Religious Liberty in
American History." Journal of Church and State 6, no. 3
(1964), 314-322.

McLoughlin, William G. "Isaac Backus and the Separation of
Church and State in America." American Historical Review
73, no. 5 (1968), 1392-1413.

Mead, Sidney E. "From Coercion to Persuasion: Another Look at
the Rise of Religious Liberty and the Emergence of
Denominationalism." Church History 25, no. 4 (1956), 317-
337.

Mead, Sidney E. The Lively Experiment: The Shaping of
Christianity in America. New York: Harper & Row, 1963.

Mecklin, John Moffatt. The Story of American Dissent. Port
Washington, N.Y.: Kennikat Press, 1970.

Meyer, Carl S. "The Development of the American Pattern in
     Church-State Relations." In Church and State Under God,
     edited by Albert G. Huegli. St. Louis, Mo.: Concordia
     Publishing House, 1964.

Miller, Glenn T. Religious Liberty in America: History and
     Prospects. Philadelphia: Westminster Press, 1976.

Miller, Helen Hill. The Case for Liberty. Chapel Hill:
     University of North Carolina Press, 1965.

Miller, Perry. "The Contribution of the Protestant Churches to
     Religious Liberty in Colonial America." Church History 4,
     no. 1 (1935), 57-66.

Miller, Perry. The Life of the Mind in America from the
     Revolution to the Civil War. New York: Harcourt, Brace and
     World, 1965.

Nichols, Roy F. Religion and American Democracy. Baton Rouge,
     La.: Louisiana State University Press, 1959.

Norman, E. R. The Conscience of the State in North America.
     Cambridge: Cambridge University Press, 1968.

Pfeffer, Leo. "The Case for Separation." In Religion in
     America, edited by John Cogley. New York: Meridian Books,
     1958.

Smith, Elwyn A. Religious Liberty in the United States: The
     Development of Church-State Thought Since the Revolutionary
     Era. Philadelphia: Fortress Press, 1972.

Sweet, William Warren. "The American Colonial Environment and
     Religious Liberty." Church History 4, no. 1 (1935), 43-56.

Sweet, William Warren. American Culture and Religion: Six
     Essays. Dallas: Southern Methodist University Press, 1951.

Sweet, William Warren. The Story of Religion in America. New
     York: Harper & Brothers, 1939.

Trent, William P. "The Period of Constitution-Making in the
     American Churches." In Essays in the Constitutional History
     of the United States in the Formative Period, 1775-1789,
     edited by J. Franklin Jameson. 1889. Reprint. New York:
     Da Capo Press, 1970.

Vance, Donald F. "The Supreme Court and the Definition of
     Religion." Ph.D. diss., Indiana University, 1970.

Wilson, John F. "Public Religion as an American Problem."
     Chap. 1 of Public Religion in American Culture.
     Philadelphia: Temple University Press, 1979.

2. RELIGIOUS LIBERTY AND DISESTABLISHMENT IN THE STATES

a. General

Adams, Willi Paul. The First American Constitutions: Republican Ideology and the Making of the State Constitutions in the Republican Era. Translated by Rita and Robert Kimber. Chapel Hill: University of North Carolina Press, 1980.

Armstrong, O. K., and Armstrong, Marjorie. Baptists Who Shaped a Nation. Nashville: Broadman Press, 1975.

Dawson, Joseph M. Baptists and the American Republic. 1956. Reprint. New York: Arno Press, 1980.

James, Sydney V. "Religion and the American Revolution: The Development of the Federal Style in the Relations Between Religion and Civil Authority." In The American and European Revolutions, 1776-1848: Sociopolitical and Ideological Aspects, edited by Jaroslaw Pelenski. Iowa City: University of Iowa Press, 1980.

Miller, Howard. "The Grammar of Liberty: Presbyterians and the First American Constitutions." Journal of Presbyterian History 54 (Spring 1976), 142-164.

Sutherland, Arthur E. "Church and State Before 1800." Chap. 11 in Constitutionalism in America: Origin and Evolution of Its Fundamental Ideals. New York: Blaisdell Publishing Co., 1965.

Wood, Gordon. The Creation of the American Republic, 1775-1787. New York: Norton, 1972.

b. New England

Bumsted, John M. "Orthodoxy in Massachusetts: The Ecclesiastical History of Freetown, 1683-1776." New England Quarterly 43, no. 2 (1970), 274-284.

Bushman, Richard. From Puritan to Yankee: Character and the Social Order in Connecticut, 1690-1765. Cambridge, Mass.: Harvard University Press, 1967.

Clark, Charles E. "Disestablishment at the Grass Roots: Curtis Coe and the Separation of Church and Town." Historical New Hampshire 36, no. 4 (1981), 280-305.

Coons, Paul W. The Achievement of Religious Liberty in Connecticut. New Haven: Yale University Press, 1936.

Cushing, John D.   "Notes on Disestablishment in Massachusetts,
    1780-1833." William and Mary Quarterly, 3d ser., 26, no. 2
    (1969), 169-190.

Estep, William R.   "New England Dissent, 1630-1833: A Review
    Article." Church History 41, no. 2 (1972), 246-252.

Goen, C. C. Revivalism and Separatism in New England, 1740-
    1800: Strict Congregationalists and Separate Baptists in the
    Great Awakening. New Haven: Yale University Press, 1962.

Ford, David B. New England's Struggles for Religious Liberty.
    Philadelphia: American Baptist Publication Society, 1896.

Greene, M. Louise. The Development of Religious Liberty in
    Connecticut. 1905. Reprint. New York: Da Capo Press,
    1970.

Hale, Robert. Early Days of Church and State in Maine.
    Bowdoin College Studies in History, no. 1. Brunswick, Me.:
    The College, 1910.

Kinney, Charles B. Church and State: The Struggle for
    Separation in New Hampshire, 1630-1900. New York: Teachers
    College, Columbia University, 1955.

Kirsch, George B. "Clerical Dismissals in Colonial and
    Revolutionary New Hampshire." Church History 49, no. 2
    (1980), 160-177.

Lauer, Paul E. Church and State in New England. 1892.
    Reprint. New York: Johnson Reprint Corp., 1973.

Lippy, Charles H. "The 1780 Massachusetts Constitution:
    Religious Establishment or Civil Religion?" Journal of
    Church and State 20, no. 3 (1978), 533-550.

Maclear, James Fulton. "The True American Union of Church and
    State in the Reconstruction of the Theocratic Tradition."
    Church History 28, no. 1 (1959), 41-62.

McLoughlin, William G. "The Balkcom Case (1782) and the
    Pietistic Theory of Separation of Church and State."
    William and Mary Quarterly, 3d ser., 24, no. 2 (1967), 267-
    283.

McLoughlin, William G. "The Bench, the Church, and the
    Republican Party in New Hampshire, 1790-1820." Historical
    New Hampshire 20, no. 2 (1965), 3-31.

McLoughlin, William G. Isaac Backus and the American Pietistic
    Tradition. Boston: Little, Brown, 1967.

McLoughlin, William G. "Massive Civil Disobedience as a
    Baptist Tactic in 1773." American Quarterly 21, no. 4
    (1969), 710-727.

McLoughlin, William G. New England Dissent, 1630-1833: The
    Baptists and the Separation of Church and State. 2 vols.
    Cambridge, Mass.: Harvard University Press, 1971.

Mansfield, John H. "New England Dissent, 1630-1833: The
    Baptists and the Separation of Church and State." American
    Journal of Legal History 17, no. 2 (1973), 185-201.

Mead, Sidney E. "Church, State, Calvinism, and Conscience."
    Perspectives in American History 3 (1969), 443-459.

Meyer, Jacob C. Church and State in Massachusetts from 1740 to
    1833: A Chapter in the History of the Development of
    Individual Freedom. Cleveland: Western Reserve University
    Press, 1930.

Miller, Howard. "The Grammar of Liberty: Presbyterians and the
    First American Constitutions." Journal of Presbyterian
    History 54 (Spring 1976), 142-164.

Morison, Samuel Eliot. "The Struggle Over the Adoption of the
    Constitution of Massachusetts, 1780." Massachusetts
    Historical Society, Proceedings 50 (1917), 353-412.

Noll, Mark A. "Ebenezer Devotion: Religion and Society in
    Revolutionary Connecticut." Church History 45, no. 3
    (1976), 293-307.

Peters, Ronald M. The Massachusetts Constitution of 1780: A
    Social Compact. Amherst, Mass.: University of Massachusetts
    Press, 1978.

Purcell, Richard J. Connecticut in Transition, 1775-1818. 2d
    ed. Middletown, Conn.: Wesleyan University Press, 1963.

Reed, Susan M. Church and State in Massachusetts, 1691-1740.
    University of Illinois Studies in the Social Sciences, vol.
    3, no. 4. Urbana: University of Illinois Press, 1914.

Ryan, Walter A. "The Separation of Church and State in
    Acworth, New Hampshire." Historical New Hampshire 34, no. 2
    (1979), 143-153.

Taylor, Robert J. "Construction of the Massachusetts
    Constitution." American Antiquarian Society, Proceedings 90
    (1980), 317-346.

Thorning, Joseph Francis. <u>Religious Liberty in Transition: A Study of the Removal of Constitutional Limitations on Religious Liberty as Part of the Social Progress in the Transition Period.</u> Washington, D.C.: Catholic University of America Press, 1931.

Trumbull, Benjamin. <u>A Complete History of Connecticut Civil and Ecclesiastical</u>. 2 vols. New London, Conn.: H. D. Utley, 1892.

Willingham, William F. "Grass Roots Politics in Windham, Connecticut, During the Jeffersonian Period." <u>Journal of the Early Republic</u> 1, no. 2 (1981), 127-148.

                    c.   The Middle Colonies

Andrews, Matthew Page. "Separation of Church and State in Maryland." <u>Catholic Historical Review</u> 21, no. 2 (1935), 165-176.

Bauman, Richard. <u>For the Reputation of Truth: Politics, Religion and Conflict Among Pennsylvania Quakers, 1750-1800</u>. Baltimore: Johns Hopkins University Press, 1971.

DeConte, Alexander, ed. "William Vans Murray on Freedom of Religion in the United States, 1787." <u>Maryland Historical Magazine</u> 50, no. 4 (1955), 282-290.

Ervin, Spencer. "The Established Church of Colonial Maryland." <u>Historical Magazine of the Protestant Episcopal Church</u> 24, no. 3 (1955), 232-292.

Ferguson, John DeLancey. <u>The Relation of the State to Religion in New York and New Jersey During the Colonial Period</u>. New Brunswick, N.J.: Rutgers College, 1912.

Hanley, Thomas O'Brien. <u>The American Revolution and Religion in Maryland, 1770-1800</u>. Washington, D.C.: Catholic University of America Press, 1971.

Jamison, Wallace. <u>Religion in New Jersey: A Brief History</u>. New Jersey History Series, vol. 13. Princeton, N.J.: D. Van Nostrand Co., 1964.

Lasson, Kenneth L. "Religious Freedom and the Church-State Relationship in Maryland." <u>Catholic Lawyer</u> 14 (Winter 1968), 4-36.

Pratt, John Webb. <u>Religion, Politics, and Diversity: The Church-State Theme in New York History</u>. Ithaca, N.Y.: Cornell University Press, 1967.

Rainbolt, John Corbin. "The Struggle to Define 'Religious
    Liberty' in Maryland, 1776-85." Journal of Church and State
    17, no. 3 (1975), 443-458.

Rightmyer, Nelson Waite. Maryland's Established Church.
    Baltimore: Church Historical Society for the Diocese of
    Maryland, 1956.

Vivian, Jean H. "The Poll Tax Controversy in Maryland, 1770-
    76: A Case of Taxation With Representation." Maryland
    Historical Magazine 71, no. 2 (1976), 151-176.

Werline, Albert Warwick. Problems of Church and State in
    Maryland During the Seventeenth and Eighteenth Centuries.
    South Lancaster, Mass.: College Press, 1948.

Zimmer, Anne Y. "The 'Paper War' in Maryland, 1772-73: The
    Paca-Chase Political Philosophy Tested." Maryland
    Historical Magazine 71, no. 2 (1976), 177-193.

                    d. The Southern Colonies

Bauer, Gerald. "The Quest for Religious Freedom in Virginia."
    Historical Magazine of the Protestant Episcopal Church 41,
    no. 1 (1972), 85-93.

Brinsfield, John Wesley. "The Separation of Church and State
    in Colonial South Carolina During the American Revolution."
    Ph.D. diss., Emory University, 1973.

Brydon, George M. Virginia's Mother Church and the Political
    Conditions Under Which It Grew. 2 vols. Richmond, Va.:
    Virginia Historical Society, 1947, 1952.

Buckley, Thomas Edwin. Church and State in Revolutionary
    Virginia, 1776-1787. Charlottesville: University Press of
    Virginia, 1977.

Buckley, Thomas Edwin. "Church-State Settlement in Virginia:
    The Presbyterian Contribution." Journal of Presbyterian
    History 54, no. 1 (1976), 105-119.

Conkin, Paul. "The Church Establishment in North Carolina,
    1765-1776." North Carolina Historical Review 32 (1955), 1-
    30.

Eckenrode, H. J. Separation of Church and State in Virginia: A
    Study in the Development of the Revolution. 1910. Reprint.
    New York: Da Capo Press, 1971.

Ervin, Spencer. "The Anglican Church in North Carolina."
    Historical Magazine of the Protestant Episcopal Church 25,
    no. 2 (1956), 102-161.

Freeze, Gary. "Like a House Built on Sand: The Anglican Church
    and Establishment in North Carolina, 1765-1776." Historical
    Magazine of the Protestant Episcopal Church 48, no. 4
    (1979), 405-432.

Gewehr, Wesley. The Great Awakening in Virginia, 1740-1790.
    Durham, N.C.: Duke University Press, 1930.

Green, Fletcher M. Constitutional Development in the South
    Atlantic States, 1776-1860. 1930. Reprint. New York: Da
    Capo Press, 1971.

Green, Jesse C., Jr. "The Early Virginia Argument for
    Separation of Church and State." Baptist History and
    Heritage 11, no. 1 (1976), 16-26.

Hill, A. Shrady. "The Parson's Cause." Historical Magazine of
    the Protestant Episcopal Church 46, no. 1 (1977), 5-35.

Hood, Fred J. "Revolution and Religious Liberty: The
    Conservation of the Theocratic Concept in Virginia." Church
    History 40, no. 2 (1971), 170-181.

Isaac, Rhys. "Religion and Authority: Problems of the Anglican
    Establishment in Virginia in the Era of the Great Awakening
    and the Parson's Cause." William and Mary Quarterly, 3d
    ser., 30, no. 1 (1973), 3-36.

McIlwaine, Henry R. The Struggle of Protestant Dissenters for
    Religious Toleration in Virginia. 1894. Reprint. New
    York: Johnson Reprint Corp., 1973.

Miller, Wallace Elden. "Relations of Church and State in
    Georgia, 1732-1776." Ph.D. diss., Northwestern University,
    1937.

Moore, John S. "The Struggle for Religious Freedom in
    Virginia." Baptist History and Heritage 11, no. 3 (1976),
    160-168.

Singleton, Marvin K. "Colonial Virginia as First Amendment
    Matrix: Henry, Madison, and Assessment Establishment."
    Journal of Church and State 8, no. 3 (1966), 344-364.

Strickland, Reba C. Religion and the State in Georgia in the
    Eighteenth Century. 1939. Reprint. New York: AMS Press,
    1967.

Thom, William T. "The Struggle for Religious Freedom in
    Virginia: The Baptists." Baltimore: Johns Hopkins
    University Press, 1900.

Weeks, Stephen B. Church and State in North Carolina. 1893.
    Reprint. New York: Johnson Reprint Corp., 1973.

3. THE MAKING AND INTERPRETATION OF THE CONSTITUTION

a. The Constitution and the Bill of Rights

Anastaplo, George. The Constitutionalist: Notes on the First
    Amendment. Dallas: Southern Methodist University Press,
    1971.

Antieau, Chester James. Rights of Our Fathers. Vienna, Va.:
    Coiner Publications, 1968.

Antieau, Chester James; Downey, Arthur T.; and Roberts, Edward
    C. Freedom From Federal Establishment: Formation and Early
    History of the First Amendment Religion Clauses. Milwaukee:
    Bruce Publishing Co., 1964.

Arnold, O. Carroll. Religious Freedom on Trial. Valley Forge,
    Pa.: Judson Press, 1978.

Benjamin, Walter. "Separation of Church and State: Myth and
    Reality." Journal of Church and State 11, no. 1 (1969),
    93-109.

Berns, Walter F. The First Amendment and the Future of
    American Democracy. New York: Basic Books, 1976.

Beth, Loren P. The American Theory of Church and State.
    Gainesville, Fla.: University of Florida Press, 1958.

Borden, Morton. Jews, Turks, and Infidels. Chapel Hill:
    University of North Carolina Press, 1984.

Botein, Stephen. "Church and State in Early American
    Constitutional Law." Paper delivered at a conference of the
    Philadelphia Center for Early American Studies on "The
    Creation of the American Constitution," Philadelphia, Pa.,
    October 18-20, 1984 (privately consulted: forthcoming in
    publication).

Bowser, Anita O. "The Meaning of Religion in the
    Constitution." Ph.D. diss., University of Notre Dame, 1976.

Brady, Joseph Hugh. Confusion Twice Confounded: The First
    Amendment and the Supreme Court, An Historical Study. South
    Orange, N.J.: Seton Hall University Press, 1954.

Brant, Irving N. The Bill of Rights: Its Origin and Meaning.
    1965. Reprint. New York: New American Library, 1967.

Brownfield, Allen C. "The Constitutional Intent Concerning
    Matters of Church and State." William and Mary Law Review
    5, no. 2 (1964), 174-204.

Butts, R. Freeman. The American Tradition in Religion and
    Education. Boston: Beacon Press, 1950.

Cahn, Edmond. Confronting Injustice: The Edmond Cahn Reader.
    Edited by Lenore L. Cahn. Boston: Little, Brown, 1966.

Campbell, Bruce A. "Dartmouth College as a Civil Liberties
    Case: The Formation of Constitutional Policy." Kentucky Law
    Journal 70 (1982), 643-706.

Cord, Robert. Separation of Church and State: Historical Fact
    and Current Fiction. New York: Lambeth Press, 1982.

Cornelison, Isaac. The Relation of Religion to Civil
    Government in the United States of America. 1895. Reprint.
    New York: Da Capo Press, 1970.

Curry, Patricia E. "James Madison and the Burger Court:
    Converging Views of Church-State Separation." Indiana Law
    Journal 56, no. 4 (1981), 615-636.

Fellman, David. "Religion in American Public Law." Boston
    University Law Review 44 (Summer 1964), 287-399.

Frank, Roy C. "Religious Liberty in the Constitution." In
    Church and State Under God, edited by Albert G. Huegli. St.
    Louis, Mo.: Concordia Publishing House, 1964.

Gaustad, Edwin Scott. "A Disestablished Society: Origins of
    the First Amendment." Journal of Church and State 11, no. 3
    (1969), 409-425.

Hammond, Phillip E. "The Shifting Meaning of a Wall of
    Separation: Some Notes on Church, State, and Conscience."
    Sociological Analysis 42, no. 3 (1981), 227-234.

Hillam, Ray C., ed. 'By the Hands of Wise Men': Essays on the
    United States Constitution. Provo, Utah: Brigham Young
    University Press, 1979.

Howard, A. E. Dick; Baker, John W.; and Derr, Thomas Sieger.
    Church, State, and Politics. Final Report of the 1981 Chief
    Justice Earl Warren Conference on Advocacy in the United
    States sponsored by the Roscoe Pound-American Trial Lawyers
    Foundation, Washington, D.C., [1981].

Howe, Mark DeWolfe. "Church and State in the United States."
    Harvard Law Review 64, no. 1 (1950-1951), 170-175.

Howe, Mark DeWolfe. The Garden and the Wilderness: Religion
    and Government in American Constitutional History. Chicago:
    University of Chicago Press, 1965.

Hudson, Winthrop S. "The Issue of Church and State: A
   Historical Perspective." Religion in Life 46, no. 3 (1977),
   278-288.

Hudspeth, C. M. "Separation of Church and State in America."
   Texas Law Review 33, no. 7 (1955), 1035-1056.

Huegli, Albert G., ed. Church and State Under God. St. Louis,
   Mo.: Concordia Publishing House, 1964.

Johnson, Alvin Walter, and Yost, Frank H. Separation of Church
   and State in the United States. Minneapolis: University of
   Minneapolis Press, 1948.

Katz, Wilbur G. "The Case for Religious Liberty." In Religion
   in America, edited by John Cogley. New York: Meridian
   Books, 1958.

Katz, Wilbur G. Religion and American Constitutions.
   Evanston, Ill.: Northwestern University Press, 1964.

Katz, Wilbur G. "Religion and Law in America." In Religion in
   American Life, vol. 2, Religious Perspectives in American
   Culture, edited by James Ward Smith and A. Leland Jamison.
   Princeton, N.J.: Princeton University Press, 1961.

Kauper, Paul G. "Church, State, and Freedom: A Review."
   Michigan Law Review 52, no. 6 (1954), 829-848.

Kauper, Paul G. Religion and the Constitution. Baton Rouge,
   La.: Louisiana State University Press, 1964.

Kohler, Max. "The Fathers of the Republic and Constitutional
   Establishment of Religious Liberty." In God in Freedom,
   edited by Luigi Luzzatti. New York: Macmillan, 1930.

Konvitz, Milton R. Fundamental Liberties of a Free People.
   Ithaca, N.Y.: Cornell University Press, 1957.

Kruse, Clifton B. "The Historical Meaning and Judicial
   Construction of the Establishment of Religion Clause of the
   First Amendment." Washburn Law Journal 2, no. 1 (1962), 65-
   141.

Kurland, Philip B. "The Irrelevance of the Constitution: The
   Religion Clauses of the First Amendment and the Supreme
   Court." Villanova Law Review 24, no. 1 (1978), 3-27.

Lardner, Lynford Alexander. "How Far Does the Constitution
   Separate Church and State?" American Political Science
   Review 45, no. 1 (1951), 110-132.

Levinson, Sanford. "'The Constitution' in American Civil
   Religion." 1979 Supreme Court Review, 123-151.

Levy, Leonard W. _An Establishment of Religion: The First
    Amendment's Clause on the Wall of Separation_. New York:
    Macmillan, forthcoming.

Levy, Leonard W. _Judgments: Essays on American Constitutional
    History_. Chicago: Quadrangle Books, 1972.

Littell, Franklin H. "An American Plea for Religious Liberty."
    American Review 3, no. 3 (1964), 26-43.

Malbin, Michael J. _Religion and Politics: The Intentions of
    the Authors of the First Amendment_. Washington, D.C.:
    American Enterprise Institute, 1978.

Manzullo, Donald A. _Neither Sacred Nor Profane: The Supreme
    Court and the Church_. New York: Exposition Press, 1973.

Marnell, William H. _The First Amendment: The History of
    Religious Freedom in America_. Garden City, N.Y.: Doubleday,
    1964.

Marty, Martin E. "Freedom of Religion and the First
    Amendment." _Virginia Cavalcade_ 32, no. 4 (1983), 158-171.

Mead, Sidney E. "Religion, Constitutional Federalism, Rights,
    and the Court." _Journal of Church and State_ 14, no. 2
    (1972), 191-209.

Medhurst, Martin J. "From Duche to Provoost: The Birth of
    Inaugural Prayer." _Journal of Church and State_ 24, no. 3
    (1982), 573-588.

Moehlman, Conrad H. "The Baptist View of the State." _Church
    History_ 6 (1937), 24-49.

Moehlman, Conrad H. _The Wall of Separation Between Church and
    State: An Historical Study of Recent Criticism of the
    Religious Clause of the First Amendment_. Boston: Beacon
    Press, 1951.

Morgan, Richard E. _The Supreme Court and Religion_. New York:
    Free Press, 1972.

O'Neill, James M. "The Meaning of the Establishment Clause: A
    Debate." _Buffalo Law Review_ 2, no. 2 (1953), 242-66, 272-
    278.

O'Neill, James M. _Religion and Education Under the
    Constitution_. 1949. Reprint. New York: Da Capo Press,
    1972.

Parsons, Wilfred. _The First Freedom: Consideration on Church
    and State in the United States_. New York: Declan X.
    McMullen Co., 1948.

Peterson, Walfred. _Thy Liberty in Law_. Nashville: Broadman Press, 1978.

Pfeffer, Leo. "The Case for Separation." In _Religion in America_, edited by John Cogley. New York: Meridian Books, 1958.

Pfeffer, Leo. "Church and State: Something Less Than Separation." _University of Chicago Law Review_ 19 (1951), 1-29.

Pfeffer, Leo. _Church, State, and Freedom_. rev. ed. Boston: Beacon Press, 1967.

Pfeffer, Leo. _God, Caesar, and the Constitution: The Court as Referee of Church-State Confrontation_. Boston: Beacon Press, 1975.

Pfeffer, Leo. "The Meaning of the Establishment Clause: A Debate." _Buffalo Law Review_ 2, no. 2 (1953), 225-241, 267-272.

Religion in the Constitution: A Delicate Balance. Clearinghouse Publication, no. 80. United States Commission on Civil Rights, September 1983.

Rutland, Robert A. _The Birth of the Bill of Rights, 1776-1791_. Chapel Hill: University of North Carolina Press, 1955.

Sanders, Thomas G. _Protestant Concepts of Church and State_. New York: Holt, Rinehart and Winston, 1964.

Schaff, Philip. _Church and State in the United States_. Papers of the American Historical Association 2, no. 4. 1888. Reprint. New York: Arno Press, 1972.

Schwartz, Bernard. _The Great Rights of Mankind: A History of the American Bill of Rights_. New York: Oxford University Press, 1977.

Schaffer, Thomas L. "First Amendment: History and the Courts." _Review of Politics_ 40, no. 2 (1978), 271-279.

Singleton, Marvin K. "Colonial Virginia as First Amendment Matrix: Henry, Madison, and Assessment Establishment." _Journal of Church and State_ 8, no. 3 (1966), 344-364.

Smith, Ronald A. "Freedom of Religion and the Land Ordinance of 1785." _Journal of Church and State_ 24, no. 3 (1982), 589-602.

Smylie, James H. "Protestant Clergy, the First Amendment, and Beginnings of a Constitutional Debate, 1781-1791." In _The Religion of the Republic_, edited by Elwyn A. Smith. Philadelphia: Fortress Press, 1971.

Snee, Joseph M. "Religious Disestablishment and the Fourteenth
     Amendment." Washington University Law Quarterly 1954, no. 4
     (1954), 371-407.

Stokes, Anson Phelps. Church and State in the United States.
     3 vols. New York: Harper & Brothers, 1950.

Stokes, Anson Phelps, and Pfeffer, Leo. Church and State in
     the United States. rev. ed. in 1 vol. New York: Harper &
     Row, 1964.

Sutherland, Arthur E. The Church Shall Be Free.
     Charlottesville: University Press of Virginia, 1965.

Sutherland, Arthur E. "Historians, Lawyers, and 'Establishment
     of Religion.'" In Religion and the Public Order, No. 5: An
     Annual Review of Church and State, and of Religion, Law, and
     Society, edited by Donald A. Giannella, 27-50. Institute of
     Church and State, Villanova University School of Law.
     Ithaca, N.Y.: Cornell University Press, 1969.

Swancara, Frank. The Separation of Religion and Government:
     The First Amendment, Madison's Intent, and the McCollum
     Decision -- A Study of Separationism in America. New York:
     Truth Seeker, 1950.

Torpey, William George. Judicial Doctrines of Religious Rights
     in America. Chapel Hill: University of North Carolina
     Press, 1948.

Tussman, Joseph. The Supreme Court on Church and State. New
     York: Oxford University Press, 1962.

Vance, Donald F. "The Supreme Court and the Definition of
     Religion." Ph.D. diss., Indiana University, 1970.

Van Patten, Jonathan K. "In the End is the Beginning: An
     Inquiry Into the Meaning of the Religion Clauses." St.
     Louis University Law Journal 27 (1983), 1-93.

Weclew, Robert G. "Church and State: How Much Separation?" De
     Paul Law Review 10, no. 1 (1960), 1-26.

Whipple, Leon. Our Ancient Liberties: The Story of the Origin
     and Meaning of Civil and Religious Liberty in the United
     States. 1927. Reprint. New York: Da Capo Press, 1972.

Wood, James E., Jr.; Thompson, E. Bruce; and Miller, Robert T.
     Church and State in Scripture, History, and Constitutional
     Law. Waco, Tex.: Baylor University Press, 1958.

b. The Supreme Court and History: The Problem of
Interpretation

Brest, Paul. "The Misconceived Quest for the Original
    Understanding." Boston University Law Review 60, no. 2
    (1980), 204-238.

Cornelius, William J. "Church and State -- The Mandate of the
    Establishment Clause: Wall of Separation or Benign
    Neutrality?" St. Mary's Law Journal 16, no. 1 (1984), 1-39.

Ely, John Hart. "Constitutional Interpretivism: Its Allure and
    Impossibility." Indiana Law Journal 53 (1977-1978), 399-
    448.

Emerson, Thomas I. "Colonial Intentions and Current Realities
    of the First Amendment." University of Pennsylvania Law
    Review 125, no. 4 (1977), 737-760.

Grey, Thomas C. "Do We Have an Unwritten Constitution?"
    Stanford Law Review 27 (1974-1975), 703-718.

Grey, Thomas C. "Origins of the Unwritten Constitution:
    Fundamental Law in American Revolutionary Thought."
    Stanford Law Review 30 (1978), 843-893.

Jacobsohn, Gary. "E. T.: The Extra-Textual in Constitutional
    Interpretation." Constitutional Commentary 1, no. 1 (1984),
    21-42.

Kelly, Alfred H. "Clio and the Court: An Illicit Love Affair."
    1965 Supreme Court Review, 119-158.

Kurland, Philip B. "The Irrelevance of the Constitution: The
    Religion Clauses of the First Amendment and the Supreme
    Court." Villanova Law Review 24, no. 1 (1978), 3-27.

Maltz, Earl. "Some New Thoughts on an Old Problem -- The Role
    of the Intent of the Framers in Constitutional Theory."
    Boston University Law Review 63, no. 4 (1983), 811-851.

Powell, H. Jefferson. "The Original Understanding of Original
    Intent." Harvard Law Review 98, no. 5 (1985), 885-948.

Sandalow, Terrance. "Constitutional Interpretation."
    Michigan Law Review 79 (1981), 1033-1072.

Schlag, Pierre. "Framers Intent: The Illegitimate Uses of
    History." University of Puget Sound Law Review 8, no. 2
    (1985), 283-330.

Tushnet, Mark V. "Following the Rules Laid Down: A Critique of
    Interpretivism and Neutral Principles." Harvard Law Review
    96, no. 4 (1983), 781-827.

4.　POLITICS, THE CONSTITUTION, AND THE FOUNDING FATHERS

Benson, C. Randolph. _Thomas Jefferson as Social Scientist_.
Rutherford, N.J.: Fairleigh Dickinson University Press,
1971.

Boller, Paul F., Jr. _George Washington and Religion_. Dallas:
Southern Methodist University Press, 1963.

Boller, Paul F., Jr. "George Washington and Religious
Liberty." _William and Mary Quarterly_, 3d ser., 17, no. 4
(1960), 486-506.

Borden, Morton. "Federalists, Antifederalists, and Religious
Freedom." _Journal of Church and State_ 21, no. 3 (1979),
469-482.

Brant, Irving. _James Madison_. 6 vols. Indianapolis: Bobbs-
Merrill, 1941-1961.

Brant, Irving. "The Madison Heritage." _New York University
Law Review_ 35 (1960), 882-902.

Brant, Irving. "Madison on the Separation of Church and
State." _William and Mary Quarterly_, 3d ser., 8, no. 1
(1951), 3-24.

Drakeman, Donald. "Religion and the Republic: James Madison
and the First Amendment." _Journal of Church and State_ 25,
no. 3 (1984), 31-54.

Commager, Henry Steele. _Jefferson, Nationalism, and the
Enlightenment_. New York: George Braziller, 1975.

Edwards, Rem B. _A Return to Moral and Religious Philosophy in
Early America_. Washington, D.C.: University Press of
America, 1982.

Foote, Henry Wilder. _Thomas Jefferson: Champion of Religious
Freedom, Advocate of Christian Morals_. Boston: Beacon
Press, 1947.

Gurley, James Lafayette. "Thomas Jefferson's Philosophy and
Theology: As Related to His Political Principles, Including
Separation of Church and State." Ph.D. diss, University of
Michigan, 1975.

Hansen, Joel F. "Jefferson and the Church-State Wall: A
Historical Examination of the Man and the Metaphor."
Brigham Young University Law Review 1978, 645-674.

Healey, Robert M. _Jefferson on Religion in Public Education_.
New Haven: Yale University Press, 1962.

Hooker, Richard J. "John Dickinson on Church and State."
    American Literature 16 (1944-1945), 82-98.

Hunt, Gaillard. "James Madison and Religious Liberty." Annual
    Report of the American Historical Association for 1901 1,
    163-171.

Huntley, William B. "Jefferson's Public and Private Religion."
    South Atlantic Quarterly 79, no. 3 (1980), 286-301.

Kessler, Sanford. "Locke's Influence on Jefferson's 'Bill for
    Establishing Religious Freedom.'" Journal of Church and
    State 25, no. 2 (1983), 231-252.

Koch, Adrienne. Jefferson and Madison: The Great
    Collaboration. New York: Knopf, 1950.

Koch, Adrienne. The Philosophy of Thomas Jefferson. New York:
    Columbia University Press, 1943.

Levy, Leonard W. Jefferson and Civil Liberties: The Darker
    Side. New York: New York Times Book Co., 1973.

Little, David. "Thomas Jefferson's Religious Views and Their
    Influence on the Supreme Court's Interpretation of the First
    Amendment." Catholic University of America Law Review 26
    (Fall 1976), 57-72.

Mabee, Charles. "Thomas Jefferson's Anti-Clerical Bible."
    Historical Magazine of the Protestant Episcopal Church 48,
    no. 4 (1979), 473-481.

McCants, David A. "The Authenticity of James Maury's Account
    of Patrick Henry's Speech in the Parson's Cause." Southern
    Speech Communications Journal 42 (Fall 1976), 20-34.

Mead, Sidney E. "Neither Church Nor State: Reflections on
    James Madison's 'Line of Separation.'" Journal of Church
    and State 10, no. 3 (1968), 349-378.

Mott, Royden J. "Sources of Jefferson's Ecclesiastical Views."
    Church History 3, no. 4 (1934), 267-284.

Nichols, James Hastings. "John Witherspoon on Church and
    State." In Calvinism and the Political Order, edited by
    George L. Hunt. Philadelphia: Westminster Press, 1965.

O'Brien, Charles F. "The Religious Issue in the Presidential
    Campaign of 1800." Essex Institute Historical Collections
    107, no. 1 (1971), 82-93.

Pearson, Samuel C. "Nature's God: A Reassessment of the
    Religion of the Founding Fathers." Religion in Life 46, no.
    2 (1977), 152-165.

Ploch, W. M.   "Thomas Jefferson, Author of the Statute of
     Virginia for Religious Freedom." <u>Jurist</u> 3 (1943), 182-230.

Sandler, S. Gerald.   "Lockean Ideas in Thomas Jefferson's <u>Bill</u>
     <u>for Establishing Religious Freedom</u>." <u>Journal of the History</u>
     <u>of Ideas</u> 21 (January-March 1960), 110-116.

Sanford, Charles B.   <u>The Religious Life of Thomas Jefferson</u>.
     Charlottesville: University Press of Virginia, 1984.

Sanford, Charles B.   <u>Thomas Jefferson and His Library: A Study</u>
     <u>of His Literary Interests and of the Religious Attitudes</u>
     <u>Revealed by Relevant Tiles in His Library</u>. Hamden, Conn.:
     Archon Books, 1977.

Schulz, Constance B.   "'Of Bigotry in Politics and Religion':
     Jefferson's Religion, the Federalist Press, and the
     Syllabus." <u>Virginia Magazine of History and Biography</u> 9,
     no. 1 (1983), 73-91.

Schulz, Constance B.   "The Radical Religious Ideas of Thomas
     Jefferson and John Adams: A Comparison." Ph.D. diss.,
     University of Cincinnati, 1973.

Swancara, Frank.   <u>Thomas Jefferson Versus Religious Oppression</u>.
     New York: University Books, 1969.

Thompson, Peggy.   "Jefferson Trimmed the Bible to His Taste."
     <u>Smithsonian</u> 14, no. 6 (1983), 139-145, 147-148.

Trainor, M. Rosaleen.   "Thomas Jefferson on Freedom of
     Conscience." Ph.D. diss., St. John's University, 1966.

Weber, Paul J.   "James Madison and Religious Equality: The
     Perfect Separation." <u>Review of Politics</u> 44, no. 2 (1982),
     163-186.

          5.   THE WORKING OUT OF SEPARATION: DISESTABLISHMENT,
                    VOLUNTARYISM, AND THE DENOMINATIONS

Adams, James Luther.   "The Voluntary Principle in the Forming
     of American Religion." In <u>The Religion of the Republic</u>,
     edited by Elwyn A. Smith. Philadelphia: Fortress Press,
     1971.

Ahlstrom, Sydney.   "Religion, Revolution, and the Rise of
     Modern Nationalism: Reflections on the American Experience."
     <u>Church History</u> 44, no. 4 (1975), 492-504.

Bellah, Robert N.   "Cultural Pluralism and Religious
    Particularism." In Freedom of Religion in America:
    Historical Roots, Philosophical Concepts, and Contemporary
    Problems, edited by Henry B. Clark II. New Brunswick, N.J.:
    Transaction Books, 1982.

Bodo, John R.   The Protestant Clergy and Public Issues, 1812-
    1848. Princeton, N.J.: Princeton University Press, 1954.

Bowden, Henry Warner. "Philip Schaff and Sectarianism: The
    Americanization of a European Viewpoint." Journal of Church
    and State 8, no. 1 (1966), 97-106.

Cherry, Conrad. "Nation, Church, and Private Religion: The
    Emergence of an American Pattern." Journal of Church and
    State 14, no. 2 (1972), 223-233.

Clark, Henry B., II, ed. Freedom of Religion in America:
    Historical Roots, Philosophical Concepts, and Contemporary
    Problems. New Brunswick, N.J.: Transaction Books, 1982.

Commager, Henry Steele. "Religion and Politics in American
    History." In Religion and Politics, edited by James E.
    Wood, Jr. Waco, Tex.: Baylor University Press, 1983.

Commager, Henry Steele. "The Significance of Freedom of
    Religion in American History." In Freedom of Religion in
    America: Historical Roots, Philosophical Concepts, and
    Contemporary Problems, edited by Henry B. Clark II. New
    Brunswick, N.J.: Transaction Books, 1982.

Handy, Robert T. A Christian America: Protestant Hopes and
    Historical Realities. New York: Oxford University Press,
    1971.

Hatch, Nathan O. The Sacred Cause of Liberty: Republican
    Thought and the Millennium in Revolutionary New England.
    New Haven: Yale University Press, 1977.

Hudson, Winthrop S. The Great Tradition of the American
    Churches. New York: Harper & Brothers, 1953.

Humphrey, Edward F. Nationalism and Religion in America, 1774-
    1789. 1924. Reissued. New York: Russell and Russell,
    1965.

Jameson, J. Franklin. The American Revolution Considered as a
    Social Movement. Princeton, N.J.: Princeton University
    Press, 1926.

Kelly, George Armstrong. Politics and Religious Consciousness
    in America. New Brunswick, N.J.: Transaction Books, 1984.

Lee, Robert, and Marty, Martin E., eds. Religion and Social
    Conflict. New York: Oxford University Press, 1964.

Littell, Franklin H. <u>From State Church to Pluralism: A Protestant Interpretation of Religion in American History</u>. Garden City, N.Y.: Doubleday & Co., Anchor Books, 1962.

Littell, Franklin H. "Religious Liberty in a Pluralistic Society." <u>Journal of Church and State</u> 8, no. 3 (1966), 430-444.

McClellan, James. "Christianity and the Common Law." Chap. 3 in <u>Joseph Story and the American Constitution</u>. Norman, Okla.: University of Oklahoma Press, 1971.

McLoughlin, William G. "The Role of Religion in the Revolution: Liberty of Conscience and Cultural Cohesion in the New Nation." In <u>Essays on the American Revolution</u>, edited by S. G. Kurtz and J. H. Hutson. Chapel Hill: University of North Carolina Press, 1973.

Marty, Martin E. "Living with Establishment and Disestablishment in Nineteenth-Century Anglo-America." <u>Journal of Church and State</u> 18, no. 1 (1976), 61-77.

Mead, Sidney E. "The Fact of Pluralism and the Persistence of Sectarianism." In <u>The Religion of the Republic</u>, edited by Elwyn A. Smith. Philadelphia: Fortress Press, 1971.

Mead, Sidney E. "From Coercion to Persuasion: Another Look at the Rise of Religious Liberty and the Emergence of Denominationalism." <u>Church History</u> 25, no. 4 (1956), 317-337.

Mead, Sidney E. <u>The Lively Experiment: The Shaping of Christianity in America</u>. New York: Harper & Row, 1963.

Mead, Sidney E. <u>The Nation With the Soul of a Church</u>. New York: Harper & Row, 1975.

Mead, Sidney E. "The Theology of the Republic and the Orthodox Mind." <u>Journal of the American Academy of Religion</u> 44, no. 1 (1976), 105-113.

Miller, Glenn T. <u>Religious Liberty in America: History and Prospects</u>. Philadelphia: Westminster Press, 1976.

Miller, Perry. "The Location of American Religious Freedom." In <u>Religion and Freedom of Thought</u>. Garden City, N.Y.: Doubleday, 1954.

Miller, William Lee. "American Religion and American Political Attitudes." In <u>Religion in American Life</u>, vol. 2, <u>Religious Perspectives in American Culture</u>, edited by James Ward Smith and A. Leland Jamison. Princeton, N.J.: Princeton University Press, 1961.

Morgan, Richard E. The Supreme Court and Religion. New York:
     Free Press, 1972.

Niebuhr, H. Richard. Social Sources of Denominationalism.
     Hamden, Conn.: Shoestring Press, 1954.

Niebuhr, Reinhold. "A Note on Pluralism." In Religion in
     America, edited by John Cogley. New York: Meridian Books,
     1958.

Niebuhr, Reinhold, and Heimert, Alan. A Nation So Conceived:
     Reflections on the History of America From Its Early Visions
     to Its Present Power. New York: Scribner's Sons, 1963.

Pfeffer, Leo. "Freedom and Separation: America's Contribution
     to Civilization." Journal of Church and State 2, no. 2
     (1960), 100-111.

Pfeffer, Leo. "The Deity in American Constitutional History."
     Journal of Church and State 23, no. 2 (1981), 215-239.

Richey, Russell E., ed. Denominationalism. Nashville:
     Abingdon Press, 1977.

Robertson, D. B., ed. Voluntary Associations: A Study of
     Groups in Free Societies. Richmond, Va.: John Knox Press,
     1966.

Smith, Elwyn A. Religious Liberty in the United States: The
     Development of Church-State Thought Since the Revolutionary
     Era. Philadelphia: Fortress Press, 1972.

Smith, Elwyn A. "The Voluntary Establishment of Religion." In
     The Religion of the Republic, edited by Elwyn A. Smith.
     Philadelphia: Fortress Press, 1971.

Smylie, John. "National Ethos and the Church." Theology Today
     20, no. 3 (1963), 313-321.

Spiegel, Jayson. "Christianity as Part of the Common Law."
     North Carolina Central Library Journal 14 (Spring 1984),
     494-516.

Wilson, John F. Public Religion in American Culture.
     Philadelphia: Temple University Press, 1979.

6. RESOURCES

a. Documents and Sources

Blakely, William A. American State Papers and Related
Documents on Freedom of Religion. 4th rev. ed. Washington,
D.C.: Review and Herald Press, 1949.

Blau, Joseph L. Cornerstones of Religious Freedom in America.
Boston: Beacon Press, 1949.

Cousins, Norman, ed. In God We Trust: The Religious Beliefs
and Ideas of the American Founding Fathers. New York:
Harper Brothers, 1958.

Documentary History of the Constitution of the United States of
America, 1786-1870. 5 vols. 1894-1900. Reprint. New
York: Johnson Reprint Co., 1965.

Documents Illustrative of the Formation of the Union of the
American States. Washington, D.C.: Government Printing
Office, 1927.

Eidelberg, Paul. "Provisions in the State Constitutions
Respecting Religion, Morality, Education, and the Qualities
Required of Statesmen." Appendix 2 in The Philosophy of the
American Constitution: A Reinterpretation of the Intentions
of the Founding Fathers. New York: Free Press, 1968.

Elliot, Jonathan, ed. The Debates in the Several State
Conventions on the Adoption of the Federal Constitution. 5
vols. 1836. Reprint. New York: Burt Franklin, n.d.

Farrand, Max, ed. The Records of the Federal Convention of
1787. 1911. rev. ed. 4 vols. New Haven: Yale University
Press, 1937.

Hall, Verna M., comp. Christian History of the Constitution of
the United States of America. Edited by Joseph A.
Montgomery. 2 vols. San Francisco: American Christian
Constitution Press, 1960, 1962.

Handlin, Oscar, and Handlin, Mary, eds. The Popular Sources of
Political Authority: Documents on the Massachusetts
Constitution of 1780. Cambridge, Mass.: Harvard University
Press, Belknap Press, 1966.

Horwitz, Morton. "Documents of Constitutional Development."
Law Library Journal 69 (August 1976), 295-299.

James, Charles F. Documentary History of the Struggle for
Religious Liberty in Virginia. 1900. Reprint. New York:
Da Capo Press, 1971.

Jensen, Merrill, and Becker, Robert A., eds. The Documentary
    History of the Ratification of the Constitution. Madison,
    Wis.: State Historical Society of Wisconsin, 1976 -.

Kettleborough, Charles, comp. and ed. The State Constitutions
    and the Federal Constitution and Organic Laws of the
    Territories and Other Colonial Dependencies of the United
    States of America. Indianapolis, Ind.: B. F. Bowen and Co.,
    1908.

Konvitz, Milton R. Bill of Rights Reader: Leading
    Constitutional Cases. 5th ed. rev. Ithaca, N.Y.: Cornell
    University Press, 1973.

Lewis, John Donald, ed. Anti-Federalists Versus Federalists:
    Selected Documents. San Francisco: Chandler Publishing Co.,
    1967.

McLoughlin, William G. "Introduction." In Isaac Backus on
    Church, State, and Calvinism, Pamphlets, 1754-1780, 1-61.
    Cambridge, Mass.: Harvard University Press, John Harvard
    Library, 1968.

Moehlman, Conrad H., comp. The American Constitutions and
    Religion: Religious References in the Charters of the
    Thirteen Colonies and the Constitutions of the Forty-Eight
    States, A Source Book on Church and State in the United
    States. Berne, Ind., 1938.

Morison, Samuel Eliot. Sources and Documents Illustrating the
    American Revolution, 1764-1788, and the Formation of the
    Federal Constitution. 2d ed. New York: Oxford University
    Press, 1962.

Perry, Richard L., ed. Sources of Our Liberties: Documentary
    Origins of Individual Liberties in the United States
    Constitution and Bill of Rights. Chicago: American Bar
    Foundation, 1959.

Poore, Benjamin P., ed. The Federal and State Constitutions,
    Colonial Charters, and Other Organized Laws of the U.S.
    Compiled Under an Order of the United States Senate. 2d ed.
    2 vols. 1878. Reprint. New York: Burt Franklin, 1972.

Powell, Milton B. The Voluntary Church: American Religious
    Life (1740-1860) Seen Through the Eyes of European Visitors.
    New York: Macmillan, 1967.

Odegard, Peter. Religion and Politics. Dobbs Ferry, N.Y.:
    Oceana Publications, 1960.

Prescott, Arthur Taylor. Drafting the Federal Constitution: A
    Rearrangement of Madison's Notes. University, La.:
    Louisiana State University Press, 1941.

Schwartz, Bernard. <u>The Bill of Rights: A Documentary History</u>.
2 vols. New York, Toronto, London, Sydney: Chelsea House
Publishers in association with McGraw Hill Book Co., 1971.

Thorpe, Francis Newton, comp. <u>The Federal and State
Constitutions, Colonial Charters, and Other Organic Laws of
the States, Territories, and Colonies Now or Heretofore
Forming the United States of America</u>. Washington, D.C.:
Government Printing Office, 1909.

Wilson, John F. <u>Church and State in American History</u>. Boston:
D. C. Heath, 1965.

b. Bibliographies

Brunkow, Robert deV., ed. <u>Religion and Society in North
America: An Annotated Bibliography</u>. Santa Barbara, Calif.:
Clio Press, 1983.

Gephart, Ronald M., comp. <u>Periodical Literature on the
American Revolution: Historical Research and Changing
Interpretations, 1895-1970</u>. Washington, D.C.: Library of
Congress, General Reference and Bibliographical Division,
1971.

Hall, Kermit L. <u>A Comprehensive Bibliography of American
Constitutional and Legal History, 1896-1979</u>. vols. 1-5.
Millwood, N.Y.: Kraus International Publications, 1984.

<u>Journal of Church and State</u>. Each issue contains a listing of
recent doctoral dissertations on religion and politics.

Lanoue, George R. <u>A Bibliography of Doctoral Dissertations
Undertaken in American and Canadian Universities, 1940-1962,
on Religion and Politics</u>. New York: National Council of
Churches, 1963.

McCarrick, Earlean M. <u>U.S. Constitution: A Guide to
Information Sources.</u> American Government and History
Information Guide Series, vol. 4. Detroit, Mich.: Gale
Research Co., 1980.

Mason, Alpheus Thomas, and Stephenson, D. Grier, Jr., comps.
<u>American Constitutional Development</u>. Arlington Heights,
Ill.: AHM Publishing Corp., 1977.

Menendez, Albert J. <u>Church-State Relations: An Annotated
Bibliography</u>. New York: Garland Publishing, 1976.

Millett, Stephen M., comp. <u>A Selected Bibliography of American
Constitutional History</u>. Santa Barbara, Calif.: Clio Books,
1975.

Shy, John, ed. The American Revolution. Goldentree
    Bibliographies in American History Series. Northbrook,
    Ill.: AHM Publishing Corp., 1973.

Smith, Dwight, ed. Era of the American Revolution: A
    Bicentennial Bibliography. Santa Barbara, Calif.: American
    Bibliographical Center, ABC-Clio Press, 1975.

6

Religion, Politics, and the Rise of the Denomination in Early Nineteenth-Century America

John R. Fitzmier

The opening years of the nineteenth century represent a critical stage of development in the relationship between religious institutions and civil governments in America. With the Revolution long past, the Constitution finally in place, and Jefferson triumphant, experimentation began, particularly in New England, concerning the possible ways to develop this relationship within the constraints of the state and federal system. In these turbulent initial decades of the century, Jeffersonian republicanism developed into Jacksonian democracy, and the frontier became a dominant feature of American society. With respect to church life, the ecclesiastical hegemony of New England Congregationalism was shaken by political and religious dissenters while popular Protestantism explored new structures of religious order. The result was the pattern of denominationalism which became the definitive characteristic of nineteenth-century American Protestantism.

If it is true that the popular mind appropriates myths to help explain complex and paradoxical cultural events—especially events which shape the identity of individuals and groups—Americans were blessed with a myth-maker of monumental proportions in the person of Lyman Beecher. Variously described as clergyman, theologian, revivalist, and social reformer, Beecher functioned as the grand promoter of popular, evangelical, middle-class culture in early nineteenth-century America. In his *Autobiography*, a pastiche of reminiscences that he dictated in his seventy-fifth year, Beecher, perhaps unwittingly, set a course for the writing of American religious history that would remain virtually unchanged for a century and a half. Three well-known vignettes, all set forth in the mythic idiom that characterized Beecher's understanding of his era, have cast long shadows on the religious historiography of antebellum America. The first myth concerns Beecher's recollections of the religious revival at Yale College; the second, Beecher's initially negative reaction to the disestablishment of Connecticut Congregationalism in

1819; the third, his subsequent conviction that this separation of church and state was the best thing that ever happened to American Christianity. This essay will examine these three elements of the larger Beecher mythos that together have dominated a considerable literature on this subject.

YALE AND THE SECOND GREAT AWAKENING

In the spring of 1795, sophomore Lyman Beecher encountered a species of religious skepticism at Yale College that was quite foreign to the Connecticut he knew as the Land of Steady Habits. If Beecher's memory served him correctly, raucous students traversed the campus and "called each other Voltaire, Rousseau, D'Alembert." In Beecher's mind, these jests were symptomatic of a pervasive "infidelity" that prevailed in the college. Believing that the stodgy clerics of the faculty were "afraid of free discussion," this new breed of undergraduate carried on as if its skepticism had already become the intellectual standard of the day. Beecher's first myth, then, begins at this supposed nadir of Connecticut orthodoxy and promptly introduces a hero figure, Yale's President, Timothy Dwight. As a traditionalist and a respected leader of Connecticut Federalists, Dwight aggressively struck back at student infidelity. According to Beecher, Dwight required his seniors to debate with him the proposition "Is the Bible the Word of God?" Of course, Dwight soundly thrashed the opposition. He "heard all they had to say, answered them, and there was an end." Henceforth, said Beecher, "all infidelity skulked and hid its head" (p. 27).

This story has been the starting point for most historical treatments—both hagiographic and scholarly—of the Second Great Awakening. Noted twentieth-century historians such as Charles Roy Keller, Sidney Mead, William Clebsch, and Stephen Berk have adopted Beecher's account, and have assumed that his partisan ruminations were in fact an accurate representation of the entire national experience. In these accounts, Dwight inevitably plays the part of the champion of New England orthodoxy, rescuing it from the maw of French (or, as Dwight believed, Jeffersonian) infidelity. Dwight puts an end to student skepticism, he increases the membership in the college church, he transforms Yale into a "little temple of prayer," he rallies bright young men under the banner of the Standing Order, and he inaugurates what some have termed the "Protestant Counter-Reformation in America." Perhaps the best example of how this thesis has been uncritically accepted is to be found in Jerald C. Brauer's *Protestantism in America: A Narrative History*. In a chapter entitled "Revivalism to the Rescue," Brauer summarized three decades of American revivals with the claim, "So revivalism came to the Church's rescue. . . . It defeated deism and indifference, it overcame the problem of space, and won thousands of members for the voluntary churches" (p. 116).

In 1963, this historiographical pattern was broken by an article whose intent, oddly enough, was to rehabilitate the reputation of Ezra Stiles, the thinly veiled antagonist to Dwight in Beecher's legend. Edmund S. Morgan, in his "Ezra Stiles and Timothy Dwight," carefully scrutinized the Beecher story, and found the historical facts of the Beecher myth to be specious. First, Morgan showed that Dwight's ostensibly progressive handling of the situation was, in fact, quite traditional. Previous Yale presidents had confronted similar student assaults on orthodoxy, and responded with similar methods. Dwight's choice of the senior disputation topic, for instance, was hardly novel: Ezra Stiles had participated in a similar disputation on Divine Revelation as early as 1750. Moreover, Morgan's analysis of contemporary church records indicates "that the revival spread from other churches to the college, and not vice versa" (p. 109). With this single article, then, Edmund Morgan implicitly suggested a broad program of revisions aimed at the traditional interpretation of the Second Great Awakening.

Many scholars have subsequently taken Morgan's lead, and the revisionist historiography they have developed runs along three distinct lines of inquiry. The first concerns the political aspects of the declension thesis. The second treats the regional revivals that took place outside New England and began before Dwight's success at Yale. The third analyzes several of New England's theological movements—notably the New Divinity and Unitarianism—that developed during the period of the Second Awakening.

The Politics of Revival

Sidney Mead, in his landmark *Nathaniel W. Taylor, 1786–1858: A Connecticut Liberal*, concluded that the origins of the Awakening—especially in Connecticut—were distinctly political. According to his thesis, the revolutionary and constitutional periods had left New England Protestantism debilitated. Moreover, with Jefferson's accession to the presidency in 1800, New England Congregationalists—nearly all of whom were ardent Federalists— found themselves at a severe political disadvantage. In order to bolster their position—that is, to maintain the hegemony of the religious establishment, the Congregational Standing Order—they contrived and deployed revivals to win the political consciences, if not the souls, of New England's populace. As John R. Bodo later argued, these New England "theocrats" responded to their loss of status with something more than a system of doctrine: theirs was a complete program of political action.

Interestingly enough, this popular interpretation has functioned much like the "declension thesis" that long dominated the historiography of New England Puritanism. Like its seventeenth-century counterpart, this nineteenth-century declension thesis maintains that the New England ministerial elite sought to increase their failing influence through the leverage of congregational renewal. According to proponents of this theory, the ministers' formula for success was simple: fill the pews, preach aggressively, revive the churches and, as a matter of course, the Standing Order's power will be consolidated.

The Mead thesis, though moderately popular, was revised by a group of young social historians who, unlike Mead, were not concerned with intellectual history. The notion that the revival was a Federalist political tool was first questioned by Richard Birdsall. In "The Second Great Awakening and the New England Social Order," Birdsall claimed that the Awakening, contrary to Mead's interpretation, was a religious movement whose genesis was on a popular level. Individual religious beliefs, not the "ecclesiastical statesmanship of such major clergymen as Dwight, Beecher, and Taylor" (p. 345), were responsible for Connecticut's revived religious sensibilities. This shift in emphasis away from Federalist elites and toward Connecticut's growing middle classes functioned as a clarion call to other revisionists, who have now thoroughly reworked the standard thesis. Richard Shiels, for example, in an unpublished doctoral dissertation, and later in "The Second Great Awakening in Connecticut: A Critique of the Traditional Interpretation," argued that the leaders of the revivals, even in Connecticut, were for the most part not political figures. Though Shiels recognized that Dwight was one of the Awakening's guiding lights, he also argued that he was one of only a few men to wield both political and religious influence. Like Birdsall, Shiels concluded that the engines of revivalism were to be found in lay voluntary societies, such as the *Connecticut Evangelical Magazine* and local missionary groups, and not in the machinations of the Calvinist-Federalists. This revisionist literature has opened a new avenue to the study of the Second Awakening: instead of explaining both the Awakening and its attendant theological developments as an attempt to bolster failing Federalism, the two phenomena are now considered separately.

Revivals outside New England

The popularity of Beecher's account of his religious experience at Yale led to a preoccupation with Dwight's battle with infidelity. But Connecticut was not the only location of Second Awakening revivals, nor was it the first. Popular revivals had occurred on the frontier prior to Dwight's Yale harvests. These elements of the Second Awakening attracted scholarly attention prior to Morgan's proposed revisions. One of the earliest scholarly works in the field was brought out by Catharine C. Cleveland in 1916, *The Great Revival of the West, 1797–1805*. But despite its scholarly tone, essentially it was a pietistic account. Others like it continued to be published. Typical of this genre was Arthur B. Strickland's *The Great American Revival: A Case Study in the History of Evangelism with Implications for Today*. Strickland made an appeal that accurately reflected the "religion to the rescue" theme that was a common operating assumption among historians. The introduction to Strickland's monograph claimed, "A national revival of religion is long over-due in America. . . . It is good men and women who will bring in a good age. It is personal and pastoral evangelism which is to bring the renaissance of the church and the desired change in society" (p. 6). Revivalism, it appeared, was seen as a panacea for America's pressing social and political ills.

The historiography of the period took a swing toward a more critical stance with the 1958 publication of Bernard Weisberger's *They Gathered at the River: The Story of the Great Revivalists and Their Impact Upon Religion in America*. Weisberger's narrative account assessed the awakenings of both the eighteenth and nineteenth centuries, and examined the careers of Charles G. Finney, Dwight L. Moody, and Billy Sunday. In this it was one of the first critical treatments of the American revival tradition as a whole. Critical appraisals of the camp meetings also appeared. The historiography of this topic had long been dominated by another set of autobiographies, those of Finney and the "backwoods preacher," Peter Cartwright. Dickson D. Bruce, Jr., writing as a cultural anthropologist, studied the songs and spirituals used in camp meetings to assess "plain-folks religious activities and expressions on their own terms." (p. 9) Bruce found that the camp meeting, contrary to its popular image as the haven for religious cranks and evangelistic pitchmen, offered frontier folk a means of entry into the stable community of the saints in an otherwise chaotic environment.

The development of social history and the increased popularity of circumscribed studies of particular regions and locales forced other changes in revivalist historiography. John B. Boles's *The Great Revival, 1787–1805: The Origins of the Southern Evangelical Mind* was typical of this approach. Acknowledging that previous accounts focused too exclusively on Kentucky's Cumberland Valley and on the bizarre psychological components of frontier revivals, such as the barks and the jerks, Boles set out to "reconstruct the multifaceted religious mind of the southern evangelicals" (p. xi). He observed that southern evangelical groups were "individualistic, conversion-oriented, provincial, and anti-institutional," and, moreover, "took comparatively little notice of political and social matters" (p. 194). Boles went on to claim that these elements of the Great Revival "soon characterized the southern religious outlook" (p. 195). Whereas northern Protestantism produced a plethora of theologians and competing schools of theology, Boles claimed that the south, though perhaps the most religious region in America, "could boast no great theologians" (p. 195).

Though this last claim may have some merit, several monographs indicate that the southern evangelical mind was fertile indeed. Theodore Dwight Bozeman's *Protestants in an Age of Science* and E. Brooks Holifield's *Gentlemen Theologians* demonstrate that southern theologians deserve serious attention. Often assumed to have eschewed Enlightenment thought, many adopted its substance, at least in modified form. The Scottish Common Sense school of philosophy, introduced through John Witherspoon and later operative at Princeton Theological Seminary, was the medium through which American evangelicals appropriated the otherwise threatening systems associated with such men as Berkeley and Hume. Thus prepared with a nuanced version of the scientific method, Holifield's southern gentlemen bear strong resemblance to nineteenth-century Catholic neo-Thomists for whom natural reason functioned amicably alongside revealed truth. These "Christian Baconians," Holifield argues, concluded that natural reason, honestly applied to the conscience, could approximate the fundamental principles taught in scripture. Holifield's perceptions are borne out in subsequent studies of the development of American Fundamentalism, notably that of George Marsden, in which the importance of Common Sense philosophy is again underscored.

Donald Mathews's comprehensive assessment of southern evangelical religion became available only in 1977. *Religion in the Old South* focused attention not on theology or doctrine, but on the institutions upon which southern Protestantism had its greatest effects: self-identity, the family, and social class. Mathews concluded that southern evangelicalism enabled lower- and middle-class citizens—and especially blacks—to achieve individual security, group identity and social solidarity, all of which became rungs on a ladder that would become, in time, a route to social respectability.

Evangelical religion was tied to the initial emancipation and eventual political enfranchisement of both American blacks and women. Accounts of these relationships are but one element of a larger literature concerning the evangelical roots of America's social reform movements. Gilbert Barnes's *The Antislavery Impulse, 1830–1844* and Alice Felt Tyler's encyclopedic *Freedom's Ferment* began to map the various cultural effects of religion on American society. But it remained for Timothy L. Smith to give a detailed explanation of how particular evangelical doctrines gave rise to the system of social ethics that energized America's "great century" of social reform. In his enormously influential *Revivalism and Social Reform*, Smith argued that the Wesleyan doctrines of entire sanctification and perfectionism were the theological keys to understanding a broad range of reform movements including temperance, sabbatarianism, abolitionism, missions, and women's rights. Though scholars dispute Smith's claim that Arminian theology, and not one or more versions of American Calvinism, gave rise to the reforming societies, his work forced subsequent historians to give careful attention to both the social and theological aspects of this important American epoch.

Scholarly analysis of a particular figure frequently spawns reappraisals of the larger events in which that figure participated. In the fall of 1981, in commemoration of the sesquicentennial of Charles G. Finney's Rochester revivals, a group of scholars convened to discuss American Evangelicalism. The conference culminated in a published volume that contained work on Finney himself, as well as articles on the relationship of Evangelicalism to particular social groups (the American Indian, black slaves, and women) and religious movements (millennialism, fundamentalism, and popular twentieth-century evangelicalism). The volume was edited by Leonard I. Sweet, whose excellent historiographical essay, "The Evangelical Tradition in America," introduced the other articles. Sweet's essay, though centered on Evangelicalism, is wide-ranging and inclusive. Rather than choosing to treat Evangelicals apart from other movements, Sweet addressed Evangelicalism's relationship to the full range of American social, political, and religious phenomena. Replete with over three hundred notes, most of which contain multiple citations, Sweet's essay represents the single best historiographical essay on American Evangelicalism yet published.

Theological Ferment in New England

A proliferation of theological dissent and a differentiation of religious behavior took place in the decades of the late eighteenth and early nineteenth centuries that would eventuate in the multiplication of Protestant denominations. In New England particularly, preoccupation with refinement of doctrine played an important role in the attempt to secure a lasting resolution of the church-state question. Two of these traditions are worthy of attention here. The first, the New Divinity movement, was centered at Yale. The second, Unitarianism, flourished at Harvard.

As theological heirs to Jonathan Edwards, the so-called "New Divinity" men have increasingly attracted scholarly attention. This is due in part to the evangelistic role they played in the Second Awakening. But the New Divinity's lasting contribution to American religious culture—and especially to early nineteenth-century revivalism—is to be found in its distinctive system of theological and social ethics. New Divinity theologians, despite their preoccupation with metaphysics, were responsible for the popularization of the notion of disinterested benevolence. Despite Timothy Smith's contention, this Calvinist ethic, injected into a cultural milieu pervaded by a voluntaristic spirit, helped to ignite America's passion for social reform.

Historians generally concur on the makeup and beliefs of the Liberal and Old Calvinist segments of Congregationalism, but the New Divinity men have defied comparable analysis. Although theirs was a broad religious movement which issued in an extensive cultural agenda, scholars have often assessed it in strictly theological terms. Analysis invariably begins with considerations of the theology of Jonathan Edwards and moves to the work of his disciples, Samuel Hopkins and Joseph Bellamy. Adding to the limitations posed by strictly theological analysis of the movement is the dominating influence of the work of two scholars within the historiography. Both men found the New Divinity program seriously flawed, arriving at this conclusion by way of different historiographical routes.

Joseph Haroutunian viewed the New Divinity movement from the perspective of Jonathan Edwards's theology. In *Piety Versus Moralism* he argued that the New Divinity was responsible for a major alteration in American Calvinism. He proposed that, sensing the coming demise of their cherished system, New Divinity theologians offered an apologia for their mentor's version of the tradition. Hopkins and Bellamy, among others, greatly modified Edwards's theology. But according to Haroutunian, the disciples "lacked either his profound piety, his intellectual vigor, or both." Haroutunian took the high ground of Edwards's version of Calvinism; from this perspective the history of subsequent New England theology appeared to be simply, "the history of a degradation" (p. xxii).

Sidney Mead's *Nathaniel W. Taylor* also used the New Divinity as a foil against which to examine another American theological tradition. Mead took as his vantage point Lyman Beecher and Nathaniel W. Taylor. While these New Haven thinkers were advocating progressive theology and social reform, the New Divinity men, claimed Mead, were lost in rural backwaters, spinning metaphysical webs that would entangle American theology for decades.

Whereas Haroutunian had observed that the New Divinity men lacked their mentor's piety, Mead believed that their failings were in poetics. The history of New Divinity theology could be written, he claimed "in terms of the extraction by these unimaginative men of hard and sober metaphysical entities from Edwards's writings" (p. 16). Since the publication of Mead's work in 1942, the New Divinity men have been known as America's metaphysical preachers.

Within the last decade several scholars have begun an extensive revision of the prevailing negative views of the New Divinity movement. In an attempt to emend Haroutunian's *Piety Versus Moralism*, William Breitenbach has argued that Edwards's heirs represent a more traditional alignment of "Piety and Moralism." Similarly, Stephen Berk, in his *Calvinism Versus Democracy*, claimed that the New Divinity movement included not only metaphysicians but also less scholastic ministers. Berk characterized this latter group as the "evangelical" wing of the New Divinity, and placed Timothy Dwight at its head.

These interpretations all presuppose that the New Divinity movement, although to some degree internally diverse, promulgated a formal body of divinity—something best referred to as a school of theology. This assumption, however, has been the subject of continuing scholarly debate.

As early as 1851 Charles Hodge, architect of the Princeton Theology, charged that New Divinity men were nothing more than a "little coterie" of New England divines. Hodge's observation drew quick fire from the man reputed to be the last of the "consistent Calvinists," Edwards Amasa Park. In his response to Hodge, Park formulated a doctrinal definition of the New Divinity which, until recently, has remained a dominant element in the historiography. Most scholars now acknowledge the presence of a unique theological tradition alternately called Edwardseanism, the New Divinity movement, Hopkinsianism, or New England theology, that flourished from Edwards's time through at least the first quarter of the nineteenth century.

Positing such a theological tradition, however, does not solve the problem of determining whether or not a particular theologian belonged to the group. One limitation of this approach is that the identification of particular ministers as New Divinity men has rested solely upon their doctrinal affirmations. This compounds the larger challenge of identifying the cultural and political ethics of the New Divinity men and the larger movement they represented.

The monolithic view of New Divinity doctrine has itself undergone some revision. As Dorus Rudisill's *The Doctrine of the Atonement in Jonathan Edwards and His Successors* makes evident, the New Divinity movement was theologically diverse. Edwards, Hopkins, Bellamy, and West, it appears, disagreed in their interpretation of Christ's atonement. It is, therefore, problematic to argue that there existed a glossary of definitions or a canon of doctrines that defined the boundaries of New Divinity theology. Recent work has further clarified the roles of both the New Divinity movement and its offspring, the New Haven Theology. In their work, Robert Ferm, Mark Noll, Richard Birdsall, Anthony Cecil, and Earl Pope utilize several types of analysis—theological, social, and political—to great advantage. The older, exclusively doctrinal analysis can now be situated in a fuller context.

Joseph A. Conforti has produced the best of this growing literature. His *Samuel Hopkins and the New Divinity Movement* is a fine example of multi-faceted analysis. Combining a graceful narrative biography with careful attention to sociohistorical data, Conforti puts Hopkins—the prototypical metaphysician of Mead's thesis—in an intelligible cultural context. From this vantage point, the author traces the notion of benevolence from Edwards's "benevolence to Being in general" to Hopkins's more pragmatic "disinterested benevolence," thus offering a useful exploration of how New Divinity theological ethics were translated into concrete social policy. In effect, Conforti's work has significantly revised the Haroutunian/Mead images of the logic-chopping, hyper-Calvinism of the New Divinity men.

In addition to his interpretation of Hopkins, Conforti identifies fifty-six New England ministers and theologians who aligned themselves with the New Divinity movement. Conforti suggests that careful analysis of this group, including considerations of their educational, economic, and social backgrounds, will enable subsequent interpreters to better understand the development of Edwardseanism and its relationship to nineteenth-century social reform.

Conforti's volume is an intellectual biography similar in genre to Mead's *Nathaniel W. Taylor* and Marie Caskey's *Chariot of Fire: Religion and the Beecher Family.* Such studies greatly enhance the historiography of the period. Unfortunately, however, a host of major religious figures of the period, from Whitefield to Dwight and from Finney to Hodge, have not been as well served.

The theological ferment which fostered the New Divinity movement produced other theological realignments within New England Congregationalism. The complex development of Edwardseanism centered on Yale, but New England's other premier center of theology, Harvard, was also the setting of a new movement. In 1803, the death of David Tappan—a moderate Calvinist—left the Hollis Professorship of Divinity vacant. Two years of bitter infighting among Harvard's leaders followed, a political and theological battle which was resolved with the appointment of Henry Ware, an avowed Unitarian. With a liberal in Harvard's most prestigious chair of theology, and with the subsequent flight of many of Harvard's orthodox professors to the newly formed seminary at Andover, the nation's oldest institution of higher learning fell to the Unitarians.

The development of Unitarianism in America, a story that reaches back at least to the Great Awakening, has been analyzed in Conrad Wright's *The Beginnings of Unitarianism in America.* Wright ably traces the history of American Arminianism—the target of much of Jonathan Edwards's work—and indicates how the anti-trinitarian party coalesced and developed over time. Though Wright only treated the roots of Unitarian thinking, ending his narrative at the point of the Harvard takeover, other scholars have explored the movement's subsequent development. Daniel Walker Howe's *The Uni-*

tarian Conscience: Harvard Moral Philosophy, 1805–1861, for instance, claims to be neither a denominational history of Unitarianism, nor an institutional study of Harvard itself. Sensitive to the ethical dilemmas faced by unitarian moralists, particularly the question of slavery, Howe offers a fine account of the theological mind of this, perhaps New England's most prolific movement. Unitarian contributions to the development of American theology and belles lettres, as well as the emergence of the Bostonian Unitarian elite all find ample treatment in Howe's work.

Howe also touches on one of the most fascinating issues of the period, that of the political alignments of the Unitarians. With the exception of a group of successful merchants from Salem, New England Unitarians were Federalist nearly to a man, a fact that suggests an interesting case study in the history of the American church-state question. As has been noted, the historiography of the period has focused on the vociferous religious leaders of the Standing Order, such as Timothy Dwight. Yet Dwight's vision of American godliness— best understood as a total religious outlook, defined through social, political, and cultural parameters—obviously defined Unitarianism as a species of infidelity. Thus Dwight was forced to exclude his political allies, the Unitarians, from his religious account of a virtuous America.

But the paradox does not end there. To further complicate matters, the revivalist tradition which formed a part of the Standing Order—and which was very strong in Dwight and Beecher—was also very evident within New England's separatist traditions. But these products of revivalism, especially the Baptists, were themselves energetic Republican partisans. Thus, many evangelicals who shared Dwight's religious program for the nation, became his political enemies. These lines of fracture within New England's Standing Order, though treated by Howe and others, represent areas of inquiry that deserve further scholarly attention.

THE DISASTER OF DISESTABLISHMENT

A second vignette from Beecher's *Autobiography*, focusing on events that occurred almost two decades after the Yale revival, further popularized Beecher's interpretation of the religious and political events of the day. In 1818, a year after Dwight's death, Congregationalism was officially disestablished in Connecticut. Though Massachusetts Congregationalism would maintain its privileged position for another fifteen years, the fall of Connecticut's Standing Order marked the start of the era in which the modern interpretation of the separation of church and state was dominant.

Lyman Beecher was horrified at the news of the demise of the Standing Order. One of his children reported "seeing father, the day after the election, sitting on one of the old-fashioned rush-bottomed kitchen chairs, his head drooping on his breast, his arms hanging down." When asked what troubled him, Beecher answered, "The Church of God." Of that fateful day he would say, "It was as dark a day as ever I saw. The odium thrown upon the ministry was inconceivable. The injury done to the cause of Christ, as we then supposed, was irreparable" (p. 252).

Beecher's conclusion that American Christianity had been dealt a near-fatal blow may appear to be nothing more than the exaggerated grief of a defeated man. Yet to the Federalists, Republicans, Congregationalists, Dissenters, and skeptics who actually waged the political battle, the stakes were high indeed. The disestablishment question was hotly debated in state and local politics, making it the most prominent political issue of the period.

Several monographs offer particularly useful discussions of disestablishment from the perspective of New England Federalism. Richard Purcell's *Connecticut in Transition, 1775–1818*, first published in 1918, remains a fine account of the fall of Connecticut's Standing Order. Beginning with descriptions of Connecticut's religious minorities, Purcell outlined the complaints of these dissident groups, giving particular attention to Connecticut's notorious certificate law. This legislation stipulated that Congregational churches receive financial support from local tax coffers and required dissenting congregations to depend entirely on private charitable gifts. Connecticut's dissenters were thus forced to support two religions: their taxes kept the Congregationalist hegemony intact while their own institutions were supported by their personal gifts. The bitterness engendered by the certificate law fueled further resentment over other political and economic privileges of the Standing Order. These grievances formed the backdrop against which Purcell told the complex story of the rising opposition to Connecticut Federalism and the political events which finally led to its demise.

In *Federalists in Dissent, Imagery and Ideology in Jeffersonian America*, Linda K. Kerber examined the Federalist world view at the opening of the nineteenth century. Kerber claimed that Federalist imagery found its center of gravity in Augustan Rome. Horatio Greenough's statue of Washington robed in a Roman toga symbolized the Federalist mind: like Augustus, the Federalists would create a civilization and build an empire fraught with religious symbolism.

Having sketched the outlines of Federalist ideology, Kerber explored a series of cultural issues over which the Federalists and Republicans were diametrically opposed: slavery, the method of scientific inquiry, educational and legal philosophy, and the institutions of social order. Kerber's analysis of these circumscribed arenas of conflict led her to a larger observation about the breadth of the Federalist vision of America. In the words of one Federalist newspaper, "There is . . . a strong connection between literature, morality, politics and religion" (p. 173). The Standing Order offered citizens an integrated way of life, not merely a set of disparate political, social, and religious commitments. Given this insight, the magnitude of Beecher's sense of loss becomes far more intelligible.

Linda Kerber appraised the Federalist ethos dialectically, in relation to its Republican nemesis. But David H. Fischer's *The Revolution of American Conservatism: The Federalist Party in the Era of Jeffersonian Democracy* assessed the development of distinct ideologies within Federalism itself. Fischer found that Federalism underwent significant changes in response to the political tactics of the Jeffersonians. He argued that these shifts corresponded to the differences between "Old School Federalists" such as George Cabot and John Jay and "Young Federalists" like Harrison Gray Otis and John Quincy Adams.

Fischer found one trend among the Federalists that is particularly noteworthy for historians of religion. The "younger generation of Federalist leaders . . . returned to Christianity, with an evangelical enthusiasm rarely in evidence among gentlemen of the old school" (p. 48). Yet contrary to the "revival to the rescue thesis," Young Federalists converted to Christianity for strictly personal reasons, with little regard for the political ramifications. "In a world where class conflict was added to class consciousness, where the acceleration of change was a constant, evangelical Christianity was a haven of assurance, a sanctuary from social strife" (p. 49).

Religious alignments among the Republicans are the subject of another large literature. Though less concerned with political developments, several studies explore the relationship between orthodox Christianity and seventeenth- and eighteenth-century skepticism. Two monographs, both published in the 1930s, examined the development of the "rational religion" to which many Republicans adhered. G. Adolph Koch's *Republican Religion: The American Revolution and the Cult of Reason* tells the story "of the rise, the short-lived triumph, and the collapse of an intellectual movement reflected on this side of the Atlantic in the last three decades of the eighteenth century" (p. 292). The Republican political victories in Connecticut and Massachusetts notwithstanding, Koch argued that the victor of the religious confrontation between Republican reason and Christian revelation was New England orthodoxy. In the years that Standing Order ministers were lamenting the decline of orthodoxy, their system—unbeknownst to them—was gaining ascendency over rational religion. From Koch's point of view, the dismal prognosis articulated in Dwight's *The Triumph of Infidelity* was inaccurate: traditional Christianity had overcome its first real challenge. Though more sensitive to the intellectual development of rational religion, much the same assessment was rendered by Herbert M. Morais in *Deism in Eighteenth Century America.*

The political histories of Purcell, Kerber, and Fischer, on one hand, and the religious studies of Koch and Morais, on the other, left a curious lacuna in the history of disestablishment in New England. The former authors mapped the political decline of the Federalists, the latter, their long-term religious ascendency. Missing was a detailed account of the groups which embraced evangelical Christianity and yet voted with the Republicans.

In 1971, William G. McLoughlin's *New England Dissent, 1630–1833: The Baptists and the Separation of Church and State* filled this gap. In two volumes, totaling nearly 1300 pages, McLoughlin charted the history of the American Baptist movement. Beginning with the rise of antipaedobaptist theology, he traced the history of the Baptists and their allies—the Quakers and Anglicans—through the Puritan commonwealth, the Great Awakening, the Revolution, and the era of disestablishment.

The broad aim of McLoughlin's work was to explain "how two self-images—the Puritan and the Evangelical protest—came into conflict in the middle of the eighteenth century and how the latter gradually replaced the former" (p. xx). In rendering his account, he offered several revisionistic insights into the complex development of the Baptist movement in America. Traditional interpretations argued that the modern notion of the separation of church and state sprang from one of two sources; the rationalistic spirit of the Enlightenment as mediated through Jefferson and Madison, or the radical Anabaptist tradition as conceived in the Protestant Reformation. McLoughlin argued, however, that religious liberty was the result of innumerable local confrontations. The town meeting and the congregational meeting, not the rarified atmosphere of philosophical debate, were the real locus of American religious liberty.

According to McLoughlin, local circumstances occasioned not only the theory of religious toleration, but also its political implementation. Traditionally, historians have fallen into two distinct schools of interpretation concerning the Baptists' self-conscious attempts to secure religious liberty. Many, including Perry Miller, argued that American religious dissenters did not win their liberty, but had it thrust upon them by the democratic ethos of the early national period. Other historians, many of whom wrote from within the Baptist tradition, argued that the Baptists achieved liberty by means of direct political action. McLoughlin steered a middle course between these alternatives, arguing that Baptist liberties "were neither so fortuitous as Perry Miller implied nor so triumphant and inevitable as his predecessors had said" (p. 1277).

Although Lyman Beecher played only a small part in McLoughlin's narrative, *New England Dissent*, perhaps more than any other work, helps us understand the political dimensions of his mythology. Its description of the broad-based struggle to overthrow the Standing Order shows how disastrous disestablishment was to the Congregational mind. Sitting in his kitchen on that fateful day, Beecher understood perfectly the parameters of his defeat: the Standing Order had not merely suffered a temporary setback, it lay in ruins, never to rise again. Puritanism and all its cultural relics had been replaced by the vibrant new ethos of American evangelicalism.

VOLUNTARISM AND DENOMINATIONALISM

Despite the "odium thrown upon the ministry," Lyman Beecher lived to experience the surprising revivification of New England Congregationalism. Within days of disestablishment in Connecticut, Beecher's sense of loss was transformed to an almost euphoric feeling of victory. As he put it, though "he suffered what no tongue can tell," he soon discovered that disestablishment was "the best thing that ever happened to the State of Connecticut. It cut the churches loose from dependence on state support. It threw them wholly on their own resources and on God." Though it initially appeared to Beecher that ministers had "lost their influence," he would later claim, "the fact is, they have gained. By voluntary efforts, societies, missions, and revivals, they exert a deeper influence than ever they could by queues and shoe-buckles, and cocked hats, and gold-headed canes" (pp. 252–253).

The first two Beecher vignettes described in this essay were skewed along the lines of Beecher's partisanship. In the first case, Beecher's attachment to President Dwight and his fear of European infidelity led him to enlarge the significance of the Yale revival. In the second, his fondness for ministerial privilege and his fear of disestablishment caused him to lament their final demise. But in this third scene, Beecher seems to have accurately assessed the situation and realistically interpreted its significance. In an era of voluntarism, disestablishment had cast Congregationalism into a field of determined competitors. And to Beecher's surprise, his beloved Congregationalism fared remarkably well.

The large and diversified literature assessing America's denominations—unlike the historiography of revivalism and disestablishment—has developed in something of a concentric pattern. At the center of this genre stand scores of denominational histories. Many of these works—Charles Hodge's *Constitutional History of the Presbyterian Church*, for example—were written from within the tradition they attempted to assess, making them liable to the partisan interpretation that plagued Beecher's recollections. But despite their natural biases such works represent invaluable sources of detailed information about particular traditions. Moreover, the prevalence of periodic self-examinations often allows readers to detect interesting trends and developments within a denomination's self-consciousness.

Surrounding this core of primary source documentation is a body of secondary interpretation that relates developments within particular denominations to larger cultural issues. Much of this work has appeared in periodicals that are dedicated to particular traditions, such as the *Journal of Presbyterian History*, the *Historical Magazine of the Protestant Episcopal Church, Methodist History*, or the *Wesleyan Theological Journal*. In addition to these subject-specific journals, monographs such as George Marsden's *The Evangelical Mind and the New School Presbyterian Experience*, and the previously cited works of Howe, Wright, and McLoughlin offer broader treatments of social and cultural issues within particular denominations.

To a remarkable degree, the internal history of America's major denominations can be traced by examining their respective theological seminaries. Doctrinal developments among New England Congregationalists and middle-states Presbyterians have been assessed by studies of seminaries that promulgated variations of the Reformed theological tradition. These include Leonard Woods's *History of Andover Theological Seminary*, Roland Bainton's *Yale and the Ministry*, George H. Williams's *Harvard Divinity School*, Mark Noll's *The Princeton Theology* and Lefferts Loetscher's *The Broadening Church*. Although the Lutherans played a negligible role in New England, the prodigious writings of two German-Reformed theologians, John W. Nevin and Philip Schaff, led to important assessments of cognate schools of theology. James Hastings Nichols's *The Mercersburg Theology*, proves helpful in this respect.

The outside circle of this concentric pattern is comprised of a body of literature that examines denominationalism as a unique religious phenomenon. Comprised mostly of articles, this literature has been collected by Russell E. Richey in a useful reader entitled *Denominationalism*.

Winthrop S. Hudson's "Denominationalism as a Basis of Ecumenicity: A Seventeenth-Century Conception," Richey claimed, typifies the theological appraisal of denominationalism. Hudson argued that doctrinal differences between seventeenth-century Anglicans and English Independents should be viewed as the starting point of Protestant denominationalism. Regarding this process of differentiation as largely positive, Hudson claimed that the participants realized that no single group could "represent the whole church of Christ" (p. 22).

Many historians, including Sidney E. Mead, found this theological analysis too simplistic. In "Denominationalism: The Shape of Protestantism in America," Mead opted for a sociological analysis of the problem. Claiming that the American denomination was neither confessional nor territorial, Mead defined a denomination as a "voluntary association of like-hearted and like-minded individuals, who are united on the basis of common beliefs for the purpose of accomplishing tangible and defined objectives," one of which was "the propagation of its point of view" (p. 291). Mead noted several tendencies—all of which are best explained in sociological terms—that conditioned American Protestantism during the critical years of its development, from 1787 to 1850. In general, Mead argued, denominations attempted to erect their ecclesiology on an archetypal New Testament model, they relied heavily on the voluntary principle and the spirit of competition, they maintained their membership by means of revivalism and recruited new members by means of extensive missionary efforts and, finally, they replaced Enlightenment rationalism with fideistic evangelical pietism.

As Richey observes, either theological or sociological approaches characterized the earliest interest in denominationalism. But subsequent efforts have combined elements of both disciplines in an attempt to offer a wholistic view of the subject. His *Denominationalism* includes several essays which have adopted this approach. Timothy L. Smith and E. Franklin Frazier treat the religious and social character of ethnic and racial communities, respectively, while essays by Fred J. Hood and Richey himself probe the social sources of denominationalism within specific theological traditions.

Lyman Beecher's mythic vision has served as a framework for countless historical reflections on the relationship between church and state in America. But Beecher's interpretive vision had a purpose. In an era when both the Republic and the Church were reconfiguring at a dizzying pace, Beecher offered a series of stable images to the popular mind. In the face of widespread insecurity, this Puritan-become-Evangelical, unconscious of the change his own life represented, distilled the complexities of history. He created and broadcast vignettes of hope: like President Dwight, godly men could still convince young people to abandon infidelity. Like the disestablished Congregationalists, self-reliant believers could, with genuine hope of success, seek to establish the Kingdom of God in New England.

With varying degrees of success, Beecher attempted to transcend the vagaries of his troubled era. In their attempts to understand the religious culture that inspired Beecher's hopes and fears, historians have met with similarly mixed success. Some, like the Beecher of the Yale revival, have examined their subject through the single lens of Christian doctrine. Their accounts, however invaluable as historical theology, lack integration with the larger

cultural context from which they are drawn. But others, more like the exul-
tant Beecher who had just discovered the religious potential of voluntarism,
have added sophisticated social and political analyses to their histories of
American religion. This broader, integrated literature provides students of
the nineteenth-century church-state issue an excellent place from which to
begin their work.

BIBLIOGRAPHY

Adams, Doug. <u>Meetinghouse to Camp Meeting: Toward a History of American Free Church Worship from 1620-1835</u>. Saratoga, Calif.: Modern Liturgy/Resources Publications, 1981.

Addison, James Thayer. <u>The Episcopal Church in the United States, 1789-1931</u>. New York: Scribners, 1951.

Ahlstrom, Sydney E. "The Religious Dimensions of American Aspiration." <u>Review of Politics</u> 38 (July 1976), 332-342.

Anderson, Philip J. "William Linns, 1752-1808: American Revolutionary and Anti-Jeffersonian." <u>Journal of Presbyterian History</u> 55 (Winter 1977), 381-394.

Andres, John A., III. <u>Rebuilding the Christian Commonwealth: New England Congregationalists and Foreign Missions, 1800-1830</u>. Lexington: University Press of Kentucky, 1976.

Bainton, Roland H. <u>Yale and the Ministry: A History of Education for the Christian Ministry at Yale from the Founding in 1701</u>. New York: Harper, 1957.

Banner, Lois W. "Presbyterians and Voluntarism in the Early Republic." <u>Journal of Presbyterian History</u> 50 (Fall 1972), 107-205.

Barnes, Clifford. <u>The Antislavery Impulse, 1830-1844</u>. New York: D. Appleton-Century Co., 1933.

Barnes, Howard A. "The Idea that Caused a War: Horace Bushnell Versus Thomas Jefferson." <u>Journal of Church and State</u> 16 (Winter 1974), 73-83.

Beam, Christopher M. "Millennialism and American Nationalism, 1740-1800." <u>Journal of Presbyterian History</u> 54 (Spring 1976), 182-199.

Beasley, James R. "Emerging Republicanism and the Standing Order: The Appropriation Act Controversy in Connecticut." William and Mary Quarterly, 3d ser., 29 (October 1972), 587-610.

Beaver, R. Pierce. "American Missionary Efforts to Influence Government Indian Policy." Journal of Church and State 5 (May 1963), 77-94.

Beaver, R. Pierce. "Church, State and the Indians: Indian Missionaries in the New Nation." Journal of Church and State 4 (May 1962), 11-30.

Beecher, Lyman. The Autobiography of Lyman Beecher. Edited by Barbara M. Cross. 2 vols. Cambridge, Mass.: Harvard University Press, Belknap Press, 1961.

Bellah, Robert N. "Religion and Legitimation in the American Republic." Society 15 (May/June 1978), 16-23.

Benne, Robert, and Hefner, Philip. Defining America: A Christian Critique of the American Dream. Philadelphia: Westminster Press, 1974.

Berk, Stephen E. Calvinism Versus Democracy: Timothy Dwight and the Origins of American Evangelical Orthodoxy. Hamden, Conn.: Archon Books, 1974.

Birdsall, Richard D. "The Second Great Awakening and the New England Social Order." Church History 39 (September 1970), 345-364.

Bodo, John R. The Protestant Clergy and Public Issues, 1812-1848. Princeton, N.J.: Princeton University Press, 1954.

Boles, John B. The Great Revival, 1787-1805: The Origins of the Southern Evangelical Mind. Lexington: University Press of Kentucky, 1972.

Borden, Morton. "Federalists, Antifederalists, and Religious Freedom." Journal of Church and State 21 (Autumn 1979), 469-482.

Bowden, Henry Warner. "Philip Schaff and Sectarianism: The Americanization of a European Viewpoint." Journal of Church and State 8 (Winter 1966), 97-106.

Bozeman, Theodore Dwight. Protestants in an Age of Science: The Baconian Ideal and Antebellum American Religious Thought. Chapel Hill: University of North Carolina Press, 1977.

Brauer, Jerald C. "Conversion From Puritanism to Revivalism." Journal of Religion 58 (July 1978), 227-243.

Brauer, Jerald C. Protestantism in America: A Narrative History. Philadelphia: Westminster Press, 1953.

Brauer, Jerald C. A Reinterpretation of American Church History. Chicago: University of Chicago Press, 1968.

Breitenbach, William. "The Consistent Calvinism of the New Divinity Movement." William and Mary Quarterly, 3d ser., 41 (April 1984), 241-264.

Breitenbach, William. "Piety and Moralism: Edwards and the New Divinity." Unpublished essay delivered at the Conference on Jonathan Edwards held at Wheaton College, Wheaton, Illinois, October 1984.

Breitenbach, William. "Unregenerate Doings: Selflessness and Selfishness in New Divinity Theology." American Quarterly 34 (Winter 1982), 479-502.

Briceland, Alan V. "The Philadelphia Aurora, the New England Illuminati, and the Election of 1800." Pennsylvania Magazine of History and Biography 100 (January 1976), 3-36.

Bruce, Dickson D., Jr. And They All Sang Hallelujah: Plain-Folk Camp-Meeting Religion, 1800-1845. Knoxville: University of Tennessee Press, 1974.

Bumsted, J. M. "Religion and American Culture." Canadian Review of American Studies 11 (Spring 1980), 49-56.

Butler, Jon. "Enthusiasm Described and Decried: The Great Awakening as Interpretive Fiction." Journal of American History 69 (September 1982), 305-325.

Calhoun, Daniel H. Professional Lives in America: Structure and Aspiration. Cambridge, Mass.: Harvard University Press, 1965.

Cartwright, Peter. The Autobiography of Peter Cartwright. Edited by Charles L. Wallis. New York: Abingdon Press, 1956.

Caskey, Marie. Chariot of Fire: Religion and the Beecher Family. New Haven: Yale University Press, 1978.

Cassara, Ernest, ed. Universalism in America: A Documentary History. Boston: Beacon Press, 1971.

Cecil, Anthony C., Jr. The Theological Development of Edwards Amasa Park, Last of the Consistent Calvinists. Missoula, Mont.: Scholars Press, 1974.

Cherry, Conrad. "The Structure of Organic Thinking: Horace
   Bushnell's Approach to Language, Nature, and Nation."
   Journal of the American Academy of Religion 40 (March 1972),
   3-20.

Cherry, Conrad, ed. God's New Israel: Religious
   Interpretations of American Destiny. Englewood Cliffs,
   N.J.: Prentice-Hall, 1971.

Clark, Clifford E., Jr. Henry Ward Beecher: Spokesman for a
   Middle Class America. Urbana: University of Illinois Press,
   1978.

Clebsch, William. From Sacred to Profane in America: The Role
   of Religion in American History. New York: Harper and Row,
   1968.

Cleveland, Catharine C. The Great Revival of the West, 1797-
   1805. Chicago: University of Chicago Press, 1916.

Cobb, Sanford H. The Rise of Religious Liberty in America.
   New York: Macmillan Company, 1902.

Cole, Charles C., Jr. The Social Ideas of the Northern
   Evangelists, 1826-1860. New York: Columbia University
   Press, 1954.

Conforti, Joseph A. "The Rise of the New Divinity in Western
   Massachusetts, 1740-1800." History of Western Massachusetts
   8 (January 1980) 37-47.

Conforti, Joseph A. Samuel Hopkins and the New Divinity
   Movement: Calvinism, the Congregational Ministry, and Reform
   in New England Between the Great Awakenings. Grand Rapids:
   Eerdmans, 1981.

Cott, Nancy F. "Young Women in the Second Great Awakening in
   New England." Feminist Studies 3 (Spring 1975), 15-29.

Cross, Whitney R. The Burned-Over District: The Social and
   Intellectual History of Enthusiastic Religion in Western New
   York, 1800-1850. Ithaca, N.Y.: Cornell University Press,
   1950.

Cushing, John D. "Notes on Disestablishment in Massachusetts,
   1780-1833." William and Mary Quarterly, 3d ser., 26 (April
   1969), 169-190.

Dearmont, Nelson S. "Federalist Attitudes Toward Governmental
   Secrecy in the Age of Jefferson." Historian 37 (February
   1975), 222-240.

Deschamps, Margaret Burr. "The Presbyterians in the South
   Atlantic States, 1801-1861." Journal of Presbyterian
   History 30 (September 1952), 193-207.

Deutsch, Eberhard P. "The Real Origin of the Secession
	Movement." American Bar Association Journal 55 (December
	1969), 1134-1140.

Dexter, Franklin B. "Student Life at Yale College Under the
	First President Dwight, 1795-1817." American Antiquarian
	Society, Proceedings, n. s. 27 (October 1917), 318-335.

Drakeman, Donald L. "Religion and the Republic: James Madison
	and the First Amendment." Journal of Church and State 25
	(Autumn 1983), 427-445.

[Dwight, Timothy.] The Triumph of Infidelity. Printed in the
	World, 1788.

East, Robert A. "Economic Development and New England
	Federalism, 1803-1814." New England Quarterly 10 (September
	1937), 430-446.

Elliott, Emory. Revolutionary Writers: Literature and
	Authority in the New Republic, 1725-1810. New York: Oxford
	University Press, 1982.

Engel, J. Ronald. "Sidney Mead's Tragic Theology of the
	Republic." Journal of the American Academy of Religion 44
	(March 1976), 155-165.

Ferm, Robert L. "Jonathan Edwards the Younger and the Plan of
	Union of 1801." Journal of Presbyterian History 42
	(December 1964), 286-292.

Ferm, Robert L. Jonathan Edwards the Younger, 1745-1801:
	Colonial Pastor. Grand Rapids: Eerdmans, 1976.

Finney, Charles G. Memoirs of Charles G. Finney. New York: A.
	S. Barnes, 1876.

Fischer, David H. The Revolution of American Conservatism: The
	Federalist Party in the Era of Jeffersonian Democracy. New
	York: Harper and Row, 1965.

Foster, C. I. An Errand of Mercy: The Evangelical United
	Front, 1790-1837. Chapel Hill: University of North Carolina
	Press, 1960.

Foster, Frank H. A Genetic History of the New England
	Theology. Chicago: University of Chicago Press, 1907.

Fox, Dixon Ryan. "The Protestant Counter-Reformation in
	America." New York History 16 (January 1935), 19-35.

Frazier, E. Franklin. The Negro Church in America. New York:
	Schocken Books, 1964.

French, Roderick A. "Elihu Palmer, Radical Deist, Radical Republican: A Reconsideration of American Free Thought." Studies in Eighteenth Century Culture 8 (1978), 87-108.

Gabriel, Ralph H. "Evangelical Religion and Popular Romanticism in Early Nineteenth-Century America." Church History 19 (March 1950), 34-47.

Goen, Clarence C. "Broken Churches, Broken Nation." Church History 52 (March 1983), 21-35.

Goen, Clarence C. Revivalism and Separatism in New England, 1740-1800: Strict Congregationalists and Separate Baptists in the Great Awakening. New Haven: Yale University Press, 1962.

Good, Douglas L. "The Christian Nation in the Mind of Timothy Dwight." Fides et Historia 7 (1974), 1-18.

Greene, Evarts. "A Puritan Counter-Reformation." American Antiquarian Society, Proceedings, n. s. 42 (April 1932), 17-46.

Greene, Evarts. Religion and the State: The Making and Testing of an American Tradition. New York: New York University Press, 1941.

Greene, M. Louise. The Development of Religious Liberty in Connecticut. Boston and New York: Houghton, Mifflin, and Co., 1905.

Grenz, Stanley J. "Isaac Backus and Religious Liberty." Foundations 22 (October 1979), 352-360.

Gribbin, William. The Churches Militant: The War of 1812 and American Religion. New Haven: Yale University Press, 1973.

Gribbin, William. "The Covenant Transformed: The Jeremiad Tradition and the War of 1812." Church History 40 (September 1971), 297-305.

Gribbin, William. "Republican Religion and the American Churches in the Early National Period." Historian 35 (November 1972), 61-74.

Gribbin, William. "The War of 1812 and American Presbyterianism: Religion and Politics During the Second War With Britain." Journal of Presbyterian History 47 (December 1969), 320-339.

Griffin, Clifford S. "Religious Benevolence as Social Control, 1815-1860." Mississippi Valley Historical Review 44 (December 1957), 423-444.

Griffin, Clifford S. Their Brother's Keeper: Moral Stewardship
    in the United States, 1800-1865. New Brunswick, N.J.:
    Rutgers University Press, 1960.

Hamilton, William B. "Preachers and Professionalism." History
    of Education Quarterly 19 (Winter 1979), 515-522.

Hammond, John L. The Politics of Benevolence: Revival Religion
    and American Voting Behavior. Norwood, N.J.: Ablex, 1979.

Hammond, John L. "Revivals, Consensus, and American Political
    Culture." Journal of the American Academy of Religion 46
    (September 1978), 293-314.

Handy, Robert T. A Christian America: Protestant Hopes and
    Historical Realities. New York: Columbia University Press,
    1971.

Handy, Robert T., ed. Religion in the American Experiment: The
    Pluralistic Style. Columbia, S.C.: University of South
    Carolina Press, 1972.

Haroutunian, Joseph. Piety Versus Moralism: The Passing of the
    New England Theology. New York: Henry Holt and Co., 1932.

Hatch, Nathan O. "The Christian Movement and the Demand for a
    Theology of the People." Journal of American History 67
    (December 1980), 545-567.

Hatch, Nathan O. The Sacred Cause of Liberty: Republican
    Thought and the Millennium in Revolutionary New England.
    New Haven: Yale University Press, 1977.

Henry, Stuart C. Unvanquished Puritan: A Portrait of Lyman
    Beecher. Grand Rapids: Eerdmans, 1973.

Hodge, Charles. The Constitutional History of the Presbyterian
    Church in the United States of America. Philadelphia:
    Presbyterian Board of Publication and Sabbath-School Work,
    1851.

Hodge, Charles. "Professor Park and The Princeton Review."
    The Biblical Repertory and Princeton Review 23 (October
    1851), 674-695.

Hoffecker, W. Andrew. Piety and the Princeton Theologians:
    Archibald Alexander, Charles Hodge, and Benjamin Warfield.
    Grand Rapids: Baker Book House, 1981.

Hofstadter, Richard. The Paranoid Style in American Politics,
    And Other Essays. New York: Knopf, 1965.

Holifield, E. Brooks. The Gentlemen Theologians: American
    Theology in Southern Culture, 1795-1860. Durham, N.C.: Duke
    University Press, 1978.

Hood, Fred J. "The American Reformed Tradition in African
     Colonization and Missions." _Journal of Church and State_ 19
     (Autumn 1977), 539-555.

Hood, Fred J. _Reformed America: The Middle and Southern
     States, 1783-1837_. University, Ala.: University of Alabama
     Press, 1980.

Hovencamp, Herbert. _Science and Religion in America, 1800-
     1860_. Philadelphia: University of Pennsylvania Press, 1978.

Howard, Leon. _The Connecticut Wits_. Chicago: University of
     Chicago Press, 1943.

Howe, Daniel Walker. _The Unitarian Conscience: Harvard Moral
     Philosophy, 1805-1861_. Cambridge, Mass.: Harvard University
     Press, 1970.

Howe, Mark DeWolfe. _The Garden and the Wilderness: Religion
     and Government in American Constitutional History_. Chicago:
     University of Chicago Press, 1965.

Hudson, Winthrop S. _The Great Tradition of the American
     Churches_. New York: Harper and Brothers, 1953.

Hudson, Winthrop S. "The Issue of Church and State: A
     Historical Perspective." _Religion in Life_ 46 (Fall 1977),
     278-288.

Hudson, Winthrop S. "The Quest for Freedom Within the Church
     in Colonial America." _Journal of Church and State_ 3 (May
     1961), 6-15.

Huntly, William B. "Jefferson's Public and Private Religion."
     South Atlantic Quarterly 79 (July 1980), 286-301.

Hutchinson, William R. _The Transcendentalist Ministers: Church
     Reform in the New England Renaissance_. New Haven: Yale
     University Press, 1959.

Johnson, James E. "Charles G. Finney and Oberlin
     Perfectionism." _Journal of Presbyterian History_ 46 (March
     1968), 42-56; (June 1968), 128-138.

Johnson, James E. "Charles G. Finney and a Theology of
     Revivalism." _Church History_ 38 (September 1969), 338-358.

Johnson, Paul E. _A Shopkeeper's Millennium: Society and
     Revivals in Rochester, New York, 1815-1837_. New York: Hill
     and Wang, 1979.

Keller, Charles Roy. _The Second Great Awakening in
     Connecticut_. New Haven: Yale University Press, 1942.

Kerber, Linda K. Federalists in Dissent: Imagery and Ideology
    in Jeffersonian America. Ithaca, N.Y.: Cornell University
    Press, 1970.

Kessler, Sanford. "Tocqueville on Civil Religion and Liberal
    Democracy." Journal of Politics 39 (February 1977), 119-
    146.

Ketchem, Ralph L. "James Madison and Religion--A New
    Hypothesis." Journal of Presbyterian History 38 (June
    1960), 65-90.

Koch, Gustav Adolph. Republican Religion: The American
    Revolution and the Cult of Reason. New York: H. Holt and
    Company, 1933.

Kohn, Richard H. Eagle and Sword: The Federalists and the
    Creation of the Military Establishment in America, 1783-
    1802. New York: Free Press, 1975.

LaFontaine, Charles V. "God and Nation in Selected United
    States Presidential Inaugural Addresses, 1789-1945."
    Journal of Church and State 18 (Winter 1976), 39-60; (Autumn
    1976), 503-522.

Lane, Belden C. "Presbyterian Republicanism: Miller and the
    Eldership as an Answer to Lay Tensions." Journal of
    Presbyterian History 56 (Winter 1978), 311-324.

Leon, D. H. "'The Dogma of the Sovereignty of the People':
    Alexis de Tocqueville's Religion in America." Journal of
    Church and State 14 (Spring 1972), 279-295.

Lewis, W. David. "The Reformer as Conservative: Protestant
    Counter Subversion in the Early Republic." In The
    Development of American Culture, edited by S. Cohen and L.
    Ratner. Englewood Cliffs, N.J.: Prentice-Hall, 1970.

Lippy, Charles H. "The 1780 Massachusetts Constitution:
    Religious Establishment or Civil Religion." Journal of
    Church and State 20 (Autumn 1978), 533-549.

Littell, Franklin H. "The Basis of Religious Liberty in
    American History." Journal of Church and State 6 (Autumn
    1964), 314-332.

Littell, Franklin H. From State Church to Pluralism: A
    Protestant Interpretation of Religion in American History.
    New York: Macmillan Company, 1971.

Loetscher, Lefferts A. The Broadening Church: A Study of
    Theological Issues in the Presbyterian Church since 1869.
    Philadelphia: University of Pennsylvania Press, 1957.

Loveland, Anne C. Southern Evangelicals and the Social Order, 1800-1860. Baton Rouge: Louisiana State University Press, 1980.

McClurkin, Paul T. "Presbyterianism and New England Congregationalism." Journal of Presbyterian History 31 (December 1953), 245-256; 32 (June 1954), 109-114.

Maclear, J. F. "The Republic and the Millennium." In Religion in American History: Interpretive Essays, edited by John M. Mulder and John F. Wilson, 181-198. Englewood Cliffs, N.J.: Prentice-Hall, 1978.

McLoughlin, William G. "The Balkcom Case (1782) and the Pietistic Theory of the Separation of Church and State." William and Mary Quarterly, 3d ser., 24 (April 1967), 267-283.

McLoughlin, William G. Isaac Backus and the American Pietistic Tradition. Boston: Little, Brown and Company, 1967.

McLoughlin, William G. "Isaac Backus and the Separation of Church and State in America." American Historical Review 73 (June 1968), 1392-1413.

McLoughlin, William G. Modern Revivalism: Charles Grandison Finney to Billy Graham. New York: Ronald Press, 1959.

McLoughlin, William G. New England Dissent, 1630-1883: The Baptists and the Separation of Church and State. 2 vols. Cambridge, Mass.: Harvard University Press, 1971.

McLoughlin, William G. Revivals, Awakenings, and Reform: An Essay on Religion and Social Change in America, 1607-1977. Chicago: University of Chicago Press, 1978.

Marsden, George M. The Evangelical Mind and the New School Presbyterian Experience: A Case Study of Thought and Theology in Nineteenth-Century America. New Haven: Yale University Press, 1970.

Marsden, George M. Fundamentalism and American Culture: The Shaping of Twentieth Century Evangelicalism. New York: Oxford University Press, 1980.

Marsden, George. "Kingdom and Nation: New School Presbyterian Millennialism in the Civil War Era." Journal of Presbyterian History 46 (December 1968), 254-273.

Marty, Martin E. "Living with Establishment and Disestablishment in Nineteenth-Century Anglo-America." Journal of Church and State 18 (Winter 1980), 61-77.

Mathews, Donald G. Religion in the Old South. Chicago: University of Chicago Press, 1977.

Mathews, Donald G. "The Second Great Awakening as an
   Organizing Process, 1780-1830." In Religion in American
   History: Interpretive Essays, edited by John M. Mulder and
   John F. Wilson, 199-217. Englewood Cliffs, N.J.: Prentice-
   Hall, 1978.

Mead, Sidney E. "Denominationalism: The Shape of Protestantism
   in America." Church History 23 (December 1954), 241-320.

Mead, Sidney E. "From Coercion to Persuasion; Another Look at
   the Rise of Religious Liberty and the Emergence of
   Denominationalism." Church History 25 (December 1956), 317-
   337.

Mead, Sidney E. "Lyman Beecher and Connecticut Orthodoxy's
   Campaign Against Unitarianism." Church History 9 (1940),
   218-234.

Mead, Sidney E. Nathaniel W. Taylor, 1786-1858: A Connecticut
   Liberal. Chicago: University of Chicago Press, 1942.

Mead, Sidney E. "The Nation with the Soul of a Church."
   Church History 36 (September 1967), 262-283.

Mead, Sidney E. "Neither Church nor State: Reflection on James
   Madison's 'Line of Separation.'" Journal of Church and
   State 10 (Autumn 1968), 349-363.

Mead, Sidney E. The Old Religion in the Brave New World:
   Reflections on the Relation Between Christianity and the
   Republic. Berkeley: University of California Press, 1977.

Mead, Sidney E. "Religious Pluralism and the Character of the
   Republic." Soundings 61 (Fall 1978), 306-327.

Mead, Sidney E. "The Theology of the Republic and the Orthodox
   Mind." Journal of the American Academy of Religion 44
   (March 1976), 105-113.

Mead, Sidney E. "Thomas Jefferson's 'Fair Experiment'--
   Religious Liberty." Religion in Life 23 (Autumn 1954), 566-
   579.

Meyer, Jacob C. Church and State in Massachusetts from 1740 to
   1833: A Chapter in the History of the Development of
   Individual Freedom. Cleveland: Western Reserve University
   Press, 1930.

Miller, Perry. "The Contribution of the Protestant Churches to
   Religious Liberty in Colonial America." Church History 4
   (March 1935), 57-66.

Miller, Perry. The Life of the Mind in America From the
   Revolution to the Civil War. New York: Harcourt, Brace and
   World, 1965.

Miyakawa, T. Scott. _Protestants and Pioneers: Individualism and Conformity on the American Frontier_. Chicago: University of Chicago Press, 1964.

Moore, LeRoy. "Sidney Mead's Understanding of America." _Journal of the American Academy of Religion_ 44 (March 1976), 133-154.

Morais, Herbert M. _Deism in Eighteenth-Century America_. New York: Columbia University Press, 1934.

Morgan, Edmund S. "Ezra Stiles and Timothy Dwight." Massachusetts Historical Society, _Proceedings_ 72 (1963), 101-117.

Morrison, Howard Alexander. "The Finney Takeover and the Second Great Awakening During the Oneida Revivals of 1825-1827." _New York History_ 59 (January 1978), 27-53.

Nash, Gary. "The American Clergy and the French Revolution." _William and Mary Quarterly_, 3d ser., 22 (July 1965), 392-412.

Nelson, William E. _Dispute and Conflict Resolution in Plymouth County, Massachusetts, 1725-1825_. Chapel Hill: University of North Carolina Press, 1981.

Nichols, James Hastings. _Democracy and the Churches_. Philadelphia: Westminster Press, 1951.

Nichols, James Hastings, ed. _The Mercersburg Theology_. New York: Oxford University Press, 1966.

Niebuhr, H. Richard. _The Kingdom of God in America_. Hamden, Conn.: Shoe String Press, 1956.

Niebuhr, H. Richard. _The Social Sources of Denominationalism_. Hamden, Conn.: Shoe String Press, 1956.

Noll, Mark A. "Moses Mather (Old Calvinist) and the Evolution of Edwardseanism." _Church History_ 49 (September 1980), 273-285.

Noll, Mark A. "Protestant Theology and Social Order in Antebellum America." _Religious Studies Review_ 8 (April 1982), 133-142.

Noll, Mark A., ed. _The Princeton Theology: 1812-1921_. Grand Rapids: Baker Book House, 1983.

O'Brien, Charles F. "The Religious Issue in the Presidential Campaign of 1800." _Essex Institute Historical Collections_ 107 (January 1971), 82-93.

Ostrander, Gilman M. "New England Religions: Unitranscendentalism and Presbygationalism." *Canadian Review of American Studies* 11 (Spring 1980), 57-63.

Pearson, Samuel C., Jr. "From Church to Denomination: American Congregationalism in the Nineteenth Century." *Church History* 38 (March 1969), 67-87.

Pearson, Samuel C., Jr. "Nature's God: A Reassessment of the Religion of the Founding Fathers." *Religion in Life* 46 (Summer 1977), 152-165.

Pickman, Clifford Deborah. *Mine Eyes Have Seen the Glory: A Biography of Julia Ward Howe*. Boston: Little, Brown, and Co., Inc., 1979.

Pope, Earl A. "The Rise of the New Haven Theology." *Journal of Presbyterian History* 44 (March 1966), 24-44; (June 1966), 106-121.

Pope, Robert G. "The Myth of Declension." In *Religion in American History: Interpretive Essays*, edited by John M. Mulder and John F. Wilson, 45-56. Englewood Cliffs, N.J.: Prentice-Hall, 1978.

Potts, David B. "American Colleges in the Nineteenth Century: From Localism to Denominationalism." *History of Education Quarterly* 11 (Winter 1971), 363-380.

Purcell, Richard J. *Connecticut in Transition, 1775-1818*. 2d ed. Middletown, Conn.: Wesleyan University Press, 1963.

Riley, I. Woodbridge. "The Rise of Deism at Yale College." *American Journal of Theology* 9 (July 1905), 474-483.

Ritchey, Russell E., ed. *Denominationalism*. Nashville: Abingdon Press, 1977.

Rudisill, Dorus Paul. *The Doctrine of the Atonement in Jonathan Edwards and His Successors*. New York: Poseidon Books, 1971.

Ryan, Walter A. "The Separation of Church and State in Acworth, New Hampshire." *Historical New Hampshire* 34 (Summer 1979), 143-153.

Sandeen, Ernest R. "The Distinctiveness of American Denominationalism: A Case Study for the 1846 Evangelical Alliance." *Church History* 45 (June 1976), 222-234.

Schaff, Philip. *Church and State in the United States*. Papers of the American Historical Association 2, no. 4. 1888. Reprint. New York: Arno Press, 1972.

Scott, Donald M. From Office to Profession: The New England
     Ministry, 1750-1850. Philadelphia: University of
     Pennsylvania Press, 1978.

Shiels, Richard D. "The Second Great Awakening in Connecticut:
     A Critique of the Traditional Interpretation." Church
     History 49 (December 1980), 401-415.

Shriver, George K. "Philip Schaff: America's Destiny in the
     Unfinished Reformation." Journal of Presbyterian History 50
     (Summer 1972), 148-159.

Sisson, Daniel. The American Revolution of 1800. New York:
     Knopf, 1974.

Smelser, Marshall. "The Federalist Period as an Age of
     Passion." American Quarterly 10 (Winter 1958), 391-419.

Smelser, Marshall. "The Jacobin Phrenzy: Federalism and the
     Menace of Liberty, Equality and Fraternity." Review of
     Politics 13 (October 1951), 457-482.

Smith, Elwyn A. "The Forming of a Modern American
     Denomination." Church History 31 (March 1962), 74-99.

Smith, Elwyn A. "The Fundamental Church-State Tradition of the
     Catholic Church in the United States." Church History 38
     (December 1969), 486-505.

Smith, Elwyn A. Religious Liberty in the United States: The
     Development of Church-State Thought Since the Revolutionary
     Era. Philadelphia: Fortress Press, 1972.

Smith, Timothy L. "Congregation, State, and Denomination: The
     Forming of an American Religious Structure." William and
     Mary Quarterly, 3d ser., 25 (April 1968), 155-176.

Smith, Timothy L. "Religious Denominations as Ethnic
     Communities: A Regional Case Study." Church History 35
     (June 1966), 207-226.

Smith. Timothy L. Revivalism and Social Reform: American
     Protestantism on the Eve of the Civil War. New York:
     Abingdon Press, 1957.

Smylie, James H. "Clerical Perspectives on Deism: Paine's Age
     of Reason." Eighteenth Century Studies 6 (Winter
     1972/1973), 203-220.

Smylie, James H. "Presbyterian Clergy and the Problems of
     'Dominion' in the Revolutionary Generation." Journal of
     Presbyterian History 48 (Fall 1970), 161-175.

Snyder, Alan K. "Foundations of Liberty: The Christian
     Republicanism of Timothy Dwight and Jedidiah Morse." New
     England Quarterly 56 (September 1983), 382-397.

Stauffer, Vernon. New England and the Bavarian Illuminati.
     New York: Columbia University Press, 1918.

Stephens, Bruce M. "Watchman on the Walls of Zion: Samuel
     Miller and the Christian Ministry." Journal of Presbyterian
     History 56 (Winter 1978), 293-309.

Strickland, Arthur B. The Great American Revival: A Case Study
     in the History of Evangelism with Implications for Today.
     Cincinnati: Standard Press, 1934.

Strout, Cushing. The New Heaven and the New Earth: Political
     Religion in America. New York: Harper and Row, 1974.

Sweet, Leonard I. "The View of Man Inherent in New Measure
     Revivalism." Church History 45 (June 1976), 206-221.

Sweet, Leonard I., ed. The Evangelical Tradition in America.
     Macon, Ga.: Mercer University Press, 1984.

Sweet, William Warren. The American Churches: An
     Interpretation. New York: Abingdon-Cokesbury, 1948.

Sweet, William Warren. American Culture and Religion, Six
     Essays. Dallas: Southern Methodist University Press, 1951.

Sweet, William Warren. Religion and the Development of
     American Culture, 1765-1840. New York: C. Scribner's Sons,
     1952.

Sweet, William Warren. Revivalism in America: Its Origin,
     Growth and Decline. New York: C. Scribner's Sons, 1944.

Sweet, William Warren. "The Rise of Theological Schools in
     America." Church History 6 (September 1937), 260-273.

Swift, David E. "Samuel Hopkins: Calvinist Social Concern in
     Eighteenth-Century New England." Journal of Presbyterian
     History 47 (March 1969), 31-54.

Szasz, Ferenc M. "Daniel Webster: Architect of America's Civil
     Religion." Historical New Hampshire 34 (Fall/Winter 1979),
     223-243.

Tracy, Joseph. The Great Awakening: A History of the Revival
     of Religion in the Time of Edwards and Whitefield. Boston:
     Tappan and Dennet, 1842.

Trinterud, Leonard J. The Forming of an American Tradition: A
     Re-examination of Colonial Presbyterianism. Philadelphia:
     Westminster Press, 1949.

Tuveson, Ernest Lee. Millennium and Utopia: A Study in the
    Background of the Idea of Progress. Berkeley: University of
    California Press, 1949.

Tuveson, Ernest Lee. Redeemer Nation: The Idea of America's
    Millennial Role. Chicago: University of Chicago Press,
    1968.

Tyler, Alice Felt. Freedom's Ferment: Phases of American
    Social History to 1860. Minneapolis: University of
    Minnesota Press, 1944.

Vorpahl, Ben Merchant. "Presbyterianism and the Frontier
    Hypothesis: Tradition and Modification in the American
    Garden." Journal of Presbyterian History 45 (September
    1967), 180-192.

Weddle, David L. "The Law and the Revival: A 'New Divinity'
    for the Settlements." Church History 47 (June 1978), 196-
    214.

Weisberger, Bernard A. They Gathered At The River: The Story
    of the Great Revivalists and Their Impact Upon Religion in
    America. Boston: Little, Brown and Company, 1958.

Whitehead, John S. The Separation of College and State:
    Columbia, Dartmouth, Harvard, and Yale, 1776-1876. New
    Haven: Yale University Press, 1973.

Williams, George H., ed. The Harvard Divinity School: Its
    Place in Harvard University and in American Culture.
    Boston: Beacon Press, 1954.

Williams, Peter W. "Religion and the Old Northwest: A
    Bibliographic Essay." Old Northwest 5 (Spring 1979), 57-73.

Wimberly, Ronald C., and Christenson, James A. "Civil Religion
    and Church and State." Sociology Quarterly 21 (Winter
    1980), 35-40.

Woods, Leonard. The History of Andover Theological Seminary.
    Boston: James R. Osgood and Co., 1885.

Wright, Conrad. The Beginnings of Unitarianism in America.
    Boston: Starr King Press, 1955.

Wright, Conrad. The Liberal Christians: Essays on American
    Unitarian History. Boston: Beacon Press, 1970.

Zanger, Jules. "The Pit and the Pendulum and American
    Revivalism." Religion in Life 49 (Spring 1980), 96-105.

Zuchert, Catherine. "Not by Preaching: Tocqueville on the Role
    of Religion in American Democracy." Review of Politics 43
    (April 1981), 259-280.

7

Religion and Reform in America, 1776–1860

Louis P. Masur

Beginning in the late eighteenth century, a wave of revivals jolted the towns and villages along the frontier regions of the United States. More than anything since the Great Awakening some fifty years earlier, these revivals served to revitalize religious concerns and activities among thousands of people. By the 1830s, revivalism had become a national phenomenon. Twenty years later, revivalism and evangelicalism had been woven deep into the fabric of society both in rural areas and throughout the growing metropolises of the eastern seaboard. Commonly referred to as the Second Great Awakening, this extended period of revivalistic fervor not only shaped the denominational forms of American Protestantism but also helped transform American society and culture between the Revolution and the Civil War.

If religious revivals characterized America in the first half of the nineteenth century, so too did social reform. Men and women worked in unprecedented numbers for such causes as antislavery, temperance, peace, and education. Moral reform, tract, and missionary societies abounded. Just as the voluntary association itself marked a new approach to reform, so too did some of the solutions advocated by reformers. Middle-class Americans began to tout the schoolhouse, the penitentiary, and the asylum as institutions that promised to cure those ills that seemed to threaten the republic's survival. It should come as no surprise that this impulse toward reform was inextricably bound up with religious enthusiasm.

Evangelical Protestantism and moral reform blossomed in America at the precise moment that church-state relations in the constitutional arena were being transformed. Much has been made, for example, of disestablishment in Connecticut in 1818 and Massachusetts in 1833. But if local and federal governments created a more formal separation of church and state in the nineteenth century, they had little desire to interfere with religion in other aspects of society and polity. To many Americans in the 1830s and 1840s, secular government was inseparable from the moral government of God. Reformers, motivated by deeply held religious beliefs, saw themselves as trying to make America into a more Christian nation. Toward this end they joined voluntary associations as often as churches and felt perfectly comfortable agitating against the delivery of Sunday mail or denouncing constitutional support of slavery as anti-Christian. Despite formal disestablishment at the governmental level, evangelical Protestantism and moral reform helped strengthen the connection between religion and society in nineteenth-century America.

The theological underpinnings of the revival, which would help make reform a central concern for thousands of Americans, were articulated most simply by Charles G. Finney. "God," he declared, "has made man a moral free agent." The ideas embedded in this claim carried evangelical Protestantism far enough away from the Calvinist notion of total depravity to permit individuals to exercise choice in the business of salvation. They were free to choose good over evil, virtue over sin, righteousness over depravity. Perfectibility, in this scheme, could be attained through the power of conversion. With God's moral government ruling society, the millennium seemed assured. This complex of religious beliefs not only fueled the revivals, it also energized the moral and social reforms of the day.[1]

Before turning to these consequences we must first ask what did the revivals mean? How can we understand the origins of the Second Great Awakening? Students of religion have offered a number of perspectives on this question. Some suggest that the revivals occurred in response to the spiritual unrest of the people and a general lack of religious enthusiasm throughout the nation. Yet the reality of religious torpor is difficult to distinguish from the rhetoric of the jeremiad tradition that chronically laments a dwindling of faith. Even if we could measure the relative decline in piety, such data would not help explain why revivals occur when they do or how the process of revitalization takes place.

Another interpretation, one that has the merit of trying to link the revivals to society more generally, examines evangelical Protestantism as a response to social disorder. According to this argument, Americans apparently suffered from social strain, isolation, and anomie in ways which made them ripe for mass evangelization. The problem with this thesis is that it is extremely difficult to demonstrate the precise link between psychic disorders and the embrace of revivalism. It is equally possible that people experiencing such strain will find non-religious ways of ordering their lives. A different interpretation that is related to this social disorder argument links the revivals to a specific class, typically a middle class anxious about its status. According to this view, either a displaced or a rising middle class seizes upon the revival as an opportunity either to regain or solidify its position in the community. This analysis has the virtue of inquiring into class conflict, but it often fails to demonstrate the precise link between class and revival and neglects to take religion seriously.[2]

An analysis that shares some of the assumptions of the above interpretations links evangelical Protestantism to the rise of a capitalist society. The emergence of capitalism, according to this argument, created new relations of production that shattered long-standing paternalistic relationships. With the institutionalization of wage labor and the spatial reorganization of cities along class lines, entrepreneurs used the revival to address the social ills that plagued their communities. The revival encouraged self-discipline, order, regularity, and sobriety, qualities that were extremely desirable in a town undergoing economic and social transformation. Evangelical Protestantism replaced external with internal controls and, in so doing, contributed to the emergence of a bourgeois social order in the nineteenth century. It is important to comment that such a perspective need not reduce religion simply to part of a capitalist conspiracy; it merely illuminates the compatibility between evangelical Protestantism and the needs of a capitalist society.[3]

However we choose to interpret the Second Great Awakening, revivalism in the nineteenth century cannot be separated from reform. So reform-minded were Americans of the first half of the century that Ralph Waldo Emerson, hardly an evangelical, asked rhetorically: "What is man born for, but to be a Reformer, a Remaker of what man has made?"[4] The question reflected the faith of many antebellum Americans that evil and injustice could be eradicated, that society could be reformed, improved, even perfected. It was a question that could not be posed, however, without the deepest belief that man indeed had the capacity to make the world over again. This faith, of course, had many sources other than evangelical Protestantism. But this particular version of Protestant theology provided a foundation for the idea that man's hands were not hopelessly tied. Conversion and salvation could be achieved. Religion demanded reform of the self and then society.

If conversion centered upon an individual action, it often began and ended as a social one. Revivalism organized the rapid, total transformation of the sinner into the saved. The experience of the individual was easily projected into a belief that society, viewed as nothing more than a voluntary gathering of persons, could also be quickly purified of all social ills. Evangelical Protestantism required that individuals not only rid themselves of sin but also wage battle against a sinful, polluted world. William Goodell, a radical abolitionist, stated this connection most clearly. "The conversion of the world," he insisted, "must be nothing less than the conversion of the masses of its inhabitants, and this would involve the moral renovation of SOCIETY, as well as of the *individuals* of whom society is composed."[5] Assured that benevolence would triumph in the world, evangelicals followed their spiritual calling into social activism.

At every step, the problems reformers attacked and the ways in which they approached them bore the stamp of evangelical Protestantism. Drunkenness violated all canons of middle-class respectability and evangelicals worked tirelessly to promote temperance, viewed as a core value for a bourgeois family life. Criminality seemed less a matter of depravity than a socially conditioned deviance that could be cured through the proper moral training. Toward this end, revivalists played a key role in promoting the penitentiary, an institution designed to encourage penitence through solitude. A new generation of abolitionists increasingly denounced slavery as sin. Inspired by the evangelical injunction to renounce all evil, they demanded the immediate and unconditional emancipation of all slaves.[6] In these ways, as in many others, the revival contributed to the reform impulse of the nineteenth century. Of course, not all reformers drew sustenance from evangelical religion. Many activists came from non-evangelical and non-religious backgrounds. They did not agree on the tactics of reform nor did they share a uniform set of social and political beliefs. The web of reform contained many strands and, over time, it was stretched in a number of opposed directions. But there is little doubt that throughout the nineteenth century revivalist religion gave shape to the moral reform enterprise in America.

Scholars agree that evangelical Protestantism helped drive the engine of reform, but they offer differing interpretations of the wider motivation of social activism in nineteenth-century America. Two approaches tend to polarize discussions. Some scholars view social reform as essentially humanitarian, as the work of dedicated activists who challenged social problems and, in so doing, helped make society a better place. Advocates of this position tend to take reformers at their word and seize upon the language of benevolence, betterment, and social responsibility as evidence of the reformers' good intentions. Scholars who judge reform in humanitarian terms are in some ways like the reformers they study. Both groups share a teleology that views the world as a rational place where progress is possible if not inevitable.[7]

A second approach examines reform in terms of social control. Hardly humanitarians, reformers in the nineteenth century, according to this interpretation, were members of a middle-class elite which feared social disorder and used reforms such as the temperance crusade as a way to maintain authority in a society being rapidly transformed. Scholars working within this framework disagree as to whether or not reform ranks were filled by members of a declining, conservative elite or a rising middle class, but they believe that more than anything else reform served to legitimate a capitalist order. It did so by working to instill in people new standards of behavior that would yield discipline and order in a highly mobile, democratic society.[8]

However illuminating each may be, taken together the interpretive schemes of humanitarianism and social control present us with a false dichotomy. The former interpretation is more concerned with reformers' intentions whereas the latter evaluates the results of reform. Indeed, it is possible that both may be true. Sincere religious, humanitarian sensibilities undoubtedly motivated many reformers who would have scoffed at the idea that they were prompted by their own best interests as a class. But it may also be the case that despite the best of intentions, reform functioned as a mechanism of social order and control. One way to move beyond this dichotomy is to analyze more precisely the tension between intentions and results, the process by which reformers' dreams of perfectibility became little more than devices of control for their subjects. Possibly only in this way can we arrive at a more sophisticated assessment of reform.

At another level, the two schools of interpretation reflect a tension in evangelical reform itself. The evangelical impulse was simultaneously liberating and constraining, liberal and conservative. Belief in free moral agency helped make the moral government of God the only legitimate government. Releasing man from his obligation to obey non-Divine government suggested questioning all temporal forms of authority and, accordingly, antebellum evangelical reform indeed contained an anarchistic strain. But while Protestant piety could challenge authority and liberate the individual to reshape society, the evangelical temperament could also restrain an individual's actions. Faith in personal conversion and salvation often led evangelicals away from cooperative solutions to social problems. As a result, pressures for consensus and agreement created an almost unbearable tension in reform organizations and these societies tended to fragment and disband over time. Complacency as well could settle on those who, having declared themselves pure and the world sinful, sat back to watch the wondrous revival do its work. With its emphasis on internalized standards of behavior, on self-discipline and self-control, evangelical Protestantism could be seen not only as a humanitarian force that freed individuals to work on behalf of bettering people's lives, but simultaneously as a moral power bent on controlling those who failed to conform.[9]

Evangelical Protestantism could lead the reformer to labor both for the liberation and the control of the individual, but we must be careful not to overemphasize the individualistic basis of reform. Focusing on the rhetoric of personal conversion and salvation, scholars in the 1960s commonly portrayed nineteenth-century reformers as anti-institutional and non-political.[10]

Actually, antebellum reformers had great faith in institutional solutions to moral and social problems. Believers in the power of conversion, they recognized that institutions could play a central role in transforming the individual and society. To exert greater influence, they joined voluntary associations by the thousands. They also believed strongly in the power of the school and the home to promote virtue and order.

Revival reform further had a momentous impact on antebellum politics as evangelicals tried to exert a moral force in the political sphere. There is little doubt that during this period religious beliefs helped shape political attitudes. Students of ethno-cultural politics have demonstrated, for example, that Protestants tended to vote for the Whig party whereas Catholics voted with the Democratic party. Even more to the point is the way in which the revival reshaped local political alliances. In Rochester, New York, for example, following the revival the Whig party became the party of evangelical Protestant businessmen whereas the Democratic party contained fewer Church members and opposed the Whig attempt to coerce social behavior. Religion influenced national politics as well. Some religious leaders called for a "Christian Party in politics" and throughout the antebellum period issues such as temperance, Sabbatarianism, and anti-slavery dominated the political arena. One faction of abolitionists even began a third political organization, the Liberty party, in an attempt to allow partisans the opportunity to vote their moral beliefs. As the political life of the time demonstrates, the evangelical emphasis on individual conscience by no means preempted a belief that institutions were also crucial to reform.[11]

In numerous ways, then, religion and reform refashioned American society and culture between the Revolution and the Civil War. Reform helped to mold church-state relations by making the connection more pervasive even as it was becoming less formal. Religious beliefs and reform efforts also hastened a shift away from public, external, physical forms of discipline toward a society that valued private, internal, psychological restraints. It was toward these ends that the church, the schoolhouse, the family, and the penitentiary all pointed. Piety, sobriety, domesticity, sentimentality, and purity became core values of the middle class at a time when American society was undergoing deep economic transformation. Regardless of intentions, it is clear that evangelical Protestantism and the reform enterprise shaped and reflected these broad shifts in culture and society.

For several decades, scholars in a number of disciplines have been addressing the issues discussed briefly in this introduction. As in any field, the works range from broad, theoretical examinations of the period to detailed studies of esoteric issues and activists. There is little question that the literature on antebellum religion and social reform is exceptional in every respect.

Yet there are many problems that await future students of religion and reform. The chronological boundaries of the subject remain too narrowly defined. The majority of studies focus on the 1830s and 1840s. While during these decades revivalism and reform certainly crested in intensity, the first waves of activism came in the 1780s and 1790s. We need to examine further the issue of continuity and change over time, the process by which the conflicts of one period molded the conflicts of another. Such a view of religion and reform will serve as a necessary first step toward a much needed synthesis of the field.

Currently, we have valuable works on the role of individual denominations in various reform enterprises. Studies of the Presbyterians, Congregationalists, Baptists, and Methodists, the Unitarians and Universalists as well as the many innovative religions of the period, are quite common. We also have detailed accounts of the antislavery, temperance, peace, and education movements. But how do these many denominations and reforms fit together? What made a person a reformer and how did the multiple visions of what social reform was about hold together? What challenges faced the reformers in their crusade to transform individuals and institutions? It is also important to remember that many Americans opposed reform, often on the same religious grounds that others advocated change. Reform and anti-reform must be analyzed in conjunction with one another.

We need as well to understand better than we do the origins of social reform. Most scholars assume either that new ideas propel activism or that changing social conditions give rise to reform. One is an idealist interpretation, the other materialist. But the question that awaits further study is the relationship between ideas and structure, beliefs and material conditions. Toward this end, scholars may profit from the theoretical literature in a variety of fields including sociology, social psychology, and cultural anthropology. These disciplines should not be raided for fresh jargon but mined for alternative ways of thinking about the relationships between thought, structure, and action.

Finally, the new history of religion and reform in eighteenth- and nineteenth-century America must have a broadened geographical focus. Too many studies concentrate on either the northeast or the near frontier without trying to integrate analyses of the two highly interactive areas. Too few works take seriously the southern region of the United States where evangelical religion also helped give rise to reform. A national focus, however desirable, is not enough. England and Europe also experienced waves of revival and reform during this period. Only works that allow for this broader perspective will enable us to discover what was novel about the American experience and what was tied to currents that spread wider and deeper than previously imagined.

A wealth of sources awaits scholars who wish to pursue these questions. A revolution in the technology of publishing in the early nineteenth century made inexpensive, mass printing possible. Reform organizations took advantage of the change by publishing hundreds of thousands of books, tracts, pamphlets, newspapers, and broadsides on every imaginable topic. Much of this material has survived, but little of it is indexed by subject. For works prior to 1800 consult Charles Evans, *The American Bibliography* (New York: P. Smith, 1941–1957). Indispensable for the period 1801–1830 is Ralph Shaw and Richard Shoemaker, *American Bibliography* (New York: Scarecrow Press, 1958–1971). *The National Union Catalog: Pre-1956 Imprints* is the best source for nineteenth-century books generally.

Students of religion and reform should also consult the many periodicals published during the antebellum period. Journals such as the *Biblical Repertory and Princeton Review* (New York, 1825–1888), *The Christian Examiner* (Boston, 1824–1869), and the *Methodist Quarterly Review* (New York, 1818–1931), to name but a few, contain invaluable information on denominational approaches to reform. Fortunately, most of these periodicals are available on microfilm. A valuable guide to this literature is Jean Hoornstra and Trudy Heath, *American Periodicals, 1741–1900* (Ann Arbor: University Microfilms International, 1979). Also see Jayne K. Kribbs, *An Annotated Bibliography of American Literary Periodicals, 1741–1850* (Boston: G. K. Hall and Co., 1977).

Newspapers are also indispensable to the study of religion and reform. Penny-press papers such as the *New York Herald, Boston Daily Times*, and *Philadelphia Public Ledger*, as well as the more traditional party papers, often carried editorials about reform and reported on the meetings of reform organizations. An excellent introduction to newspapers published prior to 1820 is offered by Clarence S. Brigham, *History and Bibliography of American Newspapers, 1690–1820* (Worcester: American Antiquarian Society, 1947). Also consult *Newspapers in Microform: United States* (Washington, D.C., 1973). Reformers frequently published material devoted to specific reforms. A partial index to antislavery publications is John W. Blassingame and Mae G. Henderson, *Antislavery Newspapers and Periodicals* (Boston: G. K. Hall and Co., 1980–1984). A good guide to antislavery works generally is Dwight Lowell Dumond, *A Bibliography of Antislavery in America* (Ann Arbor: University of Michigan Press, 1961). Unfortunately, similar guides for reforms other than antislavery are not available.

In addition to books, pamphlets, periodicals, and newspapers, researchers should consult the annual reports of religious and reform organizations. The reports of the American Anti-Slavery Society, the Massachusetts Society for the Suppression of Intemperance, and the American Peace Society, to name only a few, provide rich information on membership, financing, and activities, as well as ideology. The most complete collections of annual reports are housed at the Library of Congress and the American Antiquarian Society.

No source is more cumbersome, and yet potentially rewarding, than the personal papers of activists. The manuscripts of both prominent and obscure reformers fill repositories around the country but there is no single way to identify whose papers are located where. A first step is to consult the *National Union Catalog: Manuscript Collections* (Washington, D.C.). Fortunately, there are several useful edited volumes of the letters of influential abolitionists: Walter Merrill and Louis Ruchames, *The Letters of William Lloyd Garrison, 1823–1879* (Cambridge, Massachusetts: Harvard University Press, 1971–1981); Gilbert H. Barnes and Dwight L. Dumond, *The Letters of Theodore Dwight Weld, Angelina Grimke Weld, and Sarah Grimke* (New York: Appleton-Century, 1939); Dwight L. Dumond, *The Letters of James Gillespie Birney, 1831–1857* (New York: Appleton-Century, 1938); Irving Bartlett, "New Light on Wendell Phillips: The Community of Reform, 1840–1880," *Perspectives in American History* 12 (1979), 1–232. The Phillips letters are selected from the Blagden Collection, an excellent collection of material housed at Harvard University. Comparable works for other activists are scarcer, but these letters shed light on the entire community of reform.

Finally, scholars must continue to explore new sources for the study of religion and reform. Church and court records, for example, may provide fresh perspectives. Census materials and tax lists allow us to trace the more obscure individuals who may have participated in the reform enterprise. We also need to take greater advantage of graphic sources. The thousands of photographs and drawings of the period provide rich images of society that must be decoded. These materials, of course, are often the most elusive. An example of what is available in one city can be gleaned from Harry J. Carman and Arthur W. Thompson, *A Guide to the Principal Sources for American Civilization, 1800–1900, in the City of New York* (New York: Columbia University Press, 1962).

The bibliography that follows consists of secondary works relating to religion and reform in the period roughly between the American Revolution and the Civil War. The majority of these works cluster around the antebellum period, the decades of the 1830s, 1840s, and 1850s. This bibliography is not intended as a definitive gathering of all the literature related to this broad and important topic. Such a list would quickly become unwieldy and users would have no way of distinguishing analytical from antiquarian pieces. An attempt has been made to include both historiographic milestones and definitive pieces on relatively minor aspects of reform. The bibliography is weighted heavily towards works published in the last thirty years. A dated but still useful treatment of this topic can be found in Nelson R. Burr, *A Critical Bibliography of Religion in America* (Princeton: Princeton University Press, 1961), volume 4, esp. pp. 677–693.

Specifically, this bibliography makes no attempt to exhaust two types of reference: citations to biographies and denominational accounts of reform activities. There are scores of biographies for activists both influential and obscure. These works are accessible through subject headings in card catalogs and yearly indexes to state historical journals. Local histories also yield much factual information on reform activities. Finally, official accounts of church involvement in reform movements may be found in ecclesiastical histories and denominational journals.

NOTES

1. Finney quoted in Paul E. Johnson, *A Shopkeeper's Millennium*, p. 3; Timothy Smith, *Revivalism and Social Reform;* James Moorhead, "Social Reform and the Divided Conscience of Antebellum Protestantism."

2. Whitney Cross, *The Burned-Over District;* Richard Birdsall, "The Second Great Awakening and the New England Social Order"; Donald Mathews, "The Second Great Awakening as an Organizing Process, 1780–1830"; William McLoughlin, *Revivals, Awakenings, and Reform.*

3. Paul E. Johnson, *A Shopkeeper's Millennium.*

4. Emerson quoted in George Brown Tindall, *America: A Narrative History* (New York: W. W. Norton, 1984), vol. I, 494.

5. Goodell quoted in Lewis Perry, *Radical Abolitionism*, p. 46.

6. Ian Tyrrell, *Sobering Up;* Jed Dannenbaum, *Drink and Disorder;* David Rothman, *The Discovery of the Asylum;* James Essig, *The Bonds of Wickedness;* David Brion Davis, "The Emergence of Immediatism in British and American Antislavery Thought"; Anne Loveland, "Evangelicalism and Immediate Emancipation in American Antislavery Thought."

7. Martin Wiener, "Humanitarianism or Control?"; Lois Banner, "Religious Benevolence as Social Control"; Alice Tyler, *Freedom's Ferment.*

8. Clifford Griffin, "Religious Benevolence as Social Control, 1815–1860"; W. David Lewis, "The Reformer as Conservative."

9. James Moorhead, "Social Reform and the Divided Conscience of Antebellum Protestantism"; Lewis Perry, *Radical Abolitionism.*

10. John Thomas, "Romantic Reform in America, 1815–1860."

11. Ronald Formisano, *The Birth of Mass Political Parties;* Paul E. Johnson, *A Shopkeeper's Millennium;* Bertram Wyatt-Brown, "Prelude to Abolitionism"; John Hammond, *The Politics of Benevolence;* Richard Sewell, *Ballots for Freedom.*

BIBLIOGRAPHY

Abzug, Robert H. _Passionate Liberator: Theodore Dwight Weld and the Dilemma of Reform_. New York: Oxford University Press, 1980.

Albanese, Catherine. _Corresponding Motion: Transcendental Religion and the New America_. Philadelphia: Temple University Press, 1977.

Aptheker, Herbert. "The Quakers and Negro Slavery." _Journal of Negro History_ 25 (July 1940), 331-362.

Banner, Lois W. "Religion and Reform in the Early Republic: The Role of Youth." _American Quarterly_ 23 (December 1971), 677-695.

Banner, Lois W. "Religious Benevolence as Social Control: A Critique of An Interpretation." _Journal of American History_ 60 (June 1973), 23-41.

Barnes, Gilbert H. _The Antislavery Impulse, 1830-1844_. New York: Appleton-Century-Crofts, 1933.

Bartlett, Irving H. _Wendell Phillips: Brahmin Radical_. Boston: Beacon Press, 1961.

Bartlett, Irving H., ed. "New Light on Wendell Phillips: The Community of Reform, 1840-1880." _Perspectives in American History_ 12 (1979), 1-232.

Bell, Marion. _Crusade in the City: Revivalism in Nineteenth-Century Philadelphia_. Lewisburg, Pa.: Bucknell University Press, 1977.

Bidwell, Charles. "The Moral Significance of the Common School." _History of Education Quarterly_ 6 (Fall 1966), 50-91.

Billington, Ray Allen. The Protestant Crusade, 1800-1860: A
Study of the Origins of the American Nation. New York:
Macmillan Company, 1938.

Birdsall, Richard D. "The Second Great Awakening and the New
England Social Order." Church History 39 (September 1970),
345-371.

Bodo, John R. The Protestant Clergy and Public Issues, 1812-
1848. Princeton, N.J.: Princeton University Press, 1954.

Boles, John B. The Great Revival, 1785-1805: The Origins of
the Southern Evangelical Mind. Lexington: University Press
of Kentucky, 1972.

Boles, John B. "Henry Holcombe: A Southern Baptist Reformer in
the Age of Jefferson." Georgia Historical Quarterly 54
(Summer 1970), 381-407.

Bolt, Christine, and Drescher, Seymour. Anti-Slavery,
Religion, and Reform: Essays in Memory of Roger Anstey.
Folkestone, England: W. Dawson; Hamden, Conn.: Archon Books,
1980.

Boyer, Paul. Urban Masses and Moral Order in America, 1820-
1920. Cambridge, Mass.: Harvard University Press, 1978.

Brock, Peter. Radical Pacifists in Antebellum America.
Princeton, N.J.: Princeton University Press, 1968.

Bruns, Roger. "A Quaker's Antislavery Crusade: Anthony
Benezet." Quaker History 65 (Autumn 1976), 81-92.

Bumsted, J. M. "Religion and American Culture." Canadian
Review of American Studies 11 (Spring 1980), 49-56.

Carwardine, Richard. "American Evangelical Protestantism and
the Reform Impulse." Journal of the United Reformed Church
Historical Society (Great Britain) 2 (1980), 153-160.

Carwardine, Richard. "Evangelicals, Whigs and the Election of
William Henry Harrison." Journal of American Studies 17
(April 1983), 47-75.

Carwardine, Richard. "The Second Great Awakening in the Urban
Centers: An Examination of Methodism and the 'New
Measures.'" Journal of American History 59 (September
1972), 327-340.

Carwardine, Richard. Transatlantic Revivalism: Popular
Evangelicalism in Britain and America, 1790-1865. Westport,
Conn.: Greenwood Press, 1978.

Caskey, Marie. Chariot of Fire: Religion and the Beecher
Family. New Haven: Yale University Press, 1978.

Clark, Clifford E. "The Changing Nature of Protestantism in
Mid-Nineteenth-Century America: Henry Ward Beecher's 'Seven
Lectures to Young Men.'" Journal of American History 57
(March 1970), 832-846.

Clark, Norman H. Deliver Us From Evil: An Interpretation of
American Prohibition. New York: Norton, 1976.

Cole, Charles C., Jr. "The Free Church Movement in New York
City." New York History 34 (July 1953), 284-297.

Cole, Charles C., Jr. The Social Ideas of the Northern
Evangelists, 1826-1860. New York: Columbia University
Press, 1954.

Commager, Henry Steele. Theodore Parker. Boston: Little,
Brown, 1936.

Conforti, Joseph A. "Samuel Hopkins and the Revolutionary
Antislavery Movement." Rhode Island History 38 (May 1979),
39-49.

Crandall, John C. "Patriotism and Humanitarian Reform in
Children's Literature, 1825-1860." American Quarterly 21
(Spring 1969), 3-22.

Creagh, Ronald. "The Age of Reform: A Reappraisal." Revue
Francaise d'Etudes Americaines 3 (1978), 7-18.

Cross, Whitney R. The Burned-Over District: The Social and
Intellectual History of Enthusiastic Religion in Western New
York, 1800-1850. Ithaca, N.Y.: Cornell University Press,
1950.

Culver, Raymond B. Horace Mann and Religion in the
Massachusetts Public Schools. New Haven: Yale University
Press, 1929.

Curti, Merle. The American Peace Crusade, 1815-1860. Durham,
N.C.: Duke University Press, 1929.

Dannenbaum, Jed. Drink and Disorder: Temperance Reform in
Cincinnati from the Washingtonian Revival to the WCTU.
Urbana: University of Illinois Press, 1984.

Davis, David Brion. "The Emergence of Immediatism in British
and American Antislavery Thought." Mississippi Valley
Historical Review 49 (September 1962), 109-230.

Davis, David Brion. "The Movement to Abolish Capital
Punishment in America, 1787-1861." American Historical
Review 63 (October 1957), 23-46.

Davis, David Brion. The Problem of Slavery in the Age of
     Revolution, 1770-1823. Ithaca, N.Y.: Cornell University
     Press, 1975.

Davis, David Brion. "Some Themes of Counter-Subversion: An
     Analysis of Anti-Masonic, Anti-Catholic, and Anti-Mormon
     Literature." Mississippi Valley Historical Review 47
     (September 1960), 205-224.

DeBenedetti, Charles. The Peace Reform in American History.
     Bloomington: Indiana University Press, 1980.

Diggins, John. The Lost Soul of American Politics. New York:
     Basic Books, 1984.

Dillon, Merton L. "The Abolitionists: A Decade of
     Historiography, 1959-1969." Journal of Southern History 35
     (November 1969), 500-522.

Dillon, Merton L. The Abolitionists: The Growth of a
     Dissenting Minority. DeKalb: Northern Illinois University
     Press, 1974.

Dodd, Jill Siegal. "The Working Classes and the Temperance
     Movement in Antebellum Boston." Labor History 19 (Fall
     1978), 510-531.

Doherty, Robert W. "Religion and Society: The Hicksite
     Separation of 1827." American Quarterly 17 (Spring 1965),
     63-80.

Douglas, Ann. The Feminization of American Culture. New York:
     Knopf, 1977.

Drake, Thomas. Quakers and Slavery in America. New Haven:
     Yale University Press, 1950.

Dumond, Dwight L. Antislavery: The Crusade for Freedom in
     America. Ann Arbor: University of Michigan Press, 1961.

Ekirch, Arthur A. The Idea of Progress in America, 1815-1860.
     New York: Columbia University Press, 1944.

Epstein, Barbara L. The Politics of Domesticity: Women,
     Evangelicalism, and Temperance in Nineteenth-Century
     America. Middletown, Conn.: Wesleyan University Press,
     1981.

Essig, James D. The Bonds of Wickedness: American Evangelicals
     Against Slavery, 1770-1808. Philadelphia: Temple University
     Press, 1982.

Essig, James D. "The Lord's Free Man: Charles G. Finney and
     his Abolitionism." Civil War History 24 (March 1978), 24-
     45.

Fellman, Michael. "Theodore Parker and the Abolitionist Role
    in the 1850s." Journal of American History 61 (December
    1974), 666-684.

Filler, Louis. The Crusade Against Slavery, 1830-1860. New
    York: Harper and Row, 1960.

Finkelstein, Barbara J. "The Moral Dimensions of Pedagogy:
    Teaching Behaviour in Popular Primary Schools in Nineteenth-
    Century America." American Studies 15 (1974), 79-89.

Formisano, Ronald P. The Birth of Mass Political Parties:
    Michigan, 1827-1861. Princeton, N.J.: Princeton University
    Press, 1971.

Formisano, Ronald P., and Kutolowski, Kathleen Smith.
    "Antimasonry and Masonry: The Genesis of Protest, 1826-
    1827." American Quarterly 29 (Summer 1977), 139-165.

Fortenbaugh, Robert. "American Lutheran Synods and Slavery,
    1830-1860." Journal of Religion 13 (January 1933), 72-92.

Foster, Charles I. An Errand of Mercy: The Evangelical United
    Front, 1790-1837. Chapel Hill: University of North Carolina
    Press, 1960.

Foster, Charles I. "The Urban Missionary Movement, 1814-1837."
    Pennsylvania Magazine of History and Biography 75 (January
    1951), 47-65.

Fox, Dixon Ryan. "The Protestant Counter-Reformation in
    America." New York History 33 (January 1935), 19-35.

Friedman, Lawrence J. "Confidence and Pertinacity in
    Evangelical Abolitionism: Lewis Tappan's Circle." American
    Quarterly 31 (Spring 1979), 81-106.

Friedman, Lawrence J. "The Gerrit Smith Circle: Abolitionism
    in the Burned Over District." Civil War History 26 (March
    1980), 18-38.

Friedman, Lawrence J. Gregarious Saints: Self and Community in
    American Abolitionism, 1830-1870. Cambridge: Cambridge
    University Press, 1982.

Friedman, Lawrence J. Inventors of the Promised Land. New
    York: Knopf, 1975.

Frost, William J. "The Origins of the Quaker Crusade Against
    Slavery: A Review of Recent Literature." Quaker History 67
    (Spring 1978), 42-58.

Gatell, Frank Otto. John Gorham Palfrey and the New England
    Conscience. Cambridge, Mass.: Harvard University Press,
    1963.

George, Carol V. R. "Widening the Circle: The Black Church and
the Abolitionist Crusade, 1830-1860." In Antislavery
Reconsidered: New Perspectives on the Abolitionists, edited
by Lewis Perry and Michael Fellman, 75-95. Baton Rouge:
Louisiana State University Press, 1979.

Gravely, William B. "Christian Abolitionism." In The Social
Gospel: Religion and Reform in Changing America, edited by
Ronald C. White, Jr. and C. Howard Hopkins. Philadelphia:
Temple University Press, 1976.

Gravely, William B. Gilbert Haven, Methodist Abolitionist: A
Study in Race, Religion, and Reform, 1850-1880. Nashville:
Abingdon Press, 1973.

Gribbin, William. "Antimasonry, Religious Radicalism, and the
Paranoid Style of the 1820s." History Teacher 7 (1974),
234-254.

Gribbin, William. "Republicanism, Reform, and the Sense of Sin
in Antebellum America." Cithara 14 (1974), 25-42.

Griffin, Clifford S. "The Abolitionists and Benevolent
Societies, 1831-1861." Journal of Negro History 44 (July
1959), 195-216.

Griffin, Clifford S. "Converting the Catholics: American
Benevolent Societies and the Antebellum Crasade Against the
Church." Catholic Historical Review 47 (October 1961), 325-
341.

Griffin, Clifford S. The Ferment of Reform, 1830-1860.
Arlington Heights, Ill.: AHM Publishing, 1967.

Griffin, Clifford S. "Religious Benevolence as Social Control,
1815-1860." Mississippi Valley Historical Review 44
(December 1957), 423-444.

Griffin, Clifford S. Their Brothers' Keepers: Moral
Stewardship in the United States, 1800-1865. New Brunswick,
N.J.: Rutgers University Press, 1960.

Gusfield, Joseph R. Symbolic Crusade: Status Politics and the
American Temperance Movement. Urbana: University of
Illinois Press, 1963.

Hammond, John L. The Politics of Benevolence: Revival Religion
and American Voting Behavior. Norwood, N.J.: Ablex, 1979.

Hammond, John L. "Revival Religion and Antislavery Politics."
American Sociological Review 39 (April 1974), 175-186.

Hammond, John L. "Revivals, Consensus, and American Political
Culture." Journal of the American Academy of Religion 46
(1978), 293-314.

Hampel, Robert L. "The Contexts of Antebellum Reform."
    American Quarterly 33 (Spring 1981), 93-101.

Handy, Robert T. "The Protestant Quest for a Christian
    America." Church History 22 (March 1953), 8-20.

Harris, Robert L. "Early Black Benevolent Societies, 1789-
    1830." Massachusetts Review 20 (Autumn 1979), 603-625.

Harwood, Thomas F. "British Evangelical Abolitionism and
    American Churches in the 1830s." Journal of Southern
    History 28 (August 1962), 287-306.

Hatch, Nathan O. "The Christian Movement and the Demand for a
    Theology of the People." Journal of American History 67
    (December 1980), 545-567.

Hatch, Nathan O. The Sacred Cause of Liberty: Republican
    Thought and the Millennium in Revolutionary New England.
    New Haven: Yale University Press, 1977.

Hay, Robert P. "Providence and the American Past." Indiana
    Magazine of History 65 (June 1969), 79-101.

Heale, M. J. "Humanitarianism in the Early Republic: The Moral
    Reformers of New York, 1776-1826." Journal of American
    Studies 2 (December 1968), 161-176.

Heale, M. J. "The New York Society for the Prevention of
    Pauperism, 1817-1823." New York Historical Society
    Quarterly 55 (April 1971), 153-176.

Hood, Fred. Reformed America: The Middle and Southern States,
    1783-1837. University, Ala.: University of Alabama Press,
    1980.

Horton, James Oliver. "Generations of Protest: Black Families
    and Social Reform in Antebellum Boston." New England
    Quarterly 49 (June 1976), 242-256.

Hovet, Theodore R. "Christian Revolution: Harriet Beecher
    Stowe's Response to Slavery and the Civil War." New England
    Quarterly 47 (December 1974), 535-549.

Howe, Daniel Walker. The Unitarian Conscience: Harvard Moral
    Philosophy, 1805-1861. Cambridge, Mass.: Harvard University
    Press, 1970.

Jable, J. Thomas. "Aspects of Reforms in Early Nineteenth-
    Century Pennsylvania." Pennsylvania Magazine of History and
    Biography 102 (July 1978), 344-363.

Jacob, J. R. "LaRoy Sunderland: The Alienation of an
    Abolitionist." Journal of American Studies 6 (April 1972),
    1-17.

Jensen, Richard. "Religion, Morality, and American Politics."
    Journal of Libertarian Studies 6 (Summer/Fall 1982), 321-
    332.

Jentz, John B. "The Antislavery Constituency in Jacksonian New
    York City." Civil War History 27 (June 1981), 101-122.

Johnson, James E. "Charles G. Finney and Oberlin
    Perfectionism." Journal of Presbyterian History 46 (March
    1968), 42-57; (June 1968), 128-138.

Johnson, James E. "Charles G. Finney and a Theology of
    Revivalism." Church History 38 (September 1969), 338-358.

Johnson, Paul E. A Shopkeeper's Millennium: Society and
    Revivals in Rochester, New York, 1815-1837. New York: Hill
    and Wang, 1978.

Kaestle, Carl F. Pillars of the Republic: Common Schools and
    American Society, 1780-1860. New York: Hill and Wang, 1983.

Kaestle, Carl F. "Social Change, Discipline, and the Common
    School in Early Nineteenth-Century America." Journal of
    Interdisciplinary History 9 (Summer 1978), 1-17.

Katz, Michael V. The Irony of Early School Reform: Educational
    Innovation in Mid-Nineteenth-Century Massachusetts.
    Cambridge, Mass.: Harvard University Press, 1968.

Keller, Charles Roy. The Second Great Awakening in
    Connecticut. New Haven: Yale University Press, 1942.

Klebaner, Benjamin J. "Poverty and its Relief in American
    Thought, 1815-1861." Social Service Review 38 (1964), 382-
    399.

Kraditor, Aileen S. Means and Ends in American Abolitionism:
    Garrison and His Critics on Strategy, 1834-1860. New York:
    Pantheon, 1969.

Kraut, Alan, and Field, Phyllis. "Politics versus Principles:
    The Partisan Response to 'Bible Politics' in New York
    State." Civil War History 25 (June 1979), 101-118.

Krout, John A. The Origins of Prohibition. New York: Knopf,
    1925.

Kull, Irving Stoddard. "Presbyterian Attitudes Toward
    Slavery." Church History 7 (June 1938), 101-114.

Lannie, Vincent P., and Diethorn, Bernard C. "For the Honor
    and Glory of God: The Philadelphia Bible Riots of 1840."
    History of Education Quarterly 8 (Spring 1968), 44-106.

Latner, Richard B., and Levine, Peter. "Perspectives on
    Antebellum Pietistic Politics." Reviews in American History
    4 (March 1976), 15-24.

Lesick, Lawrence T. The Lane Rebels: Evangelicalism and
    Antislavery in Antebellum America. Metuchen, N.J.:
    Scarecrow Press, 1980.

Levesque, George A. "Inherent Reformers--Inherited Orthodoxy:
    Black Baptists in Boston, 1800-1873." Journal of Negro
    History 60 (October 1975), 491-519.

Lewis, W. David. "The Reformer as Conservative: Protestant
    Counter-Subversion in the Early Republic." In The
    Development of an American Culture, edited by Stanley Coben
    and Lorman Ratner. Englewood Cliffs, N.J.: Prentice-Hall,
    1970.

Lewitt, Robert T. "Indian Missions and Antislavery Sentiment:
    A Conflict of Evangelical and Humanitarian Ideals."
    Mississippi Valley Historical Review 50 (June 1963), 39-55.

Lipset, Seymour Martin. "Religion and Politics in the American
    Past and Present." In Religion and Social Conflict, edited
    by Robert Lee and Martin Marty, 69-126. New York: Oxford
    University Press, 1964.

Lipson, Dorothy A. Freemasonry in Federalist Connecticut,
    1789-1860. Princeton, N.J.: Princeton University Press,
    1978.

Loetscher, Lefferts A. "The Problem of Christian Unity in
    Early Nineteenth-Century America." Church History 32 (March
    1963), 3-16.

Loveland, Anne C. "Domesticity and Religion in the Antebellum
    Period." Historian 39 (May 1977), 455-471.

Loveland, Anne C. "Evangelicalism and Immediate Emancipation
    in American Antislavery Thought." Journal of Southern
    History 32 (May 1966), 172-188.

Loveland, Anne C. Southern Evangelicals and the Social Order,
    1800-1860. Baton Rouge: Louisiana State University Press,
    1980.

Ludlum, David. Social Ferment in Vermont, 1791-1850. New
    York: Columbia University Press, 1939.

Luker, Ralph E. "Religion and Social Control in the
    Nineteenth-Century American City." Journal of Urban History
    2 (1976), 363-368.

MacCormac, Earl R. "The Development of Presbyterian Missionary
    Organizations, 1790-1870." Journal of Presbyterian History
    43 (September 1965), 149-173.

McElroy, James L. "Social Control and Romantic Reform in
    Antebellum America: The Case of Rochester, New York." New
    York History 58 (January 1977), 17-46.

McKivigan, John R. "The American Baptist Free Mission Society:
    Abolitionist Reaction to the 1845 Baptist Schism."
    Foundations 21 (October-December 1978), 340-355.

McKivigan, John R. "The Christian Anti-Slavery Movement of the
    Northwest." Old Northwest 1 (1979-80), 345-366.

McKivigan, John R. "Vote as you Pray and Pray as you Vote:
    Church-Oriented Abolitionism and Antislavery Politics." In
    Crusaders and Compromisers, edited by Alan M. Kraut.
    Westport, Conn.: Greenwood Press, 1983.

McKivigan, John R. The War Against Proslavery Religion:
    Abolitionism and the Northern Churches, 1830-1865. Ithaca,
    N.Y.: Cornell University Press, 1984.

Maclear, J. F. "The Evangelical Alliance and the Antislavery
    Crusade." Huntington Library Quarterly 42 (Spring 1979),
    141-164.

McLoughlin, William G. The Meaning of Henry Ward Beecher: An
    Essay on Shifting Values of Mid-Victorian America, 1840-
    1870. New York: Knopf, 1970.

McLoughlin, William G. Revivals, Awakenings, and Reform: An
    Essay on Religion and Social Change in America, 1607-1977.
    Chicago: University of Chicago Press, 1978.

Marini, Stephen. Radical Sects of Revolutionary New England.
    Cambridge, Mass.: Harvard University Press, 1982.

Marsden, George M. The Evangelical Mind and the New School
    Presbyterian Experience: A Case Study of Thought and
    Theology in Nineteenth-Century America. New Haven: Yale
    University Press, 1970.

Mathews, Donald G. "The Methodist Schism of 1844 and the
    Popularization of Antislavery Sentiment." Mid-America: An
    Historical Review 51 (January 1968), 2-23.

Mathews, Donald G. "The Second Great Awakening as an
    Organizing Process, 1780-1830." American Quarterly 21
    (Spring 1969), 23-43.

Mathews, Donald G. Slavery and Methodism: A Chapter in
    American Morality, 1780-1845. Princeton, N.J.: Princeton
    University Press, 1965.

May, Henry. The Enlightenment in America. New York: Oxford
    University Press, 1976.

Mead, Sidney E. Nathaniel William Taylor, 1786-1858: A
    Connecticut Liberal. Chicago: University of Chicago Press,
    1942.

Melder, Keith. "'Ladies Bountiful': Organized Women's
    Benevolence in Early Nineteenth-Century America." New York
    History 48 (July 1967), 231-254. Reprinted in his
    Beginnings of Sisterhood: The American Woman's Rights
    Movement, 1800-1850. New York: Schocken Books, 1977.

Meyer, Donald H. The Instructed Conscience: The Shaping of the
    American National Ethic. Philadelphia: University of
    Pennsylvania Press, 1972.

Miller, Perry. The Life of the Mind in America from the
    Revolution to the Civil War. New York: Harcourt, Brace, and
    World, 1965.

Miyakawa, T. Scott. Protestants and Pioneers: Individualism
    and Conformity on the American Frontier. Chicago:
    University of Chicago Press, 1964.

Moellering, Ralph L. Christian Conscience and Negro
    Emancipation. Philadelphia: Fortress Press, 1965.

Mohl, Raymond. "The Humane Society and Urban Reform in Early
    New York, 1787-1831." New York Historical Society Quarterly
    54 (January 1970), 30-52.

Moorhead, James H. "Between Progress and Apocalypse; A
    Reassessment of Millennialism in American Religious Thought,
    1800-1880." Journal of American History 71 (December 1984),
    524-542.

Moorhead, James H. "Social Reform and the Divided Conscience
    of Antebellum Protestantism." Church History 48 (December
    1979), 416-430.

Murray, Andrew F. "Bright Delusion: Presbyterians and African
    Colonization." Journal of Presbyterian History 58 (Fall
    1980), 224-237.

Noll, Mark A. "Protestant Theology and Social Order in
    Antebellum America." Religious Studies Review 8 (April
    1982), 133-142.

Nye, Russell. Fettered Freedom: Civil Liberties and the Slave
    Controvery. East Lansing: Michigan State University Press,
    1949.

Osofsky, Gilbert. "Abolitionists, Irish Immigrants, and the
    Dilemmas of Romantic Nationalism." American Historical
    Review 80 (October 1975), 889-912.

Perry, Lewis. "Adin Ballou's Hopedale Community and the
    Theology of Anti-Slavery." Church History 39 (September
    1970), 372-389.

Perry, Lewis. Childhood, Marriage, and Reform: Henry Clarke
    Wright, 1797-1870. Chicago: University of Chicago Press,
    1980.

Perry, Lewis. Radical Abolitionism: Anarchy and the Government
    of God in Antislavery Thought. Ithaca, N.Y.: Cornell
    University Press, 1973.

Perry, Lewis. "Versions of Anarchism in the Antislavery
    Movement." American Quarterly 20 (Winter 1968), 768-782.

Phelps, Christina. The Anglo-American Peace Movement in the
    Mid-Nineteenth Century. New York: Columbia University
    Press, 1930.

Posey, Walter B. "The Slavery Question in the Presbyterian
    Church of the Old Southwest." Journal of Southern History
    15 (August 1949), 311-324.

Post, Albert. Popular Free Thought in America, 1825-1830.
    New York: Columbia University Press, 1943.

Pritchard, Linda K. "The Burned-Over District Reconsidered: A
    Portent of Evolving Religious Pluralism in the United
    States." Social Science History 8 (Summer 1984), 243-266.

Purifoy, Lewis M. "The Methodist Antislavery Tradition, 1784-
    1844." Methodist History 4 (July 1966), 3-16.

Ratner, Lorman. Powder Keg: Northern Opposition to the
    Antislavery Movement, 1831-1840. New York: Basic Books,
    1968.

Richards, Leonard. "Gentlemen of Property and Standing": Anti-
    Abolition Mobs in Jacksonian America. New York: Oxford
    University Press, 1970.

Rodgers, James. "The Religious Origins of American Radicalism
    and the Ideological Roots of Intellectual Communities."
    Revue Francaise d'Etudes Americaines 2 (1976), 23-29.

Rorabaugh, W. J. The Alcoholic Republic: An American
    Tradition. New York: Oxford University Press, 1979.

Rothman, David J. The Discovery of the Asylum: Social Order
    and Disorder in the New Republic. Boston: Little, Brown,
    1971.

Rowe, David L. "A New Perspective on the Burned-Over District:
The Millerites in Upstate New York." Church History 47
(December 1978), 408-420.

Ryan, Mary P. Cradle of the Middle Class: The Family in Oneida
County, New York, 1790-1865. Cambridge: Cambridge
University Press, 1981.

Saum, Lewis O. "Providence in the Popular Mind of Pre-Civil
War America." Indiana Magazine of History 72 (December
1976), 315-346.

Schlesinger, Arthur M., Jr. The Age of Jackson. Boston:
Little, Brown, 1945.

Scott, Donald M. "Abolition as a Sacred Vocation." In
Antislavery Reconsidered: New Perspectives on the
Abolitionists, edited by Lewis Perry and Michael Fellman,
51-74. Baton Rouge: Louisiana State University Press, 1979.

Sewell, Richard H. Ballots for Freedom: Antislavery Politics
in the United States, 1837-1860. New York: Oxford
University Press, 1976.

Singleton, Gregory H. "'Mere Middle-Class Institutions': Urban
Protestantism in Nineteenth-Century America." Journal of
Social History 6 (Summer 1973), 489-504.

Singleton, Gregory H. "Protestant Voluntary Organizations and
the Shaping of Victorian America." American Quarterly 27
(December 1975), 549-560.

Smith, Timothy L. "Protestant Schooling and American
Nationality, 1800-1850." Journal of American History 53
(March 1967), 679-695.

Smith, Timothy L. Revivalism and Social Reform in Mid-
Nineteenth-Century America. New York: Abingdon Press, 1957.

Smith-Rosenberg, Carroll. Religion and the Rise of the
American City: The New York City Mission Movement, 1812-
1870. Ithaca, N.Y.: Cornell University Press, 1971.

Sokolow, Jayme A. "Revolution and Reform: The Antebellum
Jewish Abolitionists." Journal of Ethnic Studies 9 (Spring
1981), 27-41.

Sorin, Gerald. Abolitionism: A New Perspective. New York:
Praeger, 1972.

Sorin, Gerald. The New York Abolitionists: A Case Study of
Political Radicalism. Westport, Conn.: Greenwood Press,
1971.

Staiger, C. Bruce. "Abolitionism and the Presbyterian Schism
    of 1837-1838." Mississippi Valley Historical Review 36
    (December 1949), 391-414.

Stange, Douglas C. "Abolitionism as Maleficience: Southern
    Unitarians versus 'Puritan Fanaticism,' 1831-1860." Harvard
    Library Bulletin 26 (April 1978), 146-171.

Stange, Douglas C. "Abolition or Treason: The Unitarian Elite
    Defends Law, Order, and the Union." Harvard Library
    Bulletin 28 (April 1980), 152-170.

Stange, Douglas C. Patterns of Antislavery Among American
    Unitarians, 1831-1860. Rutherford, N.J.: Fairleigh
    Dickinson University Press, 1977.

Stange, Douglas C. Radicalism for Humanity: A Study of
    Lutheran Abolitionism. St. Louis: O. Slave, 1970.

Staudenraus, Philip J. The African Colonization Movement,
    1816-1865. New York: Columbia University Press, 1961.

Stewart, James B. "The Aims and Impact of Garrisonian
    Abolitionism, 1840-1860." Civil War History 15 (September
    1969), 197-209.

Stewart, James B. "Evangelicalism and the Radical Strain in
    Southern Antislavery Thought During the 1820s." Journal of
    Southern History 39 (August 1973), 379-396.

Stewart, James B. Holy Warriors: The Abolitionists and
    American Slavery. New York: Hill and Wang, 1976.

Stewart, James B. Joshua Giddings and the Tactics of Radical
    Politics, 1795-1864. Cleveland: Case Western Reserve
    University Press, 1969.

Stewart, James B. "Peaceful Hopes and Violent Expectations:
    The Evolution of Reforming and Radical Abolitionism, 1831-
    1837." Civil War History 17 (December 1971), 293-309.

Stirn, James R. "Urgent Gradualism: The Case of the American
    Union for the Relief and Improvement of the Colored Race."
    Civil War History 25 (December 1979), 309-328.

Sweeney, Kevin. "Rum, Romanism, Representation, and Reform:
    Coalition Politics in Massachusetts, 1847-1853." Civil War
    History 22 (June 1976), 116-137.

Sweet, Leonard I. "The View of Man Inherent in the New Measure
    Revivalism." Church History 45 (June 1976), 206-221.

Sweet, William Warren. Religion in the Development of American
    Culture, 1765-1840. New York: Scribner's Sons, 1952.

Taylor, Richard S. "Beyond Immediate Emancipation: Jonathan Blanchard, Abolitionism, and the Emergence of American Fundamentalism." Civil War History 27 (September 1981), 260-274.

Thomas, John L. "Antislavery and Utopia." In The Antislavery Vanguard, edited by Martin Duberman, 240-269. Princeton, N.J.: Princeton University Press, 1965.

Thomas, John L. The Liberator: William Lloyd Garrison. Boston: Little, Brown, 1963.

Thomas, John L. "Romantic Reform in America, 1815-1860." American Quarterly 17 (Winter 1965), 656-681.

Thompson, J. Earl, Jr. "Abolitionism and Theological Education at Andover." New England Quarterly 47 (June 1974), 238-261.

Thompson, J. Earl, Jr. "Lyman Beecher's Long Road to Conservative Abolitionism." Church History 42 (March 1973), 89-109.

Thompson, J. Earl, Jr. "Slavery and Presbyterianism in the Revolutionary Era." Journal of Presbyterian History 54 (Summer 1976), 121-141.

Tyack, David. "The Kingdom of God and the Common School: Protestant Ministers and the Educational Awakening in the West." Harvard Educational Review 36 (Fall 1960), 447-469.

Tyler, Alice Felt. Freedom's Ferment: Phases of American Social History from the Colonial Period to the Outbreak of the Civil War. Minneapolis: University of Minnesota Press, 1944.

Tyrell, Alexander. "Making the Millennium: The Mid-Nineteenth Century Peace Movement." Historical Journal 21 (March 1978), 75-95.

Tyrell, Ian R. Sobering Up: From Temperance to Prohibition in Antebellum America, 1800-1860. Westport, Conn.: Greenwood Press, 1979.

Upton, James M. "The Shakers as Pacifists in the Period Between 1812 and the Civil War." Filson Club Historical Quarterly 47 (July 1973), 267-283.

Walker, Peter F. Moral Choices: Memory, Desire, and Imagination in Nineteenth-Century Abolition. Baton Rouge: Louisiana State University Press, 1978.

Walters, Ronald G. American Reformers, 1815-1860. New York: Hill and Wang, 1978.

Walters, Ronald G. The Antislavery Appeal: American
   Abolitionism after 1830. Baltimore: Johns Hopkins
   University Press, 1976.

Welter, Rush. The Mind of America, 1820-1860. New York:
   Columbia University Press, 1975.

Wiener, Martin J., ed. "Humanitarianism or Control? A
   Symposium on Aspects of Nineteenth-Century Social Reform in
   Britain and America." Rice University Studies 67 (Winter
   1981), 1-84.

Wilson, Major L. "Paradox Lost: Order and Progress in
   Evangelical Thought of Mid-Nineteenth-Century America."
   Church History 44 (September 1975), 352-366.

Wilson, Major L. "Time and the Religious Dialogue in Mid-
   Nineteenth-Century America." Midwest Quarterly 21 (1980),
   175-195.

Wood, Gordon S. "Evangelical America and Early Mormonism."
   New York History 61 (October 1980), 359-386.

Wyatt-Brown, Bertram. Lewis Tappan and the Evangelical War
   Against Slavery. Cleveland: Case Western Reserve
   University, 1969.

Wyatt-Brown, Bertram. "Prelude to Abolitionism: Sabbatarian
   Politics and the Rise of the Second Party System." Journal
   of American History 58 (September 1971), 316-345.

York, Robert. George B.Cheever: Religious and Social Reformer,
   1807-1890. Orono, Me.: University of Maine Press, 1955.

8

Communitarian Experiments, New Religions, and the Political Culture

John L. Merrill

A bibliographical volume on church-state relations in American history might treat the topic of communitarian societies in various ways. One approach would be to focus on how the legal and political structures of federal, state, and local governments were brought to bear on the religious dimensions of the numerous communities that developed in America in the late eighteenth and nineteenth centuries. Surely this is a legitimate and valuable approach to the topic, for it would tell much about the extent to which the political structures could tolerate and accommodate religious beliefs and practices that fell outside the mainstream of American religion. Still more informative would be a holistic consideration of the communitarian groups as societies embodying their own political as well as religious structures. Such an approach would also include assessment of the degree to which these mini-commonwealths were accommodated within the larger commonwealth's own structures of religious and political authority.

While not neglecting these viewpoints, the focus of this bibliographic essay is on the new religions and communitarian societies as alternative visions of how American society should best be structured. To adopt such an approach is to take the broadest view of the subject, as well as to take the intention, purpose, and self-understanding of the majority of the communitarians seriously as they attempted to provide a solution to the ills and disharmonies perceived to exist in American society. In this perspective their purpose was to suggest by way of concrete example arrangements alternative to the mainstream culture.

The suggestion of alternative visions for America could be seriously entertained up through the antebellum period; for as long as the social structures of the nation were not yet firmly set, it seemed feasible to consider initiating, through the example of prototypical communities, a radical departure from traditional patterns of religious and civil authority. While the more popular antebellum reform movements focused on piecemeal changes in the political and religious life of the nation, the communitarian approach commended itself to those who thought that the existing ills of society were too great to be remedied by such partial solutions, yet who rejected the idea of change through a revolutionary overthrow of the existing structures. Though proportionately few citizens were actual participants in any of these experiments, many more were sympathetic observers. And there was much to observe, for by the Civil War, over 140 communities had been ventured.

In a sense, the American communitarian tradition has its roots in the earliest settlements on the continent. Kenneth Lockridge, for example, characterized colonial Dedham, Massachusetts, in its first half-century, as "a utopian commune," calling it no less so than the famed nineteenth-century experiments of Amana, Brook Farm, and Oneida (*A New England Town: The First Hundred Years*, New York: W. W. Norton, 1970, p. 1). Furthermore, as Robert Fogarty observes in his *Dictionary of American Communal and Utopian History*, "There is a body of literature which suggests that the whole of American life has been utopian and experimental" (p. 237), H. Richard Niebuhr's *The Kingdom of God in America* (Hamden, Conn.: Shoe String Press, 1956), Charles L. Sanford's *The Quest for Paradise* (Urbana, Ill.: University of Illinois Press, 1961), and Ernest Tuveson's *Redeemer Nation* (Chicago: University of Chicago Press, 1968) being among the more notable examples.

While such a view is not without value, especially as it helps draw attention to some of the distinctive features of American history, if pressed too far it obscures recognition of the notable range of differences *within* American culture. Furthermore, while the American venture may be broadly utopian in that its goals have not been derived simply from the example of any already existing society, but from ideals of what ought to be, the mainstream of American society has not sought to realize these goals through the means of small communities with socialistic systems.

Taking a more strict definition of our subject matter, by asking with Fogarty whether a given group "organized its economic affairs, its living arrangements, [and] its practical life around cooperative or communal principles," (*Dictionary*, p. ix), it may be said that the communitarian tradition in America had its origins in the migration to America of persecuted European pietistic religious sects of the late seventeenth and eighteenth centuries. Among the first such recorded groups were the short-lived Labadist Colony and the Society of the Woman in the Wilderness, while the Ephratans and Moravians, who proved more durable, immigrated in the eighteenth century. These groups may have found the New World more hospitable to their religious beliefs and practices than the Old, yet cultural and linguistic barriers reinforced their sense of distinctiveness and encouraged the development of a communal form of life. Furthermore, unsuccessful at restructuring the society of their native land and unable to exert a direct influence on the social and religious life of their new surroundings, their remaining alternative was the communitarian strategy of seeking influence through example.

It is important to note, however, that unlike the later secular communitarians, the communal practices of these sects were seldom, if ever, a part of their original beliefs, but were tendencies that were intensified by external circumstances, and were finally realized for pragmatic rather than intrinsic reasons. Their primary focus was on spiritual rather than earthly things, on their relation to the divine rather than to one another. The form their human relationships took regarding, for example, the relations of the sexes, the family, and the ownership of property was intended to facilitate the achievement of their otherworldly objectives. Thus, while the later secular and other more earthly minded religious utopians of the nineteenth century believed that the pietistic communities had much to teach them, what they learned was not necessarily what these pietists had been most concerned to teach.

Though the pietistic communities were generally long-lived, these same language and cultural barriers kept them from acquiring American-born proselytes, and their common practice of celibacy further kept their numbers from becoming very large. The Shakers mark something of a shift in this communitarian tradition, for while pietistic in nature and European in derivation, their English-speaking origins allowed them to make a much greater impact on American society. By the time the Shakers had organized themselves into a communistic society in 1787, thirteen years after the arrival of their founder Mother Ann Lee, the leadership had passed into the hands of native-born Americans. Though ascetic and otherworldly in nature and celibate in practice, they were able to grow in numbers and influence due to their ability to recruit new members, particularly from the ranks of those stirred by the religious revivals of the period. The Oneida society formed in the 1840s represents a further shift away from the older communitarianism, for it showed an interest in both worlds and a more active concern for how to perfect American society. It, too, was rooted in the Christian tradition, but was itself a product of the evangelical revivals and perfectionist theology. Accordingly, what it drew from that tradition was markedly different. Though a carefully disciplined society, it lacked the stark simplicity and ascetic quality that marked most of the earlier religious groups.

Oneida had its own distinctive religious beliefs, which were originally conceived as the raison d'être of the group's existence, but what interested outsiders most about Oneida and its fellow religious communities was their communal social organization. In consequence, these groups tended to accentuate this aspect of their lives, emphasizing what most attracted the out-side world. Here, then, the stress was not on how civil and religious relations were structured within these societies, but simply on the secular, sociopoliti-cal arrangements of the group and on how they might be instructive for the rest of American society. Arthur Bestor finds it telling that when the Rappites completed construction of their third communal village in 1825 (twenty years after this religious sect's organization into a communal society), they chose not to name their village Harmony, as they had the first two, but Economy, in keeping with the new interest in the economic aspects of communal life (*Backwoods Utopias*, p. 40). Similarly he notes that in the first half of the nineteenth century, the Shakers "gradually shifted their emphasis from the-ology to social reform" (p. 41). And when John Humphrey Noyes, leader of the Oneida Community, wrote his *History of American Socialisms* in 1870, his interest was not in promoting the distinctive beliefs of his society, but in pointing out commonalities among the different communitarian ventures and in arguing that their fundamental form of social and economic organization was a distinctive truth in itself, which should be adopted by Americans generally, quite apart from considerations of the truth of specific religious beliefs.

In addition to Oneida, a number of other religiously motivated commu-nities rooted in American soil were initiated in the 1840s. Hopedale was founded by the Universalist minister Adin Ballou, while Brook Farm and Fruitlands were inspired by New England Unitarians and Transcendentalists. These groups occupied something of a middle ground between the overriding spiritual focus of the pietists and the worldly orientation of the secular com-munitarians. As Ronald Walters observes, "Oneida, Brook Farm and Hope-dale represent a native American midpoint between two types of commu-nitarianism originating in Europe: that of the German and Shaker pietists and the secular variety of Robert Owen and Charles Fourier" (*American Reform-ers*, p. 60).

This is, indeed, one way to slice up the communitarian pie, but there are no simple and clear lines of division. Differences between the Shakers and the pietist groups of Continental origin have already been noted—differences which position the Shakers closer to Oneida. Likewise, there are dissimilari-ties between Oneida and other American creations like Hopedale, Brook Farm, and Fruitlands. For while each was characterized by a distinctive religious tone, only at Oneida could it be said that adherence to specific religious doctrines and practices was an integral and defining feature of the community. The unbroken continuity between Brook Farm's early years as a Transcendentalist community and its later years as a Fourierist phalanx indi-cates that its religious character was of a more diffuse nature than that of

Oneida or the pietist communities. Conversely, this point should also serve to illustrate that the so-called secular utopian societies were not necessarily lacking in religious influences, and that their own doctrines taken as a set constituted something of an alternative religious vision. The similarities between Brook Farm and Oneida were sufficient to prompt Noyes to claim, somewhat fancifully, that the spirit of Brook Farm lived on in his own community, noting that its demise in the late 1840s was concurrent with the beginnings of Oneida.

It would be easy to exaggerate or oversimplify the nature of the trend away from ascetic, otherworldly religious communities (which lacked a vision for the whole of American society and adopted communistic practices out of expediency more than as a matter of principle) toward thisworldly, secular communities (which held to their communal practices as a model for the whole of society). Throughout the nineteenth century, pietist sects continued to emigrate to America, there to form communitarian societies. The Amana Society and the Bishop Hill Colony, both begun in the 1840s, were only two of the more important of these groups. Likewise, the first secular communitarian ventures developed before Oneida was formed or any of the other notable religiously inspired indigenous American communities were begun. Robert Owen's "new view of society," which he brought to America from England in 1824 and presented before Congress twice the following year, produced a wave of excitement across the land, resulting in the formation of a half dozen or so Owenite communities before the decade was over. Many Americans, however, believed that Owen's version of life in community lacked an appreciation of the importance of the Christian faith. Though he did provide for freedom of worship in his communities, formal religion itself did not have an active part to play in his ideal reconstruction of society. Indeed, here was a case where contemporary observers thought that the views of a "secular" communitarian approximated an alternative religion. Particularly disturbing was Owen's thoroughgoing environmentalism, which seemed to deny original sin and the need for renovation of the heart. Owen himself, on occasion, called his doctrines a "new religion," for which he claimed, before Congress, "the full and complete protection which the American Constitution freely offers to mental and religious liberty" (*Robert Owen in the United States*, p. 43).

The second and largest wave of secular utopianism came in the 1840s with the dissemination of the ideas of the Frenchman Charles Fourier by such American disciples as Albert Brisbane and Parke Godwin. While Owen had taught that people are formed by their environment, Fourier theorized that the environment must be formed to mesh with a fixed human nature, which present civilization had stifled and misshapen. Fourier's theory was notably less rationalistic than Owen's, and more amenable to the American religious temper. Noyes observed that Owenism was "limited and local, chiefly because it was thoroughly non-religious and even anti-religious" (*History*, p. 103), while he believed that the greater success of Fourierism was in large part due to its ability to ally itself with popular religion. Remarking on one of the National Conventions of the Fourierists, Noyes noted that "the letters and addresses abounded in quotations from scripture, always laboring to identify Fourierism with Christianity" (p. 228).

An important theme that characterizes and unites nearly all of the various communitarian ventures is that of millennialism. The belief in an imminent return of Christ was fundamental for the pietistic groups, and it is perhaps fair to say that this hope was, in part, responsible for their formation into communal societies. This was, they felt, the most appropriate way to live in preparation for the return of Christ. The communitarian new religions of the Shakers and Oneida marked a shift toward a spiritualized understanding of the millennium and Christ's reign on earth; and their communal organization was, thus, an attempted enactment of how life was to be lived in the millennial age.

The secular communitarians likewise adopted their own version of Christian millennialism. Parke Godwin believed that Fourier's doctrine of Association was the key that would open the gates of millennial blessing. The Kingdom of God was to be sought through "the harmony of the passions in associative unity," and the result would be the conquest of "false philosophy and national indigence and spurious civilization." Linking Fourier's principles to the widespread belief in America as a redeemer nation, Godwin further suggested that "the peculiar history of this nation convinces us that it has been prepared by Providence for the working out of glorious issues," and that Fourierism would be the means through which America would effect these blessings (quoted in Noyes, *History*, p. 220). Robert Owen's utopian doctrines were similarly millennial in tone. At one point in his career, he interpreted the coming of his "new religion" in terms of the apocalyptic prophecy of Christ: "And then shall they see the son of man (OR TRUTH) coming in a cloud with power and glory. And when these things begin to come to pass, then look up and lift up your heads, for your redemption (FROM CRIME AND MISERY) draweth nigh" (quoted in John Harrison, *Quest for the New Moral World*, p. 92).

Concerning their attitudes toward the American government, many of the communitarian societies had ambiguous feelings. On the one hand, they appreciated it since it provided, for the most part, a hospitable seedbed in which these new versions of life in community could grow and prove themselves before the rest of the world. But on the other, this government really had no role to play once these mustard seed communities had grown to a position of predominance in the American landscape, and at this point it would best be replaced by another. The government itself perceived this potential threat to its fundamental principles, and, consequently, its attitude toward these communities was ambiguous. So long as these groups remained small, they could be accommodated by the outside society and flourish under the federalist system of government with its promise of religious liberty, but when they grew to more threatening proportions, as the Mormons most clearly demonstrate, attitudes changed. Even the Harmonists, whose members never exceeded eight hundred, found their application for a charter from the state of Pennsylvania rejected on grounds that the ideals and practices of their community were subversive to those of American society.

Central to the communitarian outlook, in any case, was a distrust of the effectiveness of appeal to secular authority as a means of bringing about the desired social order. Communitarians advocated influence through example, rather than through political agitation, and believed that the present order needed to be replaced, not simply modified. The earliest pietist groups, of course, held this view in the extreme, claiming that the world had gone so badly awry that only the return of Christ could set things in proper order. Thus, the only choice for the saints, in order to keep themselves pure, was to withdraw from this evil world. Though these early groups, such as Ephrata, were not very optimistic about effecting change through example, a more positive view gradually took hold and came to characterize the communitarian outlook.

Concerning their own forms of government and polity, the communitarian groups varied widely. In general, the religious groups were authoritarian in nature, most being under the guidance of a charismatic leader. Such was the case with Johann Conrad Beissel of Ephrata, George Rapp of the Harmonists, Eric Jansson of Bishop Hill Colony, Christian Metz of the Amana Society, and John Humphrey Noyes of Oneida. Though such communities were, in principle, based on values and ideals that transcended their embodiment in any single person, their group membership was closely defined by allegiance to a charismatic leader, and the departure of that leader frequently meant the decline and eventual demise of the group itself. Such was the case for Ephrata, Bishop Hill, Oneida, and, to a lesser degree, Harmony and Amana. Unless the group was able to find a worthy successor to its founder, as the Mormons discovered in Brigham Young an able heir to the martyred Joseph Smith, it was in serious danger of disintegration. The case of the Shakers is somewhat distinct, in that their founder, Ann Lee, died before the group assumed its communal form. Leadership from Joseph Meacham in particular helped it survive its early years. While the group maintained its allegiance to

Mother Ann Lee and her revelations, its government assumed a hierarchical form where control was strict but not exercised through the unmediated power of a single individual.

In these religious societies, the distinction between temporal and spiritual spheres of communal life and government was not clear-cut. Rapp delegated the oversight of some aspects of temporal affairs to another, and the Amana and Shaker societies made a similar distinction in distributing responsibility among their ruling elders, but the spiritual leadership always clearly outranked the temporal. As for the secular communities, very few of them were overtly opposed to institutional religion. Most left their members free to practice whatever religion they might choose, provided, of course, the religious beliefs and practices did not clash with the fundamental values, ideals, and vision of life upon which the community was predicated. To the extent that these guiding ideals and values may be said to be of an implicitly religious nature, there was no distinction in the life and government of these communities between those aspects of life which were tacitly religious and those which were not. The model for "church and state" relations within these secular communities, then, might, by some stretch, be said to resemble that exemplified by the American nation itself, which, while allowing freedom of worship for a range of religious beliefs and practices, was not without its own implicit form of public religion in terms of a set of values and ideals shared by its loyal citizens.

Leadership in the secular communities was, almost without exception, nonauthoritarian in form and lacking in a charismatic figure. Even New Harmony, which was initiated through the direct efforts of Robert Owen, was far from being dominated by its founder. And this was in keeping with Owen's principles, for he advocated a constitutional and democratic form of government. Indeed, decentralized and nonhierarchical democratic governments were the norm for the secular colonies. Some former Owenites expressed their dissatisfaction with the lack of distinctly religious values and the absence of an authoritarian and strongly group-centered life by joining the ranks of the Shakers, among the more notable being Frederick Evans. Others, however, thought the solution to the ills of Owen's project lay in a move in the opposite direction. Such were the sentiments of Josiah Warren, who left the Owenites to form the anarchistic colonies of Equity and Modern Times.

Concerning forms of economic organization, the religious groups tended to practice a more thoroughgoing communism than the secular ones. This difference is particularly noteworthy in that nearly all the religious groups began simply as religious congregations and only later adopted communism of property and other communitarian practices. Except for the Mormons, the major religious groups considered below all practiced community of property and goods, while neither the Fourierist nor Owenite communities completely abolished private property nor provided for its members on the basis of need. Owen in principle favored community of property and goods, but he was not willing to risk his entire fortune on the New Harmony venture. Other Owenite communities likewise tended to be sponsored by one or a small number of investors. Those members who lacked capital to invest in the enterprise were expected to supply the difference through extra labor. The Fourierist phalanxes, as the communities were called, were more properly joint-stock companies, where the stockholders were not required to be participants. Community profits were to be distributed in varying proportions to investors and workers, with skilled labor receiving a higher percentage than unskilled.

In other aspects besides economics, the religious communities were similarly characterized by a higher degree of collectivization. The nuclear family was in most cases perceived as a threat to group loyalty, and the policy of celibacy as maintained by the Ephratans, Harmonists, and Shakers helped strengthen group cohesion and commitment. Noyes's unique solution at Oneida was not to institute celibacy, but to extend communalism to persons through a practice known as "complex marriage." This practice, he believed, not only avoided the problem of divided loyalties which accompanied "exclusive love," but actually served to strengthen group ties. Noyes frequently claimed that the primary goal of the communitarian movement was *"the enlargement of home—the extension of family union beyond the little man-and-wife circle to large corporations,"* and that "home on the large scale . . . is heaven" (*History*, pp. 23, 292). Through the use of common dining halls and frequent group meetings these communities did indeed become a kind of family for their members. Even at Amana, where celibacy was merely recommended and traditional family units were maintained, collective dairies, kitchens, and dining halls served to promote larger group unity. The Rappites had their own celibate households, averaging five or six in membership, which prepared their own meals. The Shaker colonies were each composed of several "families," ranging from thirty to ninety members, each of which approached economic self-sufficiency.

By contrast, the secular communities made little headway in abolishing the traditional family unit, though Owen, for example, was hardly a strong supporter of marriage and family life. In general, these communities made fewer demands on their members in terms of commitment, shared values, and common practices, and their way of life did not depart as radically from that of the surrounding American society as that of their religious counterparts. While roughly five of every six secular communities disbanded within ten years of their establishment, three in four of the religious societies persisted for over a decade. The durability of the religious communities proved to be an inspiration to the secular communitarian theorist who strove to distill the communitarian philosophy into a more generally palatable form, purged of its religious peculiarities and excessive restraints on individual freedom. In reality, however, these were frequently the features that contributed to a community's success.

In the larger view, even where the communitarian ventures were successful in terms of longevity and a modest realization of their goals, their success must be qualified, for the result was not that for which the communitarians had hoped. American society was not, in fact, transformed by the shining example of the successful communities. While the American federalist system was particularly amenable to the experimental implementations of utopian ideals through small communities, not everyone concluded that what worked on a small scale for a select, dedicated, and homogeneous group of people would necessarily work when applied to the whole society. An aged Thomas Jefferson gave expression to this skepticism when he replied in a letter to one communitarian:

That, in the principle of a communion of property, small societies may exist in habits of virtue, order, industry, and peace, and consequently in a state of as much happiness as Heaven has been pleased to deal out to imperfect humanity, I can readily conceive, and indeed, have seen its proofs in various small societies which have been constituted on that principle. But I do not feel authorized to conclude from these that an extended society, like that of the United States, or of an individual State, could be governed happily on the same principle (*The Writings of Thomas Jefferson*, vol. 15, Washington, D.C.: Thomas Jefferson Memorial Association, 1903, pp. 399–400).

The growth of industry and development of economies of scale after the Civil War hindered small communities from being economically self-sufficient and prosperous; and the solidification of the existing authority structures in American political and religious life rendered the communitarian approach to social reform increasingly unrealistic. Communal ventures were attempted in the late nineteenth and twentieth centuries as frequently as they had been in the previous decades, but seldom with the hope of providing a model for the reform of American society at large. Rather, they provided a means of retreat and withdrawal from a society with which members were still dissatisfied but no longer had any hope of changing.

The citations listed below focus on the well known and better researched communities of the estimated 143 that were founded in America before the Civil War. The most complete and thorough listing of American communitarian groups is Otochiko Okugawa's "Annotated List of Communal and Utopian Societies, 1787–1919," appended to Fogarty's *Dictionary of American Communal and Utopian History*. The *Dictionary*, itself, is a valuable reference work, containing a brief description of a significant number of these groups and a particularly worthwhile collection of biographical sketches of nearly all the notable utopian leaders of the period. Also included is a bibliographic essay and selected bibliography covering communities founded throughout the span of American history. Ralph Albertson's *Survey of Mutualistic Communistic Societies* is another useful source for sketches of the various communities. Bestor's *Backwoods Utopias* includes a helpful checklist of communities founded before the Civil War as well as an important bibliographic essay. Though in need of updating, the bibliographic essays found in the second volume of Donald Egbert and Stow Persons's *Socialism and American Life*, which cover nine of the major groups, remain unparalleled in their thoroughness. For a selection of writings on communitarian ventures worldwide, viewed primarily from a social sciences perspective, see Hyman Mariampolski's "Communes and Utopias." Rosabeth Kanter's bibliography in *Commitment and Community* is also helpful for its listing of historical and sociological sources relevant to the American scene.

Of the writings of surveys of American utopias there is no end; many of them are more valuable for what they tell of the cultural attitudes existing at the time they were written than for what they tell about the communities themselves. Few recent studies are as useful as the classic texts by Noyes, Charles Nordhoff, and William Hinds, with Noyes's *History of American Socialisms* being surely one of the most penetrating and perceptive studies ever published. Noyes's emphasis on the Owenite and Fourierist phases is complemented by Nordhoff's primary focus on the religious communities in his *Communistic Societies of the United States*. Hinds's *American Communities* is the most comprehensive, if least imaginative, of the three. Among modern studies, Bestor's *Backwoods Utopias* is indispensable, not only for its treatment of the Owenite phase, but for its opening remarks on American communitarianism as a movement. The second edition of this work also includes Bestor's excellent essay on "Patent-Office Models of the Good Society." A less useful but popular survey is Mark Holloway's *Heavens on Earth*. Two well-written chapters in Walters's *American Reformers* are devoted to a synthesis of much of the best scholarship on the antebellum communitarians. Special mention should also be made of Carol Weisbrod's *Boundaries of Utopia*, which studies the relations between five nineteenth-century communities and the American legal system.

Among the comparative studies listed below, Kanter's works deserve special mention. Most important is her *Commitment and Community*, which, from a sociological viewpoint, compares the nineteenth-century communal ventures with those of the 1960s. Her focus is on isolating the group structures and commitment mechanisms which made for a successful community, and though written with an eye for "lessons" from the past, her analysis has broad-ranging relevance. Charles Erasmus's sociological study *In Search of the Common Good*, which places the communitarians in transhistorical and worldwide perspective, devotes a chapter to a concise comparative analysis of the structures and practices of the major nineteenth-century American communes. The broader significance of the various sexual practices of the religious communities has been of special interest to scholars, and the recent works by Lawrence Foster and Louis Kern are particularly fine studies of the Shakers, Mormons, and Oneida Community from this angle. Fuller treatment of this important topic is given in the chapter on gender issues included in this volume. Ira Mandelker's *Religion, Society, and Utopia* provides a Weberian analysis of religious utopias, with primary attention given to the efforts of the Oneida Community to transcend what Weber theorized to be an inevitable tension between religion and the world. Finally, Dolores Hayden's *Seven American Utopias* deserves notice as it marks a new departure by exploring the significance of architectural design for understanding the social dynamics and ideologies of the various communities.

The Ephrata Colony, formally known as The Solitary Brethern of the Community of the Seventh Day Baptists, was founded in 1732 by Johann Conrad Beissel, and dissolved in 1770, two years after his death. The bibliography by Eugene Doll and Anneliese Funke provides an exhaustive listing of printed sources for the colony and covers manuscript collections and secondary accounts as well. The bibliography contained in Walter Klein's lively but carefully researched biography of Beissel is also helpful. A recent brief study of another leading figure at Ephrata, Israel Eckerlin, is located in Klaus Wust's *Saint-Adventurers of the Virginia Frontier*. The older studies on Ephrata by Julius Sachse and Oswald Seidensticker remain essential; a manuscript English translation of the latter is housed with the Germantown Historical Society.

George Rapp's Harmony Society, founded in 1805, is given thorough treatment by the numerous publications of Karl Arndt. His *George Rapp's Harmony Society, 1785–1847*, is the definitive study of the colony in its several locations in western Pennsylvania and southwestern Indiana. *George Rapp's Successors and Material Heirs, 1847–1917*, continues the narrative beyond Rapp's death to the Society's dissolution. Both volumes contain helpful bibliographies, and the latter includes a "Survey of the Harmony Society Archives at Economy, Pennsylvania." The earlier studies by John Bole, John Duss, and Aaron Williams are still worthwhile.

The Amana Society, also called the Society of True Inspiration, was, like Ephrata and Harmony, German pietist in origin. These followers of Christian Metz first emigrated to western New York in 1842, and a dozen years later moved to Iowa, where the Society would remain until its formal dissolution in 1932. Diane Barthel's *Amana* is an excellent sociological study of the Society's gradual secularization while Bertha Shambaugh provides the standard history written in a more traditional vein. Extensive manuscript sources are housed at Amana.

After tangling with the Lutheran State Church of Sweden over his perfectionist theology, Eric Jansson and his twelve hundred followers departed in 1846 to establish the pietist community of Bishop Hill, Illinois. Paul Elmen's *Wheat Flour Messiah* is a recent study of this colorful figure who was shot, four years after emigrating, by a disgruntled follower. Olov Isaksson and Sören Hallgren, as well as Michael Mikkelson, give useful accounts of the colony itself, which survived its leader by twelve years.

While many of the pietist groups believed that God could inspire and guide his present-day prophets by imparting to them new words, the communities designated below by the heading "Communitarian New Religions" constitute departures from previous beliefs or practices significant enough to warrant viewing them as discontinuous with the religious context in which they emerged. In the case of the Shakers, Mother Ann Lee claimed to be the female incarnation of the Godhead, and her revelations constituted the basis upon which the Society was built. By nearly all accounts, the Shakers, or the Society of Believers in Christ's Second Appearing, were the most successful and durable of the communitarian ventures. As Noyes observed, "Their success has been the 'specie basis' that has upheld all the paper theories, and counteracted the failures, of the French and English schools" (*History*, p. 670). The literature by and about the Shakers is vast, and Mary Richmond's two-volumed annotated bibliography *Shaker Literature* is a comprehensive listing of printed sources. She also includes locations and descriptions of the various manuscript collections. Kermit Pike's *A Guide to Shaker Manuscripts* is a catalog of the holdings of the largest manuscript depository. The *Shaker Quarterly* is also useful for its frequent bibliographic listings.

The leading scholar of the Shakers is Edward Deming Andrews, and his *The People Called Shakers* is the standard introduction to the subject. Still noteworthy, however, is the earlier survey by Marguerite Melcher. Henri Desroche's *The American Shakers* places the movement within the context of European social and religious radicalism. Though perhaps not entirely successful, Desroche argues that Shakerism, as a response to the nascent industrialism of Manchester, England, is a predecessor to modern socialism. Stephen Marini's *Radical Sects of Revolutionary New England* is an important study which treats the early Shakers within the context of other radical American religious movements of the day. The study of the Philadelphian black Shaker, Rebecca Cox Jackson, by Richard Williams and the edition of her autobiographical writings by Jean Humez provide an interesting counter-example to the common view of the Shakers as a strictly white rural phenomenon. Concerning Shaker expansion in the midwest, the standard work remains Richard McNemar's *The Kentucky Revival.* Noyes's *History* devotes relatively little space to the Shakers, but the chapter he includes provides a valuable account of the movement during its spiritualist phase. Literature written by Shakers themselves is extensive and only a representative sampling has been included here. Diane Sasson's *The Shaker Spiritual Narrative* is important for the attention it gives to the tension between the ideals of Shakerism and the values of the surrounding American society as manifested in these narratives.

Not listed below, but nonetheless worthy of mention, is the New Jerusalem Colony of Jemima Wilkinson. Sometimes regarded as an indigenous American version of Mother Ann Lee, the story of this unusual and obscure woman and the late eighteenth-century sect she founded is told in Herbert Wisbey's *Pioneer Prophetess: Jemima Wilkinson, The Publick Universal Friend* (Ithaca, N.Y.: Cornell University Press, 1964).

Unlike the founders of the Shakers and Mormons, Noyes never claimed extra-biblical revelations for support of his teachings. His millennial and perfectionist message may be seen as the logical extension of contempory currents of thought, but the practices that he initiated among the Oneida Community, based on what these doctrines implied, are sufficiently distinct to warrant the consideration of his venture as something of a new religion.

Unfortunately, many of the manuscript sources for the Oneida Community have been destroyed, while the remaining materials, housed in the Mansion House on the Oneida grounds, are not available to the public. The most complete record of printed sources on the group is Lester Wells's annotated bibliography. Two collections of primary materials dealing with the group's founder and leader are the compilations by his son George Wallingford Noyes. John Humphrey Noyes's own autobiographical account of the religious development of his early years, *Confessions of John H. Noyes: Part I* is invaluable. Part II, intended to deal with the formation of his social ideas, was never published.

Noyes himself showed a remarkable degree of self-understanding and psychological acuity concerning the dynamics of his community, and subsequent historians have followed in this vein with their own analyses. The recent studies by Robert Thomas employ psychohistory, as does Ernest Sandeen in his "John Humphrey Noyes and the New Adam." An important determinant of the success of communitarian ventures lay in the nature of the leadership, and Olin Spencer's essay on "The Oneida Community and the Instability of Charismatic Authority" analyzes the breakup of the Community in 1881 using social theories derived from Max Weber. Looking at membership composition, Fogarty's "Oneida: A Utopian Search for Religious Security" concludes that a primary appeal of the group lay in the security it offered to those discomfited by the uncertainties of American life. Studies dealing with the sexual practices of the Community have already been noted. The best traditional secondary account of Noyes remains Robert Parker's *A Yankee Saint*, while a standard treatment of the history of Oneida is Maren Lockwood Carden's sociological study *Oneida: Utopian Community to Modern Corporation*.

The Church of Jesus Christ of Latter-day Saints belongs somewhat on the fringe of communitarian phenomena. In their manifestation of group-mindedness, close adherence to their Prophet's leadership and teachings, subsequent separation into a mini-commonwealth within the larger American society, and attempt at economic self-sufficiency, the Mormons demonstrated many of the attributes of communitarianism. Only at isolated points in the movement's history, however, were communitarian ventures undertaken which involved corporate ownership of property, and these were limited experiments in which the whole group did not participate. Sheer numbers militated against a thoroughgoing communitarian outlook, and the decentralization entailed in the establishment of dozens of small communities might well have been regarded as detrimental to the unity of a movement which, in its early stages, was rapidly changing and highly protean.

Essential to an understanding of the Mormons is a knowledge of such standard works as the Book of Mormon, *The Pearl of Great Price*, and *The Doctrine and Covenants of the Church of Latter-day Saints* (a record of the revelations given to Joseph Smith and subsequent Church leaders). The *Journal of Discourses* provides twenty-six volumes of sermon texts of nineteenth-century leaders. Among the various bibliographies included below, several are particularly noteworthy. Chad Flake's massive *A Mormon Bibliography* is a record of all known printed sources by and about the Latter-day Saints printed during the Church's first century, while Davis Bitton's *Guide to Mormon Diaries and Autobiographies* provides an annotated listing of nearly three thousand manuscripts and their locations. The 62-page bibliography included in James Allen and Glen Leonard's *The Story of the Latter-day Saints* is probably the most useful annotated listing of secondary sources. For a record of current publications, see the annual listings by Chad Flake in *Brigham Young University Studies* and the tri-annual compilations titled "Among the Mormons" found in *Dialogue: A Journal of Mormon Thought*.

An indispensable documentary history of Mormonism's early period is Joseph Smith's *History of the Church of Jesus Christ of Latter-day Saints.* Of more recent vintage is a single-volume edition of primary materials by William Mulder and Russell Mortensen. Among the recent scholarly general histories of Mormonism is Leonard Arrington and Davis Bitton's *The Mormon Experience.* Valuable recent works on Mormon history from a cultural perspective include Mark Leone's *The Roots of Modern Mormonism* and Klaus Hansen's *Mormonism and the American Experience.* A classic analysis of Mormon beliefs and institutions by a sociologist is Thomas O'Dea's *The Mormons.* Marvin Hill and James Allen's *Mormonism and American Culture* provides an excellent anthology of articles by leading scholars in the field, while Mark McKiernan, Alma Blair, and Paul Edwards's *The Restoration Movement* is a useful collection of thirteen previously unpublished essays.

Fawn Brodie's *No Man Knows My History,* first published forty years ago, has, at least among non-Mormons, been the standard biography of Joseph Smith. Brodie provoked controversy by arguing that the Book of Mormon was a product of Joseph Smith's imaginative genius and that Mormonism itself could be understood as a product of the cultural context in which it arose. Richard Bushman gives a more sympathetic treatment of the Prophet's early life in *Joseph Smith and the Beginnings of Mormonism,* arguing, after an insightful delineation of the social and cultural conditions of Smith's upstate New York, that Joseph Smith was a man who outgrew his culture. In her excellent study *Mormonism: The Story of a New Religious Tradition,* Jan Shipps contends that Mormonism represents more than simply a move toward early Christian primitivism; it constitutes a break with the Christian tradition in the same way that Christianity broke with Judaism. Employing a history of religions approach, her study takes the broadest view and places Mormonism within the perspective of world religions and cultures.

For an orientation to Mormonism and church-state issues broadly conceived, John Wilson's suggestive essay "Some Comparative Perspectives on the Early Mormon Movement and the Church-State Question, 1830–1845" is a good place to begin. Klaus Hansen's *Quest for Empire* is an important study of the Mormon attempt to establish a political kingdom of God through the auspices of a secret central committee established by Joseph Smith. Bruce Flanders's *Nauvoo: Kingdom on the Mississippi* looks at the political and economic life of the Mormons in their final location prior to the Prophet's assassination and their subsequent migration to the Far West. The standard treatment of Mormon economic life for the Utah period is Leonard Arrington's *Great Basin Kingdom.* His recent biography, *Brigham Young: American Moses,* is the best study of Joseph Smith's successor. Arrington shows that, for Young, there was no distinction between church and state and that in his efforts to preserve his followers from a corrupt Gentile world and build group solidarity, Young's goals of economic self-sufficiency and cooperation were at variance with the individualistic values held by the larger American society. The communitarian experiments initiated by Young's "Second United Order of Enoch" in 1874 had their precedents in the settlements Joseph Smith established at Kirtland, Ohio, and Independence, Missouri, on the authority of revelations given him in 1832. The story of these ventures, along with other cooperative practices of the Mormons throughout their history, is told in *Building the City of God*, by Arrington, Feramorz Fox, and Dean May.

The topic of Mormon polygamy has traditionally been a focal point of church-state studies. Though the practice was outlawed by President Lincoln prior to the Civil War, not until much later was enforcement attempted. For an introduction to this subject, see Gustive Larson's *The "Americanization" of Utah for Statehood*. For a more broadly conceived study of Mormon polygamy, Foster's *Religion and Sexuality*, noted earlier, is excellent.

The heading of "Utopian Experiments" designates, roughly, those communities that did not prominently display an overtly religious orientation and motivation, but which were undertaken primarily as social experiments, being trial enactments of the preconceived vision of one or more social theorists. The Hopedale Community, founded in 1842 by Universalist minister Adin Ballou, is the most distinctly Christian of the groups listed here. Its continuance for a quarter-century also makes it the longest-lived. As the articles by Lewis Perry and Richard Rollins indicate, this society, organized on joint-stock principles, was composed of "Practical Christians" animated by the reform interests of the day. Fruitlands, founded in 1843 by Bronson Alcott and others, was a particularly small colony which survived less than two years but remains, along with Brook Farm, one of the notable testaments to transcendentalist ideals translated into a communal context. Brook Farm, famous in its own right for its distinguished members and visitors, also became, two years after its founding in 1841, the leading American Fourierist phalanx. Edith Curtis's *A Season in Utopia* provides a narrative history of the colony, while Henry Sams has edited a fine collection of primary documents. Lindsay Swift's *Brook Farm* contains entertaining vignettes of the notables associated with the community. For a biography of one of Brook Farm's leaders, see Charles Crowe's *George Ripley*. Unfortunately, few studies have been made of the numerous other Fourierist phalanxes, although Noyes's *History of American Socialisms* contains a valuable collection of primary materials for many, including the prominent North American and Wisconsin communities. The articles by Charles Guarneri are solid recent studies of Fourierism in America. Nicholas Riasanovsky has written an excellent guide to Fourier's system of thought, while Bestor's article on Albert Brisbane does justice to Fourier's leading disciple.

Concerning Owenism in America, Bestor's *Backwoods Utopias* remains the definitive work. Included is a bibliographic essay with extensive references to primary and secondary sources, as well as locations of manuscript collections. The best biography of Robert Owen is John Harrison's *Quest for a New Moral World*, which includes an extensive bibliography of writings by and about Owen. For a description of the leading Owenite community of New Harmony, see the studies by William Wilson and George Lockwood. Another English reformer, who had close ties with Owen, was Frances Wright. Alice Perkins and Theresa Wolfson's biography *Frances Wright* provides a good starting place for a study of this early feminist, who was prominent in the communitarian movement and who founded the interracial community of Nashoba.

BIBLIOGRAPHY

1. GENERAL WORKS

a. Historical Treatments

Albertson, Ralph. A Survey of Mutualistic Communistic
Communities in America. 1936. Reprint. New York: AMS
Press, 1973.

Bestor, Arthur Eugene, Jr. Backwoods Utopias: The Sectarian
and Owenite Phases of Communitarian Socialism in America,
1663-1829. 2d ed. Philadelphia: University of Pennsylvania
Press, 1970.

Brown, Ira V. "Watchers of the Second Coming: The Millenarian
Tradition in America." Mississippi Valley Historical Review
39 (December 1952), 441-458.

Cross, Whitney R. The Burned-Over District: The Social and
Intellectual History of Enthusiastic Religion in Western New
York, 1800-1850. Ithaca, N.Y.: Cornell University Press,
1950.

Durnbaugh, Donald F. "Work and Hope: The Spirituality of the
Radical Pietist Communitarians." Church History 39 (March
1970), 72-90.

Egbert, Donald Drew, and Persons, Stow, eds. Socialism and
American Life. 2 vols. Princeton, N.J.: Princeton
University Press, 1952.

Fellman, Michael. The Unbounded Frame: Freedom and Community
in Nineteenth Century American Utopianism. Westport, Conn.:
Greenwood Press, 1973.

Fogarty, Robert S. Dictionary of American Communal and Utopian
History. Westport, Conn.: Greenwood Press, 1980.

Fogarty, Robert S., ed. American Utopianism. Itasca, Ill.: F.
E. Peacock, 1972.

Fried, Albert, ed. Socialism in America: From the Shakers to
the Third International: A Documentary History. Garden
City, N.Y.: Doubleday Anchor, 1970.

Fryer, Judith. "American Eves in American Edens." American
Scholar 44 (Winter 1974-1975), 78-99.

Guimond, James. "Nineteenth-Century American Millennial
Experience." Shaker Quarterly 13 (Spring 1973), 3-15;
(Summer 1973), 42-55.

Harrison, John F. C. The Second Coming: Popular
Millenarianism, 1780-1850. London: Routledge & Kegan Paul,
1979.

Hatch, Nathan O. "Sola Scriptura and Novus Ordo Seculorum."
In The Bible in America: Essays in Cultural History, edited
by Nathan O. Hatch and Mark A. Noll. New York: Oxford
University Press, 1982.

Hinds, William A. American Communities and Cooperative
Colonies. 3d ed. Chicago: C. H. Kerr and Co., 1908.

Holloway, Mark. Heavens on Earth: Utopian Communities in
America, 1680-1880. 2d ed. New York: Dover Publications,
1966.

Kent, Alexander, comp. "Cooperative Communities in the United
States." Bulletin of the Department of Labor 35 (July
1901), 563-646.

Lawson, Donna. Brothers and Sisters All Over This Land:
America's First Communes. New York: Praeger Publishers,
1972.

Ludlum, David M. "Social Architects." Chapter 8 in Social
Ferment in Vermont: 1791-1850. New York: Columbia
University Press, 1939.

Manuel, Frank E., and Manuel, Fritzie P. Utopian Thought in
the Western World. Cambridge, Mass.: Harvard University
Press, Belknap Press, 1979.

Manuel, Frank E., ed. Utopias and Utopian Thought. Boston:
Houghton Mifflin, 1965.

Meynen, Emil, ed. Bibliography on German Settlement in
Colonial North America. Leipzig: Harrossowitz, 1937.

Moment, Gairdner B., and Kraushaar, Otto F., eds. Utopias: The
American Experience. Metuchen, N.J.: Scarecrow Press, 1980.

Nordhoff, Charles. The Communistic Societies of the United
     States, From Personal Visit and Observation. 1875.
     Reprint. New York: Dover, 1960.

Noyes, John Humphrey. History of American Socialisms.
     Philadelphia: J. B. Lippincott and Co., 1870.

Parrington, Vernon L., Jr. American Dreams: A Study of
     American Utopias. 2d ed. New York: Russell & Russell,
     1964.

Rexroth, Kenneth. Communalism: From Its Origins to the
     Twentieth Century. New York: Seabury Press, 1974.

Rhodes, H. V. Utopia in American Political Thought. Tucson,
     Ariz.: University of Arizona Press, 1967.

Smith, David E. "Millenarian Scholarship in America."
     American Quarterly 17 (Autumn 1965), 535-549.

Sweet, Leonard I. "Millennialism in America: Recent Studies."
     Theological Studies 40 (September 1979), 510-531.

Sweetland, James H. "Federal Sources for the Study of
     Collective Communities." Government Publications Review 7A,
     no. 2 (1980), 129-138.

Thomas, John L. "Anti-Slavery and Utopia." In The Anti-
     Slavery Vanguard, edited by Martin Duberman. Princeton,
     N.J.: Princeton University Press, 1965.

Thomas, John L. "Romantic Reform in America, 1815-1865."
     American Quarterly 17 (Winter 1965), 656-681.

Tyler, Alice F. Freedom's Ferment: Phases of American Social
     History to 1860. Minneapolis: University of Minnesota
     Press, 1944.

Veysey, Laurence, ed. The Perfectionists: Radical Social
     Thought in the North, 1815-1860. New York: John Wiley and
     Sons, 1973.

Walters, Ronald G. American Reformers, 1815-1860. New York:
     Hill and Wang, 1978.

Weisbrod, Carol. The Boundaries of Utopia. New York: Pantheon
     Books, 1980.

b. Comparative Studies

Alexander, Peter, and Gill, Rodger, eds. Utopias. London:
     Gerald Duckworth and Co., 1984.

Bennett, John W. "Communes and Communitarianism." Theory and
    Society 2 (Spring 1975), 63-94.

Cavan, Ruth Shoule, and Das, Man Singh, eds. Communes:
    Historical and Contemporary. New Delhi: Vikas Publishing
    House, 1979.

Erasmus, Charles J. In Search of the Common Good: Utopian
    Experiments Past and Future. New York: Free Press, 1977.

Foster, Lawrence. Religion and Sexuality: Three American
    Communal Experiments of the Nineteenth Century. New York:
    Oxford University Press, 1981.

Goodwin, Barbara. Social Science and Utopia: Nineteenth-
    Century Models of Social Harmony. Hassocks, England:
    Harvester Press, 1978.

Hayden, Dolores. Seven American Utopias: The Architecture of
    Communitarian Socialism, 1790-1975. Cambridge, Mass.:
    M.I.T. Press, 1976.

Hostetler, John A. Communitarian Societies. New York: Holt,
    Rinehart and Winston, 1974.

Kanter, Rosabeth Moss. Commitment and Community, Communes and
    Utopias in Sociological Perspective. Cambridge, Mass.:
    Harvard University Press, 1972.

Kanter, Rosabeth Moss. "Utopian Communities." Sociological
    Inquiry 43, nos. 3-4 (1973), 263-290.

Kanter, Rosabeth Moss, ed. Communes: Creating and Managing the
    Collective Life. New York: Harper & Row, 1973.

Kephart, William M. Extraordinary Groups: The Sociology of
    Unconventional Life-Styles. New York: St. Martin's Press,
    1976.

Kern, Louis. An Ordered Love: Sex Roles and Sexuality in
    Victorian Utopias--the Shakers, the Mormons, and the Oneida
    Community. Chapel Hill: University of North Carolina Press,
    1981.

LaBarre, Weston. "Materials for a History of Studies of Crisis
    Cults: A Bibliographical Essay." Current Anthropology 12
    (February 1971), 3-44.

Levitas, R. "Sociology and Utopia." Sociology 13 (January
    1979), 19-33.

Mandelker, Ira L. Religion, Society, and Utopia in Nineteenth-
    Century America. Amherst, Mass.: University of
    Massachusetts Press, 1984.

Mariampolski, Hyman, ed. "Communes and Utopias, Past and Present: A Bibliography of Post-1945 Studies." Bulletin of Bibliography 36 (July-September 1979), 119-127, 143.

Melville, Keith. Communes in the Counter Culture: Origins, Theories, Styles of Life. New York: William Morrow, 1972.

Muncy, Raymond Lee. Sex and Marriage in Utopian Communities: Nineteenth-Century America. Bloomington, Ind.: Indiana University Press, 1973.

Redekop, Calvin. "A New Look at Sect Development." Journal for the Scientific Study of Religion 13 (September 1974), 345-352.

Richter, Peyton E., ed. Utopias: Social Ideals and Communal Experiments. Boston: Holbrook Press, 1971.

Schwartz, Hillel. "The End of the Beginning: Millenarian Studies, 1969-75." Religious Studies Review 2 (July 1976), 1-15.

Stephan, Karen H., and Stephan, G. Edward. "Religion and the Survival of Utopian Communities." Journal for the Scientific Study of Religion 12 (March 1973), 89-100.

Thrupp, Sylvia L., ed. Millennial Dreams in Action. New York: Schocken, 1970.

Wallace, Anthony F. C. "Revitalization Movements: Some Theoretical Considerations for Their Comparative Study." American Anthropologist 38 (April 1956), 264-281.

Waltman, Jerold L. "Federalism, Communitarianism, and Current Realities." Potomac Review 22-23 (1982), 31-48.

Whitworth, John McKelvie. God's Blueprints: A Sociological Study of Three Utopian Sects. Boston: Routledge & Kegan Paul, 1975.

2. TRADITIONAL PIETISTIC COMMUNITARIAN GROUPS

a. Ephrata

Aurand, A. Monroe, Jr. Historical Account of the Ephrata Cloister and the Seventh Day Baptist Society. Harrisburg, Pa.: Aurand Press, 1940.

Doll, Eugene E. "Social and Economic Organization in Two Pennsylvania German Religious Communities." American Journal of Sociology 57 (September 1951), 168-177.

Doll, Eugene E., and Funke, Anneliese. The Ephrata Cloisters:
     An Annotated Bibliography. Bibliographies on German
     American History, no. 3. Philadelphia: Carl Schurz Memorial
     Foundation, 1944.

Ernst, James E. Ephrata, A History. Allentown, Pa.:
     Schlecters, 1963.

Klein, Walter C. Johann Conrad Beissel, Mystic and Martinet,
     1690-1768. Philadelphia: University of Pennsylvania Press,
     1942.

Lamech, Brother, and Agrippa, Brother. Chronicon Ephratense: A
     History of the Community of Seventh Day Baptists at Ephrata,
     Lancaster County, Pennsylvania. Translated by J. Max Hark.
     1889. Reprint. New York: Burt Franklin, 1972.

Randolph, Corliss F. "The German Seventh-Day Baptists." In
     Seventh Day Baptists in Europe and America, vol. 2., edited
     by the Seventh Day Baptist General Conference, 933-1257.
     Plainfield, N.J.: American Sabbath Tract Society, 1910.

Reichman, Felix, and Doll, Eugene E., eds. Ephrata As Seen by
     Contemporaries. Allentown, Pa.: Pennsylvania German
     Folklore Society, 1952.

Sachse, Julius F. The German Sectarians of Pennsylvania, 1708-
     1800: A Critical and Legendary History of the Ephrata
     Cloister and the Dunkers. 2 vols. Philadelphia: The
     author, 1899-1900.

Seidensticker, Oswald W. Ephrata, eine americanische
     Klostergeschichte. Cincinnati: Meckenborg & Rosenthal,
     1883.

Williams, Edwin M. "The Monastic Orders of Provincial
     Ephrata." In Lancaster County, Pennsylvania: A History,
     vol. 1, edited by H. M. J. Klein and E. Melvin Williams,
     384-476. New York: Lewis Historical Publishing Company,
     1924.

Wust, Klaus. The Saint-Adventurers of the Virginia Frontier.
     Edinburg, Va.: Shenandoah History, 1977.

                         b. Harmony

Arndt, Karl J. R. George Rapp's Harmony Society, 1785-1847.
     2d ed. Rutherford, N.J.: Fairleigh Dickinson University
     Press, 1972.

Arndt, Karl J. R. George Rapp's Successors and Material Heirs,
     1847-1916. Rutherford, N.J.: Fairleigh Dickinson University
     Press, 1971.

Arndt, Karl J. R.   "Rapp's Harmony Society as an Institution
  'Calculated to Undermine and Destroy Those Fundamental
  Principles of Free Government, Which Have Conspicuously
  Distinguished Us From All the Nations of the Earth.'"
  Western Pennsylvania Historical Magazine 63 (October 1980),
  359-366.

Arndt, Karl J. R., comp. and ed.   A Documentary History of the
  Indiana Decade of the Harmony Society, 1814-1824.   2 vols.
  Indianapolis: Indiana Historical Society, 1975-1978.

Arndt, Karl J. R., comp. and ed.   Economy on the Ohio, 1826-
  1834: George Rapp's Third Harmony, A Documentary History.
  Worcester, Mass.: Harmony Society Press, 1984.

Arndt, Karl J. R., comp. and ed.   George Rapp's Separatists,
  1700-1803: The German Prelude to Rapp's American Harmony
  Society, A Documentary History.   Worcester, Mass.: Harmony
  Society Press, 1980.

Arndt, Karl J. R., comp. and ed.   Harmony on the
  Connoquenessing: George Rapp's First American Harmony, 1803-
  1815.   Worcester, Mass.: Harmony Society Press, 1980.

Arndt, Karl J. R., comp. and ed.   Harmony on the Wabash in
  Transition, 1824-1826: A Documentary History.   Worcester,
  Mass.: Harmony Society Press, 1982.

Bole, John A.   The Harmony Society: A Chapter in German
  American Culture History.   1904.   Reprint.   New York: AMS
  Press, 1973.

Douglas, Paul H.   "The Material Culture of the Harmony
  Society."   Pennsylvania Folklife 24, no. 3 (1975), 2-16.

Duss, John A.   The Harmonists: A Personal History.   1943.
  Reprint.   Philadelphia: Porcupine Press, 1973.

Friesen, Gerhard K., ed.   "An Additional Source on the Harmony
  Society of Economy, Pennsylvania."   Western Pennsylvania
  Historical Magazine 61 (October 1978), 301-314.

Knoedler, Christiana F.   The Harmony Society: A 19th Century
  Utopia.   New York: Vantage Press, 1954.

Kring, Hilda Adam.   The Harmonists, A Folk-Cultural Approach.
  ATLA Monograph Series, no. 3.   Metuchen, N.J.: Scarecrow
  Press, 1973.

Pitzer, Donald E., and Elliott, Josephine M.   "New Harmony's
  First Utopians, 1814-1824."   Indiana Magazine of History 75
  (September 1979), 224-300.

Trautmann, Frederic, ed. and trans. "Western Pennsylvania
     Through a German's Eyes: The Travels of Franz von Loher."
     Western Pennsylvania Historical Magazine 65 (July 1982),
     221-237.

Williams, Aaron. The Harmony Society at Economy, Pennsylvania,
     Founded by George Rapp, A.D. 1805. 1866. Reprint. New
     York: Augustus Kelly, 1970.

                         c. Amana

Andelson, Jonathan G. "The Double Bind and Social Change in
     Communal Amana." Human Relations 34 (February 1981), 111-
     125.

Andelson, Jonathan G. "Routinization of Behavior in a
     Charismatic Leader." American Ethnologist 7 (November
     1980), 716-733.

Barthel, Diane L. Amana: From Pietist Sect to American
     Community. Lincoln: University of Nebraska Press, 1984.

Christen, Wallace. Inspirationist Mysticism: The Amana
     Community. Lockport, Ill.: Ogren Press, 1975.

Perkins, William Rufus, and Wick, Barthinius. History of the
     Amana Society. 1891. Reprint. New York: Arno Press, 1975.

Shambaugh, Bertha M. Amana That Was and Amana That Is. 1932.
     Reprint. New York: Arno Press, 1976.

Yambura, Barbara S., and Bodine, Eunice W. A Change and a
     Parting: My Story of Amana. Ames: Iowa State University
     Press, 1960.

                       d. Bishop Hill

Elmen, Paul. "Bishop Hill: Utopia on the Prairie." Chicago
     History 5 (Spring 1976), 45-52.

Elmen, Paul. Wheat Flour Messiah. Carbondale, Ill.: Southern
     Illinois University Press, 1976.

Isaksson, Olov, and Hallgren, Sören. Bishop Hill, Illinois: A
     Utopia on the Prairie. Translated by Albert Read.
     Stockholm: LT Publishing House, 1969.

Mikkelsen, Michael Andrew. The Bishop Hill Colony: A Religious
     Communistic Settlement in Henry County, Illinois. 1892.
     Reprint. Philadelphia: Porcupine Press, 1973.

Norton, John E., ed. "'For It Flows with Milk and Honey'; Two Immigrant Letters About Bishop Hill." _Swedish Pioneer Historical Quarterly_ 24 (July 1973), 163-179.

Wright, Rochelle. "Stuart Engstrand and Bishop Hill." _Swedish Pioneer Historical Quarterly_ 28 (July 1977), 192-204.

e. Other Pietist Communities

Dobbs, Catherine R. _Freedom's Will: The Society of the Separatists of Zoar_. New York: William-Frederick Press, 1947.

Gollin, Gillian Lindt. _Moravians in Two Worlds: A Study of Changing Communities_. New York: Columbia University Press, 1967.

Grant, H. Roger. "The Society of Bethel: A Visitor's Account." _Missouri Historical Review_ 68 (January 1974), 223-231.

Hendricks, Robert J. _Bethel and Aurora: An Experiment in Communism as Practical Christianity with Some Account of Past and Present Ventures in Collective Living_. 1933. Reprint. New York: AMS Press, 1971.

James, Bartlett B. _The Labadist Colony in Maryland_. 1899. Reprint. Baltimore: Johns Hopkins University Press, 1974.

Landis, George B. "The Society of Separatists of Zoar, Ohio." American Historical Association, _Annual Report_ (1898), 163-220.

Levering, Joseph Mortimer. _A History of Bethlehem, Pennsylvania, 1741-1872, with Some Account of Its Founders and Their Early Activity in America_. 1903. Reprint. New York: AMS Press, 1971.

Morhart, Hilda Dischinger. _The Zoar Story_. Dover, Ohio: Seibert Printing Co., 1967.

Randall, E. O. _History of the Zoar Society, From Its Commencement to Its Conclusion: A Sociological Study in Communism_. 1904. Reprint. New York: AMS Press, 1971.

Sessler, Jacob John. _Communal Pietism among Early American Moravians_. New York: H. Holt and Co., 1933.

3. COMMUNITARIAN NEW RELIGIONS

a. Shakers

Andrews, Edward Deming. The People Called Shakers: A Search
    for the Perfect Society. 2d ed. New York: Dover, 1963.

Andrews, Edward Deming, and Andrews, Faith. "The Shaker
    Children's Order." In Winterthur Portfolio 8, edited by Ian
    M. G. Quimby. Charlottesville, Va.: University Press of
    Virginia, 1973.

Andrews, Edward Deming, and Andrews, Faith. "The Shakers and
    the Law." Chapter 3 in Work and Worship: The Economic Order
    of the Shakers. Greenwich, Conn.: New York Graphic Society,
    1974.

Bainbridge, William Sims. "Shaker Demographics, 1840-1900."
    Journal for the Scientific Study of Religion 21 (December
    1982), 352-365.

[Bishop, Rufus, and Wells, Seth Y., eds.] Testimonies of the
    Life, Character, Revelations and Doctrines of Our Ever
    Blessed Mother Ann Lee and the Elders with Her. Hancock,
    Mass.: J. Talcott & J. Deming, 1816.

Brewer, Priscilla J. "Emerson, Lane, and the Shakers: A Case
    of Converging Ideologies." New England Quarterly 55 (June
    1982), 254-275.

Brown, Thomas. An Account of the People Called Shakers. 1812.
    Reprint. New York: AMS Press, 1972.

Campion, Nardi Reeder. Ann the Word: The Life of Mother Ann
    Lee, Founder of the Shakers. Boston: Little, Brown, 1976.

Clark, Thomas D., and Ham, F. Gerald. Pleasant Hill and Its
    Shakers. Pleasant Hill, Ky.: Shakertown Press, 1968.

Desroche, Henri. The American Shakers: From Neo-Christianity
    to Presocialism. Translated and edited by John K. Savacool.
    Amherst, Mass.: University of Massachusetts Press, 1971.

Evans, Frederick W. Autobiography of a Shaker and Revelation
    of the Apocalypse. 1888. Reprint. Philadelphia: Porcupine
    Press, 1973.

Evans, Frederick W. Shakers; Compendium of the Origin,
    History, Principles, Rules and Regulations, Government and
    Doctrine of the United Society of Believers in Christ's
    Second Appearing. 4th ed. 1867. Reprint. New York: AMS
    Press, 1975.

[Green, Calvin, and Wells, Seth Y.] A Summary View of the
   Millennial Church or United Society of Believers (Commonly
   Called Shakers). Albany, N.Y.: Packard & Van Benthuysen,
   1823.

Horgan, Edward R. The Shaker Holy Land: A Community Portrait.
   Harvard, Mass.: Harvard Common Press, 1982.

Jackson, Rebecca. Gifts of Power: The Writings of Rebecca
   Jackson, Black Visionary, Shaker Eldress. Edited by Jean
   McMahon Humez. Amherst, Mass.: University of Massachusetts
   Press, 1981.

Johnson, Theodore, ed. "The 'Millennial Laws' of 1821."
   Shaker Quarterly 7 (Summer 1967), 35-43.

Johnson, Theodore, ed. "Rules and Orders for the Church of
   Christ's Second Appearing . . . 1860." Shaker Quarterly 11
   (Winter 1971), 139-165.

Klein, Janice. "Ann Lee and Mary Baker Eddy: The Parenting of
   New Religions." Journal of Psychohistory 6 (Winter 1979),
   361-375.

MacLean, John Patterson. Shakers of Ohio. 1907.
   Philadelphia: Porcupine Press, 1974.

McNemar, Richard. The Kentucky Revival. 4th ed. 1846.
   Reprint. New York: AMS Press, 1974.

Marini, Stephen A. Radical Sects of Revolutionary New England.
   Cambridge, Mass.: Harvard University Press, 1982.

Meader, Robert F. W. "The Shakers and the Mormons." Shaker
   Quarterly 2 (Fall 1962), 83-96.

Melcher, Marguerite Fellows. The Shaker Adventure. 1941.
   Reprint. Cleveland: Press of Western Reserve University,
   1960.

Morgan, John H. "Religious Communism: The Shaker Experiment in
   Christian Community." Shaker Quarterly 12 (Winter 1973),
   119-131.

Morse, Flo, ed. The Shakers and the World's People. New York:
   Dodd, Mead, 1980.

Neal, Julia. By Their Fruits: The Story of Shakerism in South
   Union, Kentucky. 1947. Reprint. Philadelphia: Porcupine
   Press, 1974.

Neal, Julia. The Kentucky Shakers. Lexington, Ky.: University
   Press of Kentucky, 1977.

Paterwick, Stephen. "The Effect of the Civil War on Shaker
    Societies." Historical Journal of Western Massachusetts 2
    (January 1973), 6-26.

Patterson, Daniel W. The Shaker Spiritual. Princeton, N.J.:
    Princeton University Press, 1979.

Piercy, Caroline B. The Valley of God's Pleasure: A Saga of
    the North Union Community. New York: Stratford House, 1951.

Pike, Kermit J., ed. A Guide to Shaker Manuscripts in the
    Library of Western Reserve Historical Society. Cleveland:
    Western Reserve Historical Society, 1974.

Proper, David R., ed. "Bibliography of Shaker Periodical
    Literature." Shaker Quarterly 4 (Winter 1964), 130-142; 5
    (Spring 1965), 26-32; 5 (Winter 1965), 141-144; 8 (Winter
    1968), 107-110; 10 (Winter 1970), 138-140; 13 (Spring 1973),
    33-36.

Ray, Mary Lyn. "A Reappraisal of Shaker Furniture and
    Society." In Winterthur Portfolio 8, edited by Ian M. G.
    Quimby. Charlottesville, Va.: University Press of Virginia,
    1973.

Richmond, Mary L. Shaker Literature: A Bibliography. 2 vols.
    Hanover, N.H.: University Press of New England, 1977.

Rourke, Constance. "The Shakers." In her The Roots of
    American Culture and Other Essays. Edited by Van Wyck
    Brooks. New York: Harcourt Brace, 1942.

Sasson, Diane. The Shaker Spiritual Narrative. Knoxville,
    Tenn.: University of Tennessee Press, 1983.

Sears, Clara Endicott, comp. Gleanings from Old Shaker
    Journals. 1916. Reprint. Westport, Conn.: Hyperion Press,
    1975.

Society of Believers at Pleasant Hill, Kentucky. Account of
    Some of the Proceedings of the Legislatures of the States of
    Kentucky and New Hampshire . . . in Relation to the People
    Called Shakers. 1828. Reprint. New York: Egbert, Hovey &
    King, 1846.

Thomas, Samuel W., and Young, Mary Lawrence. "The Development
    of Shakertown at Pleasant Hill, Kentucky." Filson Club
    History Quarterly 49 (July 1975), 231-255.

Upton, James M. "The Shakers as Pacifists in the Period
    Between 1812 and the Civil War." Filson Club History
    Quarterly 47 (July 1973), 267-283.

Upton, Richard F. "Franklin Pierce and the Shakers: A
     Subchapter in the Struggle for Religious Liberty."
     Historical New Hampshire 23 (Summer 1968), 3-18.

White, Anna, and Taylor, Leila S. Shakerism: Its Meaning and
     Message. 1904. Reprint. New York: AMS Press, 1972.

Williams, Richard E. Called and Chosen: The Story of Mother
     Rebecca Jackson and the Philadelphia Shakers. Metuchen,
     N.J.: Scarecrow Press, 1981.

Yoder, Don. "The Spiritual Lineage of Shakerism."
     Pennsylvania Folklife 27 (Spring 1978), 2-14.

[Youngs, Benjamin Seth.] The Testimony of Christ's Second
     Appearing. Lebanon, Ohio: John McClean, 1808.

                         b. Oneida

Achorn, Erik. "Mary Cragin, Perfectionist Saint: Noyes' Theory
     and Experiments." New England Quarterly 28 (December 1955),
     490-518.

Carden, Maren Lockwood. Oneida: Utopian Community to Modern
     Corporation. Baltimore: Johns Hopkins University Press,
     1969.

DeMaria, Richard. Communal Love at Oneida: A Perfectionist
     Vision of Authority, Property, and Sexual Order. New York:
     Edwin Mellen, 1978.

Dixon, William Hepworth. Spiritual Wives. 2 vols.
     Philadelphia: J. B. Lippincott, 1868.

Estlake, Allan [Abel Easton]. The Oneida Community: A Record
     of an Attempt to Carry out the Principles of Christian
     Unselfishness and Scientific Race Improvement. London:
     George Redway, 1900.

Fogarty, Robert S. "Oneida: A Utopian Search for Religious
     Security." Labor History 14 (Spring 1973), 202-227.

Griffin, Clifford S. "Making Noyes." Reviews in American
     History 5 (December 1977), 518-523.

Lockwood, Maren. "The Experimental Utopia in America." In
     Utopias and Utopian Thought, edited by Frank E. Manuel.
     Boston: Houghton Mifflin, 1965.

Noyes, George Wallingford, ed. John Humphrey Noyes, The Putney
     Community. Oneida, N.Y.: The editor, 1931.

Noyes, George Wallingford, ed. The Religious Experience of
     John Humphrey Noyes. New York: Macmillan, 1923.

Noyes, John Humphrey. The Berean: A Manual for the Help of
    Those Who Seek the Faith of the Primitive Church. Putney,
    Vt.: Office of the Spiritual Magazine, 1847.

Noyes, John Humphrey. Confessions of John H. Noyes: Part I:
    Confessions of Religious Experience, Including a History of
    Modern Perfectionism. Oneida Reserve, N.Y.: Leonard, 1849.

Noyes, Pierrepont B. My Father's House: An Oneida Boyhood.
    New York: Farrar & Reinhart, 1937.

Olin, Spencer C., Jr. "The Oneida Community and the
    Instability of Charismatic Authority." Journal of American
    History 67 (September 1980), 285-300.

Oneida Community. Bible Communism: A Compilation of the Annual
    Reports and Other Publications of the Oneida Association and
    Its Branches. 1853. Reprint. Philadelphia: Porcupine
    Press, 1973.

Oneida Community. Handbook of the Oneida Community, 1867 &
    1871. 1867, 1871. Reprint. New York: AMS Press, 1976.

Parker, Robert A. A Yankee Saint: John Humphrey Noyes and the
    Oneida Community. New York: G. P. Putnam's Sons, 1935.

Robertson, Constance Noyes. Oneida Community Profiles.
    Syracuse, N.Y.: Syracuse University Press, 1977.

Robertson, Constance Noyes. Oneida Community: The Breakup,
    1876-1881. Syracuse, N.Y.: Syracuse University Press, 1972.

Robertson, Constance Noyes, ed. Oneida Community: An
    Autobiography, 1851-1876. Syracuse, N.Y.: Syracuse
    University Press, 1970.

Sandeen, Ernest R. "John Humphrey Noyes as the New Adam."
    Church History 40 (March 1971), 82-90.

Sibley, Mulford Q. "Oneida's Challenge to American Culture."
    In Studies in American Culture, edited by Joseph J. Kwait.
    Minneapolis: University of Minnesota Press, 1960.

Thomas, Robert D. "John Humphrey Noyes and the Oneida
    Community: A 19th-Century American Father and his Family."
    Psychohistory Review 6, nos. 2-3 (1977-1978), 68-87.

Thomas, Robert D. The Man Who Would Be Perfect: John Humphrey
    Noyes and the Utopian Impulse. Philadelphia: University of
    Pennsylvania Press, 1977.

Wells, Lester G. The Oneida Community Collection in the
    Syracuse University Library. Syracuse, N.Y.: Syracuse
    University Library, 1961.

c. Mormons

Alexander, Thomas G. "The Place of Joseph Smith in the
  Development of American Religion: A Historiographical
  Inquiry." Journal of Mormon History 5 (1978), 3-17.

Alexander, Thomas G., and Allen, James B. "The Mormons in the
  Mountain West: A Selected Bibliography." Arizona and the
  West 9 (Winter 1967), 365-384.

Allen, Edward J. The Second United Order Among the Mormons.
  New York: Columbia University Press, 1936.

Allen, James B. "Ecclesiastical Influence on Local Government
  in the Territory of Utah." Arizona and the West 8 (Spring
  1966), 35-48.

Allen, James B. "Emergence of a Fundamental: The Expanding
  Role of Joseph Smith's First Vision in Mormon Religious
  Thought." Journal of Mormon History 7 (1980), 43-61.

Allen, James B., and Arrington, Leonard J. "Mormon Origins in
  New York: An Introductory Analysis." Brigham Young
  University Studies 9 (Spring 1969), 241-274.

Allen, James B., and Leonard, Glen M. The Story of the Latter-
  day Saints. Salt Lake City: Deseret Book Company, 1976.

Anderson, Richard. Joseph Smith's New England Heritage. Salt
  Lake City: Deseret Book Company, 1971.

Arrington, Leonard J. Brigham Young: American Moses. New
  York: Knopf, 1985.

Arrington, Leonard J. Great Basin Kingdom: An Economic History
  of the Latter-day Saints, 1830-1900. Cambridge, Mass.:
  Harvard University Press, 1958.

Arrington, Leonard J. "Mormonism: From Its New York
  Beginnings." Dialogue: A Journal of Mormon Thought 13 (Fall
  1980), 120-135.

Arrington, Leonard J., and Bitton, Davis. The Mormon
  Experience: A History of the Latter-day Saints. New York:
  Knopf, 1979.

Arrington, Leonard J.; Fox, Feramorz Y.; and May, Dean L.
  Building the City of God: Community and Cooperation among
  the Mormons. Salt Lake City: Deseret Book Company, 1976.

Bergera, Gary James. "The Orson Pratt-Brigham Young
  Controversies: Conflict Within the Quorums, 1853-1868."
  Dialogue: A Journal of Mormon Thought 13 (Summer 1980), 7-
  49.

Bitton, Davis, ed. <u>Guide to Mormon Diaries and
  Autobiographies</u>. Provo, Utah: Brigham Young University
  Press, 1977.

Blanke, Gustav H., with Lynn, Karen. "'God's Base of
  Operations': Mormon Variations on the American Sense of
  Mission." <u>Brigham Young University Studies</u> 20 (Fall 1979),
  83-92.

Brodie, Fawn. <u>No Man Knows My History: The Life of Joseph
  Smith, The Mormon Prophet</u>. 2d ed. New York: Knopf, 1971.

Bush, Lester E., Jr. "Mormonism's Negro Doctrine: An
  Historical Overview." <u>Dialogue: A Journal of Mormon Thought</u>
  8 (Spring 1973), 11-68.

Bushman, Richard L. "The Book of Mormon and the American
  Revolution." <u>Brigham Young University Studies</u> 17 (Fall
  1976), 3-20.

Bushman, Richard L. <u>Joseph Smith and the Beginnings of
  Mormonism</u>. Urbana, Ill.: University of Illinois Press,
  1984.

Bushman, Richard L. "Mormon Persecutions in Missouri, 1833."
  <u>Brigham Young University Studies</u> 3 (Autumn 1960), 11-20.

Clark, James R. "The Kingdom of God, the Council of Fifty and
  the State of Deseret." <u>Utah Historical Quarterly</u> 26 (April
  1958), 130-148.

Crawley, Peter, ed. "A Bibliography of the Church in New York,
  Ohio, and Missouri." <u>Brigham Young University Studies</u> 12
  (Summer 1972), 465-537.

Creer, Leland H. "The Evolution of Government in Early Utah."
  <u>Utah Historical Quarterly</u> 27 (January 1958), 23-44.

Davis, David Brion. "The New England Origins of Mormonism."
  <u>New England Quarterly</u> 26 (June 1953), 147-160.

Davis, David Brion. "Some Themes of Counter-Subversion: An
  Analysis of Anti-Masonic, Anti-Catholic, and Anti-Mormon
  Literature." <u>Mississippi Valley Historical Review</u> 47
  (September 1960), 205-224.

DePillis, Mario S. "The Development of Mormon
  Communitarianism, 1826-1846." Ph.D. diss., Yale University,
  1961.

DePillis, Mario S. "The Quest for Religious Authority and the
  Rise of Mormonism." <u>Dialogue: A Journal of Mormon Thought</u> 1
  (Spring 1966), 68-88.

DePillis, Mario S. "The Social Sources of Mormonism." Church History 37 (March 1968), 50-79.

Ehat, Andrew F. "'It Seems Like Heaven Began on Earth': Joseph Smith and the Constitution of the Kingdom of God." Brigham Young University Studies 20 (Spring 1980), 253-279.

Eriksen, Ephraim E. The Psychological and Ethical Aspects of Mormon Group Life. 1922. Reprint. Salt Lake City: University of Utah Press, 1974.

Flake, Chad, ed. A Mormon Bibliography, 1830-1930: Books, Pamphlets, Periodicals, and Broadsides Relating to the First Century of Mormonism. Salt Lake City: University of Utah Press, 1978.

Flanders, Robert B. "The Kingdom of God in Illinois: Politics in Utopia." Dialogue: A Journal of Mormon Thought 5 (Spring 1970), 26-36.

Flanders, Robert B. Nauvoo: Kingdom on the Mississippi. Urbana, Ill.: University of Illinois Press, 1965.

Foster, Lawrence. "James Strang: The Prophet Who Failed." Church History 50 (June 1981), 182-192.

Gager, John G. "Early Mormonism and Early Christianity: Some Parallels and Their Consequences For the Study of New Religions." Journal of Mormon History 9 (1982), 53-60.

Gardner, Hamilton. "Communism Among the Mormons." Quarterly Journal of Economics 37 (November 1922), 134-174.

Geddes, J. A. The United Order among the Mormons (Missouri Phase). Salt Lake City: Deseret News Press, 1924.

Hansen, Klaus J. Mormonism and the American Experience. Chicago: University of Chicago Press, 1981.

Hansen, Klaus J. Quest for Empire: The Political Kingdom of God and the Council of Fifty in Mormon History. East Lansing, Mich.: Michigan State University Press, 1967.

Hickman, Martin B. "The Political Legacy of Joseph Smith." Dialogue: A Journal of Mormon Thought 3 (Autumn 1968), 22-36.

Hill, Donna. Joseph Smith: The First Mormon. Garden City, N.Y.: Doubleday, 1977.

Hill, Marvin S. "Cultural Crisis in the Mormon Kingdom: A Reconsideration of the Causes of Kirtland Dissent." Church History 49 (September 1980), 286-297.

Hill, Marvin S.   "Joseph Smith's New York Reputation
     Reappraised." Brigham Young University Studies 10 (Spring
     1970), 283-314.

Hill, Marvin S.   "Mormon Religion in Nauvoo: Some Reflections."
     Utah Historical Quarterly 44 (Spring 1976), 170-180.

Hill, Marvin S.   "A Note on Joseph Smith's First Vision and Its
     Import in the Shaping of Early Mormonism." Dialogue: A
     Journal of Mormon Thought 12 (Spring 1979), 90-99.

Hill, Marvin S.   "Quest for Refuge: An Hypothesis as to the
     Social Origins and Nature of the Mormon Political Kingdom."
     Journal of Mormon History 2 (1975), 3-20.

Hill, Marvin S.   "The Rise of Mormonism in the Burned-Over
     District: Another View." New York History 61 (October
     1980), 411-430.

Hill, Marvin S.   "The Shaping of the Mormon Mind in New England
     and New York." Brigham Young University Studies 9 (Spring
     1969), 351-372.

Hill, Marvin S., and Allen, James B., eds. Mormonism and
     American Culture. New York: Harper & Row, 1972.

Jensen, Therald N.   "Mormon Theory of Church and State." Ph.D.
     diss., University of Chicago, 1938.

Jessee, Dean C., ed.   "Joseph Smith's 19 July 1840 Discourse."
     Brigham Young University Studies 19 (Spring 1979), 390-394.

Journal of Discourses. 26 vols. 1854-1886. Reprint. Los
     Angeles: General Printing & Lithograph, 1961.

Larson, Gustive O.   The "Americanization" of Utah for
     Statehood. San Marino, Calif.: Huntington Library, 1971.

Leone, Mark. The Roots of Modern Mormonism. Cambridge, Mass.:
     Harvard University Press, 1979.

Lyon, T. Edgar.   "Doctrinal Development of the Church During
     the Nauvoo Sojourn, 1839-1846." Brigham Young University
     Studies 15 (Summer 1975), 435-446.

McKiernan, F. Mark; Blair, Alma R.; and Edwards, Paul M., eds.
     The Restoration Movement: Essays in Mormon History.
     Lawrence, Kans.: Coronado Press, 1972.

May, Dean L.   "The Making of Saints: The Mormon Town as a
     Setting for the Study of Cultural Change." Utah Historical
     Quarterly 45 (Winter 1977), 75-92.

Melville, James Keith. "Brigham Young's Ideal Society: The
  Kingdom of God." Brigham Young University Studies 10
  (Summer 1970), 488-490.

Melville, James Keith. Conflict and Compromise: The Mormons in
  Mid-Nineteenth-Century Politics. Provo, Utah: Brigham Young
  University Press, 1975.

Melville, James Keith. "Theory and Practice of Church and
  State During the Brigham Young Era." Brigham Young
  University Studies 3 (Autumn 1960), 33-55.

Michaelsen, Robert S. "Thomas F. O'Dea on the Mormons:
  Retrospect and Assessment." Dialogue: A Journal of Mormon
  Thought 11 (Spring 1978), 44-57.

Mulder, William A., and Mortensen, A. Russell, eds. Among the
  Mormons: Historic Accounts by Contemporary Observers. 1958.
  Reprint. Lincoln: University of Nebraska Press, 1973.

Oaks, Dallin H. "The Suppression of the Nauvoo Expositor."
  Utah Law Review 9 (Winter 1965), 862-903.

O'Dea, Thomas F. The Mormons. Chicago: University of Chicago
  Press, 1957.

Paul, Rodman W. "The Mormons as a Theme in Western Historical
  Writing." Journal of American History 54 (December 1967),
  511-523.

Poll, Richard D. "The Mormon Question Enters National
  Politics, 1850-1856." Utah Historical Quarterly 25 (April
  1957), 117-131.

Poll, Richard D. "Nauvoo and the New Mormon History: A
  Bibliographical Survey." Journal of Mormon History 5
  (1978), 3-17.

Pollock, Gordon Douglas. "In Search of Security: The Mormons
  and the Kingdom of God on Earth, 1830-1844." Ph.D. diss.,
  Queens University, Ontario, Canada, 1977.

Quaife, Milo M. The Kingdom of Saint James: A Narrative of the
  Mormons. New Haven, Conn.: Yale University Press, 1930.

Quinn, D. Michael. "The Evolution of the Presiding Quorums of
  the LDS Church." Journal of Mormon History 1 (1974), 21-38.

Quinn, D. Michael. "The Mormon Succession Crisis of 1844."
  Brigham Young University Studies 16 (Winter 1976), 187-233.

Roberts, Brigham H. A Comprehensive History of the Church of
  Jesus Christ of Latter-day Saints, Century I. 6 vols.
  1905-1915. Reprint. Salt Lake City: Deseret News Press,
  1930.

Robertson, R. J., Jr. "The Mormon Experience in Missouri,
   1830-1839." Missouri Historical Review 68 (April-July
   1974), 280-298.

Schweikart, Larry. "The Mormon Connection: Lincoln, the
   Saints, and the Crisis of Equality." Western Humanities
   Review 34 (Winter 1980), 1-22.

Shipps, Jan. Mormonism: The Story of a New Religious
   Tradition. Urbana, Ill.: University of Illinois Press,
   1985.

Shipps, JoAnn (Jan). "The Mormons in Politics: The First
   Hundred Years." Ph.D. diss., University of Colorado, 1965.

Shipps, Jan. "The Prophet Puzzle: Suggestions Leading Toward a
   More Comprehensive Interpretation of Joseph Smith." Journal
   of Mormon History 1 (1974), 3-20.

Smith, Joseph, Jr. History of the Church of Jesus Christ of
   Latter-day Saints: Period I, History of Joseph Smith, the
   Prophet. Edited by B. H. Roberts. 6 vols. 2d ed. Salt
   Lake City: Deseret Book Company, 1955.

Smith, Timothy L. "The Book of Mormon in a Biblical Culture."
   Journal of Mormon History 7 (1980), 3-21.

Strout, Cushing. "Peculiar People in the Land." Chapter 8 in
   The New Heavens and New Earth: Political Religion in
   America. New York: Harper & Row, 1974.

Taggart, Stephen. Mormonism's Negro Policy: Social and
   Historical Origins. Salt Lake City: University of Utah
   Press, 1970.

Underwood, Grant. "Early Mormon Millenarianism: Another Look."
   Church History 54 (June 1985), 215-229.

Walters, Wesley P., and Bushman, Richard L. "Roundtable: The
   Question of the Palmyra Revival." Dialogue: A Journal of
   Mormon Thought 4 (Spring 1969), 59-100.

Warner, Edward Allen. "Mormon Theodemocracy: Theocratic and
   Democratic Elements in Early Latter-day Saint Ideology,
   1827-1846." Ph.D. diss., University of Iowa, 1973.

Weeks, Robert P. "A Utopian Kingdom in the American Grain."
   Wisconsin Magazine of History 61 (Autumn 1977), 2-20.

Williams, J. D. "Separation of Church and State in Mormon
   Theory and Practice." Dialogue: A Journal of Mormon Thought
   1 (Summer 1966), 30-54.

Wilson, John F. "Some Comparative Perspectives on the Early
    Mormon Movement and the Church-State Question, 1830-1845."
    Journal of Mormon History 8 (1981), 63-77.

Wood, Gordon. "Evangelical America and Early Mormonism." New
    York History 61 (October 1980), 359-86.

                    4. UTOPIAN EXPERIMENTS

                      a. Hopedale

Ballou, Adin. Autobiography of Adin Ballou, 1803-1890. Edited
    by William S. Heywood. Lowell, Mass.: Vox Populi Press,
    1896.

Ballou, Adin. History of the Hopedale Community: From Its
    Inception to Its Virtual Submergence in the Hopedale Parish.
    Edited by William S. Heywood. 1897. Reprint.
    Philadelphia: Porcupine Press, 1972.

Perry, Lewis. "Adin Ballou's Hopedale Community and the
    Theology of Antislavery." Church History 39 (September
    1970), 372-389.

Perry, Lewis. Radical Abolitionism: Anarchy and the Government
    of God in Antislavery Thought. Ithaca, N.Y.: Cornell
    University Press, 1973.

Rollins, Richard M. "Adin Ballou and the Perfectionist's
    Dilemma." Journal of Church and State 17 (Autumn 1975),
    459-476.

                      b. Fruitlands

Francis, Richard. "Circumstances and Salvation: The Ideology
    of the Fruitlands Utopia." American Quarterly 25 (May
    1973), 202-234.

Sears, Clara Endicott. Bronson Alcott's Fruitlands. Boston:
    Houghton Mifflin, 1915. Reprinted as Sears, Clara Endicott,
    comp. Bronson Alcott's Fruitlands, With "Transcendental
    Wild Oats," by Louisa M. Alcott. Philadelphia: Porcupine
    Press, 1975.

Shepard, Odell. Peddler's Progress: The Life of Bronson
    Alcott. Boston: Little, Brown, 1937.

c. Fourierist Communities

Belz, Herman J. "The North American Phalanx: Experiment in Socialism." New Jersey Historical Society, Proceedings 81 (October 1963), 215-247.

Bestor, Arthur E., Jr. "Albert Brisbane--Propagandist for Socialism in the 1840's." New York History 28 (April 1947), 128-158.

Bestor, Arthur E., Jr. "American Phalanxes: Fourierist Socialism in the United States." Ph.D. diss., Yale University, 1938.

Brisbane, Albert. Social Destiny of Man: Or, Association and Reorganization of Industry. 1840. Reprint. New York: Burt Franklin, 1968.

Brisbane, Redelia. Albert Brisbane: A Mental Biography, with a Character Study. 1893. Reprint. New York: Burt Franklin, 1969.

Carlson, Oliver. Brisbane: A Candid Biography. New York: Stackpole Sons, 1937.

Codman, John Thomas. Brook Farm: Historic and Personal Memoirs. Boston: Arena Publishing Co., 1894.

Crowe, Charles. George Ripley: Transcendentalist and Utopian Socialist. Athens, Ga.: University of Georgia Press, 1967.

Curtis, Edith Roelker. A Season in Utopia: The Story of Brook Farm. New York: Thomas Nelson and Sons, 1961.

Dwight, Marianne. Letters from Brook Farm, 1844-1847. Edited by Amy L. Reed. 1928. Reprint. Philadelphia: Porcupine Press, 1973.

Expose of the Condition and Progress of the North American Phalanx . . . Intended to Set Forth the Principles, Aims and Character of the Phalanx, in its Relations to the General Subject of Social Reform. 1853. Reprint. Philadelphia: Porcupine Press, 1974.

Fourier, Francois Marie Charles. Design For Utopia: Selected Writings of Charles Fourier. Edited by Charles Gide. Translated by Julia Franklin. 1901. Reprint. New York: Schocken Books, 1971.

Fourier, Francois Marie Charles. The Utopian Vision of Charles Fourier: Selected Texts on Work, Love, and Passionate Attraction. Edited and translated by Jonathan Beecher and Richard Bienvenu. Boston: Beacon Press, 1971.

Francis, Richard. "The Ideology of Brook Farm." In <u>Studies in the American Renaissance, 1977</u>, edited by Joel Myerson. Boston: Twayne Publishers, 1978.

Godwin, Parke. <u>A Popular View of the Doctrines of Charles Fourier</u>. 1844. Reprint. Philadelphia: Porcupine Press, 1972.

Golemba, Henry L. <u>George Ripley</u>. Twayne's United States Authors Series, no. 281. Boston: Twayne Publishers, 1977.

Greene, Mand Honeyman. "Raritan Bay Union, Eagleswood, New Jersey." New Jersey Historical Society, <u>Proceedings</u> 67 (January 1950), 2-19.

Guarneri, Carl J. "The Associationists: Forging a Christian Socialism in Antebellum America." <u>Church History</u> 52 (March 1983), 36-49.

Guarneri, Carl J. "Importing Fourierism to America." <u>Journal of the History of Ideas</u> 43 (October-December 1982), 581-594.

Guarneri, Carl J. "Two Utopian Socialist Plans for Emancipation in Antebellum Louisiana." <u>Louisiana History</u> 24 (Winter 1983), 5-24.

Haraszti, Zoltan, ed. <u>The Idyll of Brook Farm, As Revealed by Unpublished Letters in the Boston Public Library</u>. Boston: Trustees of the Public Library, 1937.

Jones, Russell M. "Victor Considérant's American Experience (1852-1869)." <u>French-American Review</u> 1, nos. 1-2 (1976-1977), 65-94, 124-150.

Jordan, Philip D. "The Iowa Pioneer Phalanx." <u>Palimpsest</u> 16 (July 1935), 211-225.

Kirchmann, George. "Unsettled Utopias: The North American Phalanx and the Raritan Bay Union." <u>New Jersey History</u> 97, no. 1 (1979), 25-36.

Manuel, Frank E. "Charles Fourier: The Burgeoning of Instinct." Chapter 5 in <u>The Prophets of Paris</u>. Cambridge, Mass.: Harvard University Press, 1962.

Matthews, James W., ed. "An Early Brook Farm Letter." <u>New England Quarterly</u> 53 (June 1980), 226-230.

Myerson, Joel, ed. "James Burrill Curtis and Brook Farm." <u>New England Quarterly</u> 51 (September 1978), 396-423.

Riasanovsky, Nicholas V. <u>The Teaching of Charles Fourier</u>. Berkeley and Los Angeles: University of California Press, 1969.

Robinson, David. "The Political Odyssey of William Henry
    Channing." American Quarterly 34 (Summer 1982), 165-184.

Sams, Henry W., ed. Autobiography of Brook Farm. Engelwood
    Cliffs, N.J.: Prentice-Hall, 1958.

Sokolow, Jayme A. "Culture and Utopia: The Raritan Bay Union."
    New Jersey History 94 (Summer-Autumn 1976), 89-100.

Spencer, Michael C. Charles Fourier. Boston: Twayne
    Publishers, 1981.

Swift, Lindsay. Brook Farm: Its Members, Scholars, and
    Visitors. 1900. Reprint. Secaucus, N.J.: Citadel Press,
    1973.

Wennerstein, John R. "Parke Godwin, Utopian Socialism, and the
    Politics of Antislavery." New-York Historical Society
    Quarterly 60 (July-October 1976), 107-127.

Zonderman, David A., ed. "George Ripley's Unpublished Lecture
    on Charles Fourier." In Studies in the American
    Renaissance, 1982, edited by Joel Myerson. Boston: Twayne
    Publishers, 1983.

d. Owenite Communitarianism

Armytage, W. H. G. "William Maclure, 1763-1840: A British
    Interpretation." Indiana Magazine of History 47 (March
    1951), 1-20.

Bestor, Arthur, ed. Education and Reform at New Harmony:
    Correspondence of William Maclure and Marie Duclos
    Fretageot, 1820-1830. Indianapolis: Indiana Historical
    Society, 1948.

Brown, Paul. Twelve Months in New Harmony, Presenting a
    Faithful Account of the Principal Occurrences That Have
    Taken Place There During That Period. 1827. Reprint.
    Philadelphia: Porcupine Press, 1973.

Carmony, Donald F., and Elliott, Josephine M. "New Harmony,
    Indiana: Robert Owen's Seedbed for Utopia." Indiana
    Magazine of History 76 (September 1980), 161-261.

Egerton, John. "Nashoba: Frances Wright's Experiment in
    'Practical Equality.'" Chapter 2 in Visions of Utopia:
    Nashoba, Rugby, Ruskin and the "New Communities" in
    Tennessee's Past. Knoxville, Tenn.: University of Tennessee
    Press, 1977.

Harrison, John F. C. Quest for the New Moral World: Robert
    Owen and the Owenites in Britain and America. New York:
    Charles Scribner's Sons, 1969.

Harrison, John F. C., ed. <u>Utopianism and Education: Robert Owen and the Owenites</u>. New York: Teachers College Press, 1969.

Hermann, Janet Sharp. <u>The Pursuit of a Dream</u>. New York: Oxford University Press, 1981.

Indiana Historical Commission. <u>New Harmony as Seen by Participants and Travelers</u>. Philadelphia: Porcupine Press, 1975.

Jones, Arnita Ament. "From Utopia to Reform." <u>History Today</u> (Great Britain) 26 (June 1976), 393-401.

Lane, Margaret. "Frances Wright (1795-1852): The Great Experiment." <u>Contemporary Review</u> (Great Britain) 218, no. 1260 (1971), 7-14.

Leopold, Richard W. <u>Robert Dale Owen: A Biography</u>. Cambridge, Mass.: Harvard University Press, 1940.

Lockwood, George B. <u>The New Harmony Movement</u>. New York: D. Appleton, 1905.

Morris, James M. "Communes and Cooperatives: Cincinnati's Early Experiments in Social Reform." <u>Cincinnati Historical Society Bulletin</u> 33, no. 1 (1975), 57-80.

Owen, Robert. <u>The Life of Robert Owen</u>. 1857-1858. Reprint. New York: Augustus Kelley, 1967.

Owen, Robert. <u>A New View of Society: Or, Essays on the Formation of Human Character</u>. 1813. Reprint. New York: Augustus Kelley, 1967.

Owen, Robert. <u>Robert Owen in the United States</u>. Edited by Oakley C. Johnson. New York: Humanities Press, 1970.

Owen, Robert. <u>Robert Owen's New-Harmony Addresses</u>. Compiled by Donald K. Ennis. Evansville, Ind.: Scholars Portable Publications, 1977.

Owen, Robert Dale. <u>Robert Dale Owen's Travel Journal, 1827</u>. Edited by Josephine M. Elliott. Indiana Historical Society Publications, vol. 25, no. 4. Indianapolis: Indiana Historical Society, 1977.

Owen, Robert Dale. <u>To Holland and To New Harmony, Robert Dale Owen's Travel Journal, 1825-1826</u>. Edited by Josephine M. Elliott. Indiana Historical Society Publications, vol. 23, no. 4. Indianapolis: Indiana Historical Society, 1969.

Payne-Gaposchkin, Cecilia Helena, ed. "The Nashoba Plan for
    Removing the Evil of Slavery: Letters of Frances and Camilla
    Wright, 1820-1829." Harvard Library Bulletin 23 (July
    1975), 221-251; (October 1975) 429-461.

Perkins, Alice J. G., and Wolfson, Theresa. Frances Wright:
    Free Enquirer. New York: Harper & Brothers, 1939.

Pitzer, Donald E., ed. Robert Owen's American Legacy.
    Proceedings of the Robert Owen Bicentennial Conference.
    Indianapolis: Indiana Historical Society, 1972.

Podmore, Frank. Robert Owen. 1906. Reprint. New York:
    Augustus Kelley, 1968.

Pollard, Sidney, and Salt, John. Robert Owen, Prophet of the
    Poor. Essays in Honour of the Two Hundredth Anniversary of
    his Birth. London: Macmillan, 1971.

Waterman, William A. Frances Wright. 1924. Reprint. New
    York: AMS Press, 1972.

Wilson, William E. The Angel and the Serpent: The Story of New
    Harmony. Bloomington, Ind.: Indiana University Press, 1964.

                        e.   Others

Block, Marguerite Beck. The New Church in the New World: A
    Study of Swedenborgianism in America. 1932. Reprint. New
    York: Octagon Books, 1969.

Bonney, Margaret Atherton. "The Salubria Story." Palimpsest
    56 (March-April 1975), 34-45.

Buchstein, Frederick D. "Josiah Warren: The Peaceful
    Revolution." Cincinnati Historical Society Bulletin 32,
    nos. 1-2 (1974), 61-71.

Grant, H. Roger. "Utopia at Communia." Palimpsest 61
    (January-February 1980), 12-17.

Hawley, C. A. "A Communistic Swedenborgian Colony in Iowa."
    Iowa Journal of History and Politics 33 (January 1935), 3-
    26.

Johnson, Christopher. Utopian Communities in France: Cabet and
    the Icarians, 1839-1851. Ithaca, N.Y.: Cornell University
    Press, 1974.

McBee, Alice E. From Utopia to Florence: The Study of a
    Transcendentalist Community in Northampton, Massachusetts,
    1830-1852. 1947. Reprint. Philadelphia: Porcupine Press,
    1975.

Martin, James J. "Native American Anarchist Origins in the Era of Nineteenth Century Reform." Part 1 in Men Against the State: Expositors of Individualist Anarchism in America. DeKalb, Ill.: Adrien Allen Associates, 1953.

Pease, William H., and Pease, Jane H. Black Utopia: Negro Communal Experiments in America. Madison, Wis.: State Historical Society of Wisconsin, 1963.

Rose, Willie Lee. Rehearsal for Reconstruction: The Port Royal Experiment. Indianapolis: Bobbs-Merrill, 1964.

Shaw, Albert. Icaria: A Chapter in the History of Communism. 1884. Reprint. Philadelphia: Porcupine Press, 1973.

Sheffeld, Charles Arthur, ed. History of Florence, Massachusetts. Including a Complete Account of the Northampton Association of Education and Industry. Florence, Mass.: The editor, 1895.

Wheeler, Wayne; Hernon, Peter; and Sweetland, James H. "Icarian Communism: A Preliminary Exploration in Historiography, Bibliography and Social Theory." International Review of Modern Sociology 6 (1976), 127-137.

Wittke, Carl. The Utopian Communist: A Biography of Wilhelm Weitling, Nineteenth-Century Reformer. Baton Rouge, La.: Louisiana State University Press, 1950.

9

Church-State Issues in Education: The Colonial Pattern and the Nineteenth Century to 1870

John W. Lowe, Jr.

The history of American education cannot be understood apart from the history of American religion. Undoubtedly, formal education in America owes its genesis to the American churches and has been integrally involved with them throughout its history. Yet, neither American education nor American religion can be fully understood without attention to the relation of both to the state. The triangular relationship of education, church, and state has existed since the founding of the American republic, with antecedents in the charters of the colonies and the actions of their founders.

The importance of education in the colonies is undisputed, though to understand colonial education means looking beyond the formal schools into what Lawrence Cremin has called the "ecology of education." While older histories typically dealt only with the schools and equated education with schooling, Cremin and others like him have asserted that education occurs in many settings, including schools, church, and state programs among others, and that these settings together form a system. Cremin's interpretation and historical studies of American education can be found in his projected three-volume history, of which two volumes have appeared. The first, *American Education: The Colonial Experience, 1607–1783*, deals with colonial education. The second, *American Education: The National Experience, 1783–1876*, covers the subject from the adoption of the Constitution to the centennial of the nation. Cremin has also written a much abbreviated history entitled *Traditions of American Education*. Other educational histories are discussed in Douglas Sloan's review, "Historiography and the History of Education."

Religion, like education, was an important factor in the colonies and the early years of the republic. In both cases, some scholars have taken the institutional approach, looking at the religious history of America as the history of churches. Others, however, have investigated the influence of re-

ligion and the churches on American society and culture. William Warren
Sweet was among the first to write religious histories of America in this way;
see his *Religion in Colonial America* and *Religion in the Development of
American Culture, 1765–1840*. In both, Sweet discusses education as
important to religion. Other American religious historians have also dealt
with education; see especially Sidney Mead, *The Lively Experiment*, and
Robert T. Handy, *A Christian America: Protestant Hopes and Historical
Realities*. All of these studies deal primarily with Christianity, and more
specifically with Protestantism as it developed and sought hegemony in
America. Two other noteworthy histories look at religion in specific eras of
American history. They are Perry Miller, *Errand Into the Wilderness*, and
Douglas Sloan, *The Great Awakening and American Education*. In the first,
Miller's essays explore the educational aspects of westward migration to the
New World; while in the second, more strictly educational history, Sloan
discusses the circuit riding of the Great Awakening. Religious histories gener-
ally attempt to integrate the story of education, both the development of
church education and of what is now called public education, into their
narratives.

American education and religion first developed under colonial charters
and state constitutions. The framers of the federal constitution were sensitive
to the issues involving education and the systems of education in the various
colonies as well as their established policies regarding religion. Other chapters in this volume discuss in detail the development of the constitutional and
legal provisions concerning religious freedom and religious establishments at
both state and federal levels. (See especially chapters 5 and 10.) The federal
constitution, of course, made education the responsibility of the individual
states. It was far into the nineteenth century before the federal government
set up a department of education with regulatory powers.

Among the books which enumerate state and federal constitutional provisions regarding religion and education are *Federal and State Constitutions,
Colonial Charters and Other Organic Laws*, edited by Francis N. Thorpe,
which prints the constitutions and charters of all the states in its seven
volumes, and Herbert L. Searles, *State Constitutional and Legislative Provisions and Supreme Court Decisions Relating to Sectarian Religious Influence in Tax-Supported Universities, Colleges, and Public Schools*. Three
other particularly useful volumes covering various aspects of church and
state in education as related to constitutions are Conrad Henry Moehlman,
The American Constitutions and Religion; Lawrence Byrnes, *Religion and
Public Education* (especially chapter 2), and *Religion, Government, and
Education*, edited by William W. Brickman and Stanley Lehrer.

The relation of church and state in the context of education can be found in every colony. In Pennsylvania, William Penn's Frame of Government, passed by the General Assembly in 1682, contained a call for the education of children and the ordering and erecting of "public schools." This was reiterated in the provisional Constitution of Pennsylvania in 1776 and the Pennsylvania Constitution of 1790. Yet it was not until 1834 that Pennsylvania passed a law establishing a public education system for elementary-aged children. From the founding of the colony of Pennsylvania until 1834, the church had taken responsibility for establishing and supporting schools. While many of these were private, others were operated for all children with support from the church and the community, or from tuition and special gifts. Many denominations were so involved in supporting schools that they actively opposed laws which advocated public schools, and some of the denominational school systems in Pennsylvania did not close until much later in the nineteenth century.

In Virginia, discussion of education centered on positions backed by two future presidents, Thomas Jefferson and James Madison. Paralleling their disagreement over the federal constitution, Jefferson and Madison disagreed on the shape of education in Virginia. Jefferson advocated and drew up plans for a state education system. The single element of the plan realized in his lifetime was the University of Virginia, though the state eventually acquired a public education system. Madison, while respecting the need for education, feared that the proposals for the Virginia constitution favored the Church of England. The debates between Jefferson and Madison are well documented in Jefferson's "Act for Establishing Religious Freedom" and Madison's "Memorial and Remonstrance," both widely reproduced. A good source for Jefferson's educational views, in particular, is R. M. Healey, *Jefferson on Religion and Public Education.*

Massachusetts led the way in establishing the New England pattern of education. Almost from the moment that the Pilgrims set foot in America, they were concerned with education, as numerous documents attest. One of these is the Mayflower Compact, with its stipulation that the minister's duty is to catechize and teach. Since the Puritans retained an established church on the English pattern, responsibility for teaching and for organizing and regulating the schools fell to it. Although the schools were primarily for the privileged and not truly public schools in the modern sense, they were important in the development of the educational system and in them were foreshadowed church-state issues later to become significant.

Massachusetts also led the way in higher education. With the founding of Harvard College in 1636 by the Massachusetts Puritans, an important segment of American higher education began to develop. With the college came an emphasis upon religion and education. Most of the early American colleges were at least in part designed to train clergy, who, as mentioned before, were also expected to teach. Harvard was followed by Yale, William and Mary, the College of New Jersey (now Princeton), and Kings (now Columbia). Histories of each of these schools have been written in the nineteenth and twentieth centuries. More general histories of higher education include: John S. Brubacher and Willis Rudy, *Higher Education in Transition: An American History: 1626–1956;* Jurgen Herbst, *From Crisis to Crisis: American College Government, 1636–1819;* Frederick Rudolph, *The American College and University;* and John Whitehead, *The Separation of College and State.* Lawrence Cremin's two volumes, mentioned earlier, also contain valuable chapters on higher education. These works cover not only the early history and development of American colleges but also trace higher education well into the contemporary era.

Seminaries and divinity schools were later founded along with the colleges and universities. While the seminaries were an important aspect of American religious education (and even American education taken as a whole), tensions between church and state did not figure strongly in theological education. It was well understood that seminaries were the province of the church and seldom in their early history did the state attempt to exert any control. While some states with established churches may have given tax funds to seminaries, generally the seminaries have resisted involvement with the state. The history of the seminaries and divinity schools can be found both in the sources mentioned on higher education and in accounts of individual institutions.

In the early history of education, the interests of church and state seldom came into conflict. Colonial church-state patterns were usually of three kinds. In New England, each colony had settled, or established, churches which received tax support and special privileges from the colony. In the Middle Atlantic colonies, there was effective separation of church and state. In the southern colonies, church and state were relatively independent with preferential treatment given to the Church of England. Thus, schools in New England enjoyed the support of the state through the established church, while schools in the other colonies were not, generally, financially supported in the same way. Accordingly, education in the early period was primarily for the children of the privileged who could afford to pay tuition or private tutors. Gradually this changed and churches and individuals began to set up schools open to all. This still meant, however, that children would only go to school from the age of about six to perhaps twelve or fourteen. The objective was to teach the rudiments of reading, writing, and morals, using the Bible or other biblically centered materials. In the *New England Primer* or the *Hornbook* the pervasiveness of religious instruction in the early schools is evident. Following this primary education, most young men were apprenticed out to learn trades, went to work in family businesses, or, if fortunate, went on to one of the colleges. This education, it should be noted, was seldom available to girls or to blacks or American Indians. As Cremin has indicated, it was a pattern of education universally accepted in the colonies which survived many challenges and innovations before it was broken.

Yet the educational ideal changed over time, so that by the time the Northwest Ordinances were adopted, the state was beginning to take some responsibility for education. The Northwest Ordinance of 1785 reserved lot number 16 of every new township for maintaining public schools. And the Northwest Ordinance of 1787 went even further in making explicit the presumed relationship of church, state, and education when it declared: "Religion, morality, and knowledge, being necessary to good government and the happiness of mankind, schools and the means of education shall forever be encouraged." It was these provisions which advanced the cause of public education in the western states while some of the eastern states still resisted the very concept. Yet this granting of land and acknowledgement of the triangular relationship of church, state, and education did not result in the rapid increase of public schools even in the west. Many of the schools still were built and supported by the churches. Interestingly enough, although delegates to the Continental Congress provided for education in the northwest, they could not agree upon education in the colonies themselves and therefore left the provision of education in the Constitution to the states.

Education in the colonies contained an aspect which is not adequately discussed in histories of education per se. This is what we now call religious education. It is not easy to separate early educational efforts into "secular" and "religious" strands. Since the church sponsored both in many towns, the curriculum materials were primarily biblical, and the minister frequently also taught school, the histories of religious education also illuminate early educational endeavors more generally. Puritan educational efforts, particularly those among New Englanders (later Congregationalists) are discussed by Sandford Fleming in *Children and Puritanism*. Similar treatments of Methodist schools are found in A. W. Cummings, *Early Schools of Methodism*, and Sylvanus M. Duvall, *The Methodist Episcopal Church and Education up to 1869*, while Episcopal efforts are described by Clifton H. Brewer in *A History of Religious Education in the Episcopal Church to 1835*. The Quakers, while not so numerous as other denominations, were leaders in the field, and sought to promote universal education, though their efforts were largely restricted to Pennsylvania, New Jersey, and Maryland. Their work is described in *Quaker Education in the Colony and State of New Jersey: A Source Book*, edited by Thomas H. Woody, and in Woody's *Early Quaker Education in Pennsylvania*.

Two studies which discuss the educational activity of denominations later in the nineteenth century are Edith C. Magruder, *A Historical Study of the Educational Agencies of the Southern Baptist Convention, 1845–1945,* and Lewis J. Sherill, *Presbyterian Parochial Schools, 1846–1870.* The Magruder book is more on the order of a history of religious education among the Southern Baptists. The Sherill book, however, discusses the rise and continuation of Presbyterian parochial schools in the midst of efforts for universal public education.

Other sources on religious education further indicate how the educational programs of the churches, especially the Protestant churches through their Sunday Schools, were part of a larger educational ideal. Robert W. Lynn discusses the relations of public education and Sunday Schools in *Protestant Strategies in Education.* Similar in extent, but more probing in discussing educational relationships, is William B. Kennedy's *The Shaping of Protestant Education.* The relationship of public education to the Sunday School is described by Robert W. Lynn and Elliott Wright in *The Big Little School: Two Hundred Years of the Sunday School.* The weekday schools and Sunday Schools were not in competition with one another, as these sources point out, but were part of a larger plan in which each was complementary to the other. Both were considered part of religious education since much that was done in the weekday school was an extension of church activities, including religious exercises and the use of the Bible as a text book. (Modern textbooks would not appear for a long time yet.) In the period from the end of the Revolutionary War until the beginning of the Civil War, religious education would diminish in the schools: see the chronicle by William K. Dunn, *What Happened to Religious Education? The Decline of Religious Teaching in the Public Elementary School, 1776–1861.* A more general history of church efforts in education is Herbert B. Adams, *The Church and Popular Education.* Adams also reviews the effects of the change from church-sponsored education to public education sponsored by the state.

The colonial patterns of education were already changing by the time of the American Revolution, but change occurred much more rapidly following the birth of the new nation. The adoption of the federal constitution, economic growth and political relationships in the new nation, westward expansion, and the challenges of uniting areas and states with different views led to new theories concerning education. No longer would the fortunate receive education while the common people received none. Universal education became an ideal which would foster the development of the common or public school. Heightened revival activity was one agent of this process as it led churches to see the necessity of establishing their presence and spreading their educational programs across the new frontiers. Charles I. Foster discusses one aspect of how they acted upon this perception in *An Errand of*

Mercy: The Evangelical United Front, 1790–1837. Another perspective on the churches' missionary activity is Oliver Wendell Elsbree, *The Rise of the Missionary Spirit in America*, while Benajah H. Carroll discusses the anti-missionary forces in *The Genesis of American Anti-Missionism*.

The involvement of the churches with different states, including the rise of state educational efforts, is documented in a number of sources. Charles C. Cole, Jr., looks at Northern Evangelists and their involvement in such issues in *The Social Ideas of the Northern Evangelists, 1826–1860*. John R. Bodo, *The Protestant Clergy and Public Issues, 1812–1848*, analyzes the rise of the common school and the Protestant clergy's reactions, while Frank T. Carleton, *Economic Influences Upon Educational Progress in the United States, 1820–1850*, reflects on the role of economics in the rise of public education. Ray A. Billington, *The Protestant Crusade, 1800–1860*, sees a direct connection between the rise of the common school and attempts to recreate America as a Christian nation through the instrumentality of the schools. But while the ideal was universal education in common schools, not everyone was involved. Some chose not to be associated with the common schools and continued to support their private and parochial schools. Others, such as the American Indians and the blacks of the slave South, were excluded from the common schools. Robert F. Berkhofer, Jr., has detailed the aims of United States education for the Indians in *Salvation and the Savage: An Analysis of Protestant Missions and American Indian Response, 1787–1862*. Thomas L. Webber, *Deep Like the Rivers: Education in the Slave Quarter Community, 1831–1865*, describes how the denial of education led to a separate education system on the slave plantations of the South. The treatment of the Indians and the slavery question entailed church-state issues which divided both the churches and the nation in the eighteenth and nineteenth centuries. Moreover, the churches were openly at odds with the state over the education of Indians and slaves. One result of this situation was that while the common school was becoming established in New England and the mid-Atlantic states, the South proved slower to follow suit.

The concept of the common school is one of the great educational innovations of the American education system. Who should receive credit for it and when it became generally accepted are subject to discussion, although most educational historians look to Horace Mann of Massachusetts and Henry Barnard of Connecticut as outstanding leaders in the common school movement. The promotion of the common school, though, came largely from the churches as did the major opposition. That the common school triumphed as the educational ideal was due to an alliance of church and state in which the common school proponents used both the pulpit and the statehouse to promote their cause. While elements of the common school movement can be found in various states before 1800, it was largely after that date that it became the primary educational institution for the young in America. It is with the common school, also, that issues of conflict between church and state begin to arise.

Massachusetts became the first state with an official body for the control of public education when it set up the Massachusetts State Board of Education in 1836. Horace Mann became the Board's first Secretary. While his position was thought by many to be advisory, Mann used it to promote the common school, to suggest curriculum, to advise careful selection of teachers, and to compare the American and European educational systems. At times, his convictions and suggestions, often put forward in his annual reports as Secretary, brought challenges from educators and clergy alike. One subject of debate was whether the Massachusetts common schools were too secular and neglected the spiritual education of youth. Of course, Mann himself saw the Bible and moral education as an essential part of the curriculum, but he felt it was possible to find a common core in the Bible and morals that all religious persuasions could accept. Readings based on this core should be included, he thought, in the curriculum. Others disagreed with him, notably Matthew Hale Smith, who took a more conservative position in *The Bible, the Rod, and Religion in the Common Schools*. Several letters between Mann and Smith indicative of their views were published as pamphlets. Their debate and other relevant issues are set out in Raymond B. Culver, *Horace Mann and Religion in the Massachusetts Common Schools*. Mann's side of the argument and his views on education and religion are also found in *Life and Works of Horace Mann*, edited by his wife, Mary Peabody Mann.

Mann's influence in Massachusetts is paralleled by the influence of Henry Barnard on the common schools of Connecticut and Rhode Island. Barnard published and edited three influential journals: the *American Journal of Education*, the *Connecticut Common School Journal*, and the *Journal of the Rhode Island Institute of Instruction*. He was more theologically conservative than his colleague Mann. He was also more outspoken in advocating that the study of the Bible be a part of the common school curriculum and in recommending that Christian teachers be employed by the common schools. Barnard's Congregationalist background and his religious ideals permeate his writings. Unfortunately, Bernard C. Steiner's *Life of Henry Barnard*, useful though it is, fails to deal adequately with the social philosophy which certainly lay behind Barnard's decision to become and remain an educator. This aspect of his life is dealt with by Merle Curti, *The Social Ideas of American Educators*, who also devotes a chapter to Mann.

While Mann and Barnard are two of the better known advocates of the common school, its proponents can be found in every state of the Union in the early 1800s. In Pennsylvania, one advocate was Thaddeus Stevens. Common school advocates in Ohio were led by Calvin Stowe, Samuel Lewis, and Samuel Galloway; in Indiana by Caleb Mills; in Illinois by Ninian W. Edwards; in Michigan by John D. Pierce and Isaac E. Crary; in Kentucky by Robert J. Breckinridge; and in North Carolina by Calvin H. Wilet. The California common school movement was led by John Swett. Many of these men were ordained ministers, some of whom had left the pulpit to enter education as college or seminary presidents and faculty members. An early article that describes the role of the clergy in promoting the common schools is William C. Fowler, "The Clergy and Popular Education," written in 1868.

Among the many histories of the common school movement which deal with its evolution as a national movement are Lawrence A. Cremin, *The American Common School, An Historical Conception;* Paul Monroe, *Founding of the American Public School System;* and Edward H. Reisner, *Evolution of the Common School.* A foreign view, written closer to the founding of the schools, is Francis Adams, *Free School System of the United States,* published in 1875. None of these books, however, deals to any great extent with strictly church-state issues and church-state problems raised by the founding of the common schools. Also, none deals with the continuation of private schools or the rise of parochial school systems. These topics are covered, however, in numerous state histories of the common schools and in various histories of the church-state question.

Church-state issues in education in the New England colonies and states are the subject of several volumes. Raymond B. Culver, *Horace Mann and Religion in the Massachusetts Common Schools,* an article by Aaron B. Seidman, "Church and State in the Early Years of the Massachusetts Bay Colony," and two additional books, Jacob C. Meyer, *Church and State in Massachusetts from 1740 to 1833,* and Sherman M. Smith, *The Relation of the State to Religious Education in Massachusetts,* describe the common school movement and conflicts of church and state in education in Massachusetts. Mary Paul Mason, *Church-State Relationships in Education in Connecticut, 1633–1953,* gives similar treatment to the issues and problems in that state. The struggle over education in New Hampshire is rehearsed by Charles B. Kinney, *Church and State: The Struggle for Separation in New Hampshire, 1635–1900.*

The reluctance of New York to adopt common schools has led many writers to focus on its particular form of the interaction of church, state, and education. Immigration into the state, especially into New York City from Ireland, was partly responsible for the conflict. Immigrants were largely Catholic in faith and saw the common schools as a threat to Catholic teachings and beliefs. So alongside the common schools in New York City there grew up a Catholic parochial system which enjoyed, to some extent, the support of the state and general populace. This support turned to anger and bloodshed, however, when Governor William Seward suggested that public tax funds be used in support of the Catholic parochial schools. Riots broke out, Seward was severely censured by the press, and even Catholic leaders hesitated to support the proposal out of fear that the state might exert control of their schools. The most complete account of the New York school riots which expresses these tensions is Vincent P. Lannie, *Public Money and Parochial Education: Bishop Hughes, Governor Seward, and the New York School Controversy.* The result of the struggle was a split in the religious community and a setback for the common schools. Furthermore, Protestants reinforced their anti-Catholic feelings and resolved to make the common schools Protestant. This story is told in William O. Bourne, *History of the Public School Society of the City of New York,* and Arthur J. Hall, *Religious Education in the Public Schools of the State and City of New York.* A work dealing with earlier church-state issues in both New York and New Jersey is J. DeLancey Ferguson, *The Relation of the State to Religion in New York and New Jersey During the Colonial Period.* A more contemporary, though abbreviated, source for New York City's experience (as well as the relations of public and parochial schools in other cities and states) is David B. Tyack, *The One Best System.* An additional source for New Jersey educational history is Nelson R. Burr, *Education in New Jersey, 1630–1871.*

Although Pennsylvania was founded as one of only three colonies with full religious liberty and espoused the principle of religious liberty in its constitutions, it, too, experienced struggles between church and state over educational concerns and issues. Though no history really tells the complete story of church-state issues in Pennsylvania, several histories give insight into some of the educational issues. Samuel E. Weber, *The Charity School Movement in Colonial Pennsylvania, 1754–1763,* tells the story of a broadly based movement for the education of children during the colonial era which was opposed by some churches who thought it not religious enough. A more complete history of colonial education in Pennsylvania is Martin Grove Brumbaugh, *An Educational Struggle in Colonial Pennsylvania,* which includes the role of the church and the early state in the education of youth. The most inclusive history of Pennsylvania education is James Pyle Wickersham, *A History of Education in Pennsylvania.* Wickersham details the support and opposition of the churches to the common school laws, the parochial systems of Pennsylvania, and the beginnings of religion and education as public school issues. No history of church-state issues in Pennsylvania covers what are called "the Philadelphia Bible riots," which occurred when the Catholic church refused to allow the King James version to be read by

Catholic children attending public schools, but Vincent P. Lannie and Bernard Diethorn provide a useful account in "For the Honor and Glory of God."

The southern states, including Maryland, have been the focus of several general histories such as Charles W. Dabney, *Universal Education in the South*, and Edgar W. Knight, *Public Education in the South*. The idea of the common school took longer to implement in the South. Numerous reasons might be given for this, including the slave and plantation systems, the more genteel culture, and the somewhat isolated position of the southern colonies from New England, where the common school movement was strongest. None of these, however, is an adequate explanation. State educational histories give better explanations for the individual states. The situation in Virginia is described in two sources: Sadie Bell, *The Church, the State and Education in Virginia*, and J. L. Blair Buck, *The Development of Public Schools in Virginia, 1607–1952*. North Carolina's church-state issues with regard to education are discussed in Luther L. Gobbel, *Church and State Relationships in Education in North Carolina Since 1776*, and Charles L. Raper, *The Church and Private Schools of North Carolina*. The issues in Maryland differ somewhat from those in other southern states. Founded by a Catholic to assure religious freedom for his co-religionists, its educational system remained empathetic to Catholics longer than in most other states. This is not to say that Maryland did not experience church-state issues or educational struggles. These are investigated in Leo Joseph McCormick, *Church-State Relationships in Education in Maryland*.

Two other church-state histories written about earlier periods are still valuable in sensing how church-state issues developed in America. One is Reba C. Strickland, *Religion and the State in Georgia in the Eighteenth Century*. The other is France V. Scholes, *Church and State in New Mexico, 1610–1650*. While neither of these sources focuses much on education, each gives insights into how these states dealt with church-state issues.

The investigations of the common school movement previously mentioned are primarily from an American Protestant viewpoint. Because the majority of Americans were Protestant, politics and education were largely controlled by that persuasion in various ways. Therefore, the common schools reflected a Protestant American ideal. Some of the Protestant parochial systems had begun in the colonial period. They did not directly threaten the curriculum of the common schools, which was implicitly Protestant. The Catholic parochial schools which began in the 1800s, however, were new and threatening to Protestant America. When one considers the long history of animosity between Protestants and Catholics in Europe, it is not surprising to find that hostility transplanted to America. Indeed, some of the Catholic migrations were made to escape Protestant persecutions. These immigrants presented a new problem for the common schools since the children came from homes where English was not spoken, grew up with different customs and holidays, and did not generally value education highly. Catholic children also were accustomed to a version of the Bible other than the King James. They were taught a different version of the Lord's Prayer. And they were encouraged to resist Protestant teachings such as they found in textbooks and the curriculum of the common schools. In every state or city where there were large numbers of Catholics, or to which many had migrated, a Catholic parochial system eventually developed. As with the common schools, it developed sooner in some areas than in others. J. A. Burns has written two volumes on the history of Catholic education in America: *The Catholic School System in the United States* and *The Growth and Development of the Catholic School System in the United States*. (The latter is largely an update and revision of the former.) Burns later co-authored a volume with B. J. Kohlbrenner entitled *A History of Catholic Education in the United States*. Other volumes investigating church, state, and education from the Catholic perspective are James M. O'Neill, *Catholicism and American Freedom*, and *Catholic Education in America, A Documentary History*, edited by Neil G. McCluskey. An article by Vincent P. Lannie, "Alienation in America: The Immigrant Catholic and Public Education in pre-Civil War America," further investigates the immigrant Catholic response to public education.

Jewish believers also had difficulty with the Protestant influence in the common schools, though they were a smaller minority than the Catholics. Jewish Americans set up Hebrew schools in which to educate their children and to dispel the Protestantism of the common schools. Lloyd P. Gartner has investigated the Jewish response in "Temples of Liberty Unpolluted: American Jews and the Public Schools, 1840–1875." Gartner has also surveyed Jewish education in *Jewish Education in the United States*, as has Judah Pilch, *A History of Jewish Education in the United States*. These histories add fullness to a story which has often neglected minority religious faiths in America.

Many of the church-state issues which confront the educational community in the twentieth century originated much earlier. Bible reading, prayer in the schools, use of religious materials as part of the curriculum, tax support for private and parochial schools, compulsory education, use of school facilities by religious groups—these are a few of the issues that have their roots in the colonial period and nineteenth century. That they did not become major educational issues until the twentieth century may be due to two factors. First, until late into the nineteenth century, education was thought to be a local and state responsibility. States could make laws which affected their educational systems without concern for recourse to federal courts or agencies. Thus, many of the Bible-reading concerns were dealt with locally and did not become national issues. Second, the United States Supreme Court had not yet applied the fourteenth Amendment to state issues surrounding the First Amendment freedoms. So no church-state issue went beyond local court jurisdiction, or at least beyond a state Supreme Court. The modern period of church-state issues in education did not begin until controversies over the reading of the Bible in public schools were settled by Supreme Courts in the states of Maine, Wisconsin, and Ohio. These controversies reached a crisis about 1870.

The problem in Ohio began in Cincinnati as early as 1830. The Bible was read in the schools and religious exercises were practiced. But these were challenged by Catholics under the leadership of Archbishop Purcell. The main objection was the use of the King James version of the Bible. Accommodations were made including the dropping of Bible reading from the schools. This led a group of citizens to call a citywide meeting with the goal of putting Bible reading back into the schools. The group prepared a legal case against the city school board and began to take it through the courts. It reached the Superior Court and then the Supreme Court of Ohio, where Bible reading was declared unconstitutional in the state. Full records of the citizen's meeting and the court actions have been preserved and articles written about the case include Martha L. Edwards, "A Problem of Church and State in the 1870's"; Nancy R. Hamant, "Religion in the Cincinnati Schools, 1830–1900"; Harold M. Helfman, "The Cincinnati Bible War, 1869–1870"; and F. Michael Perko, "The Building Up of Zion: Religion and Education in Nineteenth Century Cincinnati." The Bible reading case in Maine was judged in the Supreme Court of Maine in 1855. It did not, however, have the far-reaching repercussions of the Ohio decision or of the decision in Wisconsin. Many of the Bible-reading laws and court cases are compiled in *The Bible in the Public Schools: Opinions of Individuals and of the Press, and Judicial Decisions*, which was published in 1870, along with numerous other books, pamphlets, and articles in this bibliography.

The Ohio and Wisconsin cases are the dividing points between colonial and nineteenth-century education and twentieth-century education. They set the earlier period off from the recent educational context for church and state in which litigation has become a common means for settling issues. No longer would the community decide on the role of the church in public education. Instead, the courts would rule on the constitutionality of religious issues with regard to public schools. Coincidentally, during this same period, the federal Office of Education was formed and William Torrey Harris became United States Commissioner of Education. Public education was now a national issue and not just an ideal to be discussed and implemented locally.

There are many resources which discuss church-state issues in education. Few are limited to the colonial period or the early nineteenth century. Most general histories include reference to only the most important church-state issues. One nineteenth-century publication, Philip Schaff, *Church and State in the United States*, though it refers only briefly to religion in the public schools, is nevertheless an important source for understanding church-state issues. Twentieth-century sources for church-state issues in education which include good sections on colonial and nineteenth-century patterns are Walter S. Athearn, *Religious Education and American Democracy;* David W. Beggs III and R. Bruce McQuigg, *America's Schools and Churches: Partners in Conflict;* Joseph Henry Crooker, *Religious Freedom in American Education;* Robert Michaelson, *Piety in the Public School;* James M. O'Neill, *Religion and Education Under the Constitution;* Edwin H. Rian, *Christianity and American Education;* and Daniel Ullmann, *Amendments to the Constitution of the United States, Non-Sectarian and Universal Education.* Of these, Michaelson and Rian are the most useful and carry the story up to the mid-twentieth century.

One source of information on church-state issues in education only touched on earlier consists of the numerous educational periodicals published in the nineteenth century. There is room here to mention only some of the more important. Two were entitled the *American Journal of Education.* The first was published in Boston between 1826 and 1830. The second, with Henry Barnard as editor, was published from 1855 to 1881. Horace Mann edited the *Common School Journal* from 1839 to 1848. William Holmes McGuffey, of *McGuffey Reader* fame, was associated with the *Common School Advocate*, the *Western Monthly Magazine*, and the *Western School Journal.* In Pennsylvania, the *Common School Journal of the State of Pennsylvania* appeared in 1844 with James Wickersham as editor and was replaced by the *Pennsylvania School Journal* in 1852. Other states also had educational publications which discussed such issues as Bible reading and religious exercises in the public schools, moral education, and other issues relating to church and state. It is remarkable that nearly every educational publication in the colonial and nineteenth-century periods contained articles on both religion in education and church-state issues in education.

A final word might be said about archival resources. The Russell Library at Teachers College in New York City contains many resources in both its archives and stacks. Near to Teachers College are the Burke Library of Union Theological Seminary and the Butler Library of Columbia University, whose holdings supplement the Russell collections. In Philadelphia, the archives and collections of several libraries contain information on Church-state issues, among them the Library of the Pennsylvania Historical Society, the Free

Public Library of Philadelphia, the Library of Temple University, and the Libraries of the University of Pennsylvania. Materials relating to Horace Mann are in collections at the Massachusetts Historical Society in Boston and at Antioch College, Yellow Springs, Ohio. The Henry Barnard materials are at the Connecticut Historical Society in Hartford. There are also extensive materials at the Johns Hopkins University in Baltimore, Maryland, which promoted studies of church-state issues in education at the end of the nineteenth century. The library of Catholic University in Washington, D.C., contains extensive materials on Catholic education. Jewish materials on education are found in the library of Jewish Theological Seminary in New York City and items concerning issues of church and state as they relate to Judaism are at the American Jewish Congress in the same city. Historical societies and archives in individual states also contain useful materials.

The colonial pattern of education which was, by and large, an education for males and for the privileged, gave way in the nineteenth century to the rise of the common school. With the common school, control of the educational process and responsibility for education passed from the church to the state. This brought conflict between church and state which has lasted into the twentieth century. The patterns and issues of church-state interaction and conflict which arose with these changes in American education in the nineteenth century remain as a challenge to education in the twentieth. That subject will be the focus of the continuation of this essay in the second volume of the series.

BIBLIOGRAPHY

Adams, Francis. Free School System of the United States. London: Chapman and Hall, 1875.

Adams, Herbert B. The Church and Popular Education. Baltimore: Johns Hopkins Press, 1900.

Adams, William. Christianity and Civil Government. A Discourse Delivered on Sabbath Evening, November 10, 1850. New York: Baker and Scribner, 1851.

Alviella, Goblet d'. "L'état et l'église aux Etats-Unis." Revue de Belgique 13 (1881), 325-340.

American General Committee of the City and County of New York. The Bible in the Public Schools. New York, 1858.

Anderson, W. C., and Haight, Fletcher M. Review of Dr. Scott's Bible and Politics in the Light of Religion and the Law. San Francisco: Towne and Bacon, 1859.

Angus, David L. "Detroit's Great School Wars: Religion and Politics in a Frontier City, 1842-1853." Michigan Academian 12 (Winter 1980), 261-280.

Athearn, Walter S. Religious Education and American Democracy. Boston: Pilgrim Press, 1917.

Atwater, Lyman H. "The State in Relation to Morality, Religion, and Education." Princeton Review (March 1878), 395-422.

Aydelol, B. P. Report on the Study of the Bible in Common Schools. Cincinnati: N. S. Johnson, 1837.

Backus, Simon. <u>A Dissertation on the Right and Obligation of the Civil Magistrate to Take Care of the Interest of Religion, and Provide for Its Support; In Which the Arguments in Confirmation of Said Right and Obligation, Both From Reason and the Sacred Scriptures, are Adduced: The Usual Objections Examined, -- Together with Several Corollaries Deduced from the Subject</u>. Middletown, Conn.: T. and J. B. Dunning, 1804.

Barnard, Henry. "Religious and Moral Training." <u>American Journal of Education</u> 10 (1861), 166-186.

Bartlett, Samuel Colcord. <u>Christianity in the College</u>. Baccalaureate Sermon, Dartmouth College, June 20, 1886. Hanover, N.H.: Dartmouth Press, 1886.

Beale, Howard K. <u>History of Freedom of Teaching in American Schools</u>. New York: Charles Scribner's Sons, 1941.

Beecher, Lyman. <u>A Plea for the West</u>. 2d ed. Cincinnati: Truman and Smith, 1835.

Beggs, David W., III, and McQuigg, R. Bruce. <u>America's Schools and Churches: Partners in Conflict</u>. Bloomington, Ind.: Indiana University Press, 1965.

Bell, Sadie. <u>The Church, the State, and Education in Virginia</u>. Philadelphia: Published by the author, 1930.

Berkhofer, Robert F. Jr. <u>Salvation and the Savage: An Analysis of Protestant Missions and American Indian Response, 1787-1862</u>. Lexington: University of Kentucky Press, 1965.

"Bible and the Public Schools." <u>Law Magazine and Review</u> 30 (September 1870), 48-59.

<u>The Bible in the Public Schools: Arguments in the Case of John D. Minor et al. vs. The Board of Education of the City of Cincinnati et al. (Superior Court of Cincinnati) With the Opinions and Decision of the Court</u>. Cincinnati: Robert Clarke & Co., 1870.

<u>The Bible in the Public Schools: Opinions of Individuals and of the Press, and Judicial Decisions</u>. New York: J. W. Schermerhorn & Co., 1870.

<u>The Bible in the Public Schools: Opinions of the Supreme Court of Ohio, in the Case of John D. Minor et al. vs. The Board of Education of Cincinnati et al.</u> Cincinnati: Robert Clarke & Co., 1873.

"The Bible in the Schools." <u>Nation</u>, 18 November 1869, 430-431.

The Bible in the Schools. Argument of Richard H. Dana, Jr.,
    Esq., and Opinion of the Supreme Court of Maine, In the
    Cases of Laurence Donahoe vs. Richards et al., and Bridget
    Donahoe, by Her Next Friend, vs. the Same. Boston:
    Massachusetts Sabbath School Society, 1855.

Bidwell, Charles E. "The Moral Significance of the Common
    School." History of Education Quarterly 6 (Fall 1966), 50-
    91.

Billington, Ray A. The Protestant Crusade, 1800-1860. New
    York: Macmillan, 1938.

Board of Education. Report of the Committee on the Annual
    Apportionment on the Communications of the County
    Superintendent, Relative to the Use of the Bible in the
    Public Schools of the City of New York. New York: Office of
    the Morning News, 1844.

Bodo, John R. The Protestant Clergy and Public Issues, 1812-
    1848. Princeton, N.J.: Princeton University Press, 1954.

Bourne, William O. History of the Public School Society of the
    City of New York. New York: Wood, 1870.

Brand, W. F. Christ's Kingdom Not of This World. The Church
    Viewed in Its Relation to the State. A Sermon. Baltimore:
    James S. Waters, 1862.

Breckinridge, Robert J. Denominational Secular Education:
    Remarks Introductory to a Tract. Philadelphia: C. Sherman,
    1854.

Breckinridge, Robert J. A Plea for the Restoration of the
    Scripture to the Schools. Baltimore: Matchett & Neilson,
    1839.

Brewer, Clifton H. A History of Religious Education in the
    Episcopal Church to 1835. New Haven: Yale University Press,
    1924.

Brickman, William W., and Lehrer, Stanley, eds. Religion,
    Government, and Education. New York: Society for the
    Advancement of Education, 1961.

Brooks, Charles. An Appeal to the Legislatures of the United
    States in Relation to Public Schools. Cambridge, Mass.: J.
    Wilson and Son, 1867.

Brooks, Charles. A Lecture Delivered Before the American
    Institute of Instruction, at Montpelier, Vt., August 16,
    1849, on the Duties of Legislatures in Relation to Public
    Schools in the United States. Boston: Ticknor, Reed, and
    Fields, 1850.

Brooks, Charles. School Reform or Teachers Seminaries; A Lecture Delivered Before the American Institute of Instruction at Worcester, August 25, 1837. Boston: I. R. Butts, 1837.

Brooks, Charles. Some Reasons for the Immediate Establishment of a National System of Education for the United States. New York: Loyal Publication Society, 1865.

Brooks, Charles. Two Lectures: I. History of the Introduction of State Normal Schools in America. II. A Prospective System of National Education for the United States. Boston: J. Wilson and Son, 1864.

Brownson, Orestes A. "Public and Parochial Schools." Brownson's Quarterly Review (July 1859), 324-342.

Brownson, Orestes A. "Schools and Education." Brownson's Quarterly Review (July 1854), 354-376.

Brubacher, John S., and Rudy, Willis. Higher Education in Transition: An American History: 1635-1956. New York: Harper, 1958.

Brumbaugh, Martin Grove. An Educational Struggle in Colonial Pennsylvania. N.p.: Wickersham Press, 1898.

Buck, J. L. Blair. The Development of Public Schools in Virginia, 1607-1952. Richmond: Commonwealth of Virginia, State Board of Education, 1952.

Burns, J. A. The Catholic School System in the United States. New York: Benziger Brothers, 1908.

Burns, J. A. The Growth and Development of the Catholic School System in the United States. New York: Benziger Brothers, 1912.

Burns, J. A., and Kohlbrenner, B. J. A History of Catholic Education in the United States. New York: Benziger Brothers, 1937.

Burr, Nelson R. Education in New Jersey, 1630-1871. Princeton, N.J.: Princeton University Press, 1942.

Bushnell, Horace. "Christianity and Common Schools." Common School Journal of Connecticut 2 (January 1840), 102-103.

Byrnes, Lawrence. Religion and Public Education. New York: Harper & Row, 1975.

Cady, D. R. "Ought Our Present System of Public Education to Be Sustained?" Congregational Quarterly, 2d ser., 2 (October 1870), 524-532.

Calam, J. _Parsons and Pedagogues: The S.P.G. Adventure in American Education_. New York: Columbia University Press, 1971.

Carleton, Frank T. _Economic Influences Upon Educational Progress in the United States, 1820-1850_. Madison: University of Wisconsin Press, 1908.

Carll, M. M. _A Report of the State of Education in Pennsylvania . . . Also An Address on the Moral and Political Importance of General Education_. Philadelphia: Garden and Thompson, 1830.

Carroll, Benajah H. _The Genesis of American Anti-Missionism_. Louisville: Baptist Book Concern, 1902.

Carter, James G. _Essays upon Popular Education. Containing a Particular Examination of the Schools of Massachusetts, and an Outline of an Institution for the Education of Educators_. Boston: Bowles and Dearborn, 1826.

Cavell, Jean Moore. "Religious Education Among People of Germanic Origin in Colonial Pennsylvania." Pennsylvania German Society, _Proceedings and Addresses_ 36 (1929), 30-45.

Central Committee for Protecting and Perpetuating the Separation of Church and State. _To the People of the State of New York; Appeals, Nos. 1-5_. New York: n.p., 1885-1886.

Chadbourne, P. A. _The Prominence of the Religious Element in Education_. Hartford: Case, Lockwood and Company, 1857.

Cheever, George B. _Address Before the New England Society of the City of New York_. New York: John S. Taylor & Co., 1843.

Cheever, George B. _Right of the Bible in Our Public Schools_. New York: R. Carter & Bros., 1859.

Cincinnati Citizens. _The Bible in the Public Schools. Proceedings and Addresses at the Mass Meeting, Pike's Music Hall, Cincinnati, Tuesday Evening, September 28, 1869; With a Sketch of the Anti-Bible Movement_. Cincinnati: Gazette, 1869.

Clark, Frederick G. _The Church and the Civil Government_. New York: John A. Gray & Greene, 1865.

Clark, Rufus W. _The Question of the Hour: The Bible and the School Fund._ Boston: Lee and Shepherd, 1870.

Clebsch, William A. _From Sacred to Profane in America: The Role of Religion in American History_. New York: Harper & Row, 1968.

Cobb, Sanford H. The Rise of Religious Liberty in America: A History. New York: Macmillan, 1902.

Cole, Charles C., Jr. The Social Ideas of the Northern Evangelists, 1826-1860. New York: Columbia University Press, 1954.

Coles, Abraham. Religious Education in its Relation to Public Schools and Sunday Schools. The Indivisibility of the School Fund. Newark, N.J.: Jennings Brothers, 1868.

Colwell, Stephen. The Position of Christianity in the United States in its Relations with our Political Institutions, and Specially with Reference to Religious Instruction in the Public Schools. Philadelphia: Lippincott, Grambo & Co., 1854.

Common Schools. Remarks on the School Law of the Last Session of the Legislature: and Information Concerning the Common Schools of Massachusetts, New York, South Carolina, etc., etc. Philadelphia: n.p., 1826.

Constitution and Addresses of the National Association for the Amendment of the Constitution of the United States. Published by the Committee. Philadelphia: Jas. B. Rodgers, 1864.

Coxe, A. C. "Theology in the Public Schools." North American Review 132 (March 1881), 211-222.

Cremin, Lawrence A. The American Common School, An Historic Conception. New York: Teachers College, Columbia University, 1951.

Cremin, Lawrence A. American Education: The Colonial Experience, 1607-1783. New York: Harper & Row, 1970.

Cremin, Lawrence A. American Education: The National Experience, 1783-1876. New York: Harper & Row, 1980.

Cremin, Lawrence A. Traditions of American Education. New York: Basic Books, 1977.

Crime Increasing and Our School Tax Wasted. Newark, N.J.: A. Stephen Holbrook, 1857.

Crooker, Joseph Henry. Religious Freedom in American Education. Boston: American Unitarian Association, 1903.

Cross, R. D. "Origins of Catholic Parochial Schools in America." American Benedictine Review 16, no. 2 (1965), 194-209.

Culver, Raymond B. Horace Mann and Religion in the
    Massachusetts Public Schools. New Haven: Yale University
    Press, 1929.

Cummings, A. W. Early Schools of Methodism. New York:
    Phillips and Hunt, 1886.

Curti, Merle. The Growth of American Thought. New York:
    Harper & Brothers, 1943.

Curti, Merle. The Social Ideas of American Educators. Totowa,
    N.J.: Littlefield, Adams and Co., 1978.

Dabney, Charles W. Universal Education in the South. 2 vols.
    Chapel Hill: University of North Carolina Press, 1936.

Dabney, Robert L. "Secularized Education." Princeton Review
    (September 1879), 377-400.

DeLancey, William Heathcote. A Charge to the Clergy of the
    Diocese of Western New York, Delivered August 15, 1855, at
    the Opening of the Convention in Christ Church, Binghamton,
    on the Avenues of Infidelity. Being the Third Charge.
    Geneva, N.Y.: S. H. Porter, 1855.

Dexter, Franklin B. Documentary History of Yale University.
    New Haven: Yale University Press, 1916.

Dix, Morgan. Christian Education the Remedy for the Growing
    Ungodliness of the Times. Boston: E. P. Dutton, 1866.

Dunbar, Willis. "Public Versus Private Control of Higher
    Education in Michigan, 1817-1855." Mississippi Valley
    Historical Review 22 (December 1935), 385-406.

Dunn, William K. What Happened to Religious Education? The
    Decline of Religious Teaching in the Public Elementary
    School, 1776-1861. Baltimore: Johns Hopkins Press, 1958.

DuVall, Sylvanus M. The Methodist Episcopal Church and
    Education up to 1869. New York: Teachers College, Columbia
    University Press, 1929.

Edwards, Martha L. "A Problem of Church and State in the
    1870's." Mississippi Valley Historical Review 11 (June
    1924), 37-53.

Elsbree, Oliver Wendell. The Rise of the Missionary Spirit in
    America, 1790-1815. Williamsport, Pa.: Williamsport
    Printing and Binding Co., 1928.

Emerson, George B. Moral Education. Boston: William B. Fowle
    and N. Capen, 1842.

Ferguson, J. DeLancey. The Relation of the State to Religion
in New York and New Jersey During the Colonial Period. New
Brunswick, N.J.: Rutgers College, 1912.

Fleming, Sandford. Children and Puritans: The Place of
Children in the Life and Thought of the New England
Churches, 1620-1847. New Haven: Yale University Press,
1933.

Foster, Charles I. An Errand of Mercy: The Evangelical United
Front, 1790-1837. Chapel Hill: University of North Carolina
Press, 1960.

Fowler, William C. "The Clergy and Popular Education."
American Journal of Education 17 (January 1868), 211-224.

Franklin, Benjamin. Proposals Relating to the Education of
Youth in Pennsylvania. Philadelphia: n.p., 1749.

Gabriel, Ralph H. "Evangelical Religion and Popular
Romanticism in Early Nineteenth Century America." Church
History 19 (March 1950), 34-47.

Gartner, Lloyd P. Jewish Education in the United States: A
Documentary History. New York: Teachers College Press,
1969.

Gartner, Lloyd P. "Temples of Liberty Unpolluted: American
Jews and the Public Schools, 1840-1875." In A Bicentennial
Festschrift for Jacob Rader Marcus, edited by Wallace Korn.
New York: KTAV Publishing House, 1976.

Gobbel, Luther L. Church and State Relationships in Education
in North Carolina Since 1776. Durham, N.C.: Duke University
Press, 1938.

Greaves, R. L. The Puritan Revolution and Educational Thought:
Background for Reform. New Brunswick, N.J.: Rutgers
University Press, 1970.

Greene, Evarts B. "A Puritan Counter-Reformation." American
Antiquarian Society, Proceedings, n.s. 42 (April 1932), 17-
46. Reprint. Worcester, Mass.: American Antiquarian
Society, 1933.

Greene, Evarts B. The Revolutionary Generation, 1763-1790.
New York: Macmillan, 1943.

Greene, S. S. A Report on Object Teaching. Boston:
Massachusetts Teachers' Association, 1865.

Guilday, Peter. The National Pastorals of the American
Hierarchy, 1792-1919. Westminster, Md.: Newman Press, 1954.

Hall, Arthur J. <u>Religious Education in the Public Schools of the State and City of New York</u>. Chicago: University of Chicago Press, 1914.

Halsey, L. J. <u>Thoughts for the Times; Or The Bible as a Classic. The Bible Adapted to Childhood, The Bible in the Common School, The Bible the Palladium of Our Country, The Bible and the Church of Rome; Being a Discourse Delivered in the Chestnut Street Church, Louisville, Ky., February 4th, 1855</u>. Louisville: J. F. Brennan, 1855.

Hamant, Nancy R. "Religion in the Cincinnati Schools, 1830-1900." <u>Historical and Philosophical Society of Ohio Bulletin</u> 21 (1963), 239-251.

Handy, Robert T. <u>A Christian America: Protestant Hopes and Historical Realities</u>. New York: Oxford University Press, 1971.

Hansen, Arthur J. <u>Liberalism and American Education in the Eighteenth Century.</u> New York: Macmillan, 1926.

Hassenger, R., ed. <u>The Shape of Catholic Higher Education</u>. Chicago: University of Chicago Press, 1967.

Healey, Robert M. <u>Jefferson on Public Education</u>. New Haven: Yale University Press, 1962.

Helfman, Harold M. "The Cincinnati Bible War, 1869-1870." <u>Ohio State Archaeological and Historical Quarterly</u> 60 (1951), 369-373.

Herbst, Jurgen. <u>From Crisis to Crisis: American College Government, 1636-1819</u>. Cambridge, Mass.: Harvard University Press, 1982.

Holtz, Adrian Augustus. <u>A Study of the Moral and Religious Elements in American Education up to 1800</u>. Menasha, Wis.: George Banta Publishing Company, 1917.

Howe, Mark A. DeWolfe. <u>Classic Shades</u>. Boston: Little, Brown and Co., 1928.

Hughes, F. W. <u>Decisions of the Superintendent of Common Schools of Pennsylvania, with Explanatory Instructions and Revised Forms</u>. Harrisburg, Pa.: Theo. Fenn & Co., 1852.

Hurlbut, Elisha P. <u>A Secular View of Religion in the State and the Bible in Public Schools</u>. Albany, N.Y.: J. Munsell, 1870.

James, Edmund S. Address on the Subject of Education,
     Delivered to the Members of the Legislature of Pennsylvania,
     in the Hall of the House of Representatives, on Monday
     Evening, January 13, 1834. Harrisburg, Pa.: Henry Welsh,
     1834.

Kennedy, William B. The Shaping of Protestant Education. New
     York: Association Press, 1966.

Kiddle, Henry, and Schem, A. J. Cyclopedia of Education. New
     York: E. Steiger and Co., 1883.

Kinney, Charles B., Jr. Church and State: The Struggle for
     Separation in New Hampshire, 1630-1900. New York: Teachers
     College, Columbia University, 1955.

Klain, Zora, ed. Educational Activities of New England
     Quakers: A Source Book. Philadelphia: Westbrook Publishing
     Company, 1928.

Knight, Edgar W. Public Education in the South. Boston: Ginn
     and Company, 1922.

Knox, Samuel. An Essay on the Best System of Liberal
     Education. Philadelphia: n.p., 1797.

Lannie, Vincent P. "Alienation in America: The Immigrant
     Catholic and Public Education in Pre-Civil War America."
     Review of Politics 32, no. 4 (1970), 503-521.

Lannie, Vincent P. Public Money and Parochial Education:
     Bishop Hughes, Governor Seward, and the New York School
     Controversy. Cleveland: Press of Case Western Reserve
     University, 1968.

Lannie, Vincent P., and Diethorn, Bernard. "For the Honor and
     Glory of God: The Philadelphia Bible Riots of 1840."
     History of Education Quarterly 8 (Spring 1968), 44-106.

Lazerson, Marvin. "Understanding American Catholic Educational
     History." History of Education Quarterly 16 (Fall 1977),
     297-310.

Leland, John. The Connecticut Dissenters' Strong Box, No. 1.
     New London, Conn.: Charles Holt, 1802.

Lewis, Frank G. A Sketch of the History of Baptist Education
     in Pennsylvania. Chester, Pa.: Crozier Theological
     Seminary, 1919.

Limbert, Paul M. Denominational Policies in the Support and
     Supervision of Higher Education. New York: Teachers
     College, Columbia University, 1929.

Lunt, William P. _Moral Education_. Quincy, Mass.: John A.
     Green, 1838.

Lynn, Robert W. _Protestant Strategies in Education_. New York:
     Association Press, 1964.

Lynn, Robert W., and Wright, Elliott. _The Big Little School:
     Two Hundred Years of the Sunday School_. New York: Harper &
     Row, 1971.

McClelland, J. H. _The School Question. A Lecture on Education_.
     Pittsburgh: J. T. Shryock, 1859.

McCluskey, Neil G., ed. _Catholic Education in America: A
     Documentary History_. Classics in Education, no. 21.
     Teachers College, Columbia University, 1964.

McCormick, Leo Joseph. _Church-State Relationships in Education
     in Maryland_. Washington, D.C.: Catholic University of
     America Press, 1942.

McQuaid, B. J. _Christian Free Schools. The Subject Discussed_.
     Rochester, N.Y.: A. C. Burrough, 1872.

Magruder, Edith C. _A Historical Study of the Educational
     Agencies of the Southern Baptist Convention, 1845-1945_. New
     York: Teachers College, Columbia University, 1951.

Mahoney, Charles J. _The Relation of the State to Religious
     Education in Early New York, 1633-1825_. Washington, D.C.:
     Catholic University Press, 1941.

Mann, Horace. _Answer to the "Rejoinder" of Twenty-Nine Boston
     Schoolmasters, Part of the "Thirty-One" Who Published
     "Remarks" on the Seventh Annual Report of the Secretary of
     the Massachusetts School Board_. Boston: William B. Fowle
     and Nahum Capen, 1845.

Mann, Horace. _The Common School Controversy: Consisting of
     Three Letters of the Secretary of the Board of Education of
     the State of Massachusetts in Reply to Charges Preferred
     Against the Board by the Editor of the Christian Witness and
     by Edward A. Newton, Esq_. Boston: J. N. Bradley and Co.,
     1844.

Mann, Horace. _A Few Thoughts for a Young Man_. Boston: n.p.,
     1850.

Mann, Horace. _Life and Works of Horace Mann_. Edited by Mary
     Peabody Mann and George Combe Mann. 5 vols. Boston: Lee
     and Shepherd, 1891.

Mann, Horace. _Twelve Annual Reports of the Board of Education
     Together with the Twelve Annual Reports of the Secretary of
     the Board_. Boston: Dutton and Wentworth, 1838-1848.

Mason, Mary Paul. Church-State Relationships in Education in
    Connecticut, 1633-1953. Washington, D.C.: Catholic
    University of America Press, 1953.

Mayo, Amory Dwight. Religion in the Common Schools.
    Cincinnati: R. Clarke and Co., 1869.

Mayo, Amory Dwight. A School Without a Bible, and a Government
    Without a God. N.p., ?1870.

Mayo, Amory Dwight, and Vickers, T. The Bible in the Public
    Schools. New York: J. W. Schermerhorn & Co., 1870.

Mead, Sidney E. The Lively Experiment: The Shaping of
    Christianity in America. New York: Harper & Row, 1963.

Meriwether, Colyer. Our Colonial Curriculum. Washington,
    D.C.: Capitol Publishing Company, 1907.

Meyer, Jacob C. Church and State in Massachusetts from 1740 to
    1833: A Chapter in the History of the Development of
    Individual Freedom. 1930. Reprint. New York: Russell and
    Russell, 1968.

Michaelson, Robert. "Common School, Common Religion? A Case
    Study in Church-State Relations, Cincinnati, 1869-70."
    Church History 38 (June 1969), 206-217.

Michaelson, Robert. Piety in the Public School. New York:
    Macmillan, 1970.

Middlekauff, Robert. "Before the Public School: Education in
    Colonial America." Current History 62 (June 1972), 279-281,
    307.

Miller, Perry. Errand Into the Wilderness. Cambridge, Mass.:
    Harvard University Press, 1956.

Miller, Perry. The Life of the Mind in America From the
    Revolution to the Civil War. New York: Harcourt, Brace, &
    World, 1965.

Moehlman, Conrad Henry. The American Constitutions and
    Religion: Religious References in the Charters of the
    Thirteen Colonies and the Constitutions of the Forty-Eight
    States, A Source Book on Church and State in the United
    States. Berne, Ind., 1938.

Monroe, Paul. Founding of the American Public School System.
    New York: Macmillan, 1940.

Morgan, Gilbert. Report on Public Instruction in Pennsylvania.
    Philadelphia: E. G. Dorsey, 1836.

A Native American. _An Appeal to the Members Elect of the Legislature of the State of New York_. N.p., 1837.

The New England Primer. Edited by Paul L. Ford. New York: Dodd, Mead, and Company, 1896.

O'Neill, James Milton. _Catholicism and American Freedom_. New York: Harper & Brothers, 1952.

O'Neill, James Milton. _Religion and Education Under the Constitution_. New York: Harper & Brothers, 1949.

Ong, W. J. _The Presence of the Word_. New Haven: Yale University Press, 1967.

Packard, Frederick Adolphus. _The Question: Will the Christian Religion Be Recognized as the Basis of Public Instruction in Massachusetts? Discussed in Four Letters to the Rev. Dr. Humphrey, President of Amherst College_. Boston: Whippell and Damrell, 1839.

Packard, Frederick Adolphus. _Thoughts on the Condition and Prospects of Popular Education in the United States_. Philadelphia: A. Waldie, 1836.

Patterson, R. _The Free Thinkers and the Free Schools_. Reprinted from the _Congregational Review_, March 1870. Chicago: Church, Goodman, and Donnelley, 1870.

Patterson, R. _The Rights of Tyrannies in Our Republic_. Reprinted from the _Congregational Review_, May 1870. Chicago: Church, Goodman, and Donnelley, 1870.

Peabody, Andrew P. _The Bible in the Public Schools_. Boston: Massachusetts Bible Society, n.d.

Perko, F. Michael. "The Building Up of Zion: Religion and Education in Nineteenth Century Cincinnati." _Queen City Heritage_ (Cincinnati Historical Society) 38 (Summer 1980), 96-114.

Peters, Richard. _Sermon on Education_. Philadelphia: Benjamin Franklin and D. Hall, 1751.

Phelps, Vergil V. "The Pastor and Teacher in New England." _Harvard Theological Review_ 4 (1911), 388-399.

Pilch, Judah, ed. _A History of Jewish Education in the United States_. New York: American Association for Jewish Education, 1969.

Porter, David H. _Religion and the State. A Discourse Delivered in the First Presbyterian Church, Savannah, Georgia, July 4, 1858_. Savannah, Ga.: John M. Cooper & Co., 1858.

Potts, David B. "American Colleges in the Nineteenth Century:
    From Localism to Denominationalism." History of Education
    Quarterly 11 (Winter 1971), 363-380.

Power, Edward J. A History of Catholic Higher Education in the
    United States. Milwaukee, Wis.: Bruce Publishing Company,
    1958.

Purcell, Richard J. "The Irish Educational Contribution to
    Colonial Pennsylvania." Catholic Educational Review 37
    (September 1939), 425-439.

Puritan Club. Notions on Religion and Politics. Boston:
    Dutton and Wentworth, 1826.

Rainsford, G. N. Congress and Higher Education in the
    Nineteenth Century. Knoxville: University of Tennessee
    Press, 1972.

Randall, Henry S. Decision of the State Superintendent of
    Schools, on the Right to Compel Catholic Children to Attend
    Prayers, and to Read or Commit Portions of the Bible, as
    School Exercises, Oct. 27, 1853. New York: n.p., 1853.

Raper, Charles L. The Church and Private Schools of North
    Carolina: An Historical Study. Greensboro, N.C.: Stone,
    1898.

Ravitch, Diane. The Great School Wars. New York: Basic Books,
    1974.

Reisner, Edward H. Evolution of the Common School. New York:
    Macmillan, 1930.

Reisner, Edward H. Nationalism and Education Since 1789. New
    York: Macmillan, 1922.

Remarks on the School Law of the Last Session of the
    Legislature. Philadelphia: n.p., 1826.

Report of the Minority of the Committee on By-Laws, Rules and
    Regulations of the Board of Education, Against the Adoption
    of By-Laws Compelling the Reading of the Bible in the Public
    Schools, by Penalties and Forfeitures. New York: Wynkoop,
    Hallenbeck, & Thomas, 1859.

Report on the Subject of Education, Read in the Senate, of
    Pennsylvania, March 1, 1822. [Harrisburg, Pa.]: C. Mowry
    [1822].

Rian, Edwin H. Christianity and American Education. San
    Antonio, Tex.: Naylor Company, 1949.

Rudd, George R.   The Bible in our Public Schools. A Sermon
    Preached Before the Presbytery of Lyons, N.Y., September 13,
    1870, In Which Is Found A Brief Reply to Dr. Spear's
    Argument for Excluding the Bible from our Public Schools.
    Lyons, N.Y.: Office of the Republican, 1870.

Rudolph, Frederick.   The American College and University, A
    History. New York: Knopf, 1962.

Ruettman, Johann J.   Kirche und Staat in Nordamerika.   Zurich,
    Switzerland: Burkli, 1871.

Rush, Benjamin.   A Defense of the Use of the Bible as a School
    Book. Concord, N.H.: George Hough, 1806.

Rush, Benjamin.   A Plan for the Establishment of Public Schools
    and the Diffusion of Knowledge in Pennsylvania: To Which Are
    Added Thoughts Upon the Mode of Education Proper in a
    Republic. Philadelphia: Thomas Dobson, 1786.

Schaff, Philip.   Church and State in the United States. Papers
    of the American Historical Association 2, no. 4. 1888.
    Reprint. New York: Arno Press, 1972.

Schneider, Carl E.   The German Church on the American Frontier.
    St. Louis: Eden Publishing House, 1939.

Scholes, France V.   Church and State in New Mexico, 1610-1650.
    Historical Society of New Mexico Publications in History,
    vol. 7. Albuquerque: University of New Mexico Press, 1937.

Scholte, H. P., ed.   De vereeniging van kerk en staat in Nieuw-
    Engeland. Amsterdam, Netherlands: Hoogkame, 1841.

Scott, W. A.   The Bible and Politics: Or, An Humble Plea for
    Equal, Perfect, Absolute Religious Freedom, and Against All
    Sectarianism in Our Public Schools. San Francisco: H. H.
    Bancroft and Co., 1859.

Searles, Herbert L.   State Constitutional and Legislative
    Provisions and Supreme Court Decisions Relating to Sectarian
    Religious Influence in Tax-Supported Universities, Colleges,
    and Public Schools. National Council on Religion in Higher
    Education, n.d.

Seelye, Julius H.   "The Bible in Schools." Bibliotheca Sacra
    13 (October 1856), 725-743.

Seidman, Aaron.   "Church and State in the Early Years of the
    Massachusetts Bay Colony." New England Colony 18 (1945),
    211-233.

Shea, John Gilmary.   "Catholic Free Schools in the United
    States." American Catholic Quarterly Review 21 (Fall 1969),
    523-543.

Sherill, Lewis J. Presbyterian Parochial Schools, 1846-1870.
    New Haven: Yale University Press, 1932.

Sloan, Douglas. The Great Awakening and American Education: A
    Documentary History. New York: Teachers College Press,
    1972.

Sloan, Douglas. "Harmony, Chaos, and Consensus: The American
    College Curriculum." Teachers College Record 73 (1971),
    221-251.

Sloan, Douglas. The Scottish Enlightenment and the American
    College Ideal. New York: Teachers College Press, 1971.

Smith, Asa D. People's College: An Address. New York:
    Wynkoop, Hallenbeck, & Thomas, 1859.

Smith, Matthew Hale. The Bible, the Rod, and Religion in
    Common Schools. Boston: Redding and Co., 1847.

Smith, Samuel H. Remarks on Education. Philadelphia: John
    Ormrod, 1798.

Smith, Sherman M. The Relation of the State to Religious
    Education in Massachusetts. Syracuse, N.Y.: Syracuse
    University Press, 1926.

Smith, Timothy L. "Protestant Schooling and American
    Nationality, 1800-1850." Journal of American History 53
    (March 1967), 1679-1695.

Smythe, W. Herbert. The Bible and the Common Schools, or The
    Question Settled. Detroit: John H. Caine & Co.; New York:
    Pott & Amery and E. P. Dutton & Co.; Chicago: Mitchell &
    Clarke, 1870.

"Some Considerations for Protestant Controversialists."
    Nation, 7 April 1870, 219-220.

Spear, Samuel T. The Bible in Public Schools: A Sermon
    Preached by Rev. Samuel T. Spear, D.D. in the South
    Presbyterian Church, of Brooklyn, April 24th, 1870. New
    York: William C. Martin, 1870.

Steiner, Bernard C. Life of Henry Barnard, The First United
    States Commissioner of Education, 1867-1870. Washington,
    D.C.: Government Printing Office, 1919.

Stewart, George, Jr. A History of Religious Education in
    Connecticut to the Middle of the Nineteenth Century. New
    Haven: Yale University Press, 1924.

Stowe, Calvin E. The Religious Element in Education. Boston:
    William D. Ticknor & Co., 1844.

Strickland, Reba C. Religion and the State in Georgia in the Eighteenth Century. New York: Columbia University Press, 1939.

Sweet, William Warren. Religion in Colonial America. New York: Charles Scribner's Sons, 1951.

Sweet, William Warren. Religion in the Development of American Culture, 1765-1840. New York: Charles Scribner's Sons, 1952.

Temple, C. M. Speech of C. M. Temple; Delivered in the Massachusetts House of Representatives, on the Subject of Requiring the Bible to be Daily Read in All the Public Schools of the Commonwealth. Worcester, Mass.: Edward R. Fiske, 1855.

Tewksbury, Donald G. The Founding of American Colleges and Universities Before the Civil War. New York: Teachers College, Columbia University, 1932.

Thompson, Joseph P. Shall Our Common Schools Be Destroyed? An Argument Against Perverting the School-Fund to Sectarian Uses. New York: Edward O. Jenkins, 1870.

Thorpe, Francis N., ed. Federal and State Constitutions, Colonial Charters and Other Organic Laws. 7 vols. Washington, D.C.: Government Printing Office, 1909.

Tompkins, Arnold. The Philosophy of Teaching. Boston: Ginn & Co., 1895.

Troen, Selwyn K. The Public and the Schools: Shaping the St. Louis School System, 1836-1929. Columbia, Mo.: University of Missouri Press, 1975.

Trott, Nicholas. The Laws of the British Plantations in America, Relating to the Church and the Clergy, Religion and Learning. London: Clarke, 1725.

Tyack, David B. "The Kingdom of God and the Common School." Harvard Educational Review 36 (Fall 1966), 447-469.

Tyack, David B. The One Best System: A History of American Urban Education. Cambridge, Mass.: Harvard University Press, 1974.

Tyack, David B. "Onward Christian Soldiers." In History and Education: The Educational Uses of the Past, edited by Paul Nash, 212-255. New York: Random House, 1970.

Tyack, David B., and Hansot, Elisabeth. Managers of Virtue: Public School Leadership in America, 1820-1980. New York: Basic Books, 1982.

Tyler, William S. A History of Amherst College. New York:
Frederick H. Hitchcock, 1895.

Ullmann, Daniel. Amendments to the Constitution of the United
States. Non-Sectarian and Universal Education. New York;
Baker & Godwin, 1876.

Van Rensselaer, Cortland. Characteristics of an Old-Fashioned
Education. Philadelphia: C. Sherman, 1853.

Watts, Isaac. Divine and Moral Songs for the Use of Children.
London: John Van Vorrst, 1850.

Webber, Thomas L. Deep Like the Rivers: Education in the Slave
Quarter Community, 1831-1865. New York: W. W. Norton, 1978.

Weber, Samuel Edwin. The Charity School Movement in Colonial
Pennsylvania, 1754-1763. Philadelphia: William J. Campbell,
1905.

Webster, Daniel. Webster's Speech. A Defence of the Christian
Religion and of the Religious Instruction of the Young.
Delivered in the Supreme Court of the United States,
February 10, 1844. In the Case of Stephen Girard's Will.
New York: Mark H. Newman, 1844.

Westerhoff, John H., III. McGuffey and His Readers: Piety,
Morality, and Education in Nineteenth-Century America.
Nashville: Abingdon Press, 1978.

Whitehead, John S. The Separation of College and State:
Columbia, Dartmouth, Harvard, and Yale, 1776-1876. New
Haven: Yale University Press, 1973.

Wickersham, James Pyle. A History of Education in
Pennsylvania, Private and Public, Elementary and Higher,
From the Time the Swedes Settled on the Delaware to the
Present Day. Lancaster, Pa.: Inquirer Publishing Company,
1886.

Winslow, O. E. Meetinghouse Hill, 1630-1783. New York:
Macmillan, 1952.

Woody, Thomas S. Early Quaker Education in Pennsylvania. New
York: Teachers College, Columbia University, 1920.

Woody, Thomas S., ed. Quaker Education in the Colony and State
of New Jersey: A Source Book. Philadelphia: University of
Pennsylvania Press, 1923.

Wright, Louis Booker. The Cultural Life of the American
Colonies, 1607-1763. New York: Harper & Row, 1957.

Wright, Louis Booker. Culture on the Moving Frontier. 1955.
Reprint. New York: Harper & Brothers, 1961.

10

Church-State Issues and the Law: 1607–1870

Daniel R. Ernst

The legal history of church-state relations is a promising field of study for American cultural historians. In every age, religion and law have acted as cultural systems, providing men and women with ways of organizing and interpreting their experiences and of explaining and defending their actions. Yet in this process the two cultural systems have not always been equally important, and their relative importance has changed dramatically from one era to the next. I suspect that over the course of American history, religious beliefs have become less important in shaping how people have interpreted the actions of those around them, and legal rules have become more important. Only by studying the interplay between these two cultural systems can we fully understand so fundamental a change.

Consider the case of Alvan Stewart, a New York lawyer and reformer. On Sunday, July 15, 1838, Stewart lectured on temperance and circulated a petition calling for the reform of the state's liquor laws. Several days later he was arrested for violating a statute which prohibited "servile laboring or working" on Sunday. Angered by the rough treatment he received from the arresting constable and convinced that the justice of the peace who ordered his arrest had maliciously sought to curtail his reform efforts, Stewart sued the two men for assault and battery and false imprisonment. Failing in the trial court, he appealed to the Supreme Court of Judicature in July 1839.[1]

To win his case, Stewart had to show that the justice of the peace had no authority to order his arrest. Demonstrating that the justice had misunderstood the law would not be enough: Stewart had to show that the justice's "decision was so gross as to afford evidence, per se, of the influence of bad motives."[2]

In his lengthy argument before the court, Stewart repeatedly and laboriously listed the disastrous consequences for religious liberty which he claimed would follow from upholding the justice's authority in this case. If the warrant's allegations were sufficient to give the justice jurisdiction, he argued, then so would allegations that Stewart had written on the Sabbath, read on the Sabbath, circulated bibles on the Sabbath, and so on. If Hawley's decision were unreviewable, then "the whole magistracy of this land are armed with a power more dreadful than the Spanish Inquisition." Congregationalist justices would arrest Mormons and Baptists; Baptist justices would arrest Presbyterians, and "so it might be turned by each sect against the other." Each justice could enforce the Sabbath as he saw fit, and every justice would become a "Tom Thumb of the Law, strut[ting] his little hour on the stage, in all the potency of a Pope, pacing in flowing robes up and down the Halls of the Vatican." As the circumstances of Stewart's arrest clearly showed, the law and religion would become "cloak[s] of hypocrisy" protecting "the rankest and vilest oppression."[3]

So Stewart argued, without success. Writing for a unanimous court, Chief Justice Nelson refused to second guess the justice of the peace. Although Nelson implied that Stewart had been treated unjustly, allowing Stewart to recover would deny justices and constables the "liberal protection" they needed if the general administration of justice were to be unhampered.[4]

Viewed from the distance of a century and a half, *Stewart v. Hawley* seems more significant for the arguments Stewart overlooked than for those he made. Although Stewart maintained that the "whole system of our laws, especially on all questions affecting individual liberty and toleration, are exceedingly explicit against the exercise of all ghostly and spiritual jurisdiction in the Land," he never argued that the Sabbath law was unconstitutional. On the contrary, he implied that only the absence of appellate review prevented the act from being a legitimate protection of "peace, good order, and religion on the sabbath-day."[5] Why did Stewart stop short of challenging the statute on constitutional grounds?

Legal rules probably provide part of the answer. Under the canons of interpretation Stewart learned as a law student, the case against the statute was weak. New York's constitution guaranteed the free exercise of religion, but subject to the qualification that "the liberty of conscience hereby secured shall not be so construed as to excuse acts of licentiousness, or justify practices inconsistent with the peace or safety of this State."[6] In an earlier case the New York Supreme Court had implied that the statute was a permissible safeguard against the acts of licentiousness contemplated by the constitution.[7] Nevertheless, the question had never been squarely raised and resolved, and Stewart rarely shrank from advancing unlikely arguments, particularly if doing so afforded excellent opportunities for rhetorical pyrotechnics.

Stewart's religious beliefs are, I suspect, the more important reason for his failure to attack the constitutional validity of the Sabbath law. Like many other white, Northern, middle-class males of his day, Stewart believed that civil society was impossible without religious belief and that therefore the state should encourage religious observance. As Stewart told a Sabbath School Society in 1838, "we have no wise law, either of statute, common or constitutional, which is acknowledged by the men of this generation, but the spirit of its principle will fall within some of these holy sayings [preserved in the Bible], so that the good man is constrained to acknowledge Bible wisdom and Bible law the prototype of all human law." Indeed, "the Religion of Jesus Christ is a part of the Law of the Land," and without the "auxiliary" authority of this religion, no man would obey the decrees of courts and legislatures. Measures designed to support Christianity, such as Sabbath laws, were necessary to the survival of the nation. To argue that they impermissibly united church and state was "nothing but uncompromising, relentless infidelity."[8]

The works in the bibliography that follows take up cases like *Stewart V. Hawley*, statutes like New York's Sabbath law, and religious guarantees like that of the New York Constitution of 1821. Taken together, these studies tell us much about the changing pattern of Americans' assumptions about the proper relations between church and state. They also show that Alvan Stewart's was an intermediate position in a larger transformation in American thinking about the sources of legitimate governmental authority.

The zealous English men and women who settled New England were no liberals. Because they embraced an organic notion of the community and believed that government was indispensable in a world of sinful, depraved, and fallen men and women, they erected a government that sought to subordinate self-interest to the concerns of the community. But if government was necessary, what ensured that the earthly, if presumably sainted, rulers would abide by the terms of their social compact with the ruled? To assuage such doubts, Puritan leaders maintained that God actively participated in the formation and execution of the social compact. "Just as the covenant between God and man was an agreement to terms, but terms dictated by absolute moral standards and not by the convenience of the contractors, so the articles of the social compact are first good, just, and honest in themselves, not from the compact."[9]

The implications of such reasoning explain much more than the self-confidence with which Massachusetts Puritans punished religious dissenters in the celebrated trials of Anne Hutchinson, the Antinomians, and the Quakers. Religious significance invested every governmental act, so that a complete history of the relationship between their religion and their law properly embraces their punishment of crimes we now consider secular and their regulation of the family, to name only the two most studied aspects of Puritan governance.[10]

But regardless of the theoretical soundness of the theological and political reasoning of the Puritan leaders, in practice their fellow colonists needed a more certain aid for determining proper conduct than the contemplation of scripture or the ad hoc judgment of a magistrate. For this reason Thomas Lechford saw "not a little degree of pride and dangerous improvidence" in the magistrates' "pretence that the Word of God is sufficient to rule us," and Thomas Hooker thought that to entrust magistrates with undefined discretion would be "a course which wants both safety and warrant." Such concerns produced the first Massachusetts codes, and, as we shall see, reappeared whenever public officials invoked religious sanction as direct authority for specific governmental programs.[11]

The seventeenth-century colonies which practiced toleration turned their backs on the added authority which the traditional connections between church and state had brought to civil governors. As a result, they experienced much more social turbulence than did those with a single established religion. Thus, one historian has found that "by setting itself against the prevalent cultural axiom which held that the basis of civil cohesion and magisterial authority was a positive and official relationship between church and state, Rhode Island suffered the throes which commonly accompany basic social and political innovation."[12]

The throes Rhode Island endured spread throughout colonial America as religious diversity in the colonies grew. In part this diversity was the product of the increasing number and variety of churches. In 1650, only four colonies had two or more denominations; by 1750 all colonies had at least three denominations, while New Jersey, Pennsylvania, and South Carolina had seven and New York had eight. Diversity also resulted from the splits in existing churches wrought by the Great Awakening, the growing popularity of deism and religious rationalism, and a religious "indifferentism" that left an unprecedented proportion of the population without regular affiliation with an organized faith.[13]

As religious variety and colonial prosperity simultaneously flourished, the seventeenth-century assumption that a peaceful body politic required that its members unite in worship appeared to be disproved. Perry Miller identified one result: "In a world where the ancient landmarks were fading, where the will of God was becoming ambiguous to man's reading, the one remaining certainty, the one institution which could plead at least the excuse of utility, was the organized rights of Englishmen, exercised and protected in an elective assembly."[14] The secularization of government went hand in hand with a growing desire to see rights and obligations established by representative authorities and fixed in written documents, and this spreading legal positivism limited the range of governmental action that could be justified solely by the religious beliefs of public officials.[15]

Another, narrower legal consequence of growing religious diversity was a trend toward multiple establishments in church-state relations. Colonies which had once levied a regular tax for a single church moved to a system under which the state supported all recognized religious institutions equally. By the first years of the Revolution six states had statutory or constitutional provisions authorizing general assessments in support of religious groups. This fell short of an establishment of religion per se because some faiths—those of Jews, radical religious communities, and Indians, for example—received no support, but it had become the only politically viable way to employ the fiscal powers of the state in support of religion.[16]

The years 1780 to 1810 saw a successful attack on this system of multiple establishment everywhere outside of New England. The crucial controversy starting the new trend away from general assessments was the struggle over Jefferson's "Bill for Religious Freedom" in the Virginia legislature between 1779 and 1785. A combination of favorable circumstances explains why foes of general assessments succeeded in Virginia first: Virginians' experience of Anglican domination had soured them on establishments in general; Virginian dissenters were numerous and active; many members of Virginia's elite were cosmopolitan and deistic. In New England, dissenters were far fewer and had fared better under multiple establishment, and the region's religious liberals had no quarrel with a Congregationalism that tolerated its unitarian wing. As a result, general assessments persisted in Connecticut until 1818, in New Hampshire until 1819, and in Massachusetts until 1833.[17]

Despite the widespread abolition of general assessment provisions, complete separation of church and state remained a radical idea in the federal and early national periods. Disestablishment meant an end to even impartial tax support of churches, but it did not prevent state governments from supporting religion through other means. Thus, in 1811 James Kent wrote that the framers of New York's constitutional guarantee of religious liberty sought "only to banish test oaths, disabilities and the burdens, and sometimes the oppressions, of church establishments; and to secure to the people of this state, freedom from coercion, and an equality of right, on the subject of religion." They never intended to "withdraw religion in general, and with it the best sanctions of moral and social obligation from all consideration and notice of the law."[18] For this reason, references to God in the preambles of state constitutions and acts incorporating church property evoked little controversy, although they contradicted the principle of pure voluntaryism in religious affairs. As Mark DeWolfe Howe observed, such provisions constituted "a de facto establishment of religion," and, as William McLoughlin subsequently noted, this endorsement of Protestantism provided "the cultural cohesion needed for the new nation."[19]

Beyond this general understanding, however, consensus broke down, and debate over the propriety of specific forms of "friendly aid" to Christianity could evoke strong passions. Most public assemblies (including the Congress which enacted the First Amendment) appointed chaplains, but at least James Madison disapproved of the practice.[20] State governors and Presidents Washington, Adams, and Madison proclaimed or (in Madison's case) designated days of public worship, but some, such as Thomas Cooper, objected to the practice and Jefferson explicitly refused to continue it. And although Article 6, Section 3, of the U.S. Constitution prohibited religious tests for the officers of national government, the abolition of test oaths in many states came only after prolonged struggles.[21]

Given this backdrop of consensus and conflict, the proper interpretation of the First Amendment is no easy task. Most scholars now agree that those who framed the First Amendment viewed it more as a federalism provision, limiting the power of the national government, than as a libertarian provision, guaranteeing protection of religious liberty from violation by public agencies. Many thought the amendment superfluous, because under the Constitution the national government possessed only enumerated powers, and these did not include authority to legislate in religious affairs. Nevertheless, those who feared that Congress might establish a national religion or tamper with the establishment of the New England states sought and won the guarantee. The First Amendment left all authority over the subject of religion exclusively to the states. Although it provided for a radical separation of church and state at the national level, the aim of many who supported it was to support the religious accommodations of the individual states.[22]

In *Everson v. Board of Education* (1947) the Supreme Court recast the establishment clause as a guarantee against infringements of religious liberty by state government.[23] Since *Everson*, the Supreme Court has embarked on the logically implausible course of seeking to resolve disputes over state aid to religion by invoking the intentions of the authors of an amendment not intended to reach the states. Scholars whose inquiries have been guided by the Court's ostensible reliance on "the Framers' intent" have reached exactly opposite conclusions on the significance of the historical record for any given governmental policy. For example, Michael Malbin's review of the legislative history of the First Amendment argues that the Framers only intended to prevent Congress from creating a single establishment, so that recent programs to aid parochial schools should be deemed constitutional, so long as they do not discriminate for or against particular sects. In contrast, Leonard Levy more cautiously concludes that, by "a preponderance of the whole evidence," *Everson*'s interpretation of the establishment clause as prohibiting even impartial aid to religion is "historically the more accurate one."[24]

Future scholars would do well to follow the example of Justice Brennan in his dissenting opinion in *Lynch v. Donnelly* (1984), the case that upheld the annual sponsorship of a crèche by Pawtucket, Rhode Island. "The intent of the Framers with respect to the public display of nativity scenes is virtually impossible to discern," he wrote, "primarily because the widespread celebration of Christmas did not emerge in its present form until well into the nineteenth century." Given this fact, Brennan suggested a more feasible historical inquiry: at the time of the adoption of the Constitution, was the public celebration of Christmas an important element in the competition among denominations for the allegiance of their followers, so that state interference with the practice would upset "the benign regime of competitive disorder among all denominations" which the religion clauses were intended to ensure? If historians are to be enlisted in lawyers' struggles over constitutional interpretation, then such an open-ended inquiry into the purposes and presuppositions of those who framed the First Amendment would be truer to the standards of their profession than a quixotic search for the Framers' "intentions."[25]

For historians who search the past for cultural artifacts, not legal precedents, the writings and decisions of the jurists who interpreted the religious guarantees of the first constitutions reveal a general consensus that the principles of Christianity should guide public officials. The most revealing writings concerned the commonly repeated maxim that Christianity was part of the common law. In two posthumously published writings, an appendix to his *Reports of Cases Determined in the General Court* and a letter to Major John Cartwright, Thomas Jefferson took issue with the maxim. He traced the erroneous interpretation to a seventeenth-century law commentator who, Jefferson argued, misinterpreted a fifteenth-century precedent. He then traced the error forward to his favorite bête noire, Lord Mansfield, who wrote that "the essential principles of revealed religion are part of the common law." Jefferson responded with a classic, positivistic critique: Mansfield "leaves us at our peril to find out what, in the opinion of the judge, and according to the measures of his foot or his faith, are those *essential* principles of revealed religion, obligatory on us as a part of the common law."[26]

To the defense of a Christian common law rushed Supreme Court Justice Joseph Story. In a short article published in 1833 he reviewed Jefferson's precedents, concluding that the seventeenth-century commentator interpreted them properly and that later decisions were good authority for the maxim. And in his monumental *Commentaries on the Constitution*, also published in 1833, he took up the issue of religious liberty at length. With uncharacteristic passion, Story blasted the establishment of the Church of England, which he believed Blackstone had defended "with the unsuspecting satisfaction of a bigot." But Story also argued that England's tyrannical attempt to force the consciences of other men was a very different thing from unbiased attempts to aid religion. At the time of the adoption of the First Amendment, he continued,

the general, if not the universal, sentiment in America was, that Christianity ought to receive encouragement from the state, so far as was not incompatible with the private rights of conscience, and the freedom of religious worship. An attempt to level all religions, and to hold all in utter indifference, would have created universal disapprobation, if not universal indignation.[27]

Story believed that states had to sponsor Christianity "as a matter of sound policy, as well as revealed truth," because for him Christianity was the indispensable fount of the "personal, social, and benevolent virtues" that made civil government possible. Writing in the year in which his home state, Massachusetts, ended its system of multiple establishment, he warned, "It yet remains a problem to be solved in human affairs, whether any free government can be permanent, where the public worship of God, and the support of religion, constitute no part of the policy or duty of the state."[28]

Story's defense of a general alliance between church and state represents a stream of thought that persisted well into the nineteenth century.[29] As we have seen, Alvan Stewart considered Christianity "that power which stands behind the constitution and laws and sets them all in motion."[30] Kent, speaking for the New York Supreme Court, thought that an attack on Christianity endangered "the essential interests of civil society" by destroying moral discipline.[31] Pennsylvania's Supreme Court unequivocally resolved that "no free government now exists in the world, unless where Christianity is acknowledged, and is the religion of the country. Christianity is part of the common law of this state. . . . It is the purest system of morality, the firmest auxiliary, and the only support of all human laws."[32] And Tocqueville found that for Americans, "the ideas of Christianity and liberty are so completely mingled that it is almost impossible to get them to conceive of the one without the other."[33]

In fact, as late as 1857 at least one reputable legal thinker could take a more conservative stand than Story's. In that year the lawyer and Protestant Episcopal bishop, John Henry Hopkins, denied that Hindus, Buddhists, and Muslims had religious rights under the Constitution and argued that, despite the prohibition of religious tests in Article VI, the oath for national office could not be consistently taken by non-Christians. Story, in contrast, thought that the rights of conscience were "beyond the just reach of any human power" and that the Constitutional prohibition of religious tests permitted "the Catholic and the Protestant, the Calvinist and the Arminian, the Jew and the Infidel" to "sit down at the common table of the national councils, without any inquisition into their faith, or mode of worship."[34]

But if Story represented one tradition of thought about religion and government, many in the next generation repudiated and ridiculed his conclusions. Story had come of age when the legal profession was the preserve of elites, when many still deferred to the wisdom of their social betters, and when legal rules were crafted by judges, not extruded by the press of interest groups in state legislatures. Such a world could still tolerate the belief (which had been dogma in Puritan times) that the law embodied consensual moral values. In the fifty years after the Revolution, the advent of middle-class practitioners, an elected judiciary, greater political participation, and more active legislatures destroyed most of the elitist assumptions that had underpinned the legal conciousness of Story's generation. Unlike "the last of the old race of judges," these new Americans considered the law as nothing more than the command of a political sovereign, so that a law need not be morally right to be legitimate.[35] Legal positivism, once merely an outsider's critique of an overwhelmingly paternalistic political order, had by 1840 defined how most Americans viewed their government.[36]·

This great jurisprudential sea change could not fail to transform the law of church-state relations. A general sign of the new mood was the restatement of the old positivistic critique in more popular media, such as the comment of a Philadelphia newspaper editor, who wrote:

We do not know what is generally meant when it is said that Christianity is part of the common law of the land. It is a very indefinite expression, which may mean much, or may mean little. It is a very convenient nose of wax, that may be shaped and twisted, and pointed at the will of any one who can lay his digits upon it.

More dramatic was the unprecedentedly ridiculing tone of those who sought to loosen the ties between church and state. Thus, when in voting to uphold Pennsylvania's Sabbath law a judge wrote, "We are a Christian people and state," an editor retorted, "'A *Christian* state'! Why it has only a corporate existence. It has neither a soul to be saved, nor even a body to be baptized. . . . 'A *Christian* state'! How perfectly incongruous the conception. As well a Christian engine or a Christian clock!"[37]

We can see more specific signs of a transformation in the law of church-state relations by looking at the history of religion-related criminal prosecutions and church property disputes. After the first decades of the nineteenth century, decision-makers in the criminal justice system became increasingly reluctant to entrust judges with decisions that required them to recognize and articulate a religious consensus on their own authority. Although not all judges joined in this general sentiment, many refused the role of independent articulator of a religious consensus for their jurisdiction.

The history of prosecutions for blasphemy and for violations of Sabbath laws reflects these new scruples. Many states inherited colonial precedents and statutes prohibiting blasphemy. As late as 1811, the New York Supreme Court unanimously upheld a common-law prosecution for blasphemy in *People v. Ruggles*, without the additional authority of a statutory prohibition of the offense.[38] Later successful prosecutions, such as *Updegraph v. Commonwealth* (1824) and *Commonwealth v. Kneeland* (1838), were brought under statutes and could provoke strong dissents.[39] After 1840 prosecutions for blasphemy seem to be very rare, although no quantitative study has documented the decline.[40]

In contrast, successful prosecutions for violating Sabbath laws continued throughout the nineteenth century. These prosecutions were reconcilable with the new positivistic jurisprudence because they did not force judges to determine on their own authority that the conduct of the defendant violated religious principles. The legislature commanded the judiciary to punish proscribed actions, not speech or writings. Although, as *Stewart v. Hawley* shows, unscrupulous prosecutors might use a Sabbath law for private or partisan purposes, determining whether a defendant's conduct constituted "servile labor" was much less open-ended than divining whether it amounted to "contumeliously reproaching God, his creation, government, or final judgement of the world" (to use the statutory language considered in *Kneeland*).

In addition, judges were inclined to analogize Sabbath-law prosecutions to prosecutions for common crimes because they could easily find a "secular" purpose for the prohibition on Sunday labor. Like other measures for the protection of the health, safety and welfare of the populace, it was within the police power of the state. As a judge of the Pennsylvania Supreme Court wrote in *Specht v. Commonwealth* (1848), "It is still, essentially, but a civil regulation, made for the government of man as a member of society, and obedience to it may properly be enforced by penal sanctions. . . . It cannot be said a primary object of the act was, authoritatively, to assert the supremacy of Sunday as of Divine appointment."[41] Thus, the "secular purpose requirement" in the three-part test which the U.S. Supreme Court now applies in cases arising under the establishment clause was the product of the jurisprudential doubts of state-court judges who reviewed religiously motivated legislation.[42]

The influence of positivism can also be seen in the law of church property disputes. Such controversies often arose in the nineteenth century when a congregation split up over some doctrinal issue. Before the Civil War, courts adopted one of two approaches. Under the implied trust approach, judges awarded the property to the faction which, in their independent opinion, was theologically closest to the religious views of the congregation at the time it acquired the property. The second, "simple majority" approach awarded the property to the majority faction, a rule which got judges out of the business of drawing theological distinctions but which still substituted a court's decree for the decision of the denominational hierarchy. Under a test enunciated by the U.S. Supreme Court in *Watson v. Jones* (1871), judges limited their inquiry to determining what agency, under the procedural rules of denomination, possessed general governing authority. When they identified that agency, the courts had to enforce its decision regarding the disposition of the disputed property, regardless of the doctrines or size of the winning faction. In the years after the Civil War *Watson* became the prevailing approach, as once again, courts refused to act further in religious matters than the command of legitimate authority required.[43]

Watson heralds a new age in the law of church-state relations, one that corresponds with the growth in the power and stature of the federal government wrought by the Civil War and Reconstruction. Increasingly, federal courts would find occasion to apply and alter the positivistic church-state law as it had been articulated in the state courts, and the state courts would now, like as not, follow their lead. Long before the Supreme Court applied the religion clauses of the First Amendment to the states in *Everson*, Americans would increasingly turn to the federal government to set the boundaries between church and state. On this new level old assumptions about the religious nature of the nation and the religious rights of the individual would be tested and fashioned anew.

To minimize duplication between this bibliography and others in this volume, I have listed only secondary and primary materials which discuss the positive sources of law (statutes, judicial opinions, and constitutional provisions) and the actions of judges and legislators. As many of the works listed show, anyone seeking to understand the place of the law in church-state relations in American society and American culture must consider broader social and intellectual trends in addition to these legal sources and actions. For this reason the other bibliographies in this volume supplement in crucial ways the materials listed here.

The chronological starting point of this bibliography is the first European settlement of the area that ultimately became the United States. Most of the items describe church-state relations among the British settlers of the eastern seaboard, although several discuss other ethnic groups (such as the

Dutch) and other regions (such as Spanish Louisiana). The chronological
terminus is the year 1870; a bibliography in the second volume of this series
will list items for subsequent years. The present bibliography lists works
dealing with both periods unless they treat the pre-1870 period only in
passing.

Although witchcraft trials can provide revealing insights into the rela-
tionships between religious and legal institutions, the literature treating them
is easily accessible through recent studies and is not listed here. Consult
Steven H. Keeney, "Witchcraft in Colonial Connecticut and Massachusetts:
An Annotated Bibliography," *Bulletin of Bibliography and Magazine Notes*
33 (1976), 61–72, and the notes and bibliographic materials of John Demos,
Entertaining Satan: Witchcraft and the Culture of Early New England (New
York: Oxford University Press, 1982); Richard Weisman, *Witchcraft, Magic,
and Religion in 17th-Century Massachusetts* (Amherst: University of Massachusetts Press, 1984); and Paul Boyer and Stephen Nissenbaum, *Salem
Possessed: The Social Origins of Witchcraft* (Cambridge, Mass.: Harvard University Press, 1974). The best general bibliography of American legal history
is Kermit L. Hall, *A Comprehensive Bibliography of American Constitutional and Legal History, 1896–1979* (Milwood, N.Y.: Krauss International
Publications, 1984).

The primary materials listed here are all published and generally under-
utilized by historians: transcripts of trials involving significant church-state
issues, commentary on specific legislation or constitutional provisions, and
general discussions of religious liberty in the United States. When they exist, I
have given with each item its corresponding number in Charles Evans, *American Bibliography* (New York: Peter Smith, 1941–59); Roger P. Bristol, *Supplement to Evans' American Bibliography* (Charlottesville: University Press
of Virginia, 1970); or Ralph R. Shaw and Richard Shoemaker, *American Bibliography* (New York: Scarecrow Press, 1958–66) (22 vols.).

Wilfrid J. Ritz's *Judicial Proceedings First Published Before 1801: An
Analytical Bibliography* (Westport, Conn.: Greenwood Press, 1984), lists additional published documents for many of the trials represented in this bibliography: Anne Hutchinson and the Antinomians, pp. 155–59; the Quakers
before the Massachusetts General Court in 1659, pp. 159–62; John Checkley,
pp. 162–63; Thomas Maule, pp. 9–10; Francis Makemie, pp. 49–50; and the
church property dispute, *Macsparran v. Torrey*, pp. 39–40.

Positive legal sources affecting church-state relations are too numerous
and diverse to be listed here, although many appear in the documentary
collections included in this bibliography, such as Blakely's *American State
Papers and Related Documents on Freedom in Religion* and Howe's *Cases
on Church and State in the United States.* To find other relevant judicial
opinions, consult the *Century Edition of the American Digest* (St. Paul,

Minn.: West Publishing Co., 1897–1904) (50 vols.). For statutes, consult Lawrence Keitt, *An Annotated Bibliography of Bibliographies of Statutory Materials of the United States* (Cambridge, Mass.: Harvard University Press, 1936). For the texts of federal and state constitutions, see Francis Newton Thorpe, ed., *The Federal and State Constitutions, Colonial Charters, and Other Organic Laws of the States, Territories, and Colonies Now or Heretofore Forming the United States of America* (Washington, D.C.: Government Printing Office, 1909) (7 vols.), and William F. Swindler, ed., *Sources and Documents of United States Constitutions* (Dobbs Ferry, N.Y.: Oceana Publications, 1973–79) (11 vols.). For other materials relating to the work of constitutional conventions, see Augustus Hunt Shearer, *A List of Documentary Material Relating to State Constitutional Conventions* (Chicago: Newberry Library, 1915), and Balfour Halevy, *A Selective Bibliography on State Constitutional Revision* (2d ed. New York: National Municipal League, 1967).

The principal manuscript records for the study of the law of church-state relations are those of courts, lawyers, and judges. For court records, see Richard B. Morris, *Early American Court Records: A Publication Program* (New York: New York University School of Law, 1941); Michael G. Kammen, "Colonial Court Records and the Study of Early American History: A Bibliographical Review," *American Historical Review* 70 (1965), 732–39, and three articles by David H. Flaherty: "A Select Guide to the Manuscript Court Records of Colonial New England," *American Journal of Legal History* 11 (1967), 107–26; "A Select Guide to the Manuscript Court Records of Colonial Virginia," *American Journal of Legal History* 19 (1975), 112–37; and "The Use of Early American Court Records in Historical Research," *Law Library Journal* 69 (1976), 342–46. Useful essays discussing the problems and rewards of research in the papers of eighteenth- and nineteenth-century lawyers are Hiller B. Zobel's "Bridge of Words: 18th Century Lawyers and Papers," *Law Library Journal* 69 (1976), 303–06, and Alfred Konefsky's "Lawyers' Papers as a Source of Legal History: The 19th Century," *Law Library Journal* 69 (1976), 307–09. For the papers of the justices of the United States Supreme Court, see Adrienne deVergie and Mary Kate Kell, *Location Guide to the Manuscripts of Supreme Court Justices* (Austin: Tarlton Law Library, University of Texas School of Law, 1981) (Legal Bibliography Series, no. 24). I am aware of no guide to the papers of other federal judges or of state supreme court judges, although many of these records have been deposited in state historical societies, and are available to researchers.

NOTES

1. For a report of the case in the Supreme Judicial Court, see Stewart v. Hawley, 21 Wendell's Reports 552 (N.Y. Sup. Ct. 1839). Stewart's subsequent, unsuccessful

attempt to have the Court reconsider its decision is reported as Stewart v. Hawley, 22 Wendell's Reports 551 (N.Y. Sup. Ct. 1840).

2. Stewart v. Hawley, 21 Wendell's Reports 552, 555 (N.Y. Sup. Ct. 1839).

3. An autographic draft of Stewart's argument was incorporated into a manuscript biography undertaken by Stewart's son-in-law, Luther Marsh. The manuscript survives in Folder 265.57 of the Alvan Stewart Papers of the New York State Historical Association, Cooperstown, New York. The biography was never published. Stewart's argument is numbered as pages 19–37 of Marsh's manuscript; the quoted passages appear on pages 19–20, 22–23, 30, and 33.

4. Stewart v. Hawley, 21 Wendell's Reports 552, 557 (N.Y. Sup. Ct. 1839); Stewart v. Hawley, 22 Wendell's Reports 561, 566 (N.Y. Sup. Ct. 1840).

5. Marsh's Biography, pp. 24, 21–22, Stewart Papers.

6. The relevant provision is Article VII, Section 3 of the New York Constitution of 1821, printed in William F. Swindler, ed., *Sources and Documents of United States Constitutions*, 11 vols. (Dobbs Ferry, N.Y.: Oceana Publications, 1973–79), 7:187.

7. People v. Ruggles, 8 Johnson's Reports 290, 296–97 (N.Y. Sup. Ct. 1811).

8. Address Before the Sabbath School Society, Utica, New York, 4 July 1832, Alvan Stewart Papers, New-York Historical Society, New York, New York.

9. Perry Miller, *The New England Mind: The Seventeenth Century* (Boston: Beacon Press, 1961), pp. 416–18, 426.

10. See, for example, the works listed in Parts 10 and 11 of this bibliography.

11. Thomas Lechford, *Plain Dealing, or, News from New England* (1642; reprint ed., New York: Garrett Press, 1970), pp. 67–68; Hooker quoted in Richard B. Morris, *Studies in the History of American Law with Special Reference to the Seventeenth and Eighteenth Centuries*, 2d ed. (Philadelphia: Joseph M. Mitchell Co., 1959), pp. 36–37.

12. Theodore Dwight Bozeman, "Religious Liberty and the Problem of Order in Early Rhode Island," pp. 44–45. For the proprietary colonies, see Maxine N. Lurie, "Theory and Practice of Religious Toleration." Traditional accounts of early Virginia, which stress the colony's political turbulence despite an Anglican establishment, suggest that religious homogeneity was a necessary but insufficient precondition for social order in seventeenth-century America. This qualification may be unnecessary given the redefinition of political stability (as a condition in which "public transactions happen and will continue to happen within regular patterns and without illegal violence") recently offered by John Kukla in "Order and Chaos in Early America: Political and Social Stability in Pre-Restoration Virginia," *American Historical Review* 90 (April 1985), 275–98.

13. George Dargo, *Roots of the Republic*, pp. 84–89.

14. Perry Miller, "Religion and Society in the Early Literature: The Religious Impulse in the Founding of Virginia," *William and Mary Quarterly*, 3d ser., 6 (January 1949), 41.

For a specific example of the secularization of legal rules between 1650 and 1750, see Howard I. Kushner, "Suicide and the Law in Puritan America" (Paper presented at the New-York Historical Society's conference on "The Law in America, 1607–1861," New York, New York, May 17–18, 1985).

15. James, "Religion and the American Revolution," pp. 12, 14.

16. Dargo, *Roots of the Republic*, pp. 92–98; Leonard W. Levy, "No Establishment of Religion," p. 201.

17. Levy, "No Establishment of Religion," pp. 197–201; William McLoughlin, "Religion in the Revolution," pp. 213–28.

18. People v. Ruggles, 8 Johnson's Reports 290, 297, 296 (N.Y. Sup. Ct. 1811).

19. Mark DeWolfe Howe, *The Garden and the Wilderness*, pp. 28, 14; McLoughlin, "Religion in the Revolution," pp. 247–48, 255.

20. Levy, "No Establishment of Religion," pp. 205–09.

21. Stephen Botein, "Church and State in Early American Constitutional Law" (Paper delivered at a conference of the Philadelphia Center for Early American Studies on "The Creation of the American Constitution," Philadelphia, Pa., October 18–20, 1984: privately consulted, forthcoming in publication), pp. 6–8; Thomas Cooper, "Observations on the Fast Day." On test oaths, see Morton Borden, *Jews, Turks, and Infidels* and the works listed in Part 9 of this bibliography.

22. For the First Amendment as limitation on the national government, see Howe, *The Garden and the Wilderness*, p. 26; Levy, "No Establishment of Religion," pp. 186–87; Michael J. Malbin, *Religion and Politics*, p. 16; James, "Religion and the American Revolution," p. 26; Botein, "Church and State," p. 6.

23. Everson v. Board of Education, 330 U.S. 1 (1947), held that the establishment clause, applicable to the states through incorporation into the Fifteenth Amendment, prevented a New Jersey school board from reimbursing parents for their expenses in transporting their children to parochial schools on public buses.

24. Malbin, *Religion and Politics;* Levy, "No Establishment of Religion," pp. 169–233.

25. Lynch v. Donnelly, 104 S. Ct. 1355 (1984) (Brennan, J., dissenting).

26. Thomas Jefferson, "Whether Christianity is Part of the Common Law?" For an excellent discussion of Thomas Jefferson's religious beliefs, see Eugene R. Sheridan's introduction to Dickinson W. Adams, ed., *Jefferson's Extracts from the Gospels* (Princeton: Princeton University Press, 1983), pp. 3–42.

27. Joseph Story, "Christianity a Part of the Common Law"; idem, *Commentaries on the Constitution*, 3:729 n. 2, 726.

28. Story, *Commentaries on the Constitution*, 3:724, 723, 727.

29. Thus, Richard E. Morgan's characterization of Story's thought as "aberrational" in *The Supreme Court and Religion*, pp. 36–40, is unfair. On the specific issue of multiple establishment, however, Story's position was definitely a minority view by 1833.

30. So Stewart wrote in a draft of an address to the American Bible Society in May 1834, entitled "The Bible the Only Preservative of a Republican Form of Government." Alvan Stewart Papers, New-York Historical Society.

31. People v. Ruggles, 8 Johnson's Reports 290, 294 (N.Y. Sup. Ct. 1811).

32. Updegraph v. Commonwealth, 11 Sergeant's and Rawle's Reports 394, 406–07 (Pa. 1824).

33. Alexis de Tocqueville, *Democracy in America* (New York: Harper & Row, Publishers, 1969), p. 270.

34. John Henry Hopkins, *The American Citizen*, pp. 77–79; Story, *Commentaries*

on the Constitution, pp. 727, 731. Similarly, James Kent endorsed expansive guarantees of liberty of conscience. "The *free exercise and enjoyment of religious profession and worship,*" he wrote in his *Commentaries,* "may be considered as one of the absolute rights of individuals, recognised in our American constitutions, and secured to them by law." *Commentaries on American Law,* 7th ed. (New York: William Kent, 1851), 1:644.

35. For Story's place in the natural-law tradition of jurisprudence, see James McClellan, *Joseph Story and the American Constitution: A Study in Political and Legal Thought* (Norman: University of Oklahoma Press, 1971). For the not-so-benign neglect of Story's jurisprudence after his death in 1845, see R. Kent Newmyer, *Supreme Court Justice Joseph Story: Statesman of the Old Republic* (Chapel Hill: University of North Carolina Press, 1985), pp. 380–92.

36. I have borrowed my definition of legal positivism from Hendrik Hartog, *Public Property and Private Power: The Corporation of the City of New York in American Law, 1730–1870* (Chapel Hill: University of North Carolina Press, 1983), pp. 2–3 n. 3.
There is substantial room for differences of opinion in dating transformations like the secularization of the state and the rise of legal positivism. Based on the business of the courts of Massachusetts, William Nelson considered the Revolution the turning point for these changes in *Americanization of the Common Law.* Other historians, focussing on the growing importance of legislation, place the watershed later. See, for example, the periodization of legal consciousness in the nineteenth century suggested in Robert W. Gordon's "Legal Thought and Legal Practice in the Age of American Enterprise, 1870–1920," in *Professions and Professional Ideologies in America,* ed. Gerald L. Geison (Chapel Hill: University of North Carolina Press, 1983).

37. Both sources are quoted in Borden, *Jews, Turks, and Infidels,* pp. 100, 116–17, who found them reprinted in *The Occident,* June 1849.

38. People v. Ruggles, 8 Johnson's Reports 290 (N.Y. Sup. Ct. 1811).

39. Updegraph v. Commonwealth, 11 Sergeant's and Rawle's Reports 394 (Pa. 1824); Commonwealth v. Kneeland, 37 Mass. 206 (1838).

40. Leonard W. Levy discusses the American history of blasphemy in an epilogue to his study of the crime in Great Britain, *Treason Against God: A History of the Offense of Blasphemy* (New York: Schocken Books, 1981), pp. 331–39.

41. Specht v. Commonwealth, 8 Pennsylvania State Reports 213, 323–24 (1848); see generally, Borden, *Jews, Turks, and Infidels,* pp. 97–129.

42. The Supreme Court first articulated the test in Lemon v. Kurtzman, 408 U.S. 602, 612–13 (1971). It most recently reaffirmed its adherence to test in Grand Rapids v. Ball, 53 *United States Law Week* 5006, 5008 (1985): "First, the statute must have a secular legislative purpose; second, its principal or primary effect must be one that neither advances nor inhibits religion . . . ; finally, the statute must not foster 'an excessive government entanglement with religion.'"

43. Watson v. Jones, 80 U.S. (13 Wall.) 679 (1871); see generally Morgan, *Supreme Court and Religion,* pp. 32–36.

BIBLIOGRAPHY

1. GENERAL WORKS

a. United States

Blakely, William Addison, comp. American State Papers and Related Documents on Freedom of Religion. 4th rev. ed. Washington: Review and Herald, 1949.

Borden, Morton. Jews, Turks, and Infidels. Chapel Hill: University of North Carolina Press, 1984.

Cobb, Sanford. The Rise of Religious Liberty in America: A History. New York: Macmillan Co., 1902.

Dargo, George. "The Relations Between Church and State." Chap. 4 in Roots of the Republic: A New Perspective on Early American Constitutionalism, 77-107. New York: Praeger, 1974.

Greene, Evarts Boutell. Religion and the State: The Making and Testing of an American Tradition. New York: New York University Press, 1941.

Howe, Mark DeWolfe, comp. Cases on Church and State in the United States. Cambridge, Mass.: Harvard University Press, 1952.

Howe, Mark DeWolfe. The Garden and the Wilderness: Religion and Government in American Constitutional History. Chicago: University of Chicago Press, 1965.

Humphrey, Edward Frank. Nationalism and Religion in America, 1774-1789. Boston: Chipman Law Publishing, 1924.

Johnson, Alvin Walter, and Yost, Frank H. Separation of Church and State in the United States. Minneapolis: University of Minnesota Press, 1948.

McGrath, John J. Church and State in American Law: Cases and
    Materials. Milwaukee: Bruce Publishing Co., 1962.

Marnell, William H. The First Amendment; The History of
    Religious Freedom in America. Garden City, N.Y.: Doubleday,
    1964.

Mead, Sidney E. The Lively Experiment: The Shaping of
    Christianity in America. New York: Harper and Row, 1963.

Miller, Glenn T. Religious Liberty in America: History and
    Prospects. Philadelphia: Westminster Press, 1976.

Morgan, Richard E. The Supreme Court and Religion. New York:
    Free Press, 1972.

Pfeffer, Leo. Church, State, and Freedom. rev. ed. Boston:
    Beacon Press, 1967.

Smith, Elwyn A. Religious Liberty in the United States: The
    Development of Church-State Thought Since the Revolutionary
    Era. Philadelphia: Fortress Press, 1972.

Stokes, Anson Phelps. Church and State in the United States:
    Historical Development and Contemporary Problems of
    Religious Freedom Under the Constitution. 3 vols. New
    York: Harper and Brothers, 1950.

Stokes, Anson Phelps, and Pfeffer, Leo. Church and State in
    the United States. rev. ed. in 1 vol. New York: Harper and
    Row, 1964.

Sutherland, Arthur E. "Church and State Before 1800." Chap.
    11 in Constitutionalism in America. New York: Blaisdell
    Publishing Co., 1965.

Zollman, Carl. American Civil Church Law. New York: Columbia
    University, 1917.

                        b. States and Regions

Buckley, Thomas E. Church and State in Revolutionary Virginia,
    1776-1787. Charlottesville: University Press of Virginia,
    1977.

Eckenrode, H. J. Separation of Church and State in Virginia: A
    Study in the Development of the Revolution. 1910. Reprint.
    New York: Da Capo Press, 1971.

Ferguson, John DeLancey. The Relations of the State to
    Religion in New York and New Jersey During the Colonial
    Period. New Brunswick, N.J.: Rutgers College, 1912.

Frost, J. William. "Religious Liberty in Early Pennsylvania."
Pennsylvania Magazine of History and Biography 105 (October
1981), 419-451.

Greene, M. Louise. The Development of Religious Liberty in
Connecticut. 1905. Reprint. New York: Da Capo Press,
1970.

Greenleaf, Richard E. "The Inquisition in Eighteenth-Century
New Mexico." New Mexico Historical Review 60 (January
1985), 29-60.

Greenleaf, Richard E. "The Inquisition in Spanish Louisiana,
1762-1800." New Mexico Historical Review 50 (January 1975),
45-72.

Hale, Robert. Early Days of Church and State in Maine.
Brunswick, Me.: Bowdoin College, 1910.

Hanley, Thomas O'Brien. The American Revolution and Religion:
Maryland, 1770-1800. Washington, D.C.: Catholic University
of America Press, 1971.

Hanley, Thomas O'Brien. Their Rights and Liberties: The
Beginnings of Religious and Political Freedom in Maryland.
1959. Reprint. Chicago: Loyola University Press, 1984.

James, Charles Fenton. Documentary History of the Struggle for
Religious Liberty in Virginia. 1900. Reprint. New York:
Da Capo Press, 1971.

Kinney, Charles B., Jr. Church and State: The Struggle For
Separation in New Hampshire, 1630-1900. New York: Teachers
College, 1955.

Lauer, Paul E. "Church and State in New England." Johns
Hopkins University Studies in Historical and Political
Science 10 (February-March 1892), 81-188.

McIlwaine, Henry R. "The Struggle of Protestant Dissenters for
Religious Toleration in Virginia." Johns Hopkins University
Studies in Historical and Political Science 12 (April 1894),
171-235.

Meyer, Jacob C. Church and State in Massachusetts From 1740 to
1833: A Chapter in the Development of Individual Freedom.
Cleveland: Western Reserve University Press, 1930.

O'Neill, Charles Edwards. Church and State in French Colonial
Louisiana: Policy and Politics to 1732. New Haven: Yale
University Press, 1966.

Petrie, George. "Church and State in Early Maryland." Johns
Hopkins University Studies in Historical and Political
Science 10 (April 1892), 189-238.

Pratt, John Webb. Religion, Politics, and Diversity: The Church- State Theme in New York History. Ithaca, N.Y.: Cornell University Press, 1967.

Reed, Susan Martha. Church and State in Massachusetts, 1691-1740. Urbana: University of Illinois Press, 1914.

Scholes, France V. Church and State in New Mexico, 1610-1650. Albuquerque: University of New Mexico Press, 1937.

Scholes, France V. "The First Decade of the Inquisition in New Mexico." New Mexico Historical Review 10 (July 1935), 195-241.

Strickland, Reba Carolyn. Religion and the State in Georgia in the Eighteenth Century. New York: Columbia University Press, 1939.

Weeks, Stephen B. "The Religious Development in the Province of North Carolina." Johns Hopkins University Studies in Historical and Political Science 10 (May-June 1892), 239-306.

Werline, Albert Warwick. Problems of Church and State in Maryland During the Seventeenth and Eighteenth Centuries. South Lancaster, Mass.: College Press, 1948.

Zwierlein, Frederick J. Religion in New Netherland, 1623-1664. Reprint. New York: Da Capo Press, 1971.

c. Contemporary Writings

Forney, John Wien. Address on Religious Intolerance and Political Proscription. Washington, 1855.

Hopkins, John Henry. "The Religious Rights of the American Citizen." Chap. 4 in The American Citizen: His Rights and Duties, According to the Spirit of the Constitution of the United States, 76-96. New York: Pudney and Russell, 1857.

The Palladium of Conscience; . . . Containing Furneaux's Letters to Blackstone, Priestley's Remarks on Blackstone, Blackstone's Reply to Priestley. . . . Being a Necessary Companion for Every Lover of Religious Liberty. 1773. Reprint. New York: Da Capo Press, 1974.

Pond, Enoch. Review of Mr. Whitman's Letters to Professor Stuart on Religious Liberty. 2d ed. Boston: Pierce and Parker, 1831.

Skinner, Thomas Hartley. Religion and Liberty. A Discourse Delivered Dec. 17, 1840: The Day Appointed for Public Thanksgiving by the Governor of New York. New York: Wiley and Putnam, 1841.

Stuart, Moses. _A Letter to William E. Channing, D.D., On the Subject of Religious Liberty_. 4th ed. Boston: Perkins and Marvin, 1831.

Ward, Nathaniel. _The Simple Cobler of Aggawam in America_. 1647. Reprint. Lincoln: University of Nebraska Press, 1969.

Whitman, Bernard. _Two Letters to the Reverend Moses Stuart; On the Subject of Religious Liberty_. 2d ed. Boston: Gray and Brown, 1831.

2. RELIGION, JURISPRUDENCE, AND POLITICAL THEORY

Bozeman, Theodore Dwight. "Religious Liberty and the Problem of Order in Early Rhode Island." _New England Quarterly_ 45 (March 1972), 44-64.

Burnett, Peter Hardeman. _The Path Which Led a Protestant Lawyer to the Catholic Church_. New York: D. Appleton, 1860.

Canty-Letsome, Rosezella. "John Winthrop's Concept of Law in 17th Century New England, One Notion of Puritan Thinking." _Duquesne Law Review_ 16 (1977-1978), 331-357.

Decker, Raymond G. "The Secularization of Anglo-American Law. _Thought_ 49 (September 1974), 280-298.

Ernst, James E. _The Political Thought of Roger Williams_. Seattle: University of Washington Press, 1929.

Greenleaf, Simon. _An Examination of the Testimony of the Four Evangelists, by the Rules of Evidence Administered in Courts of Justice. With an Account of the Trial of Jesus_. Boston, 1846.

Haskins, George L. "Representative Government and the 'Bible Commonwealth' in Early Massachusetts." _Akron Law Review_ 9 (Fall 1975), 207-222.

James, Sydney V. "Ecclesiastical Authority in the Land of Roger Williams." _New England Quarterly_ 57 (September 1984), 323-346.

Jefferson, Thomas. "Whether Christianity is Part of the Common Law?" In vol. 1 of _The Writings of Thomas Jefferson_, edited by Paul Leicester Ford, 360-367. New York: G. P. Putnam's Sons, 1892.

McClellan, James. "Christianity and the Common Law." Chap. 3
    in Joseph Story and the American Constitution: A Study in
    Political and Legal Thought, 118-159. Norman: University of
    Oklahoma Press, 1971.

Miller, Perry. "Law and Morality." Chap. 4, Book 2 in The
    Life of the Mind in America From the Revolution to the Civil
    War, 186-206. New York: Harcourt, Brace and World, 1965.

Nelson, William E. Americanization of the Common Law: The
    Impact of Legal Change on Massachusetts Society, 1760-1830.
    Cambridge, Mass.: Harvard University Press, 1975.

Presser, Stephen B., and Hurley, Becky Bair. "Saving God's
    Republic: The Jurisprudence of Samuel Chase." University of
    Illinois Law Review 1984, 771-822.

Sehr, Timothy J. "Defending Orthodoxy in Massachusetts 1650-
    1652." Historical Journal of Massachusetts 9 (January
    1981), 30-40.

Simpson, Stephen. Biography of Stephen Girard with his Will
    Affixed. 2d ed. Philadelphia: Thomas L. Bonsal, 1832.

Story, Joseph. "Christianity a Part of the Common Law."
    American Jurist and Law Magazine 9 (April 1833), 346-348.

Teaford, Jon C. "Toward a Christian Nation: Religion, Law and
    Justice Strong." Journal of Presbyterian History 54 (Winter
    1976), 422-437.

Webster, Chauncey. Divine and Human Rights; or, The
    Westminster Confession and the Constitution of the United
    States Tested by the Holy Scriptures. Philadelphia: W. S.
    Young, 1845.

Weddle, David L. "The Law and the Revival: A 'New Divinity'
    for the Settlements." Church History 47 (June 1978), 196-
    214.

The Will Case; Arguments of the Defendant's Counsel and
    Judgment of the Supreme Court, United States, in Case of
    Vidal and Another, Complainants and Appellants, vs. . . .
    the Executors of Stephen Girard and Others, Defendants and
    Appellees; January Term, 1844, with the Will of Stephen
    Girard. Philadelphia, 1844.

Worden, G. B. "The Rhode Island Civil Code of 1647." In
    Saints & Revolutionaries: Essays on Early American History,
    edited by David Hall, John M. Murrin, and Thad W. Tate, 138-
    151. New York: W. W. Norton, 1984.

3. MINORITY RELIGIONS AND THE LAW

Adams, Charles Francis. The Antinomian Controversy. 1892.
    Reprint. New York: Da Capo Press, 1976.

Battis, Emery. Saints and Sectaries: Anne Hutchinson and the
    Antinomian Controversy, in the Massachusetts Bay Colony.
    Chapel Hill: University of North Carolina Press, 1962.

Buckley, Thomas E. "Church and State in Massachusetts Bay: A
    Case Study of Baptist Dissenters." Journal of Church and
    State 23 (Spring 1981), 309-322.

Cadbury, Henry J. "The King's Missive." Quaker History 63
    (Autumn 1974), 117-123.

Carroll, Kenneth L. "Quaker Opposition to the Establishment of
    a State Church in Maryland." Maryland Historical Magazine
    65 (Summer 1970), 149-170.

Chandler, Peleg W., ed. "Trial of Anne Hutchinson Before the
    General Court of Massachusetts for Sedition and Heresy." In
    vol. 1 of American Criminal Trials, 1-29. Boston, 1841.

Chandler, Peleg W., ed. "Trials of the Quakers Before the
    General Court and the Court of Assistants, Massachusetts,
    1656-1661." In vol. 1 of American Criminal Trials, 31-64.
    Boston, 1841.

Checkley, John. The Speech of Mr. John Checkley, Upon His
    Trial at Boston, in 1724. Morrisania, N.Y., 1868.

Chu, Jonathan M. "The Social Context of Religious Heterodoxy:
    The Challenge of Seventeenth-Century Quakerism to Orthodoxy
    in Massachusetts." Essex Institute Historical Collections
    118 (April 1982), 119-150.

Cohen, Ronald D. "Church and State in Seventeenth-Century
    Massachusetts: Another Look at the Antinomian Controversy."
    Journal of Church and State 12 (Autumn 1979), 475-494.

Curran, Francis X., ed. Catholics in Colonial Law. Chicago:
    Loyola University Press, 1963.

Everstine, Carl N. "Maryland's Toleration Act: An Appraisal."
    Maryland Historical Magazine 79 (Summer 1984), 99-116.

Graham, John Joseph. "The Development of the Separation of
    Church and State in the United States of America." Records
    of the American Catholic Historical Society of Philadelphia
    50 (December 1939), 81-87; 51 (March-December 1940), 1-64,
    85-172.

Hall, David. The Antinomian Controversy, 1636-38. Middletown, Conn.: Wesleyan University Press, 1968.

Heyrman, Christine Leigh. "Specters of Subversion, Societies of Friends: Dissent and the Devil in Provincial Essex County, Massachusetts." In Saints and Revolutionaries: Essays on Early American History, edited by David Hall, John M. Murrin, and Thad W. Tate, 38-74. New York: W. W. Norton, 1984.

Hughes, John, and Breckinridge, John. A Discussion: Is the Roman Catholic Religion Inimical to Civil or Religious Liberty? Is the Presbyterian Religion Inimical to Civil or Religious Liberty? 1836. Reprint. New York: Da Capo Press, 1970.

Johnson, Gerald W. The Maryland Act of Religious Toleration: An Interpretation. Baltimore: Committee for the 300th Anniversary of the Maryland Act of Religious Toleration, 1949.

Krugler, John D. "'With promise of Liberty in Religion': The Catholic Lords Baltimore and Toleration in Seventeenth-Century Maryland, 1634-1692." Maryland Historical Magazine 79 (Spring 1984), 21-43.

Lawson, John D., ed. "The Trials of the Quakers William Robinson, Marmaduke Stevenson Dyer, and Others, Massachusetts, 1659." In vol. 1 of American State Trials, 813-824. St. Louis: Thomas Law Books, 1914.

Lurie, Maxine N. "Theory and Practice of Religious Toleration in the Seventeenth Century: The Proprietary Colonies as a Case Study." Maryland Historical Magazine 79 (Summer 1984), 117-125.

McLoughlin, William G. New England Dissent, 1630-1833: The Baptists and the Separation of Church and State. 2 vols. Cambridge, Mass.: Harvard University Press, 1971.

Middleton, Arthur Pierce. "Toleration and the Established Church in Maryland." Historical Magazine of the Protestant Episcopal Church 53 (March 1984), 13-24.

Morgan, Edmund S. "The Case Against Anne Hutchinson." New England Quarterly 10 (December 1937), 635-649.

Morgan, Edmund S. Roger Williams: The Church and the State. New York: Harcourt, Brace and World, 1967.

"A Report of the Trial of Ann Hutchinson Before the Church in Boston, March, 1638." Massachusetts Historical Society, Proceedings, 2d ser., 4 (1887-1889), 159-191.

Rider, Sidney Smith. An Inquiry Concerning the Origin of the
    Clause in the Laws of Rhode Island (1719-1783)
    Disenfranchising Roman Catholics. Providence: S. S. Rider,
    1889.

Sampson, William. The Catholic Question in America: Whether a
    Roman Catholic Clergyman Be in Any Case Compellable to
    Disclose the Secrets of Auricular Confession. Decided at
    the Court of General Sessions in the City of New York.
    1813. Reprint. New York: Da Capo Press, 1974.

Slafter, Edmund Farwell. John Checkley; or the Evolution of
    Religious Tolerance in Massachusetts Bay. Boston: The
    Prince Society, 1897.

Stein, Ralph Michael. "A Sect Apart: A History of the Legal
    Troubles of the Shakers." Arizona Law Review 23 (1981),
    735-751.

Trial of Frederick Eberle and Others, at a Nisi Prius Court,
    held at Philadelphia, July 1816, Before Hon. Jasper Yeates,
    for Illegally Conspiring Together, By All Means, Lawfully
    and Unlawfully, With Their Bodies and Lives, to Prevent the
    Introduction of the English Language Into the Service of St.
    Michael's and Zion's Churches, Belonging to the German
    Lutheran Congregation in the City of Philadelphia.
    Philadelphia, 1817. [Shaw-Shoemaker 1817:42,325]

Upton, Richard F. "Franklin Pierce and the Shakers: A
    Subchapter in the Struggle for Religious Liberty."
    Historical New Hampshire 23 (Spring 1968), 3-18.

Withington, Anne Fairfax, and Schwartz, Jack. "The Political
    Trial of Anne Hutchinson." New England Quarterly 51 (June
    1978), 226-240.

4. STATE CONSTITUTIONS AND DISESTABLISHMENT

Adams, Willi Paul. The First American Constitutions:
    Republican Ideology and the Making of the State
    Constitutions in the Republican Era. Translated by Rita and
    Robert Kimber. Chapel Hill: University of North Carolina
    Press, 1980.

Bauer, Gerald. "The Quest for Religious Freedom in Virginia."
    Historical Magazine of the Protestant Episcopal Church 41
    (March 1972), 85-93.

Clark, Charles E. "Disestablishment at the Grass Roots: Curtis
    Coe and the Separation of Church and Town." Historical New
    Hampshire 36 (Winter 1981), 280-305.

Cushing, John D.   "Notes on Disestablishment in Massachusetts,
    1780-1833." William and Mary Quarterly, 3d ser., 26 (April
    1969), 169-190.

Freeze, Gary. "Like a House Built Upon Sand: The Anglican
    Church and Establishment in North Carolina." Historical
    Magazine of the Protestant Episcopal Church 48 (December
    1979), 405-432.

Green, Jesse C. "The Early Virginia Argument for Separation of
    Church and State." Baptist History and Heritage 11 (January
    1976), 16-26.

Hansen, Joel F. "Jefferson and the Church-State Wall: A
    Historical Examination of the Man and the Metaphor."
    Brigham Young University Law Review 1978, 645-674.

Hill, A. Shrady. "The Parson's Cause." Historical Magazine of
    the Protestant Episcopal Church 46 (March 1977), 5-35.

Horsnell, M. E. "Spencer Roane and the Property of Rights: A
    Post-Revolutionary View." West Virginia History 30 (July
    1969), 586-597.

Isaac, Rhys. "Religion and Authority: Problems of the Anglican
    Establishment in the Era of the Great Awakening and the
    Parson's Cause." William and Mary Quarterly, 3d ser., 30
    (January 1973), 3-36.

Kessler, Sanford. "Locke's Influence on Jefferson's 'Bill for
    Establishing Religious Freedom.'" Journal of Church and
    State 25 (Spring 1983), 231-252.

Lippy, Charles H. "The 1780 Massachusetts Constitution:
    Religious Establishment or Civil Religion?" Journal of
    Church and State 20 (Autumn 1978), 533-549.

McCants, David A. "The Authenticity of James Maury's Account
    of Patrick Henry's Speech in the Parson's Cause." Southern
    Speech Communication Journal 42 (Fall 1976), 20-34.

McLoughlin, William G. "The Role of Religion in the
    Revolution: Liberty of Conscience and Cultural Cohesion in
    the New Nation." In Essays on the American Revolution,
    edited by Stephen G. Kurtz and James H. Hutson, 197-255.
    Chapel Hill: University of North Carolina Press, 1973.

Marty, Martin E. "Living with Establishment and
    Disestablishment in Nineteenth-Century Anglo-America."
    Journal of Church and State 18 (Winter 1976), 61-77.

Miller, Howard. "The Grammar of Liberty: Presbyterians and the
    First American Constitutions." Journal of Presbyterian
    History 54 (Spring 1976), 142-164.

Plochl, Willibald M. "Thomas Jefferson, Author of the Statute of Virginia for Religious Freedom." Jurist 3 (1943), 182-230.

Rainbolt, John Corbin. "The Struggle to Define 'Religious Liberty' in Maryland, 1776-85." Journal of Church and State 17 (Autumn 1975), 443-458.

Ryan, Walter A. "The Separation of Church and State in Acworth, New Hampshire." Historical New Hampshire 34 (Summer 1979), 143-153.

Sandler, S. Gerald. "Lockean Ideas in Thomas Jefferson's Bill for Establishing Religious Freedom." Journal of the History of Ideas 21 (January-March 1960), 110-116.

Singleton, Marvin K. "Colonial Virginia as First Amendment Matrix: Henry, Madison, and Assessment Establishment." Journal of Church and State 8 (Autumn 1966), 344-364.

Swanwick, John. Considerations on an Act of the Legislature of Virginia, Entitled, An Act for the Establishment of Religious Freedom. Philadelphia: Robert Aitken, 1786. [Evans 20,017]

Vivian, Jean H. "The Poll Tax Controversy in Maryland, 1770-76: A Case of Taxation with Representation." Maryland Historical Magazine 71 (Summer 1976), 151-176.

5. FIRST AMENDMENT: FRAMERS' INTENT AND EARLY INTERPRETATIONS

Antieau, Chester James; Downey, Arthur T.; and Roberts, Edward C. Freedom From Federal Establishment; Formation and Early History of the First Amendment Religion Clauses. Milwaukee: Bruce Publishing Co., 1964.

Beth, Loren P. The American Theory of Church and State. Gainesville: University of Florida Press, 1958.

Borden, Morton. "Federalists, Antifederalists, and Religious Freedom." Journal of Church and State 21 (Autumn 1979), 469-482.

Brant, Irving. "Madison: On Separation of Church and State." William and Mary Quarterly, 3d ser., 8 (January 1951), 3-24.

Cooper, Thomas. "Observations on the Fast Day." In Political Essays, 1-3, with "A Reply" by E. P., 3-7. 2d ed. Philadelphia: R. Campbell, 1800. [Evans 37,250]

Drakeman, Donald L. "Religion and the Republic: James Madison
    and the First Amendment." Journal of Church and State 25
    (Autumn 1983), 427-445.

Gaustad, Edwin Scott. "A Disestablished Society: Origins of
    the First Amendment." Journal of Church and State 11
    (Autumn 1969), 409-425.

Greninger, Edwin T. "Thanksgiving: An American Holiday."
    Social Science 54 (Winter 1979), 3-15.

Hunt, Galliard. "James Madison and Religious Liberty." Annual
    Report of the American Historical Association for the Year
    1901 1 (1902), 163-171.

James, Sydney V. "Religion and the American Revolution: The
    Development of the Federal Style in the Relations Between
    Religion and Civil Authority." In The American and European
    Revolutions, 1776-1848: Sociopolitical and Ideological
    Aspects, edited by Jaroslaw Pelenski, 2-37. Iowa City:
    University of Iowa Press, 1980.

Klein, Rose S. "Washington's Thanksgiving Proclamations."
    American Jewish Archives 20 (November 1968), 156-162.

Kruse, Clifton. "The Historical Meaning and Judicial
    Construction of the Establishment of Religion Clause of the
    First Amendment." Washburn Law Journal 2 (Winter 1962), 65-
    144.

Levy, Leonard W. "No Establishment of Religion: The Original
    Understanding." In Judgments: Essays on American
    Constitutional History, 169-224. Chicago: Quadrangle Books,
    1972.

Malbin, Michael J. Religion and Politics: The Intentions of
    the Authors of the First Amendment. Washington, D.C.:
    American Enterprise Institute, 1978.

Mead, Sidney E. "Neither Church nor State: Reflections on
    James Madison's 'Line of Separation.'" Journal of Church
    and State 10 (Autumn 1968), 349-363.

Smith, Ronald A. "Freedom of Religion and the Land Ordinance
    of 1785." Journal of Church and State 24 (Autumn 1982),
    589-602.

Story, Joseph. Sections 1865-73 in vol. 3 of Commentaries on
    the Constitution of the United States. 3 vols. Boston:
    Hillard, Gray and Company, 1833.

Sutherland, Arthur. "Historians, Lawyers, and Establishment of
    Religion." Religion and the Public Order 5 (1969), 27-50.

Weber, Paul J. "James Madison and Religious Equality: The
    Perfect Separation." Review of Politics 44 (April 1982),
    163- 186.

Winn, Wilkins B. "The Issue of Religious Liberty in the United
    States Commercial Treaty with Colombia, 1824." The Americas
    26 (January 1970), 291-301.

6. CONSCIENTIOUS OBJECTION

Klasson, Walter. "Mennonites and War Taxes." Pennsylvania
    Mennonite Heritage 1 (1978), 17-21.

Lehman, James O. "The Mennonites of Maryland During the
    Revolutionary War." Mennonite Quarterly Review 50 (July
    1976), 200-229.

MacMaster, Richard K. "Neither Whig Nor Tory: The Peace
    Churches in the American Revolution." Fides et Historia 9
    (1977), 8-24.

Renner, Richard Wilson. "Conscientious Objection and the
    Federal Government, 1787-1792." Military Affairs 38
    (December 1974), 142-145.

Stowe, Walter Herbert. "A Study in Conscience: Some Aspects of
    the Relations of the Clergy to the State." Historical
    Magazine of the Protestant Episcopal Church 44 (December
    1975), 57-75.

Worrall, Arthur J. "Persecution, Politics and War: Roger
    Williams, Quakers, and King Philip's War." Quaker History
    66 (Autumn 1977), 73-86.

Zuber, Richard L. "Conscientious Objectors in the Confederacy:
    The Quakers of North Carolina." Quaker History 67 (Spring
    1978), 1-19.

7. SABBATARIAN LEGISLATION AND LITIGATION

Blakely, William Addison, comp. American State Papers Bearing
    on Sunday Legislation. 1911. Reprint. New York: Da Capo
    Press, 1970.

Friedenberg, Albert M. "The Jews and the American Sunday
    Laws." Publications of the American Jewish Historical
    Society 11 (1903), 101-115.

Hall, Willard. __A Plea for the Sabbath, Addressed to the Legal
Profession in the United States__. Baltimore: Baltimore
Sabbath Association, 1845.

Jable, J. Thomas. "Pennsylvania's Early Blue Laws: A Quaker
Experiment in the Suppression of Sport and Amusements, 1682-
1740." __Journal of Sport History__ 1 (1974), 107-122.

Johns, Warren L. __Dateline Sunday, U.S.A.: The Story of Three
and a Half Centuries of Sunday-Law Battles in America__.
Mountain View, Calif.: Pacific Press Publishing
Association, 1967.

Johnson, Richard M. "Report of the Committee on Post-Offices
and Post-Roads of the United States Senate." 1829.
Reprinted in __Social Theories of Jacksonian Democracy__,
edited by Joseph L. Blau, 274-281. Indianapolis: Bobbs-
Merrill Co., 1954.

Miller, Wilbur R. "Never on Sunday: Moralistic Reformers and
the Police in London and New York City, 1830-1870." In
__Police and Society__, edited by David H. Bayley, 127-148.
Beverly Hills: Sage Publications, 1977.

Ringgold, James T. __Sunday: Legal Aspects of the First Day of
the Week__. Jersey City, N.J.: Frederick D. Linn and Company,
1891.

8. CHURCH PROPERTY AND INTRA-CHURCH DISPUTES

Bailey, Raymond C. "Popular Petitions and Religion in
Eighteenth-Century Colonial Virginia." __Historical Magazine
of the Protestant Episcopal Church__ 46 (December 1977), 419-
428.

Bowler, Clara Ann. "The Litigious Career of William Cotton,
Minister." __Virginia Magazine of History and Biography__ 86
(July 1978), 281-294.

Buck, Edward. __Massachusetts Ecclesiastical Law__. rev. ed.
Boston: Congregational Publishing Society, 1865.

Clark, Charles E. "A Test of Religious Liberty: The Ministry
Land Case in Narragansett, 1668-1752." __Journal of Church
and State__ 11 (Spring 1969), 295-319.

Cohen, Sheldon S. "The Guilford Controversy." __Connecticut
Historical Society Bulletin__ 31 (April 1966), 50-54.

Dignan, Patrick J. __A History of the Legal Incorporation of
Catholic Church Property in the United States (1784-1932)__.
New York: P. J. Kenedy and Sons, 1935.

Ellis, James. **A Narrative of the Rise, Progress and Issue of the Late Law-Suits, Relative to Property Held and Devoted to Pious Uses, in the First Precinct in Rehoboth [Rhode Island]: Containing the Substance of the Records which Shew for Whose Use and Benefit the Property was Originally Intended; Together with Some Observations on Certain Constitutional Principles, which Respect the Support of Public Worship, and the Equal Protection and Establishment of All Regular Denominations of Christians**. Warren, R.I.: Nathaniel Phillips, 1795. [Evans, 28,622]

Howe, M. A. DeWolfe. "The Boston Religion." _Atlantic Monthly_ 91 (June 1903), 729-738.

Levy, Leonard W. "The Unitarian Controversy: Church, State, and Court." Chap. 3 in _The Law of the Commonwealth and Chief Justice Shaw_, 29-42. Cambridge, Mass.: Harvard University Press, 1957.

The Methodist Property Case (Circuit Court for the Southern District of New York, 17-29 May 1851). New York: Lane and Scott, 1851.

Oaks, Dallin H., and Bentley, Joseph I. "Joseph Smith and Legal Process: In the Wake of the Steamboat _Nauvoo_." _Brigham Young University Law Review_ 1976, 735-782.

Report of the Case Between the Rev. Cave Jones, and the Rector and Inhabitants of the City of New York in Communion of the Protestant Episcopal Church in the State of New York. As the Same was Argued Before the Five Judges of the Supreme Court of the State of New York. New York, 1813. [Shaw-Shoemaker 1813:76]

Report of the Presbyterian Church Case: The Commonwealth of Pennsylvania vs. Ashbel Green, and Others. Philadelphia: W. S. Martien, 1839.

Rush, Jacob. **An Address, Delivered July 8th, 1790, to the Jury in the Case of the Commonwealth against John Purdon and Others**. Philadelphia, 1791. [Evans 23,748]

Some Queries Intended to be Put to the Rev. Dr. Witherspoon, and Other Clergymen, on the Trial in the Supreme Court of Pennsylvania, Between Mr. Marshall and the Scots Presbyterian Church. Philadelphia? 1789? [Bristol B7,068]

Tisdale, W. S., ed. _The Controversy Between Senator Brooks and John [Hughes], Archbishop of New York. Growing Out of the Speech of Senator Brooks on the Church Property Bill in the N. Y. State Senate, March 6th, 1855_. New York: De Witt and Davenport, Publishers, 1855.

Weeks, Louis, and Hickey, James C. "'Implied Trust' for
    Connectional Churches: Watson v. Jones Revisited." Journal
    of Presbyterian History 54 (Winter 1976), 459-470.

Zeuner, Robert W. "The Appeal to Caesar: A History of the
    Methodist Church Property Case of 1849." Methodist History
    7 (January 1969), 3-16.

9. RELIGIOUS TESTS AND OATHS

Altfeld, E. Milton. The Jew's Struggle for Religious and Civil
    Liberty in Maryland. 1924. Reprint. New York: Da Capo
    Press, 1970.

Brackenridge, Henry Marie. Speeches on the Jew Bill, in the
    House of Delegates of Maryland. Philadelphia: J. Dobson and
    Jasper Harding, 1829.

Brinsfield, John W. "Daniel Defoe: Writer, Statesman, and
    Advocate of Religious Liberty in South Carolina." South
    Carolina Historical Magazine 76 (July 1975), 107-111.

Eitches, Edward. "Maryland's 'Jew Bill.'" American Jewish
    Historical Quarterly 60 (March 1971), 258-279.

Herttell, Thomas. The Demurrer: Or, Proofs of Error in the
    Decision of the Supreme Court of the State of New York
    Requiring Faith in Particular Religious Doctrines as a
    Legal Qualification of Witnesses. 1828. Reprint. New
    York: Da Capo Press, 1972.

Stille, Charles J. Religious Tests in Provincial Pennsylvania.
    N.p. 1885.

10. FAMILY LAW

Bandel, Betty. "What the Good Laws of Man Hath Put Asunder."
    Vermont History 46 (Fall 1978), 221-233.

Cohn, Henry S. "Connecticut's Divorce Mechanism: 1639-1969."
    American Journal of Legal History 14 (January 1970), 35-54.

Fogarty, Gerald P. "Slaves, Quakers, and Catholic Marriage in
    Colonial Maryland." Jurist 35 (Spring-Summer 1975), 142-
    161.

Weisberg, D. Kelly. "'Under Greet Temptations Heer': Women and
    Divorce in Puritan Massachusetts." Feminist Studies 2
    (1975), 183-193.

11. CRIMINAL LAW

Commager, Henry Steele. "The Blasphemy of Abner Kneeland."
New England Quarterly 8 (March 1935), 29-41.

Chandler, Peleg W., ed. "Trial of Thomas Maule Before the
Superior Court of Judicature, for a Slanderous Publication
and Blasphemy, Salem, Massachusetts, 1696." In vol. 1 of
American Criminal Trials, 141-149. Boston, 1841.

The Cry of Sodom Enquired Into; Upon Occasion of the
Arraignment and Condemnation of Benjamin Goad, for His
Prodigious Villany. Together with a Solemn Exhortation to
Tremble at God's Judgements, and to Abandon Youthful Lusts.
Cambridge, Mass., 1674. [Evans 186]

Faber, Eli. "Puritan Criminals: The Economic, Social, and
Intellectual Background to Crime in Seventeenth-Century
Massachusetts." Perspectives in American History 11 (1978),
83-144.

Flaherty, David H. "Law and the Enforcement of Morals in Early
America." Perspectives in American History 5 (1971), 203-
253.

Haskins, George Lee. Law and Authority in Early Massachusetts:
A Study in Tradition and Design. New York: MacMillan Co.,
1960.

Haskins, George Lee. "Precedents in English Ecclesiastical
Practices for Criminal Punishments in Early Massachusetts."
In Essays in Legal History in Honor of Felix Frankfurter,
edited by Morris D. Forkosch, 321-336. Indianapolis: Bobbs-
Merrill Co., 1966.

Jones, Matt Bushnell. "Thomas Maule, the Salem Quakers, and
Free Speech in Massachusetts Bay, with Bibliographical
Notes." Essex Institute Historical Collections 72 (January
1936), 1-42.

Lawson, John D., ed. "The Trial of Thomas Maule for Slander
and Blasphemy, Massachusetts, 1696." In vol. 5 of American
State Trials, 85-89. St. Louis: Thomas Law Books, 1916.

Levy, Leonard W. "Satan's Apostle and Freedom of Conscience."
Chap. 4 in The Law of the Commonwealth and Chief Justice
Shaw, 43-58. Cambridge, Mass.: Harvard University Press,
1957.

Levy, Leonard W., ed. Blasphemy in Massachusetts: Freedom of
Conscience and the Abner Kneeland Case: A Documentary
Record. New York: Da Capo Press, 1973.

Marcus, Gail Sussman. "'Due Execution of the Generall Rules of
    Righteousnesse': Criminal Procedure in New Haven Town and
    Colony, 1638-1658." In <u>Saints and Revolutionaries: Essays
    on Early American History</u>, edited by David Hall, John M.
    Murrin, and Thad W. Tate, 99-137. New York: W. W. Norton,
    1984.

Morgan, Edmund S. "The Puritans and Sex." <u>New England
    Quarterly</u> 15 (December 1942), 591-607.

Murrin, John M. "Magistrates, Sinners and a Precarious
    Liberty: Trial by Jury in Seventeenth-Century New England."
    In <u>Saints and Revolutionaries: Essays on Early American
    History</u>, edited by David Hall, John M. Murrin, and Thad W.
    Tate, 152-206. New York: W. W. Norton, 1984.

<u>A Narrative of a New and Unusual American Imprisonment of Two
    Presbyterian Ministers: And Prosecution of Mr. Francis
    Makemie One of Them, for Preaching One Sermon at the City of
    New York</u>. Boston? 1707. [Evans 1,300]

Nelson, William E. "Emerging Notions of Modern Criminal Law in
    the Revolutionary Era: An Historical Perspective." <u>New York
    University Law Review</u> 42 (May 1967), 450-482.

Oaks, Robert F. "'Things Fearful to Name': Sodomy and Buggery
    in Seventeenth-Century New England." <u>Journal of Social
    History</u> 12 (Winter 1978), 268-281.

Parkes, Henry Bamford. "Morals and Law Enforcement in Colonial
    New England." <u>New England Quarterly</u> 5 (July 1932), 431-452.

Powers, Edwin. <u>Crime and Punishment in Early Massachusetts
    1620-1692: A Documentary History</u>. Boston: Beacon Press,
    1966.

Roetger, R. W. "The Transformation of Sexual Morality in
    'Puritan' New England: Evidence from New Haven Court
    Records, 1639-1698." <u>Canadian Review of American Studies</u> 15
    (Fall 1984), 243-257.

11

Women and Religion in America, 1780–1870

Elizabeth B. Clark

The historical study of women and religion in America has been a boom industry in the last fifteen years. The topic concerns scholars from the diverse fields of religious history, social history, and women's studies; the documents exist in abundance; and the churches have long been a critical medium for women, influencing them and being changed by them in turn. Nevertheless, the lives of nineteenth-century church women are not the stuff of great battles or crises, and it was only when traditional diplomatic and political history made room for social and women's history in the 1960s and 1970s that interest began to grow. "The personal is the political," one of the most heartfelt battlecries of the women's movement, is an apt slogan for the history of churchwomen, too. Both social and women's history emphasize the lives of ordinary people, their participation in local institutions, the exercise of power on a day-to-day basis, the impact on individuals of larger movements—all this describes as well the study of women in the church.

Like other fields, women's religious history has been shaped by the imperatives of the discipline. It falls between two disciplines, religion and history. In seminaries and to some degree in religion departments, the study of women has centered around women's liberation theology in an effort to bring established churches in America to a non-sexist, full acceptance of women in all roles, and to produce a theology which would emphasize typically "female" values to replace the male-dominated, hierarchical, and authoritarian structures in place before. Born out of the women's movement, it has been an intensive effort to help redress the balance of power between male and female by reinterpreting the past and the present in women's terms. Much of the historical work on women from this quarter deals with personal spiritual experience, with the role women have played within the institutional church, and with the few women who surpassed their restrictions, and went on to become ministers, preachers, or great reformers.

On the historical side, scholars have concentrated largely on the ways in which participation in church organizations gave women the public role, the confidence, and the organizational skills to move toward inclusion in formal power structures. This excellent and important body of work has also emphasized certain aspects of women's religious experience over others—the political over the spiritual, the radical over the orthodox. Until recently, such mainstream activities as temperance and mission work have been overlooked in favor of more radical religious impulses and movements. In part this was because women's history was again tied very closely to the contemporary women's movement, which was for the most part assertively secular and had little incentive to try to document a religious past.

Actually, the study of women in religion offers a unique opportunity to work out a major conflict over the interpretation of women's past, one which arises from the clash of social and political history. Social historians have emphasized women's autonomy, their ability to exercise control within the sphere of their daily lives, and have deemphasized their legal and political disablement. Political historians, on the other hand, claim that this view of women is overly optimistic, for the salient fact is women's oppression by male-dominated institutions. In this debate the stature of women depends on which end of the telescope you look through.

But the church was an interface between the social and the political. The church in the nineteenth century provided by far the greatest range of experiences available outside the home. Women's auxiliaries, charitable and reform groups, and Sunday mornings themselves were the most acceptable way for women to participate in public life, organize, hold office; and these talents stood them in good stead later in more openly political activities. In most denominations throughout the century female volunteers were the lifeblood of the church. Nevertheless, the roles women could play were severely restricted, with positions of public authority within the church hierarchy still reserved for men. Thus, the church remained a male-dominated institution, and church life brought women disability in addition to autonomy.

In the realm of ideas, too, religion played a dual role. Religiously inspired ideas of social justice compelled and sustained women in all reform work, and moral values derived from Protestantism became the yardstick against which women measured institutions and found them wanting. But the orthodox majority, men and women both, marshaled their religious values in support of the status quo. A large block of conservative clergymen were among the most active opponents of women's movements, citing Paul as their authority. In the realm of ideas, then, as well as in the realm of active participation, the churches both freed and shackled women, helped them to expand their scope and sought to restrict them, as individual women chose different avenues for the expression of religious feeling or the expression of self.

Finally, although women were denied formal political power throughout the period covered here, they played an important part in the broader aspect of church-state relations. As this essay tries to show, a Protestant women's culture became one of the main vehicles for the formation of a middle class in America, and the single most important arbiter of values and moral standards in American life, with an influence that went far beyond women's own sphere. Further, women were deeply involved in the tremendous reform activity which flourished throughout this period. Although reform groups were privately run, functioned locally, and were not highly centralized, they performed quasi-governmental functions, many of which would later be taken over by the state. Within local communities they provided both welfare networks and a type of moral regulation. Reform groups like the abolitionists also played an important part in mobilizing public opinion to influence government policy. Women in their capacity as religious and moral advocates played a critical part in the more diffuse, informal, local political networks of the antebellum period, and in these informal networks were not powerless, although they were disenfranchised.

This bibliography attempts to bring together important recent work of all persuasions on American women and their religious history. A number of bibliographies already exist, most of them dealing with contemporary issues. Two very good examples of the historical approach are Dorothy Bass's *American Women in Church and Society, 1607–1920*, published in 1973, which includes a wide range of both nineteenth- and twentieth-century works in many areas, and Jill K. Conway's *The Female Experience in Eighteenth- and Nineteenth-Century America*, which includes primary and secondary sources as well as accompanying essays. The present bibliography, for the sake of manageability, is limited largely to works on women in the Christian tradition published since 1960, with an emphasis on the most recent. Books, articles, dissertations, theses, and an occasional unpublished paper are included, along with general works on women which have chapters or substantial sections on the religious aspect. The citations have been divided under four headings: bibliographies and general works on women and religion; family, domesticity, and the woman's sphere; women in utopian and religious communities; and women in evangelical and reform movements.

DOMESTICITY, THE FAMILY, AND THE FEMINIZATION
OF RELIGION

Domesticity

The paradox of the church as both the liberator and oppressor of women is most apparent in the scholarship on domesticity and woman's sphere, one of the great themes of women's history. Domesticity—that ideal of womanhood which emphasizes women's "natural" qualities and role in the household— was interpreted by early women's historians as an oppressive, male-imposed ideology. In her seminal piece of 1966, "The Cult of True Womanhood, 1820– 1860," Barbara Welter identified its four components as piety, purity, submissiveness, and domesticity, a listing which illustrates the convergence between domesticity and Protestant evangelicalism. In this vein Ronald Hogeland's 1975 essay shows how one group of old-school male theologians developed their very conservative model of "Ornamental Womanhood" from theological premises, and encouraged women's conformity to it. In an earlier article, "'The Female Appendage,'" Hogeland reminds us that women's culture was not monolithic, and outlines four separate styles, "Ornamental Womanhood," "Romantic Womanhood" (Barbara Welter's "true woman"), "Evangelical Womanhood," and "Radical Womanhood." But although these styles were distinct, they had in common the underlying idea of women's moral powers; Hogeland sees each style as crafted by a different group of men, both as a means of control and to bring women into conformity with their own understanding of the world.

Although Hogeland's material is fascinating, his sense of women's subservience and lack of autonomy is extreme. Nevertheless, cultural expectation, and the ideals put forward by male-dominated institutions, must have played a part in the definition of women as naturally pious. We know that women were the most active members of churches throughout the nineteenth century: to what extent was their self-image or their participation conditioned by these expectations? Pauline doctrine on the role of women in the household perfectly served the need for economic and social rearrangement of the household once the productive and domestic functions began to split. This convergence of religious teachings and social necessity makes a fascinating study of the accommodation of the sacred and the secular, the ideological and the material—submission to man and submission to God were good training for each other.

But domesticity had another face. Nancy Cott's *The Bonds of Womanhood* is a major study of evangelical domesticity which recognizes both the extent to which domesticity confined women and contributed to the development of rigid, sex-segregated spheres, and the extent to which it helped create a separate sphere in which women could move more freely. But Cott, unlike Hogeland, stresses that, while the results were mixed, domesticity was an identity of women's own making, not imposed on them by men. In this domestic sphere, piety became women's most powerful asset, what made her different. As Barbara Welter says, "Religion or piety was the core of woman's virtue, the source of her strength." Women came to be seen as "naturally" pious, with a "peculiar susceptibility" to religion—"the female breast is the natural soil of Christianity" (quoted in Barbara Epstein's *The Politics of Domesticity*, p. 82). Women's moral superiority, an idea widely accepted by both men and women, was the strongest source of women's influence in antebellum America, both in public and private life.

Family

Domesticity and piety combined to give women great power within their own families. Smith-Rosenberg's and Cott's important articles on sexuality discuss the issue of sexual control within a marriage, or what came to be seen as women's right to refuse sexual relations as a means of birth control—in Daniel Scott Smith's term, "domestic feminism." Purity and piety went hand in hand in this struggle by women to control their own bodies, their own reproductive cycles. While we know that in many couples both parties continued to enjoy conjugal relations, still the image of fleshly purity was easily available to women who chose to adopt it as a natural concomitant to their spirituality. Some churches entered the debate over erotic versus reproductive sexuality at a time when growing knowledge of birth control made sex without conception a real possibility, but the position of churches on erotic sexuality, and their role in licensing or prohibiting the spread of information about techniques of birth control, remain largely unexplored.

Woman's role is also the subject of Mary Ryan's studies of revivals and the evangelical family, "A Woman's Awakening" and *Cradle of the Middle Class*. Ryan's work is of particular interest here, because she sees both the micro- and macrocosmic implications of evangelical Protestantism. Her article on women's revivalism concludes that women not only were the most eager participants, but that they usurped the role of the minister, using their influence to persuade husbands and children to join the churches. Evangelical mothers shaped the life of the household, relying on moral suasion to help safeguard the security of the family against the growing temptations of wealth and mobility. They were also responsible for the education and moral upbringing of their children in their capacities as moral guardians, a role of tremendous authority.

In addition, Ryan's book, like Johnson's *Shopkeeper's Millennium*, deals with the larger issue of the role which the evangelical family played in the development of a middle-class culture. In "The Explosion of Family History" Ryan suggests that the evangelical family acted "in collusion" with the Protestant church to disseminate its values throughout the culture, and, indeed, the evangelical values of piety, sobriety, and monogamy, became hallmarks of the rising classes, and lessons to learn for those who would rise. As Barbara Epstein points out, the middle class was as much a cultural as an economic phenomenon, and women were in large part the makers and bearers of culture in nineteenth-century society. In fact, although all cultures are pluralist in practice, evangelical values dominated antebellum America remarkably, even shaping the ideals of many who stood outside the dominant culture. Those within insisted on cultural homogeneity with a startling fierceness, perhaps in response to changing material conditions. Cultural cohesion may have been seen as a way of holding together a society which many feared was moving too fast toward a tremendous diversity of jobs and lifestyles.

In addition to exercising influence through the family, evangelical domesticity led a number of women to active, undomestic careers of their own. Kathryn Sklar's biography of Catherine Beecher, subtitled "A Study in American Domesticity," is a wonderful account of an active public life built on a commitment to domestic piety and moral reform. Loveland's account of Phoebe Palmer's life shows how a commitment to religious work led logically into a career of public speaking. Even for the rank and file, church membership was an entree into public life. Many women, as we will see, were active in church-based reform groups, women's main sanctioned activity outside the home. Women used the dual creeds of piety and domesticity, then, to expand their opportunities both in the public and private sphere.

Feminization

For the most part, however, women still acted largely within the private sphere. Even reforms like temperance which were avidly pursued in the public forum had as their object the sanctity of the home and women's control over it. Historians of the family have varied in their interpretation of this inwardness, some seeing women's domestic role as having blocked her personal development, others seeing a potential for power in "domestic feminism." Similarly, what has come to be called the "feminization" of religion has been variously construed. This phenomenon was first named and described in three highly influential pieces; Barbara Welter's "The Feminization of Religion in Nineteenth-Century America," Nancy Cott's "Young Women in the Second Great Awakening," and Ann Douglas's *The Feminization of American Culture.* As with any "ization," the components are diverse. They include women's identification of themselves as the pious sex; women's growing participation in church life, increasing their numerical predominance in all areas except the ministry; and a greater emphasis on a merciful and loving God, a more feminine, suffering Christ, and a decline of harsh theological doctrines such as predestination and infant damnation. In sociological terms "feminization" may also signal a decline in the status of a profession when women enter in numbers, as with nursing or secondary school teaching.

The idea of the virtuous woman was somewhat new. Malmsheimer's article traces the religious bias against women as the descendants of Eve the temptress. But in the nineteenth century, as the proportion of women in congregations soared, the identification of women with the church was so strong that Christian virtues became fundamental to the definition of womanhood. Religious culture became feminized, and popular women's culture was evangelical in origin and outlook. Much of the literature in this section is devoted to explaining this development, and assessing its consequences. Most of the explanations are on the "need for control" order, stressing, like Cott, women's changed economic role: the disruption of the traditional household and the isolation of women in the home without a major productive function, or the disorientation of the working girl in her untried part. Others portray women as turning to religion to relieve the stresses of childbirth, motherhood, spinsterhood, or marriage.

Carroll Smith-Rosenberg's articles "Women and Religious Revivals" and "The Cross and the Pedestal" use anthropological analysis to explore religious revivals and women's role in them. She suggests that in the initial stage of the Second Great Awakening, revivalism had a broad appeal to men and women alike, as a way to express and contain the economic and social chaos of the transformation to capitalism. After the upheaval had begun to subside, as society began to resettle, many men returned to religious orthodoxy. But even in the newly structured American society women were still marginal, still inferior, and it is to this fact that Smith-Rosenberg attributes the persistent appeal of revivalism and unorthodox religion to women in larger numbers than to men.

While church participation did provide relief for these problems, the process should not be seen in wholly instrumental terms. Religious explanations for social unrest were still the most easily available in the early nineteenth century. Both personal anxiety and fear of disorder were cast in terms of sin or turning away from God in a culture that, while less theological, was still highly religious—cultural disorientation was easily interpreted as moral decay. Within this framework, turning to religion was more a natural response than a conscious design to regain control. Further, although women were in large measure responsible for creating their own sphere of moral action, they were also responding to pull from the world of male authority, which as Ronald Hogeland shows was actively shaping an ideal of pious, domestic womanhood to suit its own purposes. Martha Blauvelt's nuanced account of the leap in women's religious activities takes in both the influence of the culturally prescribed image of the pious woman, and the need for new ways of coping with changing material conditions.

Certainly this religious sphere enhanced women's opportunities as both Welter and Blauvelt point out: it provided strength, sisterhood, satisfying work outside the home, and defined a public role. But others are more cautious in their assessment. Nancy Cott in *The Bonds of Womanhood* and Ruether and Keller in their introduction to *Women and Religion in America* show both the beneficial and confining aspects of such a sphere: while it provided opportunity, it also reinforced social stereotypes and the ideology which had confined women to the home in the first place. Epstein and Douglas go even further in their criticism. Despite their differences, they both assume the growing female culture to be rooted in sexual antagonism and see it as a wrong turn. Epstein's important study of women's religious experience views the stages of revivalism and temperance work as women's attempts to create their own culture, a culture increasingly separate from men's. But this solution was temporary, and eventually made the imbalance between men and women worse in that it exaggerated women's special moral and domestic natures. Epstein thinks that evangelical women, unlike the true feminists who sought women's rights, never effectively challenged the sexist beliefs of their society. Even the reforms they pursued publicly (temperance, social purity) were aimed at improving conditions within the home, and provided no radical critique of the larger society. Douglas, for whom feminization is a bargain struck between the mutually needy—ministers whose influence was waning and housewives—feels even more strongly that the sentimentalization of religion and culture was a short-term bid for power which ultimately destroyed the moral fiber of American womanhood.

While this apocalyptic vision is overdrawn, the literature of feminization explores important questions about the consolidation of power: the danger of "ghettoization" through separation balanced against the importance of a distinct identity for any group seeking to improve its standing. Without pushing the parallel to class formation too hard, it may be possible to see in the pervasive rhetoric of female moral superiority the growth of a group consciousness. It is hard for anyone in a post-*Brown* generation to believe in "separate but equal," but perhaps equality was not the goal. One senses on reading their writings that many of the "naturally pious" both as women and evangelicals sought not equality but moral dominance; and for dominance, separation, despite its dangers, is necessary. The question of whether they ultimately enhanced or diminished opportunities for women will always remain open to debate.

Finally, the widespread acceptance in the nineteenth century of women's "natural" qualities raises important questions. From our vantage point we can see that the "inherent" virtues of domesticity, piety, submissiveness, were actually a cultural construct, a product of their time. That image of womanhood has lost its power for us: we can see the dangers in typing characters, and that to label qualities "natural" is bad history.

But, although women have recently protested against being assigned traditional roles based on a perceived feminine nature, within women's discourse today there is still an important strain of "natural qualities" thinking, a deeply rooted belief that women are the more feeling, more caring, more moral sex, whether through genetics or socialization. These two views of woman's nature, the nineteenth-century and the twentieth-century views, are not entirely dissimilar; both are based on a capacity for sensation, for feeling, far greater than men's. There is a continuity between nineteenth- and twentieth-century women's sense of themselves as the more suffering and the more feeling: women in both centuries are defining themselves in opposition to a male culture seen as logical, efficient, loveless, and hard, thereby gaining strength in their private spheres.

The difference between the nineteenth and the twentieth centuries is in the way women make use of their special identification with feeling and morality in the public sphere. For most of the twentieth century this view had little play. Only since the rise of the women's movement has it been acknowledged, and even then it frequently remains part of a private discourse for fear of undermining the quest for equality in the public domain or shifting the traditional emphasis on equal rights. Women in the anti-nuclear movement have most successfully parlayed their feelings of moral apartness into political power through protest against the type of morality reigning in government, a movement in which the organized churches have also played an important role. In the nineteenth century the idea of women's moral superiority, by contrast, had much more clout in the public domain. That widely accepted idea became the sanction for women's public activities, informing movements like temperance, the social purity crusade, and the women's mission movement. It gave women a moral authority, a platform from which to influence public policy, and finally served as an important rationale for giving women the vote—the guardians of virtue should help guide legislatures in protecting the home and family.

But twentieth-century feminists and historians do nineteenth-century

women a disservice if they only see women's morality as assertive, a thinly
veiled ploy to gain influence. Amanda Porterfield's book explores the idea of
a unique feminine spirituality arising from woman's special "domestic consciousness" and her heightened sense of beauty. She discusses the bit-
tersweet nature of women's religious experience, usually ignored because of
its dangerous political implications: the submissive and sacrificial nature of
women's worship in the nineteenth century, which was not entirely without
pleasure; the analogies between the relations of man and god, child and
parent, man and woman in married life; and the way in which suffering
enhances the capacity to feel. Both Porterfield and Jane Tompkins mark the
power of submission, selfless love, and docility to work conversion, a moral
ability which in the nineteenth century was seen by many evangelicals as a
power greater than any political tool. Both analyze *Uncle Tom's Cabin* in
these terms, showing that the tremendous public response to the novel was
not an acclamation of weakness but of strength, because in evangelical eyes,
the Christ-like sufferings of Uncle Tom and Little Eva achieved a victory over
evil. The success of the novel showed that the "feminine" values of submissiveness, Christian humility, prayer and love in the face of brutality, had
penetrated society, representing for many a type of power beyond the sword
or the ballot. Sklar's *Catherine Beecher* shows Beecher's emphasis on the
womanly ideal of self-sacrifice, an ideal which she made the basis of woman's
action in society: by their sacrificial nature women were redemptive agents
and the salvation of a vicious world. Advocates of women's rights stood
outside this tradition. They understood influence differently, and pursued a
more assertive course. But Christian humility was more than sheep's cloth-
ing; it was a crucial part of many women's spiritual identities, and of their
understanding of relationships of dominance in the world.

WOMEN IN UTOPIAN COMMUNITIES

General

Womanhood as a constant, as well as the "natural order" of monogamy and
the nuclear family, also come into question in the study of religious communities. Women's roles in these communities, and the relationship between the
reordering of sexual and familial relations and the society at large, have been
little studied. Until recently the only monograph on the subject was Raymond
Muncy's *Sex and Marriage in Utopian Communities* (1973). Informative but
unimaginative, it is marred by the author's patronizing attitude toward communalists and by his normative belief in traditional roles as the only fulfilling
ones for women. But in 1981 Louis Kern and Lawrence Foster each published

an excellent book on women and sexual roles in the Shaker and Oneida communities, and in Mormon Utah. The works of these two authors have by themselves virtually created a field.

The middle years of the nineteenth century saw a flowering of utopian communities. Some were small and failed quickly, but others were long lived. The movement itself received much more attention from the public than the small number of participants strictly warranted. As Foster points out, the three primary groups with which he deals had much in common. All had intellectual and social roots in the Protestant Reformation; all were perfectionists; and all had charismatic leaders. In addition, as Rosemary Ruether also concludes in "Women in Utopian Movements," they were "Janus-faced" phenomena. Deeply conservative, all were authoritarian communities whose work patterns and tightly controlled social orders contrasted with the flux of an unstable, industrializing world. Ruether points out that both men and women of the working classes were being forced into accepting wage labor and poor working conditions, thus losing the productive autonomy of farming, domestic manufacture, and craftsmanship. The religious communities appealed largely to these same people, providing an alternative way of life. But most communalists also had a forward-looking vision. They saw themselves in the vanguard, as postmillennialists embodying the new social order, a pattern for society in the years to come. The balance between conservative and millennial elements, and its influence on the way women's roles within the communities were construed, has been little discussed.

Another characteristic of religious communities was that virtually all sought to restructure sexual and familial relationships because the intense loyalties of monogamy and parenthood often conflicted with the needs of the larger group. This is in common with the secular communities. But as Barbara Taylor discusses at length in her new book *Eve and the New Jerusalem: Socialism and Feminism in the Nineteenth Century*, the secular or socialist utopias took a definite stand in favor of women's rights and equality. Religious communities by contrast eschewed talk of women's rights and tended to maintain patriarchal authority structures. Many of them, including the Oneida Perfectionists and the Mormons, maintained the inferiority of women as set out by Paul and denied women positions of leadership or spiritual authority. By contrast, the Shakers, founded by a woman, gave women the greatest formal spiritual equality, even attributing to God dual masculine and feminine natures.

The religious communities were also less innovative than the secular utopian communities in developing economic roles for women. Somewhat paradoxically, the Shakers maintained the most traditional division of labor between male and female. Although domestic work was communalized, as in most of the societies, the cooking, cleaning, and child care still fell wholly to women, while men farmed or produced handicrafts. Kern and Foster disagree over the real benefit which accrued to women in the Oneida community. For Foster, the communalization of housework and the opportunity for women to take on some traditionally male work provided women with greater chance for self-expression than their sisters outside: for Kern, the fact that housework was not also divided between men and women, and the continuing ideology of male dominance, illustrate that despite some freedoms woman's lot was not substantially improved.

The sexual arrangements of these communities also cut both ways. Nineteenth-century society as a whole was coping with the tension between procreative and erotic sexuality, and this tension can be seen just as well in the utopian societies, although they resolved the problem in radically different ways. The celibate Shakers forbad sexual activity of any kind, sparing women the trauma of repeated pregnancy and childbirth, a remedy which, however, repressed female as well as male sexuality. As several works point out, we can only see in the Shakers' frenzied dancing an expression of an urgent erotic impulse. Noyes's system of male continence, forbidding ejaculation, allowed women to gratify their sexual desires without limit, while also avoiding unwanted pregnancies, and was the basis of a rigorously planned breeding system. In Oneida even the development of emotional attachment was forbidden, especially between sexual partners, and if it occurred was vigorously rebuked by the community. The Mormons, by contrast, believed only in marital sex for the purpose of procreation, and encouraged women to bear as many children as possible. But within all these diverse sexual creeds still lurked the image of Eve the temptress, of woman as the bearer of a wicked and seductive sexuality. And in all the communities sexual activity, particularly the decision to bear or not bear children, lay within the authority of the community hierarchy, which was usually male. The same obsession with the control of powerful sexual forces that plagued society at large can be seen in the religious communities, but these groups looked not to the development of self control but to the community for control of sexuality and reproduction. In each of these societies women's options to choose sex or love or children, or to refuse them, were limited, and often decisions lay in the hands of male authorities.

Kern, both in his book and in the article "Ideology and Reality," also stresses that the Oneida Perfectionists' restructuring of sexual and family roles can be interpreted as a reimposition of patriarchal authority, an authority to which evangelical notions of the family contained at least an implicit threat. In most religious communities the concept of femininity came in for revision: the roles prescribed for women often seemed a direct attack on true womanhood. Kern's "Ideology and Reality" describes in detail how the Perfectionists tried to destroy women's "philoprogenitiveness" (a desire for children), their strong identification as wives and mothers, even mounting a campaign to destroy girls' dolls. The disruption of the nuclear family relieved women of burdens, but it also took away the possibility of a domestic sphere, American women's locus of power. Both the Oneida and the Shaker communities foreswore the ideology of romantic feminism. The exaggerated differences between "male" and "female" which characterized middle-class dress and manners were downplayed—Noyes called woman "the female man," an epithet which, while it has egalitarian overtones, ultimately holds women to a male standard of development and denies them any unique experience or identity. Women were still pious but had no corner on moral virtue, as piety was expected of all members of the community: in fact, as we have seen, in most religious communities women were thought to have a lesser spiritual capacity than men. In short, whether by design or not, these communities succeeded in taking from women the traits and responsibilities which made them powerful and unique in the larger society. Kern's article ends with a woman's revolt, not for political but for domestic rights: through the assertion of domestic power and the familiar argument that women's moral influence should be more widespread, the second generation of Perfectionist women sought to reshape Oneida to look more like America. At least to Oneida women domesticity, despite its limitations, seemed to provide greater opportunity.

Mormonism

The Mormon configuration looked quite different. In some ways the Mormons discouraged the ideals of true womanhood: Mormon men criticized the leisured and skilless Gentile women, and there were even charges that the heavy skirts and tight corsets of high fashion represented women's attempts to prevent or abort unwanted pregnancies. But unlike other sects the Mormons clearly distinguished between male and female roles in dress, behavior, and spiritual authority, and encouraged women strongly in their domestic identities. Because in Mormon theology a woman's place in the next world depended wholly on her husband, a religious imperative to marry backed the church elders' prescription for devoted wife- and motherhood.

Actually, in comparison to other religious communities, the temperate and straitlaced Mormon values bore a strong resemblance to those of Victorian middle-class America. But the Mormons abandoned one of the critical props of middle-class culture, monogamy, in favor of a polygamic society, seemingly a large deviation. Dunfey's article claims that Mormon women actively defended polygamy in the name of Victorian domestic morality as a better kind of mousetrap. Polygamy provided the social stability of monogamic marriage. At the same time it allowed all women to be married, and all to husbands of substance, a commodity in short supply when the allotment was one apiece. Further, plural wives solved the problem of the adulterous impulse, the major flaw in monogamy because of men's insatiable sexual drive.

As with the other religious communities, the question of women's real status can be argued both ways. We have seen that the Mormons were the most clearly patriarchal of the groups, with a well-developed doctrine of female inferiority. Women were denied a place in the church hierarchy, as they still are today. Mormon teaching sought to repress female sexuality by the doctrine limiting sex to procreative purposes. Polygamic marriage was an obvious source of pain particularly for first wives, and women themselves lost the exclusive power of wife and mother in a monogamic household. This breaking down of exclusive bonds by those who could afford the luxury of multiple wives benefited the community. A polygamic household was a small, self-sufficient community of women who could take care of themselves and each other during their husband's long absences on missions and church business.

But Kern, Foster, Hansen, and others argue that Mormon women in Utah achieved a de facto independence greater than their Gentile sisters. These communities of women, their patriarch frequently away, usually formed a strong sisterhood, communalized work, became highly competent in running farms and businesses, and were often more free of sexual and reproductive responsibilities. Furthermore, as will be discussed later, Mormon women had active women's societies, published a vital women's newspaper, and possessed a remarkable number of legal rights, despite the fact that many Mormons, men and women both, opposed the women's rights movement which was becoming active in the East. Iversen's article expands this argument but attaches the problematic label of "feminist" to Mormon women's defense of polygamy, even though she admits that they accepted many of the limitations of their traditional roles and that "feminism and patriarchal religion are incompatible."

This catalogue of benefits and disadvantages still tells us nothing conclusive about why women, or even why any individual woman, would have chosen to join a religious community. Paul Johnson and Sean Wilentz's paper examines personal relations and motivations in a small, rather extraordinary community in New York which grew around an Old Testament style "prophet." They raise the question of what attraction an authoritarian, strongly patriarchal community would have to Jacksonian Americans. Their answer suggests, as others have, that communities of this kind grew up as a kind of working-class rebellion against the processes of industrialization and class formation which threatened an older way of life. But they also suggest an emphatic rejection of the newly genteel, middle-class, Finneyite evangelicalism which placed women in the spiritual center and gave them the power to insist on sexual respect and equality within the home, a power to which "the Christian Gentleman," as a middle-class evangelical American has been called, had to defer. Patriarchy and authoritarianism represent a return to an older style of religion and social order. In the context of the familial relations of many religious communities, they make a world where a man's home was still his castle but he was again king.

In reverting to these patterns men were struggling to take control over their lives at the direct expense of women's newly acquired domestic and spiritual authority. The genteel canons of the emergent middle class suited not only middle-class but working-class women better than the traditional model in many ways, and it is not surprising that few truly patriarchal communities existed. Clearly neither the Oneida nor the Shaker communities fits into this blatantly patriarchal mold: in both, it can be argued, women benefited from existing arrangements. What is finally most interesting is perhaps the tremendous diversity of sexual and familial models. The prophets of evangelical piety spilled enormous amounts of ink and breath convincing America that industrialism, capitalism, monogamy, domesticity, sobriety, and self-restraint formed a seamless garment of middle-class life, that each was an integral and unalterable part of a natural order. The utopian communities in their critique of the standing order consistently rejected its sexual as well as its economic arrangements—so consistently that we can assume that in their thinking they linked the two. But the arrangements they substituted were so diverse that it is difficult in the nineteenth century to find any constant link between their economic and sexual styles of life.

EVANGELICALISM AND REFORM MOVEMENTS

General

In the heyday of reform in antebellum America, an optimistic belief in the perfectibility of humankind was the common wellspring of a widely assorted group of social movements. Women as yet had no defined public role; their most powerful private role was in their capacity as mothers and moral agents. It was these same skills which they brought to reform work. Women engaged in many and varied reform activities; the bustling female do-gooder often became a comic stereotype like Dickens's Mrs. Pardiggle ("I am a School Lady, I am a Visiting Lady, I am a Reading Lady, I am on the Local

Linen Box Committee, and many general committees, and my canvassing alone is very extensive"). Some of these activities were traditional and church-centered, while others like abolitionism moved into more pathbreaking orbits of public political activity and had an overtly feminist rationale.

There is argument about lines of descent: did women's awareness of their disabilities evolve from abolitionism or from other reform movements, and what exactly was the relationship between benevolent societies, reform societies, abolitionism, and political feminism? The most common argument has been that the experience of participation in charitable and benevolent societies helped to develop individual women's consciousness of the condition of women and their desire for status and equality, and that this, along with the administrative experience, helped benevolent activities to evolve into a more open feminism.

Anne M. Boylan's recent article "Women in Groups" gives a good overview of this problem. She distinguishes the benevolent societies clearly as far less ambitious and more ready to accept the limitations of women's place than reform societies devoted to problems like moral purity and abolitionism. She concludes, on the basis of work on women's societies in New York and Boston, that few individuals made the transition from benevolence to reform or women's rights: benevolence thrived into the 1830s, but then gave way to the reform tradition, while the feminist movement did not emerge until the 1840s. Though many women belonged to more than one group, the small degree of cross-membership or transference between *types* of associations makes it difficult to see benevolent societies as direct forerunners of the more assertive reform and rights societies.

Nancy Hewitt's *Women's Activism and Social Change* is an important examination of faction in female reform societies. By focusing on relations between local reform groups in Rochester, Hewitt revises the idea of a monolithic, sisterly structure of female benevolence, and shows rather competing views of social good at work. She divides reformers into three groups: benevolent women, largely Presbyterians and Episcopalians, seeking to ameliorate the symptoms of poverty; evangelical, perfectionist women seeking to eradicate the social conditions at the root of vice and poverty; and the "ultraists," largely Hicksite Quakers, with a radical vision of complete equality for women and blacks. Hewitt shows that class and denomination were important predictors of women's stance on reform, and that each group worked in alliance with like-minded men to achieve their divergent social goals. Lori Ginzberg's recent dissertation, "Women and the Work of Benevolence," also seeks to look behind the benevolent ideal to the complex relationship between ideology and activity. Studies of this kind show the danger of assuming too great a harmony of means and ends in women's reform movements.

Nevertheless, there is general agreement that women's experience in reform societies served as a transition between private and public womanhood. Smith-Rosenberg calls the reform spirit "unspoken feminism," and Berg and Melder agree that many feminists and women's rights activists were schooled in the reform movements, developing confidence and skills, although Berg notes that the reform movements themselves evidenced "immature" feminism in that they never understood the systemic nature of woman's inequality and believed that moral action through the benevolent societies could change the status quo.

Boylan's earlier article is an attempt to flesh out the concept of "evangelical womanhood," also the subject of Leonard Sweet's *The Minister's Wife*. She suggests that, inspired by revivalism, evangelical Protestant women in the early part of the century sought to create an ideal of womanhood which would set them apart from the newly emerging middle-class "lady," whose ornamental, leisurely, skilless life (at least in the mythology of the day) seemed ungodly and wasteful. For Boylan, the revolutionary addition to the prescription for a virtuous woman's life was the mandate for social action in accordance with her beliefs, which precipitated the explosion of reform activity. Of course, it is important to remember that throughout the century traditional and more radical reform movements existed side by side, providing women with alternative paths of public service.

One historical school of the 1950s and 1960s interpreted these programs of social action as stemming from the desire of the middle classes to impose their values on the poor and "sinful," and thereby enhance the status of their own group—"the Protestant struggle for supremacy," Keith Melder calls it. According to this theory, many reformers were engaged in a conspiracy to remake the working classes in their own image—clean, upstanding, sober citizens, good clock-watching wage-earners—thereby destroying older worker-controlled social and labor patterns. Lois Banner's important article takes issue with the idea of "social control," rejecting the notion that what passed for religious benevolence on the part of clergy and laity was really the desire to dominate. For Banner, reformers had more genuine religious and humanitarian concerns, and sought to help the wayward become spiritually and materially whole again. This article was a turning point, and since its appearance in 1973 most historians have agreed that the genuine benevolent impulse was at least one major motive for reform, and that the reciprocal relationship between the benevolent and their objects of charity was much more complex than the social control model suggested.

The social control thesis came largely out of work on groups that were dominated by men. By contrast, most of the work on women in reform movements has concentrated neither on genuine religious benevolence, nor on the desire to impose values, although both elements may be present. Women's historians have concentrated rather on the potential such movements offered for women to enlarge their spheres and develop their own capacities for organization and leadership. Certainly middle-class men and women in antebellum America shared a common evangelical culture and language, and in some cases worked side by side in the same organizations. More often, though, men and women gathered separately; this was partly for reasons of propriety, but perhaps this split in the historiography also reflects genuine differences of purpose, and shows that male and female reformers were not pursuing exactly the same ends. The strains of economic and social dependency made some degree of autonomy an important goal for many more women than men. Benevolence and its activities in part served that goal. Barbara Berg's *The Remembered Gate* examines women's mixed motives—religious zeal and compassion, the establishment of moral order, opportunity—and finds that, while all may be present, the desire for autonomy was the strongest.

Anne Firor Scott gives one of the fullest accounts of the transition to public womanhood. She elaborates the subtitle of her book, *The Southern Lady: From Pedestal to Politics, 1830–1930*, in the chapter on women's associations, important both for what it tells us about the development of women's public institutions and about the female South. Scott shows clearly how the early, narrow, benevolent associations, the only approved form of female association, were concerned solely with religious and moral problems. Gradually they broadened their vision to include poverty, hunger, illiteracy, unemployment, and other ills of the poor, until by 1916 the Methodist Missionary Council had adopted a social gospel platform advocating the abolition of child labor, prison reform, and an easing of racial tensions. The social purity movement and the Women's Christian Temperance Union (WCTU) also flourished in the South, moving beyond their first concerns to involve themselves in a formidable array of social causes. By the beginning of the twentieth century the church-based benevolent societies had given way to secular women's clubs as the main organizing unit of Southern female society.

Scott's story of the South illustrates two important nationwide trends. One is the shift in the organization of public life from religious to secular groupings. Women in the early nineteenth century sought mainly to convert others, to bring them to church and to God. As the century went on, diverse reforms focusing on social ills rather than impiety or backsliding became the rage, and the associations became less church-centered. Finally by the early twentieth century the women's clubs had taken over much reform activity, working in the name of public service rather than God. The second trend is the advance toward seeking public, legislative solutions to problems on the local, state, or national levels, a movement away from moral suasion which

Ginzberg also discusses in "Women and the Work of Benevolence." Although the line is not clear, in the antebellum period it was largely political feminists who sought legal equality: most conservative or evangelical women relied on the working of change through personal relationships mediated by God's love rather than the lawmaker's power. As the century progressed, however, even religiously oriented groups like the WCTU began to call for legislative solutions to moral problems to supplement prayer and moral suasion. This does not indicate a convergence of interest of the two groups. But the conservative reformers did begin to see legislative help in reform as desirable, a development which finally made a rapprochement over the issue of women's suffrage possible.

Dorothy Bass's " 'Their Prodigious Influence' " is one of the best examinations of the relationship between the church and women's benevolent and reform activity. Bass shows that at first evangelical clergymen welcomed women's help in reforming the licentious poor. But by the 1830s and 1840s, clergymen and others were looking askance at some of the activities of women. Smith-Rosenberg's article, "Beauty, the Beast, and the Militant Woman," shows how members of the New York Female Moral Reform Society channeled their anger and frustration at oppression and the double standard into their work, patrolling outside brothels to identify and publicly expose male customers. Both Smith-Rosenberg and Ryan see the Moral Reform Society as a bastion of protofeminist sisterhood, although Ryan points out that the strict moral code of the reformers ultimately took its toll on women as well as men in terms of sexual repression.

But Smith-Rosenberg outlines a very interesting conflict within the society triggered by the publication of a letter from Sarah Grimke in the society's newspaper. Grimke's letter was an explicit attack on the orthodox religious arguments for women's subordination. Grimke suggested that a right reading of the Bible would show women to be men's equals, and that it was up to women to assert that equality. Smith-Rosenberg comments that "Grimke's overt criticism of women's traditional role, containing as it did an attack upon the Protestant ministry and orthodox interpretations of the Bible, went far beyond the consensus of the *Advocate*'s rural subscribers," and a number of readers criticized the letter's publication. As Smith-Rosenberg interprets it, the society's more radical leadership sought an alliance with openly feminist elements, but the more conservative membership was not prepared to have its deepest beliefs tampered with—the *Advocate of Moral Reform* never again printed an openly feminist piece of writing.

Education

Education for and by women was another innovative outgrowth of the reform period. The Protestant tradition was complex. Belief in woman as

man's spiritual equal could be employed to argue the need for education, at
the least basic literacy in order to read the scriptures. The domestic ideal of
the nineteenth century, though, emphasized the acquisition of social graces
and domestic arts and condemned women's attempts at intellectual development. Popular opinion held that too much learning would lead to sickness,
madness, and even death, as well as a loss of natural womanly functions. In
the revival climate of moral striving of the 1810s and 1820s, however, a
movement for women's education led to the establishment of a number of
seminaries for the training and education of girls and women. Emma Willard's seminary at Troy, New York, and Mary Lyon's at South Hadley, Massachusetts, later Mount Holyoke College, were two of the most famous, and
were run as well as staffed by women. But women's seminaries were supported as well by male community leaders, and their boards were often
composed of the town's leading ministers, doctors, and lawyers, who enthusi-
astically contributed their time and money to women's schools.

Schools for women, however, operated on different principles and served
different functions than schools for men. Janet Wilson James's *Changing
Ideas About Women* outlines the debate over the nature of women's intellect
which shaped school curricula: the prevailing view was that women's intel-
lects were subordinate to their moral natures. Seminaries provided education
in liberal arts and tutored women in domestic and moral studies, but an
intellectually challenging curriculum and the idea of learning for its own sake
were absent from many. Women's education was instrumental, fitting them
for their part in the great remaking of society which evangelicals so desired
and expected. For Keith Melder, the seminaries were a "mask of oppression,"
purporting to create equal educational opportunities for women while actually reinforcing the social and religious basis of women's subordination.

Others such as Scott and Sklar interpret women's seminaries as subtly
subversive, working through traditional forms for the advancement of wom-
en both by creating the strong bonds of all-female institutions and by inject-
ing women into the public debate over education. Sklar's excellent book on
Catherine Beecher is the best examination of evangelical ideas on women's
education. She shows Beecher in all the complexity of her anti-feminist and
pro-woman attitudes. Beecher eschewed the idea of direct political power for
women, either through the vote or through involvement in political activities.
But she exalted woman's domestic role to the skies, and like her sister,
Harriet Beecher Stowe, used that domestic identity to the fullest in her vision
of a new society. Though one wrote novels and the other tracts, the life work
of both sisters was directed at supplanting the cold, harsh, male-dominated
religion of their father, the evangelical Lyman Beecher, with a feminized
version of Christianity. Beecher and Stowe sought to make the moral and

ethical standards of the female reformers the country's reigning religion, and to break the sway of theologians and ministers. To this end Catherine Beecher worked to create a domestic and moral science which, under the auspices of women, was to provide the ruling forms for both home and society. Despite her anti-feminist stance, then, she worked toward a theory of education and moral influence for women that would expand their public scope radically and give them in effect many of the male prerogatives which she herself formally rejected.

The women's seminaries, which had always had strong connections to the church and had stressed moral development, gave way to women's colleges in the second half of the nineteenth century. Although the new institutions still concerned themselves with the moral character of their students, they were less self-consciously Protestant. But even there women did not get the chance at an education truly equal to men's until late in the century. Another important development in education was the redefinition of teaching, formerly a male preserve, as a woman's profession, a feminization which was concomitant with a loss of status and decreased pay for teachers. Brumberg's work suggests some of the professional imperatives and consequences of this feminization, the "romantic sexism" which viewed women as the perfect vehicle for the combination of love, education, and reform which was the evangelicals' ideal.

Abolitionism and Antislavery Work

Women's part in abolitionism sprang from the same source as their reform work generally—a common compassionate concern for the innocent suffering under conditions of social evil. Originally female abolitionists cast their concern as an extension of their own domestic guardianship, focusing on the plight of mothers and children and the breaking up of families. Both Ronald Walters and Lawrence Friedman connect the antislavery debate to many of the nineteenth century's dominant themes. Walters dwells on the underlying sexual preoccupations, showing how the same fear of man's lustful erotic nature and obsession with sexual corruption that mark the social purity campaign also characterize the antislavery arguments. From this standpoint women were particularly well suited to protest slavery in their role as guardians of home and virtue; not only was slavery an institution which broke up black families, but the widely reported miscegenation between slave holders and their female slaves corrupted the white Southern family as well.

But Friedman suggests that, although women's first foothold in antislavery was their special domestic agency and the moral status which derived from the true womanly ideals of purity and piety, the idea of the woman's sphere quite quickly began to be confining. Friedman finds that within the Garrisonian wing of the antislavery movement, where women participated freely, the idea of a limited domestic role for women gradually broke down, with both male and female abolitionists coming to accept women in their moral and social capacities without the highly idealizing and limiting concept of the sphere.

Unlike others who see the rise of feminism in the sexual antagonisms of the moral reformers, Dorothy Bass in " 'Their Prodigious Influence' " credits women's experience of equality in the antislavery movement with first fostering their political consciousness. Experience and ideology both began to transform the women who were allowed to speak publicly, travel, and represent the American Anti-Slavery Society on an equal basis with men. Bass and Blanche Hersh both see the response of the churches to these newly independent female activists as a catalyst for a more vehement feminism. Many of the clergy who had encouraged women in benevolent reform were horrified at these women's assertive role, and their condemnation, added to their generally unfriendly attitude toward abolitionism, disillusioned women who had relied on the church as the source of their moral commitment. In response to such criticism many women drew back from antislavery reform, participating only in the secondary capacity sanctioned by orthodoxy.

But other women, led by the Grimkes in their anticlerical charge, freed themselves from conservative religious and social strictures and went on to work vigorously in the movement. In their personal beliefs these women traveled the path from mainstream Protestantism to liberalism, agnosticism, or even atheism in the years before the war. The Grimke sisters left the Presbyterian church to become Quakers early in their careers, but their brand of feminist abolitionism proved too strong even for their adopted Society of Friends, which ultimately expelled them. Although they had not lost their spirituality, the sisters lived out their lives without formal religious affiliation, unable to contain their social and political beliefs within the confines of an organized theology. This progression is emblematic for antislavery women: as Hersh and Lerner point out, such breaks with authority seem naturally to accompany radical political action both emotionally and intellectually. Such denominational shifts were also part of a broader trend: in addition to geographic and occupational mobility, many nineteenth-century Americans practiced religious mobility, experimenting with stricter or more liberal creeds as they sought a better fit between their sacred beliefs and their changing social ideals.

Thus we can trace in the churches' response to antislavery roots not only of feminism but of the anticlerical bias of the women's rights movement. Ellen DuBois's article, "Women's Rights and Abolition: The Nature of the

Connection," attempts to resolve the debate over the origins of feminism by suggesting that while a "caste consciousness" characterized the moral reform societies and other female reforms, it was only in abolitionism that women acquired the ideology of absolute human equality, the tactics of public activism for social change, and the ability to formulate a comprehensive critique of unjust social and religious systems. As DuBois says, "their ability to comprehend religious institutions and to distinguish them from their own profoundly religious impulses was an impressive achievement for evangelicals in an evangelical age" (p. 243)—in other words, women were coming to an appreciation of their own spirituality as separate from their identities as Presbyterians, Congregationalists, or Episcopalians. DuBois sees conflict with clerical authority as the most important issue facing the women's rights movement until after the Civil War, and the women who had honed their skills in antislavery biblical exegesis were well equipped to turn to feminist exegesis, a popular form of political discourse throughout the century. Many of the leaders of the women's rights movement came out of abolitionism, and in their massive *History of Woman Suffrage* (6 vols., New York and Rochester, 1881–[1922]), Stanton and Anthony identified antislavery work as the single most important precipitant of the ferment over women's rights.

In fact the feminist-abolitionists were the first group of women in America to move beyond the concept of a sphere, however large or important, based on distinctly womanly qualities, to an insistence on the equality promised by the Constitution. In this they were the direct heirs of Mary Wollstonecraft's "Vindication of the Rights of Women" and of the enlightened natural rights theories of the founding fathers. In their attempt to expand the definition of republicanism to include women, antislavery women in 1837 published Angelina Grimke's "Appeal to the Women of the Nominally Free States" (New York, 1837), asserting that women's duty was not solely or foremost to family. Rather, like men's, it was to "themselves, to the suffering slave, to the slaveholder, to the church, to their country, and to the world at large: and above all, to their God" (p. 3). This grand view of woman as citizen of the world necessarily made her man's equal because, as the "Appeal" pointed out, men and women had exactly the same moral capacities, the same moral rights and duties. "Are we bereft of citizenship because we are the *mothers, wives,* and *daughters* of a mighty people? Have we no country—no interest staked in the public weal—no liabilities in common peril—no partnership in a nation's guilt and shame?" (p. 19). This extraordinary vision of woman's full participation in a national political system retained piety and compassionate obligation to others as foundations of woman's existence (along with a critical new addition, the duty to self), but it freed women from the domesticity and submissiveness which were the other traits of the true woman. For the

Grimkes and other feminists morality was still the key, but woman was man's moral and hence his political equal, rather than being his moral superior and political subordinate, as decreed by evangelical domesticity. This definition of woman's moral nature remained the keystone of the suffrage arguments of one group of feminists until the passage of the Nineteenth Amendment.

In 1838, of course, such a radical reordering lay quite some distance in the future, as the two important articles by Judith Wellman and Nancy Hewitt show. Both articles examine the local political, economic, and social coalitions which influenced the fortunes of women's antislavery societies in New York state. One of the goals of the first national women's antislavery convention, held in 1837, was to "interest women in the subject of antislavery, and establish a system of operations throughout every town and village in the free states, that would exert a powerful influence in the abolition of American slavery" (Wellman, p. 114). This ambitious forecast in part came true: many local women's societies were indeed formed and over the years raised much money and sent many petitions to Congress for the cause of abolition. The manifesto of the women's third antislavery convention in particular encouraged women to sign and to solicit signatures on petitions as "our only means of direct political action" (Wellman, p. 117). In fact they were so successful that, as Hewitt relates, Senator Robert Walker of Mississippi is reported to have complained that "if the ladies and Sunday school children would let us alone, there would be but a few abolition petitions." But Wellman, who examines the petition drives in some detail, finds that although the absolute number being sent increased between 1838 and 1850, the number of women's signatures had dropped significantly by the later years.

Wellman's analysis of this drop in participation outlines a critical transition. (A note promises that her article is part of a book in progress, as it deserves to be to do justice to her thesis, one which has important implications for the study of women's exercise of political power.) Wellman suggests that in its early days abolitionism was a blend of moral and political interests, a concern for a national community pursued largely through personal, local, religiously based activity. But throughout the 1840s many abolitionists moved toward a more secular stance, and toward involvement in electoral politics at a state or national level. Despite the Grimkes' pleas for national citizenship, most antislavery women could not brave the criticism of clergymen and others to break out of their domestic, church-centered role and join their male peers in direct political action. Wellman's closing paragraph suggests that by 1850 "the very definition of citizenship itself originated no longer in the religious and cultural network of family and community life on a local level but in the newly dominant realities of life in a national state. For in a legal sense, women were not only nonvoters but nonentities. Thus, as important elements within the abolitionist movement itself shifted their perspective from a moral to a political emphasis, they also closed to women one of the few ways in which women had been able to express that sense of themselves as moral and responsible beings, as members in good standing of a community both religious and political." Unlike the transition from pre-industrial agriculture to industrial capitalism, the shift from a moral or religious to a secular or political community has been badly neglected. Wellman's argument gives a new fullness to Ann Douglas's work on feminization and the declining influence of the churches. More explicitly than Douglas, Wellman puts this decline in the context of a world becoming more overtly political, focusing increasingly on national problems and solutions. Perhaps the organization of American Protestantism, its fragmentation into denominations, made it difficult for churches to wield political power effectively at the national level. Despite their national organizations and influence, churches may have functioned more effectively locally, lacking the ability to frame issues or solutions for a national constituency which would keep their influence intact. If Wellman is right, the weakening of local networks extending outward from the churches would have cut away women's main base of power within the community.

Hewitt's article deals with the split between moral suasionists and political abolitionists, and adds to the interpretation of women's non-participation in electoral politics. Of the competing antislavery societies in Rochester, those which stayed in the American Anti-Slavery Society after its well-publicized split in 1840 were critical of the role played by the institutional churches in antislavery, believed in moral suasion rather than political abolition (although this may be misleading—the moral suasionists were strongly behind petition drives, for example, which were clearly a political tactic), and preached and practiced full equality for women. The Tappans and others who left to form their own groups split in large part over these very issues. They planned to continue to work through the organized churches and through political channels, and granted to women only an auxiliary status which consisted largely of fundraising through the sale of handicrafts at local bazaars.

What is fascinating is Hewitt's evidence that the moral suasionists tended to be predominantly rural, agricultural families with ties to radical Quakerism, quite isolated from even local centers of power. Women who stayed with the political abolitionists, conversely, came much more often from urban, merchant, Presbyterian or Unitarian families, well placed in the power structure of the community. These two groups represent within one locale and time, then, the shift Wellman speaks of between a small, local, pious, democratic community, and a more urban, commercial community, ruled by a local hierarchy with ties to state and national power structures. The parallel between political forms and womanly ideals is also striking: those from the middle-class commercial milieu which spawned the ideal of domesticity were willing to accept the limited, secondary role assigned them by male political abolitionists, while women who lived the pre-industrial, more egalitarian farm life were more likely to demand full participation. Amy Swerdlow's paper adopts a similar type of analysis. Her study finds that female abolitionists from Boston and Philadelphia were overwhelmingly both feminist and from non-evangelical denominations, while women from her New York sample tended to be both evangelicals and anti-feminists. All three articles are valuable attempts to correlate personal economic, social, and religious data with moral and political beliefs to give us insight into some of the conditions which led women to choose particular moral and political paths. It remains to be seen whether local studies of this type can be combined to form a coherent and informative whole.

The different approaches of Hewitt's two groups illustrate the reformers' chronic dilemma of whether to choose to remake old institutions or sweep them away and fashion new ones. Political abolitionists worked through existing power structures. But Hewitt makes the important point that those moral suasionists who stayed with AASS-affiliated groups cannot be seen simply as religious radicals who ignored the existence of civil government in favor of a direct appeal to the heart. Rather, she suggests that in rejecting legal and constitutional remedies, Garrisonian women were criticizing not just the legal existence of slavery but the whole institutional framework of the churches and government. Moral suasionists believed that their societies, which allowed for the equal participation of all the disenfranchised, particularly women and blacks, offered a radical alternative vision of freedom to the American people which had only to be communicated to be embraced. Both moral suasionist and political abolitionist women exercised the indirect power of the disenfranchised, but the distinct ways in which each group did so seem to have been shaped by their economic, social, and religious conditions.

Finally, Hovet's articles on Harriet Beecher Stowe's antislavery work throw a slightly different light on evangelical women. He argues that some of Stowe's sharpest antislavery arguments were attacks on the Presbyterian church itself from her status, not as a moral equal, but as an advocate of a feminine ethic of Christian love. Stowe fought for an aesthetic, warm, heart-centered religion which would repudiate the cold logic of Calvinist theological disputation. Specifically, she joined her hatred of slavery to her long struggle against inability and theological determinism, attacking the Protestant churches' use of doctrines like predestination to justify the existence of slavery. Hovet says that Stowe's message, that the church as well as the government sinned in its tolerance of slavery, was deeply revolutionary, an attempt to impose feminine values on a church she perceived as masculine and without love. Stowe's theological crusade exemplifies a strain within both the evangelical and the more liberal women's movements: the struggle of many nineteenth-century men and women to free themselves from the rigid doctrines of predestination, original sin, and infant damnation; paralleled women's struggles for autonomy within the family, the reform movements, and the women's rights movement; and provided them with a critical strength. Stowe's journey from Calvinist Presbyterianism to attendance at the Episcopal church is a statement about her public as well as private beliefs.

BIBLIOGRAPHY

1. BIBLIOGRAPHIES AND GENERAL WORKS

a. Bibliographies

Allen, Arthur. "Women and Missions: A Bibliography." Duke Divinity School Review 39 (Spring 1974), 103-104.

Bass, Dorothy. American Women in Church and Society, 1607-1920: A Bibliography. New York: Auburn Program at Union Theological Seminary, 1973.

Boyd, Sandra Hughes. "The History of Women in the Episcopal Church: A Select Annotated Bibliography." Historical Magazine of the Protestant Episcopal Church 50, no. 4 (1981), 423-433.

Brunkow, Robert deV., ed. Religion and Society in North America: An Annotated Bibliography. Santa Barbara, Calif.: ABC-Clio Information Services, 1983.

Code, J. B. "Selected Bibliography of the Religious Orders and Congregations of Women Founded Within the Present Boundaries of the United States (1727-1850)." Catholic History 23 (October 1937), 331-335; 26 (July 1940), 222-245.

Conway, Jill K. The Female Experience in Eighteenth- and Nineteenth-Century America. New York: Garland Publishing Co., 1982.

Fischer, Clare B. Breaking Through: A Bibliography of Women and Religion. Berkeley: Graduate Theological Union Library, 1980.

King, Margot. A Bibliography on Women and the Church. Saskatoon, Saskatchewan: Shannon Library, St. Thomas More College, 1975.

Kolmer, Elizabeth. "Catholic Women Religious and Women's
    History: A Survey of the Literature." American Quarterly
    30, no. 5 (1978), 639-651. Reprinted in Women in American
    Religion, edited by Janet Wilson James. Philadelphia:
    University of Pennsylvania Press, 1980.

Krichmar, Albert, et al. The Women's Rights Movement in the
    United States, 1848-1970: A Bibliography and Sourcebook.
    Metuchen, N.J.: Scarecrow Press, 1972.

Loewenberg, Bert J., and Bogin, Ruth, eds. Black Women in
    Nineteenth-Century American Life: Their Words, Their
    Thoughts, Their Feelings. University Park, Pa.:
    Pennsylvania State University Press, 1976.

Patrick, Anne E. "Women and Religion: A Survey of Significant
    Literature, 1965-1974." Theological Studies 36, no. 4
    (1975), 737-765.

Religious Books, 1876-1982. New York: R. W. Bowker Co., 1983.

"Selected Bibliography: Women, Language, and Theology." In The
    Power of Language Among the People of God: Report Received
    by the Ninety-First General Assembly (1979) of the United
    States Presbyterian Church USA. New York: Advisory Council
    on Discipleship and Worship, Presbyterian Church USA, 1979.

Thomas, Evangeline, ed. Women Religious History Sources: A
    Guide to Repositories in the U.S. New York: R. W. Bowker
    Co., 1983.

Wheat, Valerie. "The Return of the Goddess: Women and
    Religion." Booklegger Magazine 2, no. 7 (1975), 10-17.

b. General Works

Culver, Elsie. Women in the World of Religion. Garden City,
    N.Y.: Doubleday, 1967.

Driver, Anne Barstow. "Review Essay: Religion." Signs 2, no.
    2 (1976), 434-442.

Harkness, Georgia. Women in Church and Society: A Historical
    and Theological Inquiry. Nashville: Abingdon, 1972.

James, Edward T.; James, Janet Wilson; and Boyer, Paul S., eds.
    Notable American Women, 1607-1950: A Biographical
    Dictionary. Cambridge, Mass.: Harvard University Press,
    Belknap Press, 1971.

James, Janet Wilson. "An Overview." In Women in American
    Religion, edited by Janet Wilson James, 1-25. Philadelphia:
    University of Pennsylvania Press, 1980.

James, Janet Wilson. "Women and Religion." <u>American Quarterly</u>
    30, no. 5 (1978), 579-581.

Keller, Rosemary Skinner; Queen, Louise L.; and Thomas, Hilah
    F., eds. <u>Women in New Worlds: Historical Perspectives on</u>
    <u>the Wesleyan Tradition</u>, vol. 2. Nashville: Abingdon, 1982.

Mathews, Donald G. "Women's History/Everyone's History." In
    <u>Women in New Worlds: Historical Perspectives on the Wesleyan</u>
    <u>Tradition</u>, vol. 1, edited by Hilah F. Thomas and Rosemary
    Skinner Keller. Nashville: Abingdon, 1981.

Ruether, Rosemary Radford, and Keller, Rosemary Skinner, eds.
    <u>Women and Religion in America</u>, vol. 1, <u>The Nineteenth</u>
    <u>Century</u>. San Francisco: Harper & Row, 1981.

Ruether, Rosemary Radford, and McLaughlin, Eleanor, eds. <u>Women</u>
    <u>of Spirit: Female Leadership in the Jewish and Christian</u>
    <u>Traditions</u>. New York: Simon and Schuster, 1979.

Sklar, Kathryn Kish. "The Last Fifteen Years: Historians'
    Changing Views of Women in Religion and Society." In <u>Women</u>
    <u>in New Worlds: Historical Perspectives on the Wesleyan</u>
    <u>Tradition</u>, vol. 1, edited by Hilah F. Thomas and Rosemary
    Skinner Keller. Nashville: Abingdon, 1981.

Smith, Page. <u>Daughters of the Promised Land: Women in American</u>
    <u>History</u>. Boston: Little, Brown & Co., 1970.

Thomas, Hilah F., and Keller, Rosemary Skinner, eds. <u>Women in</u>
    <u>New Worlds: Historical Perspectives on the Wesleyan</u>
    <u>Tradition</u>, vol. 1. Nashville: Abingdon, 1981.

2. DOMESTICITY, FAMILY LIFE, AND WOMEN'S SPHERE

a. Domesticity

Bunkle, Phillida. "Sentimental Womanhood and Domestic
    Education, 1830-1870." <u>History of Education Quarterly</u> 14
    (Spring 1974), 13-31.

Cott, Nancy F. <u>The Bonds of Womanhood: "Woman's Sphere" in New</u>
    <u>England, 1780-1835</u>. New Haven: Yale University Press, 1977.

Cott, Nancy F. "Passionlessness: An Interpretation of
    Victorian Sexual Ideology, 1790-1850." <u>Signs</u> 4, no. 2
    (1978), 219-236.

Douglas, Ann. "Heaven Our Home: Consolation Literature in the
    Northern United States, 1830-1880." <u>American Quarterly</u> 26,
    no. 5 (1974), 496-515.

Epstein, Barbara. "Domesticity and Female Subordination."
    Chap. 3 in The Politics of Domesticity: Women,
    Evangelicalism, and Temperance in Nineteenth-Century
    America. Middletown, Conn.: Wesleyan University Press,
    1981.

Freedman, Estelle B. "Sexuality in Nineteenth-Century America:
    Behavior, Ideology, and Politics." Reviews in American
    History 10, no. 4 (1982), 196-215.

Hogeland, Ronald W. "Charles Hodge, the Association of
    Gentlemen and Ornamental Womanhood, 1825-1855." Journal of
    Presbyterian History 53, no. 3 (1975), 239-255.

Hogeland, Ronald W. "'The Female Appendage': Feminine Life-
    Styles in America, 1820-1860." Civil War History 17, no. 2
    (1971), 101-114.

James, Janet Wilson. Changing Ideas About Women in the United
    States, 1776-1825. New York: Garland Publishing, Inc.,
    1981.

Kenneally, James T. "Eve, Mary, and the Historians: American
    Catholicism and Women." In Women in American Religion,
    edited by Janet Wilson James. Philadelphia: University of
    Pennsylvania Press, 1980.

Leloudis, James L., II. "Subversion of the Feminine Ideal: The
    Southern Lady's Companion and White Male Morality in the
    Antebellum South, 1847-1854." In Women in New Worlds:
    Historical Perspectives on the Wesleyan Tradition, vol. 2,
    edited by Rosemary Skinner Keller, Louise L. Queen, and
    Hilah F. Thomas. Nashville: Abingdon, 1981.

Loveland, Anne C. "Domesticity and Religion in the Antebellum
    Period: The Career of Phoebe Palmer." The Historian 39, no.
    3 (1977), 455-471.

Meyer, Donald B. "The Troubled Souls of Females." In Women
    and Womanhood in America, edited by Ronald W. Hogeland.
    Lexington, Mass.: D. C. Heath & Co., 1973. Reprinted from
    The Positive Thinkers, New York: Doubleday & Co., 1965.

Riley, Glenda Gates. "The Subtle Subversion: Changes in the
    Traditionalist Image of the American Woman." The Historian
    32, no. 2 (1970), 210-227.

Rosenberg, Charles E. "Sexuality, Class and Role in 19th-
    Century America." American Quarterly 25, no. 2 (1973), 131-
    153.

Sizer, Sandra S. "Passion in its Place: The Domestic Image."
    Chap. 4 in Gospel Hymns and Social Religion: The Rhetoric of
    Nineteenth-Century Revivalism. Philadelphia: Temple
    University Press, 1978.

Sklar, Kathryn K. Catherine Beecher: A Study in American Domesticity. New Haven: Yale University Press, 1973.

Smith, Daniel Scott. "Family Limitation, Sexual Control and Domestic Feminism in Victorian America." Feminist Studies 1, nos. 3/4 (1973), 40-57. Reprinted in Clio's Consciousness Raised: New Perspectives on the History of Women, edited by Mary S. Hartman and Lois W. Banner. New York: Harper & Row, 1974.

Smith-Rosenberg, Carroll. "The Female World of Love and Ritual." Signs 1, no. 1 (1975), 1-29. Reprinted in her Disorderly Conduct: Visions of Gender in Victorian America. New York: Knopf, 1985.

Smith-Rosenberg, Carroll. "The Hysterical Woman: Sex Roles and Role Conflict in Nineteenth-Century America." Social Research 39, no. 4 (1972), 652-678. Reprinted in her Disorderly Conduct: Visions of Gender in Victorian America. New York: Knopf, 1985.

Thomas, Samuel J. "Catholic Journalists and the Ideal Woman in Late Victorian America." International Journal of Women's Studies (Canada) 4, no. 1 (1981), 89-100.

Waller, Altina L. Reverend Beecher and Mrs. Tilton: Sex and Class in Victorian America. Amherst, Mass.: University of Massachusetts Press, 1982.

Welter, Barbara. "Anti-Intellectualism and the American Woman: 1800-1860." Mid-America 48, no. 4 (1966), 258-270.

Welter, Barbara. "The Cult of True Womanhood, 1820-1860." American Quarterly 18, no. 2, pt. 1 (1966), 151-174.

Wills, David W. "Womanhood and Domesticity in the A.M.E. Tradition: The Influence of Daniel Alexander Payne." In Black Apostles at Home and Abroad: Afro-Americans and the Christian Mission from the Revolution to Reconstruction, edited by David W. Wills and Richard Newman. Boston: G. K. Hall, 1982.

Zaretsky, Eli. "Female Sexuality and the Catholic Confessional." Signs 6, no. 1 (1980), 176-184.

b. Family

Bloch, Ruth. "American Feminine Ideals in Transition: The Rise of the Moral Mother, 1785-1815." Feminist Studies 4, no. 2 (1978), 101-126.

Boylan, Anne M. "Sunday Schools and Changing Evangelical Views of Children in the 1820s." Church History 48, no. 3 (1979), 320-333.

Cable, Mary. "Christian Nurture." Chap. 5 in The Little
    Darlings: A History of Child Rearing in America. New York:
    Scribner's, 1975.

Degler, Carl. At Odds: Women and the Family in America from
    the Revolution to the Present. New York: Oxford University
    Press, 1980.

"The Family in Baptist History." Baptist History and Heritage
    17, no. 1 (1982), whole volume.

Frost, Jerry W. "As the Twig is Bent: Quaker Ideas of
    Childhood." Quaker History 60, no. 2 (1971), 67-87.

Gillespie, Joanna Bowen. "'The Sun in Their Domestic System':
    The Mother in Early Nineteenth-Century Methodist Sunday
    School Lore." In Women in New Worlds: Historical
    Perspectives on the Wesleyan Tradition, vol. 2, edited by
    Rosemary Skinner Keller, Louise L. Queen and Hilah F.
    Thomas. Nashville: Abingdon, 1982.

Graebner, Alan. "Birth Control and the Lutherans: The Missouri
    Synod as a Case Study." In Women in American Religion,
    edited by Janet Wilson James. Philadelphia: University of
    Pennsylvania Press, 1980.

Greven, Philip. The Protestant Temperament: Patterns of Child-
    Rearing, Religious Experience, and the Self in Early
    America. New York: Knopf, 1977.

Johnson, Paul. "The Modernization of Mayo Greenleaf Patch:
    Land, Family, and Marginality in New England, 1766-1818."
    New England Quarterly 55, no. 4 (1982), 488-516.

Johnson, Paul. A Shopkeeper's Millennium: Society and Revivals
    in Rochester, New York, 1815-1837. New York: Hill and Wang,
    1979.

McLoughlin, William G. "Evangelical Childrearing in the Age of
    Jackson: Francis Wayland's View of When and How to Subdue
    the Willfulness of Children." Journal of Social History 9,
    no. 1 (1975), 21-34.

Marietta, Jack. "Quaker Family Education in Historical
    Perspective." Quaker History 63, no. 1 (1974), 3-16.

Meckel, Richard A. "Educating a Ministry of Mothers:
    Evangelical Maternal Associations, 1815-1860." Journal of
    the Early Republic 2, no. 4 (1982), 403-423.

Mohr, James C. Abortion in America: The Origins and Evolution
    of National Policy, 1800-1900. New York: Oxford University
    Press, 1978.

O'Neill, William L. "Divorce as a Moral Issue: A Hundred Years
   of Controversy." In "Remember the Ladies": New Perspectives
   on Women in American History, edited by Carol V. R. George.
   Syracuse, N.Y.: Syracuse University Press, 1975.

O'Neill, William L. Divorce in the Progressive Era. New
   Haven: Yale University Press, 1967.

O'Neill, William L. "Divorce in the Progressive Era."
   American Quarterly 17, no. 2, pt. 1 (1965), 203-217.

Pessen, Edward. "Early Industrialization, Urbanization, and
   the American Family." Reviews in American History 10, no. 1
   (1982), 49-53.

Rose, Anne C. "Men, Women and Families." Chap. 5 in
   Transcendentalism as a Social Movement, 1830-1850. New
   Haven: Yale University Press, 1981.

Ryan, Mary. Cradle of the Middle Class: The Family in Oneida
   County, New York, 1790-1865. Cambridge: Cambridge
   University Press, 1981.

Ryan, Mary. "The Explosion of Family History." Reviews in
   American History 10, no. 4 (1982), 181-195.

Ryan, Mary P. "A Woman's Awakening: Evangelical Religion and
   the Families of Utica, New York, 1800-1840." American
   Quarterly 30, no. 5 (1978), 601-623.

Sides, Sudie Duncan. "Slave Weddings and Religion." History
   Today (Great Britain) 24, no. 2 (1974), 77-87.

Stroupe, Henry S. "'Cite Them Both to Attend the Next Church
   Conference': Social Control by North Carolina Baptist
   Churches, 1772-1908." North Carolina Historical Review 52,
   no. 2 (1975), 156-170.

c.   Women and Religious Culture: The "Feminization" of Religion

Banner, Lois W. "Women's History: Culture and Feminization."
   Reviews in American History 6, no. 2 (1978), 155-162.

Barnett, Evelyn Brooks. "The Feminization of the Black Baptist
   Church, 1890-1920." Paper delivered at the Berkshire
   Conference on Women's History, Mount Holyoke College, South
   Hadley, Mass., August 23-25, 1978. (Papers on deposit at the
   Schlesinger Library, Radcliffe College, Cambridge, Mass.)

Bass, Dorothy C. "Sex Roles, Sexual Symbolism, and Social
   Change." Radical Religion 4, no. 1 (1978), 2-27.

Blauvelt, Martha Tomhave. "Women and Revivalism." In Women and Religion in America, vol. 1, The Nineteenth Century, edited by Rosemary Radford Reuther and Rosemary Skinner Keller, 1-45. San Francisco: Harper & Row, 1981.

Cott, Nancy F. "Young Women in the Second Great Awakening." Feminist Studies 3, nos. 1/2 (1975), 15-29.

Douglas, Ann. The Feminization of American Culture. New York: Knopf, 1977.

Epstein, Barbara. The Politics of Domesticity: Women, Evangelicalism, and Temperance in Nineteenth-Century America. Middletown, Conn.: Wesleyan University Press, 1981.

Fraser, Dorothy Bass. "The Feminine Mystique, 1890-1910." Union Seminary Quarterly Review 27, no. 4 (1972), 225-239.

Gadt, Jeanette Carter. "Women and Protestant Culture: The Quaker Dissent From Puritanism." Ph.D. diss., University of California at Los Angeles, 1974.

Hewitt, Nancy A. "The Perimeters of Women's Power in American Religion." In The Evangelical Tradition in America, edited by Leonard I. Sweet. Macon, Ga.: Mercer University Press, 1984.

Kimball, Gayle. "From Motherhood to Sisterhood: The Search for Religious Imagery in Nineteenth and Twentieth Century Theology." In Beyond Androcentrism: New Essays on Women and Religion, edited by Rita M. Gross. Missoula, Mont.: Scholars Press, 1977.

Malmsheimer, Lonna M. "Daughters of Zion: New England Roots of American Feminism." New England Quarterly 50, no. 3 (1977), 484-504.

Mathews, Donald G. "An Enlightened and Refined People." Chap. 3 in Religion in the Old South. Chicago: University of Chicago Press, 1977.

Porterfield, Amanda. Feminine Spirituality in America. Philadelphia: Temple University Press, 1980.

Reynolds, David S. "The Feminization Controversy: Sexual Stereotypes and the Paradoxes of Piety in Nineteenth-Century America." New England Quarterly 53, no. 1 (1980), 96-106.

Robertson, Darrel M. "The Feminization of American Religion: An Examination of Recent Interpretations of Women and Religion in Victorian America." Christian Scholar's Review 8, no. 3 (1978), 238-246.

Ruether, Rosemary Radford. "The Cult of True Womanhood."
     Commonweal, 9 November 1973, 127-132.

Ruether, Rosemary Radford, and Keller, Rosemary Skinner.
     "Introduction." In Women and Religion in America, vol. 1,
     The Nineteenth Century, edited by the authors, viii-xiv.
     San Francisco: Harper & Row, 1981.

Schuyler, David. "Inventing a Feminine Past." New England
     Quarterly 51, no. 3 (1978), 291-308.

Shiels, Richard D. "The Feminization of American
     Congregationalism, 1730-1835." American Quarterly 33, no. 1
     (1981), 46-62.

Smith-Rosenberg, Carroll. "The Cross and the Pedestal: Women,
     Anti-Ritualism, and the Emergence of the American
     Bourgeoisie." In her Disorderly Conduct: Visions of Gender
     in Victorian America. New York: Knopf, 1985.

Smith-Rosenberg, Carroll. "Women and Religious Revivals: Anit-
     Ritualism, Liminality, and the Emergence of the American
     Bourgeoisie." In The Evangelical Tradition in America,
     edited by Leonard I. Sweet. Macon, Ga.: Mercer University
     Press, 1984.

Tompkins, Jane. "Sentimental Power: Uncle Tom's Cabin and the
     Politics of Literary History." Glyph 8 (1981).

Watkins, Bari. "Woman's World in Nineteenth-Century America."
     American Quarterly 31, no. 1 (1979), 116-127.

Welter, Barbara. "The Feminization of Religion in Nineteenth-
     Century America." In Clio's Consciousness Raised: New
     Perspectives on the History of Women, edited by Mary S.
     Hartman and Lois W. Banner. New York: Harper & Row, 1974.

3. WOMEN IN UTOPIAN AND RELIGIOUS COMMUNITIES

a. General

Achorn, Erik. "Mary Cragin, Perfectionist Saint." New England
     Quarterly 28, no. 4 (1955), 490-518.

Barnhiser, Judith Anne. " A Study of the Authority Structures
     of Three Nineteenth-Century Apostolic Communities of
     Religious Women in the United States." Ph.D. diss.,
     Catholic University of America, 1975.

Bishop, Morris. "The Great Oneida Love-In." American Heritage
     20, no. 2 (1969), 14-17, 86-92.

Boyer, Paul S. "A Joyful Noyes: Reassessing America's Utopian
    Tradition." Reviews in American History 3, no. 1 (1975),
    25-30.

Campbell, D'Ann. "Women's Life in Utopia: The Shaker
    Experiment in Sexual Equality Reappraised: 1810 to 1860."
    New England Quarterly 51, no. 1 (1978), 23-38.

Carden, Maren Lockwood. "The Experimental Utopia in America."
    Daedalus 94, no. 2 (1965), 401-418.

Carden, Maren Lockwood. Oneida: Utopian Community to Modern
    Corporation. Baltimore: Johns Hopkins University Press,
    1969.

Dalsimer, Marlyn Hartzell. "Women and Family in the Oneida
    Community, 1837-1881." Ph.D. diss., New York University,
    1975.

DeMaria, Richard. Communal Love at Oneida: A Perfectionist
    Vision of Authority, Property, and Sexual Order. New York:
    Edwin Mellen Press, 1978.

Desroche, Henri. The American Shakers: From NeoChristianity to
    Presocialism. Translated by John Savacool. Amherst, Mass.:
    University of Massachusetts Press, 1971.

Foster, Lawrence. "Free Love and Feminism: John Humphrey Noyes
    and the Oneida Community." Journal of the Early Republic 1,
    no. 2 (1981), 165-183.

Foster, Lawrence. Religion and Sexuality: Three American
    Communal Experiments of the Nineteenth Century. New York:
    Oxford University Press, 1981.

Freedman, Estelle B. "Sexuality in Nineteenth-Century America:
    Behavior, Ideology and Politics." Reviews in American
    History 10, no. 4 (1982), 196-215.

Fryer, Judith. "American Eves in American Edens." American
    Scholar 44, no. 1 (1974/5), 78-99.

Humez, Jean M. "Visionary Experience and Power: The Career of
    Rebecca Cox Jackson." In Black Apostles at Home and Abroad:
    Afro-Americans and the Christian Mission from the Revolution
    to Reconstruction, edited by David W. Wills and Richard
    Newman. Boston: G. K. Hall, 1982.

Irvin, Helen Derby. "The Machine in Utopia: Shaker Women and
    Technology." Women's Studies International Quarterly 4, no.
    3 (1981), 313-319.

James, Eleanor. "The Sanctificationists of Belton." American
    West (Texas) 2, no. 3 (1965), 65-73.

Johnson, Paul, and Wilentz, Sean. "The Kingdom of Matthias:
    Sex and Salvation in Jacksonian New York." Paper delivered
    at the Charles Warren Center, Harvard University, November
    1983.

Kephart, William. "Experimental Family Organization: An
    Historico-Cultural Report on the Oneida Community." Journal
    of Marriage and the Family 25, no. 3 (1963), 261-271.

Kern, Louis J. "Ideology and Reality: Sexuality and Women's
    Status in the Oneida Community." Radical History Review 20
    (1979), 180-204.

Kern, Louis J. An Ordered Love: Sex Roles in Victorian
    Utopias: The Shakers, the Mormons, and the Oneida Community.
    Chapel Hill: University of North Carolina Press, 1981.

Kolmerton, Carol A. "Egalitarian Promises and Inegalitarian
    Practices: Women's Roles in the American Owenite
    Communities, 1824-1828." Journal of General Education 33,
    no. 1 (1981), 31-44.

Mandelker, Ira L. "Religion, Sex, and Utopia in Nineteenth-
    Century America." Social Research 49, no. 3 (1982), 730-
    751.

May, Elaine Tyler. "Sex in Utopia: A Review Essay." New York
    History 62, no. 4 (1981), 462-467.

Muncy, Raymond Lee. Sex and Marriage in Utopian Communities:
    Nineteenth-Century America. Bloomington, Ind.: Indiana
    University Press, 1973.

Peterson, Susan. "Religious Communities of Women in the West:
    The Presentation Sisters' Adaptation to the Northern Plains
    Frontier." Journal of the West 21, no. 2 (1982), 65-70.

Procter-Smith, Marjorie. Women in Shaker Community and
    Worship: A Feminist Analysis of the Uses of Religious
    Symbolism. Lewiston, N.Y.: Edwin Mellen Press, 1985.

Robertson, Constance Noyes. Oneida Community: An
    Autobiography, 1851-1976. Syracuse, N.Y.: Syracuse
    University Press, 1970.

Robertson, Constance Noyes. Oneida Community: The Breakup,
    1876-1881. Syracuse, N.Y.: Syracuse University Press, 1972.

Roemer, Kenneth. "Sex Roles, Utopia, and Change: The Family in
    Late Nineteenth-Century Utopian Literature." American
    Studies 13, no. 2 (1972), 33-47.

Ruether, Rosemary Radford. "Women in Utopian Movements." In
     Women and Religion in America, vol. 1, The Nineteenth
     Century, edited by Rosemary Radford Ruether and Rosemary
     Skinner Keller, 46-100. San Francisco: Harper & Row, 1981.

Sandeen, Ernest R. "John Humphrey Noyes as the New Adam."
     Church History 40, no. 1 (1971), 82-90.

Taylor, Barbara. Eve and the New Jerusalem: Socialism and
     Feminism in the Nineteenth Century. New York: Pantheon
     Books, 1983.

Thomas, Robert David. "John Humphrey Noyes and the Oneida
     Community: A Nineteenth-Century American Father and His
     Family." Psychohistory Review 6, nos. 2-3 (1977-1978), 68-
     87.

Thomas, Robert David. "The Quest for Security: Love, Sex and
     Marriage." Chap. 5 in The Man Who Would Be Perfect: John
     Humphrey Noyes and the Utopian Impulse. Philadelphia:
     University of Pennsylvania Press, 1977.

Welter, Barbara. "The Feminization of American Religion." In
     Clio's Consciousness Raised: New Perspectives on the History
     of Women, edited by Mary S. Hartman and Lois W. Banner. New
     York: Harper & Row, 1974.

Wyatt, Philip R. "John Humphrey Noyes and the Stirpicultural
     Experiment." Journal of the History of Medicine and Allied
     Sciences 31, no. 1 (1976), 55-66.

b. Mormonism

Arrington, Leonard J. "Blessed Damozels: Women in Mormon
     History." Dialogue: A Journal of Mormon Thought 6, no. 2
     (1971), 22-31.

Arrington, Leonard J. "The Economic Role of Pioneer Mormon
     Women." Western Humanities Review 9, no. 2 (1955), 145-164.

Arrington, Leonard J. "Persons for All Seasons: Women in
     Mormon History." Brigham Young University Studies 20, no. 1
     (1979), 39-58.

Bachman, Danel W. "A Study of the Mormon Practice of Plural
     Marriage Before the Death of Joseph Smith." Master's
     thesis, Purdue University, 1975.

Bitton, Davis. "Mormon Polygamy: A Review Article." Journal
     of Mormon History 4 (1977), 101-118.

Bitton, Davis, and Bunker, Gary L. "Double Jeopardy: Visual
     Images of Mormon Women to 1914." Utah Historical Quarterly
     46, no. 2 (1978), 184-202.

Burgess-Olson, Vicki. "Family Structure and Dynamics in Early
    Utah Mormon Families, 1847-1885." Ph.D. diss., Northwestern
    University, 1975.

Burgess-Olson, Vicki. Sister Saints. Provo, Utah: Brigham
    Young University Press, 1978.

Bush, Lester E. "Birth Control Among the Mormons:
    Introduction to an Insistent Question." Dialogue: A Journal
    of Mormon Thought 10, no. 2 (1976), 12-44.

Bushman, Claudia L., ed. Mormon Sisters: Women in Early Utah.
    Cambridge, Mass.: Emmeline Press, Ltd., 1976.

Cairncross, John. After Polygamy Was Made a Sin: The Social
    History of Christian Polygamy. London: Routledge & Kegan
    Paul, 1974.

Campbell, Eugene E., and Campbell, Bruce L. "Divorce Among
    Mormon Polygamists: Extent and Explanations." Utah
    Historical Quarterly 46, no. 1 (1978), 4-23.

Cannon, Kenneth L., II. "Beyond the Manifesto: Polygamous
    Cohabitation Among LDS General Authorities After 1890."
    Utah Historical Quarterly 46, no. 1 (1978), 24-36.

Dunfey, Julie. "'Living the Principle' of Plural Marriage:
    Mormon Women, Utopia, and Female Sexuality in the Nineteenth
    Century." Feminist Studies 10, no. 3 (1984), 523-536.

Ellsworth, S. George, ed. Dear Ellen: Two Mormon Women and
    Their Letters. Salt Lake City: University of Utah Library,
    1974.

Foster, Lawrence. "From Frontier Activism to Neo-Victorian
    Domesticity: Mormon Women in the Nineteenth and Twentieth
    Centuries." Journal of Mormon History 6 (1979), 3-21.

Foster, Lawrence. "A Little-Known Defense of Polygamy from the
    Mormon Press in 1842." Dialogue: A Journal of Mormon
    Thought 9, no. 4 (1974), 21-34.

Foster, Lawrence. "Polygamy and the Frontier: Mormon Women in
    Early Utah." Utah Historical Quarterly 50, no. 3 (1982),
    268-289.

Foster, Lawrence. Religion and Sexuality: Three American
    Communal Experiments of the Nineteenth Century. New York:
    Oxford University Press, 1981.

Goodson, Stephanie Smith. "Plural Wives." In Mormon Sisters:
    Women in Early Utah, edited by Claudia L. Bushman.
    Cambridge, Mass.: Emmeline Press, Ltd., 1976.

Hansen, Klaus J. "Changing Perspectives on Sexuality and
    Marriage." Chap. 5 in Mormonism and the American
    Experience. Chicago: University of Chicago Press, 1981.

Hansen, Klaus J. "Mormon Sexuality and American Culture."
    Dialogue: A Journal of Mormon Thought 10, no. 2 (1976), 45-
    56.

Iversen, Joan. "Feminist Implications of Mormon Polygyny."
    Feminist Studies 10, no. 3 (1984), 505-522.

Ivins, Stanley. "Notes on Mormon Polygamy." Western
    Humanities Review 10 (Summer 1956), 229-239.

Jeffrey, Julie Roy. "If Polygamy is the Lord's Order, We Must
    Carry it Out." Chap. 6 in Frontier Women: The Trans-
    Mississippi West, 1840-1880. New York: Hill & Wang, Inc.,
    1979.

Jorgensen, Victor W., and Hardy, B. Carmon. "The Taylor-Cowley
    Affair and the Watershed of Mormon History." Utah
    Historical Quarterly 48, no. 1 (1980), 4-36.

Kern, Louis J. An Ordered Love: Sex Roles in Victorian
    Utopias: The Shakers, the Mormons, and the Oneida Community.
    Chapel Hill: University of North Carolina Press, 1981.

Kunz, Phillip R. "One Wife or Several? A Comparative Study of
    Late Nineteenth-Century Marriage in Utah." In The Mormon
    People: Their Character and Traditions, edited by Thomas G.
    Alexander. Provo, Utah: Brigham Young University Press,
    1980.

Larson, Gustive O. "An Industrial Home for Polygamous Wives."
    Utah Historical Quarterly 38, no. 3 (1970), 263-275.

Madsen, Carol C., and Whittaker, David J. "History's Sequel: A
    Source Essay on Women in Mormon History." Journal of Mormon
    History 6 (1979), 123-145.

Marquis, Kathleen. "'Diamond Cut Diamond': Mormon Women and
    the Cult of Domesticity in the Nineteenth Century."
    University of Michigan Papers in Women's Studies 2, no. 2
    (1976), 105-124.

May, Dean L. "People on the Mormon Frontier: Kanab's Families
    of 1874." Journal of Family History 1, no. 2 (1976), 169-
    192.

Mulvay, Jill C. "Eliza R. Snow and the Woman Question."
    Brigham Young University Studies 16, no. 2 (1976), 250-264.

Mulvay, Jill C. "The Liberal Shall Be Blessed: Sarah M.
    Kimball." Utah Historical Quarterly 44, no. 3 (1976), 205-
    221.

Quinn, D. Michael. "Organizational Development and Social
    Origins of the Mormon Hierarchy, 1832-1932: A
    Prosopographical Study." Master's thesis, University of
    Utah, 1973.

Smith, James E., and Kunz, Phillip R. "Polygamy and Fertility
    in Nineteenth-Century America." Population Studies 30, no.
    3 (1976), 465-480.

Thomasson, Gordon J. "The Manifesto Was a Victory." Dialogue:
    A Journal of Mormon Thought 6, no. 1 (1971), 37-45.

Thornton, Arland. "Religion and Fertility: The Case of
    Mormonism." Journal of Marriage and the Family 41, no. 1
    (1979), 131-144.

Young, Kimball. Isn't One Wife Enough? The Story of Mormon
    Polygamy. New York: Henry Holt, 1954.

4.   EVANGELICALISM AND SOCIAL REFORM MOVEMENTS

a.   General

Bacon, Margaret Hope. As the Way Opens: The Story of Quaker
    Women in America. Richmond, Ind.: Friends United Press,
    1980.

Banner, Lois W. "The Protestant Crusade: Religious Missions,
    Benevolence, and Reform in the United States, 1790-1840."
    Ph.D. diss., Columbia University, 1970.

Banner, Lois W. "Religious Benevolence as Social Control: A
    Critique of an Interpretation." Journal of American History
    60, no. 1 (1973), 23-41.

Bass, Dorothy C. "'Their Prodigious Influence': Women,
    Religion and Reform in Antebellum America." In Women of
    Spirit: Female Leadership in the Jewish and Christian
    Traditions, edited by Rosemary Radford Ruether and Eleanor
    McLaughlin, 279-300. New York: Simon & Schuster, 1979.

Berg, Barbara J. "Association." Chap. 7 in The Remembered
    Gate: Origins of American Feminism. The Woman and the City,
    1800-1860. New York: Oxford University Press, 1978.

Boylan, Anne M. "Evangelical Womanhood in the Nineteenth
    Century: The Role of Women in Sunday Schools." Feminist
    Studies 4, no. 3 (1978), 62-80.

Boylan, Anne M. "Women in Groups: An Analysis of Women's
    Benevolent Organizations in New York and Boston, 1797-1840."
    Journal of American History 71, no. 3 (1984), 497-523.

Boylan, Anne M. "Women's History: Some Axioms in Need of
     Revision." Reviews in American History 6, no. 3 (1978),
     340-347.

Brandenstein, Sherilyn. "The Colorado Cottage Home." Colorado
     Magazine 53, no. 3 (1976), 229-242.

Breault, Judith Colucci. "The Odyssey of a Humanitarian; Emily
     Howland, 1827-1929: A Biographical Analysis." Ph.D. diss.,
     University of Pennsylvania, 1974.

Brenzel, Barbara M. "Better Protestant Than Prostitute: A
     Social Portrait of a Nineteenth-Century Reform School for
     Girls." Interchange 6, no. 2 (1975), 11-22.

Brunger, Ronald A. "The Ladies Aid Societies in Michigan
     Methodism." Methodist History 5, no. 2 (1967), 31-48.

Caskey, Marie. Chariot of Fire: Religion and the Beecher
     Family. New Haven: Yale University Press, 1978.

Conway, Jill K. "Evangelical Protestantism and Its Influence
     on Women in North America, 1790-1860." Paper delivered at
     the annual meeting of the American Historical Association,
     New Orleans, 1972.

Foster, Charles H. The Rungless Ladder: Harriet Beecher Stowe
     and New England Puritanism. Durham, N.C.: Duke University
     Press, 1954.

Gifford, Carolyn DeSwarte. "Women in Social Reform Movements."
     In Women and Religion in America, vol. 1, The Nineteenth
     Century, edited by Rosemary Radford Reuther and Rosemary
     Skinner Keller, 294-340. San Francisco: Harper & Row, 1981.

Gilman, Amy. "From Widowhood to Wickedness: The Politics of
     Class and Gender in New York City Private Charity, 1799-
     1860." History of Education Quarterly 24, no. 1 (1984), 59-
     74.

Ginzberg, Lori D. "Women and the Work of Benevolence: Morality
     and Politics in the Northeastern United States, 1820-1885."
     Ph.D. diss., Yale University, 1985.

Hewitt, Nancy A. Women's Activism and Social Change:
     Rochester, New York, 1822-1872. Ithaca, N.Y.: Cornell
     University Press, 1984.

James, Janet Wilson. "Charity Work and Education, 1800-1825."
     Chap. 4 in Changing Ideas About Women in the United States,
     1776-1825. New York and London: Garland Publishing, Inc.,
     1981.

Jeffrey, Julie Roy. "Ministry Through Marriage." In Women in
    New Worlds: Historical Perspectives on the Wesleyan
    Tradition, vol. 1, edited by Hilah F. Thomas and Rosemary
    Skinner Keller. Nashville: Abingdon, 1981.

Kihlstrom, Mary F. "The Morristown Female Charitable Society."
    Journal of Presbyterian History 58, no. 3 (1980), 255-272.

Kimball, Gayle. The Religious Ideas of Harriet Beecher Stowe:
    Her Gospel of Womanhood. New York: Edwin Mellen Press,
    1982.

Lebedum, Jean. "Harriet Beecher Stowe's Interest in Sojourner
    Truth, Black Feminist." American Literature 46, no. 3
    (1973), 359-363.

Lindley, Susan Hill. "Woman's Profession in the Life and
    Thought of Catherine Beecher: A Study of Religion and
    Reform." Ph.D. diss., Duke University, 1974.

May, Cheryll Lynn. "Charitable Sisters." In Mormon Sisters:
    Women in Early Utah, edited by Claudia L. Bushman.
    Cambridge, Mass.: Emmeline Press, Ltd., 1976.

Melder, Keith. Beginnings of Sisterhood: The American Woman's
    Rights Movement, 1800-1850. New York: Schocken Books, 1977.

Melder, Keith. "'Ladies Bountiful': Organized Women's
    Benevolence in Early Nineteenth-Century America." New York
    History 48, no. 3 (1967), 231-254. Reprinted in his
    Beginnings of Sisterhood: The American Woman's Rights
    Movement, 1800-1850. New York: Schocken Books, 1977.

Ryan, Mary P. "The Power of Women's Networks: A Case Study of
    Female Moral Reform in Antebellum America." Feminist
    Studies 5, no. 1 (1979), 66-86.

Scott, Anne Firor. "The Lord Helps Those . . ." Chap. 6 in
    The Southern Lady: From Pedestal to Politics, 1830-1930.
    Chicago: Chicago University Press, 1970.

Scott, Anne Firor. "Women, Religion, and Social Change in the
    South, 1830-1930." In Religion and the Solid South, edited
    by Samuel S. Hill, Jr. Nashville: Abingdon, 1972.

Sidonia, C. Taupin. "'Christianity in the Kitchen' or a Moral
    Guide for Gourmets." American Quarterly 15, no. 1 (1963),
    85-89.

Smith, Timothy. Revivalism and Social Reform in Mid-Nineteenth
    Century America. New York: Abingdon, 1957.

Smith-Rosenberg, Carroll. "Beauty, the Beast and the Militant
    Woman: A Case Study in Sex Roles and Social Stress in
    Jacksonian America." American Quarterly 23, no. 4 (1971),
    562-584. Reprinted in her Disorderly Conduct: Visions of
    Gender in Victorian America. New York: Knopf, 1985.

Smith-Rosenberg, Carroll. "New York Female Moral Reform
    Society." Chap. 4 in Religion and the Rise of the American
    City: The New York City Mission Movement, 1812-1870.
    Ithaca, N.Y.: Cornell University Press, 1971.

Stevenson, Louise L. "Women Activists and Their Communities."
    Reviews in American History 13, no. 1 (1985), 70-75.

Sweet, Leonard I. The Minister's Wife: Her Role in Nineteenth-
    Century American Evangelism. Philadelphia: Temple
    University Press, 1983.

Thomas, John L. "Romantic Reform in America, 1815-1865."
    American Quarterly 17, no. 4 (1965), 656-681.

Treudley, Mary B. "The Benevolent Fair: A Study of Charitable
    Organizations Among Women in the First Third of the
    Nineteenth Century." Social Service Review 14, no. 3
    (1940), 509-522.

Welter, Barbara. "Defenders of the Faith: Women Novelists of
    Religious Controversy in the Nineteenth Century." In her
    Dimity Convictions. Athens, Ohio: Ohio University Press,
    1976.

b. Education

Brumberg, Joan Jacobs. "The Feminization of Teaching:
    'Romantic Sexism' and American Protestant Denominalization."
    History of Education Quarterly 23, no. 3 (1983), 379-384.

Bunkle, Phillida. "Sentimental Womanhood and Domestic
    Education, 1830-1870." History of Education Quarterly 14,
    no. 1 (1974), 13-30.

Burstyn, Joan. "Catherine Beecher and the Education of
    American Women." New England Quarterly 47, no. 3 (1974),
    386-403. Reprinted in Women's Experience in America: An
    Historical Anthology, edited by Esther Katz and Anita
    Rapone. New Brunswick, N.J.: Transaction Books, 1980.

Clement, Stephen Merrell, II. "Aspects of Student Religion at
    Vassar College, 1861-1914." Ph.D. diss., Harvard
    University, 1977.

Conway, Jill K. "Perspectives on the History of Women's
    Education in the United States." History of Education
    Quarterly 14, no. 1 (1974), 1-12.

Ginzberg, Lori D. "Women in an Evangelical Community: Oberlin, 1835-1850." Ohio History 89, no. 1 (1980), 78-88.

Gordon, Ann D. "The Young Ladies Academy of Philadelphia." In Women of America: A History, edited by Carol Ruth Berkin and Mary Beth Norton. Boston: Houghton Mifflin Co., 1979.

Green, Elizabeth Alden. Mary Lyon and Mount Holyoke: Opening the Gates. Hanover, N.H.: University Press of New England, 1979.

Farello, Elene Wilson. A History of the Education of Women in the United States. New York: Vintage Press, 1970.

Hogeland, Ronald W. "Coeducation of the Sexes at Oberlin College: A Study of Social Ideas in Mid-Nineteenth Century America." Journal of Social History 6, no. 2 (1972-73), 160-176.

James, Janet Wilson. "Charity Work and Education, 1800-1825." Chap. 4 in Changing Ideas About Women in the United States, 1776-1825. New York: Garland Publishing, Inc., 1981.

Jensen, Joan M. "Not Only Ours But Others: The Quaker Teaching Daughters of the Mid-Atlantic, 1790-1850." History of Education Quarterly 24, no. 1 (1984), 3-19.

Jones, Jacqueline. Soldiers of Light and Love: Northern Teachers and Georgia Blacks, 1865-1873. Chapel Hill: University of North Carolina Press, 1980.

Jones, Jacqueline. "Women Who Were More Than Men: Sex and Status in Freedman's Teaching." History of Education Quarterly 19, no. 1 (1979), 47-59.

Lutz, Alma. Emma Willard: Pioneer Educator of American Women. Boston: Beacon Press, 1964.

Melder, Keith. "Mask of Oppression: The Female Seminary Movement in the United States." New York History 55, no. 3 (1974), 261-279.

Melder, Keith. "Woman's High Calling: The Teaching Profession in America, 1830-1860." American Studies (Lawrence, Kansas) 13, no. 2 (1972), 19-32. Reprinted in his Beginnings of Sisterhood: The American Woman's Rights Movement, 1800-1850. New York: Schocken Books, 1977.

Miller, Page Putnam. "Women in the Vanguard of the Sunday School Movement." Journal of Presbyterian History 58, no. 3 (1980), 311-325.

Riley, Glenda. "Origins of the Argument for Improved Female Education." History of Education Quarterly 9, no. 4 (1969), 455-470.

Scott, Anne Firor. "The Ever Widening Circle: The Diffusion of
    Feminist Values from the Troy Female Seminary, 1822-1872."
    History of Education Quarterly 19 (Spring 1979), 3-25.

Scott, Anne Firor. "What, Then, Is the American: This New
    Woman?" Journal of American History 65, no. 3 (1978), 679-
    703.

Sklar, Kathryn. Catherine Beecher: A Study in American
    Domesticity. New Haven: Yale University Press, 1973.

Stock, Phyllis. Better Than Rubies: A History of Women's
    Education. New York: G. P. Putnam's Sons, 1978.

Sugg, Redding, Jr. Motherteacher: The Feminization of American
    Education. Charlottesville: University Press of Virginia,
    1978.

Vinovskis, Maris, and Bernard, Richard M. "Beyond Catherine
    Beecher: Female Education in the Antebellum Period." Signs
    3, no. 4 (1978), 856-869.

c. Abolitionism

Altschuler, Glenn C., and Saltzgaber, Jan M. Revivalism,
    Social Conscience, and Community in the Burned-Over
    District: The Trial of Rhoda Bement. Ithaca, N.Y.: Cornell
    University Press, 1983.

DuBois, Ellen. "Women's Rights and Abolition: The Nature of
    the Connection." In Antislavery Reconsidered: New
    Perspectives on the Abolitionists, edited by Lewis Perry and
    Michael Fellman. Baton Rouge: Louisiana State University
    Press, 1979.

Friedman, Lawrence J. "Distinctions of Sex." Chap. 5 in
    Gregarious Saints: Self and Community in American
    Abolitionism, 1830-1870. Cambridge: Cambridge University
    Press, 1982.

Hersh, Blanche Glassman. "'Am I Not a Woman and a Sister?':
    Abolitionist Beginnings of Nineteenth-Century Feminism." In
    Antislavery Reconsidered: New Perspectives on the
    Abolitionists, edited by Lewis Perry and Michael Fellman.
    Baton Rouge: Louisiana State University Press, 1979.

Hersh, Blanche Glassman. The Slavery of Sex: Feminist-
    Abolitionists in America. Urbana: University of Illinois
    Press, 1978.

Hewitt, Nancy. "Social Origins of Women's Antislavery Politics
     in Western New York." In Crusaders and Compromisers: Essays
     on the Relationship of the Antislavery Struggle to the
     Antebellum Party System, edited by Alan M. Kraut. Westport,
     Conn.: Greenwood Press, 1983.

Hewitt, Nancy A. Women's Activism and Social Change:
     Rochester, New York, 1822-1872. Ithaca, N.Y.: Cornell
     University Press, 1984.

Hovet, Theodore R. "Christian Revolution: Harriet Beecher
     Stowe's Response to Slavery and the Civil War." New England
     Quarterly 47, no. 4 (1974), 535-549.

Hovet, Theodore R. "The Church Diseased: Harriet Beecher
     Stowe's Attack on the Presbyterian Church." Journal of
     Presbyterian History 52, no. 2 (1974), 167-187.

Kimball, Gayle. "Harriet Beecher Stowe's Revision of New
     England Theology." Journal of Presbyterian History 58, no.
     1 (1980), 64-81.

Lerner, Gerda. "The Grimke Sisters and the Struggle Against
     Race Prejudice." Journal of Negro History 48, no. 4 (1963),
     277-291.

Lerner, Gerda. The Grimke Sisters from South Carolina: Rebels
     Against Slavery. 1967. Reprint. New York: Schocken Books,
     1971.

Lerner, Gerda. "The Political Activities of Antislavery
     Women." In her The Majority Finds Its Past. New York:
     Oxford University Press, 1979.

Lerner, Gerda, ed. "Sarah M. Grimke's 'Sisters of Charity'."
     Signs 1, no. 1 (1975), 246-256.

Lumpkin, Katherine DuPre. The Emancipation of Angelina Grimke.
     Chapel Hill: University of North Carolina Press, 1974.

Lutz, Alma. Crusade for Freedom: Women of the Antislavery
     Movement. Boston: Beacon Press, 1968.

Melder, Keith. "Forerunners of Freedom: The Grimke Sisters in
     Massachusetts, 1837-1838." Essex Institute Historical
     Collections 103, no. 3 (1967), 223-249. Reprinted in his
     Beginnings of Sisterhood: The American Woman's Rights
     Movement, 1800-1850. New York: Schocken Books, 1977.

Pease, William H., and Pease, Jane H. "Samuel J. May: Civil
     Libertarian." Cornell Library Journal 3, no. 3 (1967),
     7-25.

Swerdlow, Amy. "Abolition's Conservative Sisters: The Ladies'
    New York City Anti-Slavery Societies, 1834-1840." Paper
    delivered at the third Berkshire Conference on Women's
    History, Bryn Mawr, Pa., June 9-11, 1976. (Papers on deposit
    at the Schlesinger Library, Radcliffe College, Cambridge,
    Mass.)

Walters, Ronald G. "Distinctions of Sex." Chap. 5 in The
    Anti-Slavery Appeal: American Abolitionism After 1830.
    Baltimore: Johns Hopkins University Press, 1976.

Walters, Ronald G. "The Erotic South: Civilization and
    Sexuality in American Abolitionism." American Quarterly 25,
    no. 2 (1973), 177-201.

Wellman, Judith. "Women and Radical Reform in Antebellum
    Upstate New York: A Profile of Grassroots Female
    Abolitionists." In Clio Was a Woman: Studies in the History
    of American Women, edited by Mabel E. Deutrich and Virginia
    C. Purdy. Washington, D.C.: Howard University Press, 1980.

Wyatt-Brown, Bertram. "Conscience and Career: Young
    Abolitionists and Missionaries." In Anti-Slavery, Religion
    and Reform: Essays in Memory of Roger Anstey, edited by
    Christine Bolt and Seymour Drescher, 183-203. Folkestone,
    England: W. Dawson; Hamden, Conn.: Archon Books, 1980.

Index

Contributors

RANDALL H. BALMER, assistant professor of religion at Columbia University, holds the Ph.D. from Princeton University. He is a recipient of the Sidney E. Mead Prize from the American Society of Church History, and his work has appeared in several journals and collections of essays.

ELIZABETH B. CLARK is a graduate of the University of Michigan Law School. A doctoral candidate in history at Princeton University, she is working on a study of evangelism and the suffrage movement. In 1985–1986 she held a legal history fellowship at the University of Wisconsin–Madison Law School.

DANIEL R. ERNST is a legal history fellow at the University of Wisconsin–Madison Law School, a graduate student in the Department of History at Princeton University, a graduate of the University of Chicago Law School, and a member of the Illinois bar. He is preparing a dissertation on labor law and the transition from entrepreneurial to monopoly capitalism in America.

JOHN R. FITZMIER holds degrees from the University of Pittsburgh, Gordon Conwell Theological Seminary, and Princeton University. He has recently completed a study entitled "The Godly Federalism of Timothy Dwight, 1752–1817: Society, Doctrine, and Religion in the Life of New England's Moral Legislator." He is assistant professor of American Church History at the Divinity School of Vanderbilt University.

JOHN W. LOWE, Jr., is a doctoral candidate in the joint Doctor of Education program in Religion and Education of Union Theological Seminary and Teachers College, Columbia University. He has degrees from Juniata College, Bethany Theological Seminary, and Teachers College. His doctoral dissertation examines the compulsory Bible reading law of Pennsylvania of 1913. He has also been a pastor and religious educator with involvements in public education in many capacities.

LOUIS P. MASUR is an assistant professor of history at the University of California, Riverside. His major field is eighteenth- and nineteenth-century intellectual and cultural history and his *Rites of Execution: Capital Punishment and the Transformation of American Culture, 1776–1865* will soon be published.

JOHN L. MERRILL is a graduate of Yale Divinity School and a doctoral candidate in religion at Princeton University. He is currently at work on a study of biblical and theological hermeneutics in nineteenth-century America.

LEIGH ERIC SCHMIDT is a doctoral candidate at Princeton University in the Department of Religion. He is the author of " 'A Second and Glorious Reformation': The New Light Extremism of Andrew Croswell," published in the *William and Mary Quarterly*, as well as other articles and reviews.

MARK VALERI is assistant professor of Religious Studies at Lewis and Clark College, Portland, Oregon. He is co-author with John F. Wilson of "Scripture and Society: From Reform in the Old World to Revival in the New," in *The Bible in American Law, Politics, and Political Rhetoric*, edited by James Turner Johnson.

JOHN F. WILSON is Collord professor of religion at Princeton University, where he also directs the Project on the Church-State Issue in American Culture. The project is funded by the Lilly Endowment. A specialist in American religious history, his many publications have concerned, among other aspects of the subject, Puritanism in seventeenth-century England, Jonathan Edwards, the church-state issue, and political and civil religion in American society. He is the author of *Pulpit in Parliament* and *Public Religion in American Culture*.